圓明園 **China's Lost Imperial Garden**

The World's Most Exquisite Garden Rediscovered

By Guo Daiheng

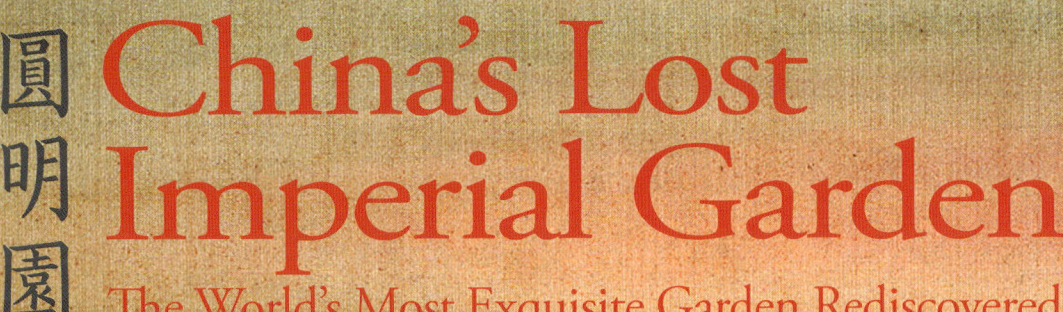

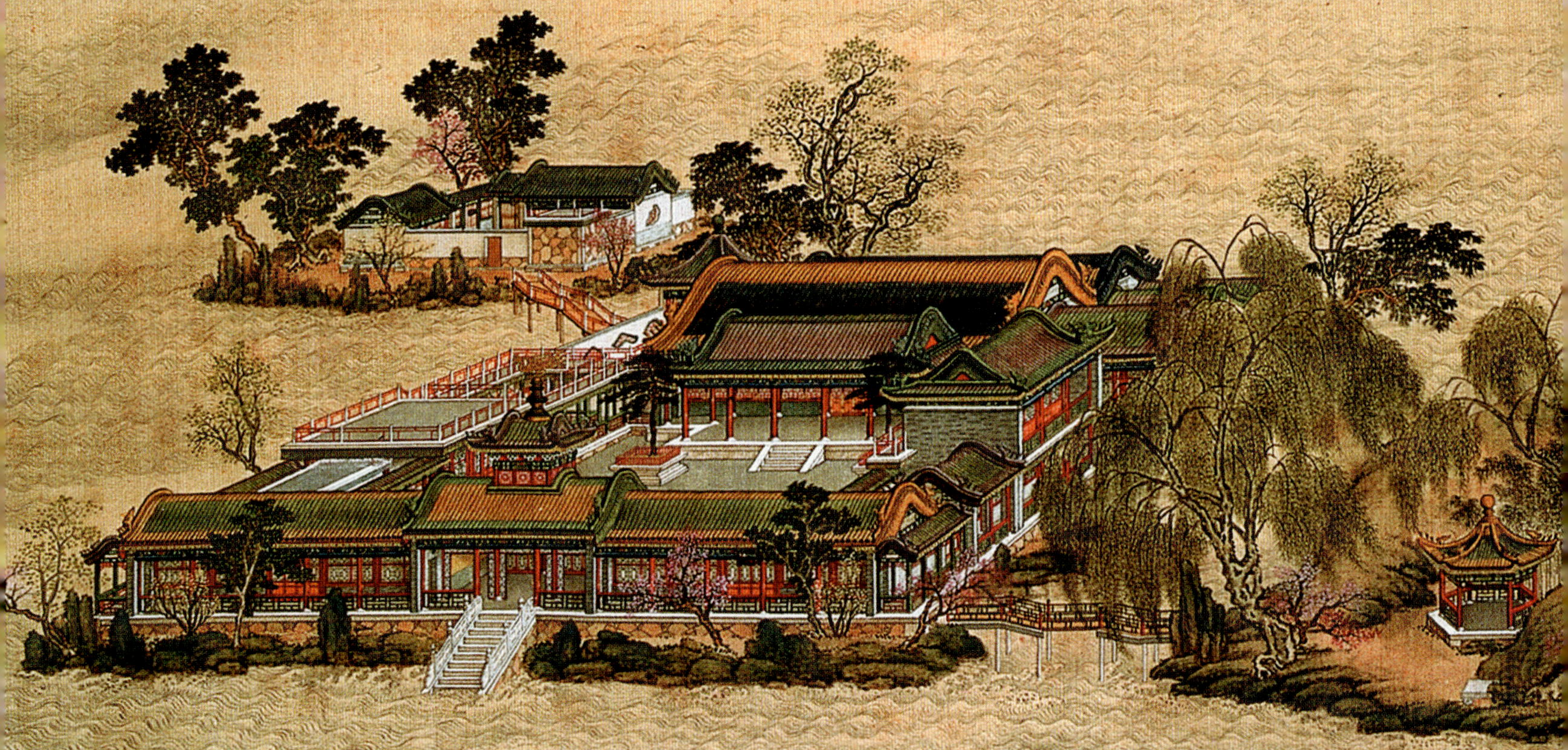

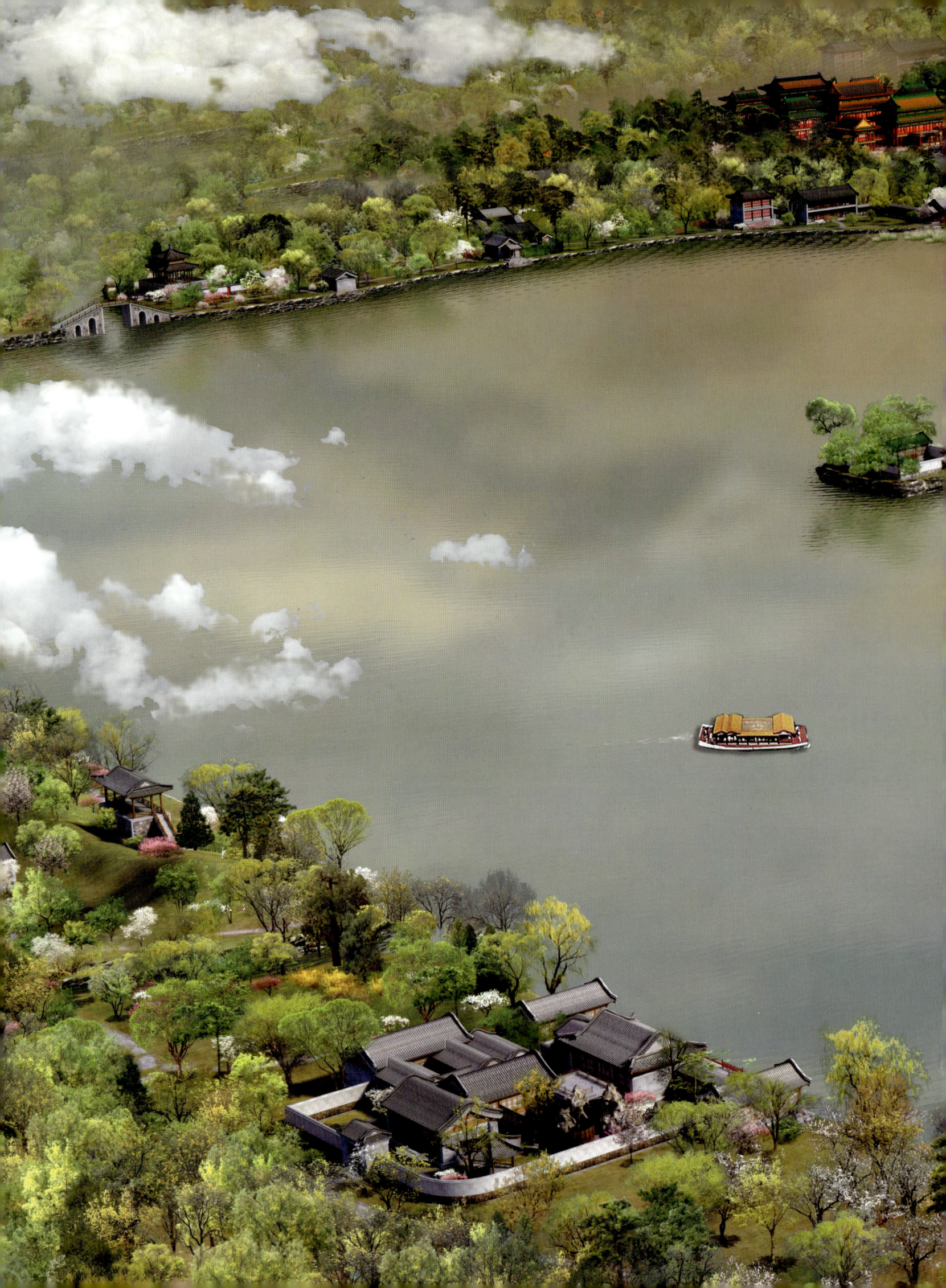

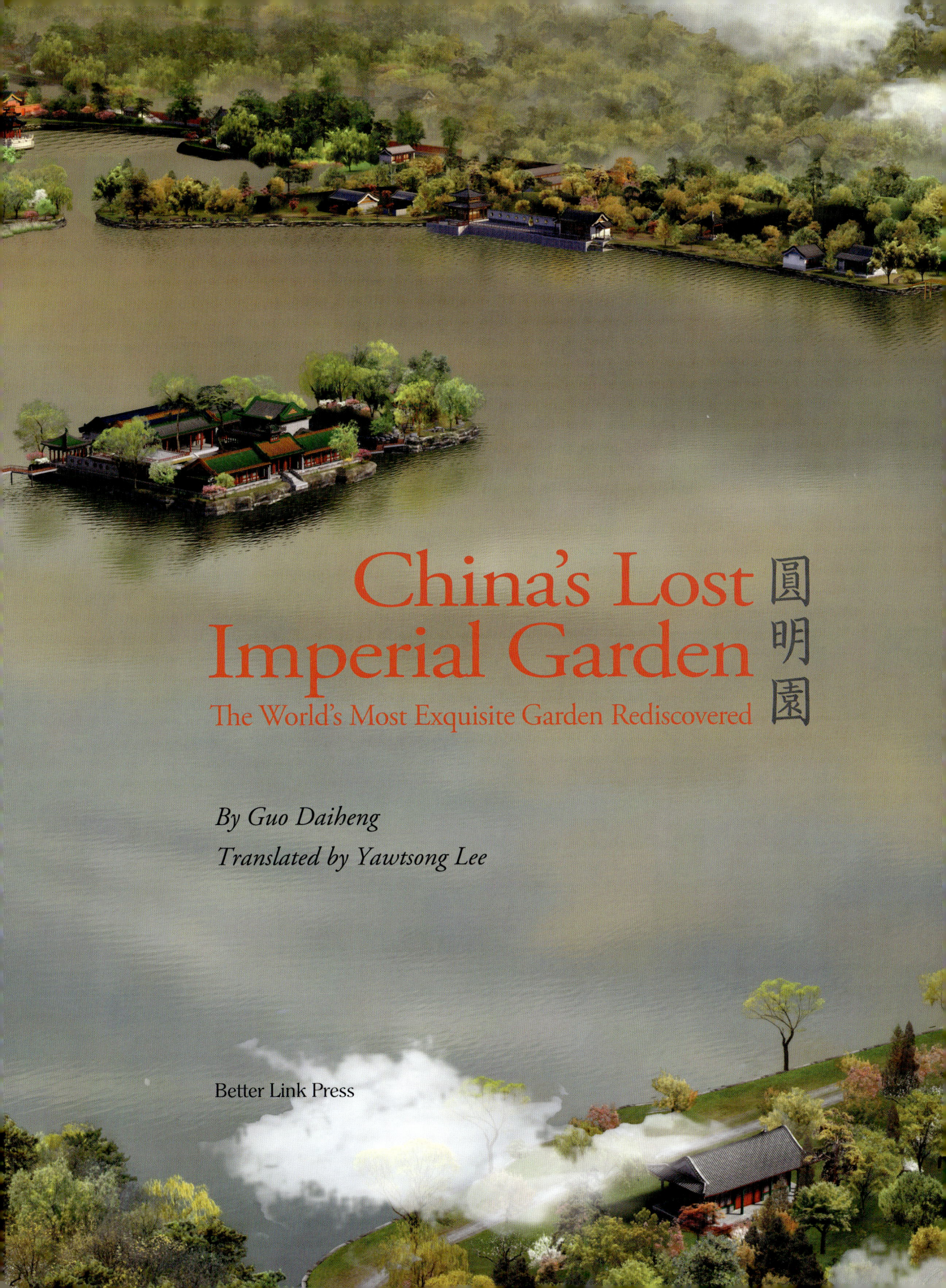

China's Lost Imperial Garden 圓明園
The World's Most Exquisite Garden Rediscovered

By Guo Daiheng

Translated by Yawtsong Lee

Better Link Press

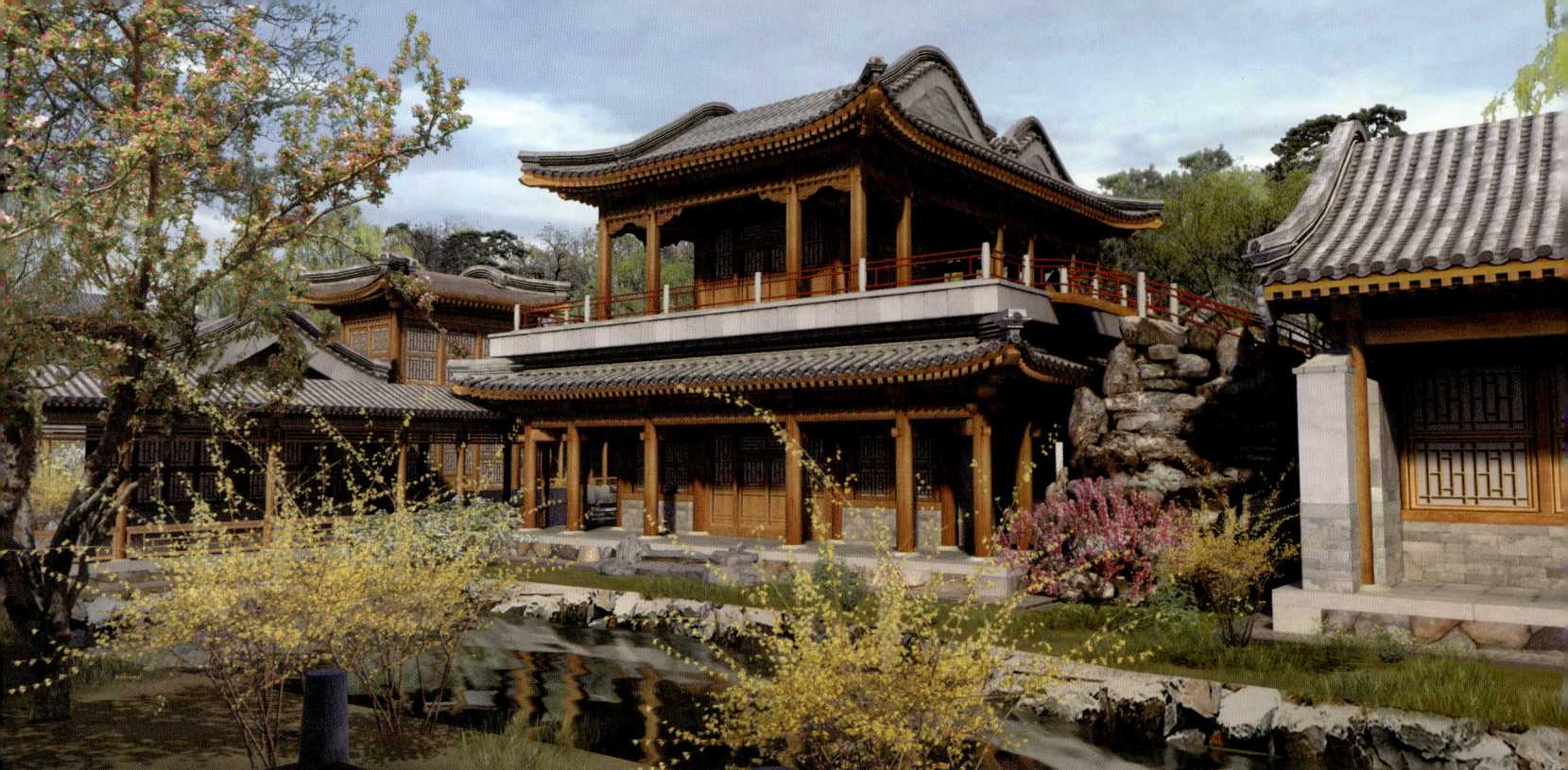

Page 1
Fig. 1   Painting of Pengdao Yaotai Complex (Complex of the Jade Terrace of Paradise Island) from the album of *Forty Scenes of the Yuan Ming Yuan*

Pages 2 and 3
Fig. 2   The panaroma of the Lake of Happiness

Above
Fig. 3   Yanshui Chenghua in Bieyou Dongtian Complex (Complex of a Whole New World within a Grotto)

Facing page
Fig. 4   Stone lions in front of Anyou Palace (Palace of Peaceful Protection)

Copyright © 2016 Shanghai Press and Publishing Development Company

All rights reserved. Unauthorized reproduction, in any manner, is prohibited.

This book is edited and designed by the Editorial Committee of *Cultural China* series

Text by Guo Daiheng
Photographs by Guo Daiheng, Quanjing
Translation by Yawtsong Lee

Cover Design: Wang Wei
Interior Design: Li Jing, Hu Bin (Yuan Yinchang Design Studio)

Assistant Editor: Cao Yue
Copy Editor: Tony Blishen
Editor: Wu Yuezhou
Editorial Director: Zhang Yicong

Senior Consultants: Sun Yong, Wu Ying, Yang Xinci
Managing Director and Publisher: Wang Youbu

ISBN: 978-1-60220-021-0

Address any comments about *China's Lost Imperial Garden: The World's Most Exquisite Garden Rediscovered* to:

Better Link Press
99 Park Ave
New York, NY 10016
USA

or

Shanghai Press and Publishing Development Company
F 7 Donghu Road, Shanghai, China (200031)
Email: comments_betterlinkpress@hotmail.com

Printed in China by Shenzhen Donnelley Printing Co., Ltd.

1   3   5   7   9   10   8   6   4   2

CONTENTS

PREFACE 9

PART I MASTERS OF THE YUAN MING YUAN 11

CHAPTER I A Garden Granted by the Emperor to Yinzhen His Fourth Son 13

CHAPTER II The Early Period of the Yuan Ming Yuan as an Imperial Garden 17

CHAPTER III Middle Period of the Yuan Ming Yuan as an Imperial Garden —the Five Gardens 21

CHAPTER IV The Late Period of the Yuan Ming Yuan—the Three Gardens 27

CHAPTER V The Inferno of 1860 31

PART II SCENERY OF THE YUAN MING YUAN 35

CHAPTER VI Public Business in Front and Private Residence in the Rear 37
  1. Zhengda Guangming Complex (Complex of Rectitude and Honor) 38
  2. Danhuai Hall (Simple Needs Hall) of the Changchun Garden (Garden of Eternal Spring) 42
  3. Qinzheng Qinxian Complex (Complex of Diligent Government) 44
  4. Jiuzhou Qingyan Complex (Complex of Nine Continents Clear and Calm) 47
  5. Hanjing Hall (Tripataka Hall) 51
  6. The Imperial Apartments of the Qichun Garden (Garden of Elegant Spring) 58

CHAPTER VII Heaven and Earth and *Ren Lun* (Human Ethics) 61
  1. Louyue Kaiyun Complex (Complex of the Engraved Moon and Unfolding Clouds) 63
  2. Hongci Yonghu Complex (Complex of Vast Compassion and Eternal Blessing) 67
  3. Changchun Xianguan Complex (Complex of Eternal Spring Immortals Hall) 71
  4. Tianran Tuhua Complex (Complex of the Nature's Own Painting) 75

CHAPTER VIII Shenfo Huyou (Protection and Blessing by the Gods and Buddha) 81
  1. Ciyun Puhu Complex (Complex of Merciful Clouds Protect All) 84
  2. Ritian Linyu Complex (Complex of Dazzling Eaves under Heaven) 85
  3. Yuedi Yunju Complex (Complex of Dwelling of the Moon, Earth, and Clouds) 86
  4. Shewei City (Sravasti) 88
  5. Guangyu Temple (Fertility Temple) 90
  6. Zhengjue Temple (Temple of Supreme Perfect Enlightenment) 91
  7. Fahui Temple (Dharma Wisdom Temple) 92
  8. Baoxiang Temple (Jeweled Image Temple) 93

CHAPTER IX Culture and Education 95
  1. Huifang Library (Library of Collected Fragrance) 97
  2. Bitong Library (Green Wutong Tree Library) 102
  3. Wuling Chunse (Spring Color at Wuling) 105
  4. Siyi Library (Library of the Four Seasons) 108
  5. Lianxi Lechu Complex (Complex of Happy Place of Lianxi) 111
  6. Wenyuan Pavilion (Pavilion of the Source of Literature) 113
  7. Dongtian Shenchu Complex (Deep in the Grotto Complex) 117

CHAPTER X Observing Farming Activities and Monitoring the Agricultural Cycle 120
  1. Xinghuachun Pavilion (Apricot Blossom Spring Pavilion) 123
  2. Beiyuan Mountain Village (Mountain Village in the Distant North) 127
  3. Danbo Ningjing Complex (Complex of Detachment and Serenity) 128
  4. Yingshui Lanxiang Complex (Complex of Water Reflections and Orchid Fragrance) 129
  5. Shuimu Mingse Complex (Complex of Sounds of Trees and Water) 130
  6. Gengyun Hall (Hall of Crop Cultivation) 131

CONTENTS

CHAPTER XI Theatrical Buildings   133
1. Shangao Shuichang Complex (Complex of High Hills and Long Waters)   134
2. Tongle Garden (Garden of Shared Pleasure)   136
3. Zhanshi Yinglü Complex (Complex of Verse and Rhyming)   146
4. Tantan Dangdang Complex (Complex of Clear Conscience and Broad Mind)   147
5. Wanfang Anhe Complex (Complex of Universal Peace and Harmony)   152

CHAPTER XII Landscape Architecture   157
1. Pengdao Yaotai Complex (Complex of the Jade Terrace of Paradise Island)   158
2. Fanghu Shengjing Complex (Complex of the Beautiful Scene of the Square Pot)   162
3. Bieyou Dongtian Complex (Complex of a Whole New World within a Grotto)   169
4. Kuoran Dagong Complex (Complex of Boundless Impartiality)   173
5. Jiexiu Mountain House (Mountain House Greeted by the Beauty of the Hills)   176
6. Qian Garden in the Changchun Garden (Garden of Eternal Spring)   177
7. Shizi Grove (Lion Grove) in the Changchun Garden   180
8. Jian Garden (Garden of Mirror) in the Changchun Garden   184
9. Qingxia Study of the Qichun Garden (Garden of Elegant Spring)   186
10. Chengxin Hall (Hall of Cleansing the Mind) of the Qichun Garden   187
11. Ten Scenes of the West Lake in the Yuan Ming Yuan   189

CHAPTER XIII Xiyang Building Complex (Complex of European Buildings)   193
1. Xie Qiqu Pavilion (Pavilion Harmonizing Surprise and Delight)   194
2. Wanhua Zhen Complex (Complex of the Maze)   199
3. Haiyan Hall (Hall of Calm Seas)   200
4. Fangwai Observatory (Observatory of Lands Beyond)   202
5. Yuanying Observatory (Immense Ocean Observatory) and Da Shuifa Fountain (Great Fountain)   204

CHAPTER XIV Market and Pleasure Grounds   209
1. Market Street   210
2. Qushui Liushang Complex (Complex of Wine Cups Floating on a Winding Channel)   214
3. Viewing Lotus Blossom in the Imperial Garden   217
4. Floating River Lanterns on Zhongyuan Festival   218

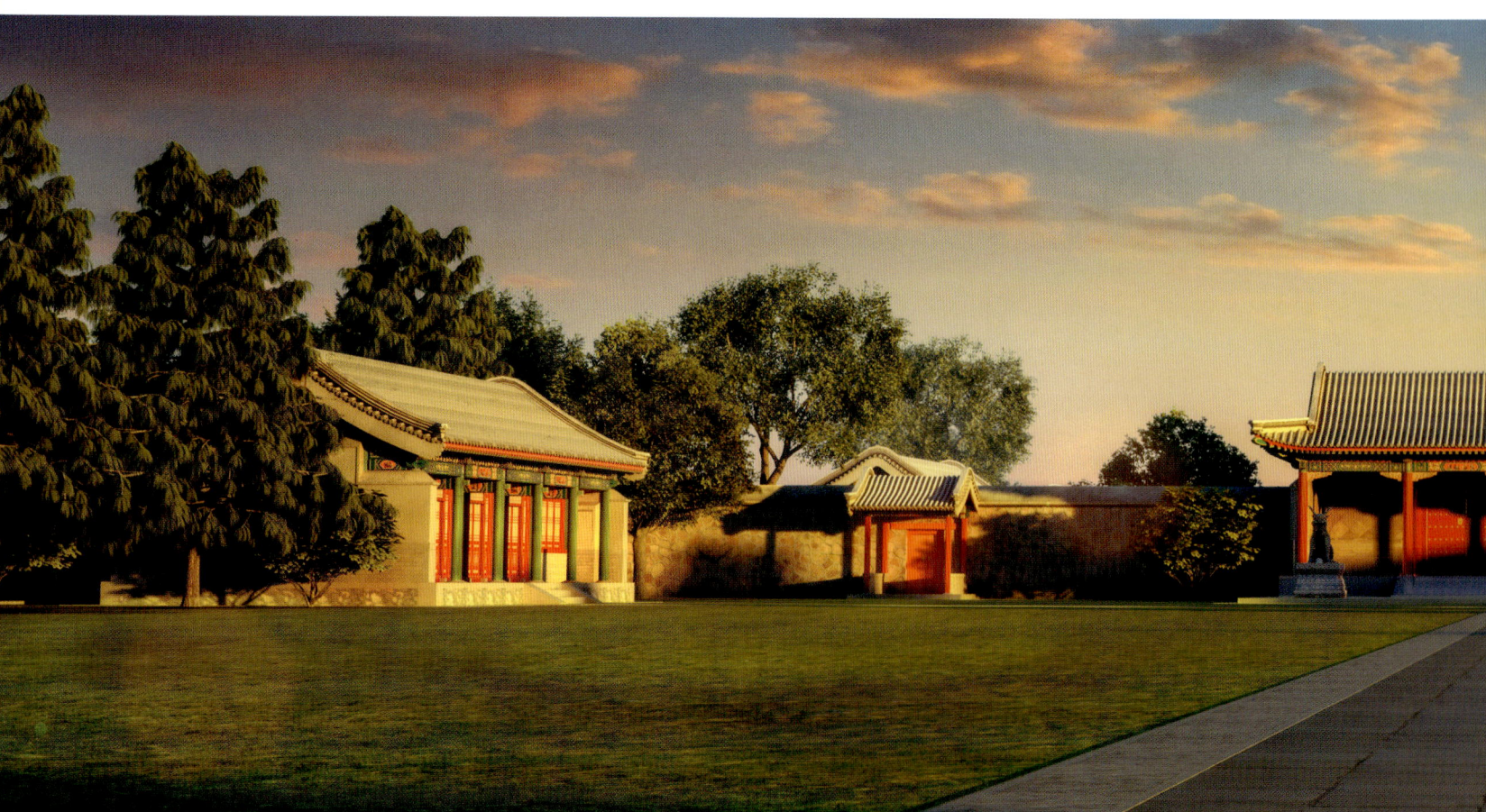

CONTENTS

    5. Dragon Boat Racing on Dragon Boat Festival   219

PART III   THE DESIGN APPROACH OF THE GARDEN CREATORS   221

CHAPTER XV   Recreating Landscape Spaces   223

CHAPTER XVI   Control of the Architectural Layout with a Grid System   224
    1. Building Groups Whose Courtyards Spread out Transversely   224
    2. Building Groups that Extend in One Direction   224
    3. Large Building Groups that Extend Longitudinally   224
    4. Cluster Type Building Groups   225
    5. 品-Shaped Building Groups   225
    6. Building Groups that Surround a Large Courtyard or a Pond   225

CHAPTER XVII   Water Courses as the Dominant Means of Transport   226

PART IV   AN ART OF GARDEN DESIGN ROOTED IN TRADITIONAL CHINESE CULTURE   233

CHAPTER XVIII   Configuration of Building Groups that Conforms to a Culture Based on Ethics   235

CHAPTER XIX   Planning the Garden with an Eye to "Centrality"   236

CHAPTER XX   Objectification of the Vision of Governance   237

CHAPTER XXI   From Aesthetic Pursuit to *Nei Sheng Wai Wang*   238

CHAPTER XXII   An Unusual Sight Removed from the Realm of Reality   239

CONCLUSION   241

APPENDICES   242
  Glossary   242
  Bibliography   250
  Dates of the Chinese Dynasties   252
  Index   253

Below
Fig. 5   The main palace gate of Yuan Ming Yuan

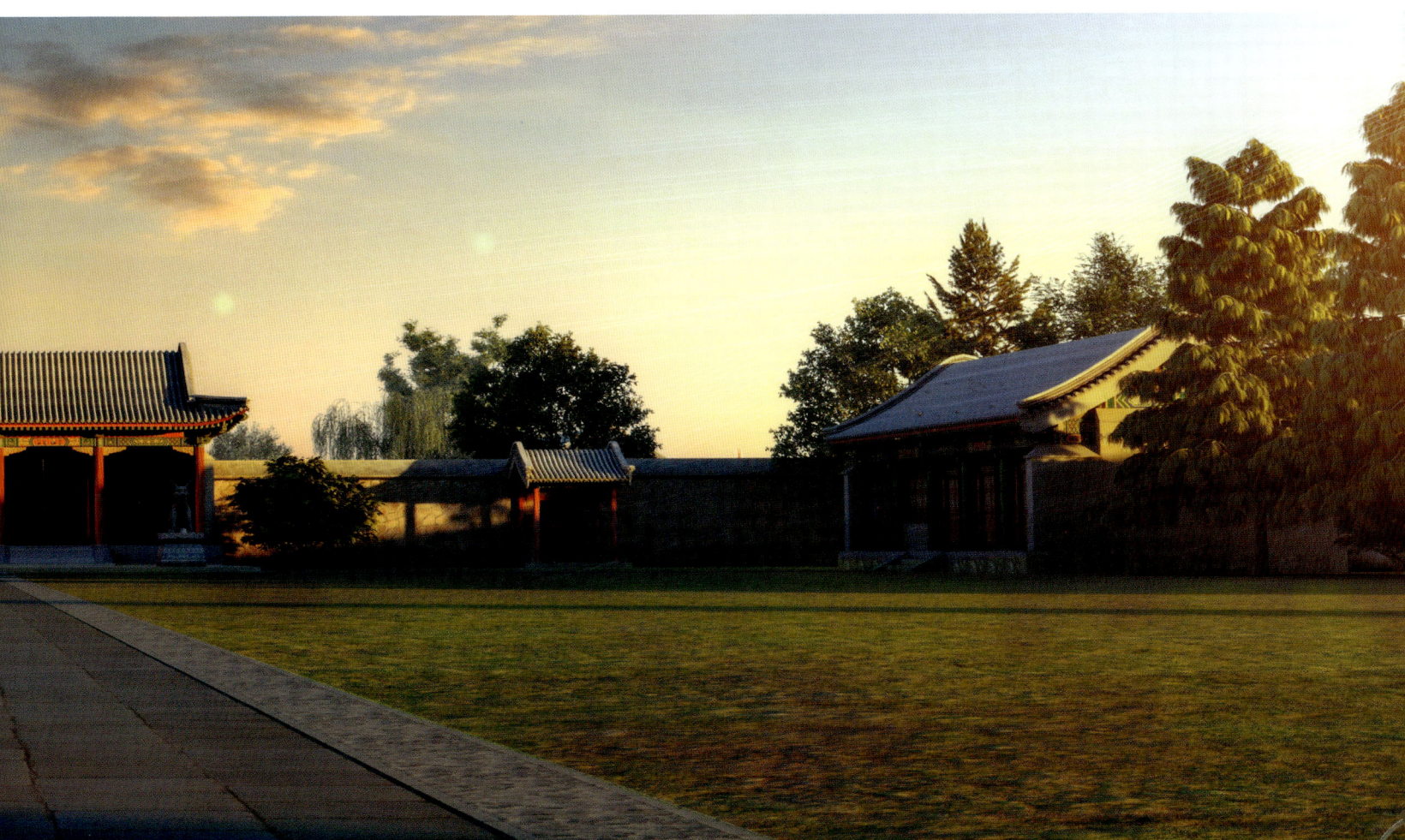

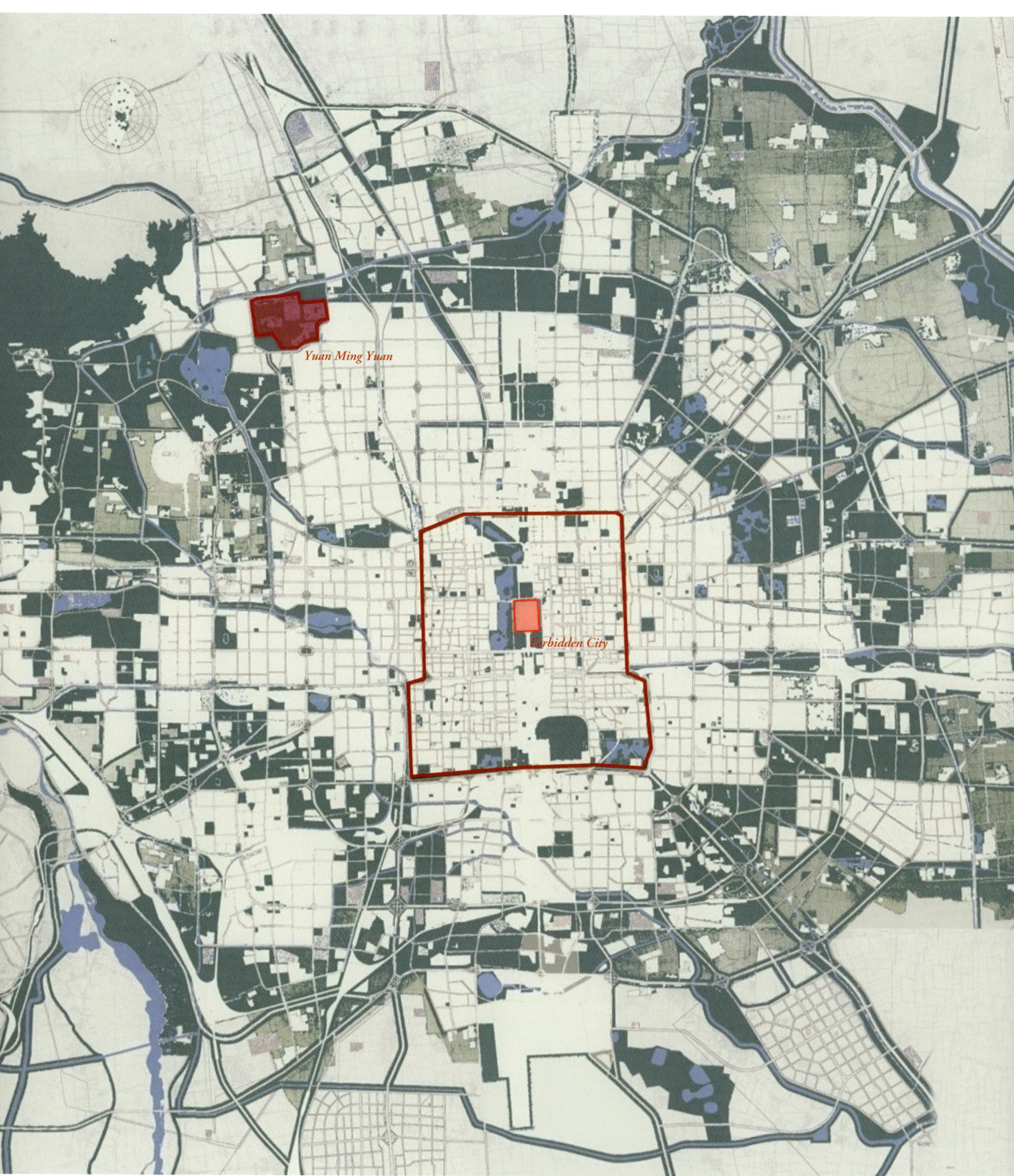

Fig. 6 Map of Yuan Ming Yuan

8 CHINA'S LOST IMPERIAL GARDEN

PREFACE

The Yuan Ming Yuan (Garden of Perfect Brightness) was an imperial garden created in China in the 18th century, at a time when the coffers of the state were full and society enjoyed stability and security (fig. 6). Because of the unique status of the occupant of the garden, the ingenuity and the best available knowhow and techniques of all the foremost designers and craftsmen of the Chinese garden went into its creation, with no expenses and resources spared. The uncommon personal cultural achievements of emperors Yongzheng and Qianlong also contributed in no small measure to the successful creation of this exquisite garden. Its dazzling variety of shape and form and color earned high praise in the world and the name of "Garden of Gardens." Its achievement in the art of garden design won worldwide renown and the Garden was acclaimed as epitomizing the best of oriental art and prompted Victor Hugo to write that "All that can be begotten of the imagination of an almost extra-human people was there." But it was burned to the ground by foreign troops that invaded China. This has left a lasting wound in the hearts and minds of the Chinese nation. Today the once glorious garden lies in ruin, with only a scattering of relics on view for visitors to this park of ruin.

In the beginning of the 20th century the Yuan Ming Yuan regained the attention of Chinese scholars, who began to search for documentation, data and relics related to the Garden both at home and abroad. Research gradually expanded but was often restricted to certain areas of it. By the end of the 20th century, our project team decided to undertake a comprehensive study of the Garden with a view to restoring its long lost glory. After fifteen years of work, during which time our researchers consulted voluminous historical literature, documentation and data, some of which were notes scribbled by garden craftsmen in haste or fragments of records maintained by officials overseeing the construction, we realized for the first time the Garden's true value. When our project team met teams conducting archaeological work in certain areas of the Garden, our team would follow up and collect data from the archaeologists. We sent out large teams to conduct surveys of exposed sites to obtain data that would help an understanding of the dimensions of the buildings that used to stand on those sites.

After several years of work, we have completed drawings that recreated the original appearances of hundreds of buildings and a large number of themed areas of the Garden and have identified the plant species and their locations. After sorting through historical data, we have been able to finally tease out little known details and clarify numerous unresolved questions; questions such as where the emperor transacted the business of government and how he did it; or where the emperor, the empress and the empress dowager lived; where the emperor's sons lived and studied; the reason for the large number of libraries and studies in the Garden; what were the distinguishing features of various buildings; what were the venues where the emperor interacted with his ministers and what differentiated these venues from others; what was the reason for the presence of large areas planted to crops; the existence of religious buildings in the Garden and how they differed from the Buddhist and Daoist temples in society; what kind of ornamental trees and flowers were planted; what were the entertainments of the emperor, the empress and their sons in the Garden; the locations of the buildings where the emperor received foreign guests and tribal leaders; the genesis of the Xiyang Building Complex (Complex of European Buildings) in the Garden and the secrets hidden in them; and the changes the Garden went through in the 150 years during which five emperors held court in the Yuan Ming Yuan.

This book answers these questions and gives an exposé of the profound historical and cultural significance of the Yuan Ming Yuan. It offers an analysis of the emperors' aesthetic visions, the garden designers' approaches and techniques and an art of garden design rooted in traditional Chinese culture. The book also contains a virtual recreation of the entire Yuan Ming Yuan with the aid of digital technology.

Through this book we are sharing with a wider public the results of our research and hope to re-present the magnificent Garden of Gardens in all its historical glory.

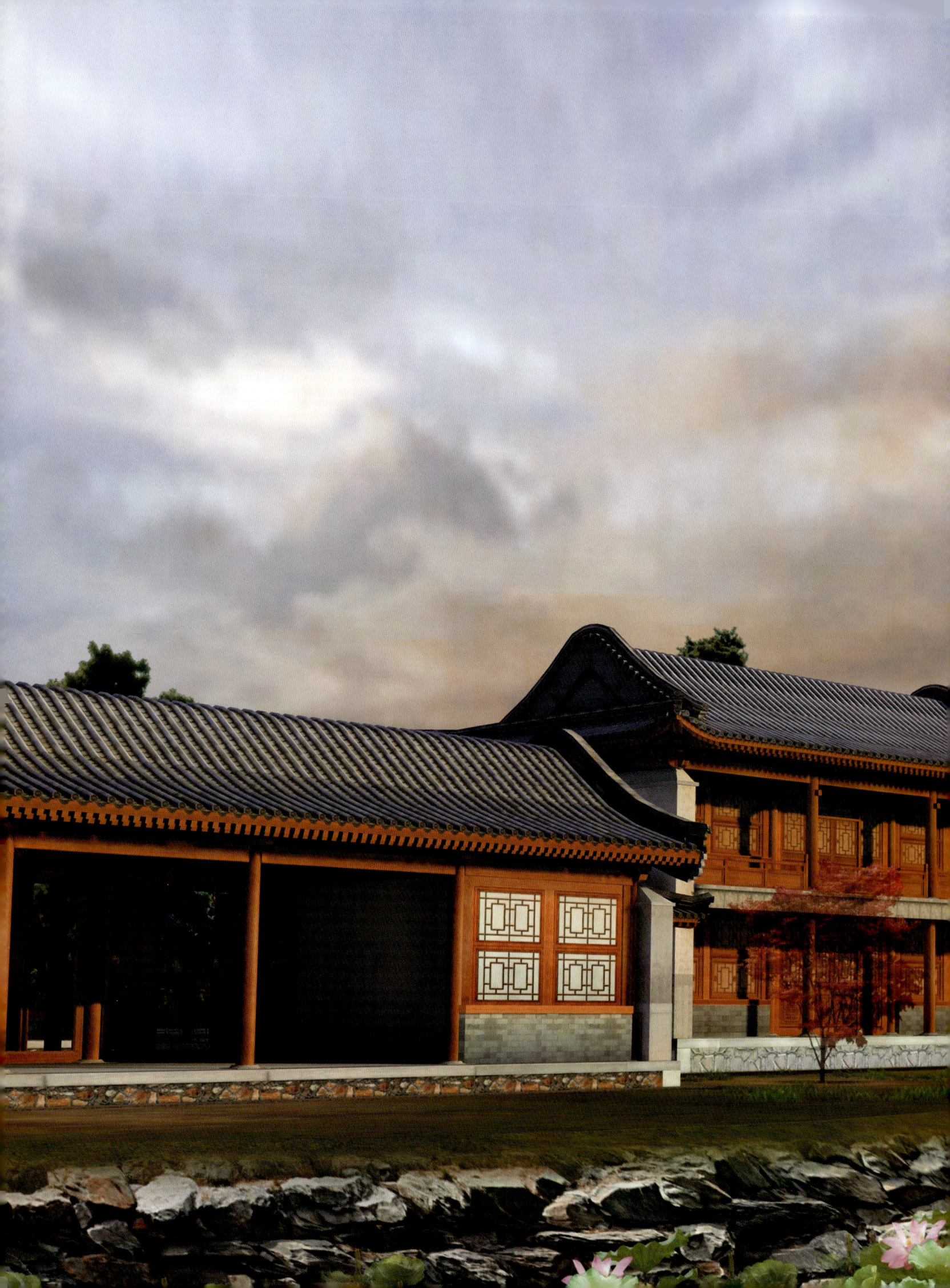

PART I
MASTERS OF THE YUAN MING YUAN

The Yuan Ming Yuan was an imperial park in China in the Qing period (1644–1911). It was situated in the suburbs of Beijing, 10 kilometers north-west of the Qing capital. Beijing, a city built at the foothills of the Yanshan Mountains, was well-endowed with natural landscapes. Since the year the Jin dynasty (1115–1234) set up its capital here and renamed it Zhongdu (the central capital) in the 12th century (1153), the Jin emperors had started building their "palaces away from the palace" in the northwest suburbs of the capital. More imperial gardens, private gardens and temples sprang up in these environs in the Yuan (1279–1368) and the Ming (1368–1644) periods. In the Qing period Emperor Kangxi built his own Changchun Garden (Joyful Spring Garden) on the ruins of a garden built for the Ming royal family. More gardens were built in the vicinity which he granted to his sons. The Yuan Ming Yuan was originally built for his fourth son, Prince Yinzhen, and later became an imperial garden.

The building of the Yuan Ming Yuan started in the 46th year of the Kangxi reign (1707). On the 13th day of the 11th month of the 61st year of the Kangxi era (1722) Yinzhen acceded to the throne and changed the era name to Yongzheng. From that date on the Yuan Ming Yuan assumed an additional function allowing the emperor to govern and give audiences from there, the Yuan Ming Yuan served that function for five emperors for 138 years until the tenth year of the Xianfeng era (1860) when it was destroyed. It became a second center of government outside of the Forbidden City. The political visions and aesthetic tastes of the emperors Yongzheng, Qianlong, Jiaqing, Daoguang and Xianfeng left their marks here. At the same time the Yuan Ming Yuan reflected the rise and fall of the Qing dynasty up to the moment when it suffered fiery destruction at the hands of British and French forces.

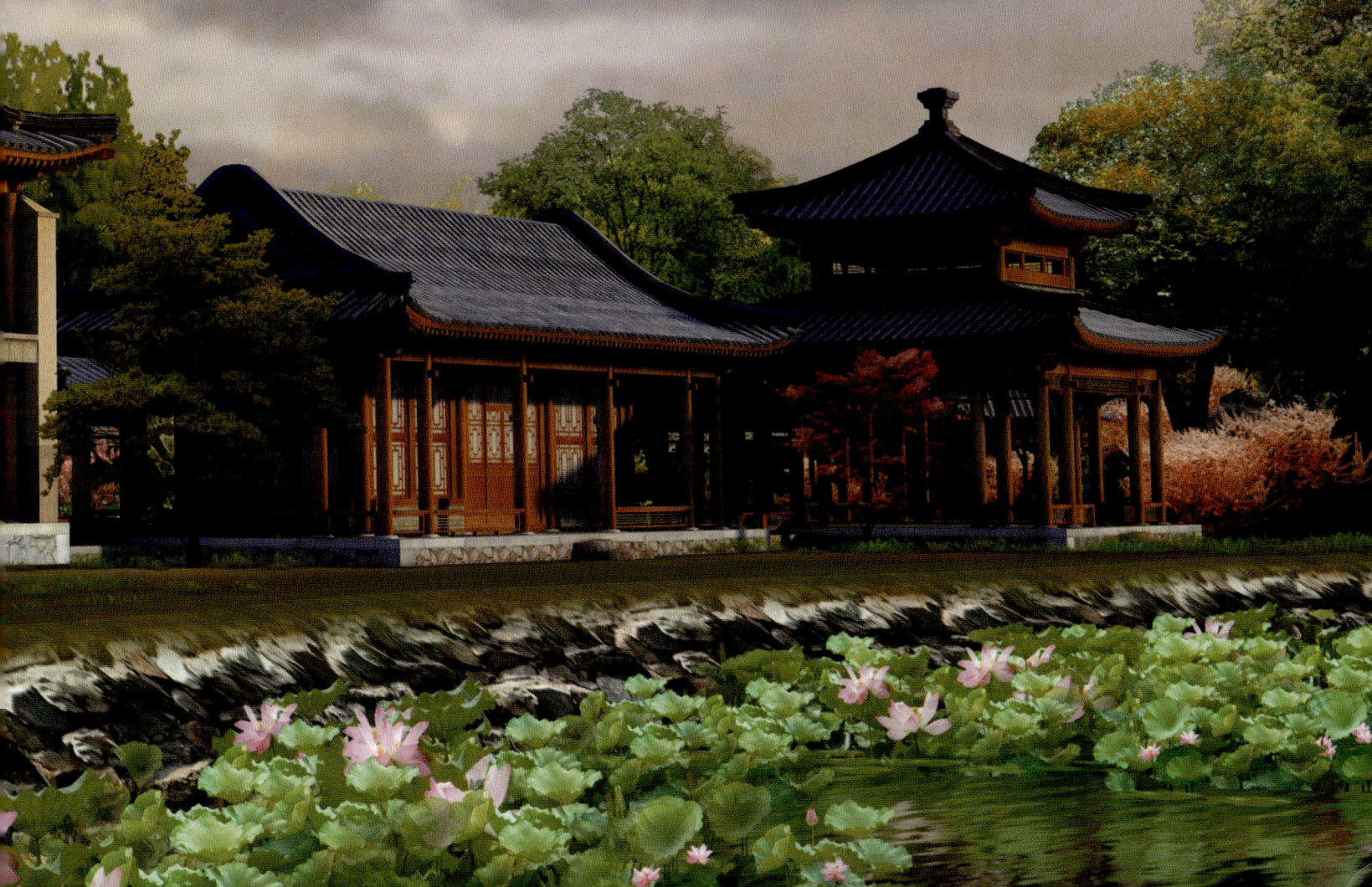

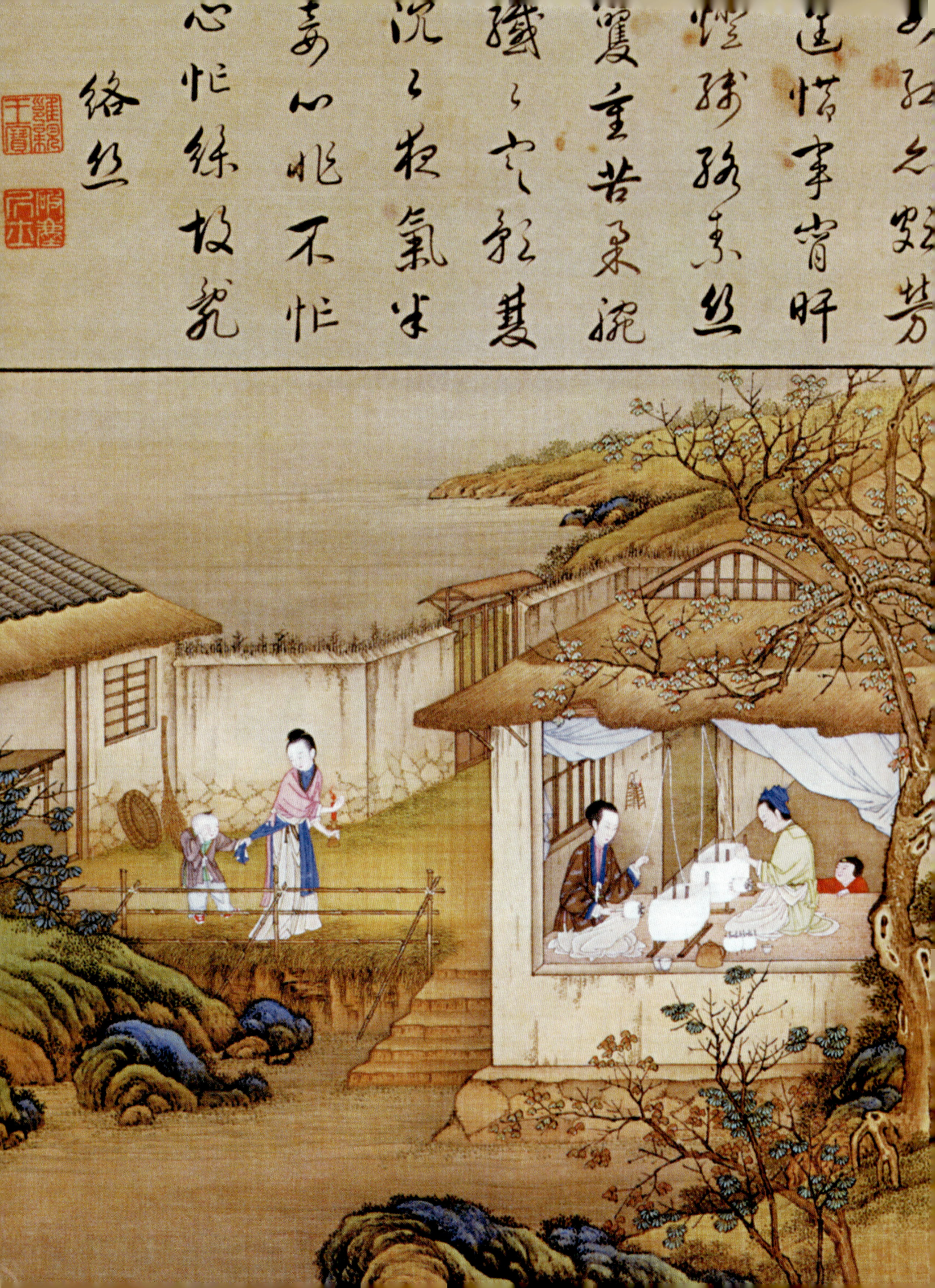

CHAPTER I
A Garden Granted by the Emperor to Yinzhen His Fourth Son

Any account of the Yuan Ming Yuan should begin from the 46th year of the Kangxi era (1707) when the emperor started building the garden to give to his fourth son Yinzhen. Emperor Kangxi had 35 sons, of whom 24 lived to adulthood. The fifth son by the name of Baoqing was made senior son after his four elder brothers died at an early age. By seniority he should have been made the crown prince, but was passed over because he was born of a concubine. The second son Yinreng, who was born in the 13th year of the Kangxi era (1674), filled the bill and was designated heir apparent when he was still in his swaddling clothes. But when the crown prince reached his adulthood, he was set against Emperor Kangxi by ambitious persons surrounding him. This led Emperor Kangxi to strip him

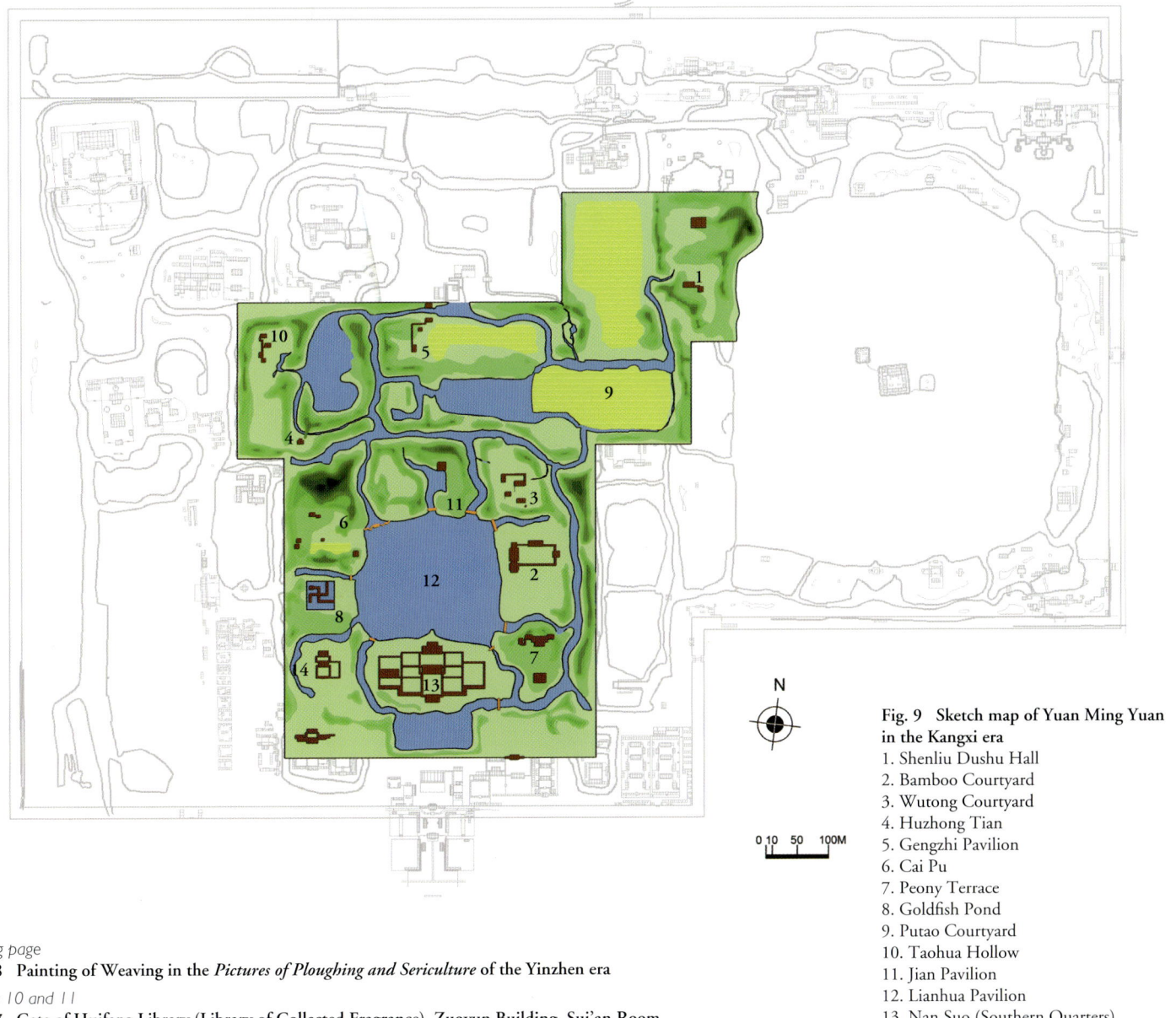

Fig. 9 Sketch map of Yuan Ming Yuan in the Kangxi era
1. Shenliu Dushu Hall
2. Bamboo Courtyard
3. Wutong Courtyard
4. Huzhong Tian
5. Gengzhi Pavilion
6. Cai Pu
7. Peony Terrace
8. Goldfish Pond
9. Putao Courtyard
10. Taohua Hollow
11. Jian Pavilion
12. Lianhua Pavilion
13. Nan Suo (Southern Quarters)
14. Xinan Suo (South-West Quarters)

Facing page
Fig. 8 Painting of Weaving in the *Pictures of Ploughing and Sericulture* of the Yinzhen era

Pages 10 and 11
Fig. 7 Gate of Huifang Library (Library of Collected Fragrance), Zuoyun Building, Sui'an Room (Contentment with One's Lot Room) and Yixiu Pavilion (Taking in the Scenery Pavilion)

of his position as crown prince in the 47th year of his reign (1708). In the intensified fight among the emperor's sons to become heir apparent, Kangxi stripped the noble titles of more than one prince and subsequently restored Yinreng as heir apparent. In the 51st year of his reign (1712) Kangxi once again removed Yinreng as crown prince. It was against this backdrop that the construction of the Yuan Ming Yuan began. Yinzhen's "Odes to 12 Scenes of the Garden"[1] described the following: Shenliu Dushu Hall (Study among Willows), Bamboo Courtyard, Wutong Courtyard (Wutong Tree Courtyard), Taohua Hollow (Peach Blossoms Hollow), Gengzhi Pavilion (Ploughing and Sericulture Pavilion), Cai Pu (Vegetable Patch), Peony Terrace, Goldfish Pond and Putao Courtyard (Grape Courtyard), all of which were known for their natural landscapes. He also mentioned groups of buildings like Huzhong Tian (Universe in a Pot), Jian Pavilion (Pavilion by a Mountain Stream) and Lianhua Pavilion (Lotus Pavilion) (fig. 9).

At the time the Yuan Ming Yuan was a garden built around "natural landscapes," where Yinzhen lived, studied and enjoyed the views; there were not many buildings. Against a backdrop of heated contests for the position of crown prince and a fraught political situation, this fourth son of the emperor with an uncertain future was not in a garden-building mood and let things be. Yinzhen commissioned a *Gengzhi Tu* (*Pictures of Ploughing and Sericulture*)[2], containing 52 illustrations. It was an edition based on the hand-colored woodblock prints of the *Gengzhi Tu* commissioned by Emperor Kangxi. He had the artists "paint the likenesses of himself and his wife"[3] into the pictures as farmers, and had the seal marks of "Yongqinwang Bao" (Prince Yong's Treasure) and "Pochen Jushi" (He Who Sees Through the Vanity of Worldly Things) impressed on the paintings (figs. 8, 10). The first seal mark indicates that the making of the book of paintings coincided with the time of Yinzhen's residence at the Yuan Ming Yuan as a prince (fig. 12). Unlike Kangxi, who as the supreme ruler

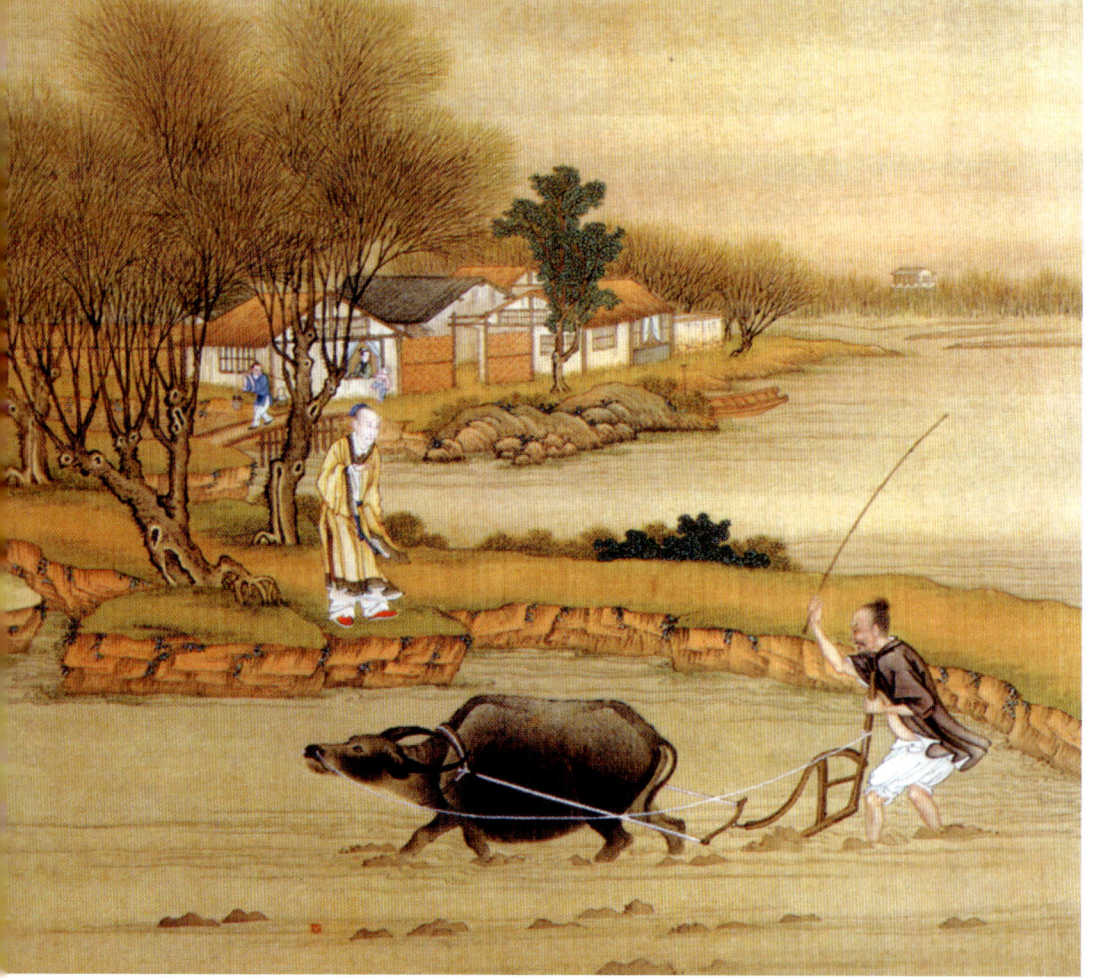

Fig. 10 Painting of Ploughing in the *Pictures of Ploughing and Sericulture* of the Yinzhen era

14   CHINA'S LOST IMPERIAL GARDEN

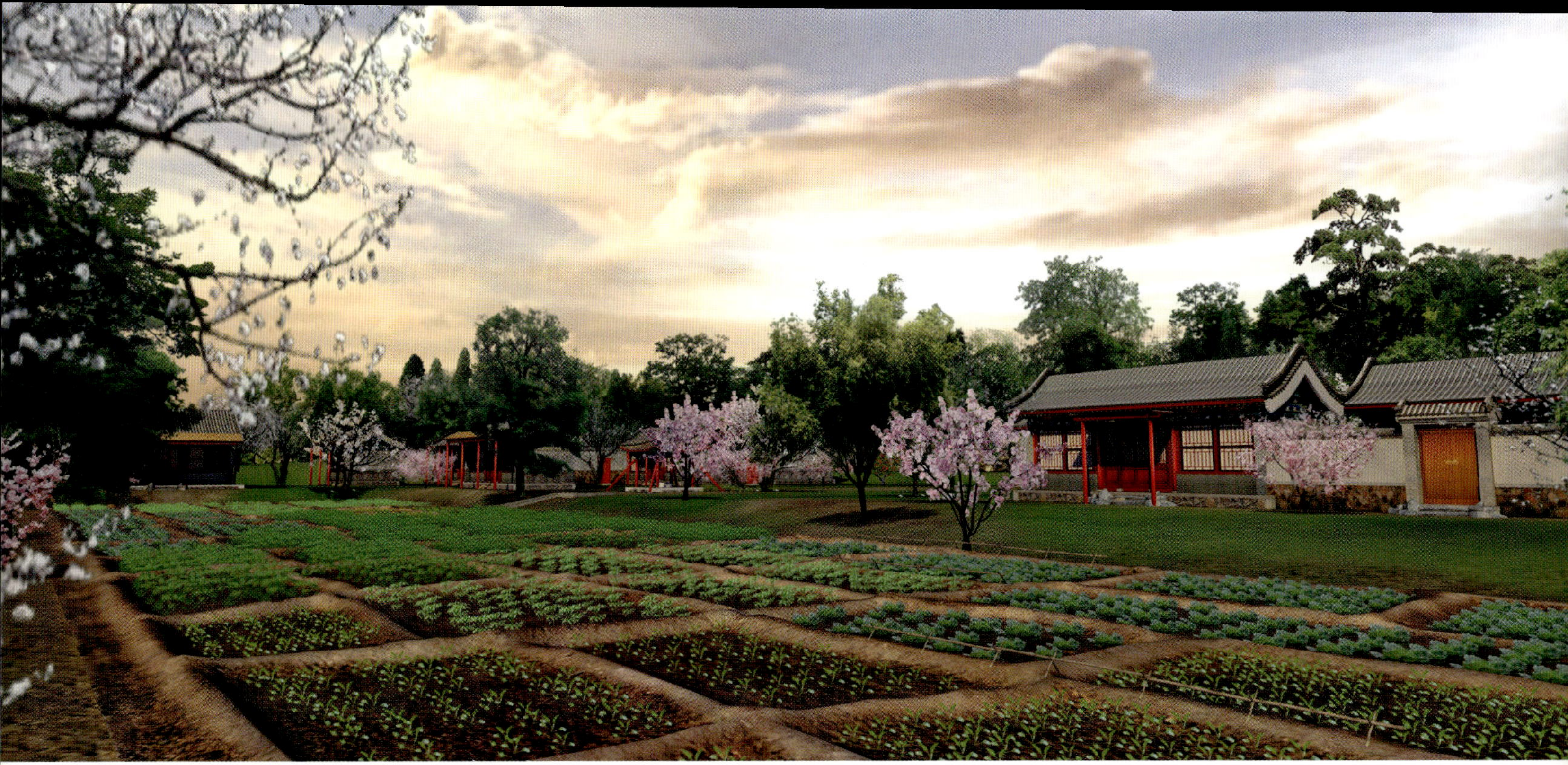

Fig. 11 Xinghuachun Pavilion (Apricot Blossom Spring Pavilion) of an earlier period

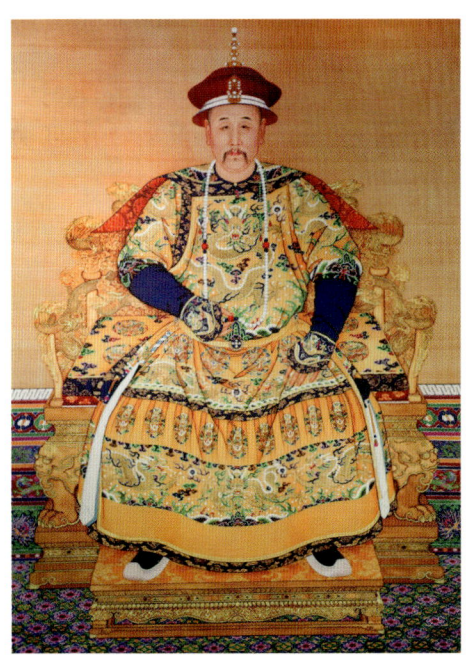

Fig. 12 Portrait of Emperor Yongzheng

was keen to assure the people that his government gave the highest priority to agriculture and sericulture, Prince Yong had something else in mind when he commissioned the paintings. His was the feeling of someone who saw an uncertain future and who saw the possibility that he was destined to become a farmer as depicted in the paintings; hence the appearance of a vegetable patch, a fish pond, a ploughing and sericulture pavilion and even a peach blossoms hollow that evoked an El Dorado out of this world (fig. 11). The second seal mark even more directly reflected the state of mind of Prince Yong, who proclaimed himself to be someone who had seen through the vanities of the world. It was an emotional statement of someone in limbo who adopted the pose of not contending for anything with anybody. He managed the Garden as one that understood that all was vanity and invited his imperial father to the Garden with a view to assuring the emperor that he had no ambitions and that he was adhering to the credo of thrift that Kangxi had been instilling in his princely sons. By so doing he fulfilled his imperial father's expectations and favorably impressed him. Therefore the early development of the Garden reflected Yinzhen's perspicacity in being able to "anticipate the emperor's wishes." The Yuan Ming Yuan of the early period was similar in style to a recluses' retreats among the private gardens.

Emperor Kangxi visited Prince Yinzhen's garden 13 times and gave it the name "Yuan Ming" or "Perfect Brightness." The word "Yuan" or "Perfect," refers to the character of the perfect gentleman; the word "Ming" or "Brightness," refers to his brightening the lives of others, as advocated by the Confucian doctrine of the mean.

---

1 *Shizong Xianhuangdi Yuzhi Wenji* (*Anthology of Emperor Yongzheng's Writings*), Volume 26, "Odes to Twelve Scenes of the Garden."
2 Now in the collection of the Palace Museum in Beijing; first published in 1933 in the *Gugong Zhoukan* (*Palace Museum Weekly*).
3 *Qingshi Tudian* (*Illustrated Dictionary of the History of the Qing Dynasty*), compiled by Zhu Chengru for the Palace Museum.

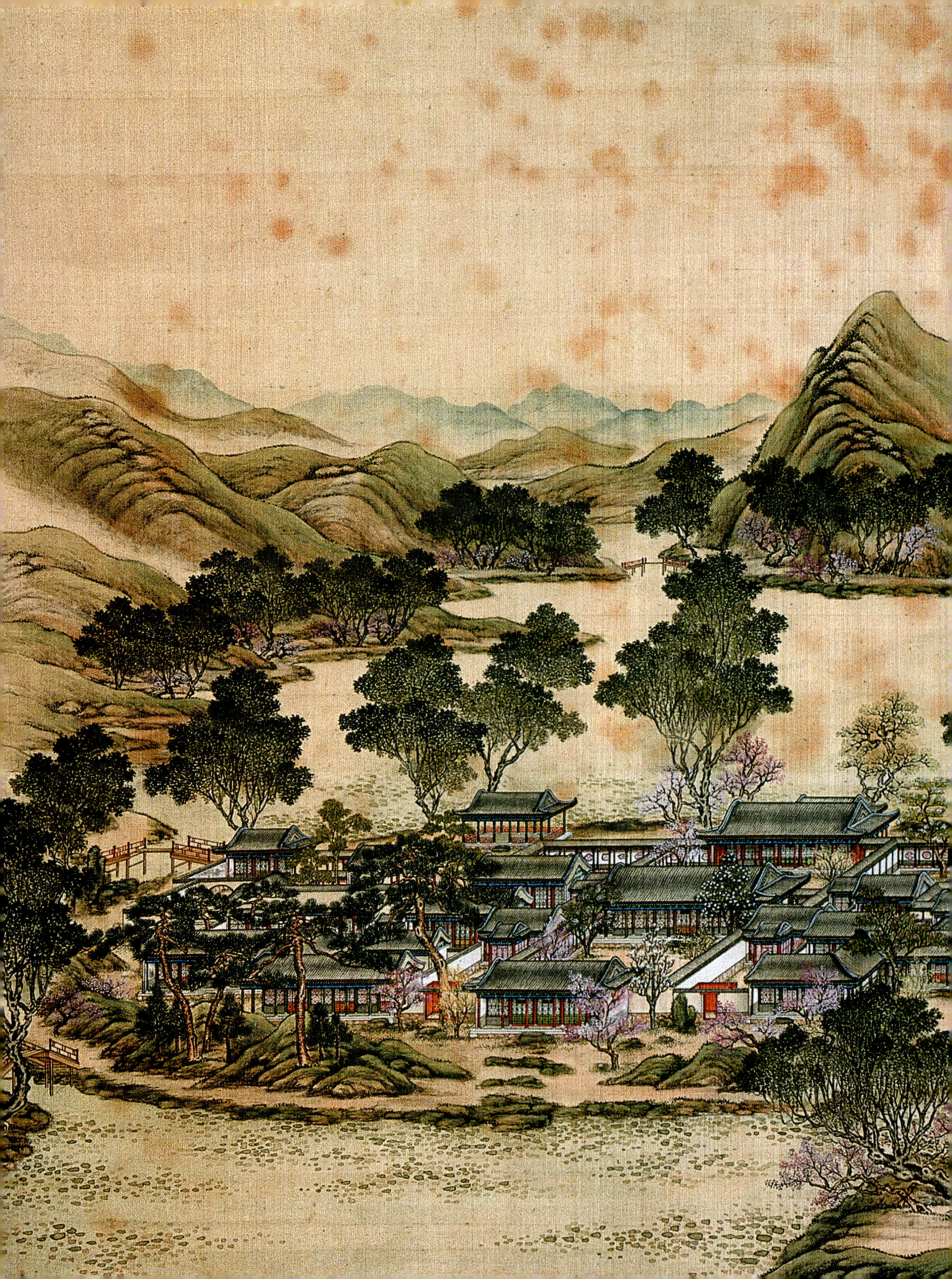

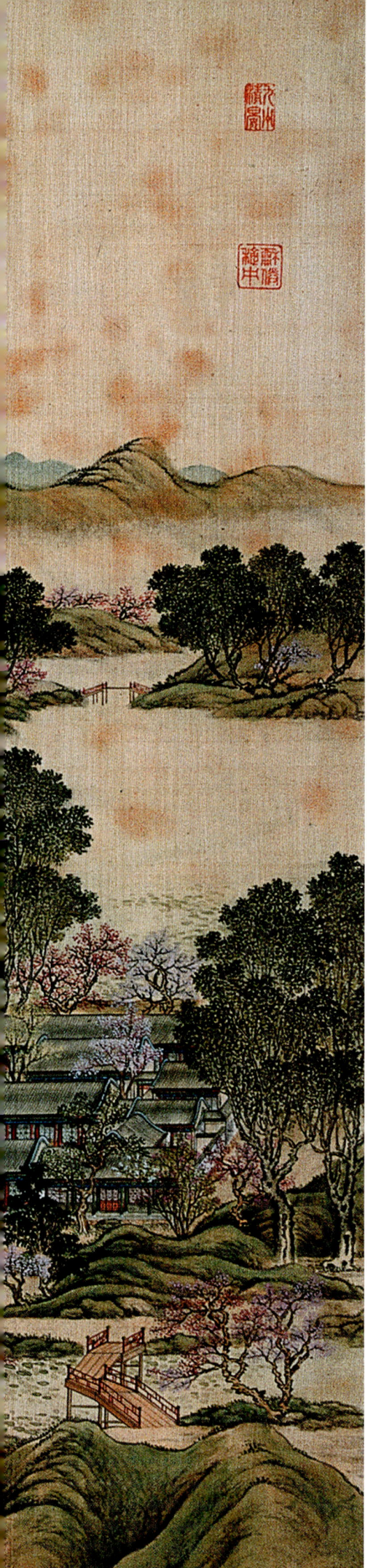

CHAPTER II
The Early Period of the Yuan Ming Yuan as an Imperial Garden

After his accession to the throne Yongzheng used the Yuan Ming Yuan for the daily business of government. He arrived in early spring and departed when winter approached, spending most of the year in the Yuan Ming Yuan transacting the business of governing the country, giving audiences to officials, discussing affairs of state and perusing memorials (fig. 14). For this purpose there had to be a transition from a private garden to an imperial park: halls for holding ceremonial events and for office use went up south of the original garden and separate areas devoted to "government work," "residential use," "agricultural use," "religious use" and "cultural activities" were developed in the Garden. By the 13th year of Yongzheng's reign (1735) the number of such areas had increased to 38 and the Yuan Ming Yuan was transformed into

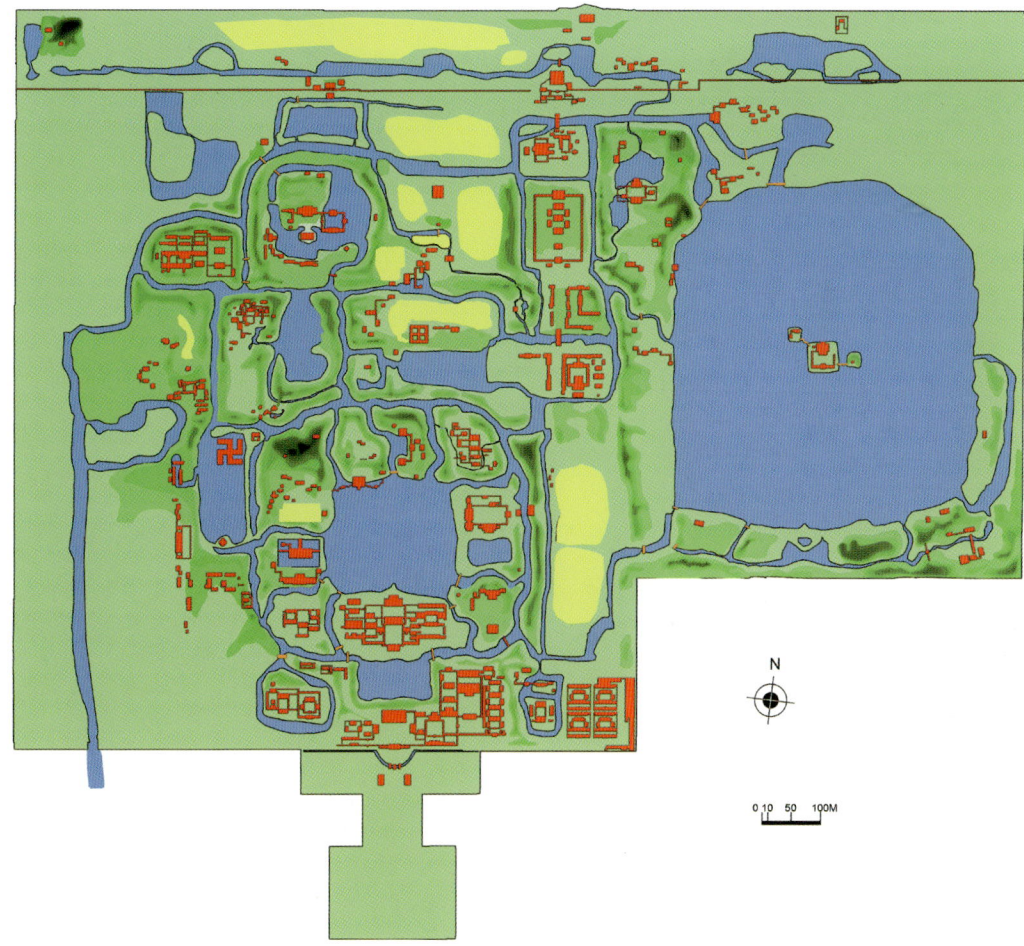

Fig. 14 Sketch map of buildings of Yuan Ming Yuan in the Yongzheng era

Left
Fig. 13 Painting of Jiuzhou Qingyan Complex (Complex of Nine Continents Clear and Calm) from the album of *Forty Scenes of the Yuan Ming Yuan*

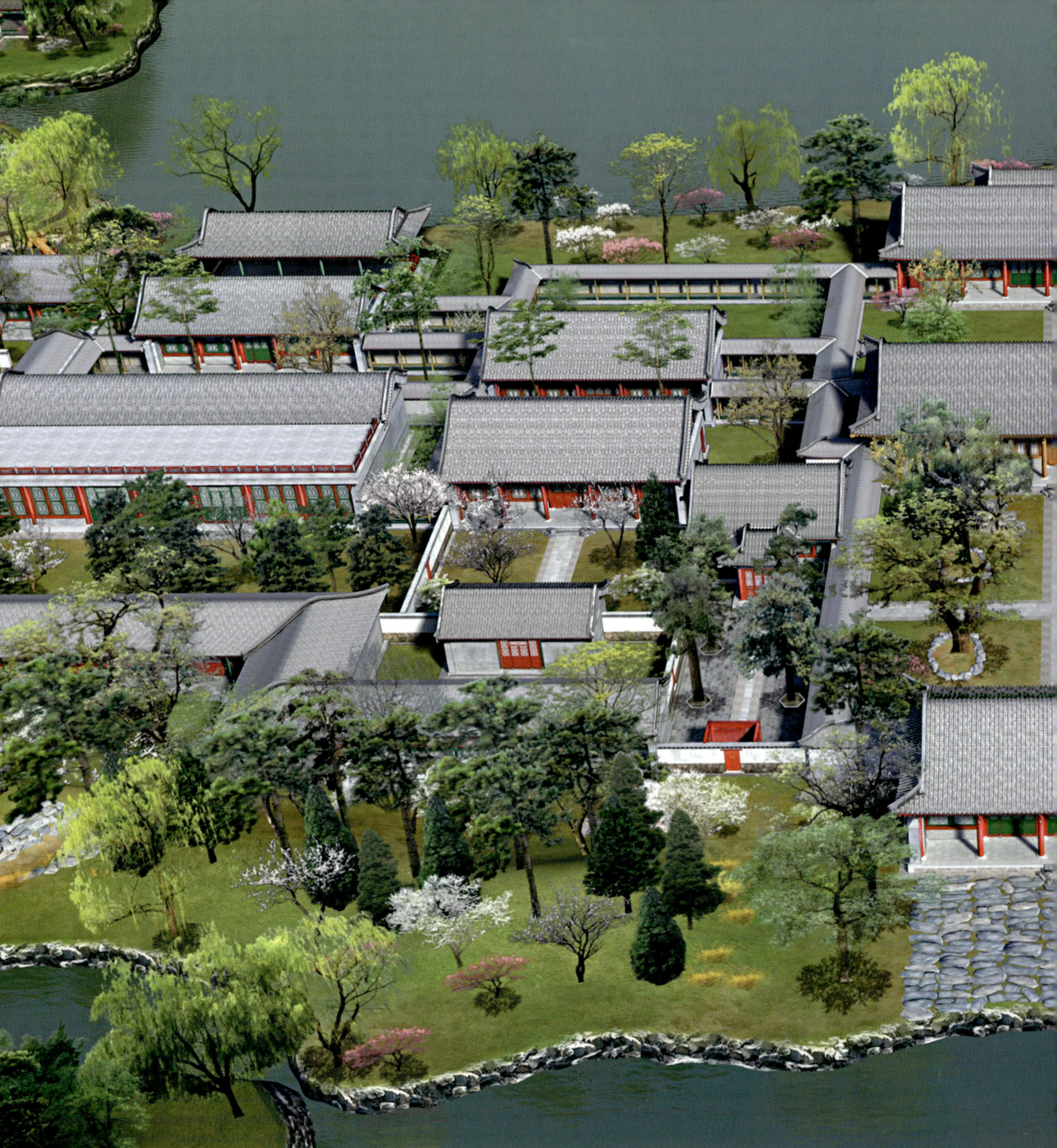

Fig 15 Themed area of Jiuzhou Qingyan Complex

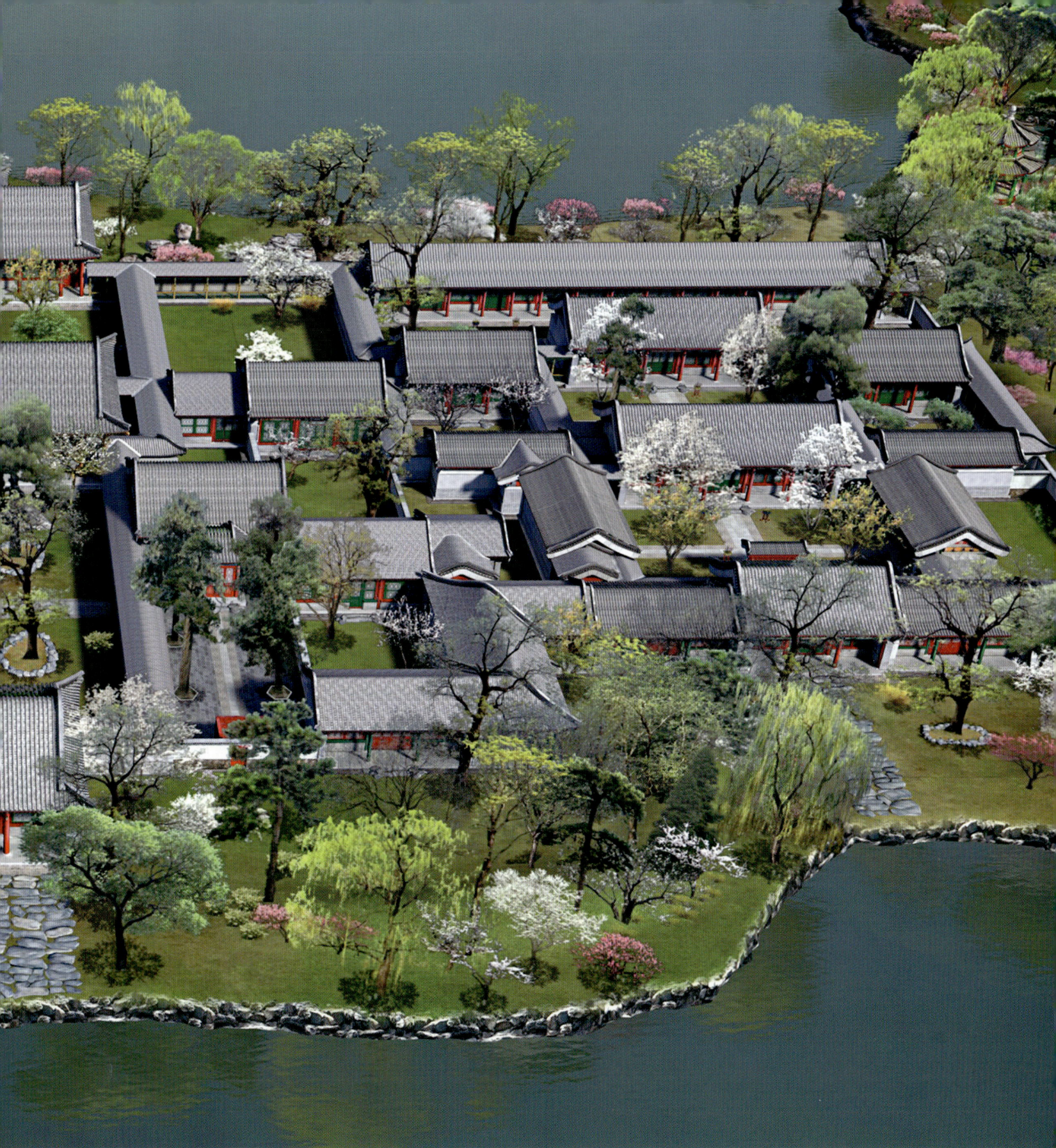

an imperial park of magnificent scale abounding in attractive vistas.

At the period the Yuan Ming Yuan's numerous landscaped complexes already had a rich cultural dimension. Nine islands were created in the middle of the garden and given the name of Jiuzhou Qingyan (Complex of Nine Continents Clear and Calm) to proclaim the supreme ruler's commitment to good governance. Mountains were thrown up in the northwest corner and a big lake excavated in the east of the Garden to symbolize the realm of ancient China (figs. 13, 15).

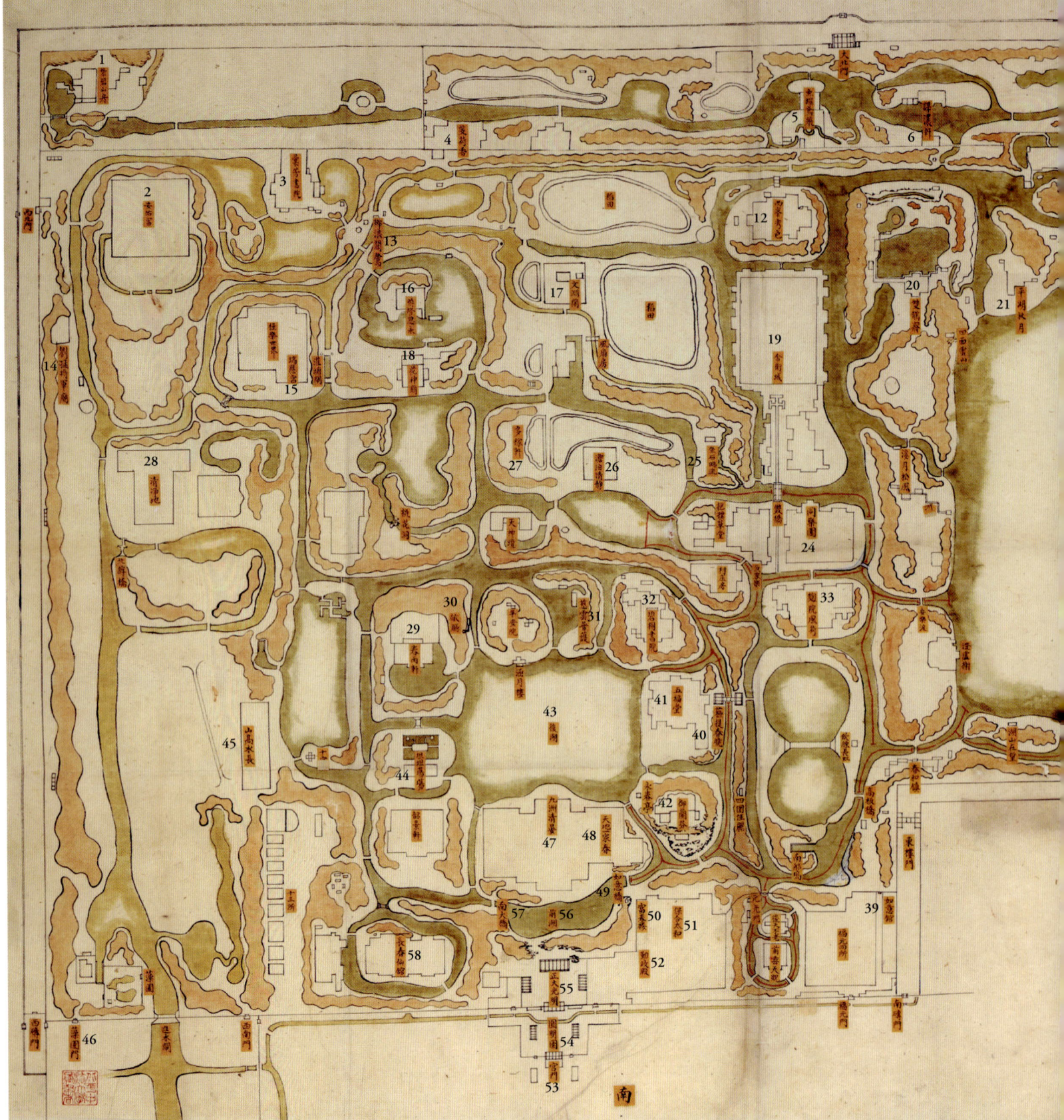

Fig. 16 Plan of Yuan Ming Yuan

1. Zibi Mountain House 2. Anyou Palace 3. Huifang Library 4. Jihexiang Pavilion 5. Yuyue Yuanfei Complex 6. Kenong Pavilion 7. Yinyue Pond 8. Ruizhu Palace 9. Fanghu Shengjing Complex 10. Santan Yinyue 11. Anlan Garden 12. Xifeng Xiuse Complex 13. Liulang Wenying (stone architectural arch) 14. Liumeng Jiangjun Temple 15. Ruiying Palace 16. Shenxiu Siyong Hall 17. Wensu Pavilion 18. Huashen Temple 19. Shewei City 20. Shuanghe Study 21. Pinghu Qiuyue Complex 22. Leifeng Xizhao Open Hall 23. Pengdao Yaotai Complex 24. Tongle Garden 25. Zuoshi Linliu Complex 26. Danbo Ningjing Complex 27. Duojia Pavilion 28. Qingjingdi Complex 29. Chunyu pavilion 30. open hall 31. Ciyun Puhu Complex 32. Bitong Library 33. Quyuan Fenghe Complex 34. Lake of Happiness 35. Xiuqing Village 36. Nanping Wanzhong Pavilion 37. Guangyu Temple 38. Jiajing Mingqin Complex 39. Ruyi Pavilion 40. Sudi Chunxiao Open Hall 41. Wufu Hall 42. Yulan Fen Hall 43. Back Lake 44. Tantan Dangdang Complex 45. Shangao Shuichang Complex 46. Zaoyuan Gate 47. Jiuzhou Qingyan Complex 48. Tiandi Yijia Chun Palace 49. Ruyi Bridge 50. Fuchun Building 51. Baohe Taihe Hall 52. Qinzheng Hall 53. Palace Gate 54. Yuan Ming Yuan 55. Zhengda Guangming Complex 56. Front Lake 57. Great South Bridge 58. Changchun Xianguan Complex

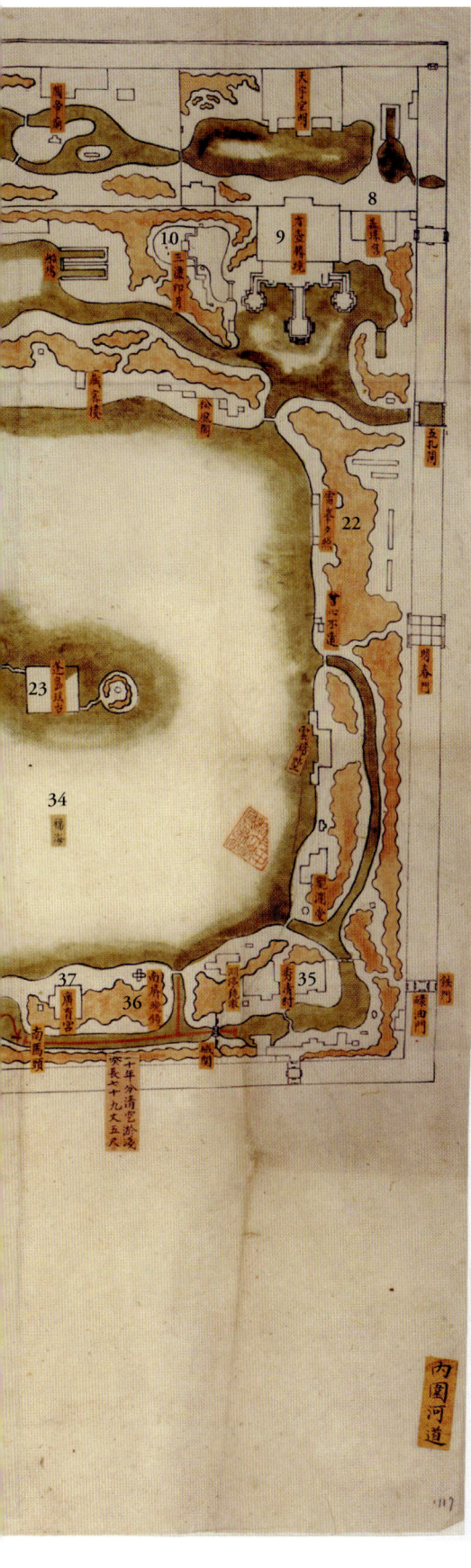

CHAPTER III
Middle Period of the Yuan Ming Yuan as an Imperial Garden—the Five Gardens

Following Emperor Yongzheng's death in 1735 Hongli succeeded to the throne in 1736 and changed the era name to Qianlong.[1] Emperor Qianlong considered the Yuan Ming Yuan already perfect in scale, in its landscapes and vistas as well as its variety of buildings and believed that nothing came close to it as an imperial pleasure park. "Later generations will certainly not desert this place to build other gardens and thus doubly consume the wealth of the people."[2] Therefore he chose to stay in the garden once occupied by his imperial father. But Emperor Qianlong was somehow not totally satisfied with the Garden and undertook some building and rebuilding. New complexes completed at his direction included the Hongci Yonghu (Complex of Vast Compassion and Eternal Blessing), the Jiajing Mingqin (Complex of a Double Mirror and the Sound of the Lute), the Fanghu Shengjing (Complex of the Beautiful Scene of the Square Pot), the Huifang Library (Library of Collected Fragrances) and the Quyuan Fenghe Complex (Complex of Distillery and Lotus Pond). The album of the *Forty Scenes of the Yuan Ming Yuan*, published in the ninth year of the Qianlong era (1744), was a comprehensive depiction of all the themed areas of the Yuan Ming Yuan[3] and adopted the new names given to the themed areas after Yongzheng's accession to the throne, thus giving a cultural dimension to the imperial garden, and adding a philosophical touch through these new names to the landscapes so much prized by the reclusive literati (figs. 16, 17). Thus the Goldfish Pond was renamed Tantan Dangdang (Clear Conscience and Broad Mind) to emphasize his commitment to clean government. The Shenliu Dushu Hall was renamed Kuoran Dagong (Hall of Boundless Impartiality) to stress that there was no room for personal desires in government.[4] The Taohua Hollow was renamed Wuling Chunse (Hollow of Spring Color at Wuling) in an allusion

---

1 Emperor Yongzheng established the practice of concealing the name of the designated heir apparent in a secret box. As early as in the first year of the Yongzheng, Hongli was confirmed as crown prince and the successor's name was put into a box hidden behind the tablet inscribed with the four characters "Zhengda Guangming" (Rectitude and Honor) hanging in the Qianqing Palace.

2 *Rixia Jiuwen Kao* (*Study of Ancient Accounts Heard in the Precincts of the Throne*), Volume 80, "Yuzhi Yuan Ming Yuan Houji" ("Later Record of the Yuan Ming Yuan").

3 Although the *Forty Scenes of the Yuan Ming Yuan* consisted of forty pictures, while the 38 vistas of the Yongzheng era and 5 added by Emperor Qianlong totaled more than that number, some of the vistas could be found in the depiction of a neighboring scene. The album therefore could rightly claim to have included all the scenes in the Yuan Ming Yuan.

4 *Zhouyi Jizhu* (*The Variorum of the Book of Changes*).

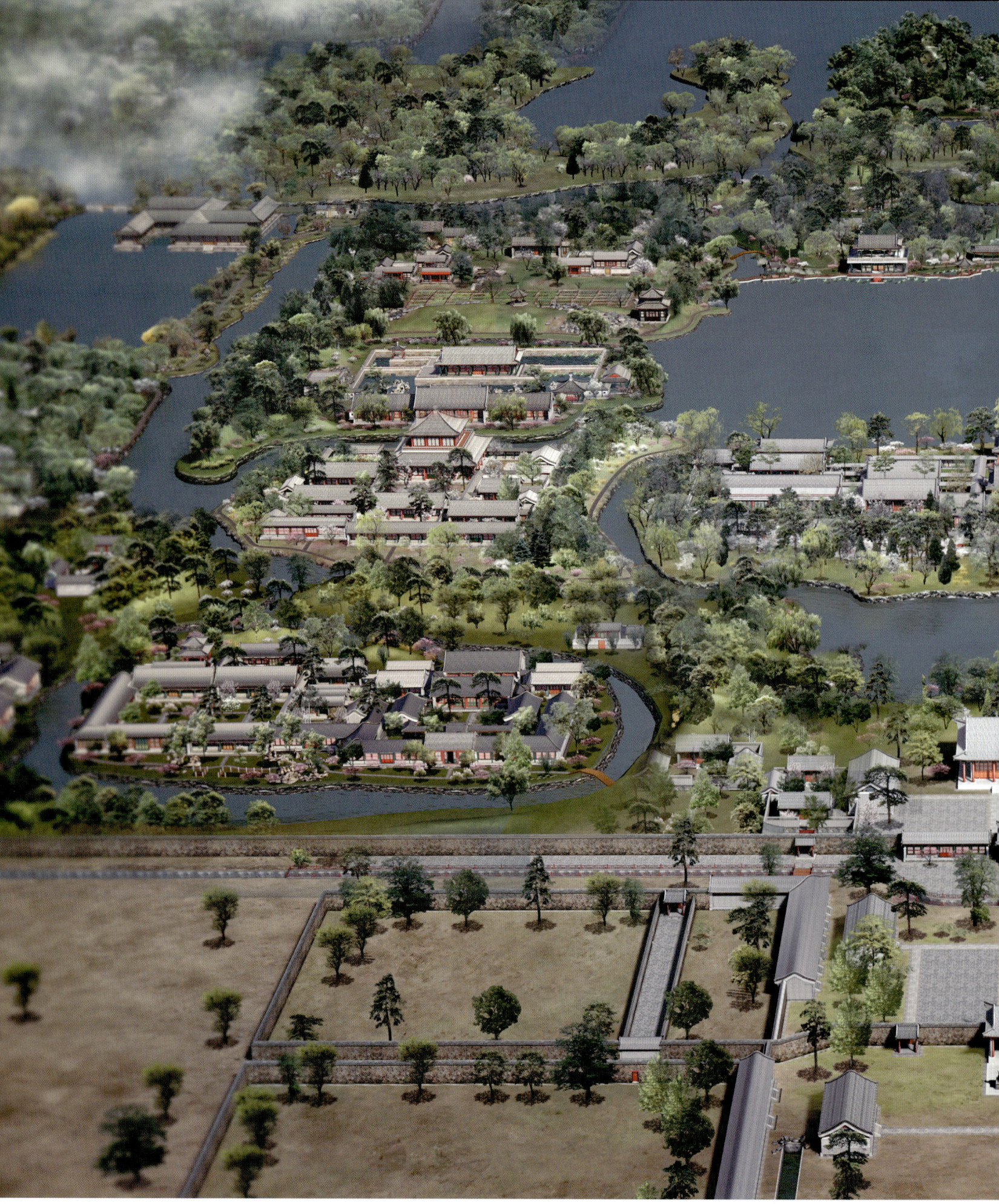

Fig. 17 Core areas of interest of Yuan Ming Yuan

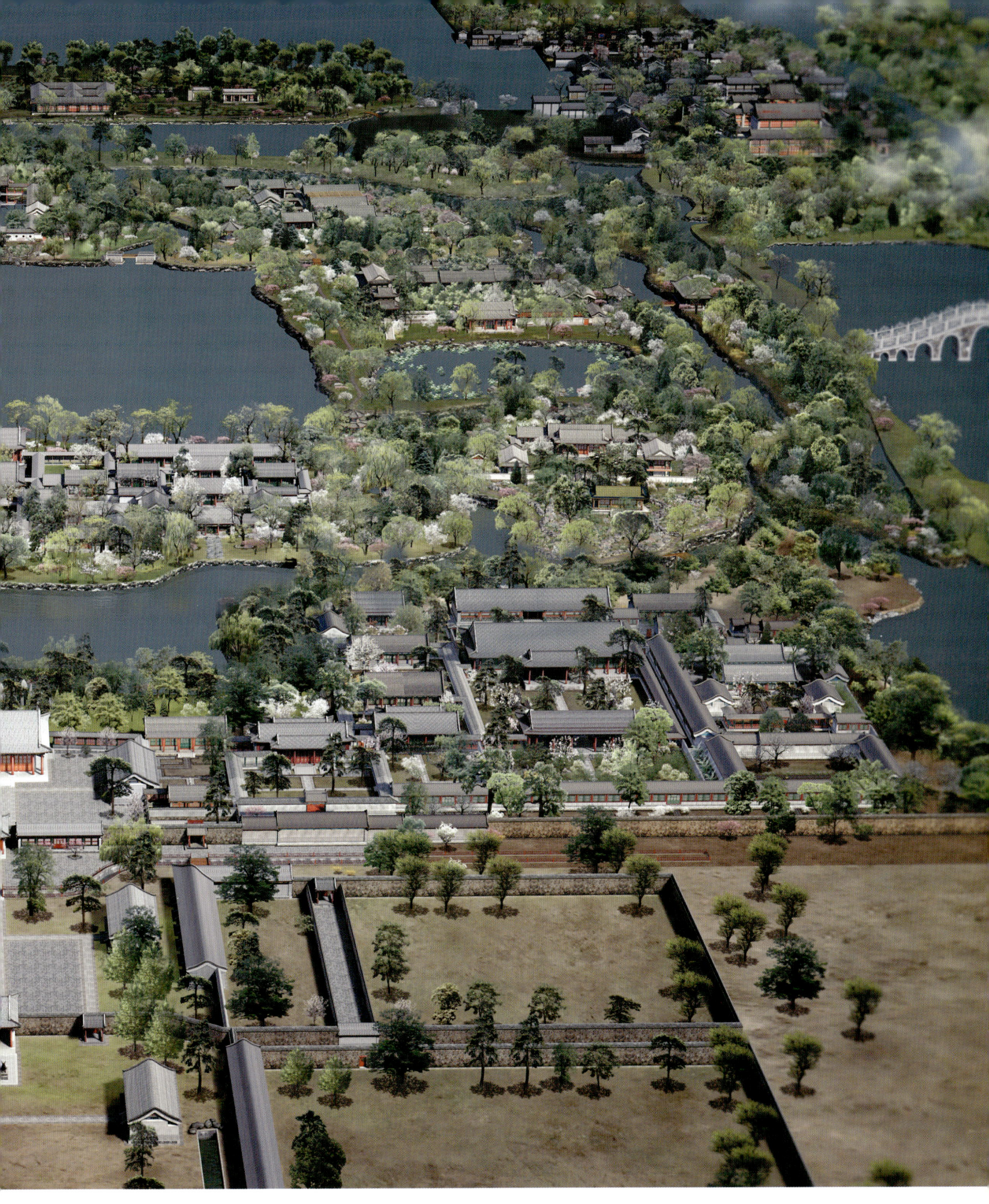

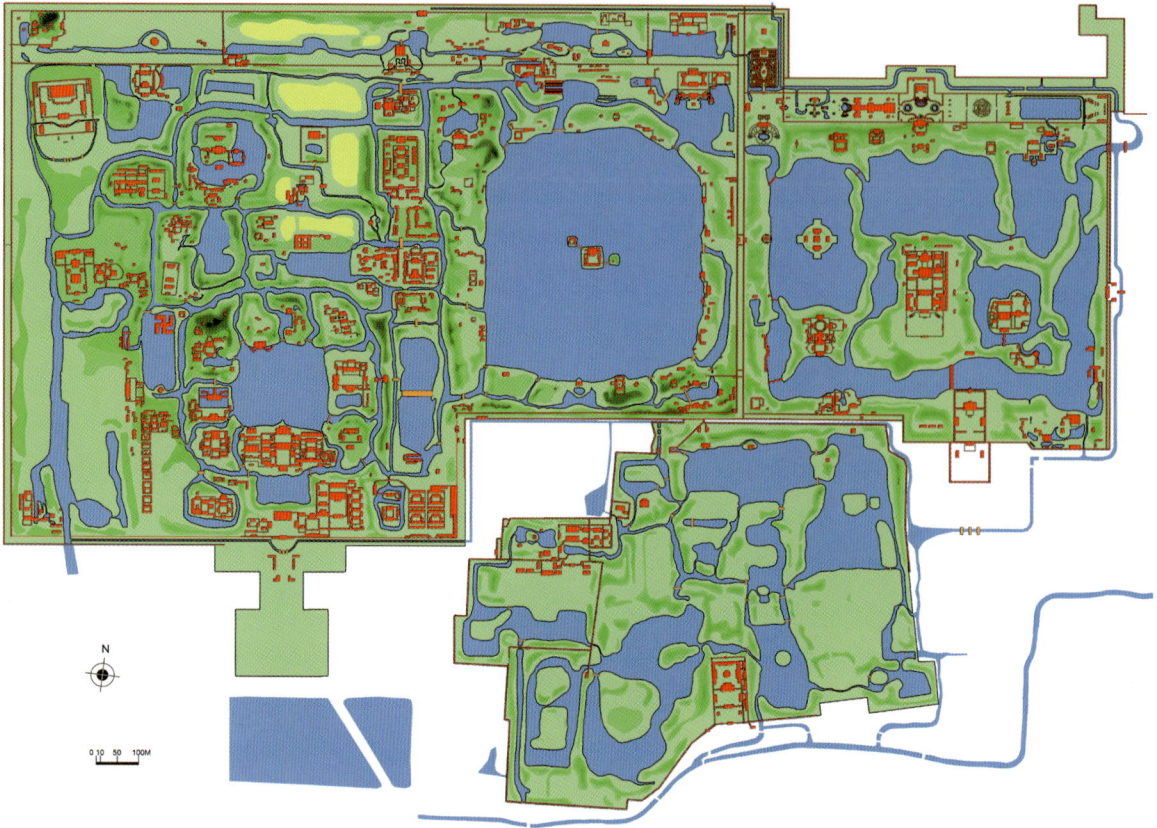

Fig. 18 Sketch map of buildings of Yuan Ming Yuan in mid-Qianlong era

to an idyllic land hidden from the outside world discovered by the people of Wuling, as described in the "Peach Blossom Spring" written by Tao Yuanmig (365–457) of the Jin period (265–420). The "Field" Character Building was renamed Danbo Ningjing Building (Building of Detachment and Serenity) in an allusion to Zhuge Liang's advice to his son: "Without detachment, there is no way to clarify one's purpose; without serenity, one will not go far."[1] The idea was not to forget to improve oneself and to pursue one's purpose in the pleasure of the garden.

In the tenth year of his reign (1745) Qianlong began planning for life after having ceded the reins of government (fig. 19). He chose a vacant space outside the east wall of the Yuan Ming Yuan on which to build a garden for his use after the 60th year of his reign (1795). This was the Changchun Yuan (Garden of Eternal Spring).

The main themed areas of the Changchun Garden included the Danhuai Hall (Simple Needs Hall) in the palace gate area, the Siyong Study, the Yulinglong Pavilion, the Haiyue Kaijin Complex (Complex of Sea of Magnanimity), the Ru Garden, the Jian Garden (Garden of Mirror), the Qian Garden, the Shizi Grove (Lion Grove) and the religious buildings Fahui Temple (Dharma Wisdom Temple) and Baoxiang Temple (Jeweled Image Temple), as well as the Xiyang Building Complex. The building groups were scattered among the islands in the garden or along the periphery of the garden separated by lakes. The Ru Garden, Jian Garden, Qian Garden and the Shizi Grove were modeled on private gardens of Jiangnan south of the Yangtze River, a reflection of Qianlong's taste for Jiangnan-style gardens acquired following his several southern tours. The set of Xiyang Building Complex was constructed because Emperor Qianlong thought there was no reason a country as large as China should not have some foreign buildings on its soil.

In the meantime Emperor Qianlong ordered that the gardens originally granted to members of the royal family in the vicinity of the Yuan Ming Yuan be taken back by the government. In the 34th

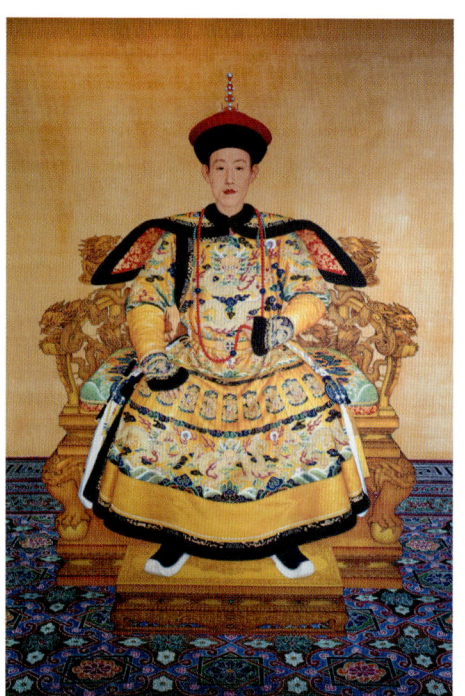

Fig. 19 Portrait of Emperor Qianlong

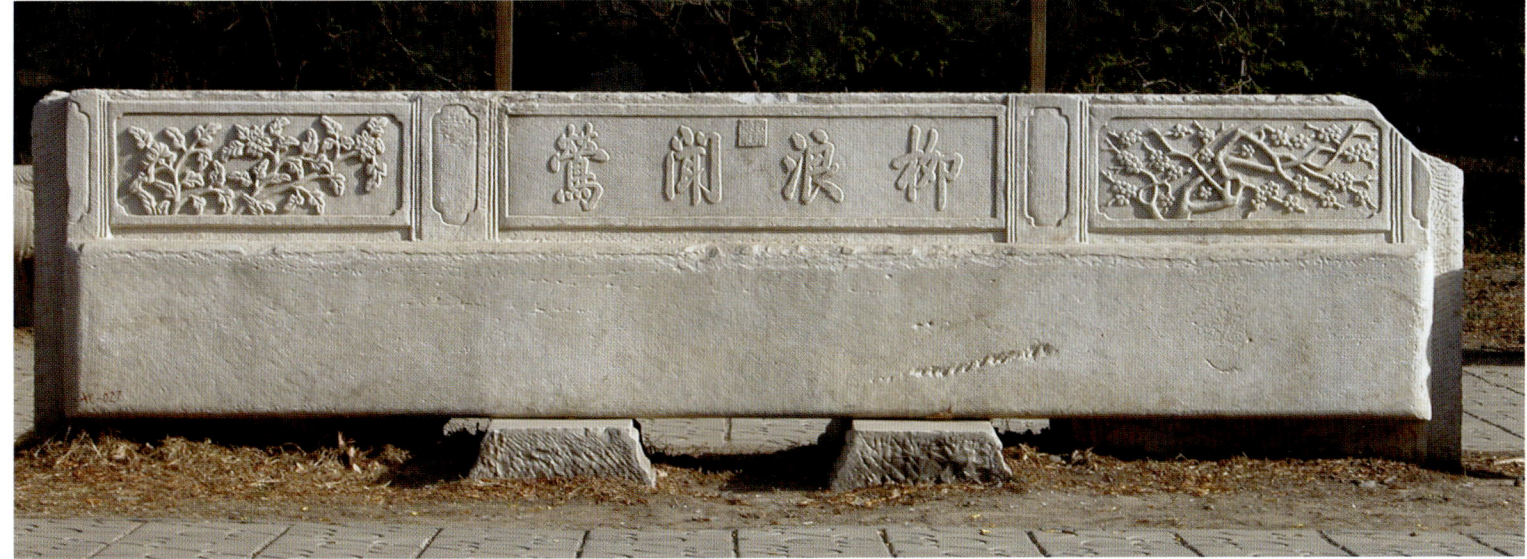

Fig. 20 Liulang Wenying of the Ten Scenes of West Lake in the Yuan Ming Yuan

year of the Qianlong era (1769) the garden of the Grand Secretary Fu Heng and his son Fu Long'an was the first to revert to the Court and was renamed Qichun Garden (Garden of Elegant Spring) the following year (1770). In the 38th year of the Qianlong era (1773) the ZhengJue Temple (Temple of Supreme Perfect Enlightenment) was built in the Qichun Garden.

In the same period the Xichun Garden and the Chunxi Courtyard (Courtyard of Harmonious Light in Spring) in the environs of the Yuan Ming Yuan were also included in the jurisdiction of the latter; this imperial park of unprecedented size was called the Five Gardens of the Yuan Ming Yuan (fig. 18).

Qianlong's rebuilding and use of the Yuan Ming Yuan was heavily influenced by his striving to be a ruler who was a sage at heart. This was conspicuously reflected in the impressive proportion of three categories of buildings in this imperial park that greatly exceeded those of other imperial park: libraries, ethics-related buildings and buildings with an agricultural theme (figs. 20, 21). In 1796 Qianlong abdicated after a reign of sixty years and chose his 15th son Yong Yan as his successor with the era name of Jiaqing.

1 *Taiping Yulan (Taiping Imperial Readings)*, Volume 459.

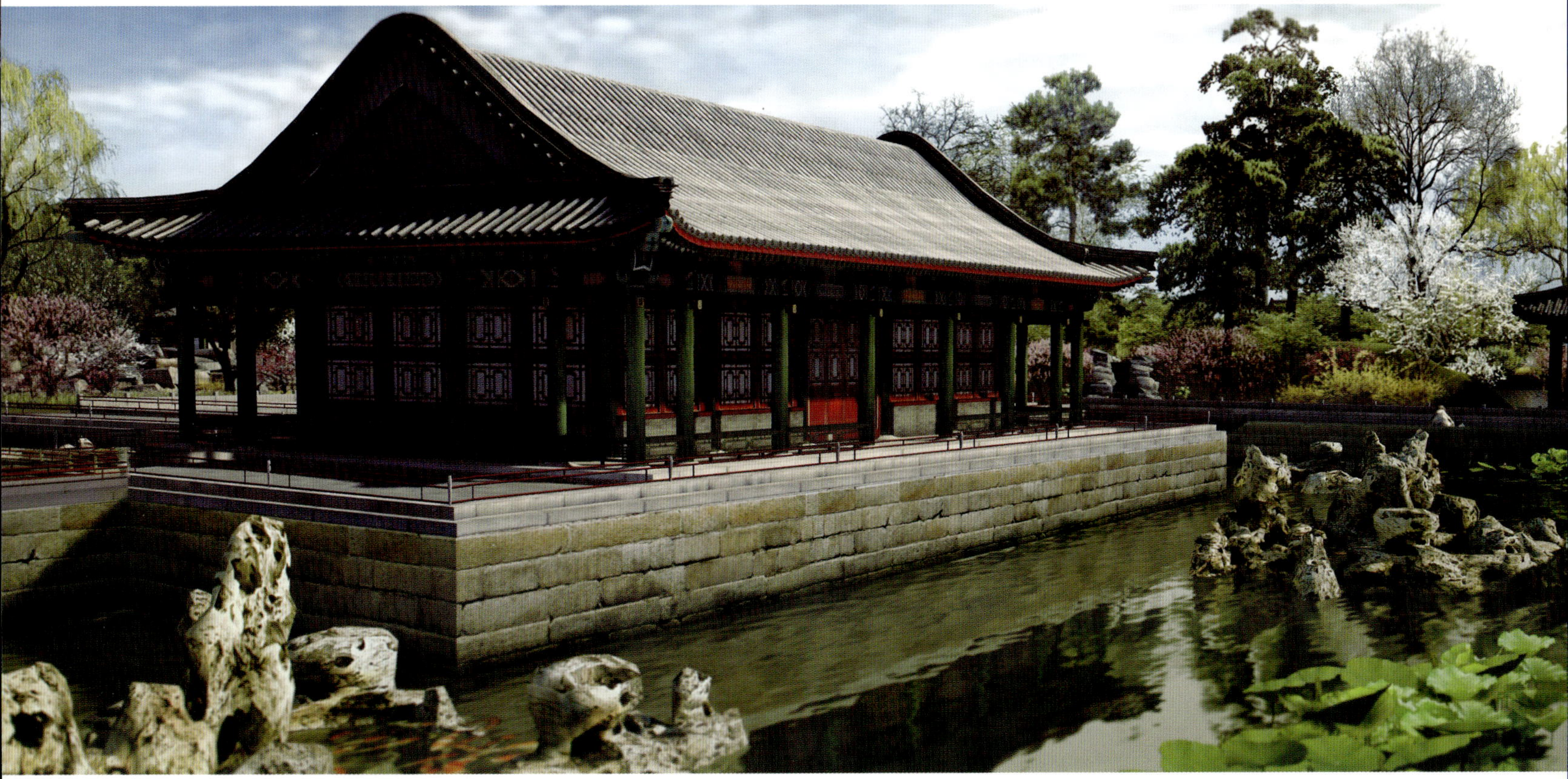

Fig. 21 The Guangfeng Jiyue Hall (Hall of Breeze and Moon after a Rain) of the Tantan Dangdang Complex

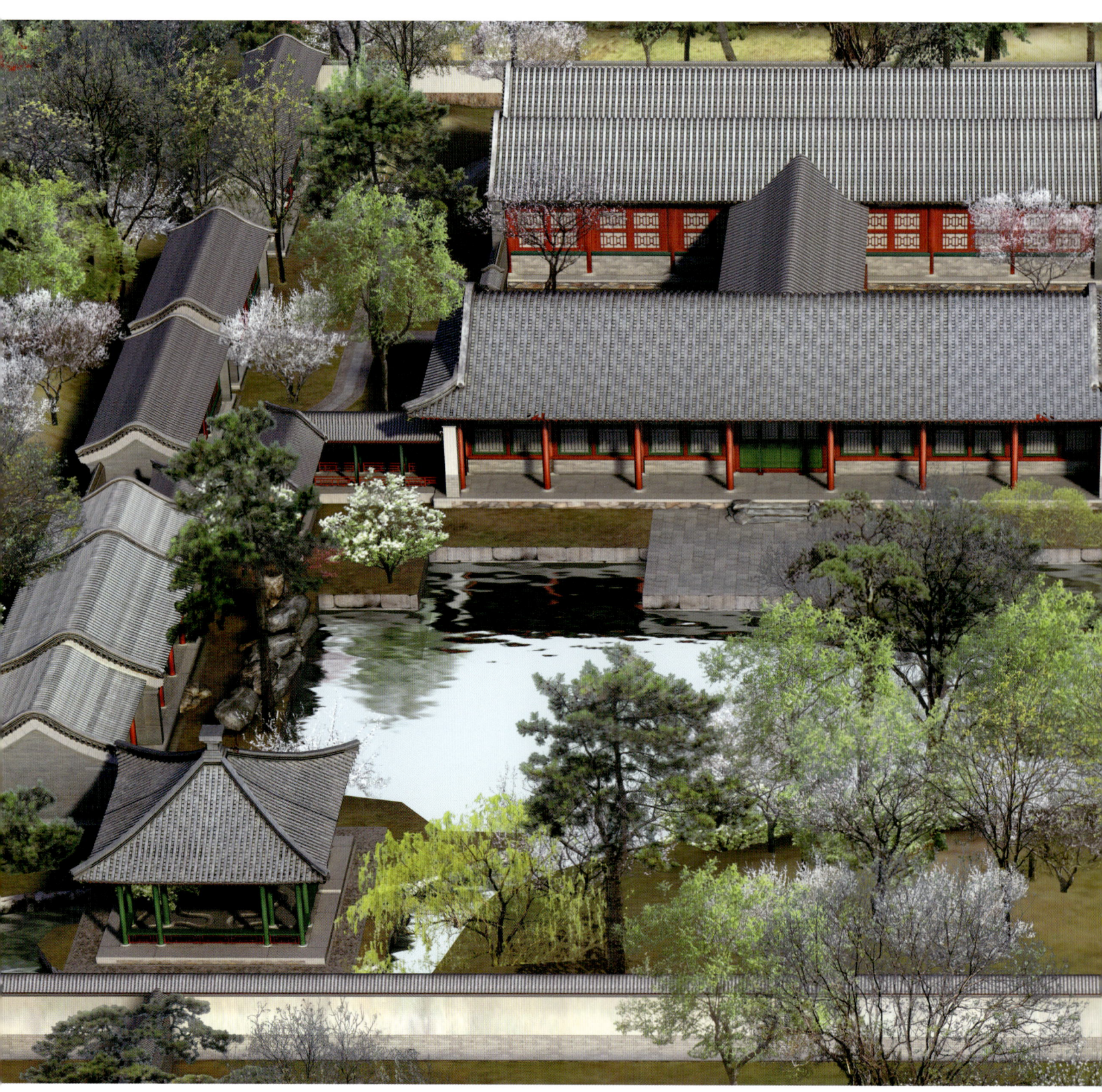

CHAPTER IV
The Late Period of the Yuan Ming Yuan—the Three Gardens

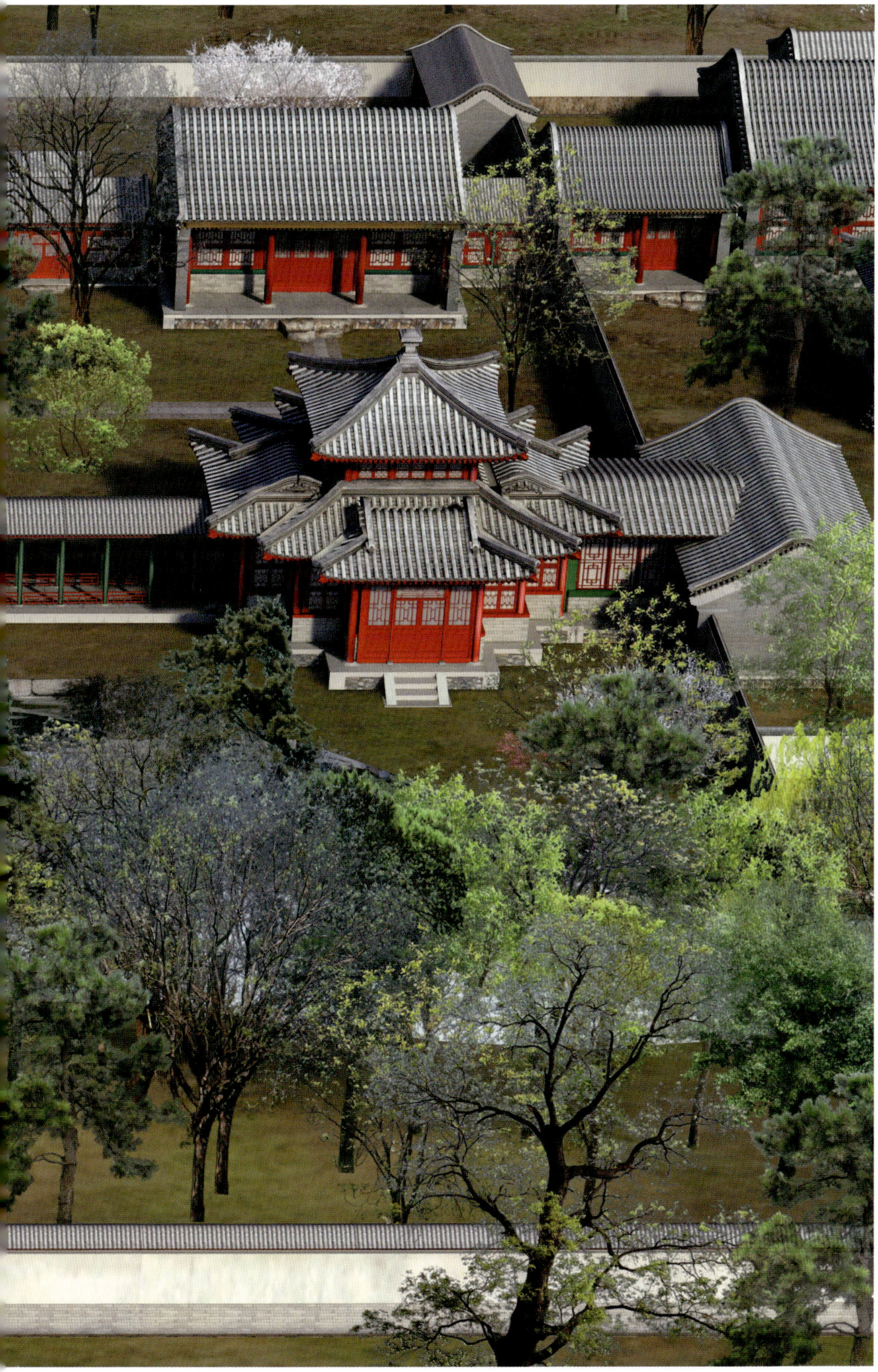

After his accession to the throne Jiaqing (fig. 23) mainly brought improvements to the Yuan Ming Yuan. Garden development overseen by him was focused in the Qichun Garden (fig. 22). A number of private gardens were taken back by the Court; some landscapes were added to the middle section of the Qichun Garden and a number of landscapes in the southwest were transformed, with the addition of the hall called Yishou Pavilion (Longevity Nurturing Pavilion) near the palace gate that served as

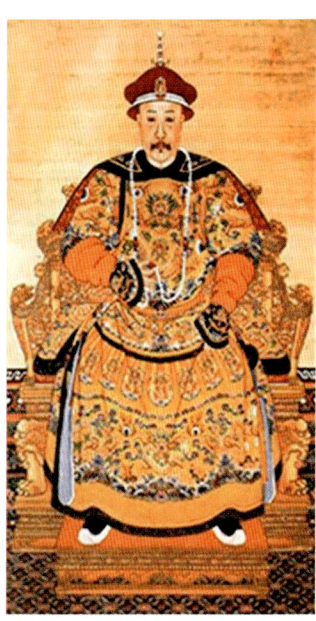

Fig. 23 Portrait of Emperor Jiaqing

Fig. 22 Qingxia Study of the Qichun Garden (Garden of Elegant Spring)

PART I MASTERS OF THE YUAN MING YUAN   27

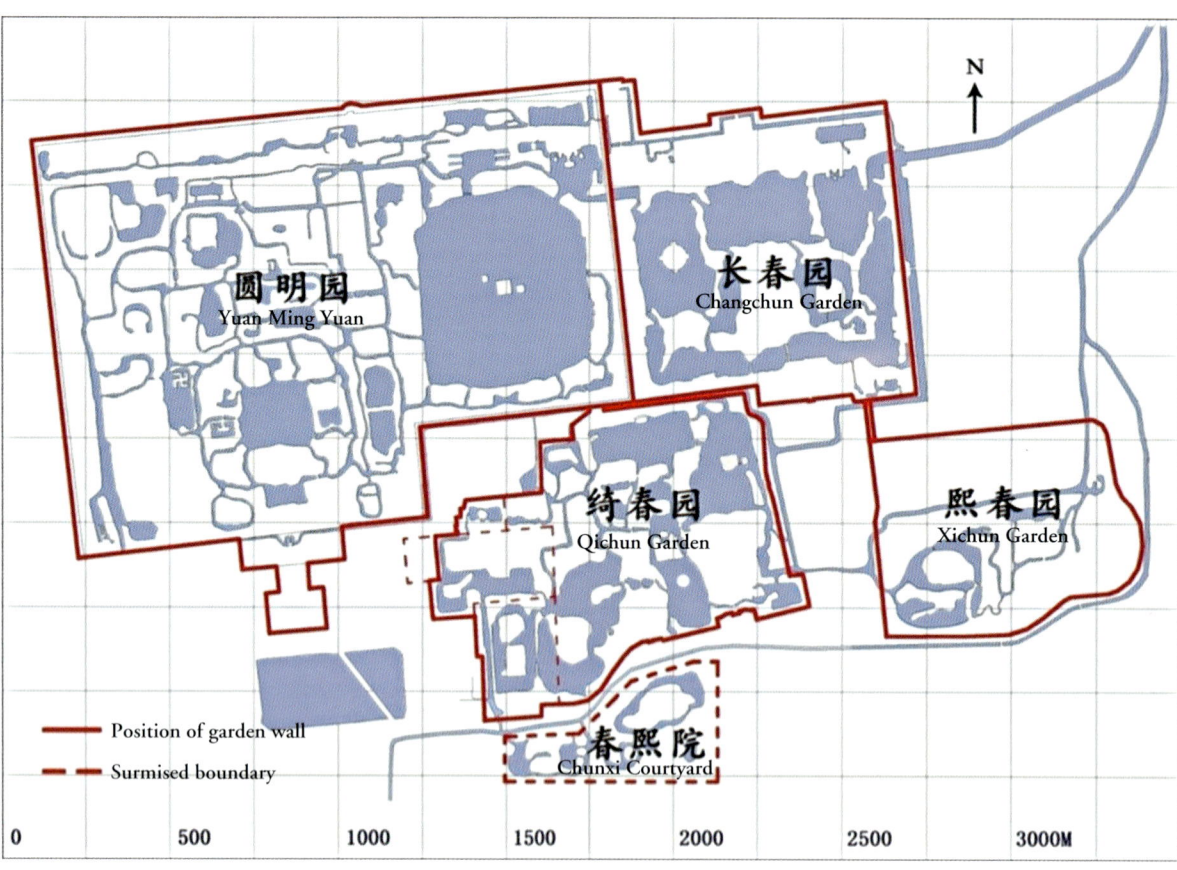

Fig. 24 Sketch map of buildings of the Five Gardens of Yuan Ming Yuan in late Qianlong era

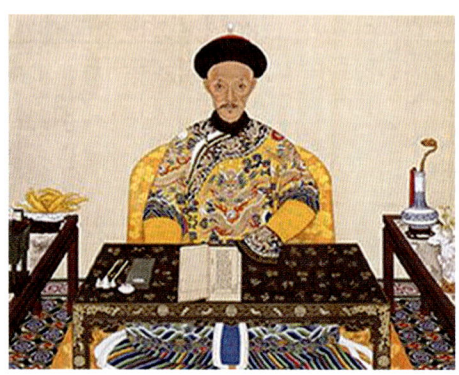

Fig. 25 Portrait of Emperor Daoguang

venue for transacting government business and the private apartments of Fuchun Hall (Blossoming Spring Hall). These additions gave the Qichun Garden the character of an imperial park (fig. 26).

In the meantime the Qichun Garden expanded to the borders of the Yuan Ming Yuan and the Changchun Garden. The three gardens were separated by their enclosure walls and communication among them was assured through gates in these walls.

Upon the death of Emperor Jiaqing in the 25th year of his reign (1821), his eldest legitimate son Minning succeeded him and assumed the era name of Daoguang (fig. 25).

In the Daoguang era China's population steadily increased[1] and with per capita arable land dwindling, the country became increasingly impoverished. Emperor Daoguang gave instructions on refraining from sensual pleasure and extravagance and made cuts among the court staff providing musical and theatrical entertainment collectively called the Nanfu (South Garden).[2] On the other hand repair and rebuilding went on year after year in the Yuan Ming Yuan.

By the first year of the Daoguang era some buildings in the imperial park in the northwest suburbs had fallen into disrepair. The Changchun Garden (Joyful Spring Garden) was in danger of collapse, this prompted the move of the empress dowager and dowager consorts to the Qichun Garden (fig. 27). The second year of the Daoguang era saw new construction and rebuilding in the Qichun Garden.

Another change in the Daoguang era was the granting of the Xichun Garden and the Chunxi Courtyard to titled princes, which

28 CHINA'S LOST IMPERIAL GARDEN

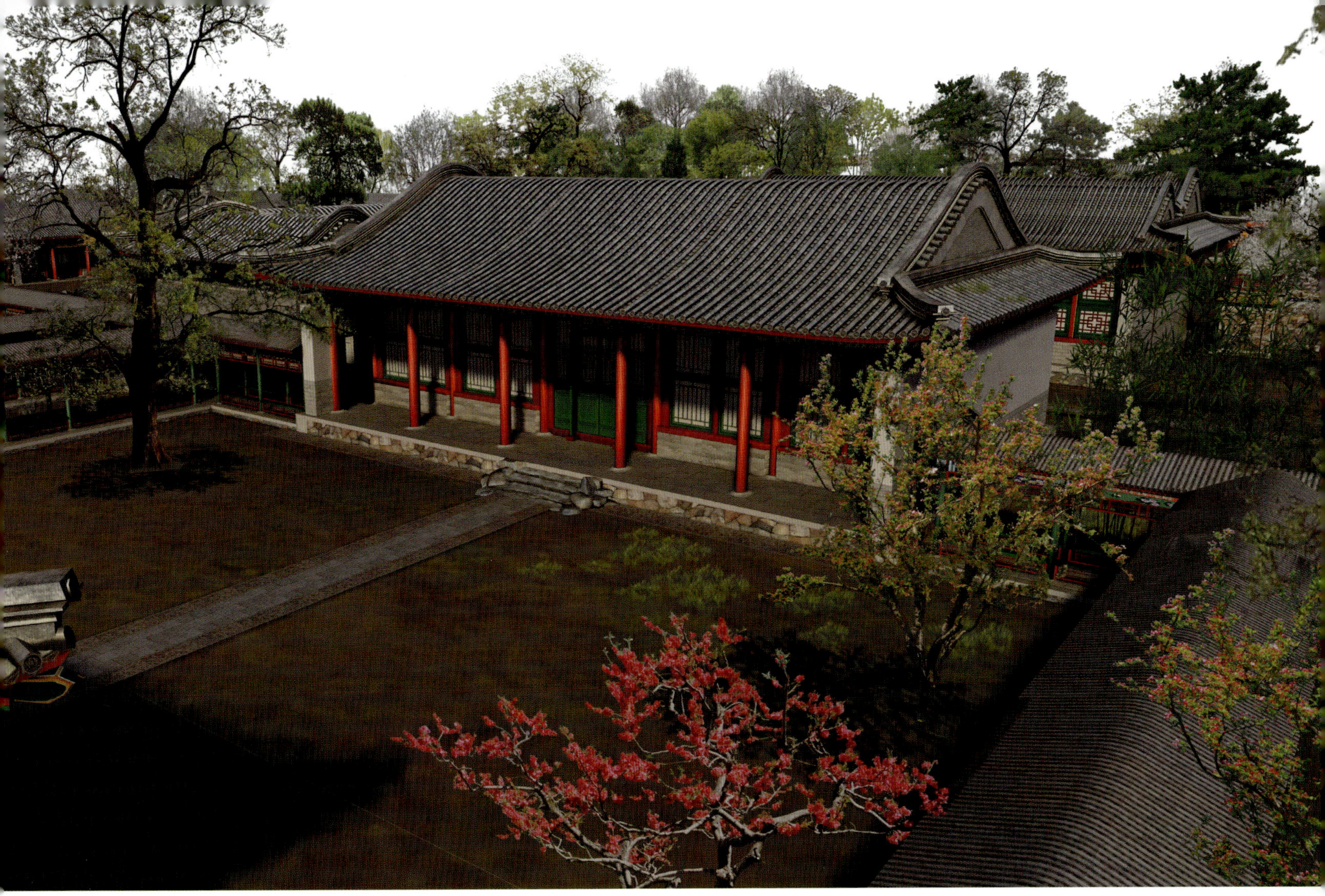

Fig. 26 Fuchun Hall of Imperial Apartments at Qichun Garden

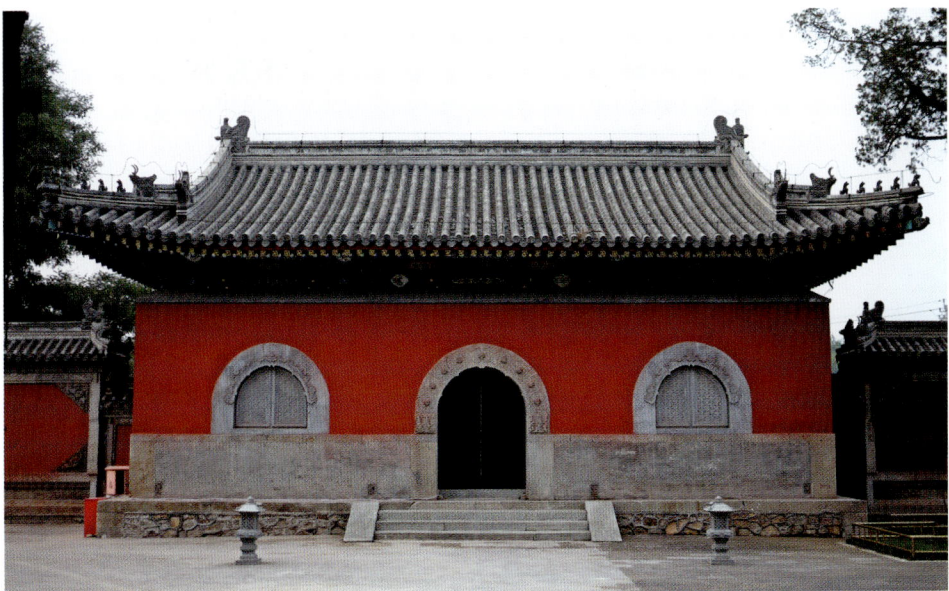

Fig. 27 Temple gateway of the Zhengjue Temple at Qichun Garden

left the Yuan Ming Yuan with only three gardens (fig. 24).

In the Xianfeng era the Qing court was beleaguered by problems both at home and abroad. Emperor Xianfeng lived in the Yuan Ming Yuan for six months in the second year of his reign and thereafter since stayed away for years. When he decided to return to the Yuan Ming Yuan in the fifth year of his reign (1855) he was met with opposition from his ministers, but that did not deter the emperor, who punished the opposing ministers and began transacting government business in the imperial garden again, citing imperial tradition and precedent. The building undertaken in this period mainly had to do with the interior remodeling of residential and government office buildings in the Yuan Ming Yuan.

1 In the Daoguang era "the population increased from 200 million of the Qianlong period to 350 million." Cf. *History of the Qing Court* published by the Forbidden City Publishing House.

2 Ibid.

PART I MASTERS OF THE YUAN MING YUAN   29

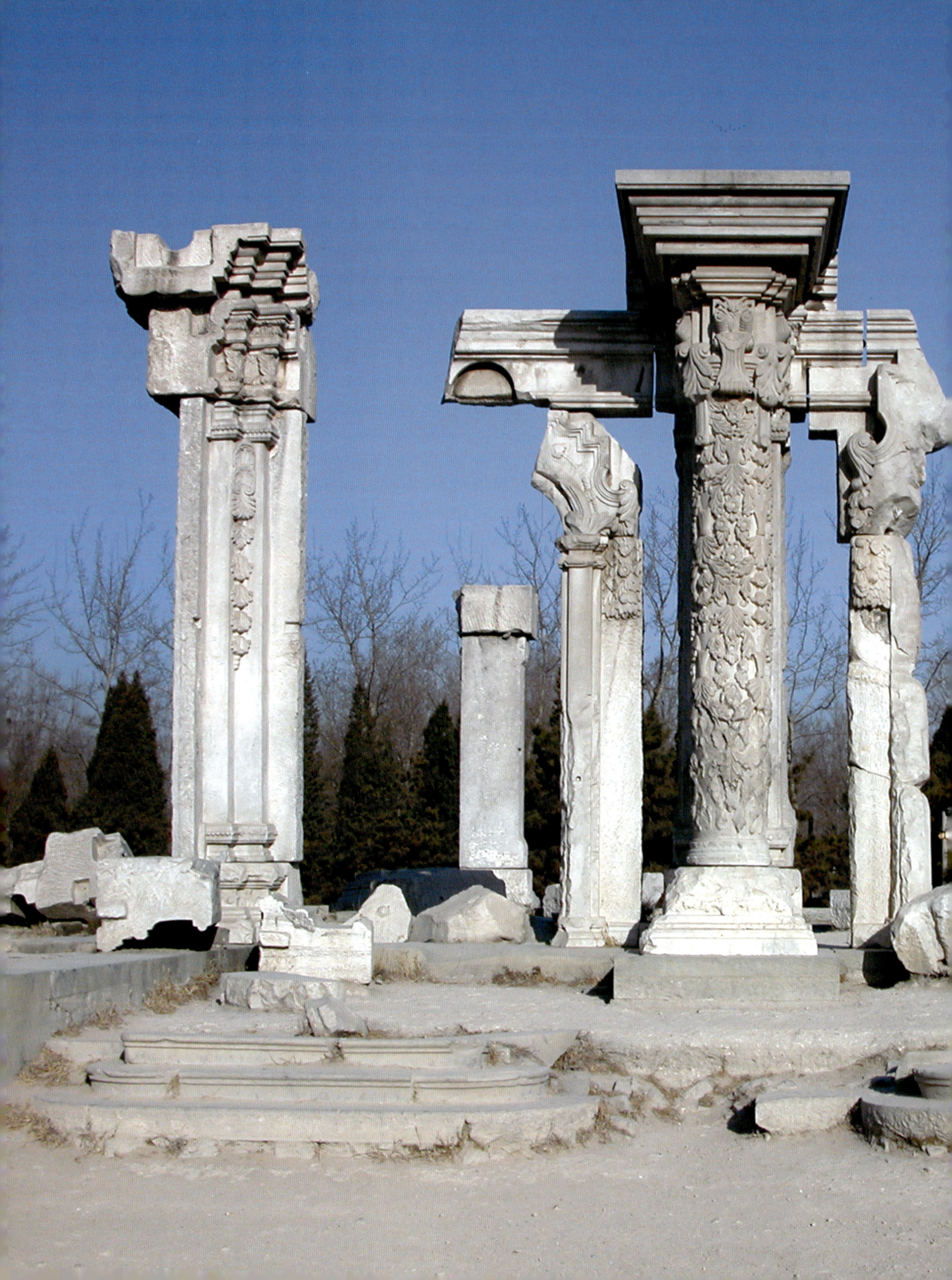

CHAPTER V
The Inferno of 1860

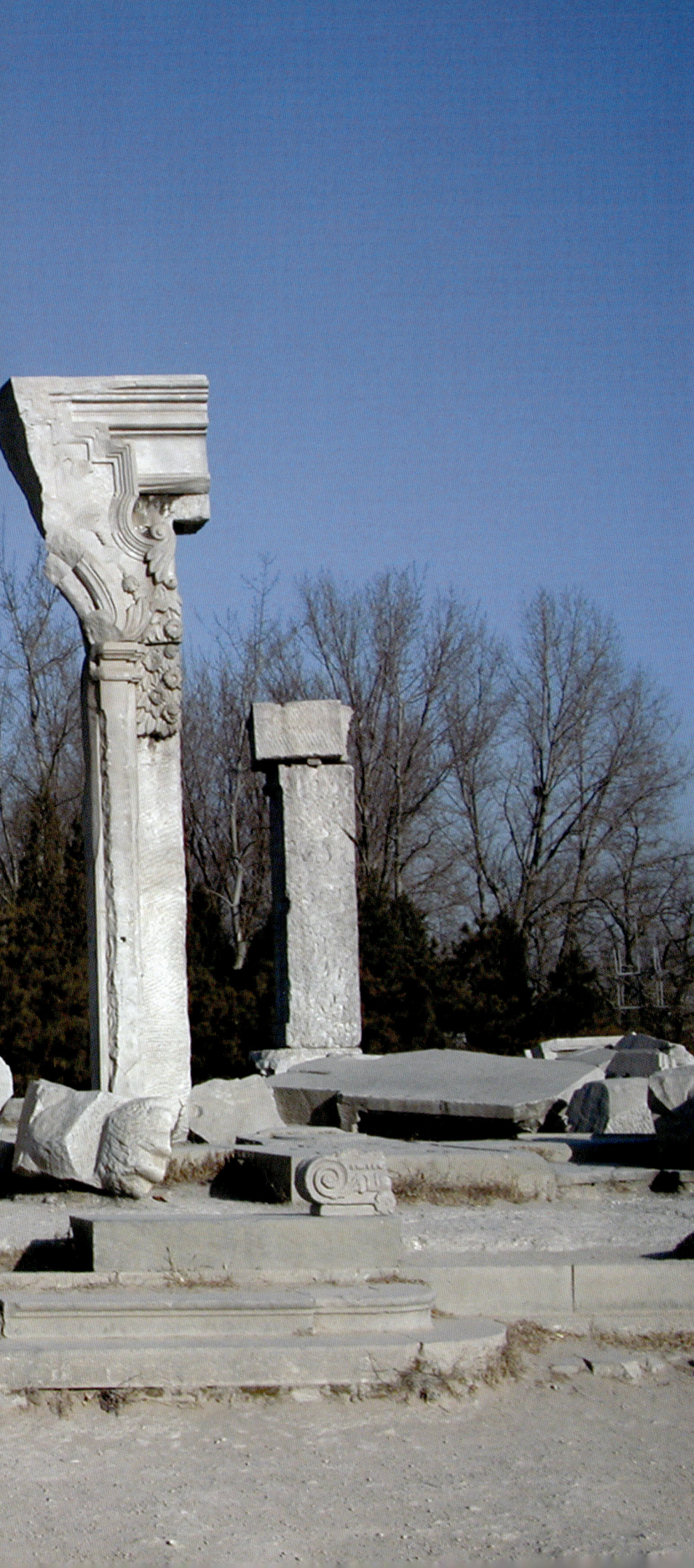

Fig. 28 Remnants of Yuanying Observatory (Immense Ocean Observatory)

In the second half of the 19th century the Qing dynasty was in steady decline due to trouble from European powers and internal turmoil. In the tenth year of the Xianfeng era (1860) British and French forces invaded Beijing, causing Emperor Xianfeng, the occupant of the Yuan Ming Yuan, to flee in a hurry, leaving only Prince Gong to stay behind to negotiate with them. After negotiations broke down, the allied invading forces headed to the Yuan Ming Yuan and began their indiscriminate plunder and unrestrained looting. After the invading forces carted away curios, rare objects, silk and embroideries, Elgin, leader of the British invasion, still unsatisfied, ordered that the Yuan Ming Yuan be burnt to the ground in order that the Qing court could be "visited with some severe punishment and signal mark of retribution (fig. 28)."

In the evening of October 6, 1860, French troops breaking into the Yuan Ming Yuan met with the resistance of about twenty armed eunuchs led by Ren Liang just inside the Churu Xianliang Gate (Gate for the Departure and Entrance of Virtue and Goodness or the second gate of a palace). After these were killed, the French commander et al. moved into the Zhengda Guangming Hall (Hall of Rectitude and Honor).[1] On October 18 the British force made the Zhengda Guangming Hall its command post and the British commander Grant ordered John Michel's division, with the greater part of the cavalry brigade, to burn down the Yuan Ming Yuan before leaving in the afternoon of October 19. R. J. L. M'Ghee, pastor to the British invading force, wrote: "A few smart riflemen soon set the Zhengda Guangming Dian in blaze; its pomp and state, and it was noble chamber, are going fast before the devouring flame; the roof must soon go in, it has been alight some time, you feel the heat a hundred yards off; there down it goes, with a terrific crash. Now for the gate and the lodges, don't leave one, no, not one—not a vestige remains of the palace of palaces,"[2] and the Yuan Ming Yuan was engulfed in a sea of fire.

On the sixth day of the ninth month of the tenth year of the Xianfeng (fig. 29) era Prince Gong wrote in his memorial to the emperor: "On the fifth day … as negotiations (with the British and French forces) were going on, flames and smoke erupted in the northwest. Soon reports came in that the barbarians with thousands of infantry and cavalry troops went to the Haidian area and set ablaze the Yuan Ming Yuan and palatial buildings in the Three Mountains area. We ascended to a high point and saw the flames still burning. It was an atrocious and heart-rending sight that defied description."[3]

According to the memorial of the fourth day of the tenth month of the tenth year of the Xianfeng

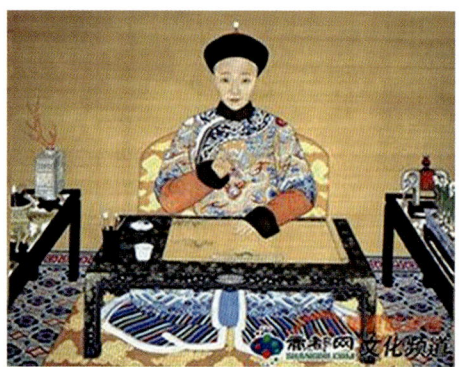

Fig. 29 Portrait of Emperor Xianfeng

era (1860) from Ming Shan of the Imperial Household Department entitled "Investigation Report of the Plunder and Torching of the Yuan Ming Yuan[4]," "the halls and buildings of the Jiuzhou Qingyan Complex, the Changchun Xianguan (Eternal Spring Immortals Hall), the Shangxia Tianguang Complex (Complex of Heavenly Light above and below), the Shangao Shuichang Complex (Complex of High Hills and Long Waters), the Tongle Garden (Garden of Shared Pleasure) and the Main East Gate were all burned to the ground on the 23rd day of the eighth month. Buildings including the Zhengda Guangming Hall in the Three Gardens were burned down on the fifth and sixth day of the ninth month, the Yulinglong Pavilion was torched on the 11th day … the (Yuan Ming Yuan's) main palace gate, the Main East Gate and the east and west waiting rooms outside the main palace gate, the offices of the six departments, the South Fruit Storeroom, the Guard of Honor duty room, the Imperial Household Department duty room … were all burned, the front and rear halls of the Archives Office and the Han Chinese Archives Office were burned, a few rooms of the Manchu Archives Office and the Imperial Architectural Design Studio, while spared by the fire, were ransacked. Only the seals have been removed in time and kept intact. Four of the six warehouses were pillaged and two were burned down."

Also according to records of the Imperial Household Department of the fifth month of the 11th year of the Xianfeng era (1861)[5] only the Zibi Mountain House (Purple Green Mountain House), the Pengdao Yaotai Complex (Complex of the Jade Terrace of Paradise Island), the Shuanghe Study (Two Herons Study) of the Kuoran Dagong Complex, the Chunyu Pavilion (Spring Rain Pavilion) and Tudi Ancestral Temple (Ancestral Temple of Land) of the Xinghuachun Pavilion (Apricot Blossom Spring Pavilion), the Qingjingdi Complex (Pure Land), the Kenong Pavilion and Guanyin Monastery of the Beiyuan Mountain Village (Mountain Village in the Distant North), the Haiyue Kaijin Complex of the Changchun Garden, the Zhengjue Temple, the River God Temple and the Huiji Ancestral Temple (Ancestral Temple of Mercy) of the Qichun Garden escaped destruction because of the relative isolation of their locations (fig. 30).

The Yuan Ming Yuan, known as the "Garden of Gardens," was thus destroyed. The outrage committed by the British and French troops shocked the world and was denounced by just-minded people. The most scathing critique was contained in the *Letter to Captain Butler* by the renowned French literary giant Victor Hugo dated November 25, 1861: "There was, in a corner of the world, a wonder of the world; this wonder

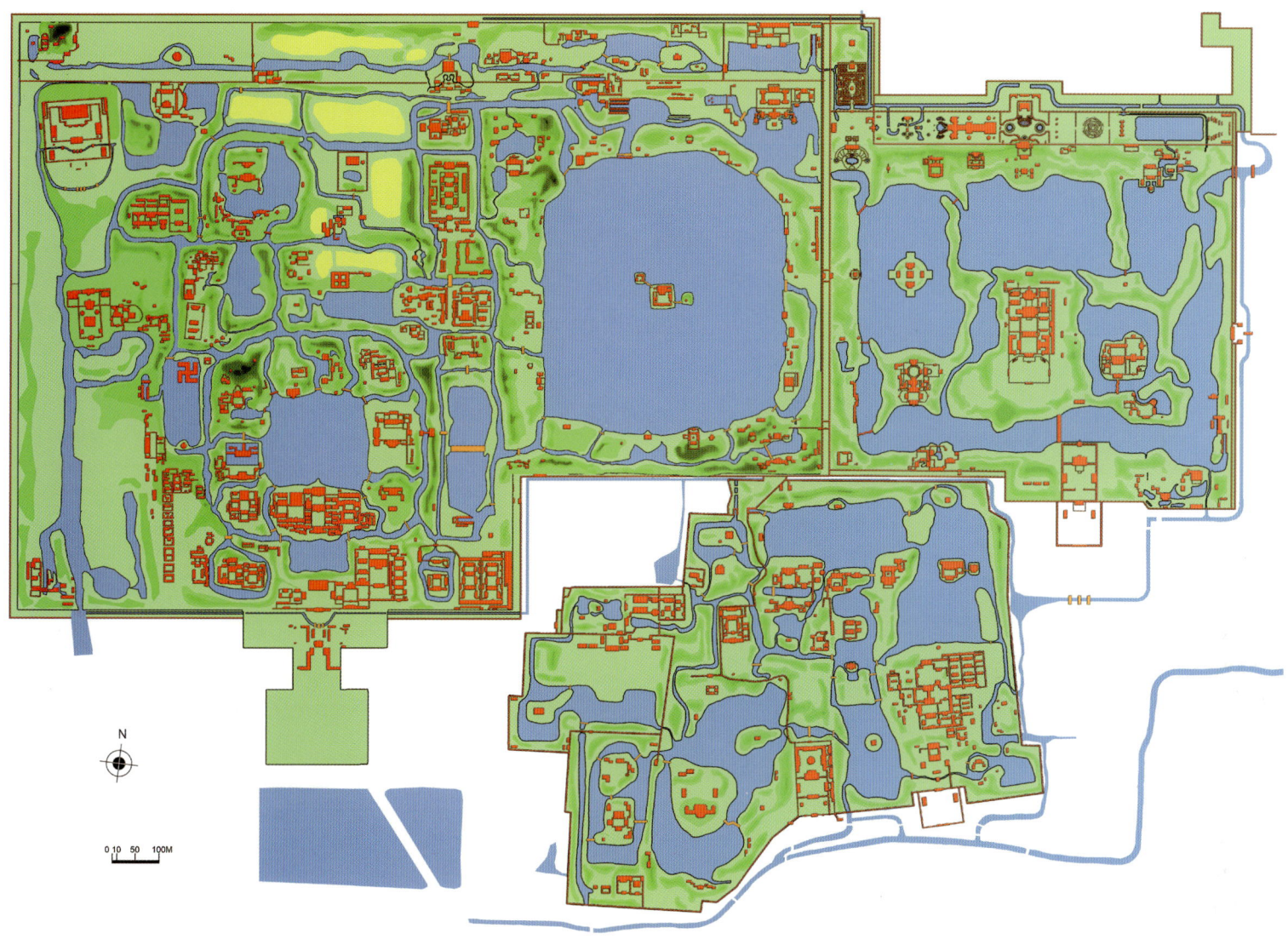

Fig. 30   Sketch map of buildings of Yuan Ming Yuan in the Daoguang era

was called the Yuan Ming Yuan. Art has two principles, the Idea, which produces European art, and the Chimera, which produces oriental art. The Yuan Ming Yuan was to chimerical art what the Parthenon is to ideal art. All that can be begotten of the imagination of an almost extra-human people was there … People spoke of the Parthenon in Greece, the pyramids in Egypt, the Coliseum in Rome, Notre-Dame in Paris, the Yuan Ming Yuan in the Orient … This wonder has disappeared … One day two bandits entered the Yuan Ming Yuan. One plundered, the other burned … Before history, one of the two bandits will be called France; the other will be called England." Victor Hugo was not alone in denouncing the barbarity of the British and French forces. Another citizen from one of the two countries whose troops committed the outrage was Guillaume Pauthier, art critic and student of Chinese art, who wrote in an article of the March 25, 1861 issue of the *Gazette des Beaux-Arts* entitled "Des Curiosités Chinoises Exposées aux Tuileries": "In addition to the unfortunate example that such an act sets for the army, it has the result of bringing discredit to the nation to which this army belongs, especially when this act takes place not as a result of a dangerous military assault, but intentionally and in cold blood … We have been in China less generous than armies that invaded our territory."

---

1 Bernard Brizay (France), *The Looting of Yuan Ming Yuan, Second Opium War,* translated and published in China in August 2005 by Zhejiang Ancient Books Publishing House.
2 Cf. R. J. L. M' Ghee, pastor to the British invading force, *How We Got into Pekin: A Narrative of the Campaign in China of 1860.*
3 *Yuan Ming Yuan*, page 563, compiled by the First Historical Archives of China, published by Shanghai Ancient Books Publishing House, May 1991.
4 Ibid., page 573.
5 Ibid., page 601.

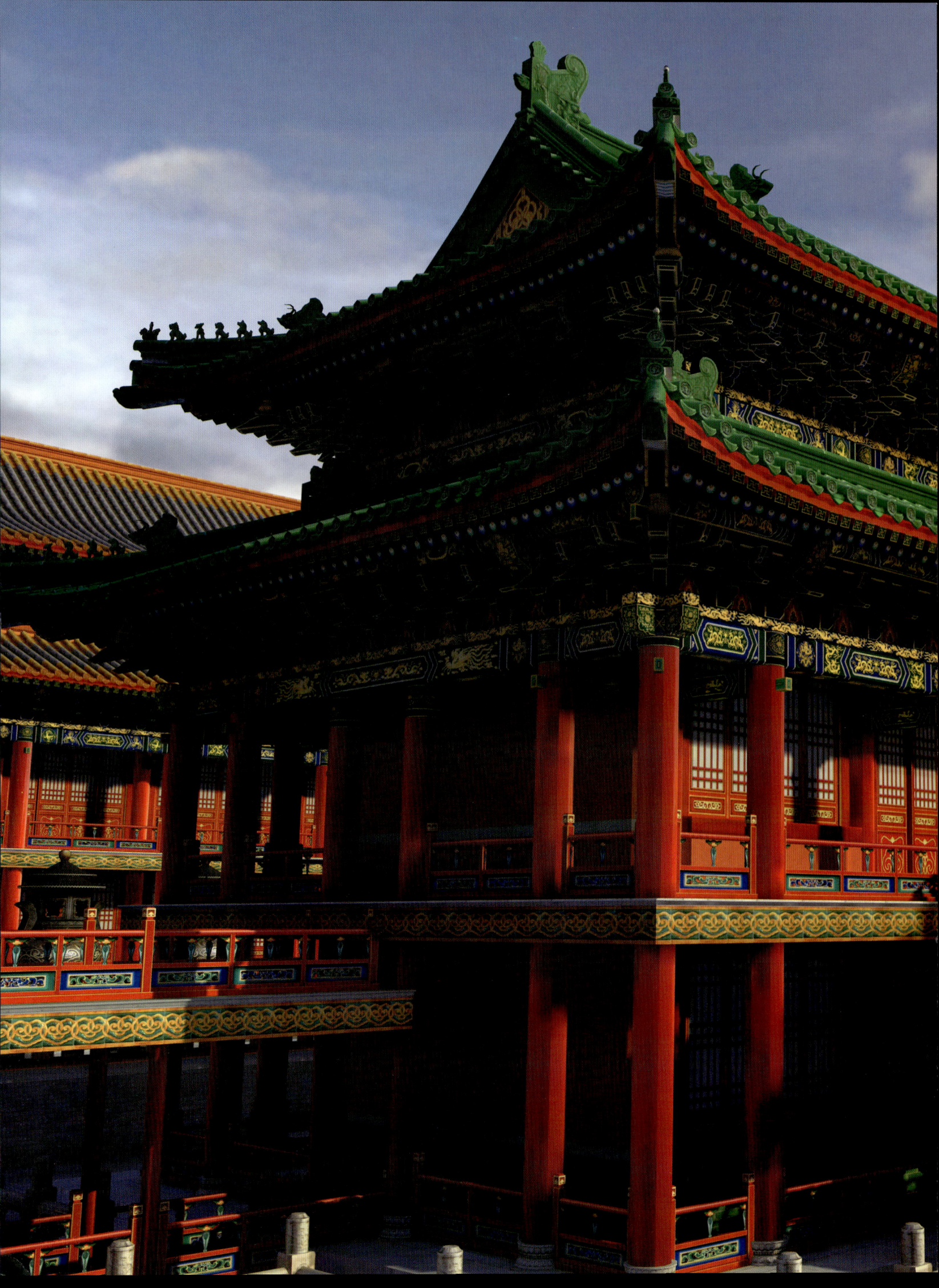

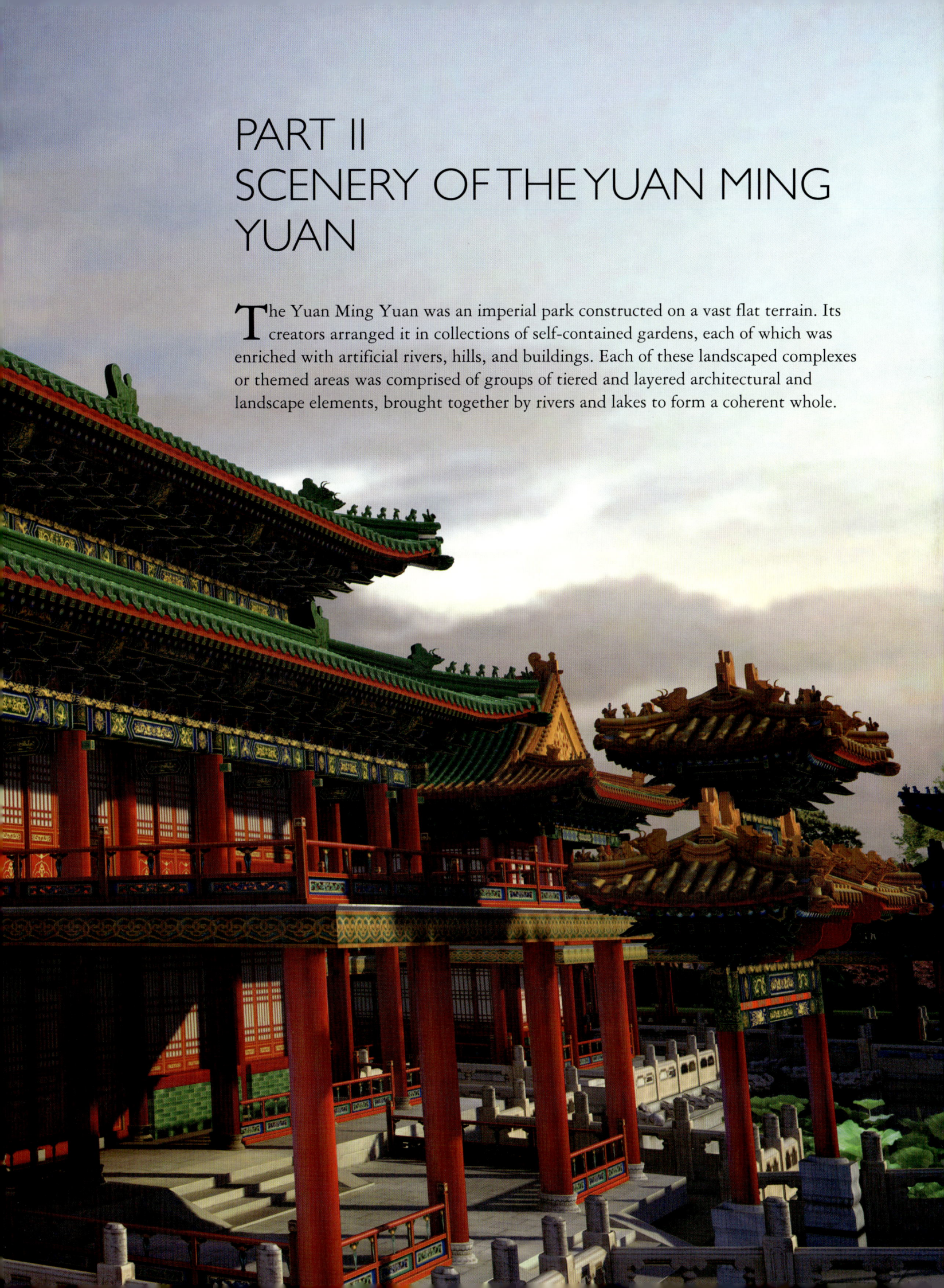

PART II
SCENERY OF THE YUAN MING YUAN

The Yuan Ming Yuan was an imperial park constructed on a vast flat terrain. Its creators arranged it in collections of self-contained gardens, each of which was enriched with artificial rivers, hills, and buildings. Each of these landscaped complexes or themed areas was comprised of groups of tiered and layered architectural and landscape elements, brought together by rivers and lakes to form a coherent whole.

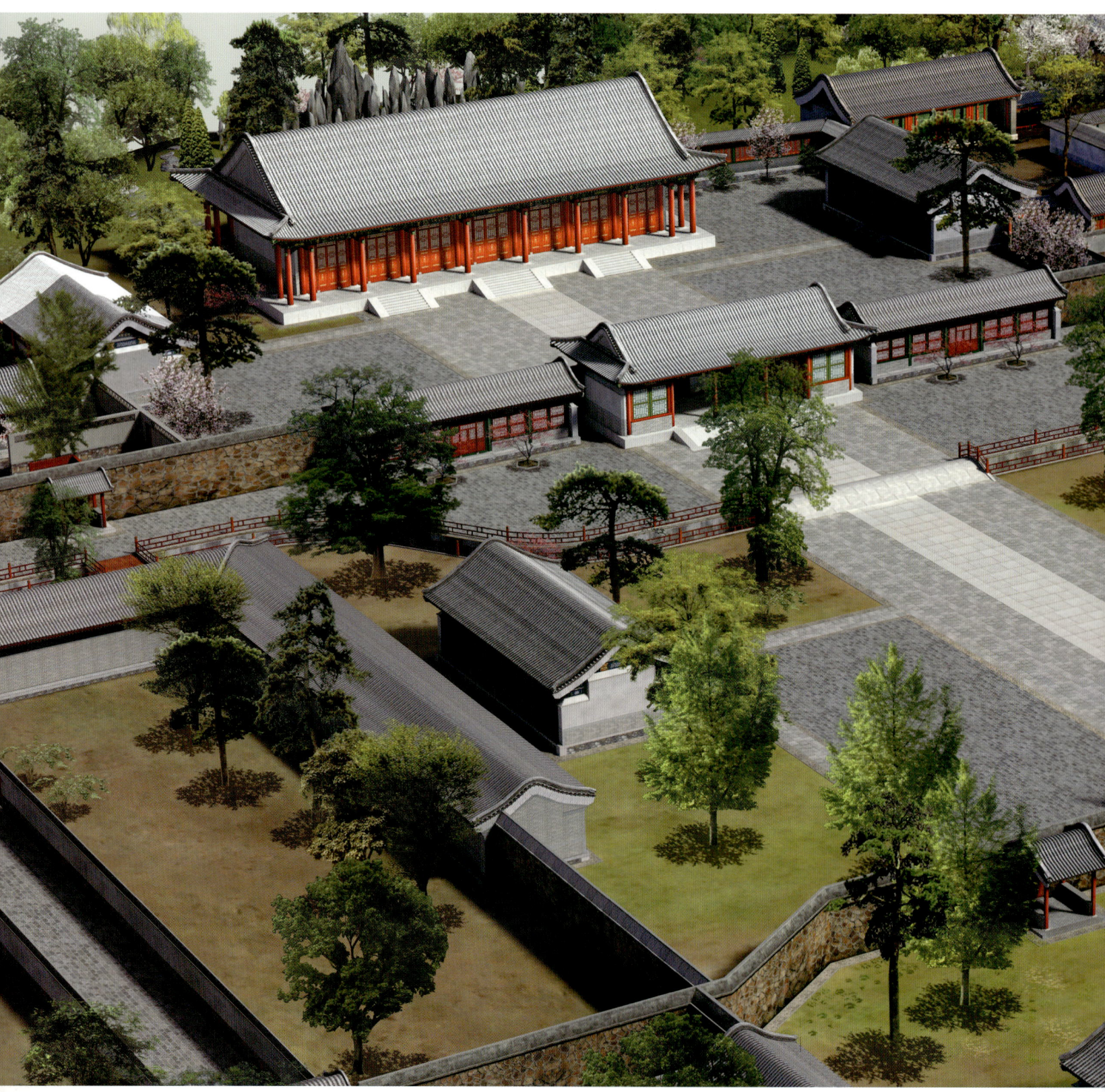

CHAPTER VI
Public Business in Front and Private Residence in the Rear

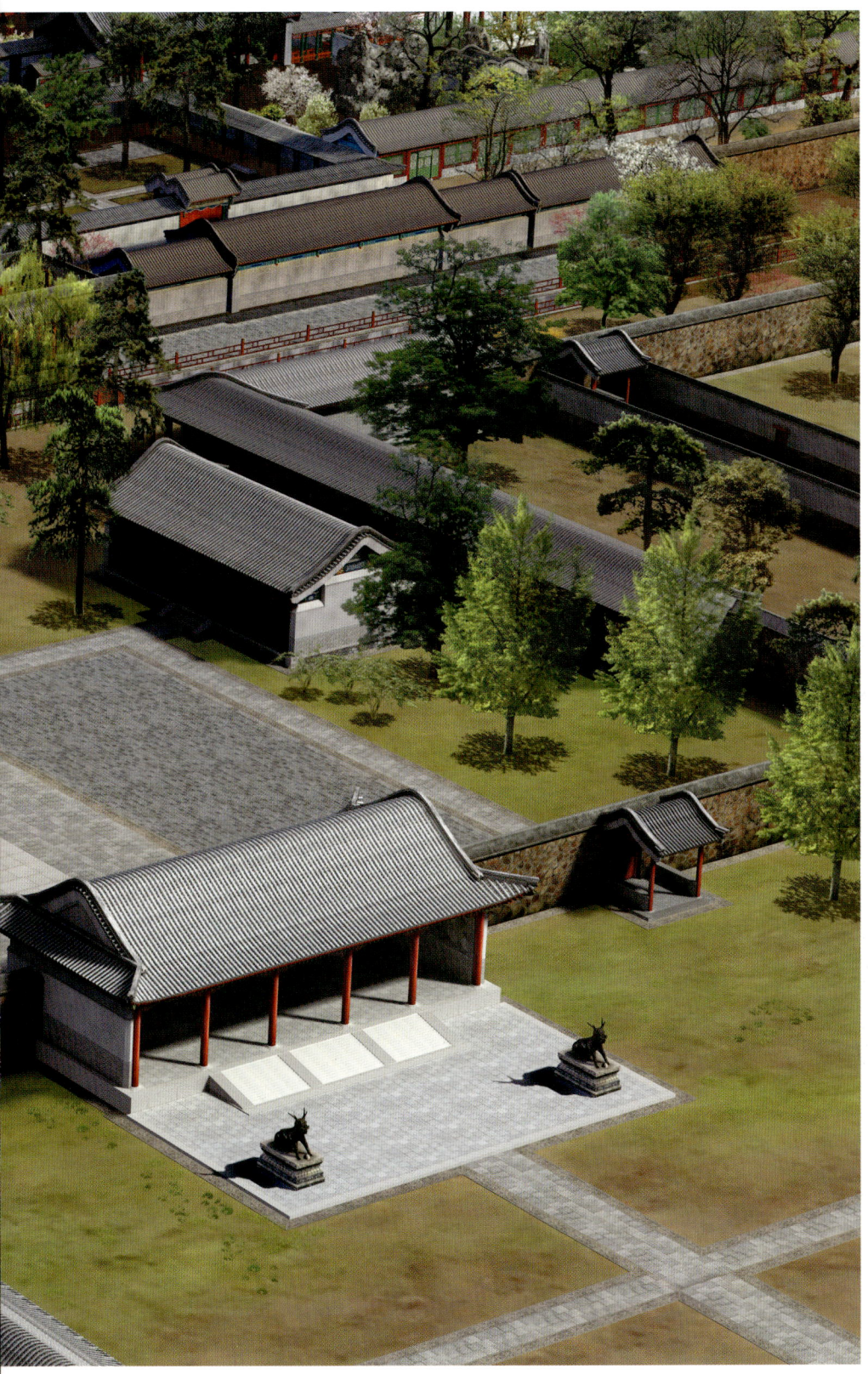

In order to meet the needs of the official business of the imperial court, receptions and ceremonies, a group of buildings centered around a large hall was constructed immediately inside the palace gate and each of the three main gardens was equipped, in the rear of the grounds, with imperial living quarters for the emperor's use. This configuration followed the age-old imperial tradition in China of the emperor having his office in the front of the compound with imperial living quarters behind. A similar plan was also followed by the common people when building their homes, with the reception hall in the front and sleeping quarters in the rear, the front hall reserved for receiving guests and hosting family gatherings and the buildings at the back for daily activities (fig. 32).

Pages 34 and 35
Fig. 31 Huiluan Hall of Fanghu Shengjing Complex

Fig. 32 Themed area of Zhengda Guangming Complex

PART II SCENERY OF THE YUAN MING YUAN 37

正大光明 Zhengda Guangming Complex (Complex of Rectitude and Honor)

The group of buildings called Zhengda Guangming served as a major venue for important ceremonial activities. The series of buildings, including the introductory space, started from the south, past a spirit wall, waiting rooms and two palace gates to finally arrive at the Hall of Zhengda Guangming (fig. 33). Behind the Hall sat an artificial hill called Shoushan (Mount of Longevity) which served as a barrier. The hall was flanked by side halls at its left and right. The strict symmetry of the buildings was relieved by a zigzagging gallery at the east side of the main hall connecting it to the eastern side hall and a small courtyard, whilst at the west side one had an unobstructed view of the lush foliage of trees and a corner of the artificial hill. Through this mix of symmetry and asymmetry and the use of artificial hills, trees and zigzag galleries to render the square-looking complex more park-like, the design conveyed the idea that Zhengda Guangming Hall was a palace located in an imperial pleasure park in contradistinction to the Main Audience Hall of the Forbidden City.

The Zhengda Guangming Hall exuded a solemn elegance, with a front that spanned seven *jian* (or bays: Chinese unit of measurement in calculating the size of buildings, a bay) and a depth of three bays; it had a porch all around the outside and topped by a hip-and-gable roof covered by gray semi-cylindrical tiles. Roof supporting beams were supported on corbel brackets. Colored pictures were painted on some of the wood elements: "The capitals ornamented with various scrolls and devices, in vivid colouring, particularly with dragons, whose feet were armed with five claws each."[1] Between the columns on the porch one could see window and door trims with a red

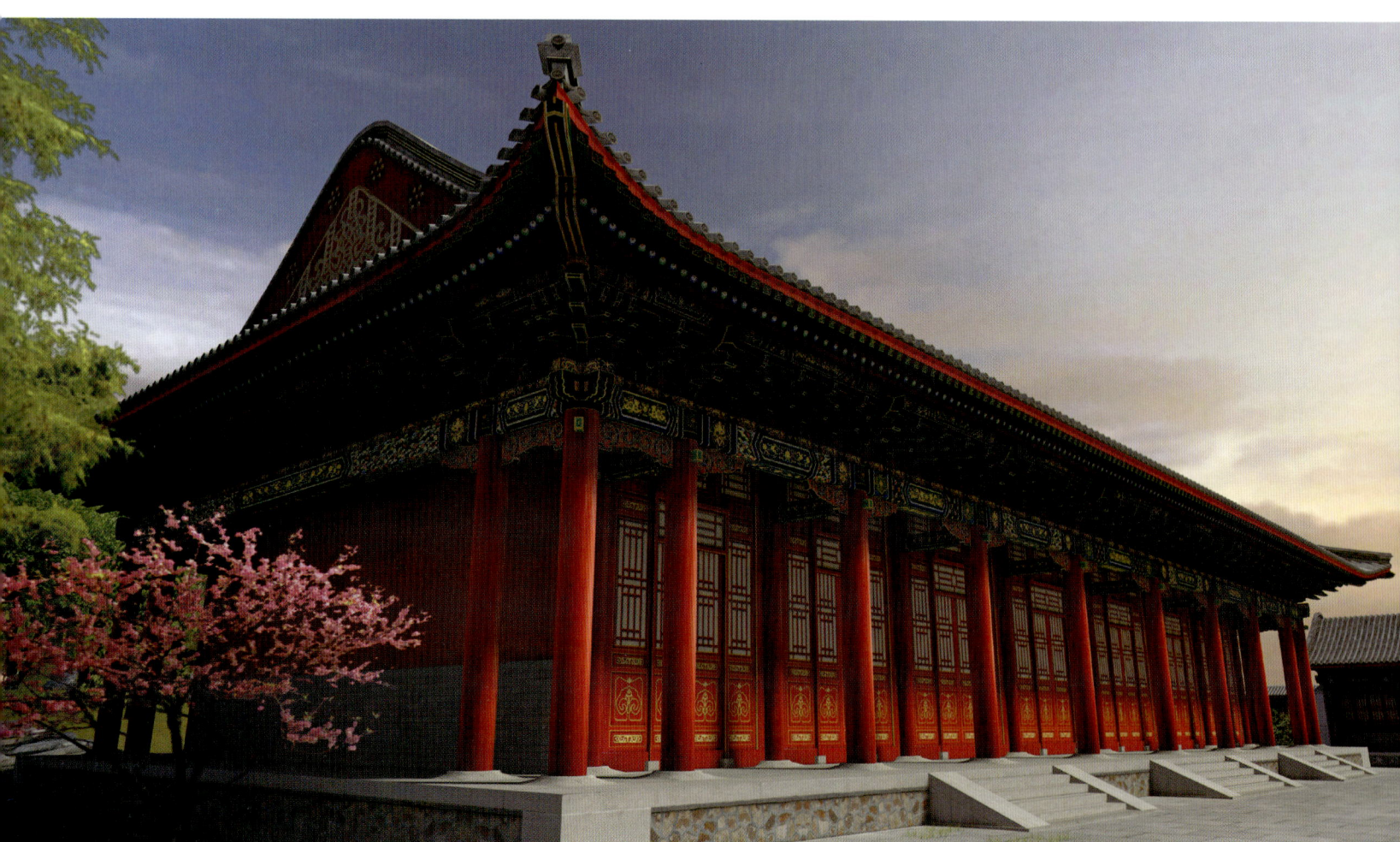

Fig. 33 Zhengda Guangming Hall

water-chestnut-flower pattern. On the eastern wall in the hall hung a copy of *Zhoushu-Wuyi* (an article in the *Book of Zhou*) in Emperor Qianlong's hand.[2] On the western wall hung a painting illustrating *Bin Feng* (Odes of Bin).[3] The main hall, seated on a raised foundation, exuded a solemn elegance (fig. 34).

The four characters "Zhengda Guangming" inscribed on the horizontal name tablet constituted a motto of the dynasty and were found on such tablets in the palaces in the Forbidden City as well as in imperial villas outside the capital, such as in the Qianqing Palace (Palace of Heavenly Purity) of the Forbidden City, the Guande Hall (Hall of Observing Virtue) of Jingshan Hill and the Qinzheng Hall (Hall of Diligent Governance) in the Bishu Mountain Resort (Imperial Summer Resort) in Chengde. In the words of the Qianlong Emperor in a poem of his, the four-character motto of the Qing imperial household, passed down through three epochs of the Qing dynasty, should be adhered to even ten thousand years thereafter.[4] The Qianlong Emperor went on to explain that *zheng* (rectitude) meant no straying from the right path in governance, *da* (broadness) meant broad-mindedness, *guang* (exhaustiveness) meant bringing to fruition what is undertaken, and *ming* (clarity) meant clear self-knowledge. The motto could be understood to be a platform for his governance of the country.

At that time, New Year, the Winter Solstice and the Wanshou Day (Longevity Day or the birthday of the emperor) were three major days of the year for festive celebration. The first two festivities

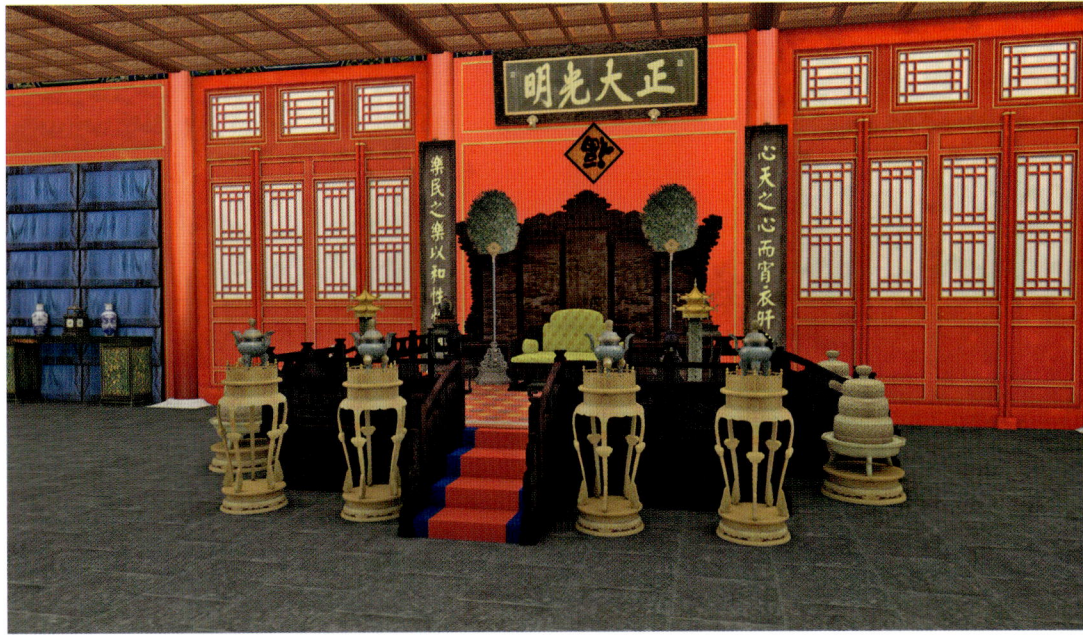

Fig. 34 Interior of Zhengda Guangming Hall

had to be held in the Forbidden City, while the Wanshou Day, if it was a decade birthday, would be observed in the Forbidden City, otherwise the emperor could choose to celebrate it away from the imperial palace. The Qianlong Emperor, whose birthday fell on August 13, had his birthday celebrations mostly in the Zhengda Guangming Hall of the Yuan Ming Yuan.

Another function of the Zhengda Guangming Hall was to serve as venue for the examination of officials. After his accession to the throne, the Qianlong Emperor took swift action to remove officials found to be incompetent or who were poorly schooled or incapable. He instituted quinquennial reviews of the performance of officials. In May of the second year of his reign (1737) the Qianlong Emperor notified his cabinet of his intention of personally designing the tests and perusing the test results. He would sort the test takers into four categories according to their test performance and decide on their promotions, demotions and transfers on that basis. According to Volume 62 of the *Huangchao Wenxian Tongkao* (*Encyclopedia of the Historical Records of the Imperial Dynasty*), an examination was held in the 33rd year (1768) of Qianlong's reign in the Zhengda Guangming Hall. It was an appraisal of officials who assumed office since the 27th year of the Qianlong reign (1763). When the test results were announced, three officials made first rank, 18 made the second rank, 30 made the third rank, 15 made the fourth rank and 2 fell short of any rank and the officials were promoted, demoted, or transferred accordingly.

The annual banquet for court officials was normally held in the

---

1 George Staunton (Great Britain): *An Authentic Account of an Embassy from the King of Great Britain to the Emperor of China*.
2 King Cheng of Zhou was young when he ascended the throne about the 11th century BCE. His uncle, Duke of Zhou, who acted as the regent, wrote the article entitled "Do Not Indulge in a Life of Ease" to counsel against indulgence in pleasure on the part of King Cheng of Zhou.
3 A painting with an agricultural theme, which inspired the works of many notable artists in Chinese antiquity. Emperor Qianlong described on numerous occasions a feeling of walking in a painting of "Odes to Bin" when he walked by fields worked by peasants.
4 *Yuzhi Shi* (*Imperial Poems*) by Emperor Qianlong, Book IV, Volume 94.

Zhengda Guangming Hall on the 16th day of January of the lunar calendar. The attendees included members of the royal family, high ministers of the court, as well as invited local leaders from across the country. Other invitees included officials working in the capital and generals at the head of military expeditions. A number of Qianlong's poems cited these occasions, showing his solicitude toward his subjects. Thus at the annual banquet for court officials in the 25th year of Qianlong's reign (1760), when tribal leaders had appeared one after the other, General Zhaohui, who had quashed the rebellion of the Dzungars and was returning with his troops, was still in Hami (Kumul) and had not yet reached the capital. In his poem *Banquet for Court Officials the Day after the Lantern Festival*,[1] the Qianlong Emperor expressed satisfaction over the defeat of the Dzungars and his concern for General Zhaohui and his troops returning from the frontier. He made a point of inviting General Zhaohui to the annual banquet for court officials held on the Lantern Festival in the 26th year of his reign (1761). On such occasions the Qianlong Emperor often gave each of his ministers a line of verse to express his affection for them.

Foreigners were invited also. In the 24th year of Qianlong's reign (1759), the attendees included legates from Kazakhstan and Russia. In the 47th year of his reign (1782) he received envoys from Korea, Ryukyu, the Lao Kingdom of Lan Xang and Siam.

Other types of banquets were sometimes also held in the Zhengda Guangming Hall. Thus according to *Qiju Zhuce* (*Chronicles of Imperial Activities*), (on the 16th day of the first month of the 13th year of Qianlong's reign, i.e. February 14, 1748) his Majesty, at the behest of the empress dowager, gave a banquet for princes' consorts, princesses and titled ladies of Mongolia in the Zhengda Guangming Hall. This shows that banquets for the emperor's close kin could also be hosted here. In another example, a banquet was held here in the 35th year of Qianlong's reign for the engagement of Kurun Princess Hejing; in the 54th year of Qianlong's reign (1789) the engagement banquet of Kurun Princess Hexiao was also held in the Zhengda Guangming Hall.[2]

The table arrangements at a banquet in the Zhengda Guangming Hall were different from the practice at a modern state banquet, where large round tables are used: the emperor sat by himself at his personal table, the princes and high ministers sat two to a table, their placement determined according to official ranks, as well as closeness and favorite status vis-a-vis the emperor. The emperor sat on his throne in the hall, facing the banquet attendees, and the latter sat facing the emperor (fig. 36).

The Zhengda Guangming Hall also served as venue for receiving foreign guests. Thus in the 58th year of Qianlong's reign (1793), a British embassy led by Lord Macartney, with Sir George Staunton as second-in-command, visited China. At the news of a British embassy dispatched to China to pay homage and tribute, the entire Qing court

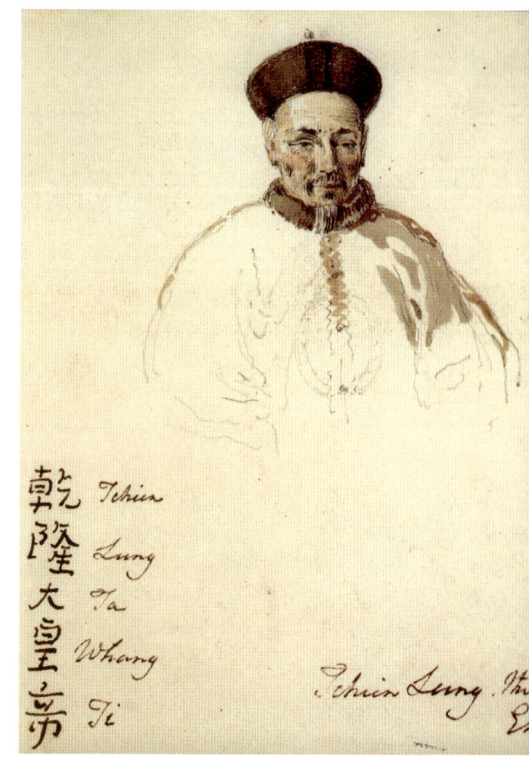

Fig. 35   Portrait of Qianlong

was overjoyed. The Qianlong Emperor felt deeply honored to be able to receive these envoys coming across the oceans as he reached an octogenarian age. The embassy arrived in Beijing in mid-August. On August 18, a Chinese official told the embassy that it should "proceed to *Yuen-in-yuen*, where a Colao of high rank was appointed by the emperor to meet (it), together with a European missionary."[3] At the time of George Maccartney's arrival at the Yuan Ming Yuan on August 23, the Qianlong Emperor was at the Bishu Mountain Resort in Chengde. Maccartney entered the Yuan Ming Yuan to set up the gifts he had brought with him for Emperor Qianlong. He was impressed by what he saw in the Yuan Ming Yuan: "This place is truly an imperial residence; the park is said to be eighteen miles round, and laid out in all the taste, variety, and magnificence which distinguish the rural scenery of Chinese gardening. There is no one very extensive contiguous building,

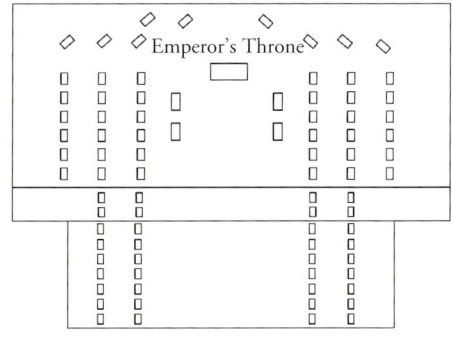
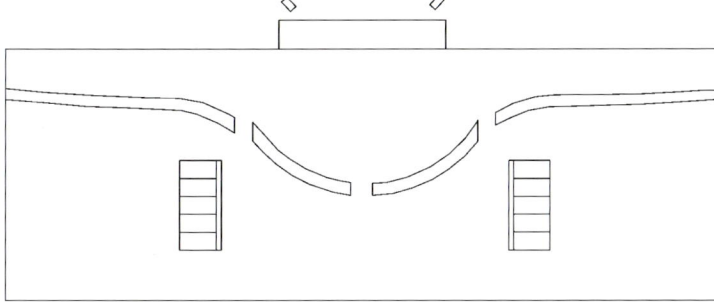

Fig. 36 Banquet seating in Zhengda Guangming Hall

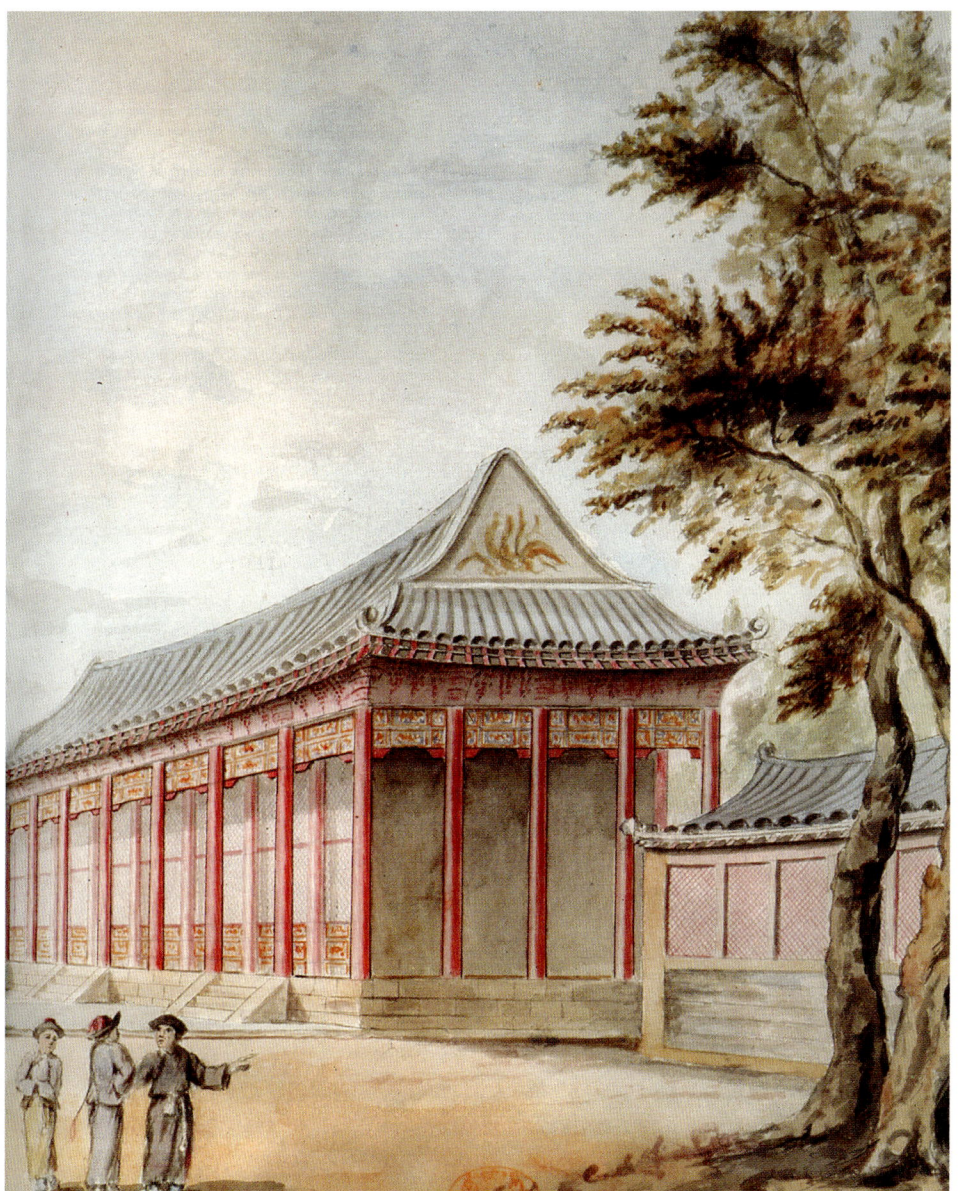

Fig. 37 Watercolor painting of Zhengda Guangming Hall by artist of Macartney's Embassy to China

but several hundreds of pavilions scattered through the grounds, and all connected together by close arbors, by passages apparently cut through stupendous rocks, or by fairy-land galleries, emerging or receding in the perspective, and so contrived as to conceal the real design of communication, and yet contribute to the general purpose and effect intended to arise from the whole. The various beauties of the spot, its lakes and rivers, together with its superb edifices, which I saw (and yet I saw but a very small part), so strongly impressed my mind at this moment that I feel incapable of describing them. I shall therefore confine myself to the great hall or Presence Chamber of the Emperor. It is one hundred and fifty feet long and sixty feet wide; there are windows on one side only, and opposite to them is the Imperial Throne of carved mahogany, and elevated by a few steps from the floor. Over the Chair of State is an inscription in Chinese:

Ching-Tha-Ouan-Ming-Foo

The translation of which signifies:

Verus, Magnus, Gloriosus. Splendidus, Felix."[4]

A member of the embassy made a water-color drawing of the Zhengda Guangming Hall (fig. 37) and a pen drawing of it, as well as a portrait of the Qianlong Emperor (fig. 35), leaving important first-hand records of the meeting.

---

1 *Yuzhi Shi*, by Emperor Qianlong, Book III, Volume 2.
2 *Daqing Gaozong Chunhuangdi Shilu* (*Chronicles of the Qianlong Emperor*).
3 *British Embassy to China 1793* by George Macartney (Original title of book unknown).
4 Ibid.

澹懷堂 Danhuai Hall (Simple Needs Hall) of the Changchun Garden (Garden of Eternal Spring)

The construction of the Changchun Garden started in the 11th year of the Qianlong era (1746) and was completed in the 35th year of his reign (1770). It was therefore the Qianlong Emperor's project from start to finish. It was built primarily for Qianlong's retired years after surrendering the reins of government. He set a target date of the 60th year of his reign, i.e. when he reached the age of 85, to retire from active governance and move to the Changchun Garden to spend his old age. The Danhuai Hall group of buildings inside the main gate to the Changchun Garden (figs. 38, 39) was used for transacting government business, while the Hanjing Hall (Tripataka Hall) group of buildings served as imperial residence. Although this garden was designed for Qianlong's use after his abdication, it had retained the model of "government business in front and private residence at the rear," and did not give the impression of a place of leisure and pleasure insulated from politics. The only difference was it did not rigorously adhere to the requirement of aligning the government office buildings in front and living quarters in back along a north-south axis. This was the only concession to the character of a royal villa away from the Forbidden City.

The gate of entrance to the

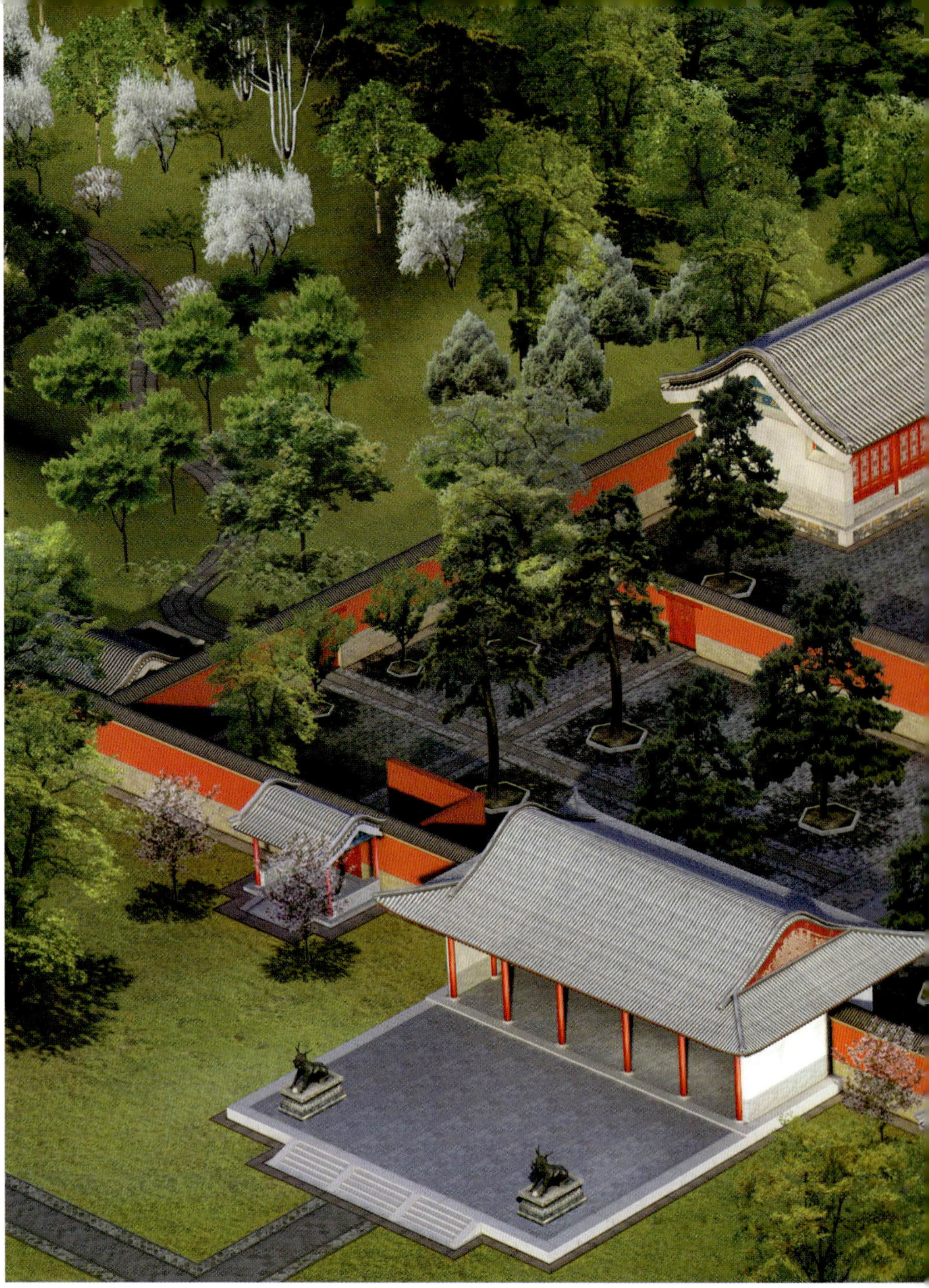

Fig. 38 Themed area of Danhuai Hall

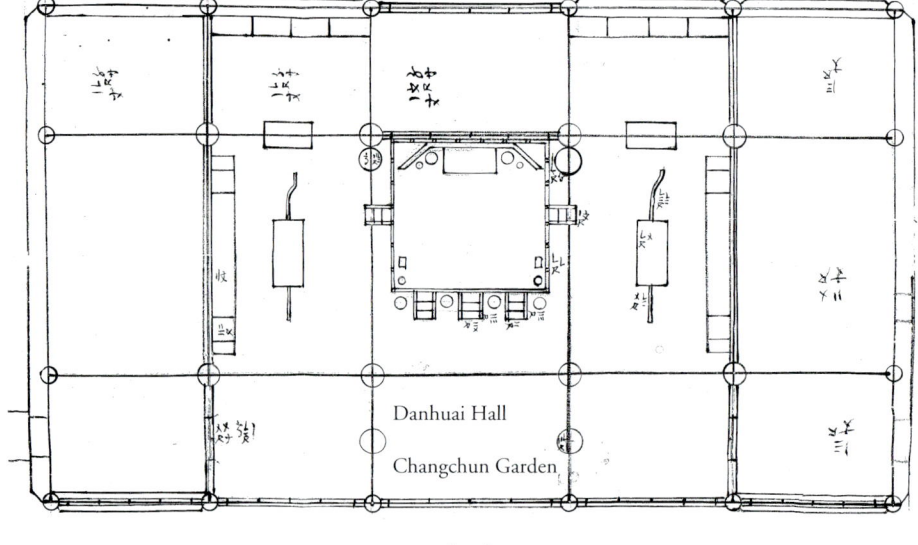

Fig. 39 Plan of Danhuai Hall

42 CHINA'S LOST IMPERIAL GARDEN

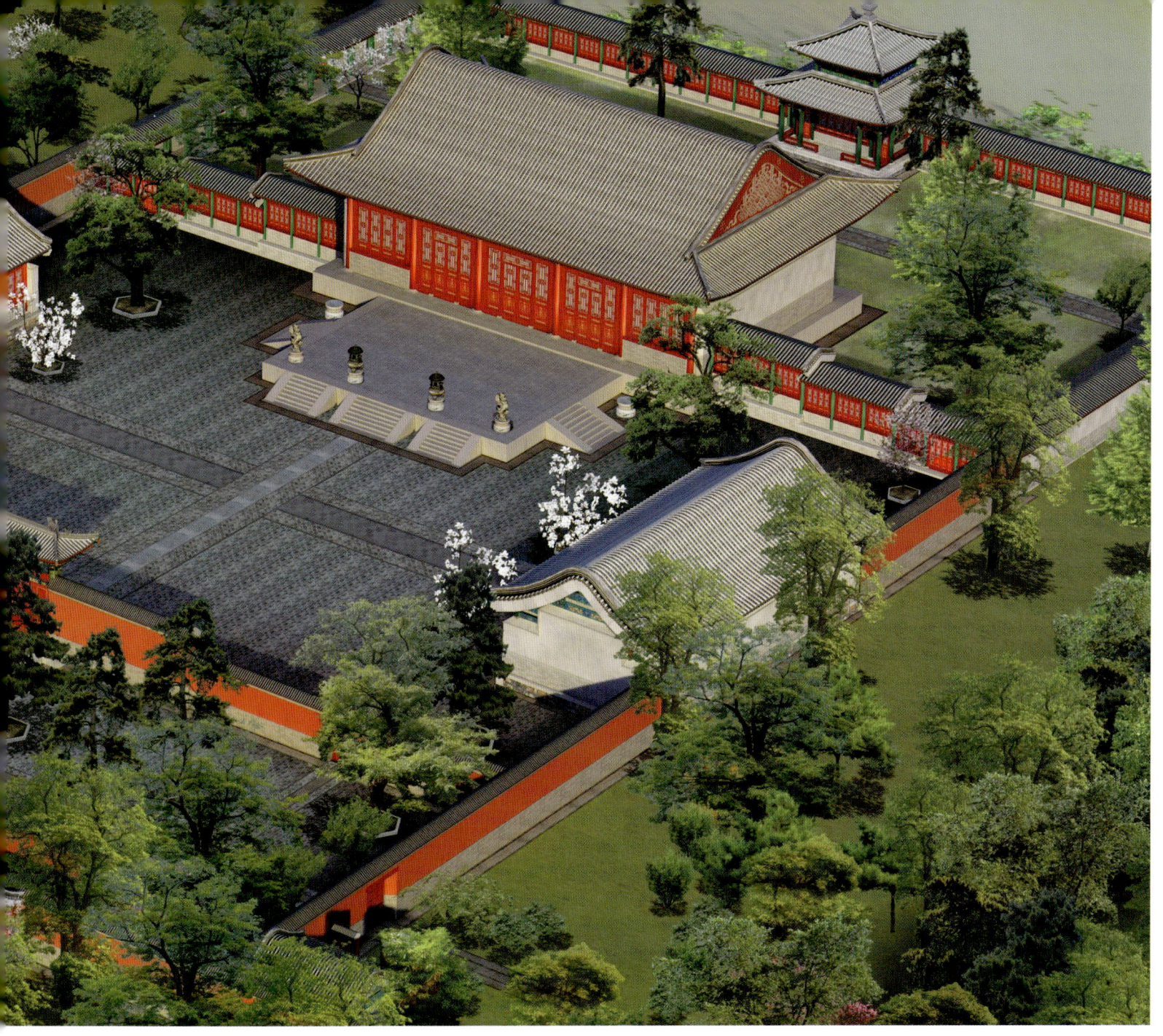

Changchun Garden was a hall of five bays. In front stood an east and a west suite of five waiting rooms each. Passing through the gate one came to an architectural arch flanked by barrier walls extending east and west. After the architectural arch one came to the main hall—Danhuai Hall, which had a raised moon terrace in front. On the east and west ends of the front courtyard stood side halls of five rooms each. Behind the main hall was a courtyard enclosed on its four sides by a gallery. A pavilion called the Zhongle Pavilion (Shared Joy Pavilion) at the north end of the courtyard sat opposite the Danhuai Hall. The stream that encircled the entire garden flowed past the pavilion behind it. The stream was overgrown with lotuses, which went into full bloom in summer and sent abroad a pleasant fragrance on the summer breeze. Here the solemnity of the front end of the complex gave way to the graces of nature.

The Danhuai Hall served also to receive envoys from China's vassals. Thus in March of the 25th year of Qianlong's reign (1760) a banquet was given here for the leaders of Hami of Xinjiang, who were then invited to the Tongle Garden in the Yuan Ming Yuan to the west, where they were regaled with tea and pastries and gifts. The Danhuai Hall was furnished with a throne that sat on a wooden platform; eight bookshelves were installed in the hall for the display of the *Gujin Tushu Jicheng* (*Complete Collection of Illustrations and Writings from the Earliest to Current Times,* also known as the *Imperial Encyclopedia*).

勤政亲贤 Qinzheng Qinxian Complex (Complex of Diligent Government)

The Qinzheng Qinxian Complex, situated to the east of the Zhengda Guangming Complex, was where the emperor attended to the business of government when he repaired to the Yuan Ming Yuan. It was a large, self-contained group of buildings, consisting of four courtyards that ran east-west (fig. 40). At its northwest an earthen hill separated it from the small lake in the rear of the Zhengda Guangming complex and at its southwest it could communicate with the Zhengda Guangming Complex through a courtyard.

The Qinzheng Hall was the westernmost group of buildings, with a front courtyard enclosed by a gallery shaped like a hollow square. The Qianlong Emperor read memorials and gave audience to his high officials here. Sometimes he also used it to receive officials of lesser rank and vassals here.[1] But activities of this nature usually took place in the morning. It was here that the Qianlong Emperor announced the designation of his 15th son Aisin Gioro Yongyan as crown prince in the 60th year of his reign (1795).[2]

In the Qianlong years the Qinzheng Qinxian Complex had a hip-and-gable roof. It was three bays wide and was flanked by two "ear rooms" or side chambers (fig. 41 on page 46). It was divided into a front space and a rear space with a wooden partition across the hall. The three bays in the middle in

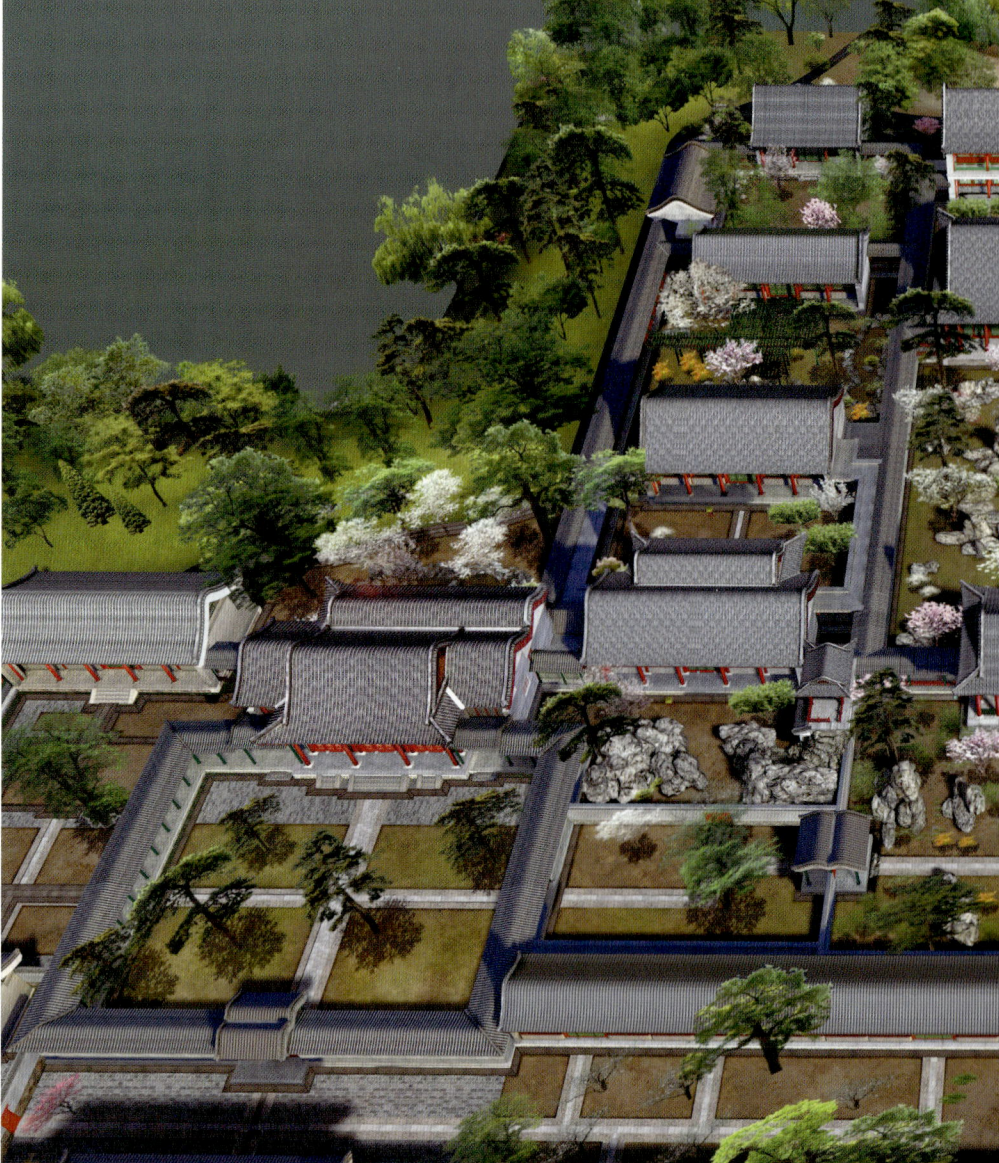

Fig. 40   Themed area of Qinzheng Qinxian

the front space, made into a single room, had at the center a throne. It was here that the emperor called in high officials for consultation. Behind the throne were windows and doors with wood trims and carvings; it had a lattice ceiling, constructed of woven wooden strips. When the high ministers came for an audience with the emperor, the latter emerged from the rear space and installed himself in the throne whilst the ministers knelt in front of the emperor (fig. 42 on page 46). The eastern "ear room" was a study. In summer the audiences normally took place in the hall, while in spring and autumn they were held in the eastern study.

The Qinzheng Qinxian Complex comprised three groups of building that ran east-west. The main hall, located in the middle of the complex, had three courtyards arranged along a north-south axis. The Fangbi Cong, five bays wide, in the first courtyard was an open hall surrounded by a gallery. The courtyard, framed by an open gallery that ran along its four sides, was equipped with an artificial hill built with lake rocks and planted with numerous flowers and trees, which accentuated the park-like atmosphere. In summer the emperor liked to read memorials and take his meals here. The Lake Tai rocks in the courtyard were gracefully shaped; some of them survive to this day. The building called Baohe Taihe Hall (Hall of

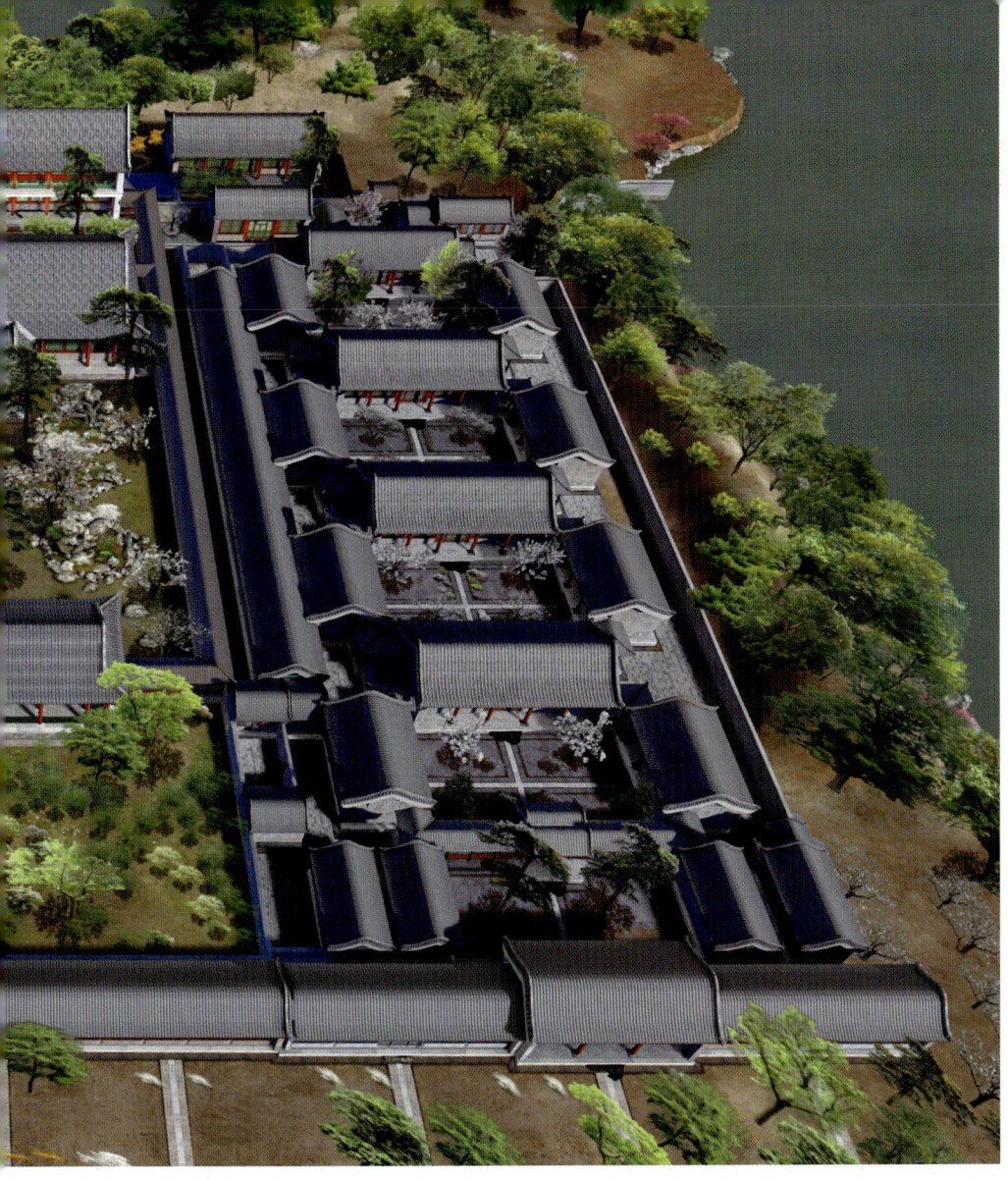

Preserving and Conserving the Primordial Harmony) in the second courtyard was the main hall, whose exterior spanned a width of nine bays. It had a front porch of three bays. Both the main hall and the porch had exquisite hip-and-gable roofs. Here banquets were given by the emperor for envoys of vassal states and high ministers. Exhibited in the hall were an oil painting by Giuseppe Castiglione, a celestial sphere and a globe. The third courtyard featured the Fuchun Building, which connected with the Baohe Taihe Hall via a winding gallery to form an "H." The Fuchun Building was furnished as a "sleeping palace" for the relaxation of the emperor. A side courtyard led to a small hill of stacked rocks at the back.

East of the main hall was a group of buildings called Jixiang Suo (Auspicious Pavilion), comprising four neatly arranged, modest-scaled *siheyuan*-style quadrangles. They were auxiliary buildings used in special circumstances such as temporary placement of coffins.

In a series of three courtyards contiguous to the Qinzheng Hall on its west figured the palace building in the south called Feiyun Pavilion (Flying Cloud Pavilion); on the north stood buildings such as Huai Qingfen (Building of Embracing Subtle Fragrance), Xiumu Jiayin Hall (Hall of Fine Shade under Handsome Tree) and Shengqiu Court (Court of Autumn Air), each of which faced south and featured a small courtyard in front. The courtyards were connected at the two ends via galleries.

The Feiyun Pavilion, of five bays, featured a overhanging gable roof with an overhanging gable and a back porch; a gallery connected it to the Qinzheng Hall at its west. It served as a small lounge in the proximity of the office. Here hung the poems composed on the occasion of the annual banquets for his ministers on the 15th day of the first lunar month. By the first year of the Jiaqing era after Qianlong's abdication, the four walls of this hall had been fully covered by these poems. One could easily imagine the good times the emperor and his retainers had in the Feiyun Pavilion.

The Huai Qingfen Building behind the Feiyun Pavilion was five bays wide, had both a front and a back porch. Its roof was characterized by a flush gable and a rounded ridge. Here the emperor took his breakfasts; thus during Qianlong's stays at the Yuan Ming Yuan in the 21st year of his reign (1756), 64 of his total of 83 breakfasts were taken at the Huai Qingfen Building. After breakfast he would go from here to the Qinzheng Hall to work. Sometimes he would read memorials and make notes on them and give audiences to officials right here.

The Xiumu Jiayin Hall and

---

1 *Qing Huidian* (*Official Journal of the Qing Dynasty*) published by Zhonghua Publishing House, 1991.
2 According to *Qiju Zhuce* (*Log of Everyday Life*), compiled by the royal secretariat, that describes the emperor's everyday life, on the third day of the ninth month of the 60th year of his reign the Qianlong Emperor convoked his sons, grandsons, noblemen and ministers to announce the installation of his 15th son Yongyan as "Prince Jia of the First Rank," or crown prince.

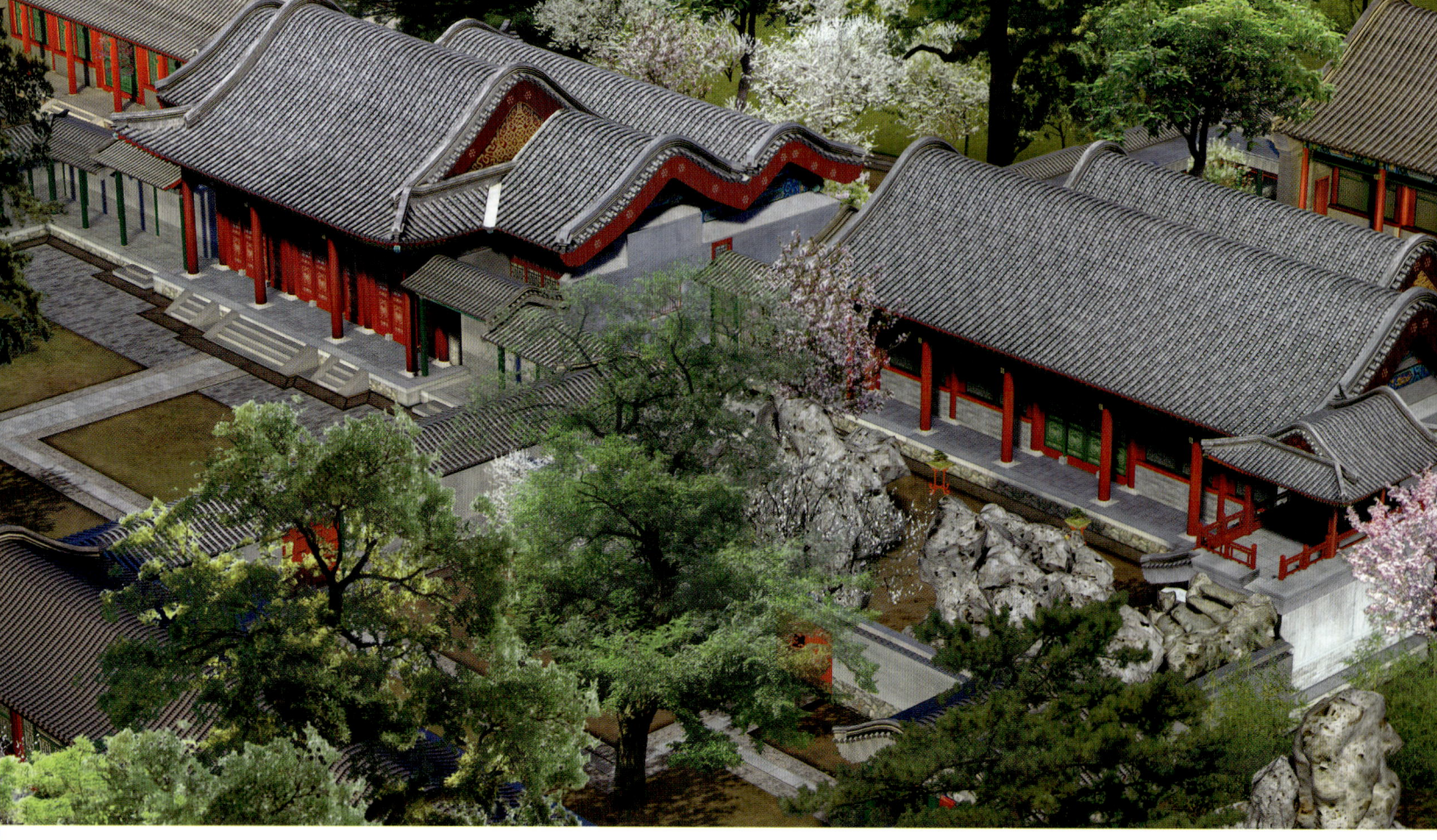

Fig. 41 Qinzheng Hall and Feiyun Pavilion

the Shengqiu Court behind the Huai Qingfen Building were both passage halls. After passing through these two small halls and crossing the Ruyi Bridge, one arrived at the imperial residence of Jiuzhou Qingyan Complex.

The concept of diligent government represented by the two characters *qin* and *zheng* served as a motto for the early emperors of the Qing dynasty and the Qianlong Emperor also prided himself on diligent government. He often felt guilty when he took advantage of some free time to enjoy the views of the Garden after attending to the business of government. This was because the Qianlong Emperor had since his childhood years been steeped in the philosophy of *nei sheng wai wang* (internalizing the virtue taught by ancient sages and externalizing them in kingly virtues and good government). Even after the accession of the Jiaqing Emperor, the retired Qianlong Emperor continued to declare that although he had ceded the reins of government he was still actively involved.

In traditional Chinese culture a good emperor not only must be diligent in governance but also be good at surrounding himself with capable and virtuous officials (*qin xian*). An emperor depended on capable and virtuous ministers to give him wise counsel and help him better distinguish right from wrong and distinguish honest officials from corrupt ones.

Fig. 42 Interior of Qinzheng Hall

九洲清晏 Jiuzhou Qingyan Complex (Complex of Nine Continents Clear and Calm)

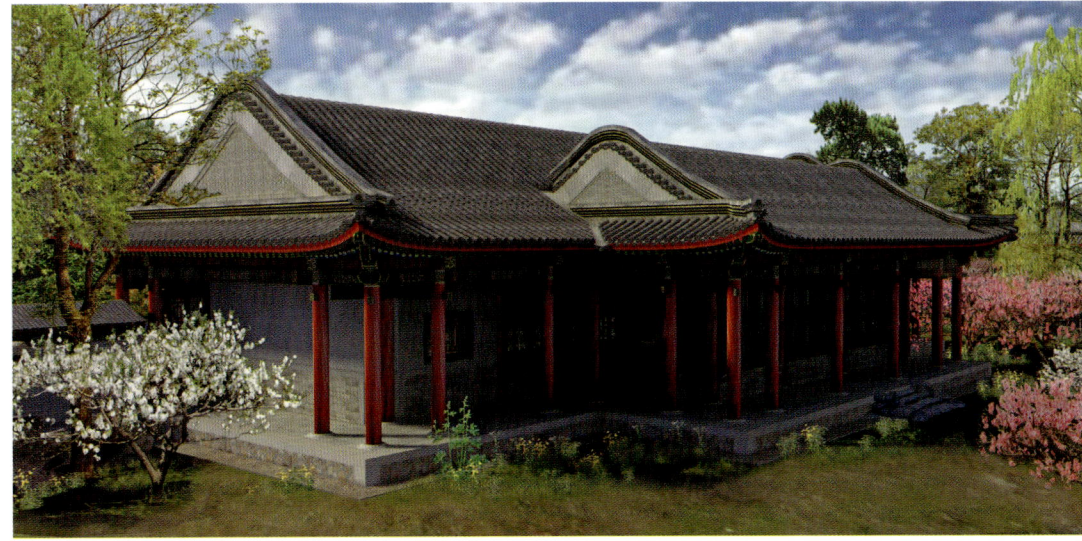

Fig. 43　Jiuzhou Qingyan Hall

The Jiuzhou Qingyan Complex, situated to the north of the Zhengda Guangming Complex, was separated from the latter by a hill called Shoushan. This group of buildings was situated on a large island, with the Front Lake to its south and the Back Lake to its north; it was bounded on its east and west by streams. It was accessible from surrounding land areas only by crossing bridges; however if one took a boat, one could directly land at docks both in front and in the rear.

The Jiuzhou Qingyan, the largest complex in the Yuan Ming Yuan, was the private apartments of the emperor, his empress and consorts. It consisted of the middle, the eastern and the western wings, with small courtyards sandwiched between them. The buildings in these courtyards predominantly faced south, with only a few side halls facing east or west (fig. 15 on pages 18 and 19).

On the middle axis were situated the Yuan Ming Yuan Hall, the Fengsan Wusi Hall (Hall of Pursuing Selflessness) and the Jiuzhou Qingyan Hall (fig. 43), all of which featured a hip-and-gable roof, signifying their higher ranking. The Yuan Ming Yuan Hall was five bays wide and featured a front and a back porch. It was once the main hall when the Yuan Ming Yuan as granted to Yongzheng when he was still a prince. When the Yuan Ming Yuan became an imperial garden, the status of the Yuan Ming Yuan Hall was equivalent to the main gate of the Jiuzhou Qingyan imperial residence. The Fengsan Wusi Hall was seven bays wide and was surrounded by a gallery; it served to host banquets for members of the imperial clan, princes and nobility in the emperor's favor. Unlike the banquets given in the Zhengda Guangming Hall, here the etiquette of the royal family was followed. In these banquets the attendees sat two to a table; they drank and recited poetry with the emperor and partook of the fine food. Thus according to the records of the family banquet held at noon on the 14th day of the first month of the 48th year of Qianlong's reign (1783), a rosewood table set before the emperor's throne had on it 32 main dishes, 4 kinds of wet or dry pastry, one dairy dish and four side dishes. The banquet was attended by princes of royal blood and titled princes, the emperor's adult and younger sons. On the tables of the princes were served 15 main dishes, 4 kinds of dry or wet pastry and 4 side dishes. After the hot food came the feast of wines. The banquet dishes were cleared from the tables and new dishes to go with the wines and *yuanxiao* (sweet dumplings made of glutinous rice flour for the Lantern Festival) were served. At this time the adult sons of the emperor drank to their father's health. The wine feast was followed by tea and pastry, after which the banquet drew to a close and the emperor's sons stepped out of the hall and gave thanks for the banquet.[1] Hierarchy was strictly observed at these banquets, even though they were attended mostly by members of the royal family. Banquets and festivities continued as before after the Qianlong Emperor retired from active governance.

On the 16th day of the first month of every year a banquet was given in the Fengsan Wusi Hall for officials of the imperial court, to which were invited those among

---

1　*Yuan Ming Yuan*, compiled by the First Historical Archives of China, published by Shanghai Ancient Books Publishing House, 1991, pages 931–932.

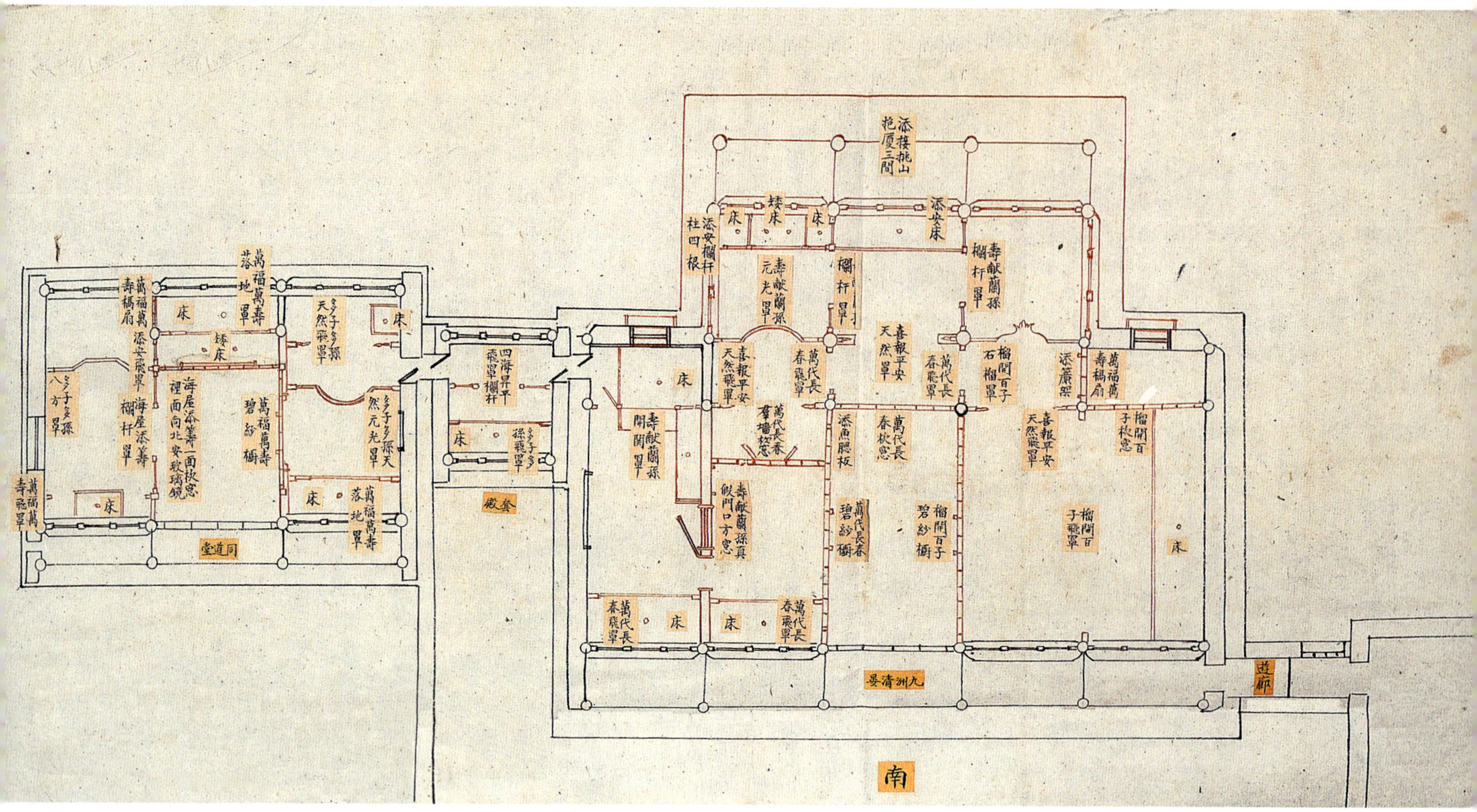

Fig. 44   Planimetric position and name of the interior of Jiuzhou Qingyan Hall

the grand secretaries and the Nine Ministers considered to be of outstanding merit by the emperor.

The Fengsan Wusi Hall was also the repository of the *Forty Scenes of the Yuan Ming Yuan* painted on silk by court painters Shen Yuan and Tang Dai in the ninth year of the Qianlong era (1744). Although it consisted of only forty paintings, the pictorial set covered almost the entirety of the Yuan Ming Yuan, with the exception of the Zibi Mountain House group of buildings in the northwest corner. This set of paintings is an authoritative historical record that helps us visualize the buildings of the Yuan Ming Yuan of the time. It gives a clear and vivid idea of the scale of the various landscaped complexes of the Garden, their environment and architectural styles.

Rooms at the east and the west end of the Fengsan Wusi Hall were furnished as Buddha chapels where the emperor could burn joss sticks.

The Jiuzhou Qingyan Hall was seven bays wide. On its north side was built a veranda of five bays. The courtyard was enclosed by a covered gallery. This was the primary imperial apartments in the Yuan Ming Yuan. The two rooms at the east end and the two at the west were two-storied inside, with a total of eight beds in them; these were for the reclining needs of the emperor and empress. The three middle rooms also served to host banquets for the emperor and his consorts (figs. 44, 45).

In the west of the Jiuzhou

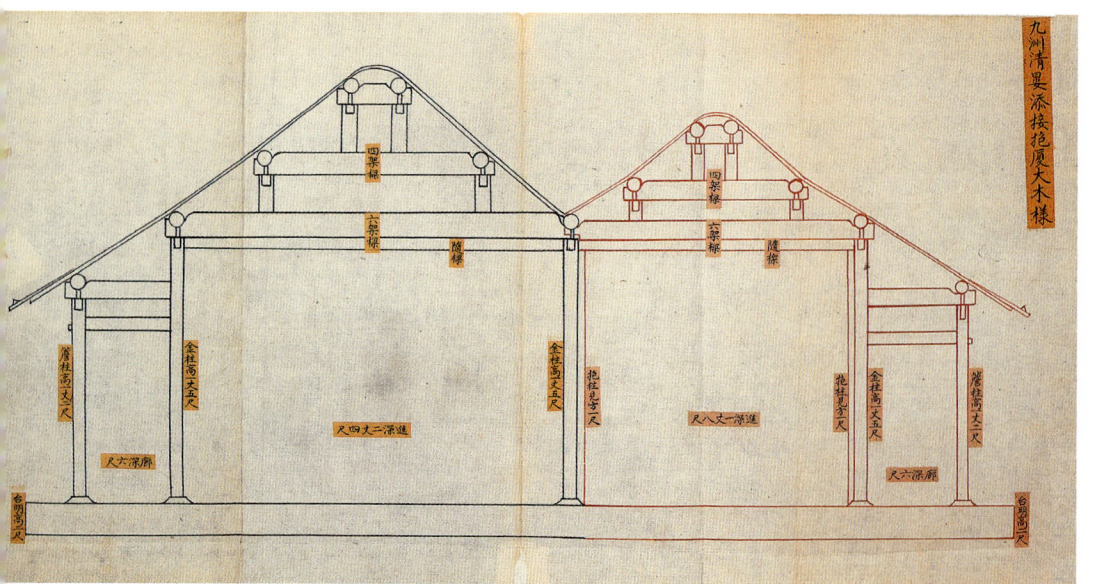

Fig. 45   Section of Jiuzhou Qingyan Hall

48   CHINA'S LOST IMPERIAL GARDEN

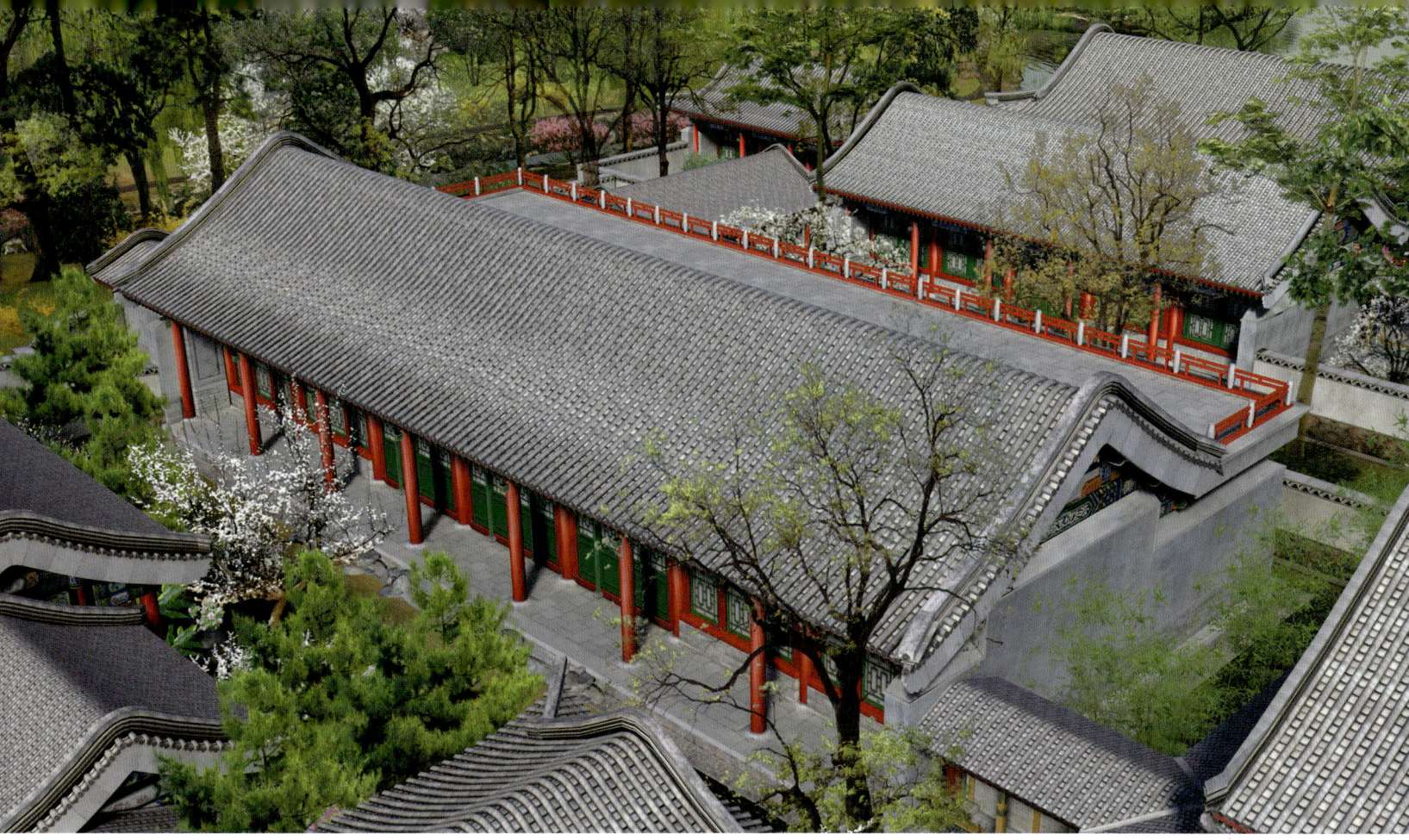

Fig. 46 Qinghui Pavilion, Imperial Apartments in West Sector of Jiuzhou Qingyan Complex

Qingyan area Qianlong built the Le Anhe, the Yiqing Shushi Hall (Hall of Books that Give Pleasure), and further west the Qinghui Pavilion (Clear Light Pavilion), the Luxiang Study (Dew Fragrance Study), the Rugu Hall (Embracing Antiquity Hall), the Songyun Building (Pine Cloud Pavilion) and the Hande Library (Virtue-Steeped Library); northernmost was the Yuanfei Yuyue Hall (Hall of Leaping Fish and Flying Kites).

The Qinghui Pavilion, with a width that spanned seven bays and a depth almost matching that of the Fengsan Wusi Hall, was the largest hall in the west of the Jiuzhou Qingyan Complex. It adjoined the Le Anhe to its east (fig. 46). It is here that small family banquets attended by the emperor and empress had been hosted since the Yongzheng era to celebrate the Lantern Festival. The Qianlong emperor feted his beloved mother here in a setting festooned with lanterns.

The Qinghui Pavilion had originally nine pine trees in front that were the same age as the Qianlong emperor. They grew robustly, as depicted in the *Forty Scenes of the Yuan Ming Yuan*. In the 28th year of Qianlong's reign (1763) the tall pines were destroyed in a fire. The accident deeply saddened Qianlong, who made several mentions of the incident in his poems. In the 30th year of his reign (1765) Qianlong proposed a redesign of the scenery in front of the Qinghui Pavilion by emulating the landscape paintings of Ni Zan (1301–1374, painter and poet) of the Yuan dynasty (1279–1368) and Huang Gongwang (1269–1354, painter of the Yuan dynasty). The front yard of the Qinghui Pavilion, only a dozen meters in depth, was of a modest scale. Part of its space was already taken up by an artificial hill, which, when framed by the tall pines, did not give an impression of overbuilding or clutter. But with the pines burned down, the artificial hill seemed out of place. The Qianlong emperor was well aware of the importance of trees to hills in Chinese garden design. After the pines were destroyed by fire, he made up for the loss by building on the hill four smaller-than-normal buildings called the Songyun Building, the Luxiang Study, the Hande Library and the Rugu Hall. These were known as the Four Vistas of the Qinghui Pavilion. These small structures, set off by the hill, appeared larger. Functionally the Songyun Building could be considered the "bed chamber," the Luxiang Study the tearoom, the Hande Library and the Rugu Hall the studies or libraries. Twenty years after the fire the place looked as visually appealing as ever.

On the east side of the main imperial residence was the Tiandi Yijia Chun Palace (Palace of Spring for One Family under Heaven and Earth), which served as residence for the imperial consorts, i.e. the empress, consorts and concubines of the emperor. In the Qing dynasty's system since the Kangxi years there were eight classes of imperial consorts, i.e. one *guanghou* (Empress), one *guangguifei* (Imperial Noble Consort), two *guifei* (Noble Consorts), four *feizi* (Consorts) and six *pin* (Imperial Concubines). Then there were the ladies-in-waiting called *guiren* (Noble Ladies), *changzai* (First Class Female Attendants) and *daying* (Choice Ladies or Second Class Female Attendants). In his life the Qianlong emperor had no less than 40 consorts[1], some of whom died early on and so there were fewer than this number of consorts at any given time. A rough idea of the configuration of the buildings in the eastern section can be formed from early pictures that have survived. There were three courtyards aligned along a central axis, featuring the entrance hall, the Tiandi Yijia Chun Palace, the Cheng'en Hall (Hall for Grace Received) and the Quanshi Ziyu Hall (Hall of Self-Entertainment with Stones in a Spring). At the two sides of the axis were two courtyards next to one another, which, together with the courtyards adjacent to the Jiuzhou Qingyan Complex, had to accommodate dozens of imperial consorts and their ladies-in-waiting. These buildings must have been stretched to their limits (fig. 47).

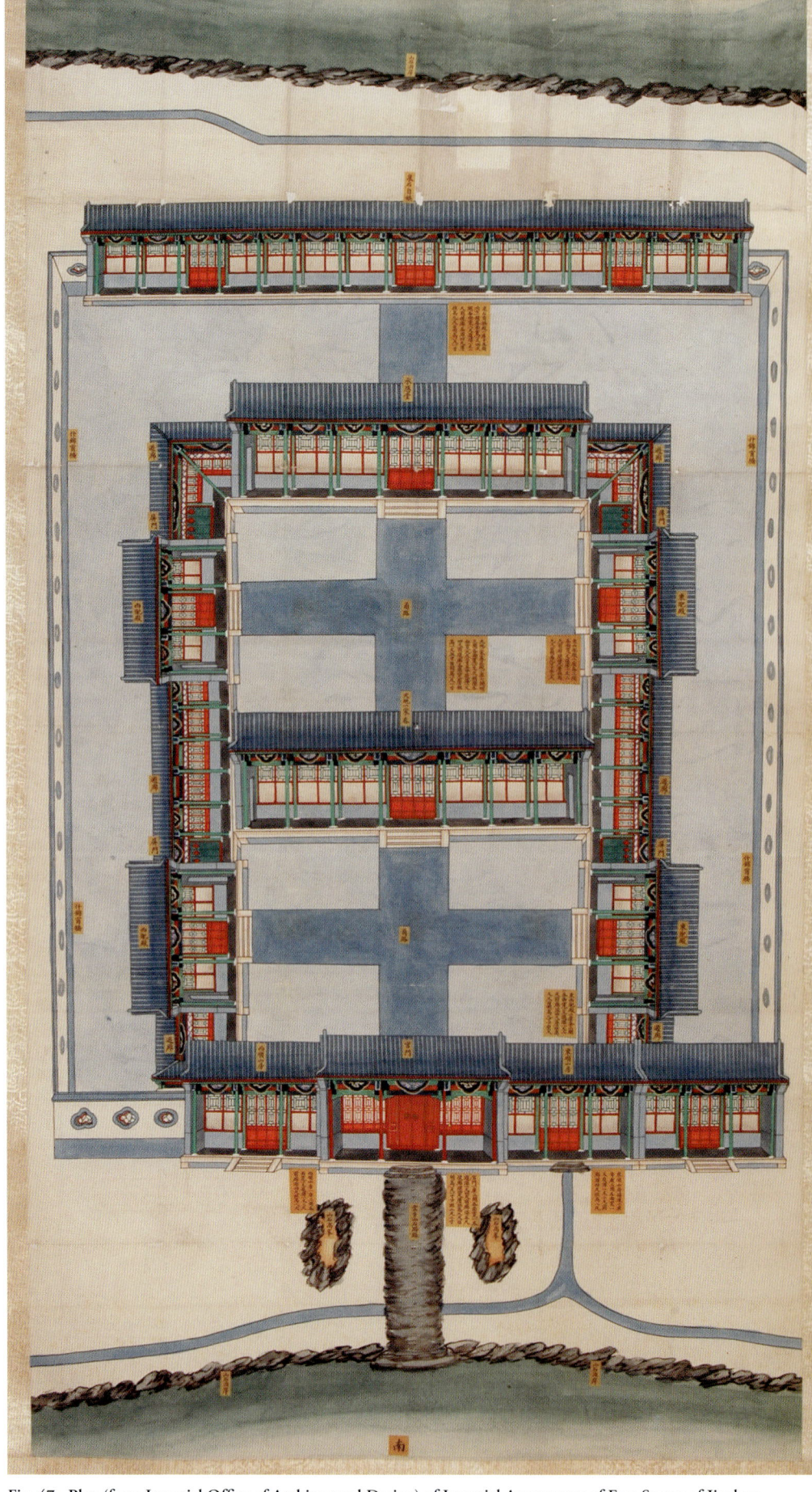

Fig. 47 Plan (from Imperial Office of Architectural Design) of Imperial Apartments of East Sector of Jiuzhou Qingyan Complex

50   CHINA'S LOST IMPERIAL GARDEN

含經堂 Hanjing Hall (Tripataka Hall)

The Hanjing Hall of the Changchun Garden was built by Emperor Qianlong for his retirement after abdicating in favor of his successor. This imperial residence was situated on a large island in the middle of the Garden and constituted the primary group of buildings in the entire Garden, with lakes, streams and other groups of buildings spread evenly around it. These buildings called the Siyong Study, Haiyue Kaijin Complex, Yulinglong Pavilion and Zelan Hall were grouped around and oriented toward the Hanjing Hall as if in homage, even though low earthen hills separated them.

The Hanjing Hall group of buildings was surrounded by earthen hills on the island on which it was located (fig. 48). Communication with the surrounding rivers and streams was made possible through a number of gaps between the hills. The group consisted of three sections: the left, the middle and the right. The middle section's gates, halls, pavilions and studies were aligned along a central axis and there were three courtyards, the front-most of which had an entrance hall of five bays fronted by a small plaza, bounded by an architectural arch on its south side and two more on its east and west sides, all decorated with glazed color tiles. Once past the gate one came to the main hall Hanjing, which was seven bays wide and furnished with both a front and a back porch and flanked by side halls of five bays on either side (east and west), all linked by galleries. The second courtyard, coming after the Hanjing Hall, comprised a main building—the Chunhua Pavilion—which was seven bays wide and three bays deep and featured also a front and a back porch; it communicated with the Hanjing Hall through winding galleries at its two sides. An artificial hill stacked with Lake Tai rocks lay athwart the courtyard, forming a sort of barrier for the Hanjing Hall. In the third courtyard stood the Yunzhen Study,

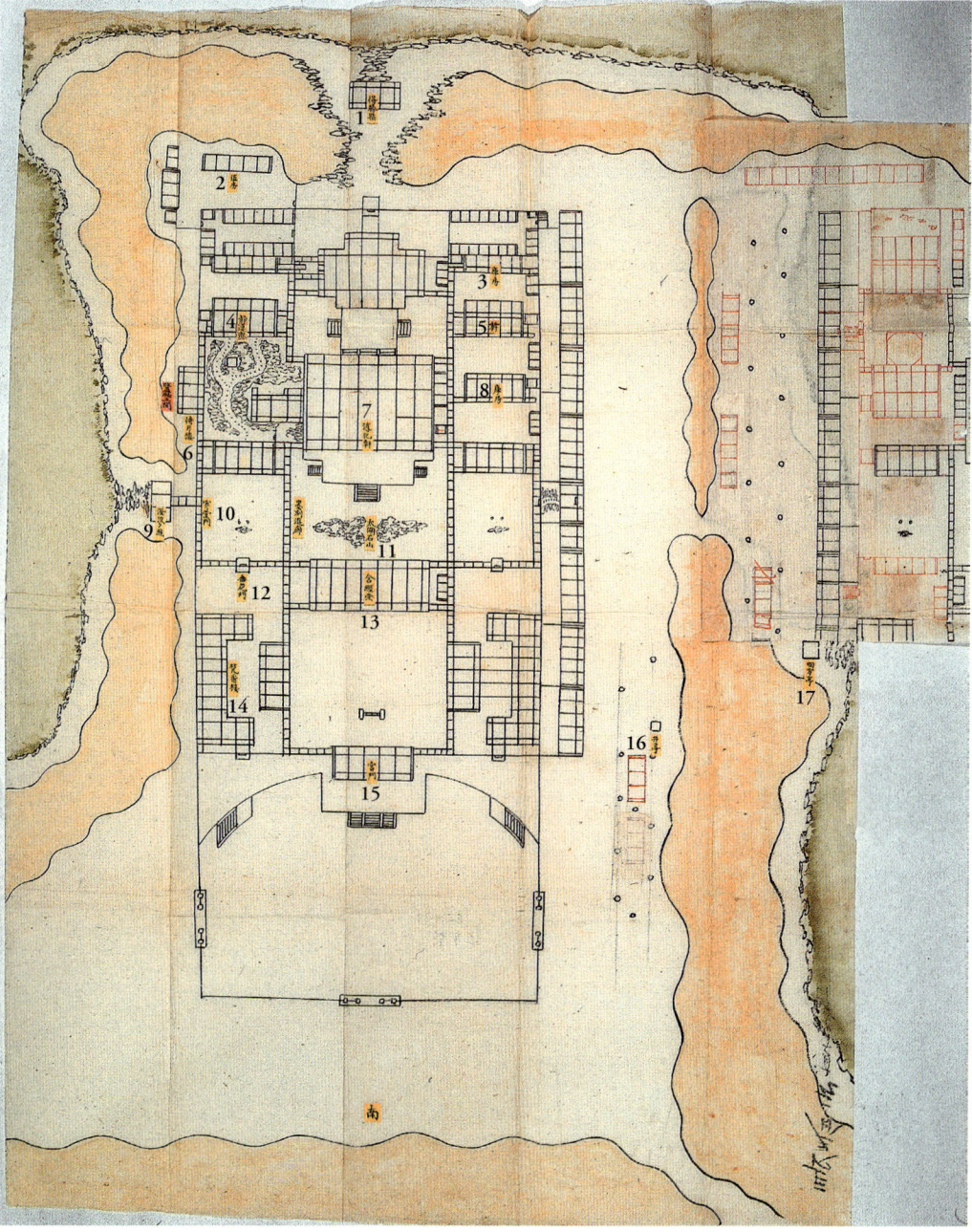

Fig. 48 Plan (from Imperial Office of Architectural Design) of Hanjing Hall in Changchun Garden
1. Deshenggai Pavilion
2. Duty room
3. Store room
4. Jinglian Study
5. Gazebo
6. Daiyue Building
7. Chunhua Pavilion
8. Store room
9. Chengbo Xizhao Pavilion
10. Connecting door
11. Lake Tai rock
12. Hanging Flowers Gate
13. Hanjing Hall
14. Fanxiang Building
15. Gate
16. Well pavilion
17. Square kiosk

---
1 Cf. *Qianlong Zhuan* (*Biography of Emperor Qianlong*) by Tang Wenji and Luo Qingsi, published by the People's Publishing House, 1994.

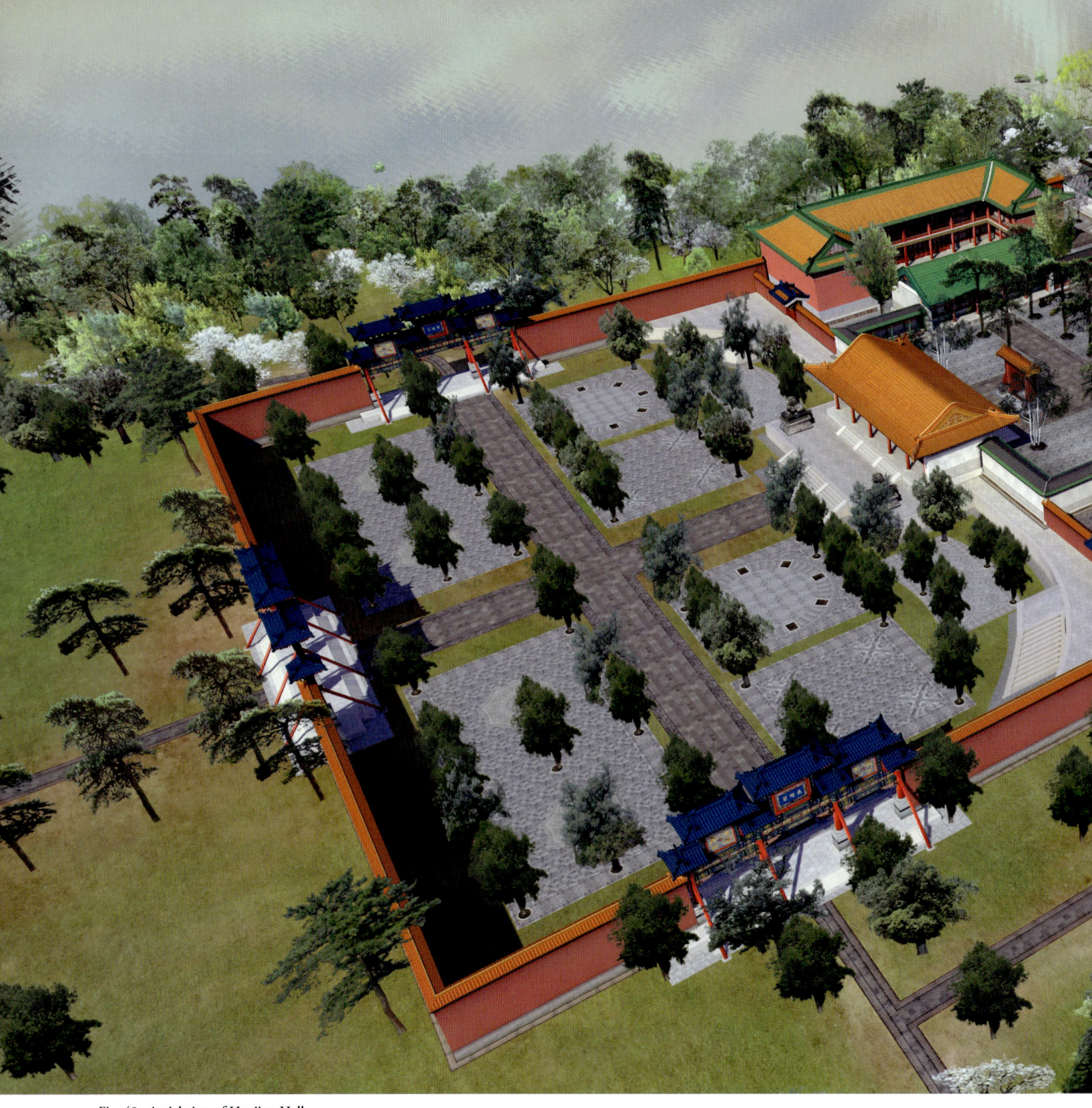

Fig. 49 Aerial view of Hanjing Hall

which was seven bays wide and featured a veranda front and back. When it was first built in the 12th year of Qianlong's reign (1747), it was located where the Chunhua Pavilion later stood. It was moved north in the 35th year of Qianlong's reign (1770) to make room for the Chunhua Pavilion. A gate in the north wall of the courtyard of the Yunzhen Study provided access to a gap between hills and the Deshenggai Pavilion (Victory Pavilion).

The west section of the Hanjing Hall group of buildings comprised five courtyards of varying sizes (fig. 49), the first of which consisted of only the Fanxiang Building (Buddhist Incense Pavilion), a U-shaped building that had an east-west orientation and was nine rooms wide and faced the west side hall of the Hanjing Hall. One passed through a Hanging Flowers Gate to access the inner courtyard,

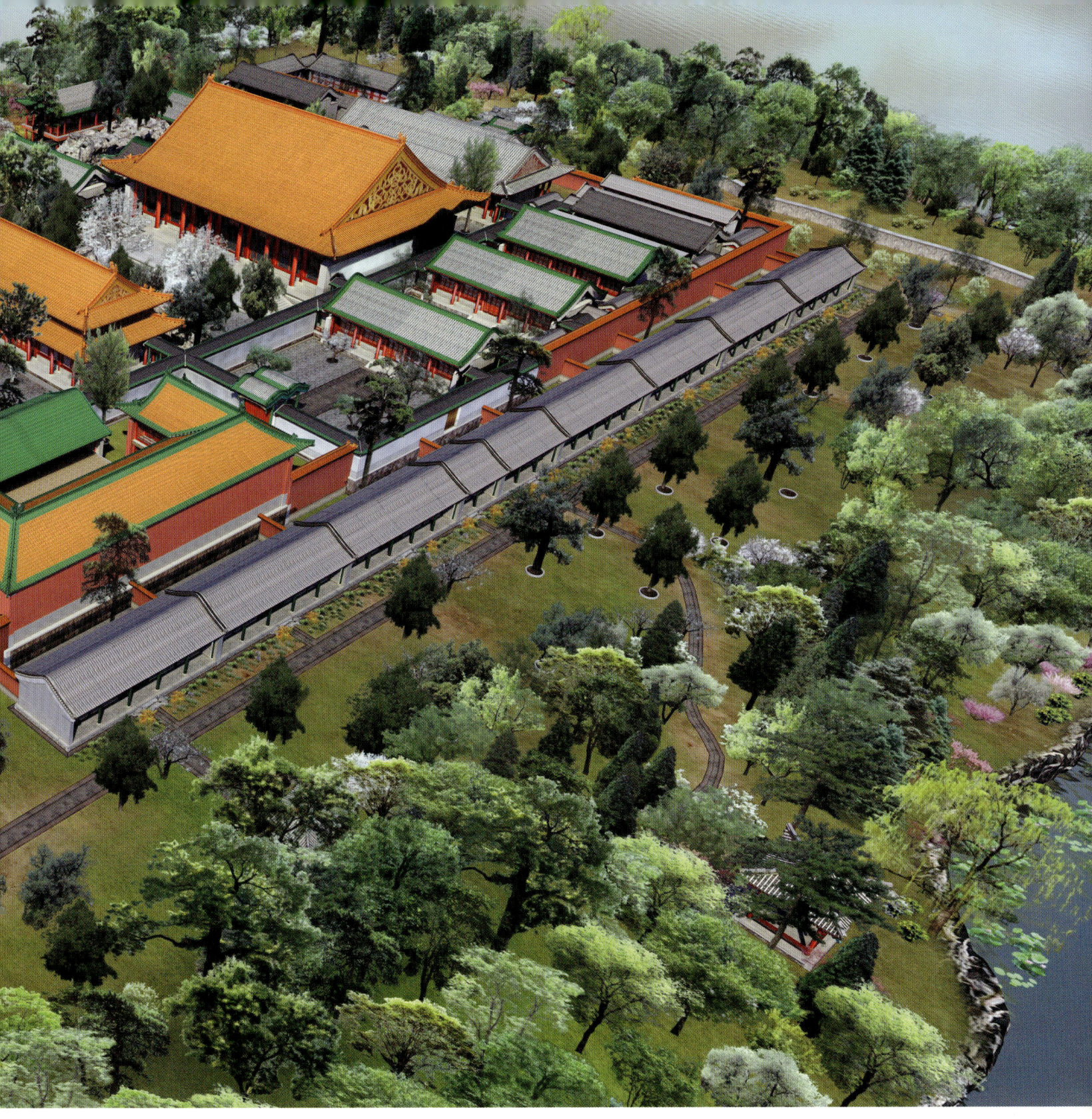

which was surrounded on three sides by a gallery; on its north side stood the Hanguang Room (Room of Lightness), five bays wide and furnished with a front and a back porch. In the west gallery of the courtyard a connecting door led to the Chengbo Xizhao Pavilion (Clear Ripples in Sunset Pavilion). The third courtyard lay against the west gable wall of the Chunhua Pavilion, against which the Sanyou Pavilion (Three Friends Pavilion) was built. The rest of the courtyard was taken up by a man-made rock-stacked hill. To the north of the hill stood the Jinglian Study (Quiet Lotus Study) and to its west the Daiyue Building (Waiting for the Moon Building). A gallery west of the hill connected these two buildings and the Hanguang Room in the front. A small square-shaped open-sided pavilion was built on the hill. The fourth courtyard was very small with only a five-bays-wide building the Lixin Building (Ordering One's

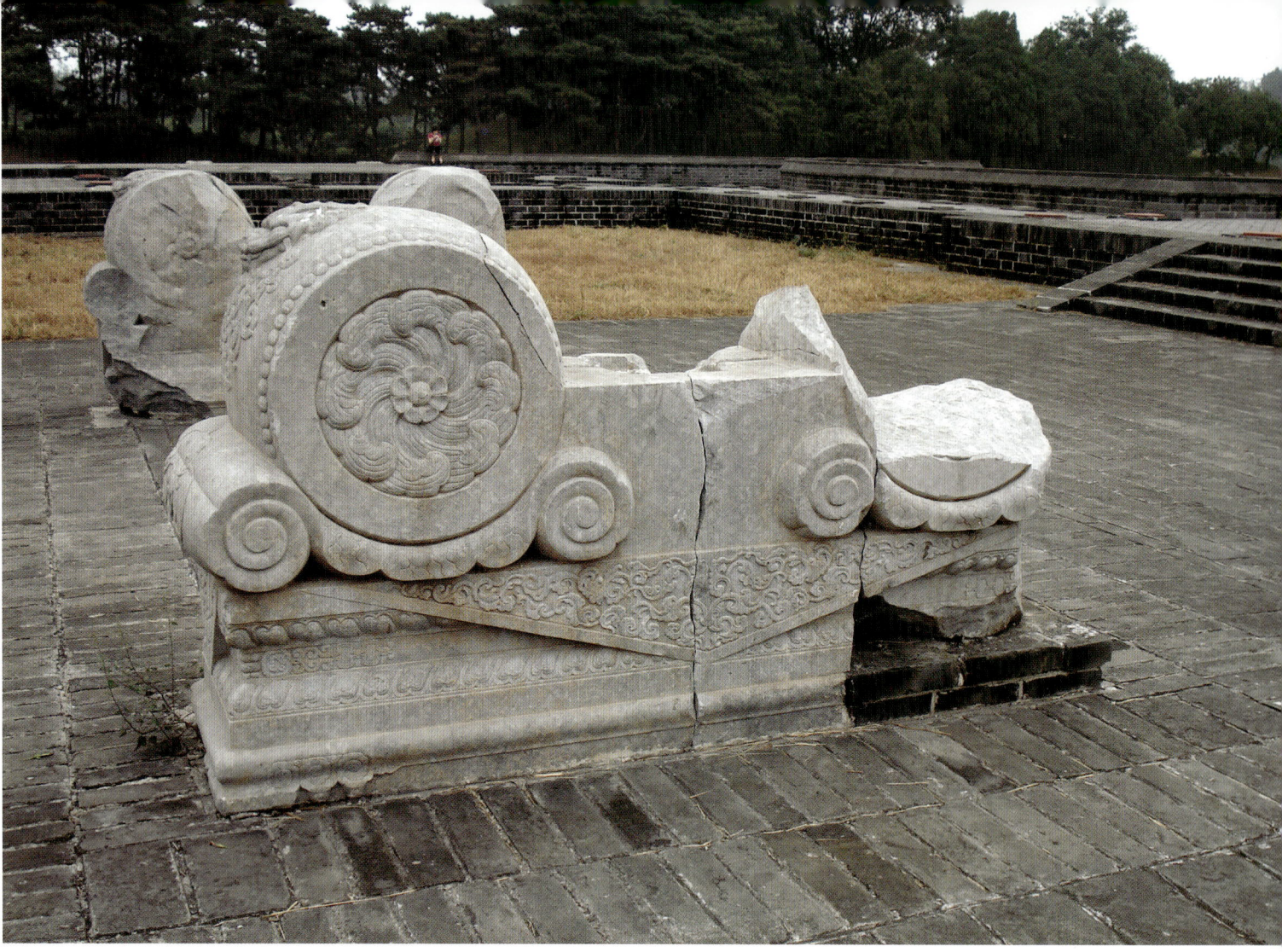

Fig. 50 Stone used to buttress Spirit Wall inside Palace Gate of Hanjing Hall

Thoughts Building). In the fifth courtyard and further back there were more than twenty duty rooms and waiting rooms.

The eastern section of the Hanjing Hall group of buildings comprised four courtyards. The first—the Xiazhu Building—and the second—the Yuanying Study (Lake Reflections Study)—had a layout similar to that of the western section. After the rebuilding overseen by Emperor Jiaqing, a Chinese opera stage, a backstage and a hall for opera viewing were installed in the back, which were not there in Qianlong's day. Outside the eastern section was a long line of shopfronts. This was the second market street in the Yuan Ming Yuan.

The Hanjing Hall and the Chunhua Pavilion stood out not only for the magnificence of their buildings but also for the ornate treatment of their spaces. A plaza was placed in front that measured 50 meters east-west and 33.7 meters north-south. Three architectural arches covered with glazed color tiles stood on the east, west and south sides of the plaza, which was divided into four rectangular spaces by two paths that crossed at right angles in the middle of the quadrangle. A number of surfaces were covered with color floor tiles. In the two north divisions of the plaza were laid a square pattern 13.9 meters across and a circular pattern 12.5 meters in diameter. It is believed that this is where felt tents were pitched[1] (fig. 51) to accommodate chieftains of nomadic tribes.

The north side of the plaza abutted the entrance hall of the Hanjing Hall, which sat on a foundation with a height of 1.6 meters. At its right and left the foundation extended south to hug the entrance hall. After one entered this gate one was met first by a spirit wall. Carved stones that used to support the spirit wall have survived to this day (fig. 50). The spirit wall, which measured 4.5 meters across, completely blocked the view of the visitor. Although the Hanjing Hall was a major imperial residential palace, it functioned as a venue for ceremonies and protocol. Archeological digging of the foundation uncovered traces of flues used in heating north of the

54 CHINA'S LOST IMPERIAL GARDEN

west outer bay (second room from the central bay) and end bay (the third from the central bay) as well near the middle of the east end bay. They suggested a setup similar to that used for the heated rooms in the palaces of the Forbidden City, which kept the interior of the buildings very warm in winter. It was cool here in summer.

A building worth mentioning near the Hanjing Hall was the Xiazhu Building east of the eastern side hall and facing it. This two-story building was actually a kind of library, which once housed the *Siku Quanshu Huiyao* (*Essentials of the Complete Library of the Four Treasuries*) for the reading pleasure of Emperor Qianlong, a bibliophile.

The Chunhua Pavilion was a palace built in the 35th year of Qianlong's reign (1770) to house the stone tablets on which the *Chunhuage Tie* (*Model Calligraphy from the Chunhua Pavilion*) of the Song dynasty (960–1279) was re-carved. The *Chunhuage Tie* of the Song dynasty is the earliest Chinese calligraphic model book and collects together choice samples of different schools of calligraphy spanning a millennium from the early Qin (221–206 BC) to the Sui (581–618) and the Tang (618–907) dynasties. The 10-volume anthology included 420 works by 103 calligraphers ranging from emperors to court ministers and famous masters. Works of renowned calligraphers from antiquity were traced on paper and transferred to stone or wood by carving before rubbings were made from the surfaces of the carved stone or wood. These rubbings were bound into the anthology entitle the *Chunhuage Tie*. This model calligraphy anthology of the Song dynasty did not survive successive wars and by the time of the Qing dynasty it was hard to find anywhere. Fortunately a good, rare copy of the model calligraphy book was kept in the Imperial Household Department of the Qing court and after careful research was recarved on stone. The stone tablets thus carved were set in the walls of the two galleries behind the Hanjing Hall and the Chunhua Pavilion was built in the courtyard between the two galleries hung with the stone tablets to house the new *Chunhuage Tie*.

It was Emperor Qianlong's intention that with the newly built pavilion, he would quietly appreciate and enjoy the beauty of calligraphy there once he reached the 60th year of his reign and the 85th year of his life.[2]

The Chunhua Pavilion was a large palatial building that was seven bays wide and three bays deep, with a frontage of 32.15 meters and a depth of 23.2 meters. The foundation above ground

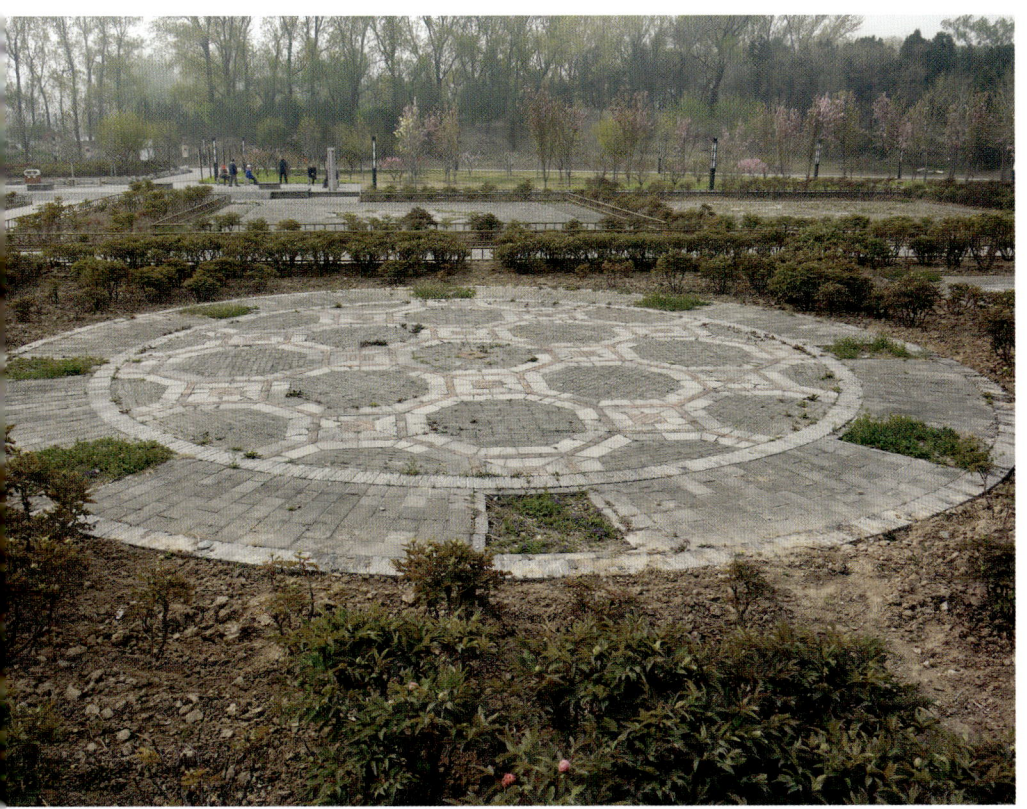

Fig. 51 Brick floral pattern in front of Hanjing Hall

---

1 Cf. *Yuan Ming Yuan Changchun Yuan Hanjing Tang Kaogu Fajue Baogao* (Archaeological Report on the Hanjing Hall of Changchun Garden of Yuan Ming Yuan) compiled by the Institute of Archaeology and Cultural Relics of Beijing.
2 Cf. *Yuzhi Shi*, by Emperor Qianlong, Volume 92 of Book III. Regrettably the "complete" original of the good copy of the *Chunhuage Tie* kept by the Imperial Household Department is no longer to be found. In recent years Volumes 6, 7 and 8 of the good-copy anthology have been bought from private collectors in the US at a cost of US $450,000 and are now in the collection of the Shanghai Museum. The Palace Museum and the National Museum of China have in their collections "complete" rubbings of the *Chunhuage Tie* from the Southern Song period (1127–1279), with an inscription in seal script at the end of every volume stating that it was traced and carved in stone on the sixth day of the 11th month of the third year of the Chunhua era on the instruction of the emperor. The Shanghai Library holds only Volume 9 of the good-copy anthology, while the Freer Gallery of Art in Washington D.C. holds the anthology with only Volume 9 missing. Between them therefore they hold the complete collection. Numerous rubbings from the Yuan, Ming and Qing dynasties have survived.

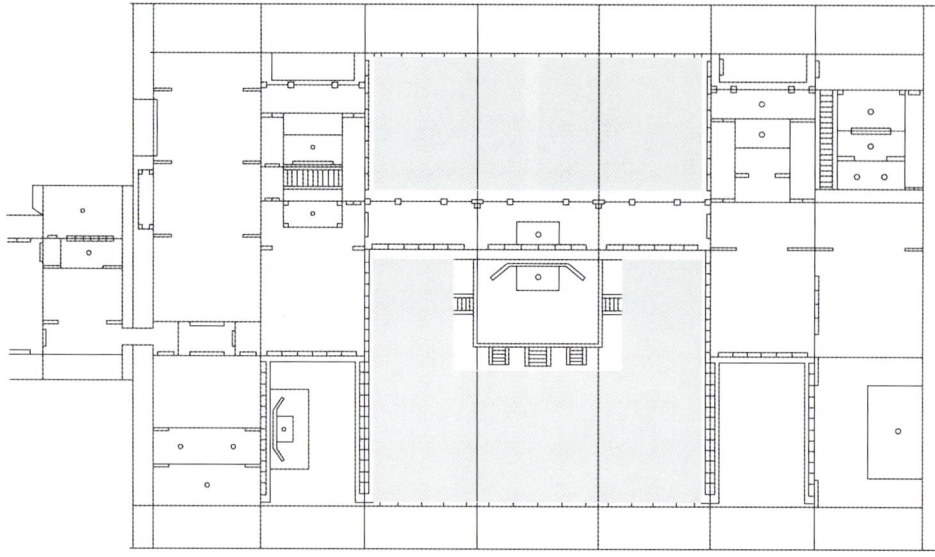

Fig. 52 Plan of main hall of Chunhua Pavilion

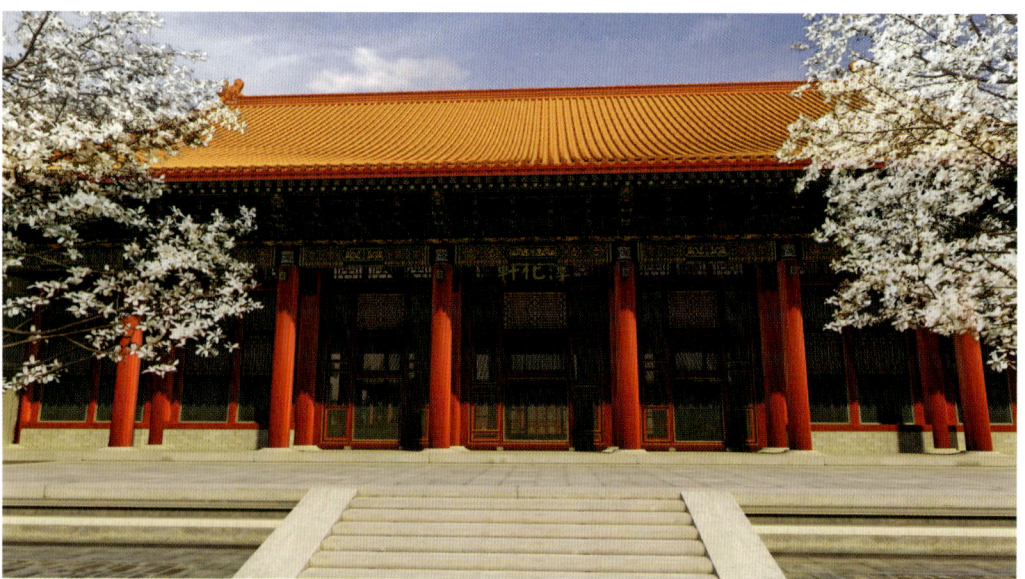

Fig. 53 Main hall of Chunhua Pavilion

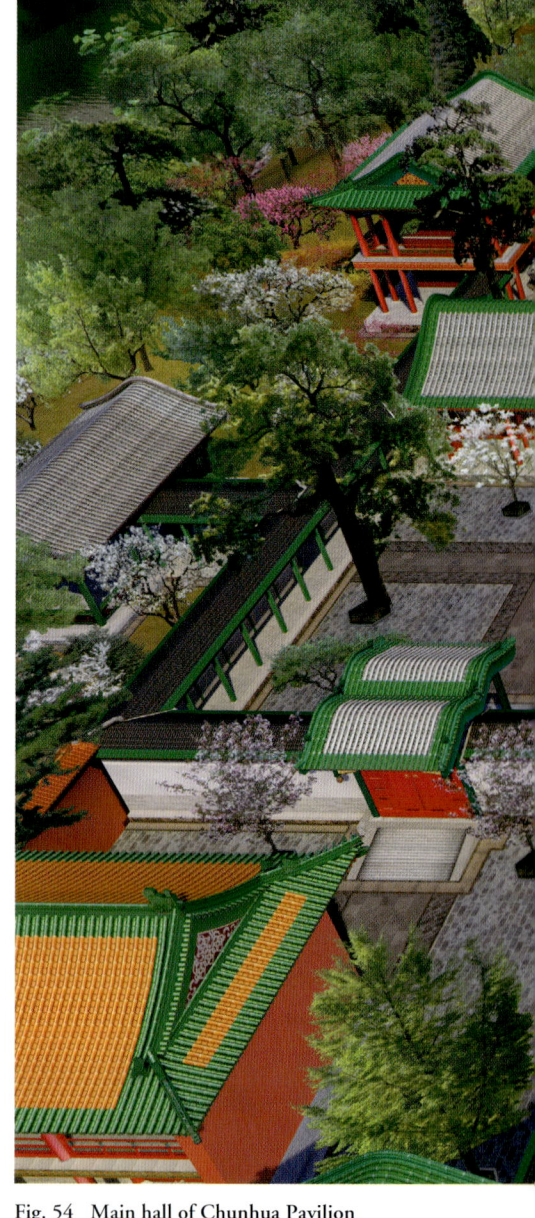

Fig. 54 Main hall of Chunhua Pavilion

measured 33.8 meters in width and 26.6 meters in depth. It featured a moon terrace in front that measured 20 meters by 6.6 meters. The central bay was 5.15 meters wide, the secondary bay (rooms next to the central hall), the outer bay and the end bay all measured 4.5 meters wide. The three bays from front to back measured 6.4 meters each. As the dimensions of the central bay exceeded the norm in similar structures, this building was more massive than other similar buildings (figs. 53, 54). The only surviving plan of the Chunhua Pavilion shows that it boasted ample interior spaces and the interior of the rooms was arranged into two stories (fig. 52).

From the north hall of the Chunhua Pavilion one stepped out of the north gate and crossed the moon terrace to arrive at the Yunzhen Study, which was seven bays wide and surrounded by a gallery, a front porch of five bays and a back porch of three bays. Its foundation above ground was 30 meters wide and its depth 21.8 meters at its deepest. In dimensions this building was smaller than the Chunhua Pavilion but it had a greater mass. Extant records show the interior of its rooms was also configured as two stories. Before the construction of the Chunhua Pavilion it must have served as the primary apartments. Archeologic work uncovered heating flues at the locations of the east and the west outer bay, which would indicate the use of the heated rooms system of heating.

The landscaping at this imperial residence was unique in the Yuan Ming Yuan. The courtyard at the west side of the Chunhua Pavilion was almost entirely taken up by a big artificial hill stacked with Lake Tai rocks and

56 CHINA'S LOST IMPERIAL GARDEN

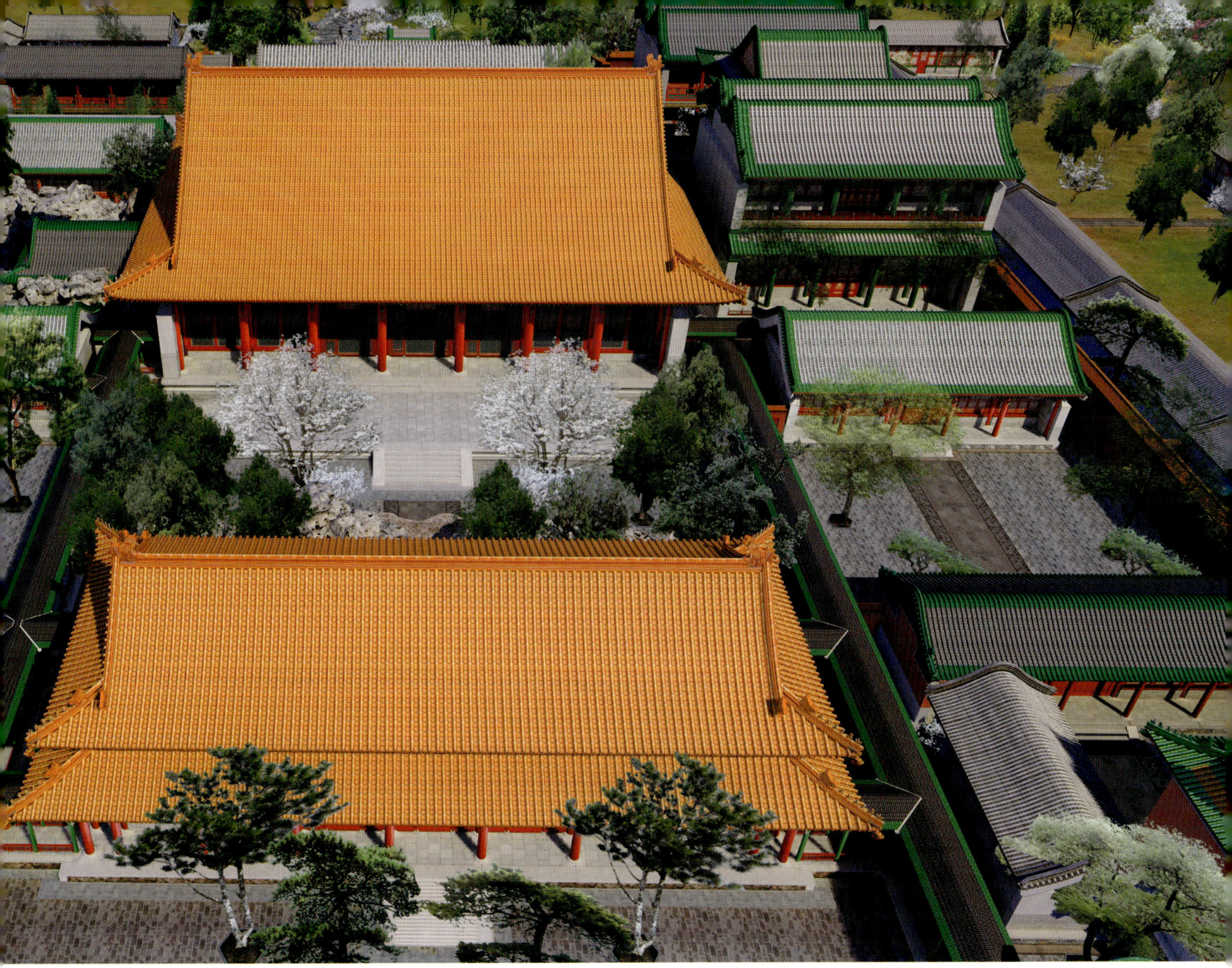

featuring stone steps, caves, cliffs and gorges (fig. 55). At the east side of the hill a small building—the Sanyou Pavilion—abutted the Chunhua Pavilion, so that there would be direct access from the Chunhua Pavilion to the courtyard through the small building and also that this small building could hide the massive gable wall of the Chunhua Pavilion and balance the taller Chunhua Pavilion and the artificial hill dwarfed by it. The pines, bamboo plants and plum trees in the garden surrounding the Sanyou Pavilion created a purifying and spiritually uplifting ambience.

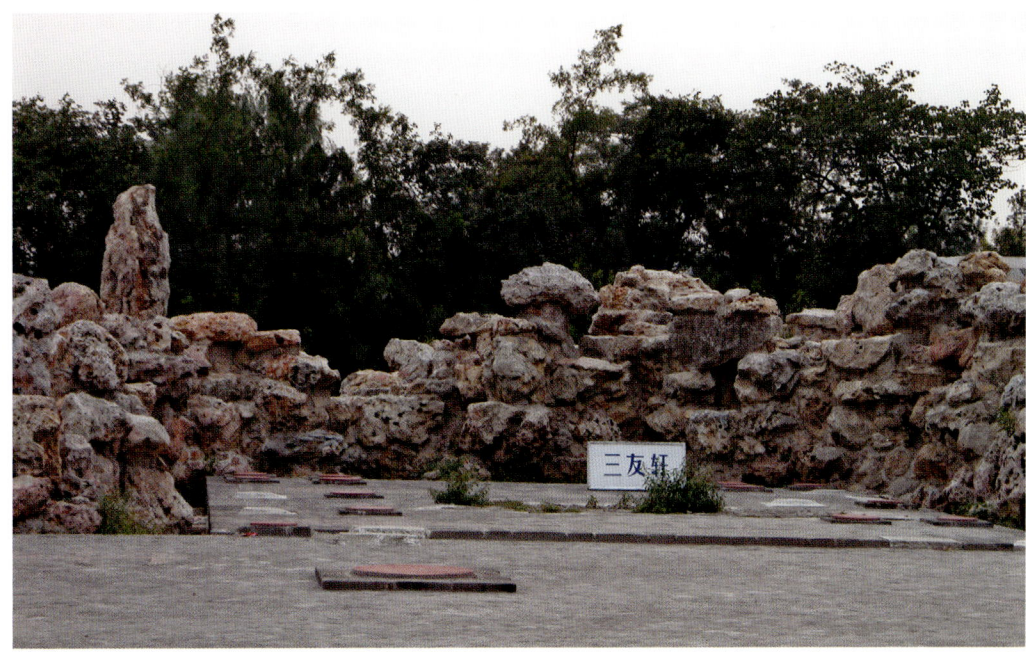

Fig. 55 Artificial hill west of Sanyou Pavilion

PART II SCENERY OF THE YUAN MING YUAN 57

綺春園 The Imperial Apartments of the Qichun Garden (Garden of Elegant Spring)

The imperial apartments of the Qichun Garden were situated behind the main hall just inside the gate and were separated from it by an earthen hill. Drawings dating from the 30th year of the Daoguang era show that the area included the inner gatehouse, the Yishou Pavilion, the Fuchun Hall, the Eastern Quarters, the Western Quarters and some garden structures (fig. 56). In the Daoguang era it became the residence of the empress dowagers, consort dowagers and other palace ladies, who moved to the Qichun Garden as a result of the grievous dilapidation of the Changchun Garden (Joyful Spring Garden), where they used to live.

The main structure amongst these apartments was the H-shaped Fuchun Hall, which was surrounded by a number of two-storied pavilions, winding galleries and waterside kiosks. The Yishou Pavilion in front of the Fuchun Hall functioned as a venue for ceremonies and protocol. The Fuchun Hall was the residence of the empress dowager; it had access through the east gate to the Eastern Quarters and Western Quarters, where consorts and concubines lived.

The Inner Gatehouse, the Yishou Pavilion, the Fuchun Hall, the connecting gallery, the rear hall and the Wenyue Building (Asking the Moon Building) of the complex were aligned along a north-south axis, at the sides of which were scattered other structures freer in architectural style, size and form. A number of artificial hills placed at various points gave the complex a bucolic air.

The Fuchun Hall was an H-shaped hall, with a width of five bays both in the front and at the back; the connecting gallery had a length of three bays. The front hall featured a hip-and-gable roof and the rear hall had a overhanging gable roof with double round ridges. The central bay of the front section, with a couch-throne placed opposite the entrance, served mainly for holding ceremonies and receiving guests. The two bays at the west end were made into one room to serve as a kind of living room for daily activities; the two bays at the east end were furnished with partitions and beds to accommodate guests. The rear section of the building, furnished with beds and lofts, was the main sleeping quarters of the building.

The Eastern Quarters and Western Quarters, quarters for persons of lower rank, were less elaborate in their furnishings; their dimensions varied according to hierarchical ranking. The two buildings were similarly configured, each comprising six courtyards. The building in the first courtyard was nine bays wide; those in the second, third and fourth courtyards were all five bays wide and the building in the fifth courtyard was seven bays wide. The tenants of these premises were all consorts, concubines, daughters and daughters-in-law of Emperor Daoguang.

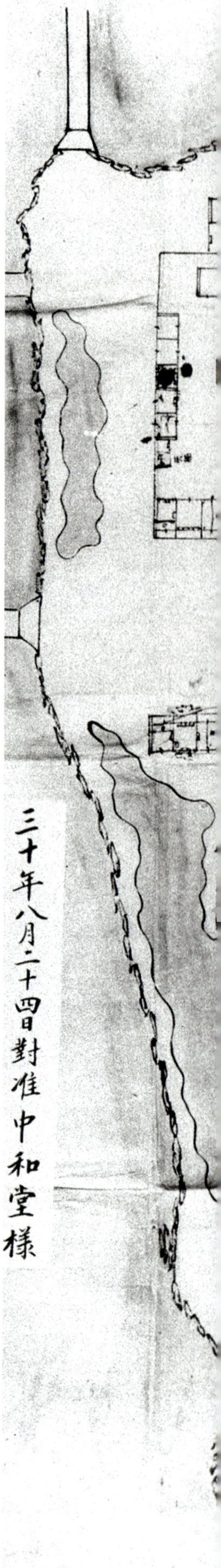

Fig. 56 General plan of the Imperial Apartments of Qichun Garden
1. Wenyue Building
2. Western Quarters
3. Eastern Quarters
4. East gate
5. Fuchun Hall
6. Side hall
7. Side hall
8. Yishou Pavilion
9. Inner Gatehouse

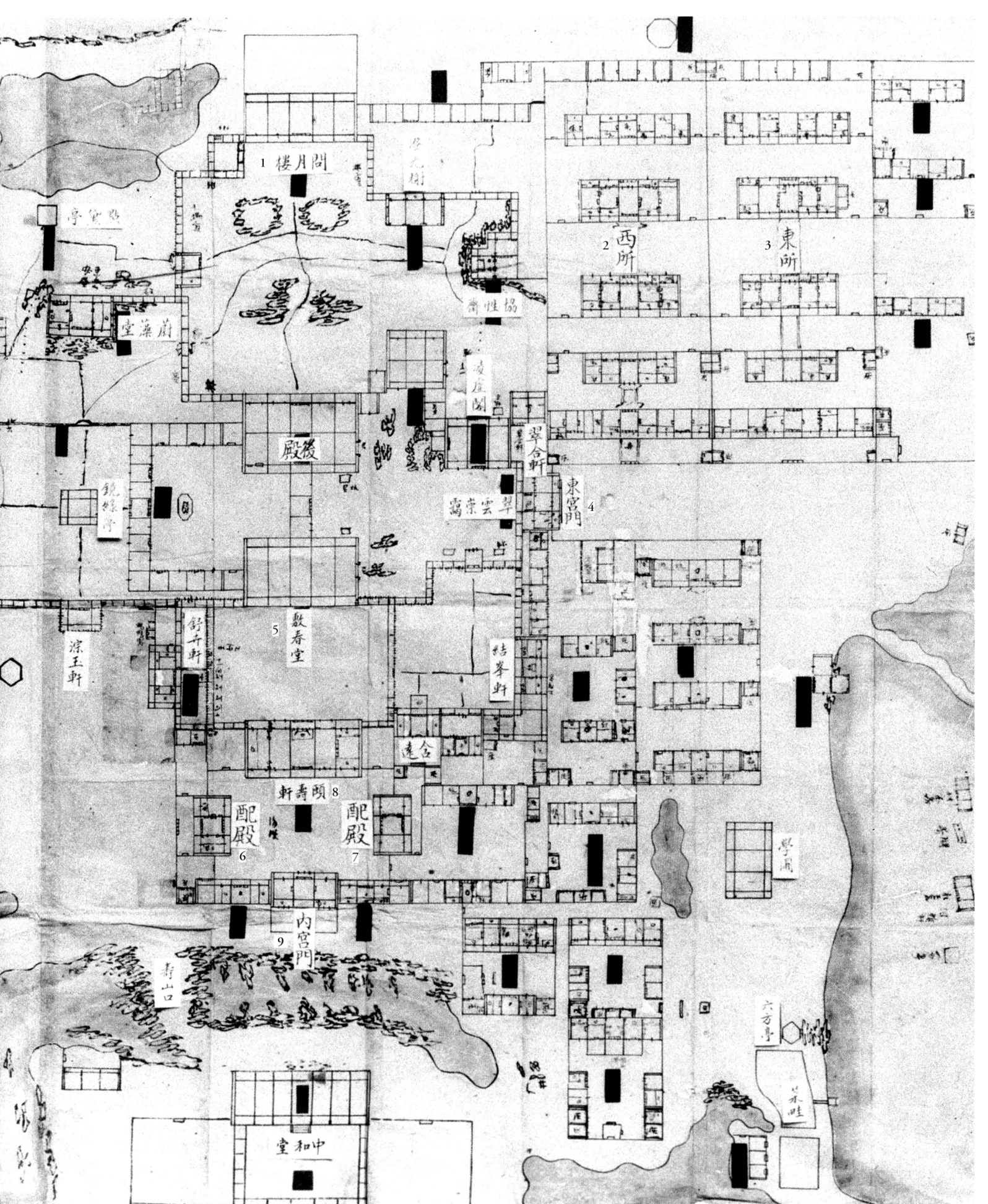

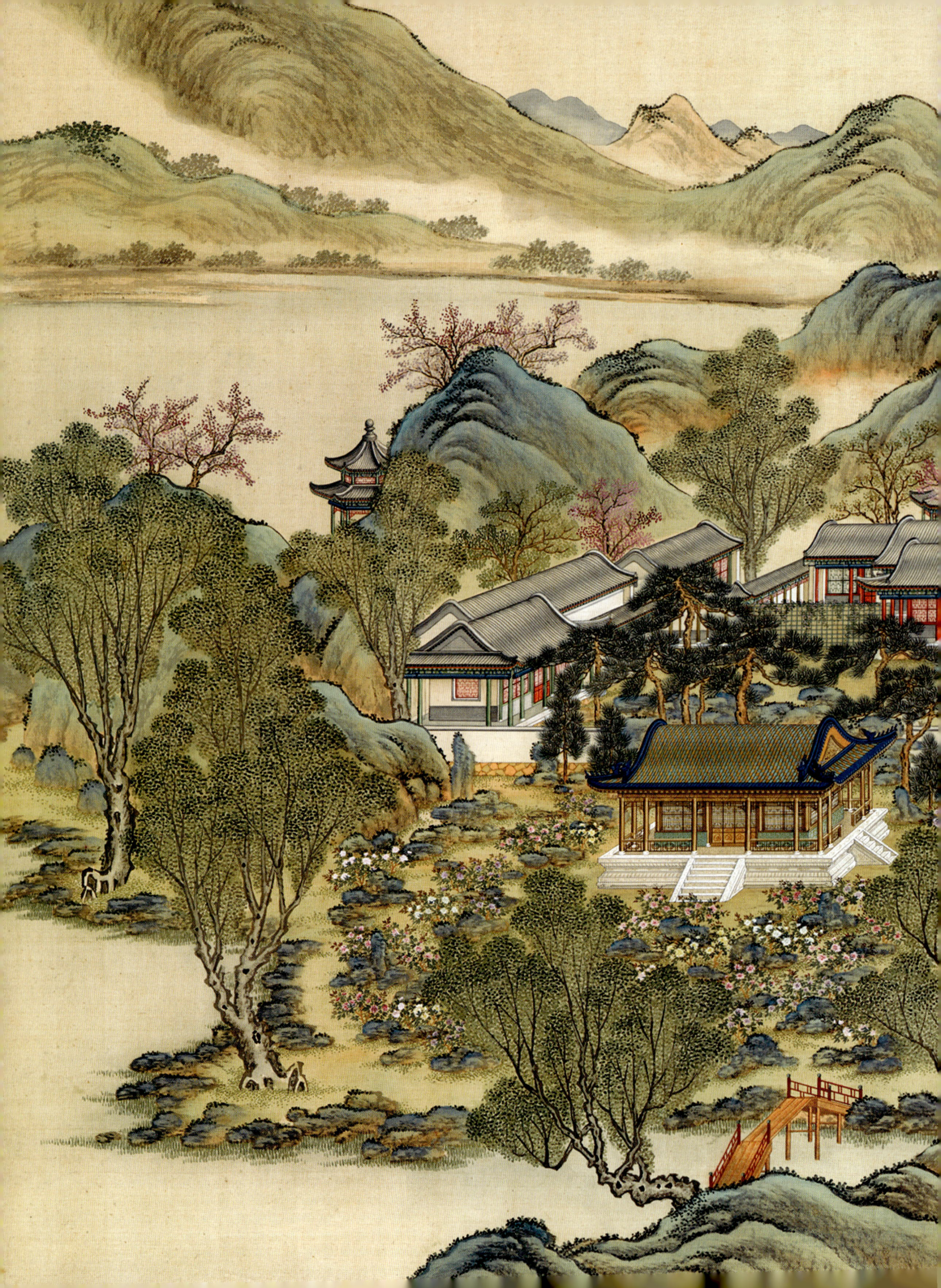

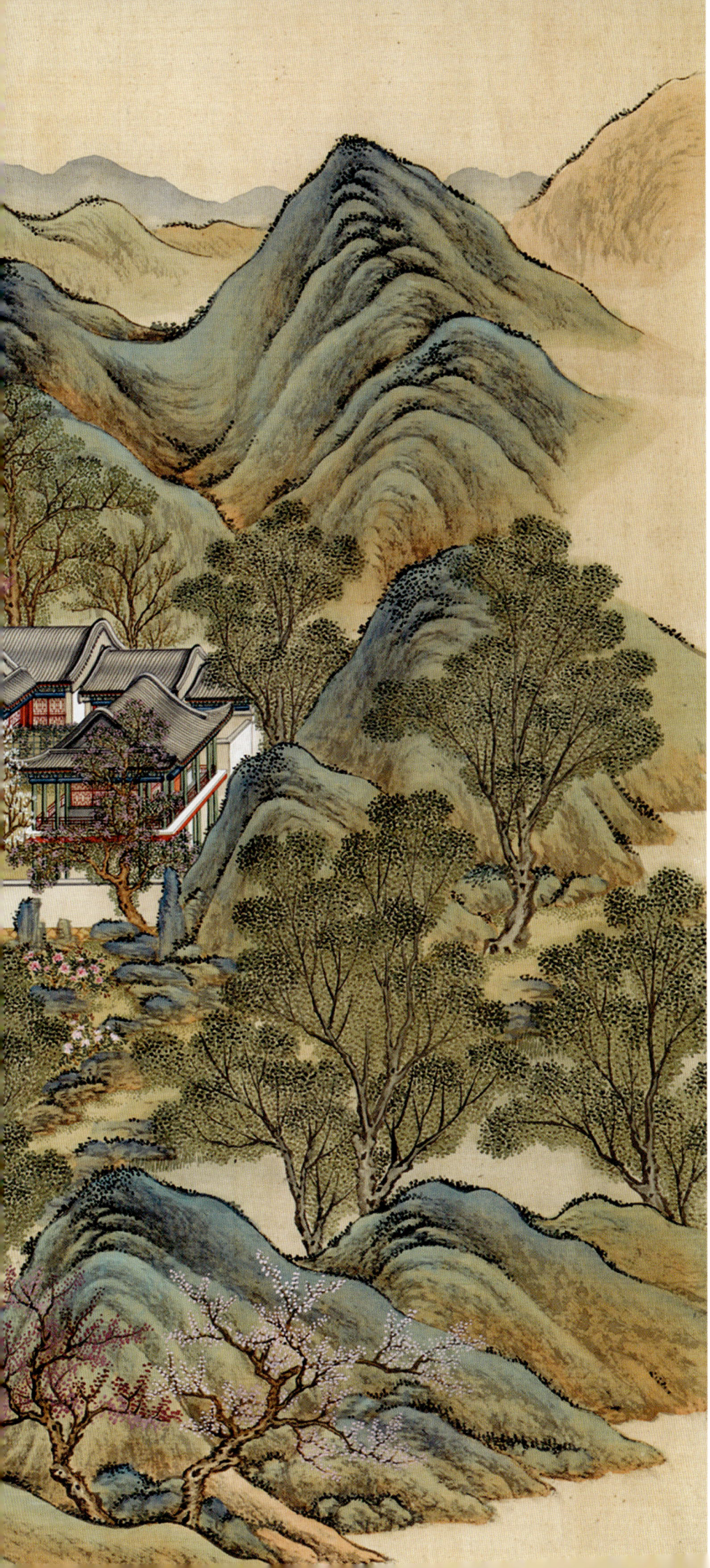

CHAPTER VII
Heaven and Earth and *Ren Lun* (Human Ethics)

Ren Lun means the norms of human relationships and the observance of propriety. It is a basic tenet of Confucian ethics with an emphasis on orderly, proper behavior among people of various statures and ages. The landscaping of the Yuan Ming Yuan reflected the moral concepts advocated by the Qing emperors (fig. 57).

Fig. 57 Louyue Kaiyun (Complex of the Engraved Moon and Unfolding Clouds) in *Forty Scenes of the Yuan Ming Yuan*

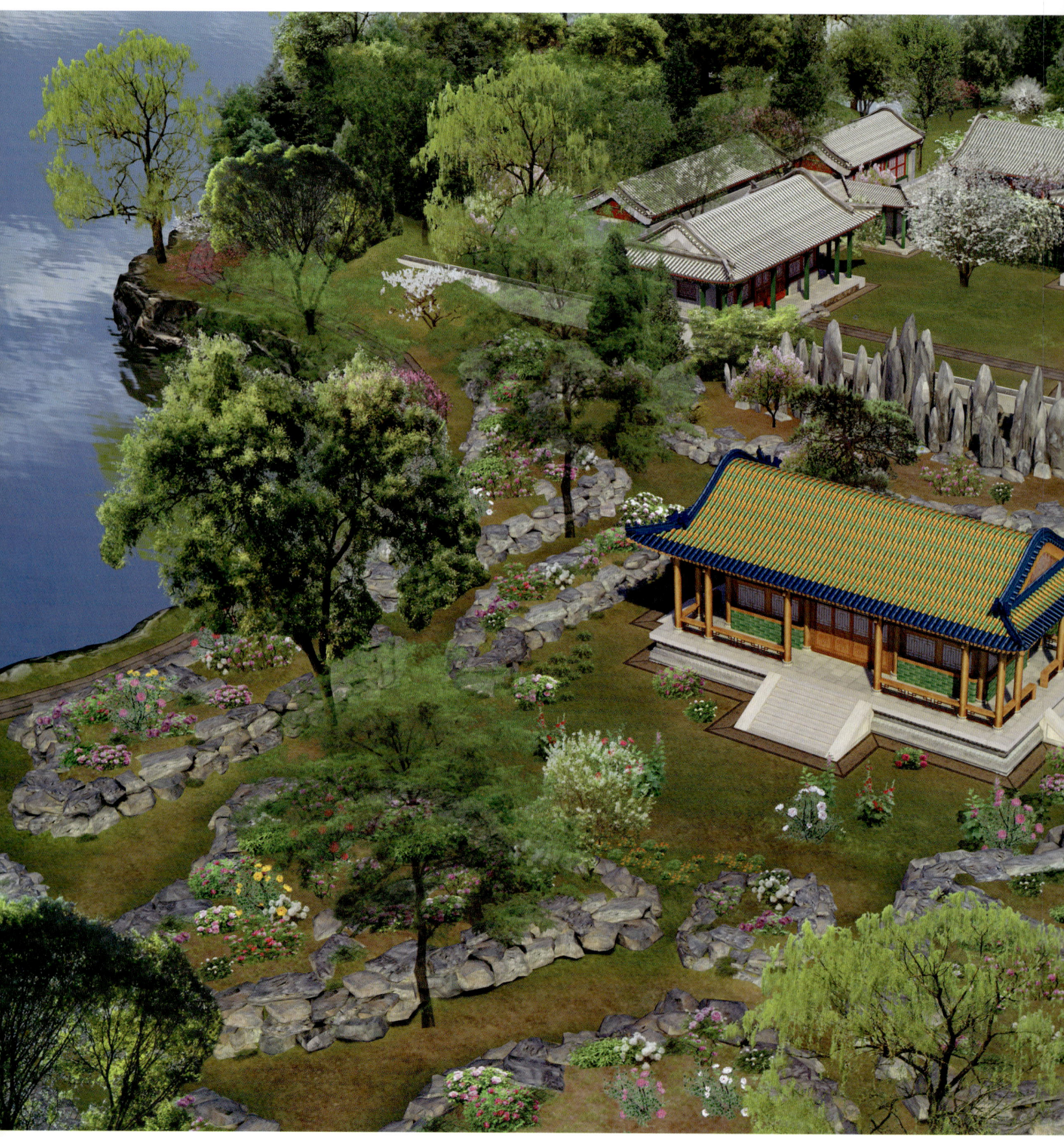

Fig. 58 Themed area of Louyue Kaiyun

镂月开云 Louyue Kaiyun Complex (Complex of the Engraved Moon and Unfolding Clouds)

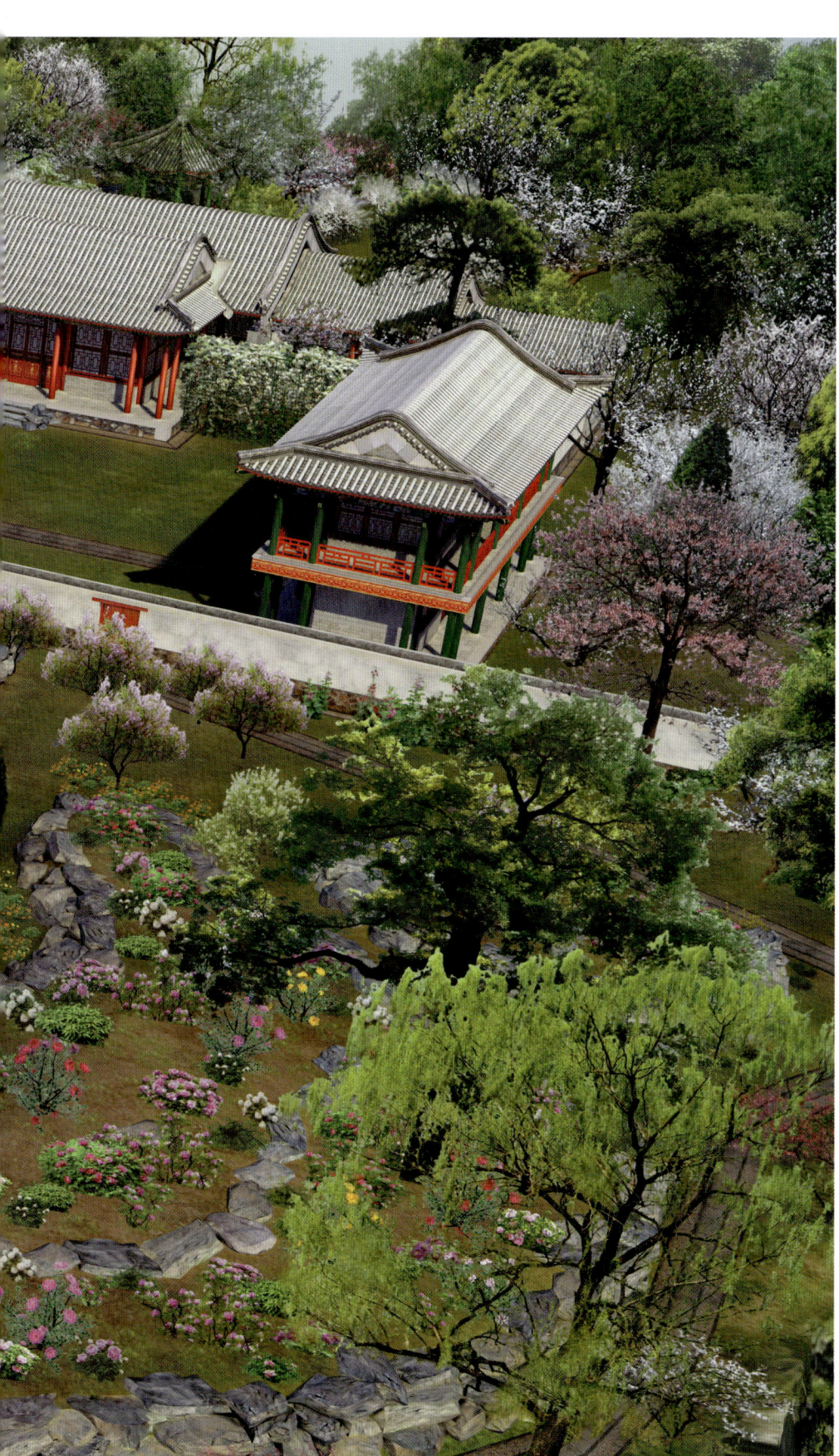

The Louyue Kaiyun Complex, known earlier as Peony Terrace was built during the reign of Emperor Kangxi. This group of buildings was noted for its peonies (fig. 58). On the 25th day of the third month of the 61st year of the Kangxi era (May 10, 1722), Yinzhen (later to become Emperor Yongzheng) invited his father Emperor Kangxi to the Peony Terrace to view the peonies. On that day Emperor Kangxi, finding his grandson Hongli (later to become Emperor Qianlong) to be uncommonly intelligent and smart, decided to take the child with him to the Forbidden City to give him personal tutoring and guidance in an effort to groom him for a great future.

Hongli had already an opportunity to demonstrate his uncommon intelligence a year before. When Yinzhen accompanied Emperor Kangxi that year on a trip to the Bishu Mountain Resort in Chengde, he brought his 11-year-old son Hongli with him. At the Guanlian Pavilion (Pavilion for Lotus Viewing) on the Ruyi Zhou (an island in the imperial summer resort) Yinzhen asked Hongli to recite passages from classic texts he had committed to memory, and Hongli did it without missing a word, greatly surprising the close aides of Emperor Kangxi. When

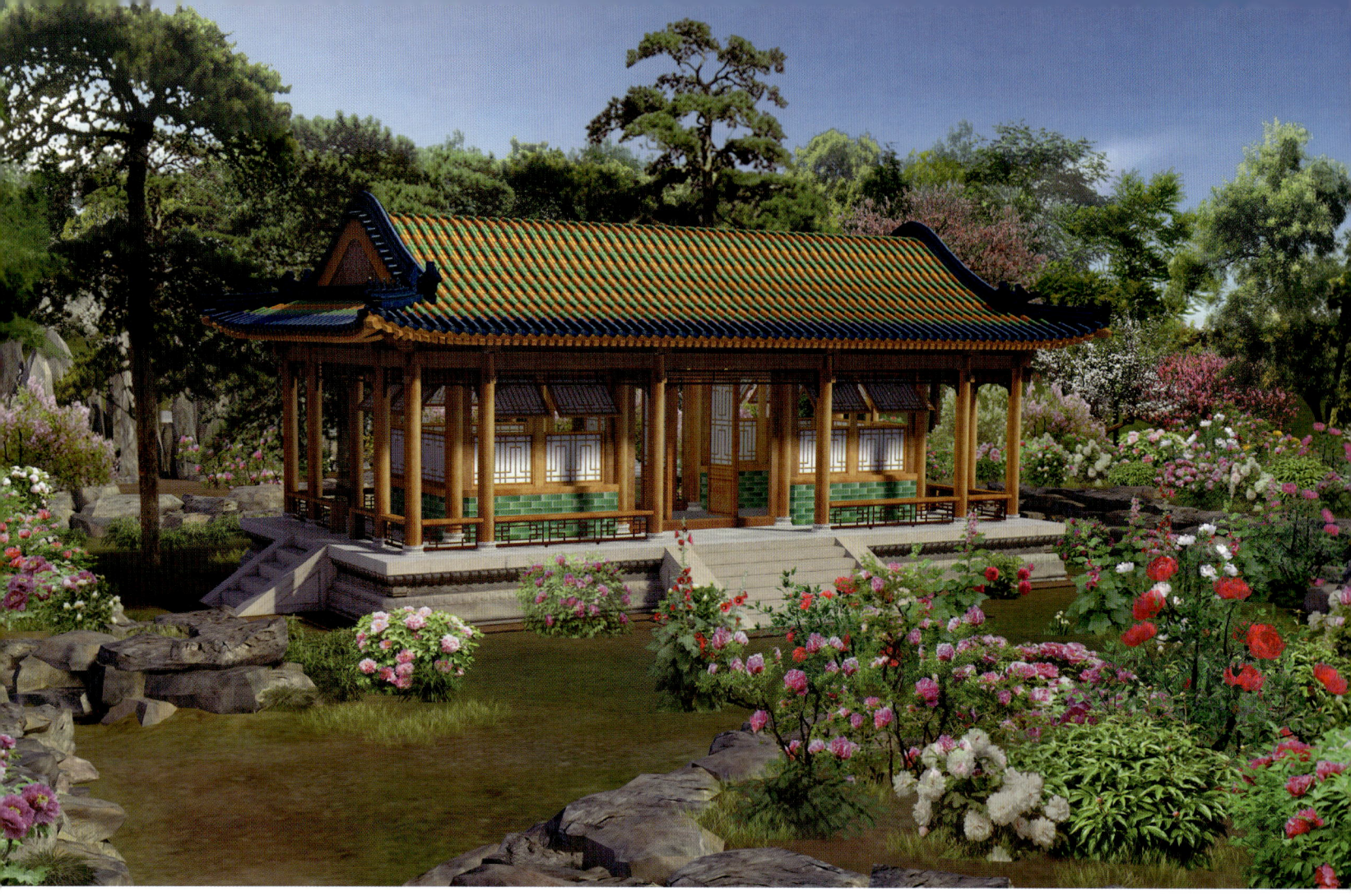

Fig. 59 Small hall made with *nanmu* wood at Peony Terrace

Emperor Kangxi saw Hongli at the Peony Terrace of the Yuan Ming Yuan the following year, he asked the lad to recite and explain the text of a famous essay by Zhou Dunyi of the Song dynasty *On the Love of the Lotus* and Hongli was able to recite it fluently and give a perceptive explanation of it, thus giving Emperor Kangxi great satisfaction. That same year Hongli followed Emperor Kangxi to the Bishu Mountain Resort in Chengde and stayed at the Wanhe Songfeng Complex (Complex of Windy Pines among a Myriad Valleys). When Yinzhen, his father, who stayed at the Shizi Garden (Lion Garden), invited Emperor Kangxi to dinner at the Shizi Garden, Hongli went along as well. At dinner Emperor Kangxi unexpectedly asked Yinzhen to bring Hongli's mother to see him. He told her that she was a "lucky person." That sentence was interpreted retrospectively by some as foreshadowing Hongli's future accession to the throne. Emperor Kangxi's education of Hongli was not solely focused on culture but also gave equal importance to martial skills, such as archery and the use of firearms. Emperor Qianlong never forgot the special affection between himself and Emperor Kangxi and made numerous mentions of it. Thus the Peony Terrace assumed a special significance in human affection and ethics.

The Louyue Kaiyun Complex was situated on the east shore of the Back Lake in the Jiuzhou (Nine Islands) area. While the Back Lake was surrounded mostly by flat terrain, the Louyue Kaiyun Complex was unique in that it had in its grounds a pile of flat rocks, with the buildings planned around it. Peonies were planted among the rocks and a pavilion was built in the middle and given the name of Peony Terrace. At the north of the terrace there was a courtyard house with living units on three sides instead of four, the main hall of which was called the Yulan Fen Hall (Hall of Orchid Scent), five bays wide, with a front porch and two "ear rooms" at its left and right. At the western end was the Yangsu Library (Cultivating the Essential Self Library) and at the eastern flank was the two-story Qiyun Building (Clouds-Lined Building). The space between the courtyard and the Peony Terrace was sprinkled with pine trees and ornamented by rock compositions.

The courtyard was surrounded by low earthen hills on its east, west and north sides, and by water beyond the hills. A small pavilion between two hills hinted at a superb view further on. In Emperor Qianlong's view, the distinct building styles of the Peony Terrace and the Yulan Fen Hall appealed to different aesthetic tastes.

The Peony Terrace was covered with green glazed tiles instead of the ubiquitous gray roof tiles used in the Nine Islands area. Its beams and pillars were made from the rare *nanmu* wood and its architraves and friezes were exquisitely decorated with wood carvings (fig. 59).

Despite his appreciation of the beauty of peonies, considered to be the King of Flowers, what weighed on Emperor Qianlong's mind were not the peonies. In good years, he would praise the beauty of peonies but he was much more concerned about agriculture and the well-being of the state. The memory associated with the Louyue Kaiyun Complex that made the deepest impression on his mind was of a gathering of the three present and future emperors at the Peony Terrace (fig. 60). It was then, he reminisced, that he, still in his early childhood, received favorable imperial notice for the first time.

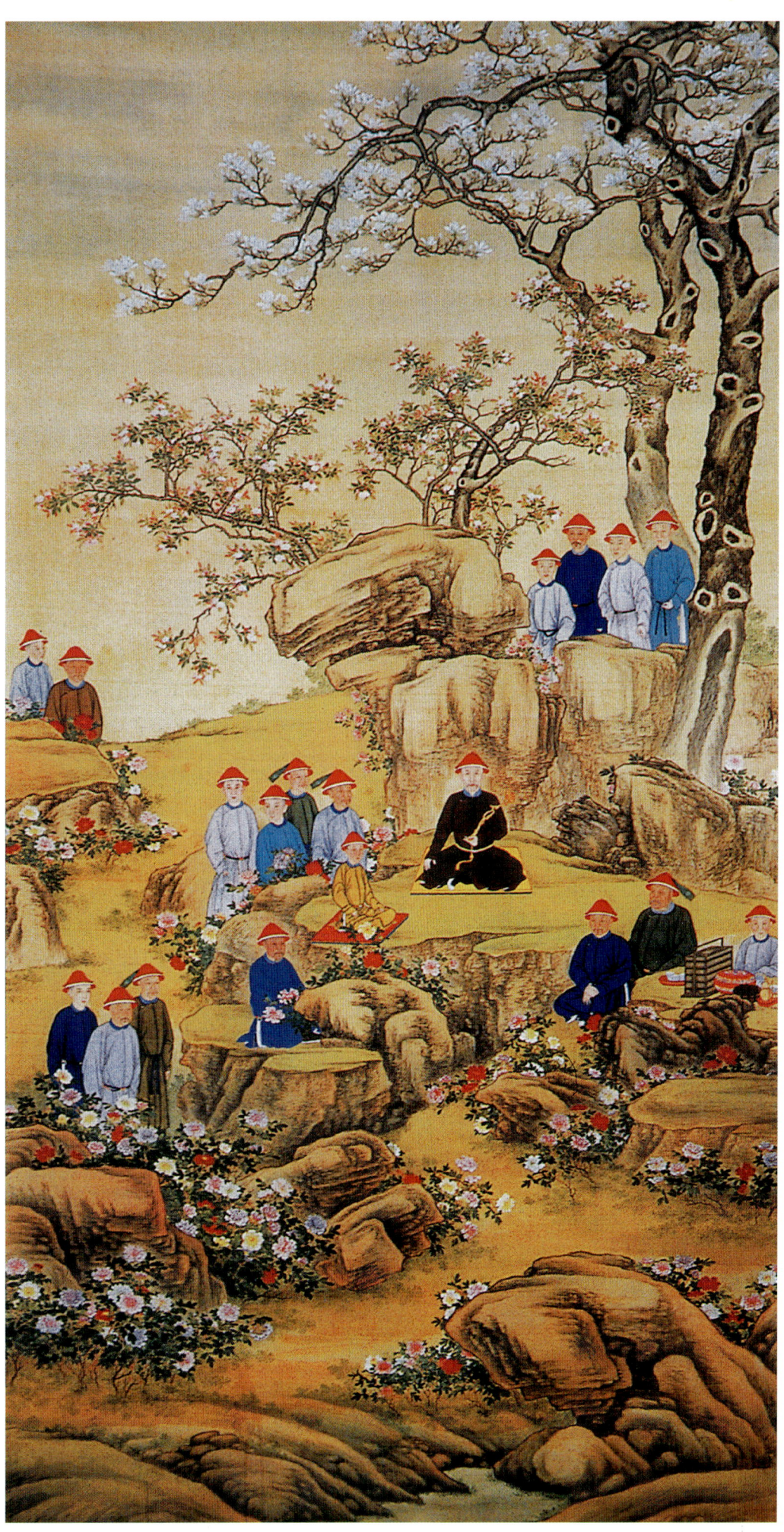

Fig. 60 *Yongzheng Appreciating Flowers*
204.1×106.6 cm
Palace Museum in Beijing
This painting featuring Yongzheng and his heir apparent Hongli depicts the famous historical meeting of the three Qing emperors Kangxi, Yongzheng and Qianlong at the Peony Terrace. In this encounter carefully engineered by his father Yinzhen, Hongli, at a tender age, met for the first time his grandfather the reigning emperor Kangxi. The three emperors' appreciation of the peony blossoms together left an indelible mark on Hongli's mind.

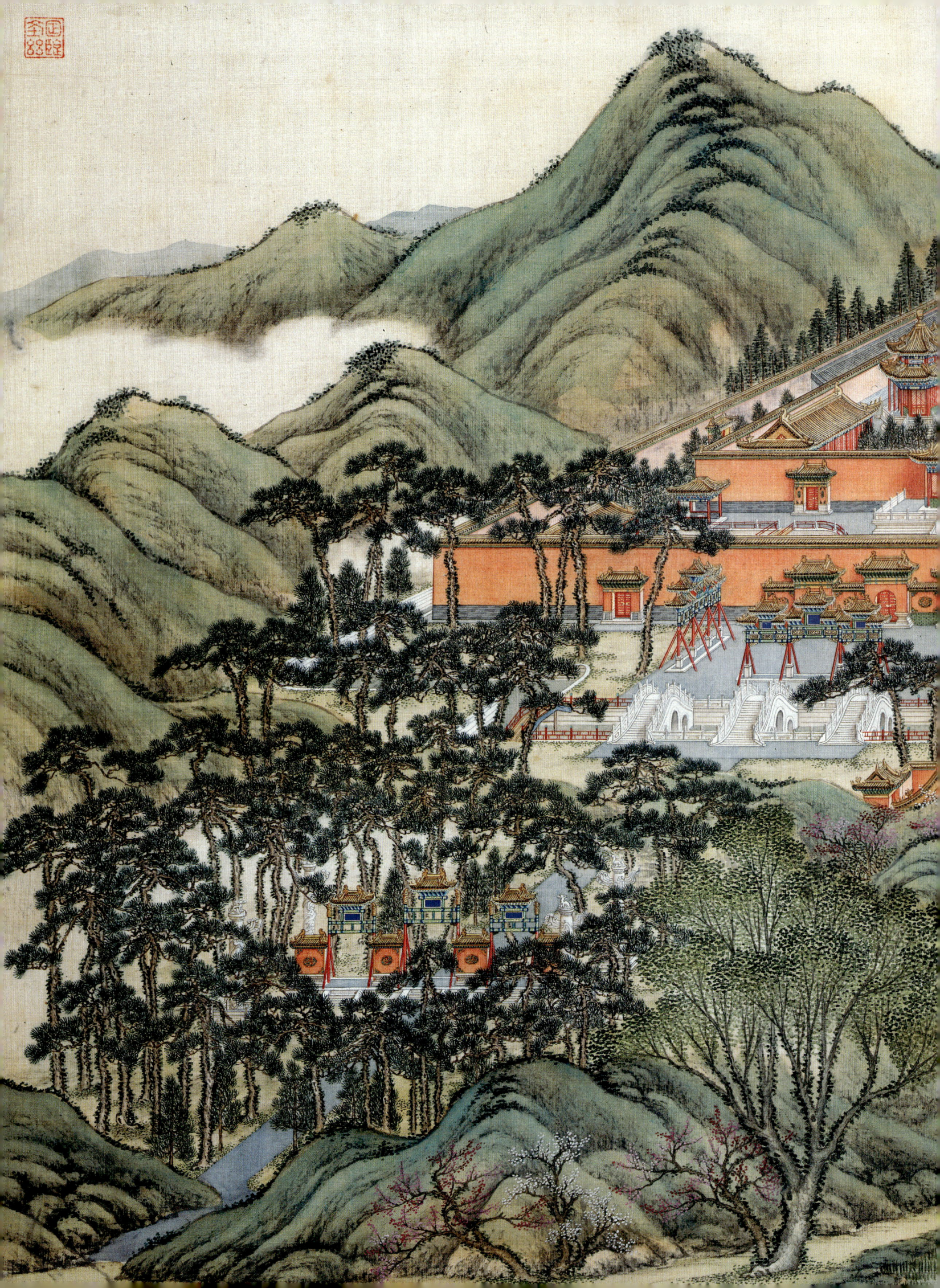

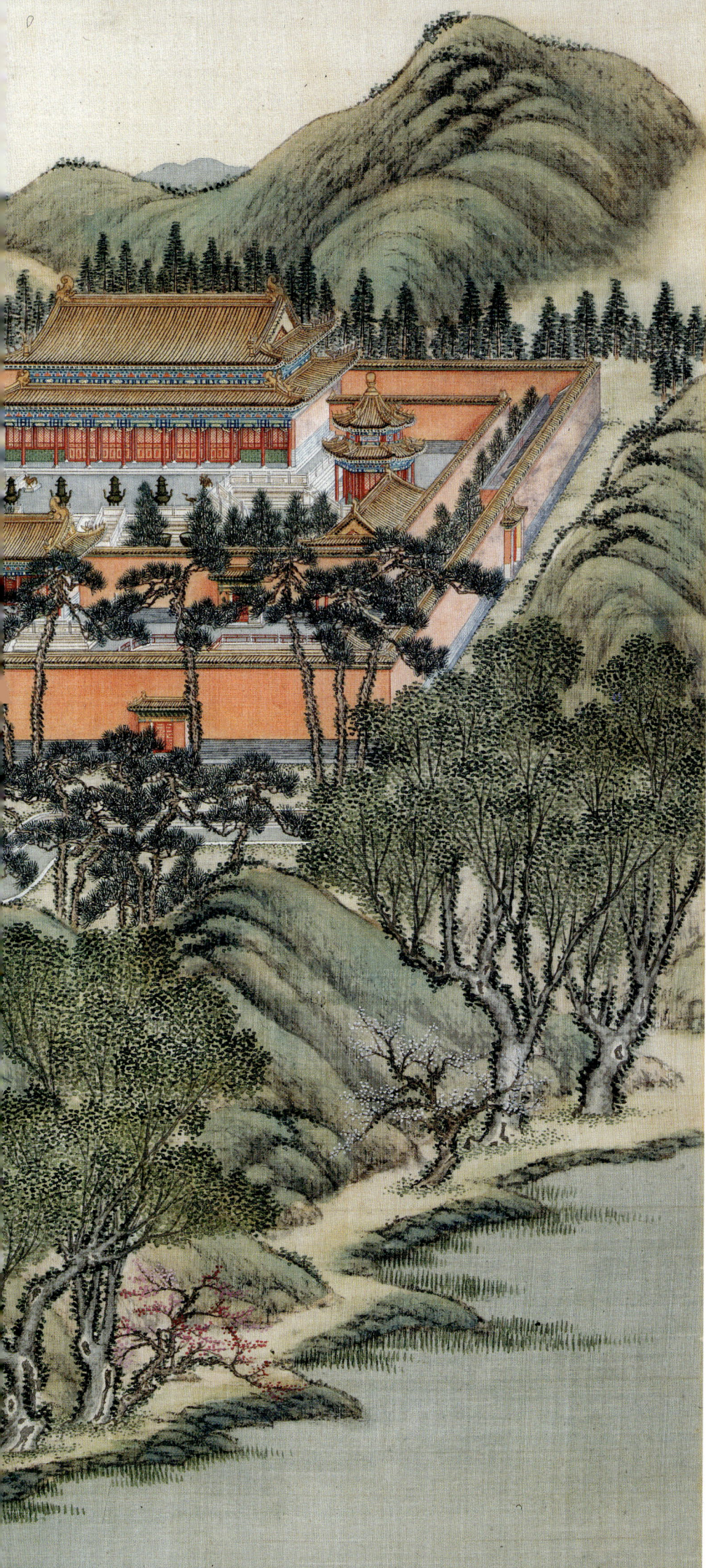

鸿慈永祜 Hongci Yonghu Complex (Complex of Vast Compassion and Eternal Blessing)

The Hongci Yonghu Complex, also known as the Anyou Palace (Palace of Peaceful Protection), was situated in the northwest corner of the Yuan Ming Yuan (fig. 61). It was a unique group of buildings—ritual buildings, and the only ancestral shrine in the imperial park. In China's classical architecture, all buildings dedicated to the deities of the heaven, earth, sun, moon, mountains, rivers and oceans as well as those used by royalty and the populace to worship their ancestors were classified as ritual buildings. The emperors of the Qing dynasty, while not of the Han ethnicity, gave unparalleled importance to the Confucian system of *li* (*li* embodies the entire spectrum of interaction with humans, nature, and even material objects).

The Palace of Peaceful Protection was a shrine to emperors Kangxi and Yongzheng. Emperor Qianlong built this palace in the Yuan Ming Yuan to mark the great contribution made by his grandfather and his father to the rule of the Qing dynasty. The uncommonly high esteem accorded by Qianlong to them was meant to ensure that the late emperors would forever bless and perpetuate the rule of the Qing royalty and

Fig. 61 Painting of the Hongci Yonghu Complex from the album *Forty Scenes of the Yuan Ming Yuan*

the act was calculated to make his practice of filial piety as the basis of good government widely known.

Extant records of Emperor Qianlong's activities of homage to his imperial grandfather and his imperial father in the Yuan Ming Yuan in the 21st year of his reign (1756) attested to his determination to set an example of filial piety. On the eighth day of the first month of that year, upon his return to the Yuan Ming Yuan from the Forbidden City, he lost no time in proceeding to the Anyou Palace to pay respects to his two ancestors. On the 15th day of the same month he went to the Anyou Palace again to kowtow (prostrate himself) before them and on the 15th day of the seventh month of the same year he went there to do so again. In addition on the first and 15th day of every month he had lamas chant sutras for the two ancestors.[1] On Qingming Day (Tomb-Sweeping Day) and anniversaries of the death of his ancestors he unfailingly went there to pay respects if he was staying at the Yuan Ming Yuan. Moreover, the addition of the Anyou Palace was symbolic in that it raised the political status of the Yuan Ming Yuan as an imperial park and palace separate from the Forbidden City.

The Hongci Yonghu Complex was a strictly ordered and symmetrical group of buildings. One started from the architectural arch and the two pairs of memorial columns in the front section, crossed the space framed by the stone bridges and the three architectural arches, past the gate in the wall to arrive at the entrance hall of the courtyard where the rites of worship took place. In this place of ancestral worship, the erection of the four memorial columns and the three architectural arches stressed the formality and dignity of the compound; the symmetry of the buildings in an enclosure added to the solemnity.

When one entered the courtyard, one was faced with the main hall of the Anyou Palace, which was flanked by two side halls, two pavilions covering tablets. A wall surrounded the buildings in this courtyard. The main hall stood nine bays wide in the square courtyard. It featured corbel brackets, a double-eave

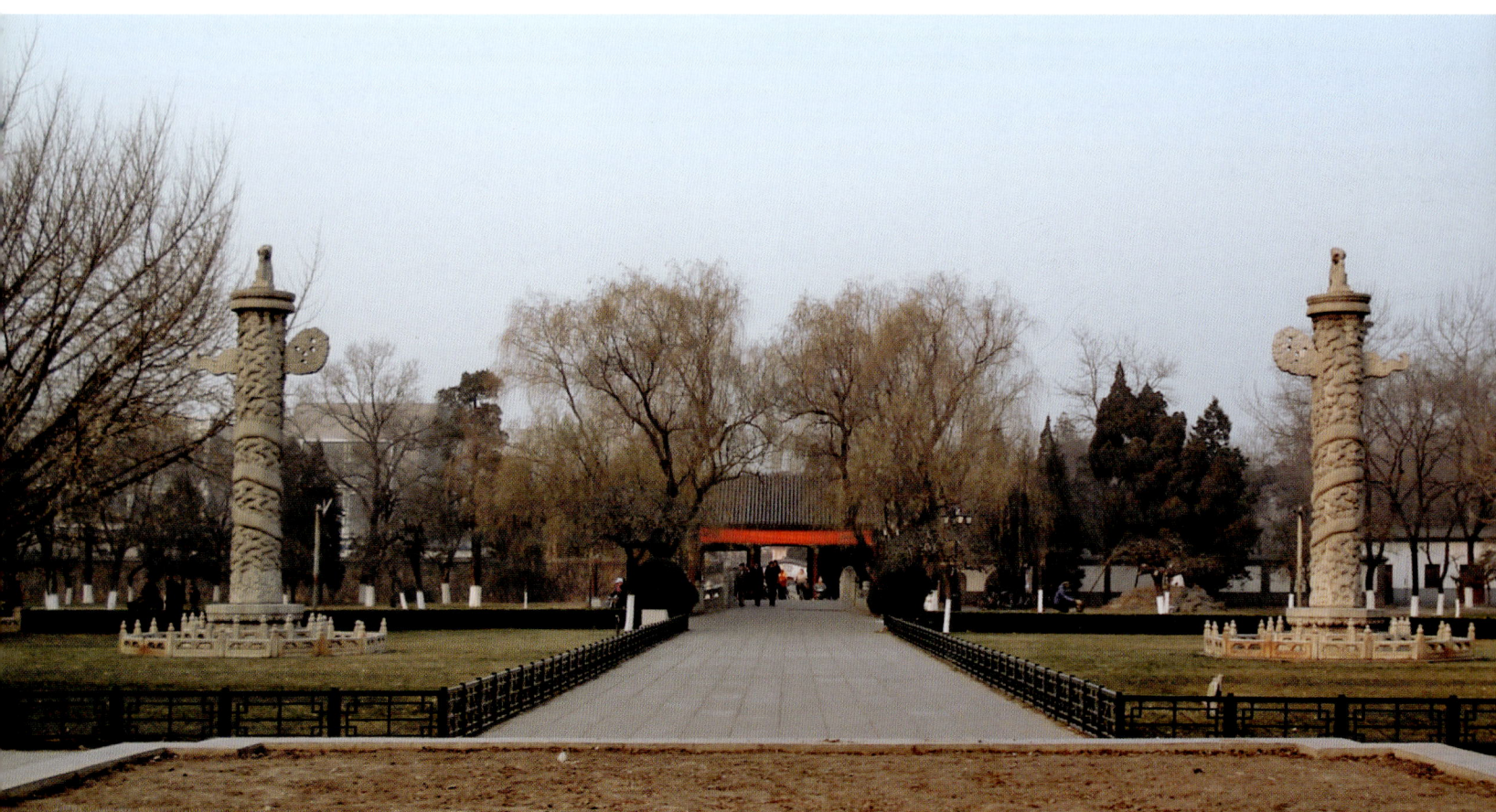

Fig. 62 *Huabiao* in the Hongci Yonghu Complex (now on campus of Beijing University)

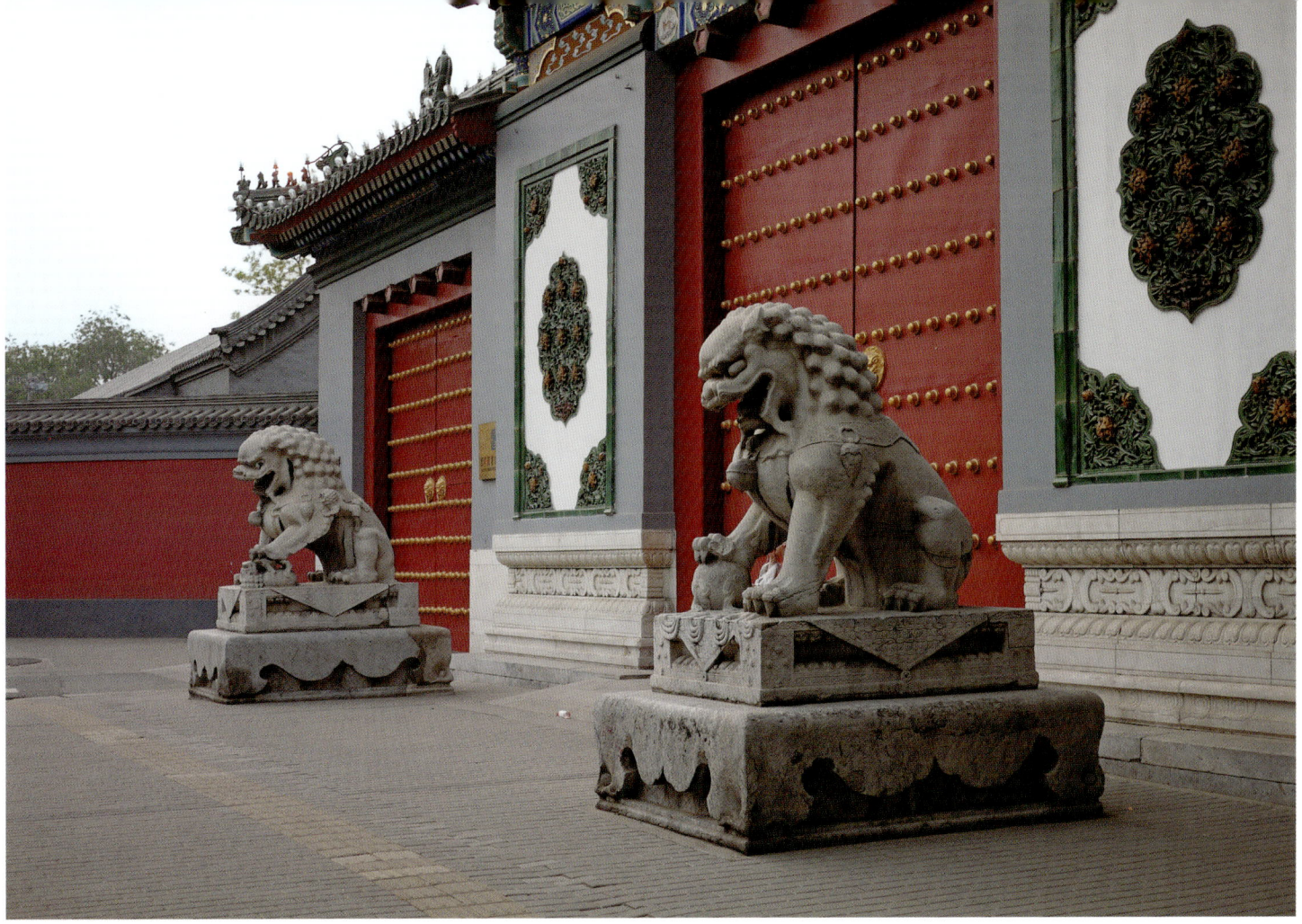

Fig. 63 Stone lions in front of Anyou Palace (now at the old building of the Beijing National Library)

roof covered with yellow glazed tiles. It sat on a foundation with a carved sumeru base; a moon terrace surrounded by a marble balustrade abutted the front of the building, which was the heart of the compound. The walled courtyard was enclosed by another outer wall, within which were a well pavilion and officials' waiting rooms on the east and on the west. Outside this larger enclosure wall stood the three architectural arches, in front of which flowed a stream called Moon River, which was straddled by three marble bridges. South of the bridges the Zhifu Hall (Achieving Trust Hall), a west-facing building of three bays, sat in a self-contained little courtyard. Further out were earthen hills and canals and another architectural arch placed in a small space framed by low hillocks. Four memorial columns stood around this architectural arch amid a grove of pine trees, giving the Anyou Palace an ambience sharply different from the surrounding grounds.

There was a magnificence to this group of buildings, all of whose structures and the enclosing walls were covered with yellow glazed tiles and featured red walls and the doors and windows were embellished with red ornamentation. Emperor Qianlong's satisfaction with this group of buildings constructed at his direction found expression in his poems. Staying in the Yuan Ming Yuan in his old age he would often, on the anniversary of the death of his grandfather, reminisce with deep emotion about the affection and trust shown by his grandfather toward him.

After the torching of the Anyou Palace by the British and French forces, one pair of the memorial columns in this complex were moved by Yanjing University (now called Beijing University) to its campus for preservation (fig. 62). The other pair of memorial columns and a pair of stone lions were removed by the Beijing Library and have been preserved in the old building of the National Library on Wenjin Street in Beijing (fig. 63).

1 Cf. *Yuan Ming Yuan*, Book I, page 86, compiled by the First Historical Archives of China, published by Shanghai Ancient Books Publishing House, 1991.

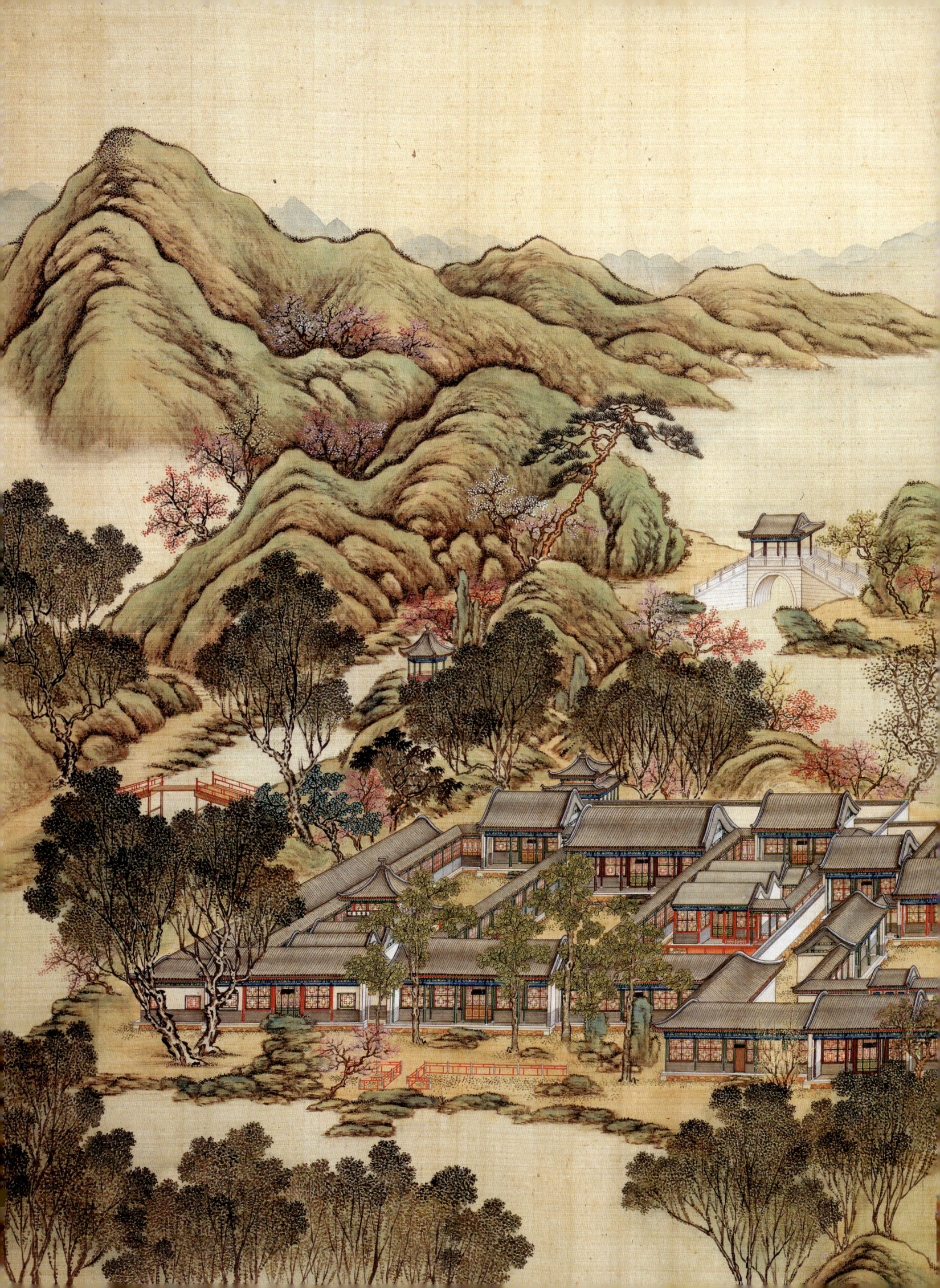

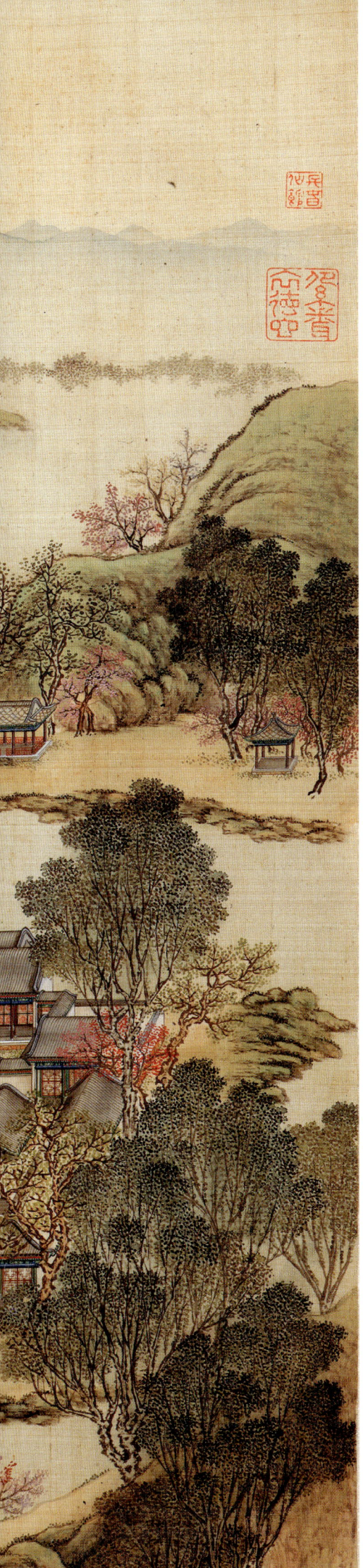

長春仙館 Changchun Xianguan Complex (Complex of Eternal Spring Immortals Hall)

The Changchun Xianguan Complex occupied by itself a small island in the southwest of the Nine Islands area. Surrounded by streams and rivers and ringed by earthen hills, it was quiet and secluded (fig. 64). This landscaped complex, built in Emperor Yongzheng's reign, served as the residence of Emperor Qianlong before his accession to the throne. Upon his enthronement this former abode for a prince was converted to a "sleeping palace" for the temporary use of his mother the empress dowager during her short stays at the Yuan Ming Yuan. When festivities were held in the imperial park, such as for the Lantern Festival, the Dragon Boat Festival, the Qixi Festival (The Night of Sevens, Magpie Festival), the Zhongyuan Festival (Ghost Festival), the Mid-Autumn Festival and the Chongyang Festival (Double Ninth Festival), the empress dowager would attend the banquets and performances of Chinese opera, view the lanterns, the flowers and the dragon boat race. The empress dowager's official residence in the Yuan Ming Yuan was the Changchun Garden (Joyful Spring Garden).

The Changchun Xianguan Complex comprised a suite of four courtyards that ran side by side from east to west, with over a hundred buildings of various sizes. The easternmost courtyard represented the main building group. When one passed through the entrance hall of the courtyard, one came to a Hanging Flowers Gate. Galleries starting at the two sides of the Hanging Flowers Gate connected the east and west side halls with the main hall called Changchun Xianguan. The main hall measured five bays and featured a front and a back porch. There was a rear hall called the Lüyin Pavilion (Green Shade Pavilion). The entrance hall was flanked by a dozen peripheral rooms.

Next to this courtyard to its west was the courtyard featuring the Mochiyun Courtyard (Courtyard of Ink Pond Clouds), then came the courtyard featuring the Linxu Guijing and the Hanbi Hall; the westernmost courtyard featured the Tengying Huacong Courtyard (Courtyard of Vine Shadows and Flowerbeds). These three courtyards were separated from one another only by two covered galleries. Between the main hall and the Mochiyun Courtyard at its west was situated a small building called the Lijing Pavilion. On the east side of the main hall was a building symmetrically opposite the Lijing pavilion; it is believed by some to be the Guxiang Study and Yi Study mentioned with fondness so many times in Emperor Qianlong's poems.

At the time when Hongli stayed there the main hall of this landscaped complex was a "sleeping palace" and the other buildings

Fig. 64 Painting of ChangcChun Xianguan Complex from the album *Forty Scenes of the Yuan Ming Yuan*

PART II SCENERY OF THE YUAN MING YUAN 71

such as the Hanbi Hall, the Guxiang Study, the Yi Study and the Sui'an Room (Contentment with One's Lot Room) were repositories of books or studies. But Hongli stayed there for only seven or eight years and most of the time the place served as the private residence of Qianlong's mother Empress Dowager Xiaosheng until the first month of the 42nd year of the Qianlong era (1777) when the empress dowager died of illness here. Therefore this was a place where Emperor Qianlong demonstrated his filial affection and respect for his mother and where fond memories abounded of their mutual affection. Every time he came here after the death of the empress dowager, he would remember with emotion the encouragement and support he received from his mother when he had to grapple with natural disasters and social upheavals as the supreme leader.

After the fire at the Jiuzhou Qingyan Complex in the 17th year of the Daoguang era (1837) the empress and consorts of Emperor Daoguang moved here.

All the buildings in this complex, with the exception of a few open-sided pavilions, featured round-ridged roofs. In this regard the Mochiyun Courtyard stood out with a building that featured a roof with triple round ridges. This architectural design that increased the depth of the building afforded greater flexibility in the portioning of interior space and served as a model for future construction of "sleeping palaces" (fig. 65).

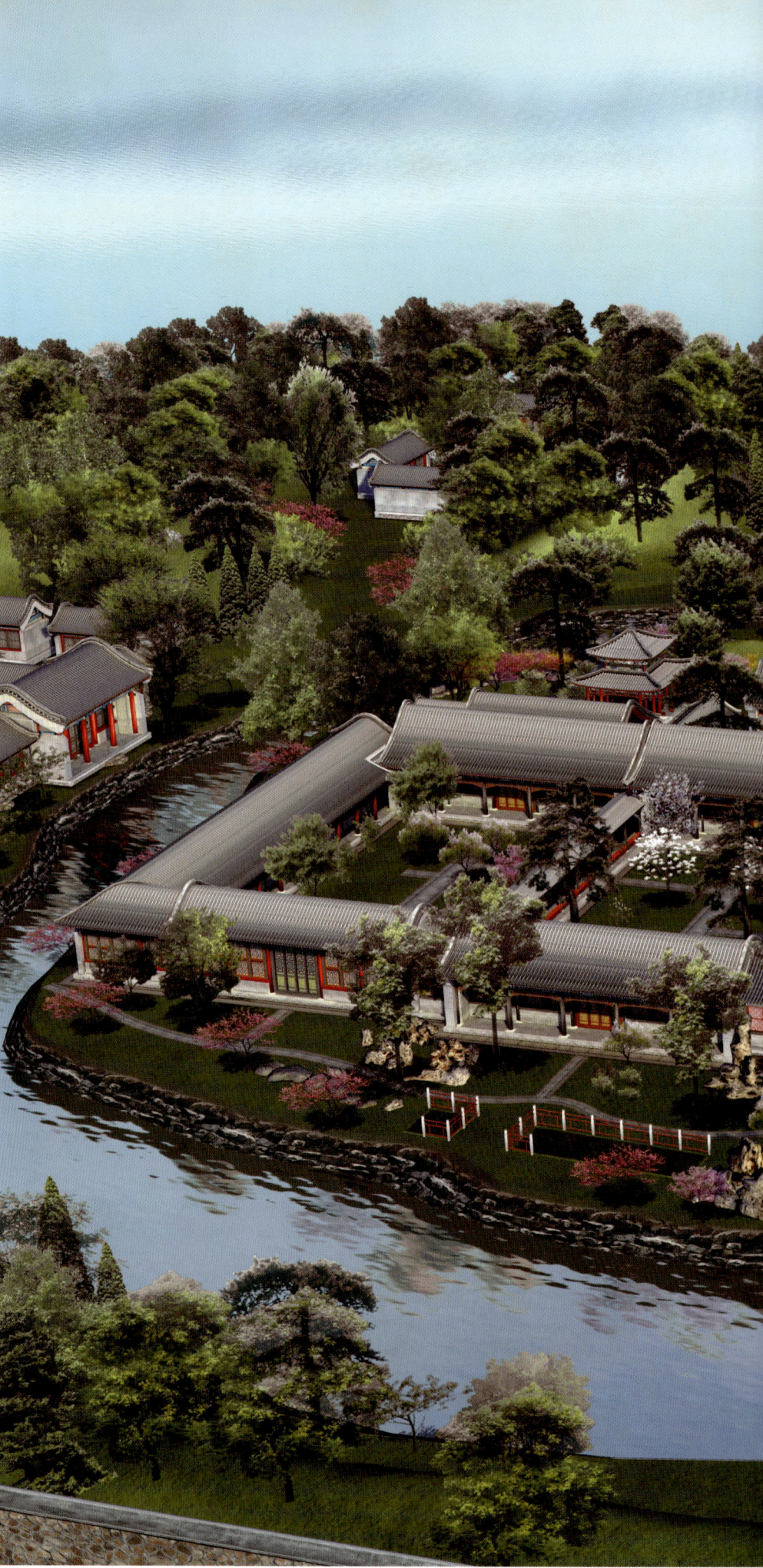

Fig. 65 Themed area of Changchun Xianguan

72 CHINA'S LOST IMPERIAL GARDEN

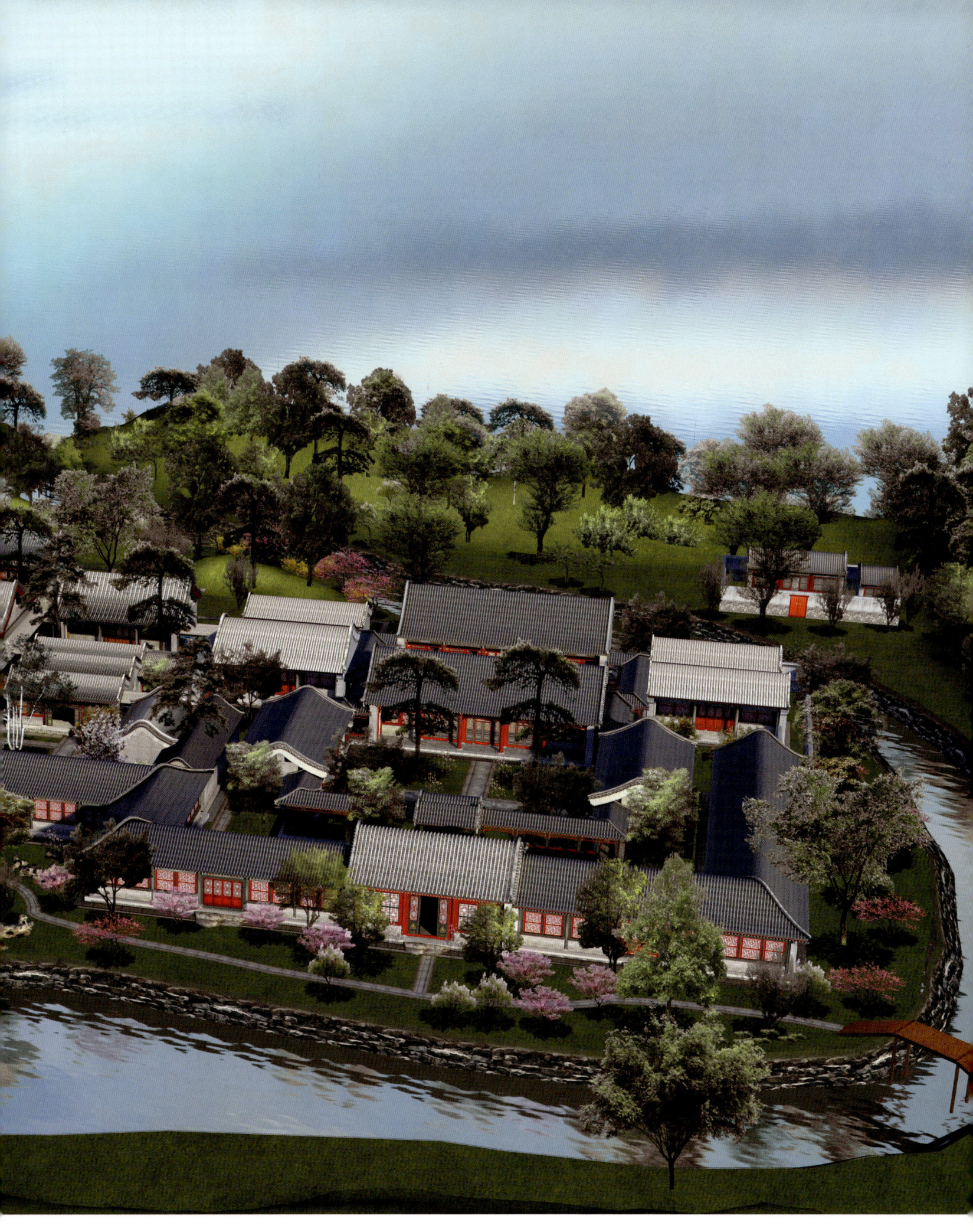

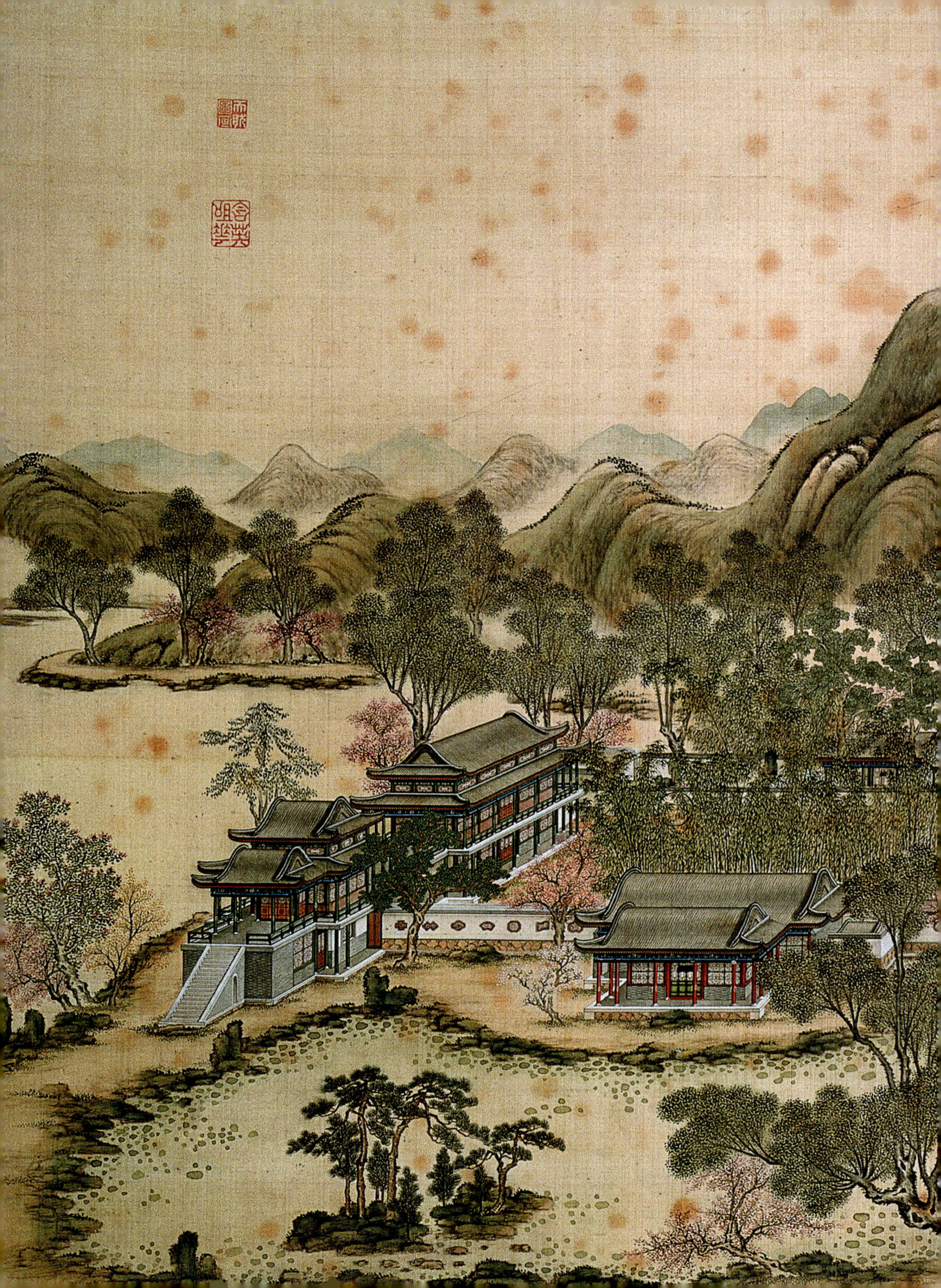

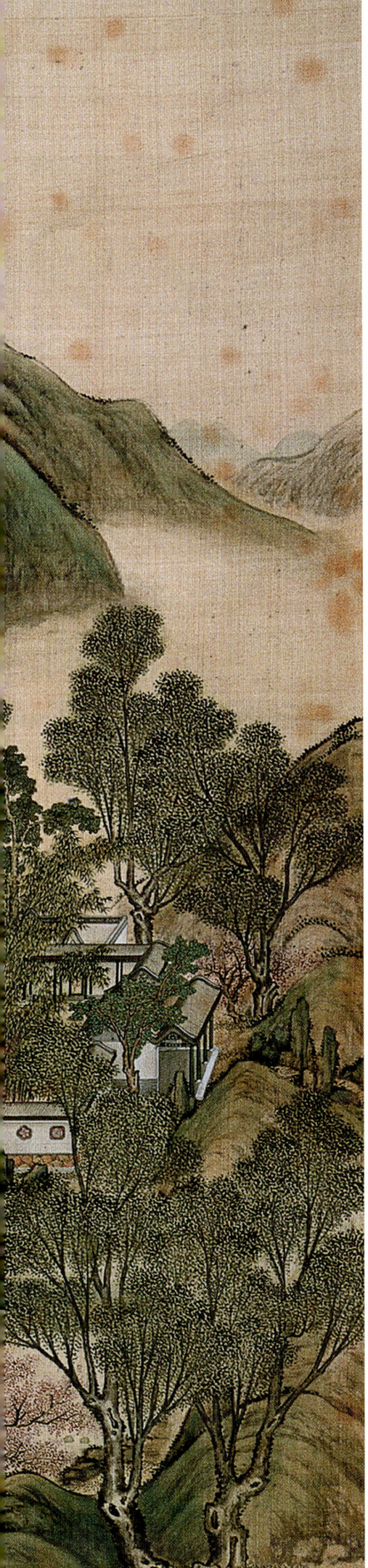

天然圖畫 Tianran Tuhua Complex (Complex of the Nature's Own Painting)

The Tianran Tuhua Complex, earlier known as the "Bamboo Garden," featured in the album of paintings *Forty Scenes of the Yuan Ming Yuan*, which shows that this was indeed a courtyard with dense groves of bamboo (fig. 67). The disposition of the various buildings in the complex showed an interesting asymmetry (fig. 66). A pond lay in front of the courtyard: "The building to the northwest of the pond is Tianran Tuhua, north of which stands the Langyin Pavilion (Verse Reciting Pavilion). Further north is the Zhuke Building, and the Wufu Hall (Five Blessings Hall) of five bays is situated to the east, with a north hall also of five bays extending behind it, called the Zhushen Hejing Hall (Hall of Dense Bamboos and Quiet Lotuses). The Jingzhi Chunshi Jia Hall (Hall of Quietly Comes the Good News of Spring) lies southeast and across the water to its east is the Sudi Chunxiao Open Hall (Open Hall of Spring Dawn on the Su Dike) (fig. 68 on pages 76 and 77)."[1] The main buildings of the Tianran Tuhua Complex were commissioned during the reign of Emperor Yongzheng. The main hall was the Wufu Hall, which, according to Emperor Qianlong, was named by his grandfather[2]. A magnolia tree, of the same age as Emperor Qianlong at the time, i.e. 75 years old, grew robustly, despite its age, in front of the Wufu Hall. Who knows but that the *wufu* or five blessings of longevity, wealth, health, virtue and good fortune might have rubbed off on it? In the 52nd year of his reign, Emperor Qianlong composed a poem in

---

1 *Rixia Jiuwen Kao*, Volume 80, 1774.
2 *Yuzhi Shi*, by Emperor Qianlong, Book II, Volume 85.

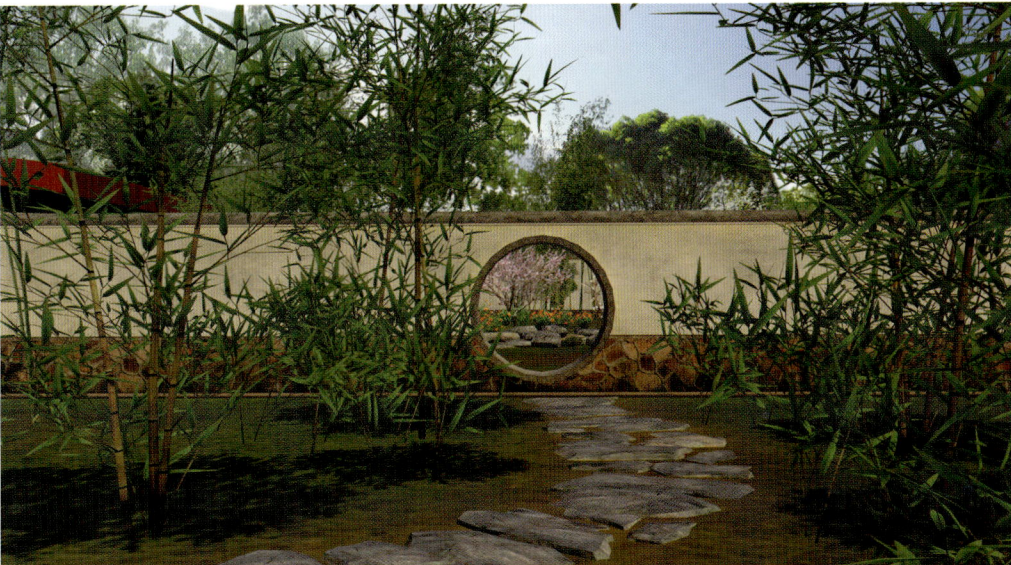

Fig. 67   Bamboo Court

Fig. 66   Painting of Tianran Tuhua Complex from the album *Forty Scenes of the Yuan Ming Yuan*

PART II   SCENERY OF THE YUAN MING YUAN

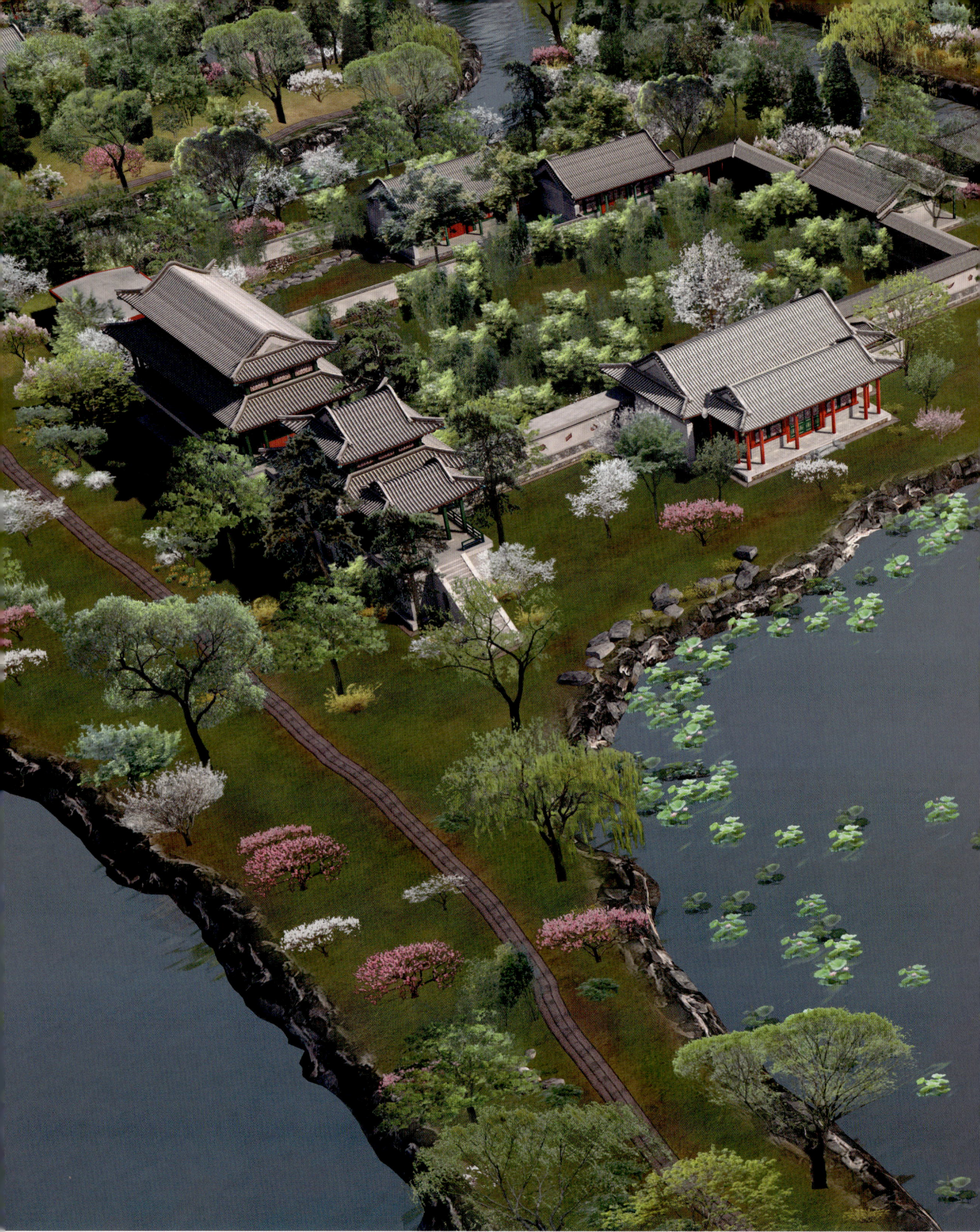

Fig. 68 Themed area of Tianran Tuhua

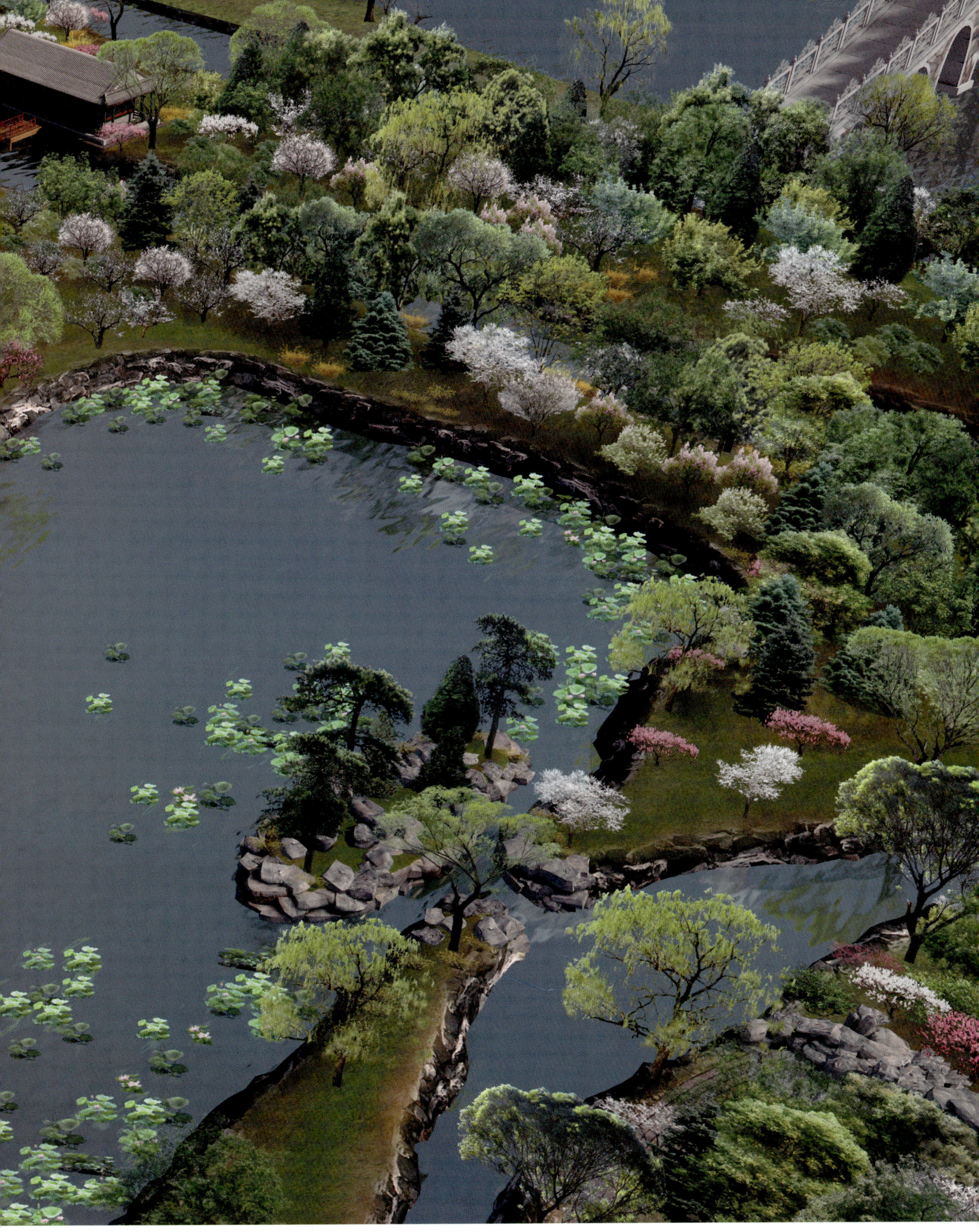

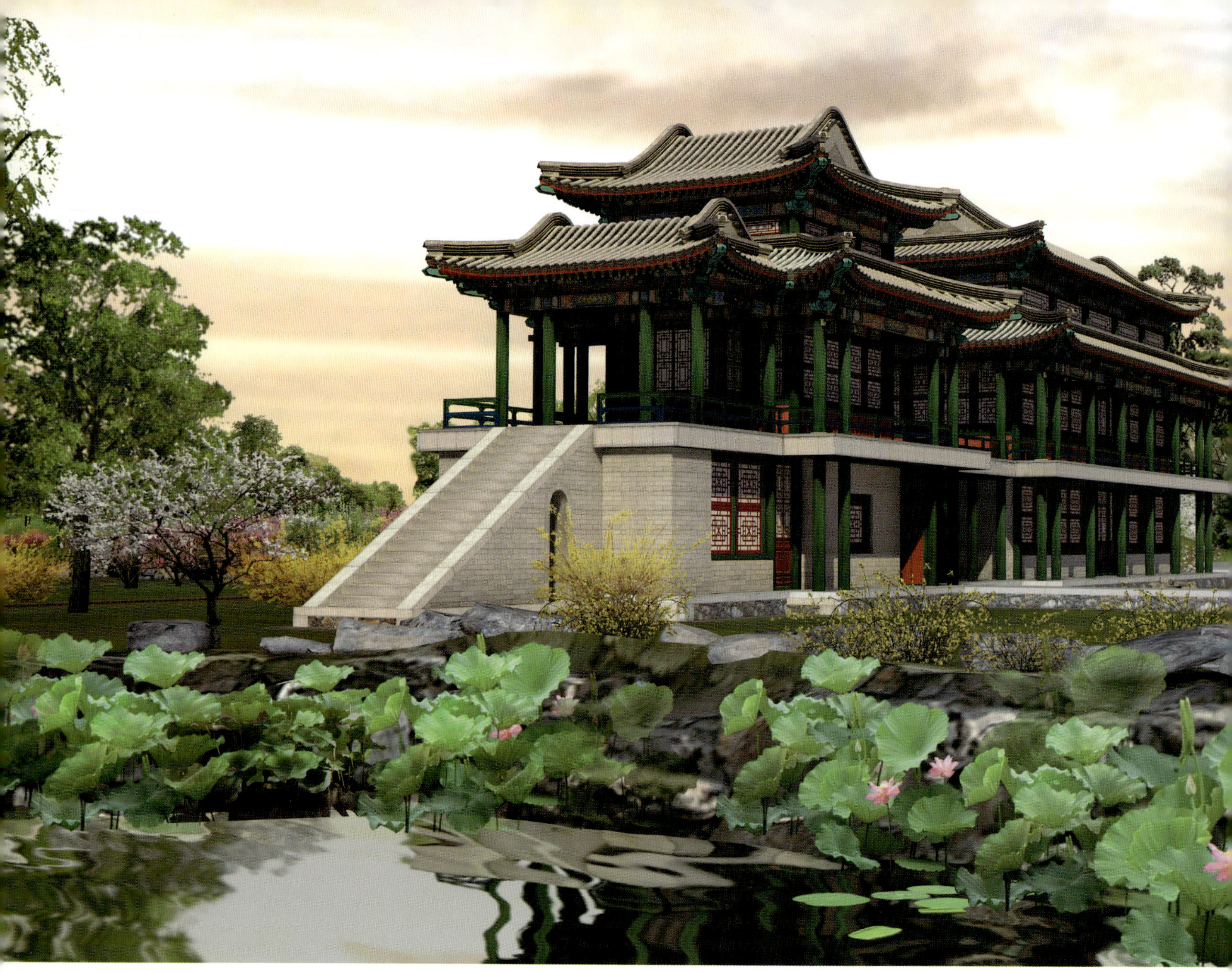

Fig. 69 Langyin Pavilion and Zhuke Building

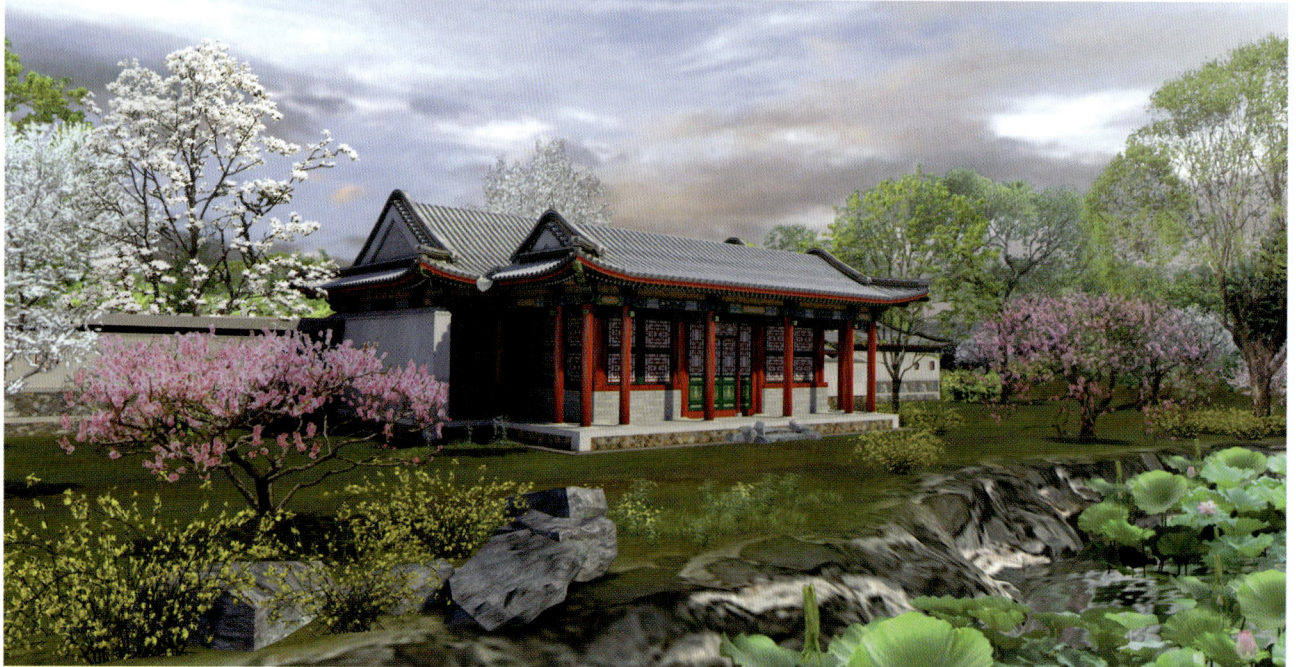

Fig. 70 Wufu Wudai Hall

78   CHINA'S LOST IMPERIAL GARDEN

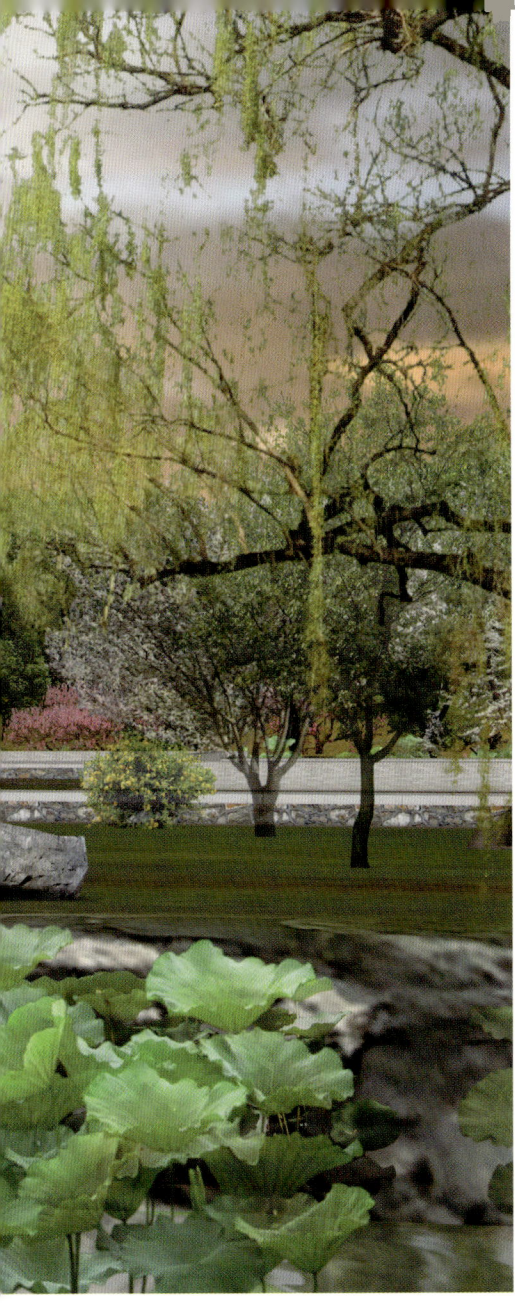

which he attributed the prosperity of that magnolia tree to the blessings of emperors Kangxi and Yongzheng.

The main hall Wufu Hall was a building with a hip-and-gable roof (fig. 70); it was five bays wide, featured a veranda that extended out from its façade. It was flanked by two "ear rooms," and a long covered gallery extending east and west featured multiform windows. The name *wufu*, or five blessings, given to the building reflected the emperor's perception of an ideal life. In the 49th year of his reign (1784) Emperor Qianlong saw the birth of a great great grandson, and with five generations of his progeny gathered around him, he considered himself the beneficiary of all five blessings and therefore decided to rename the Wufu Hall as the Wufu Wudai Hall (Five Blessings and Five Generations Hall)[1].

A gallery connected the Wufu Hall with the Langyin Pavilion to its west. The Langyin Pavilion faced south and featured a double-eave hip-and-gable roof. The graceful two-storied building had a veranda in front, also with a hip-and-gable roof—a square two-storied building known as the Tianran Tuhua. The veranda was visually appealing and its open-sided design, plus a long flight of steps leading directly to the garden below, enlivened the scene (fig. 69). This two-story building was the oldest structure in the imperial park; Emperor Qianlong recalled having seen in his childhood his father writing the three characters Langyin Pavilion on a tablet to be hung at the entrance of the building. This shows how old the building was.

The Zhuke Building stood north of the Langyin Pavilion. It was a two-storied building of five bays, had a wraparound porch and featured a double-eave hip-and-gable roof. It was the tallest building in the Nine Islands area and had an excellent view, especially of the Western Hills. Looking westward from the Zhuke Building, one was presented with the sight of hill rising behind hill, peak beyond peak, as in a landscape painting. This was how the name of Tianran Tuhua came about.

The gallery running east from the Wufu Hall made a left turn to connect with an entrance hall facing east. Another gallery extended from the north gable wall of the entrance hall. The buildings north of the bamboo grove—the Jingzhi Chunshi Jia Hall and the Zhushen Hejing Hall—framed a rectilinear courtyard densely planted with bamboos. Little islands were placed in the pond in front of the Wufu Hall and in the northeast and southeast of the pond earthen hills served as a barrier. Together they created an idyllic microenvironment, yet another painting of nature. Going out of the Wufu Hall complex through its east gate, passing through a gap between hills and crossing a stream, one came to another vista—the Quyuan Fenghe Complex. There, one was greeted by a refreshingly different sight of lotus flowers whose fragrance was wafted into one's face by the breeze.

After Qianlong's time, the pond was filled in and the little islands were gone until they were unearthed by archeologists in 2002. Fortunately the original stone embankments turned out to be in fair shape and have contributed to a better understanding and visualization of what the place looked like before its destruction.

---
1 *Yuzhi Shi*, by Emperor Qianlong, Book V, Volume 52.

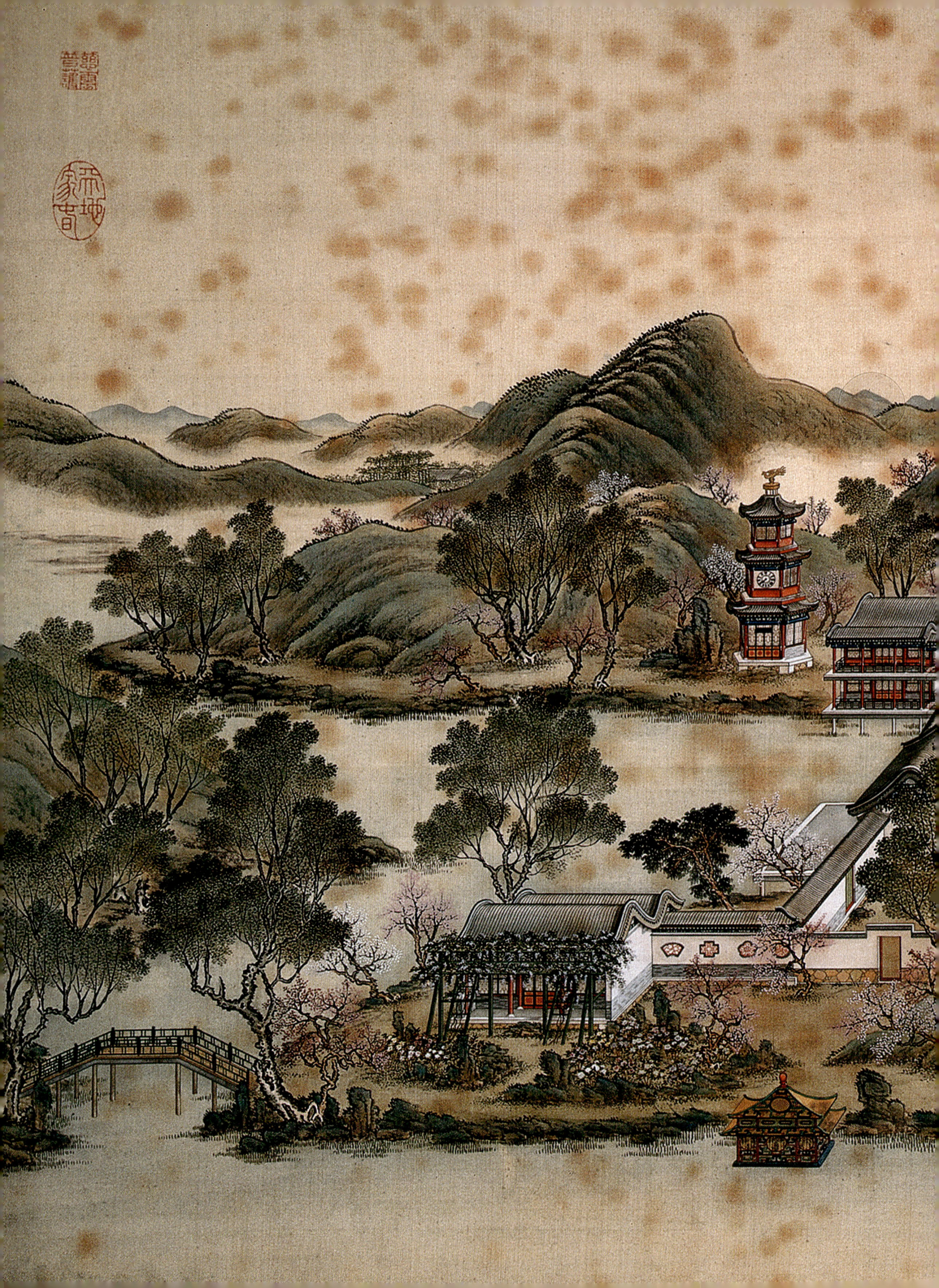

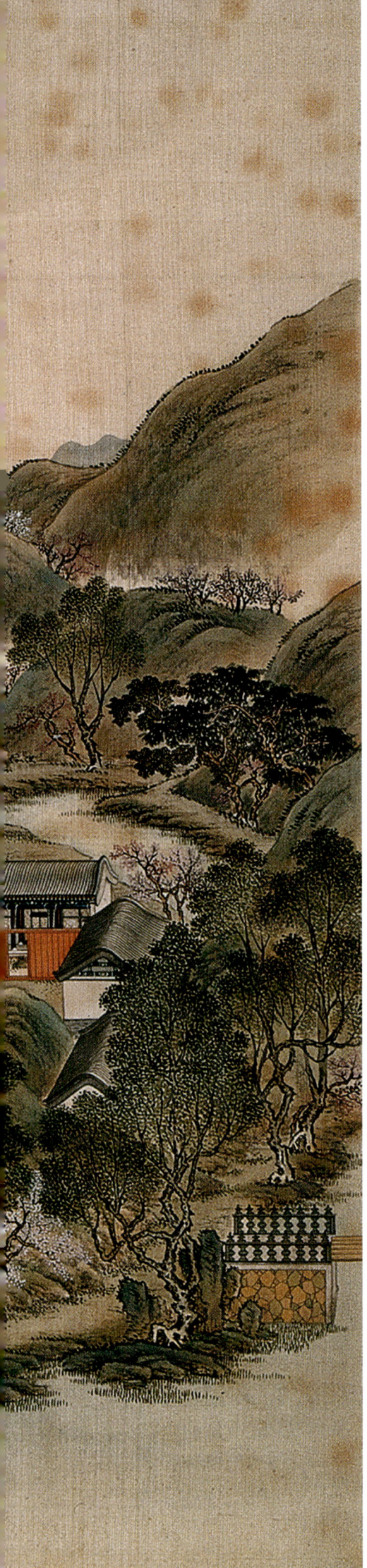

CHAPTER VIII
Shenfo Huyou (Protection and Blessing by the Gods and Buddha)

In addition to buildings for transacting official business, and for imperial repose, religious buildings were also an indispensable and integral part of the imperial parks of the Qing dynasty. The Yuan Ming Yuan was no exception. It abounded in religious buildings and ritual altars for the emperors, empresses and consorts to burn incense and worship Buddha, meeting their spiritual needs. To his subjects, the emperor had a mandate from heaven and ruled on its behalf, but when he encountered problems he couldn't solve, he was obliged to seek protection and help from the gods and Buddha. Therefore gods and Buddhist deities of all kinds and persuasions, domestic or Indian, were invited to reside in the grounds of this imperial park, which boasted not only Buddhist temples such as the Ciyun Puhu Temple (Temple of Merciful Clouds Protect All) (figs. 71 and 72 on pages 82 and 83), Ritian Linyu Temple (Temple of Dazzling Eaves under Heaven) and the Yuedi Yunju Temple (Temple of Dwelling of the Moon, Earth, and Clouds) but also shrines such as the Dou Tan, Guangyu Temple (Fertility Temple), Huashen Temple (Temple of Flower Goddesses), Liumeng Jiangjun Temple (Temple to General Liu Meng) as well shrines to Guan Yu and the Dragon King. The Changchun Garden had the Fahui and Baoxiang temples; the Qichun Garden had the Zhengjue Temple. More Buddhist chapels and retreats could be found at many scenic spots and imperial residences in the park.

When Emperor Qianlong governed from the Yuan Ming Yuan, religious activities were an important part of his spiritual life. According to records of his stay at the Yuan Ming Yuan in the 21st year of his reign (1756)[1], Emperor Qianlong stayed a total of 168 days at the Yuan Ming Yuan in that year and he took part in religious activities on 35 of those days. He unfailingly visited religious venues at major festivals and on the first and 15th days of each month. While he also attended functions at the Jingming Garden, the Dajue Temple (Temple of Enlightenment) and the Yongning Temple, the bulk of his religious observances took place inside the Yuan Ming Yuan.

---

1 *Yuan Ming Yuan*, Book II, compiled by the First Historical Archives of China, published by Shanghai Ancient Books Publishing House, 1991.

Fig. 71 Painting of Ciyun Puhu Complex from the album *Forty Scenes of the Yuan Ming Yuan*

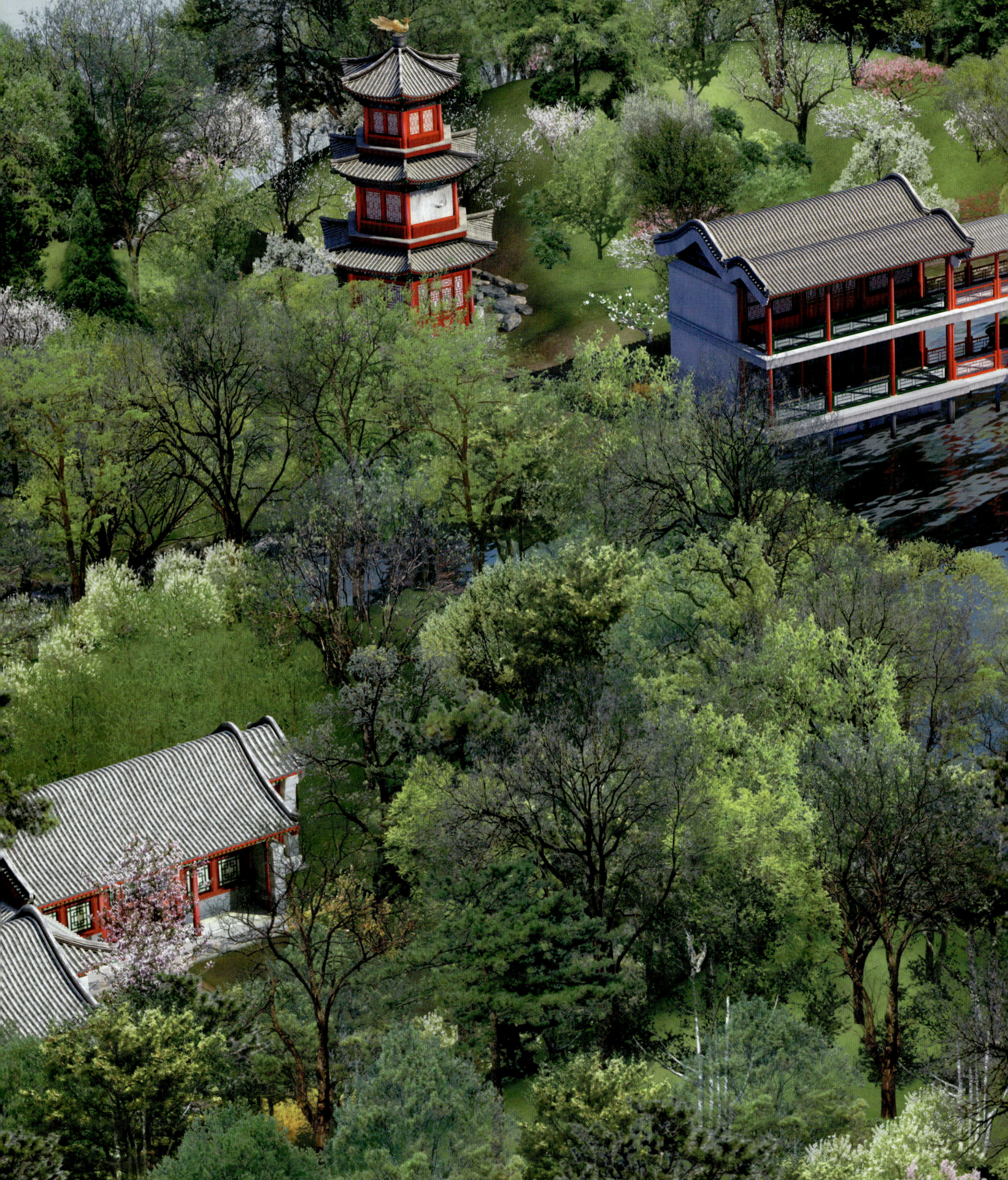

Fig. 72 Themed area of Ciyun Puhu

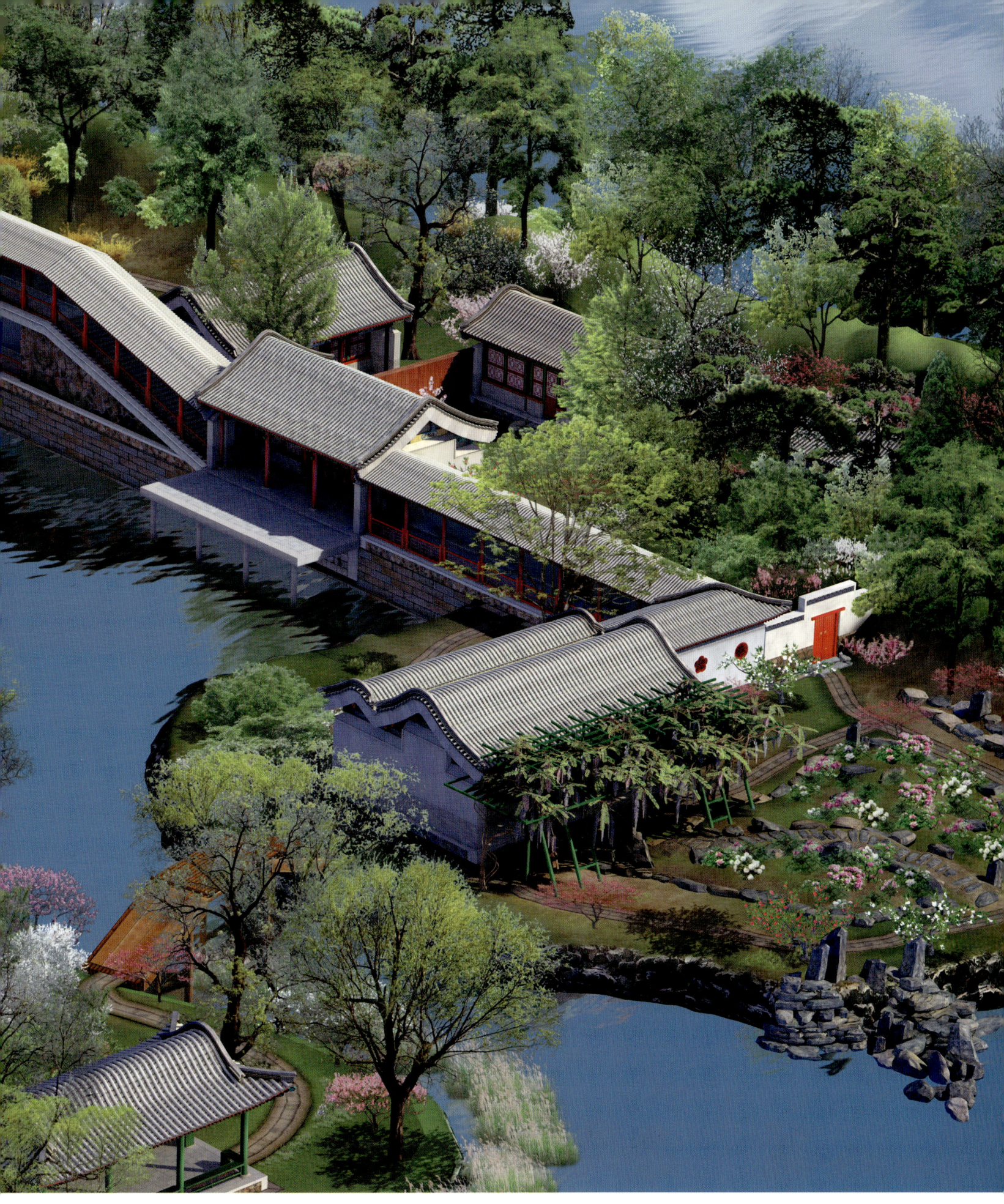

慈
雲
普
護

Ciyun Puhu Complex (Complex of Merciful Clouds Protect All)

The construction of the Ciyun Puhu Complex, situated on the north shore of the Back Lake of the Yuan Ming Yuan, was completed during the reign of Emperor Yongzheng. Grouped around the cove were a Lamaist shrine to Mandkesvara, a temple hall where Guanyin, Goddess of Mercy, was worshipped, a Daoist shrine, as well as shrines to Guan Gong, a historical military hero, and one devoted to the Dragon King. This island was thus a veritable religious melting pot. All these gods were tutelary deities who were supposed to protect and preserve the rule of the Qing royal house. Among the buildings was a bell tower with a chime clock whose tolling reminded people of the presence of these gods and deities in the park.

This religious complex in a park setting had shed the architectural attributes required by the religion concerned and was totally assimilated into its park-like environment. The front hall by the lake featured an overhanging gable roof with dual round ridges; a gallery with multiform windows extended eastward. In front of the hall could be seen a trellis for creepers, peonies, a stone embankment, and a small bridge to the right and one to the left. The bridge to the east of the hall was unique in that it had pagoda-like balusters.[1] According to Emperor Qianlong, the chiming of the bell tower was accomplished by the use of ancient Chinese water clocks. The water clocks use a series of copper vessels with a hole in the bottom and a graduated floating object inside, which tells time by the mark the out-flowing water reaches. The chiming comes from a mechanical device driven by the water clocks. The album of paintings the *Forty Scenes of the Yuan Ming Yuan* shows that the bell tower was topped by a copper phoenix, which acted as a weather vane. This bell tower attested to the achievements in science and technology in ancient China (fig. 73).

The general plan and design of this group of buildings also added to its park-like ambience. The buildings were not aligned along a central axis and instead the construction of each was adapted to the terrain on which it happened to be situated. Communication between them was accomplished through galleries. They embraced a private pond and together with a low earthen hill shaped like a carpenter's square placed north and east of it, formed a secluded mini-park. Interestingly the bell tower, set apart from the main buildings, stood opposite the little wooden bridge to its south and had a direct sight to the Jiuzhou Qingyan Hall that sat on the south side of the Back Lake, thus making a connection with the major building groups around the Back Lake. In this sense the Ciyun Puhu Complex played a significant part in the general plan of the Yuan Ming Yuan. A north-south axis ran through the palace gate, the Zhengda Guangming Complex, the Front Lake and the Jiuzhou Qingyan Complex, and went on across the Back Lake to reach the Ciyun Puhu Complex, ending at the bell tower, making this three-tiered pagoda into a sort of coda to the symphony of buildings of the imperial park.

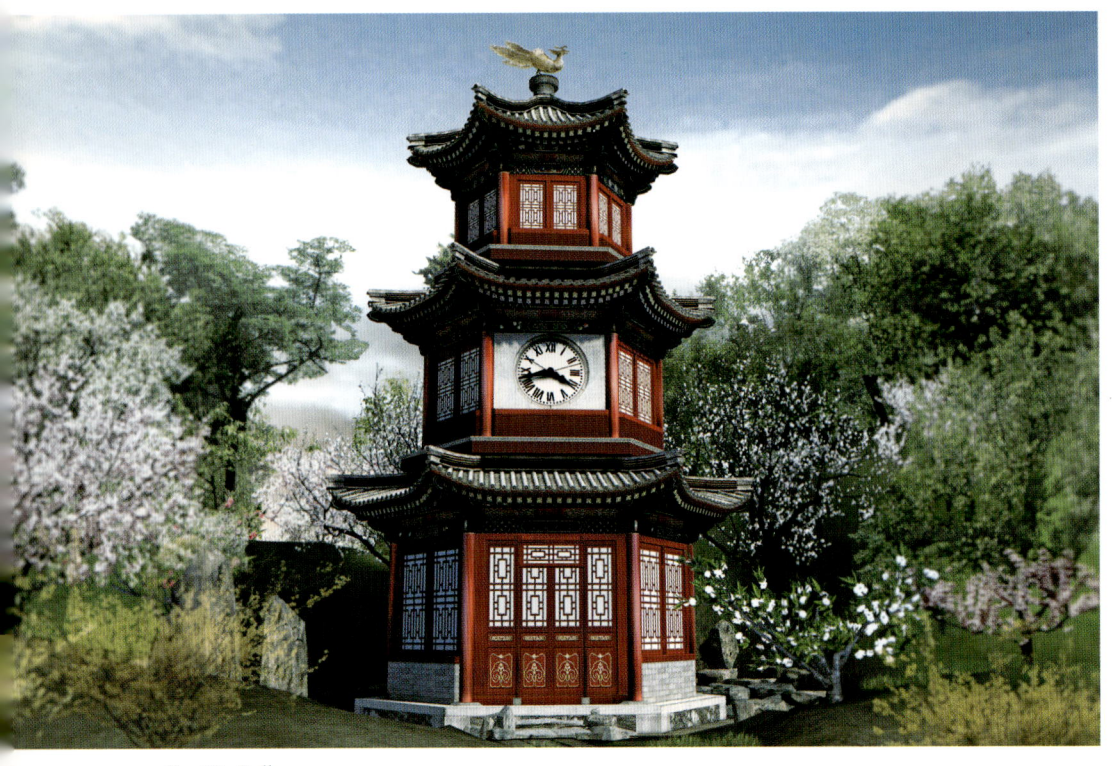

Fig. 73 Bell tower

84 CHINA'S LOST IMPERIAL GARDEN

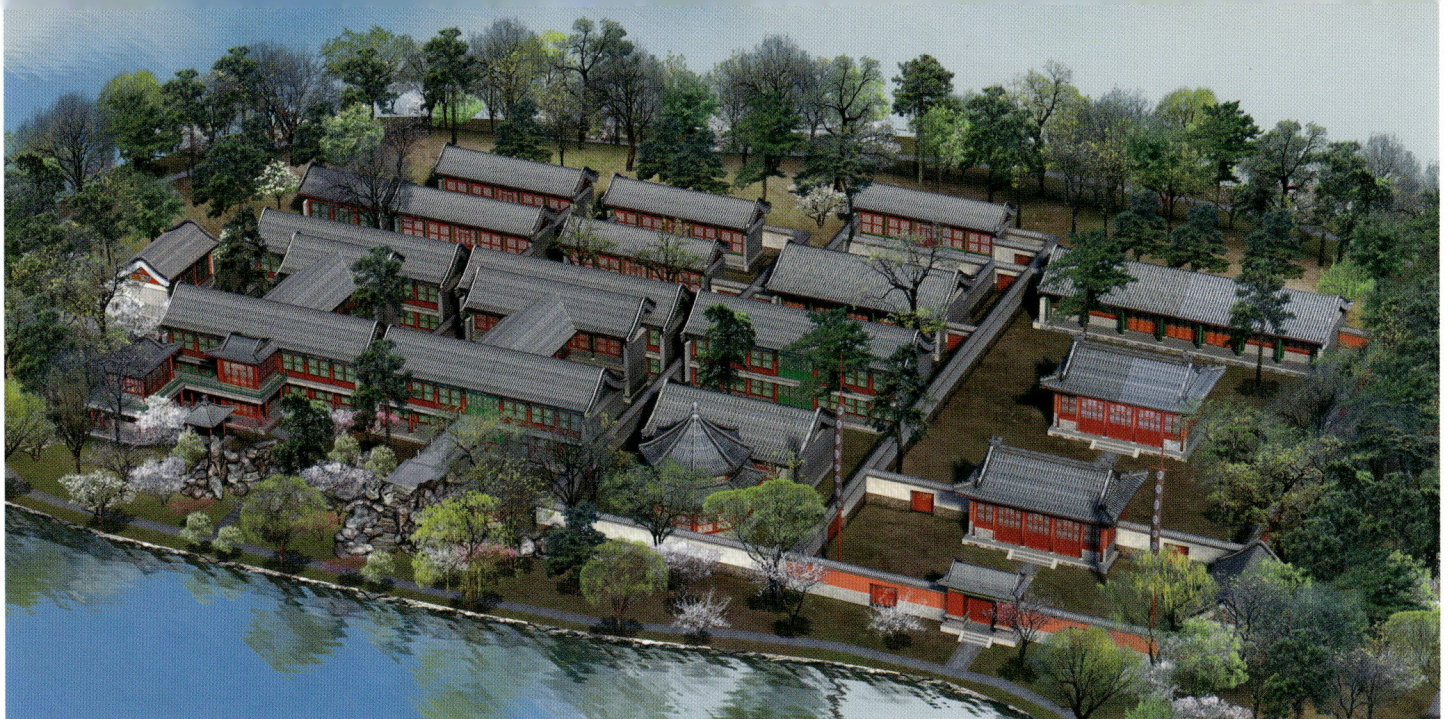

Fig. 74   Themed area of Ritian Linyu

日天琳宇 Ritian Linyu Complex (Complex of Dazzling Eaves under Heaven)

The Ritian Linyu Complex, situated in the northwest of the Nine Islands area, was formerly known as the Buddhist Complex and while it was later given the name of Ritian Linyu, the old name Buddhist Complex remained in popular usage (fig. 74). The album of paintings *Forty Scenes of the Yuan Ming Yuan* shows two groups of buildings in this complex. The group of buildings in the west comprised two two-storied structures, each of which was 14 bays wide; they were connected by a hall at ground level and a bridge at the level of the second floor. "Its specifications followed those of the Rear Buddhist Complex of the Yonghe Palace (Palace of Peace and Harmony)."[2] The design, it would appear, aimed to evoke visions of a prosperous paradise. Given that the words *linyu* (dazzling abode) meant the abode of immortals, one could imagine the reason behind Emperor Qianlong's decision to rename the Buddhist Complex "Ritian Linyu." The Buddhist Complex was built during Emperor Yongzheng's reign; his handwritten characters *Jile Shijie* (Pure Land), inscribed on the tablet hanging in the front middle building and *Yitian Xise*, inscribed on a tablet hanging in the front west building were religious allusions. Departing from the usual arrangement of buildings in a Buddhist temple consisting of a main hall and a series of courtyards, buildings in this complex lay parallel to each other and were connected by a bridging annex; there were ornamented elements such as galleries, open halls, stone lanterns and a shrine to Tai Sui—all intended to evoke a vision of paradise. Although the individual buildings were not elaborately ornamented, the overall effect was striking.

The deities worshipped in the Buddhist Complex were diverse, "in the front middle building was a shrine to Guan Yu … in the front west building was a shrine to Yuhuang Dadi (the Jade Emperor) … figures of Buddha and spirit tablets devoted to various deities are found in numerous places in the buildings."[3] There was also an altar to the Taisui.

The Ruiying Palace to the east of the Buddhist Complex was also built in the Yongzheng era. The shrine to the Dragon King was located in this building. Therefore even though this group of buildings was called Buddhist Complex and appeared to be a hallowed Buddhist establishment, it had in fact included deities other than Buddhist ones. In the view of Emperor Qianlong there was no need to distinguish between Chinese deities and those imported from India; on the first and 15th day of every month he would unfailingly come here to offer prayers to all deities, Buddhist and otherwise, and solicited their blessings.

---

1 Archeological research has found these balusters to be made by binding pieces of fired clay to a wooden stick.
2 *Rixia Jiuwen Kao*, Volume 81.
3 Ibid.

PART II   SCENERY OF THE YUAN MING YUAN

月地雲居 Yuedi Yunju Complex (Complex of Dwelling of the Moon, Earth, and Clouds)

The Yuedi Yunju Complex lay south of the Hongci Yonghu Complex. It already existed at the time of Emperor Yongzheng's reign by the name of Xianxiang Courtyard (Courtyard of Fragrance of Immortals), later changed to Lezhi Mountain Village (Mountain Village for Gladdening the Heart). In the second year of the Qianlong era (1737) it was renamed Qingjingdi and in the ninth year of Emperor Qianlong's reign (1744) it was given the name of Yuedi Yunju Complex (fig. 75). The layout of this group of buildings was typical of a temple complex even though you would not know it from its name. The main hall in the middle was modeled on the main hall of a Tibetan Buddhist temple. The main courtyard had a gatehouse of three bays, topped by a Chinese hip-and-gable roof, and called the Qingjingdi; it was flanked by two side gates. After the gatehouse one came in sight of the bell tower and the drum tower at left and right. Unlike a Han Chinese Buddhist temple this temple did not have a Tianwang Hall (Hall of Heavenly Kings). Therefore after entering the courtyard one directly faced the main hall with its double-eave pyramidal roof. It had a tablet above its threshold inscribed with the words *Miaozheng Wusheng*. Behind the main hall stood two double-eave halls in the shape

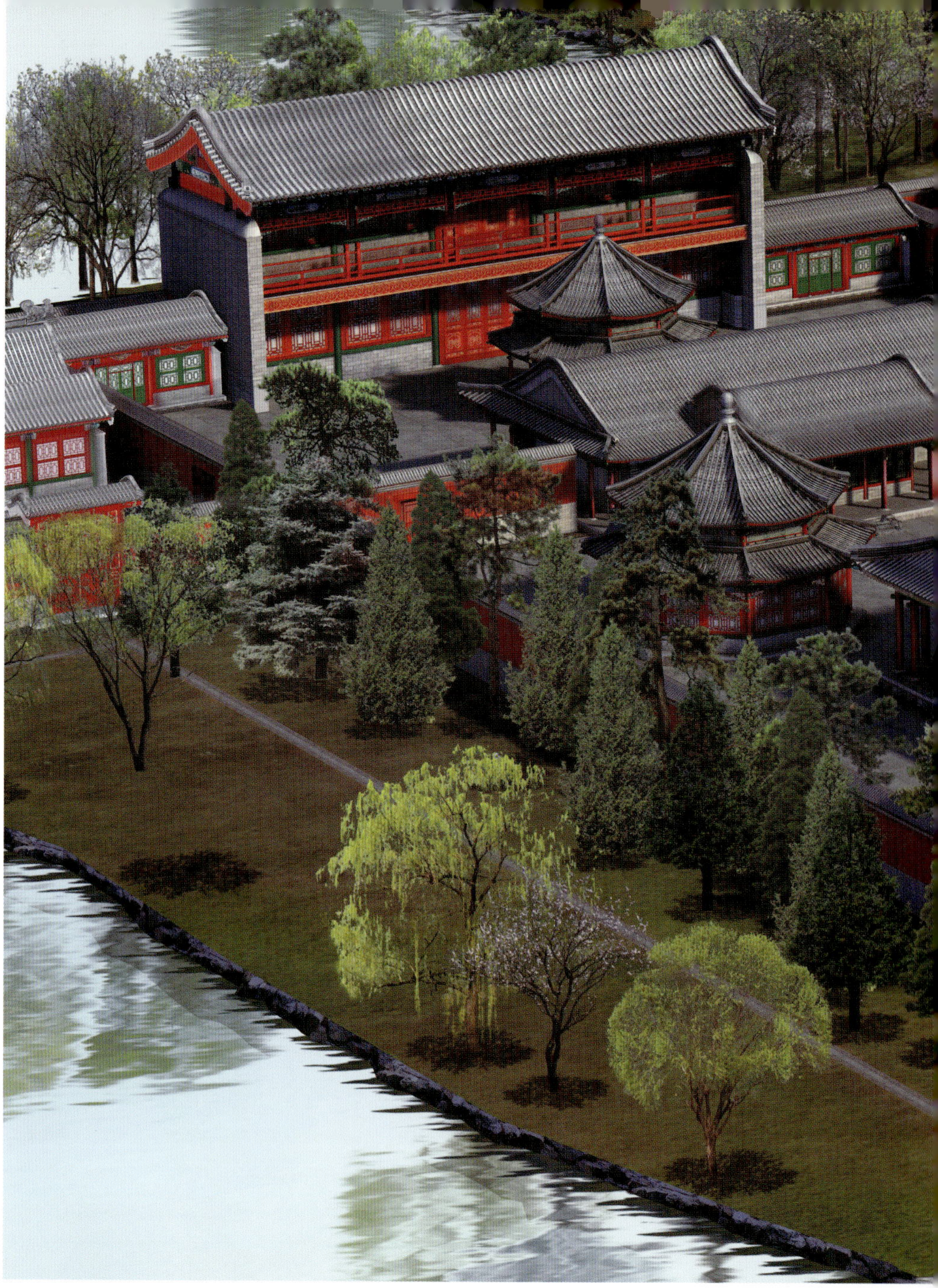

Fig. 75 Themed area of Yuedi Yunju

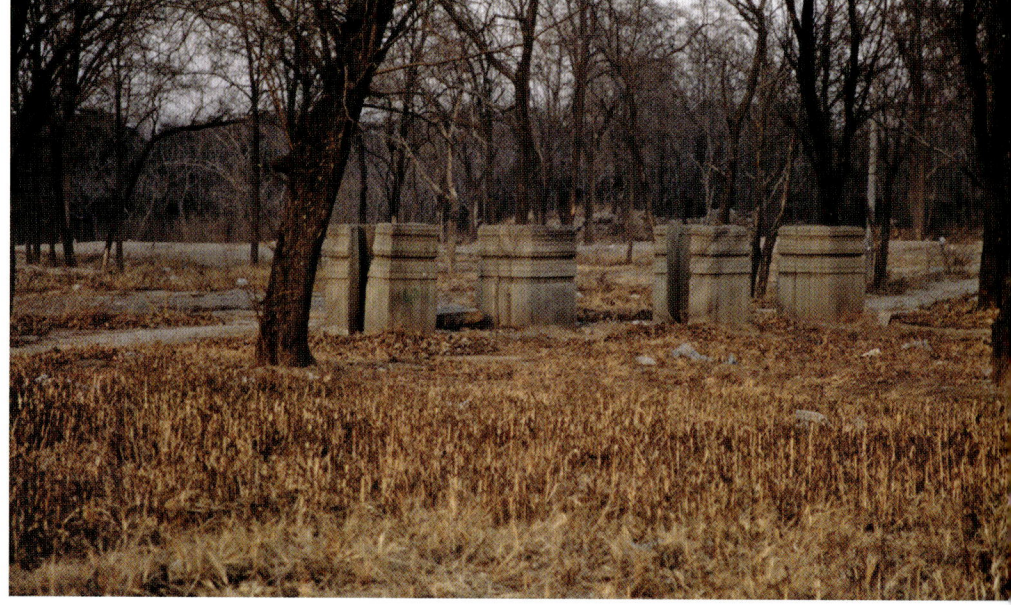

Fig. 76 Ruins

86 CHINA'S LOST IMPERIAL GARDEN

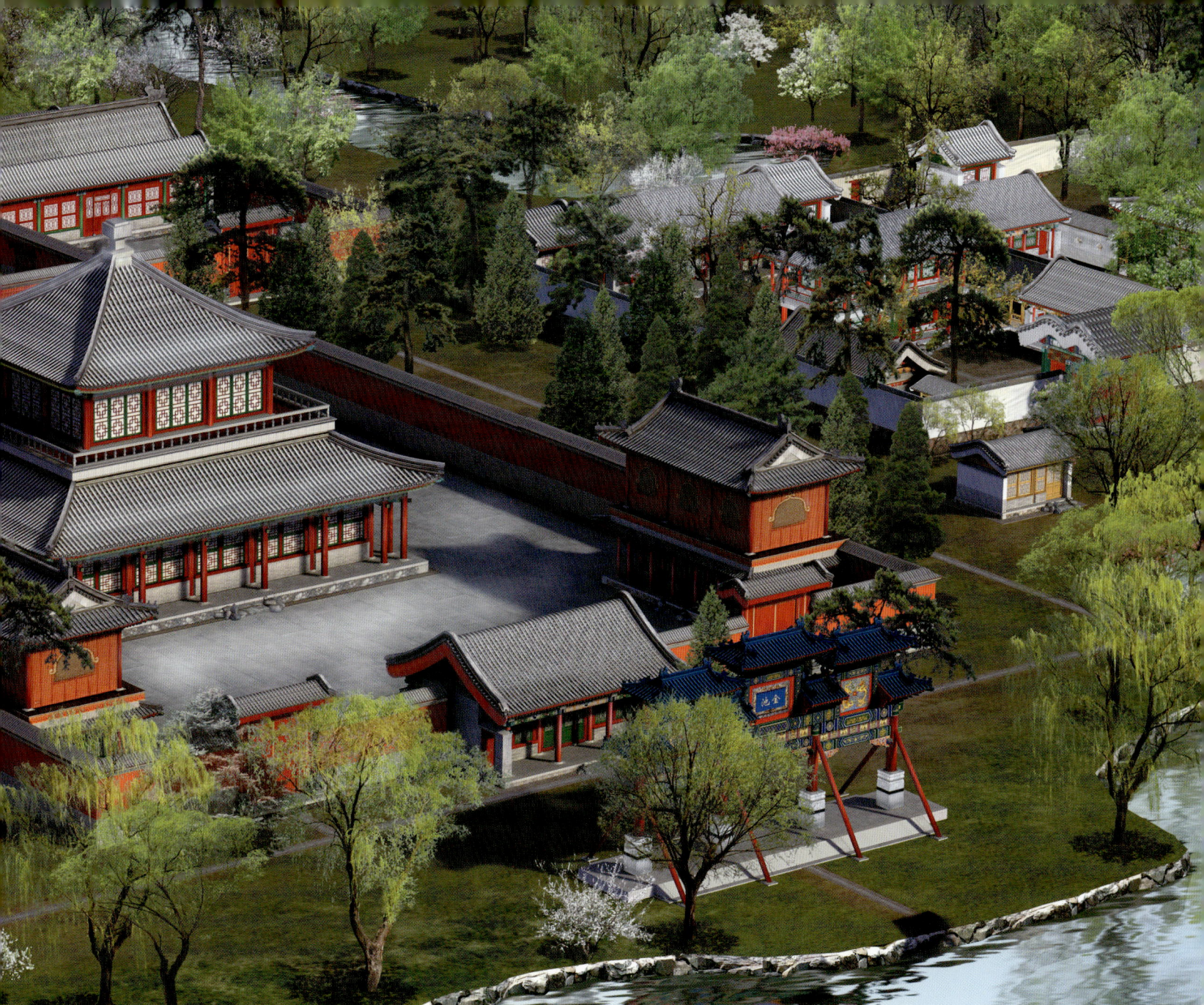

of an octagonal pavilion. After these came the hall called Lianhua Facang Hall (Lotus Facang Hall), which was flanked by two walls extending across the courtyard. There were no doors in these walls; therefore access to the rear courtyard was possible only through this hall. At the center of the rear courtyard stood the Rear Buddhist Complex, which communicated with the Lianhua Facang Hall through a connecting hall. There was another octagonal hall in this courtyard. The rear courtyard was flanked on its east and west by two identical side courtyards with their own gates to the outside; the buildings in these small courtyards were of simple construction.

To the east of this strictly symmetrical temple complex there was a secondary courtyard that was more rustic in character; it was called the Fayuan Building. This was where the emperor would rest when he visited the temple. It had a free form, with a winding fence that enclosed part of the surrounding hills into the courtyard. The buildings conformed to the terrain. The main building in this courtyard was the Fayuan Building, flanked by side halls to the east and the west. It had a Hanging Flowers Gate; a gallery went around the courtyard shaped like a square. There were a few smaller buildings sprinkled around the foot of the hill, the southernmost of which was the Jing Room (Quiet Room).

Of the Yuedi Yunju Complex only a few *jiagan shi* survived; these were stone construction pieces used to buttress the pillars of the architectural arch that used to stand in front of the entrance hall (fig. 76).

捨衛城 Shewei City (Sravasti)

The Shewei City in the Yuan Ming Yuan was a Buddhist temple built in the form of a walled city. It was the largest religious complex in the imperial park. It was situated to the north of the Tongle Garden and reached by crossing a bridge to the north section of the Market Street (fig. 78). The name Shewei is the Chinese term for Sravasti, which is a symbol of Buddhist culture. Sravasti was the capital of the Kosala Kingdom in ancient India and is a place of Buddhist pilgrimage because Shakyamuni spent 25 years here teaching Buddhist philosophy. From the plan drawing of the Shewei City (fig. 77) one sees that this walled "city" comprised three sections, the east, the middle and the west. The north and south gates were surmounted by a gate tower. The gate tower on the south gate was named Duobao Pavilion (Abundant Treasures Pavilion), which housed a shrine to Guan Yu and had a tablet hanging at its door inscribed with "Zhishen Dayong" (Consummate Skill and Great Daring), which was glowing praise for Guan Yu. The gate tower on the north gate was named Zuisheng Pavilion (Golden Light Sutra Pavilion), at whose front and back hung tablets inscribed with *Qianta Chilun* (Gandharva Holding the Wheel of the Dharma) and *Zhilin Chuiman* (Jetavana Festooned with Garlands), both associated with Buddhist culture.

Once past the main gate one was greeted by the sight of the central section of buildings enclosed in a wall. At the center of the front wall was a temple gatehouse; once past the gatehouse, one was greeted by the main hall called the Shouguo Shoumin Hall (Long Live the Country and the People Hall), which, together with the side halls on the east and on the west, formed a courtyard. Behind it were the Renci Hall (Mercy Hall) and its side halls, which formed a second courtyard. Further back was the

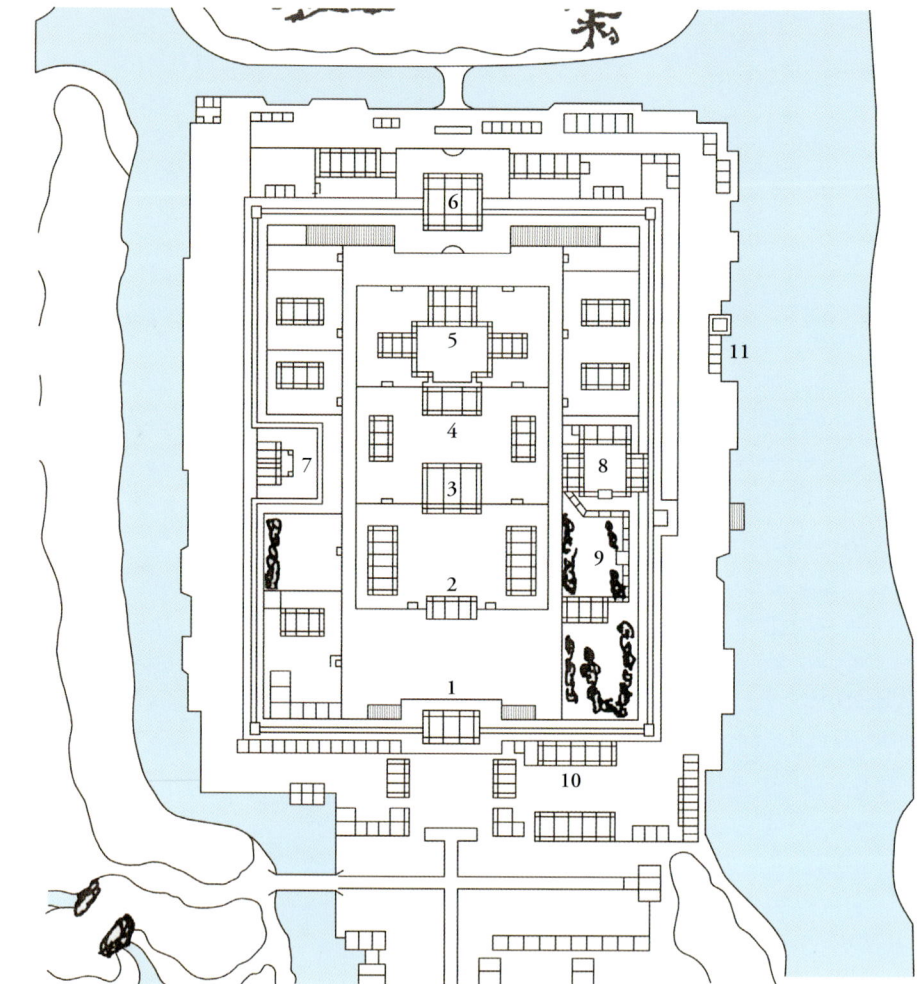

Fig. 77 Plan of Shewei City
1. Duobao Pavilion 2. Gateway of temple 3. Shouguo Shoumin Hall 4. Renci Hall 5. Pufu Palace 6. Zuisheng Pavilion 7. Sanshifo Hall 8. Zhanran Room 9. Yueji Pavilion 10. Duty Office 11. Temple of the Dragon King

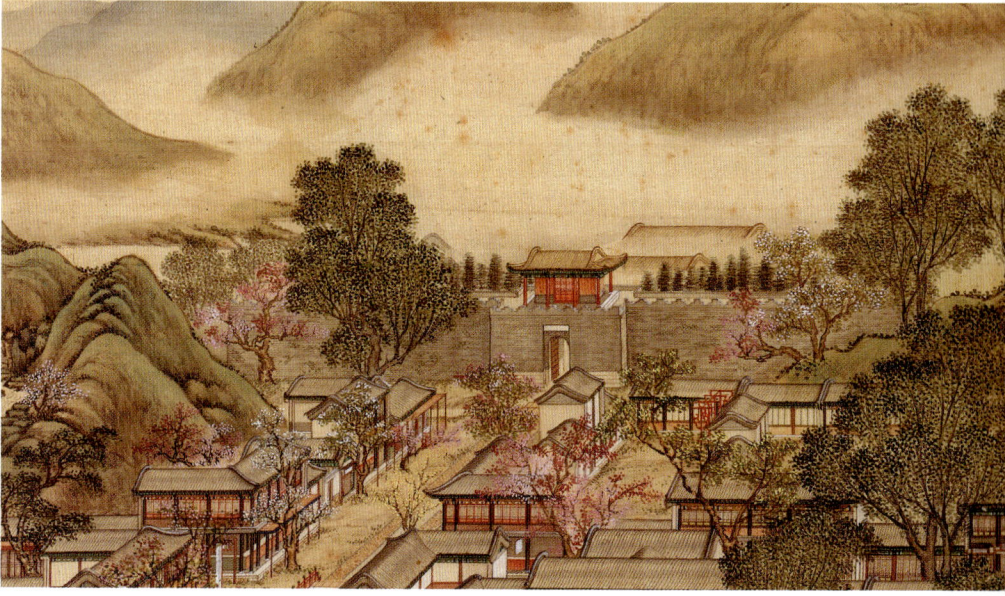

Fig. 78 Shewei City

Pufu Palace (Universal Happiness Palace) and its side halls, which formed the third courtyard. The latter courtyard was slightly different from the other two in that its side halls had a north-south orientation and the halls were interconnected by galleries. The Pufu Palace was the last building in the middle group of buildings, after which one came to the north gate. The compound in the east and the compound in the west were separated from the middle compound by walls that ran north-south. In the west compound one found the Sanshifo Hall (Buddhas of the Three Generations Hall), which had an east-west orientation, and a number of auxiliary buildings. The east compound had a small garden-like setting, embellished by pavilions, a gallery that went around the court and artificial hills. The main building in it was a library called Zhanran Room situated in the middle of the gallery. There was also a pavilion facing west called the Yueji Pavilion (Pavilion of the Joy of Clearing after Snow). Emperor Qianlong was fond of these two buildings and composed a number of poems about them.

The buildings in this walled "city" were mostly of modest scale, with ordered spaces, and densely concentrated. It was perhaps so designed to simulate urban compactness. One could see from the buildings and the names given them that the Shewei City was designed around the idea of protecting the interests of the state and of the people, as reflected in the name Shouguo Shoumin of the main hall. The shrine to Guan Yu was placed in the Duobao Pavilion

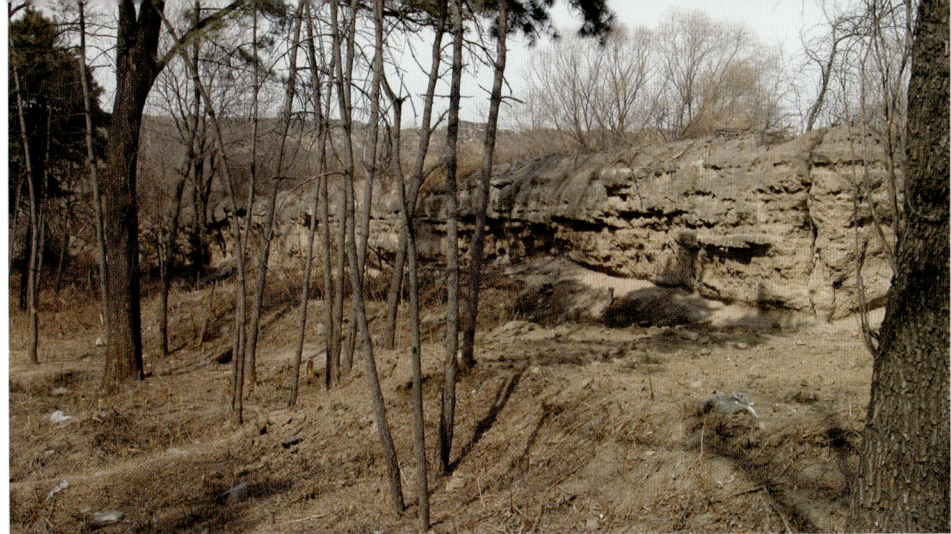

Fig. 79 Ruins of the walls of Shewei City

clearly with the same thought in mind. The emperor's concern for the country and the people was reflected in the erection of temples and shrines. From a utilitarian point of view a major function of the Shewei City was the collection of figures of Buddha. Every year on the birthday of the empress dowager, the rich and powerful from all parts of the country would naturally offer gifts of Buddha figures and precious stones, and this little mock city turned out to be most suited for storing these gifts and Buddha figures.

The French Jesuit Jean-Denis Attiret gave this most vivid account of the Sravasti: "From the emperor's private dwelling a road leads almost straight to a little township in the very midst of these park grounds. It measures a quarter of a *lieue* (one kilometer) on each side, and has gates at the four points of the compass, towers, walls with crenellated parapets, it has its streets, squares and temples, its halls, shops, courts of law and palaces, and even a harbor. In a word, everything to be found in the capital one may find here in little ... Perhaps you ask what purpose all this serves? The chief motive has been to create for the emperor a condensed picture of the bustling life in a great city when he wishes to see this."[1]

The Shewei City measured 110 meters from east to west and 150 meters from north to south. These dimensions were already impressive; when the height of its walls was taken into consideration, the mass of this complex of buildings stood out from the rest. The Market Street in front of it was unequalled in the Qing period as far as a mock city street was concerned. Commerce is a product of city living. Without a street scene the imperial park would have felt different; this Market Street was just the right accent to make a difference.

A surprising wedding was achieved of the concept of hallowed Buddhist grounds with bustling street life, and it amused the emperor. A Zen state of mind would probably have no difficulty resolving the conflict of virtue and evil. Maybe this was a reflection of the emperor's Zen practice.

Remnants of tamped earth used in the walls of the Shewei City can still be seen in the ruins of the walled complex (fig. 79).

---

1 *Gardens of China*, by Osvald Sirén (Sweden), 1949, page 124.

廣育宮 Guangyu Temple (Fertility Temple)

The Guangyu Temple, situated on the south shore of the Lake of Happiness, was built after Emperor Yongzheng's accession to the throne. It was erected on a small hill, diagonally opposite the Jiajing Mingqin Pavilion. After the gate one needed to ascend a small hill to access the courtyard at its top. In a departure from the south-facing norm of a temple, this temple faced north. It had a main hall flanked by side halls. On the north face of the hill a flight of stone steps led down to the south shore of the Lake of Happiness. Remnants of the steps and of the entrance gate have survived (figs. 80, 81).

The Guangyu Temple was devoted to Bixia Yuanjun (Goddess of Mount Tai). The worship of the Goddess of Mount Tai was already widespread in the Ming dynasty, with five well-known shrines dedicated to her located around Beijing. On the first and 15th day of every month on the lunar calendar, men and women would flock to those places of worship because it was the popular belief that Goddess of Mount Tai was omnipotent, being able to protect and bless agriculture, commerce, travel and marriage as well as cure people of illnesses, and more importantly, ensure fertility in women and watch over the wellbeing of children. The inclusion of a shrine to the Goddess of Mount Tai in the Yuan Ming Yuan served the same purpose, i.e. to give the female residents there a venue where they could pray for prosperous progeny for the royal house. On site was a sculpture of a Wawa Hill (Hill Full of Children), which had been moved there from the Guanyin Hall of the Yonghe Palace, "it was a giant wood sculpture that spanned the entire width of the back wall of the Guanyin Hall … On a stone

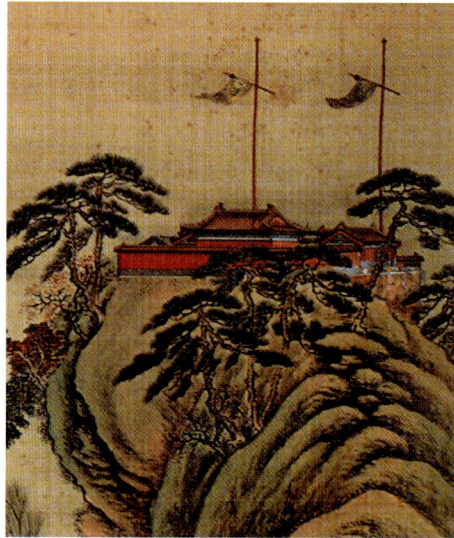

Fig. 80 Painting of Guanyu Temple from the album *Forty Scenes of the Yuan Ming Yuan*

terrace surrounded by trees sat a figure of Guanyin (Goddess of Compassion, Mercy and Kindness), the hill was populated with sculpted naked children. When the Wanfu Pavilion was under renovation, the Wawa Hill was disassembled and moved to the Guangyu Temple of the Yuan Ming Yuan."[1] This happened around the 15th year of the Qianlong era (1750); the deities residing in the temple and the ornamentation in it revolved around this theme. In the Yuan Ming Yuan motifs of *Liukai Baizi* (Pomegranate with its Many Seeds, metaphor for a hundred children), *Duozi Duosun* (Prosperous Progeny) and *Zisun Wandai* (Lineage Spanning Ten Thousand Generations) were ever present in the ornaments and structures of the imperial park.

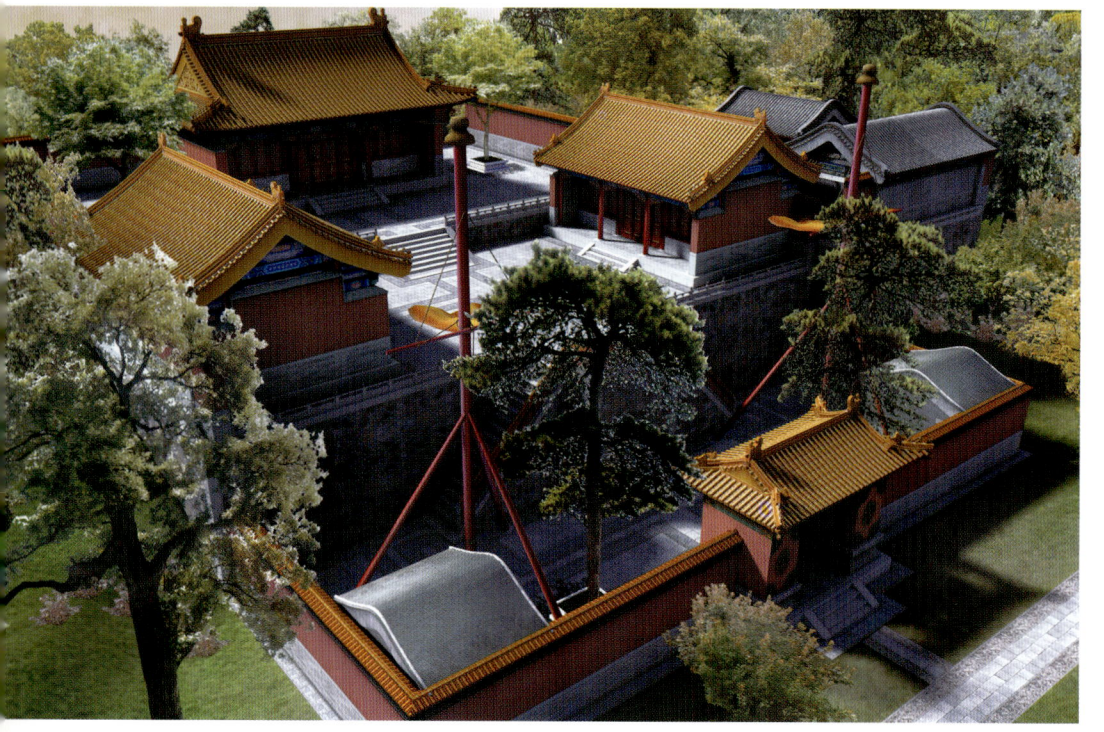

Fig. 81 Themed area of Guangyu Temple

正
覺
寺
Zhengjue Temple (Temple of Supreme Perfect Enlightenment)

The Zhengjue Temple, situated on the south border of the Qichun Garden, was built in the 38th year of the Qianlong era (1773). It was spared in the torching of the Yuan Ming Yuan by the British and French forces and has survived to this day (fig. 83).

The Zhengjue Temple was a Lamaist temple. A central axis ran through the temple gatehouse, the Tianwang Hall, the Mahavira Hall, the Wenshu Hall (Hall of Manjusri) and the Cangjing Building (Building of Scriptures). To the two sides stood the bell tower, the drum tower, the east and west side halls and the east and west corner halls. A side courtyard and a few auxiliary buildings lay to the east. The Wenshu Hall was unique in that it had an octagonal shape; while the hall itself has been preserved to this day, the Manjusri Bodhisattva that used to be enshrined in it has not survived the ravages of time (fig. 82).

Emperor Qianlong had a well-thought out religious policy. In the first year of the Jiaqing era after his abdication he composed a poem in four seven-character lines entitled *Xiaoxiang Chuang*, adding a long note of explanation at the end, saying that "Mongolia is devoutly Buddhist and the propagation of the Gelug school of Tibetan Buddhism is intended to pacify Mongolia. A great deal is at stake on this question." The Xiaoxiang Chuang was originally the name of a little structure in the Shizi Grove of the Changchun Garden. The word *chuang* means in traditional Chinese architecture a stone structure carved with quotations from Buddhist scriptures. The Xiaoxiang Chuang Hall in the Shizi Grove was however not made of stone but of wood and might have been a repository for Buddhist classics in its time.

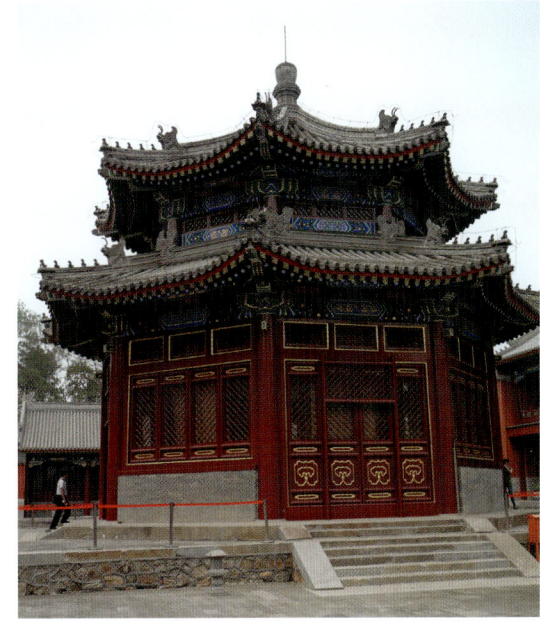

Fig. 82 Wenshu Hall

---

1 *Yonghegong Manlu* (*Random Notes on the Yonghe Palace*), by Wei Kaizhao, published by Henan People's Publishing House, 1985, pages 54–55.

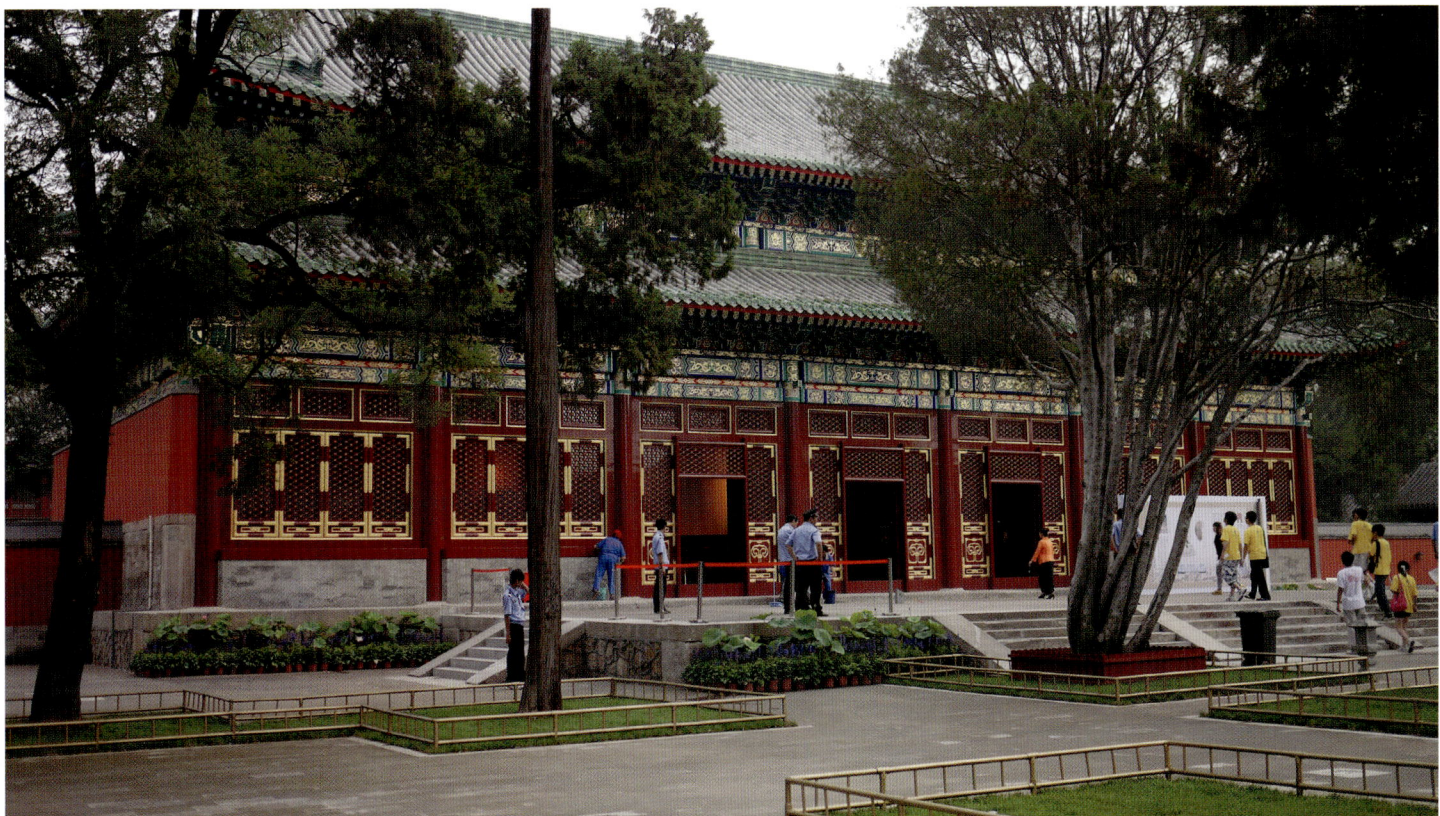

Fig. 83 Main Hall of Zhengjue Temple

法慧寺 Fahui Temple (Dharma Wisdom Temple)

The Fahui Temple was situated east of the Haiyue Kaijin Complex of the Changchun Garden and south of the Xiyang Building section. It had hills in the background and a body of water in front. This drawing from the Imperial Office of Architecture Design (fig. 85) shows that the middle section comprised three halls of five bays. The dimension of the bays remained constant from one hall to the other. The temple gatehouse called the Fuyou Daqian (Gate of Blessed is the World) stood to the south. Between the main hall Fahui Temple and the rear hall Guangming Xinghai (Hall of Brightness and Ocean of Original Nature) two U-shaped buildings facing each other on an east-west axis framed an inner courtyard, and therefore acquired the name Simianyan Building (Quadrangle Building). The main hall and the rear hall, connected by two porches attached to their respective central rooms, formed an H-shaped cross-section. A small three-bay structure contiguous to the west gable wall of the rear hall had a courtyard of its own, called the Jingyu Library (Quiet Pleasure Library), west of which stood a square courtyard enclosed by a gallery, featuring a pagoda at its center. The pagoda Duobao Liuli Pagoda (Abundant Treasures Pagoda with Glazed Tiles) had three stories, the topmost of which had a round cross-section and was surmounted by triple eaves, each covered with glazed tiles of a different color—blue, yellow and green from top to third eave. The second story was octagonal in cross-section and was topped by double eaves, covered respectively with purple and slate-colored glazed tiles. The pagoda had a square cross-section at its ground level, and its double eaves were covered with yellow and jade-green glazed tiles. The pagoda was 23.55 meters tall, with a square base whose sides measured only 5.5 meters, somewhat on the modest side, but the multi-color glazed tiles that ornamented it were visually appealing (fig. 84).

To the west of the temple a trail led to a small gate that gave access to the vistas in the west and north of the Changchun Garden.

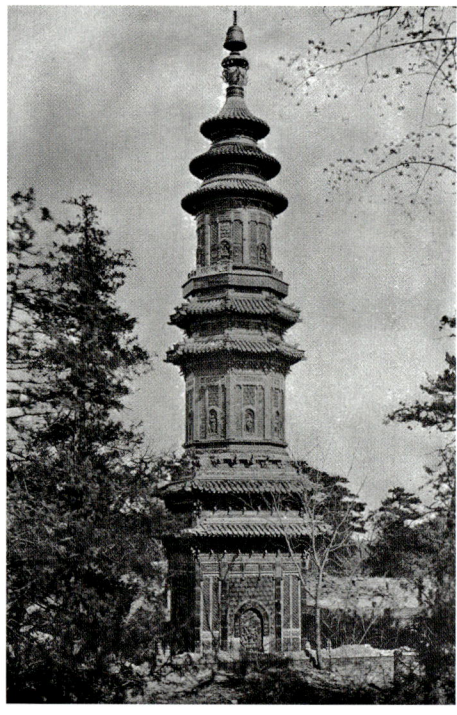

Fig. 84 Duobao Liuli Pagoda at Fahui Temple

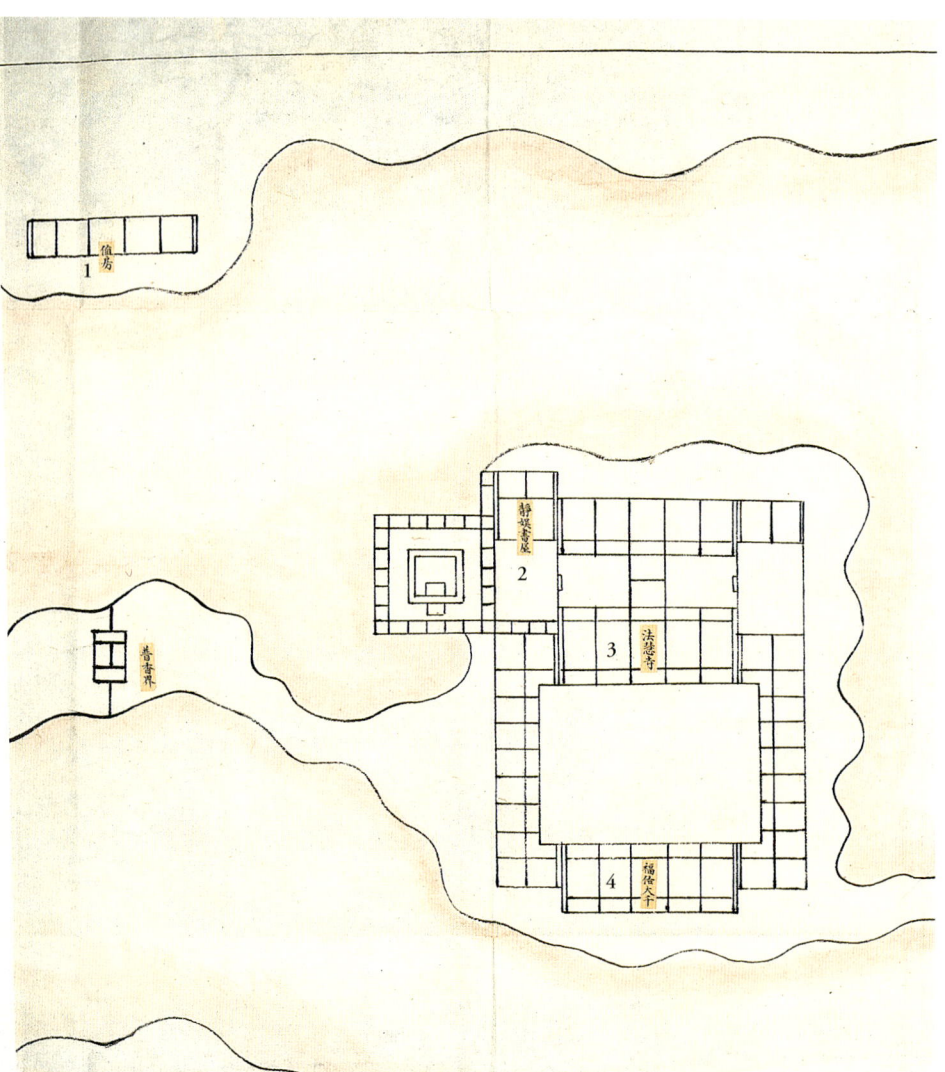

Fig. 85 Plan of Fahui Temple in Changchun Garden
1. Duty room 2. Jingyu Library 3. Fahui Temple 4. Fuyou Daqian

寶相寺 Baoxiang Temple (Jeweled Image Temple)

"To the east of the Fahui Temple lies the Baoxiang Temple, whose gatehouse faces south. It features the Chengguang Pavilion (Pure Light Pavilion), behind which stands the Tanfei Pavilion (Clouds Pavilion). In the rear on a raised foundation stands the Xianda Yuanjing Hall (Hall of Display of Great Perfect Mirror Wisdom)"[1].

The layout of the Baoxiang Temple complex was perfectly symmetrical. It sat on a terrain that inclined from north to south. The compact suite of four courtyards climbed with the rising terrain. While not very large, the complex had an interesting layering of spaces (fig. 86). Available drawings show that the temple gatehouse was flanked by two flights of steps. The gatehouse was raised above normal ground. Once in the gate one was greeted by the Chengguang Pavilion, which was five bays wide and was dedicated to the Jade Emperor).

After the Chengguang Pavilion came a courtyard at the north end of which stood the two-storied Tanfei Pavilion. The upper floor of the pavilion was open-sided and was three bays wide; a door-tunnel beneath led to a flight of steps that took one to a terrace, on which stood the five-bay main hall named Xianda Yuanjing Hall. A three-bay porch, with a terrace in front, jutted out from the middle of the south façade. The temple complex used a layout that departed from the norm: its courtyards were all made very shallow to accentuate the grandeur of the main hall, which dominated the complex from high ground.

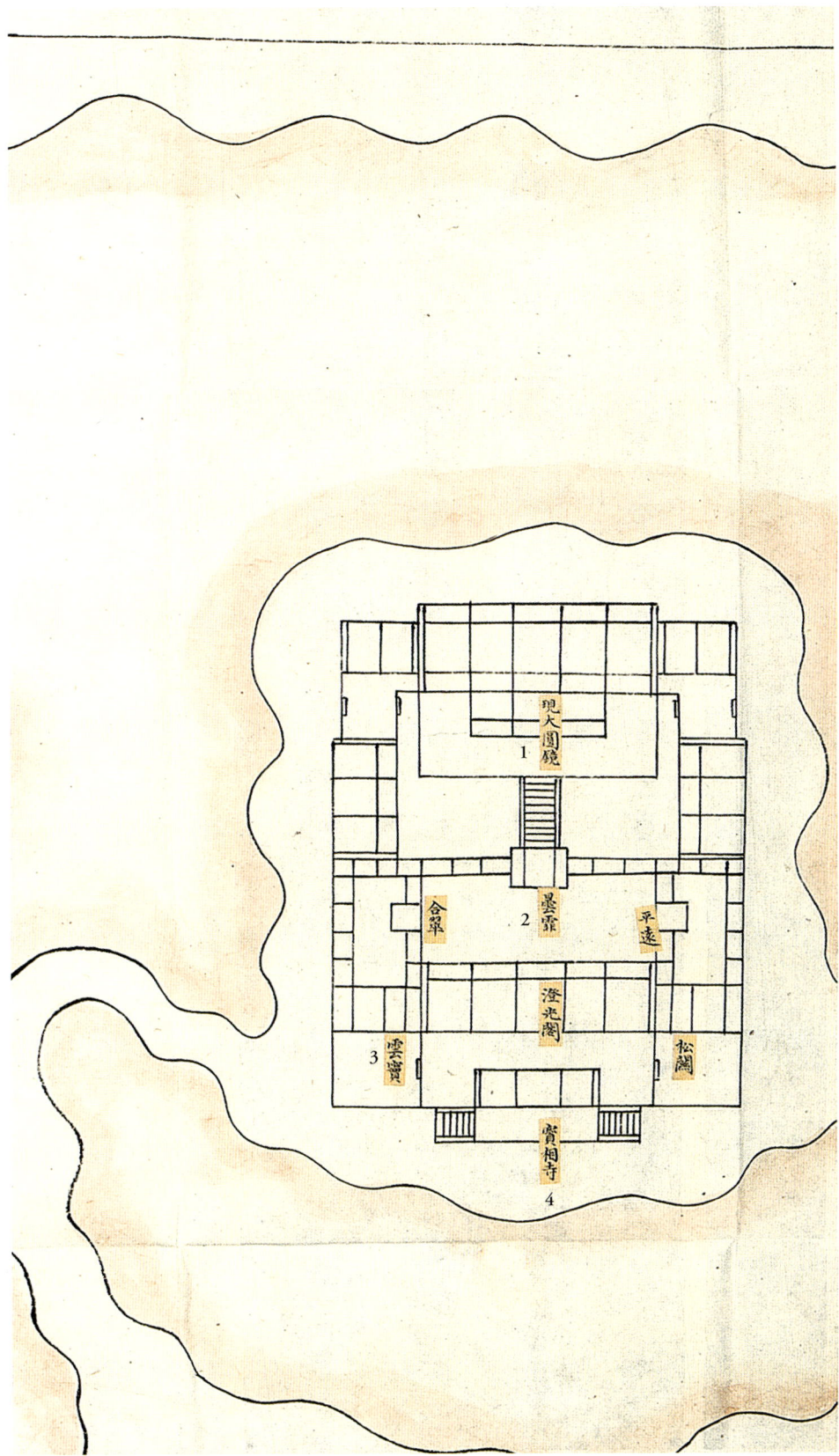

Fig. 86 Plan of Baoxiang Temple in Changchun Garden
1. Xianda Yuanjing Hall 2. Tanfei Pavilion 3. Chengguang Pavilion 4. Gate of Baoxiang Temple

---
1 *Rixia Jiuwen Kao*, Volume 83.

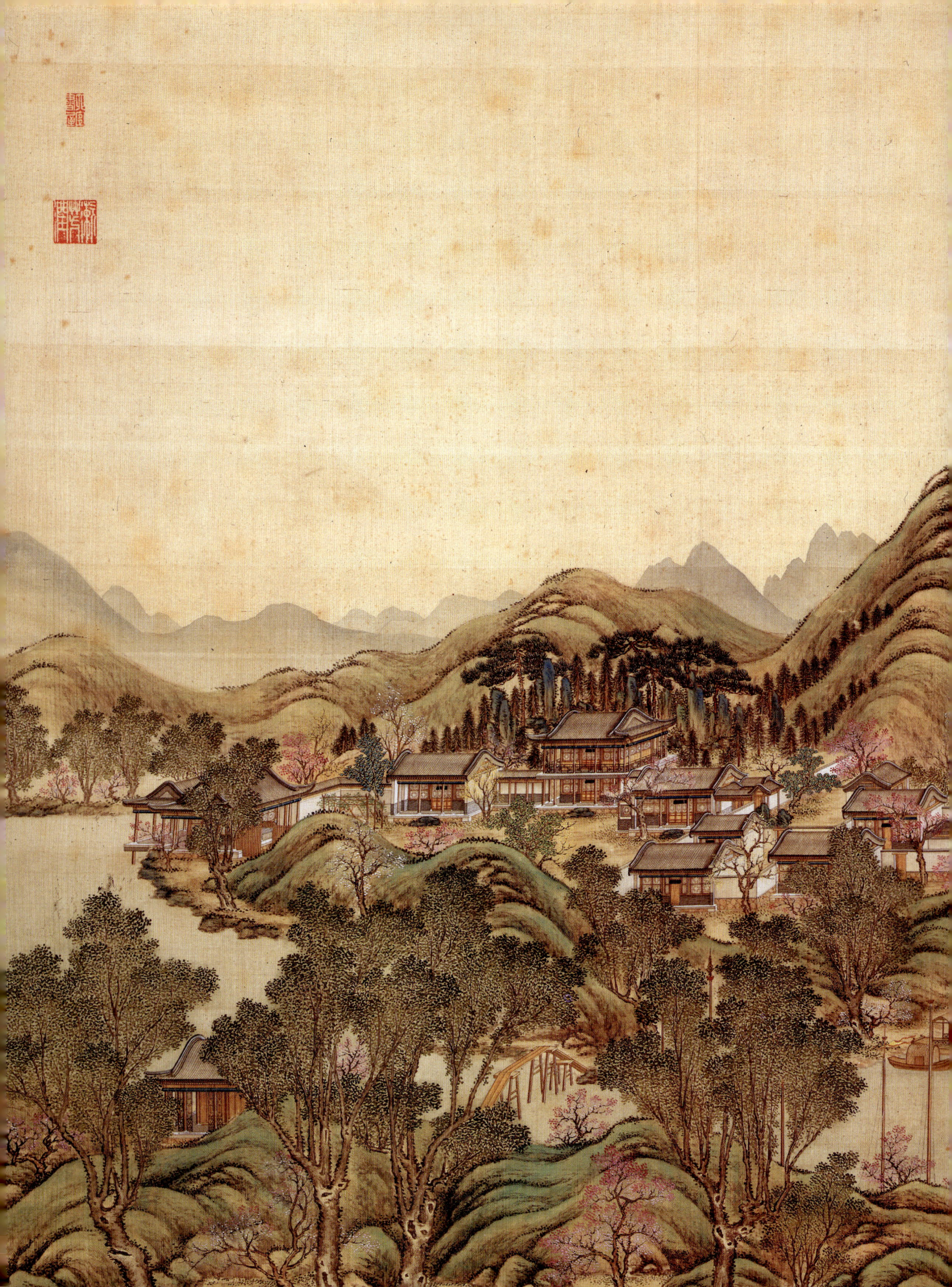

CHAPTER IX
Culture and Education

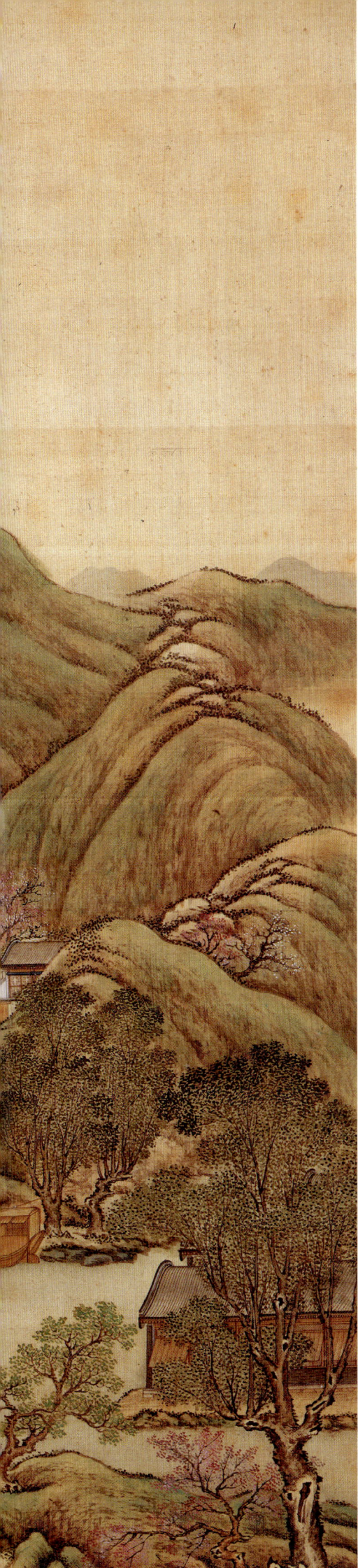

Academies, libraries and studies abounded in the Yuan Ming Yuan. Some were designated as studies for the emperor's reading pleasure; others, while their names did not give any hint of study or books, were actually places where the emperor's children studied. One such example was the Dongtian Shenchu Complex (Deep in the Grotto Complex). When the emperor's sons reached the age of six they started attending the *Shangshu Fang* or the Palace School for Princes. They realized that familiarizing themselves with the Confucian canon would give them wisdom to prepare them for governance. The Jiuzhou Qingyan Complex of the Yuan Ming Yuan was the private residence of the emperor and the empress. In one of his poems, Emperor Qianlong wrote about his eating late and rising early all in order to read more and his belief that reading was indispensable for achieving the vision, of himself, his father and his son, of bringing peace and calm to the nine continents of his realm.

Besides those complexes explicitly named academies in the Yuan Ming Yuan, dozens of buildings had names that had to do with studying; examples included 27 buildings with *shuwu* or library in their names, including the Changchun Library (Eternal Spring Library) in the Jiuzhou Qingyan Complex, the Yangsu Library in the Louyue Kaiyun Complex, the Weizhen Library (True Flavor Library) in the Lianxi Lechu Complex (Complex of Happy Place of Lianxi), Zhanxu Library (Hollowness Belying Profundity Library) in the Beiyuan Mountain Village section and the Yiran Library (Serene Contentment Library) in the Jiexiu Mountain House area (Mountain House Greeted by the Beauty of the Hills). In addition the Weiyu Library (Rich Flavor Library) of the Tripataka Hall, the Pinshi Hall (Poetry Appreciation Hall) of the Wuling Chunse area, the Zuojing Pavilion (Books as Pillow Pavilion) of the Siyi Library (Library of the Four Seasons) (fig. 87), the Rugu Hall, the Kaiyi Pavilion (Improvement by Reading Pavilion), the Xuming Room (Clarity by Cleansing Room) and the Yiqing Shushi Hall were all places for reading and learning. Reading enables one to be well versed in ancient canon and tap modern knowledge, to explore the mysteries of the world, instill integrity and to perceive the essence of things.

Fig. 87 Painting of Siyi Library from the album *Forty Scenes of the Yuan Ming Yuan*

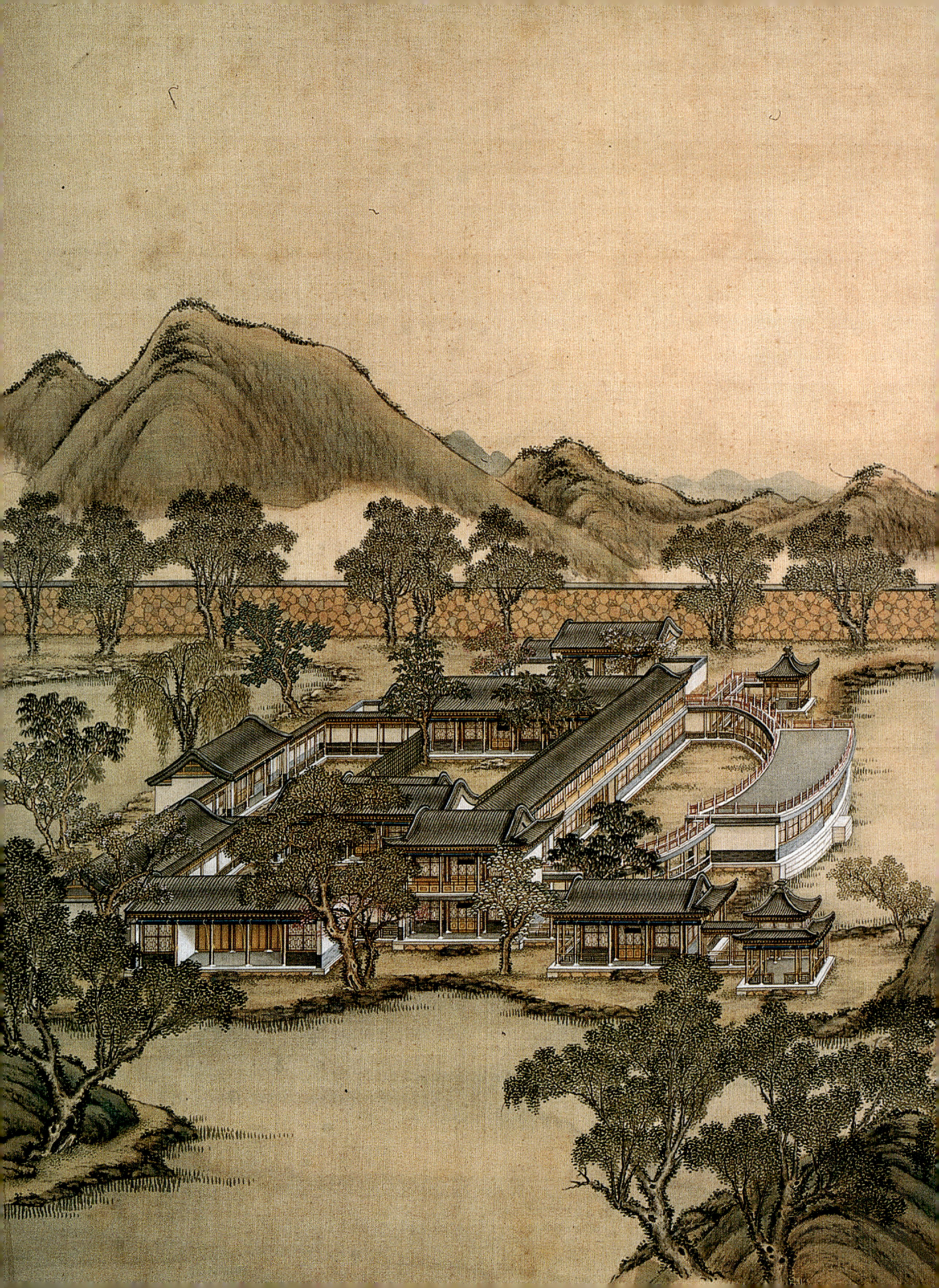

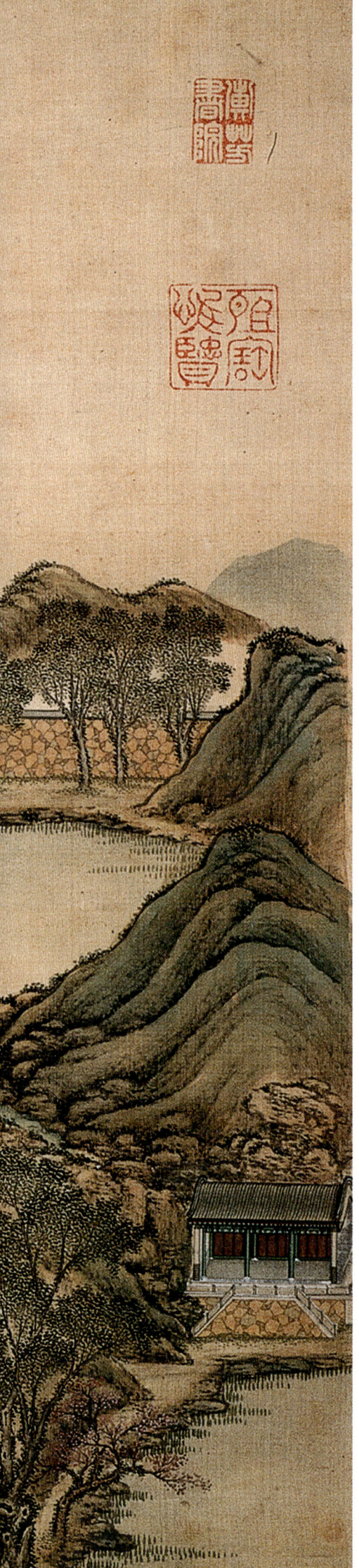

匯芳書院 Huifang Library (Library of Collected Fragrance)

Reading and associating with the wise were an important part in an emperor's political life. The two were often inseparable. The emperor read together with his learned ministers for the purpose of fostering virtuous and capable officials. *Huifang* (collecting all that is fragrant) in the name of this compound means gathering the wise around him and benefiting from the wisdom of many. This was the meaning of the name of the Huifang Library in the Yuan Ming Yuan.

The Huifang Library was built in the seventh year of the Qianlong era (1742). It was situated in the northwest of the Yuan Ming Yuan (fig. 88) on a peninsula where hills and streams met. It was in a more relaxed environment than the Nine Islands area to its south, which boasted much more vistas and attractions. Although accessible via streams and bridges, it was sufficiently isolated from the other sections of the imperial park.

In plan the buildings in this group were aligned along a north-south axis that strung together the main buildings, from north to south, the Hanyuan Study (Mirror Reflection of the World Study), the Shuzao Pavilion (Display of Literary Talent Pavilion) and the main hall of the Huifang Library. These three buildings were uniformly five bays wide, with variations only in depth. The Shuzao Pavilion featured a porch on it north façade while the other two were buildings with front and back galleries and a roof with a round ridge. There was no left-right symmetry on the two sides of the central axis and the buildings on the two sides were architecturally dissimilar. The west side was relatively simple, with galleries and side halls in the front and back courtyards; a bamboo fence was added in the courtyard of the Hanyuan Study. The east side was more elaborately developed, with the two-storied Zhuoyun Building (Lofty clouds Building) and Cuizhao Building (Green Glow Building) that were a dozen bays wide. To their east stood the Meiyue Pavilion (Crescent Moon Pavilion) with a very unique shape surrounded by small pavilions.

One of the attractive qualities of this complex was the variety in its arrangement of space, with buildings interestingly distributed and courtyards of distinct shapes and sizes and man-made structures and nature pleasingly reconciled. The quiet and seclusion calmed and pleased, making it a favorite spot for Emperor Qianlong.

The Yuan Ming Yuan was distinguished by the variety of its layouts and full use was made

Fig. 88 Painting of Huifang Library from the album *Forty Scenes of the Yuan Ming Yuan*

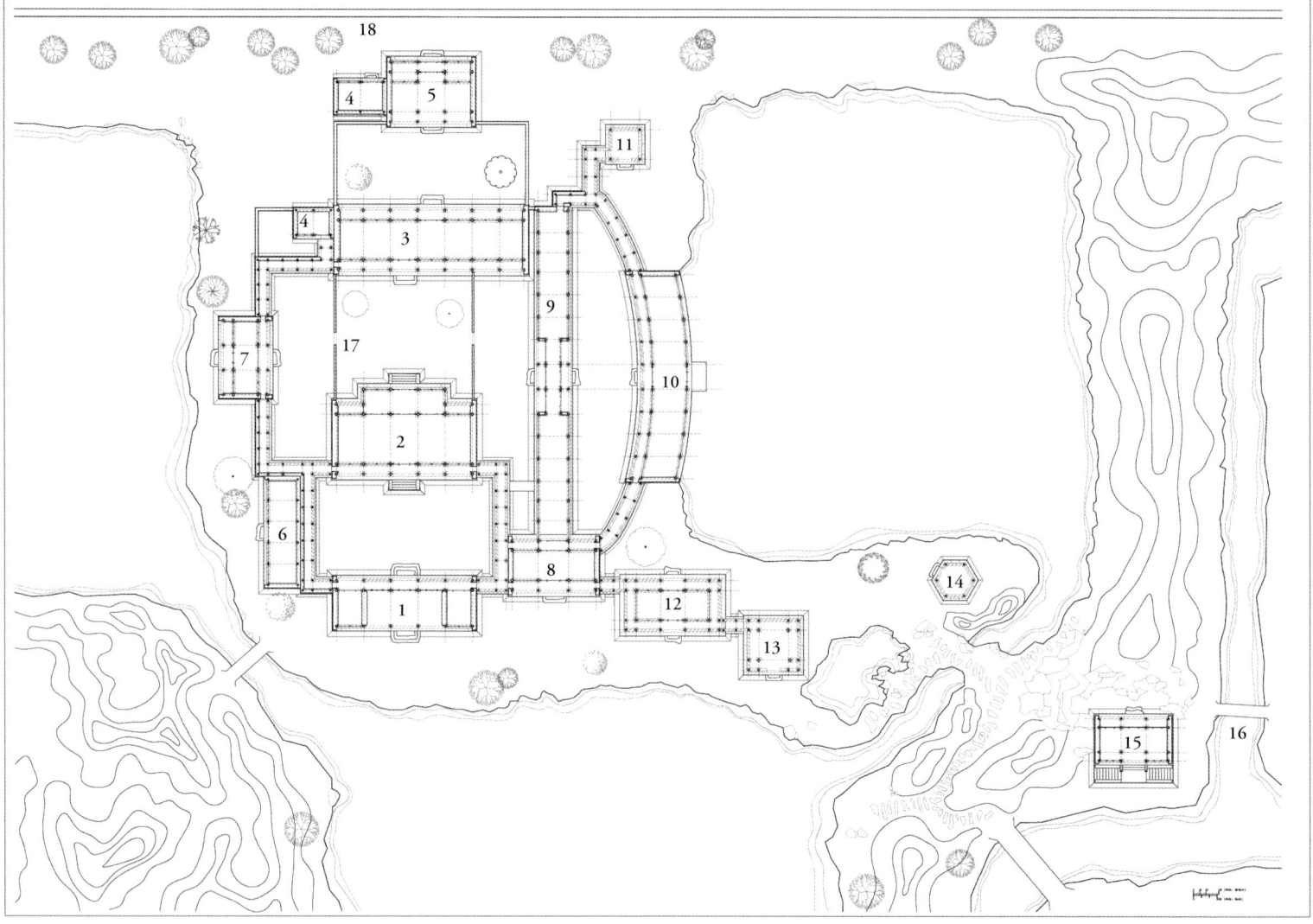

Fig. 89 Plan of Huifang Library
1. Huifang Library 2. Shuzao Pavilion 3. Hanyuan Study 4. Ear room 5. Rear building
6. Southwest hall 7. Cuizhao Pavilion 8. Zhuoyun Building 9. Zhushen Hejing Building
10. Meiyue Pavilion 11. Xiuyun Pavilion 12. Sui'an Room 13. Yixiu Pavilion 14. Yanshang Pavilion
15. Wenjin Pavilion 16. Duanqiao Canxue 17. Fence 18. North enclosure wall

of the flexibility and variability peculiar to the creative process of crafting traditional Chinese gardens. While variety arose from the need to seek certain specific forms and shapes or from functional requirements, in most cases the creators adapted the traditional gardens and courts to the natural setting and the local hills and streams and terrain. The design of the Huifang Library was one of the most successful examples of this approach.

The entire complex was divided into two parts by the Zhuoyun Building (fig. 89). The western part comprised three courtyards that conformed to the norm, the only departure from the norm being the small porch of the main building Shuzao Pavilion, which was a minor variation to differentiate the main building. But in the eastern part, which included the Zhuoyun Building, the architectural style was freer. There was the crescent-shaped Meiyue Pavilion and three small pavilions with dissimilar roofs, closely conforming to the terrain and the surrounding hills and streams. The three courtyards in the western half, and the individual buildings in them, all ran in a north-south direction. The Zhuoyun Building and the Meiyue Pavilion however ran east-west. This east-west axis extended eastward into a body of water that was hemmed in on all four sides, with only an outlet in its southeast corner that gave access to the area of water on the outside. The Meiyue Pavilion's protrusion into this little lake was intended to highlight its "water affinity," and create a perfect union with that natural environment.

The Wenjin Pavilion (Pavilion for Asking Directions to the Ford), which predated the Huifang Library on the peninsula, was kept after the latter was built to function as a sort of introductory space into the Library from the exterior. It became the main link between the Library and the rest of the Yuan Ming Yuan. Once past the Wenjin Pavilion, one was greeted by the sight of a small hill, at various heights of which stood the hexagonal Yanshang Pavilion (Transferred Favors Pavilion), the quadrangular double-eave pavilion Yixiu Pavilion (Taking in the Scenery Pavilion) and the Sui'an Room that was three bays wide and topped by a Chinese hip-and-gable roof. When one approached this point from the middle part of the Yuan Ming Yuan, one climbed over a hill and was greeted by the sight of a number of pavilions of different shapes, which announced the proximity of the library. Then one spotted this open structure of three bays, named "Wenjin" (literally asking where the ford is), an expression with possibly the deep meaning that through the study in this Library a way would be pointed out to the emperor to a ford of safe crossing as he steered the ship of state (fig. 90).

In the Huifang Library tall two-storied buildings, an arc-shaped veranda, galleries and pavilions of a rich variety of shapes and forms were integrated into a pleasing, lively whole, and a fine balance was maintained between the main and secondary buildings (fig. 91 on pages 100 and 101).

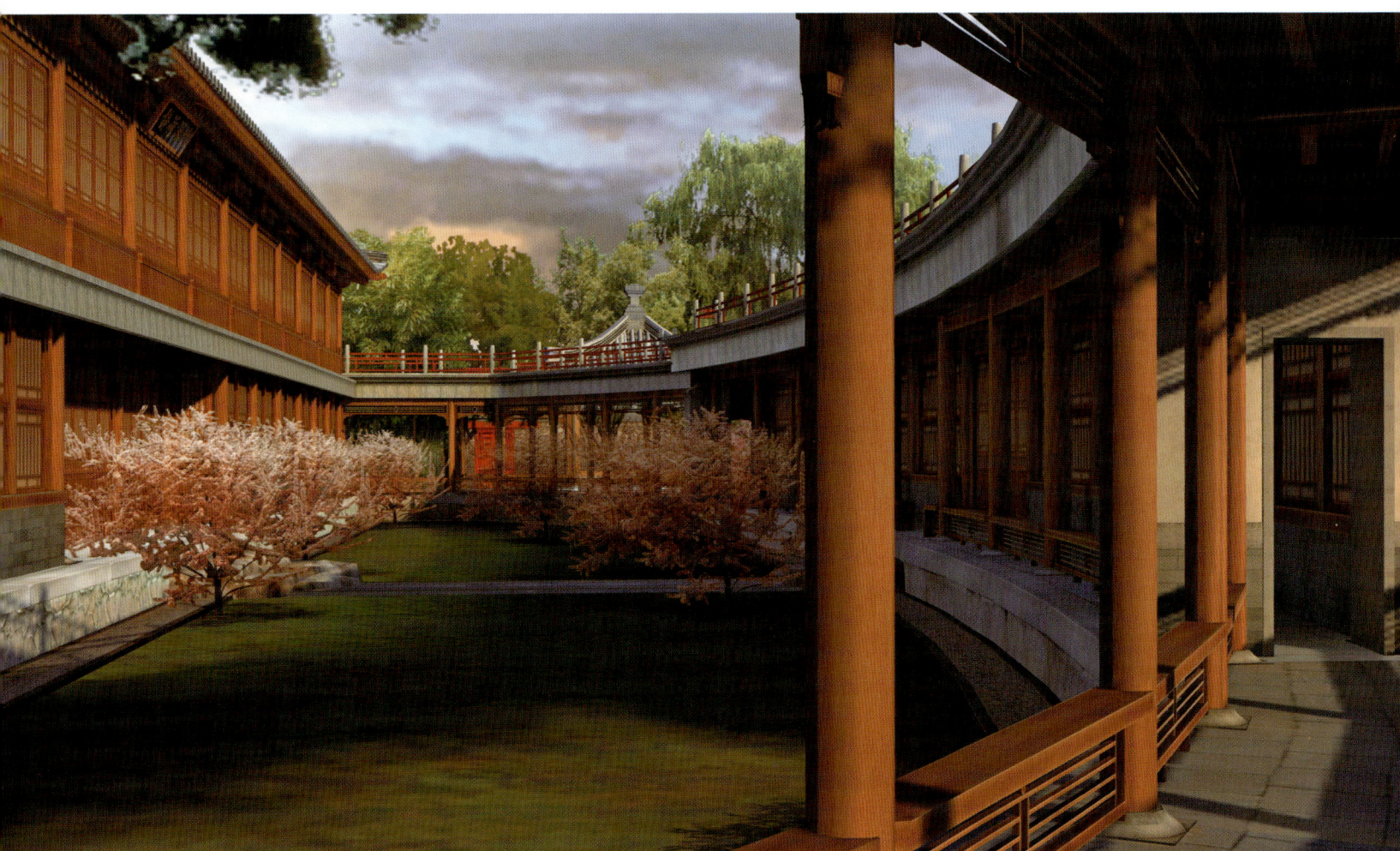

Fig. 90 Lush Bamboo and Pure Lotus Building and Meiyue Pavilion

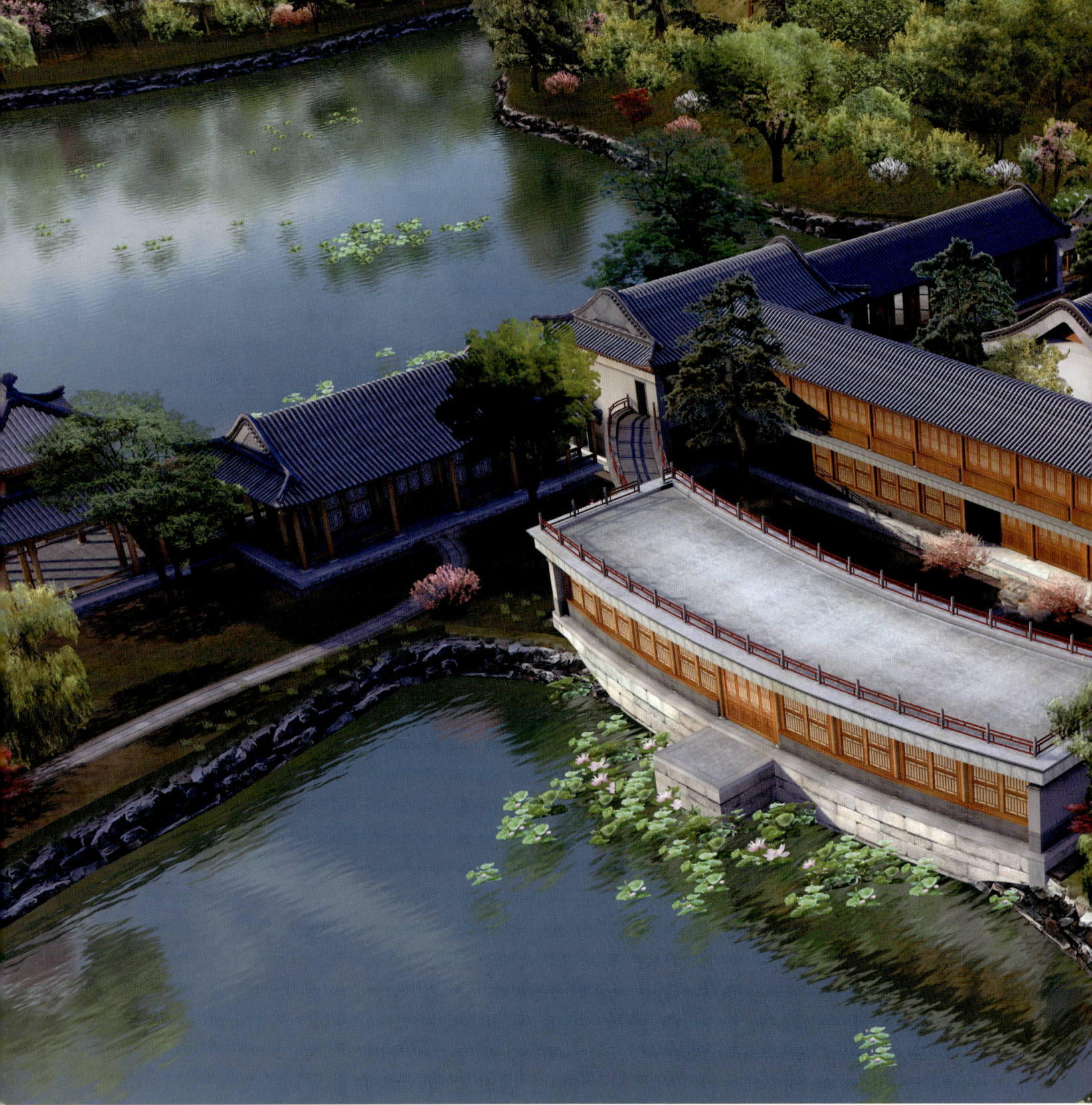

Fig. 91 Scene on east side of Huifang Library

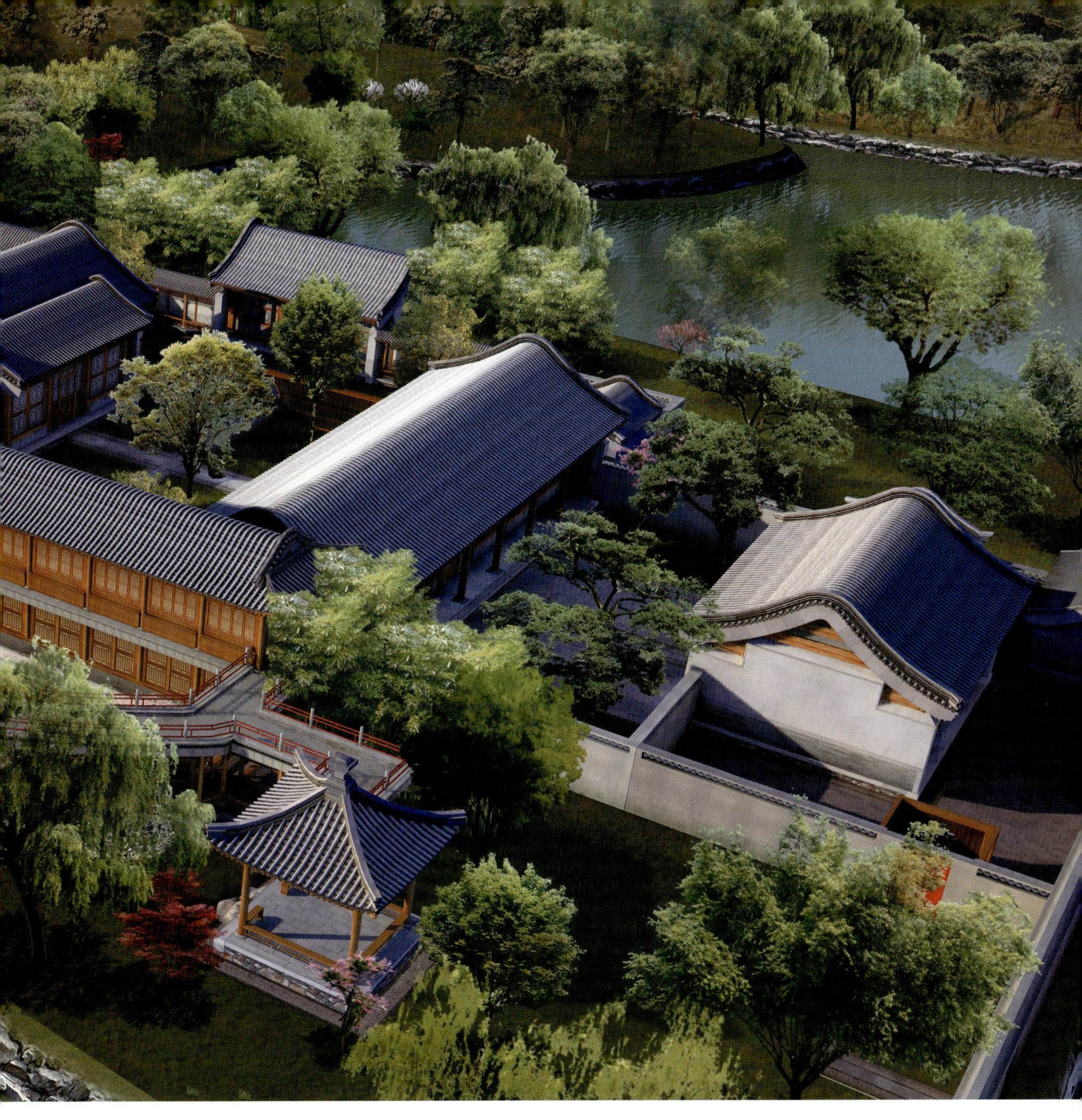

碧桐書院 Bitong Library (Green Wutong Tree Library)

The Bitong Library (fig. 92) was situated north of the Tianran Tuhua Complex. The album *Forty Scenes of the Yuan Ming Yuan* shows a dozen buildings here of various sizes. These were uniformly topped by a round-ridge roof with overhanging eaves. They were roughly divided into a main section and a secondary section, but variety was sought. The buildings on the right were the primary ones; they formed, from front to back, three courtyards, and had a north-south orientation. The main halls were placed in the third courtyard; galleries extended west from the west end of the two halls to connect with a small pavilion of three bays that faced east. A very narrow stream hugged the courtyard; this was the stream mentioned in a prefatory note to one of Emperor Qianlong's poems: "It has a flat bridge in front and a narrow stream winding around it." This narrow stream started from the foot of the little waterfall in the northwest and flowed south, rounded the small hall in the south before turning north, past a patch of flower-beds, the connection galleries west of the main hall, turning west to flow behind the main hall and connect with the waterfall in the west (fig. 93). Archeologists have unearthed next to the main hall a long, narrow cistern built with stone slabs and topped with a sun-shading wooden awning. This cooled the main hall considerably. Historical drawings show a very long rectangular cistern in the complex, with a bridge across it. Stone component parts of the cistern have been preserved among the ruins.

In the left section the buildings formed four courtyards of varying sizes and shapes. Most buildings in these courtyards were three bays wide, but their orientations varied. East of the main section a scattering of small buildings dotted the landscape.

The Library was circled by a stream and ringed by hills, which ensured its quiet and seclusion and suited it for reading and verse making. That's why Emperor Qianlong wrote in that prefatory note to his poem: "Every time I hear the dripping of rain I am moved to verse making."

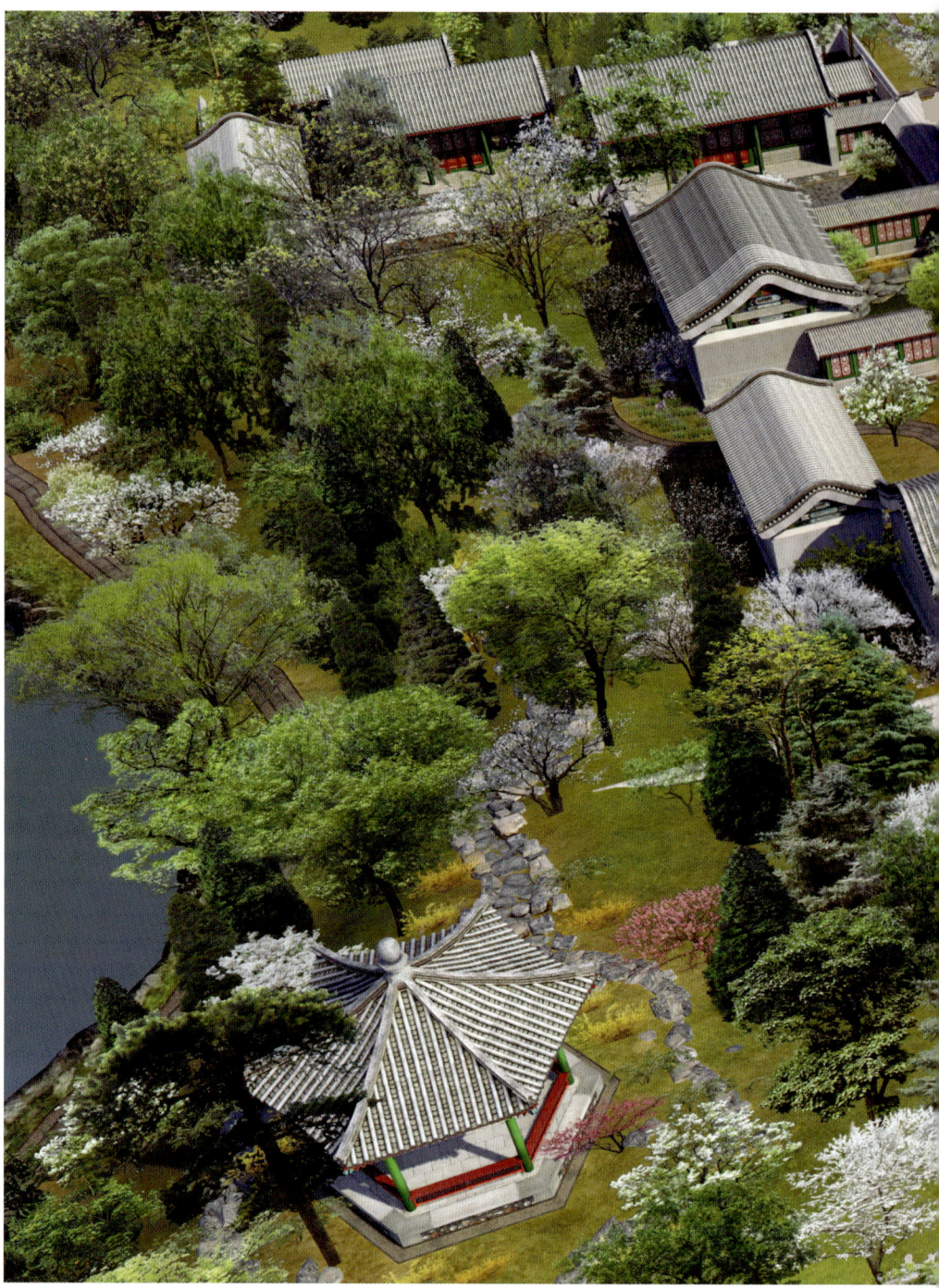

102 CHINA'S LOST IMPERIAL GARDEN

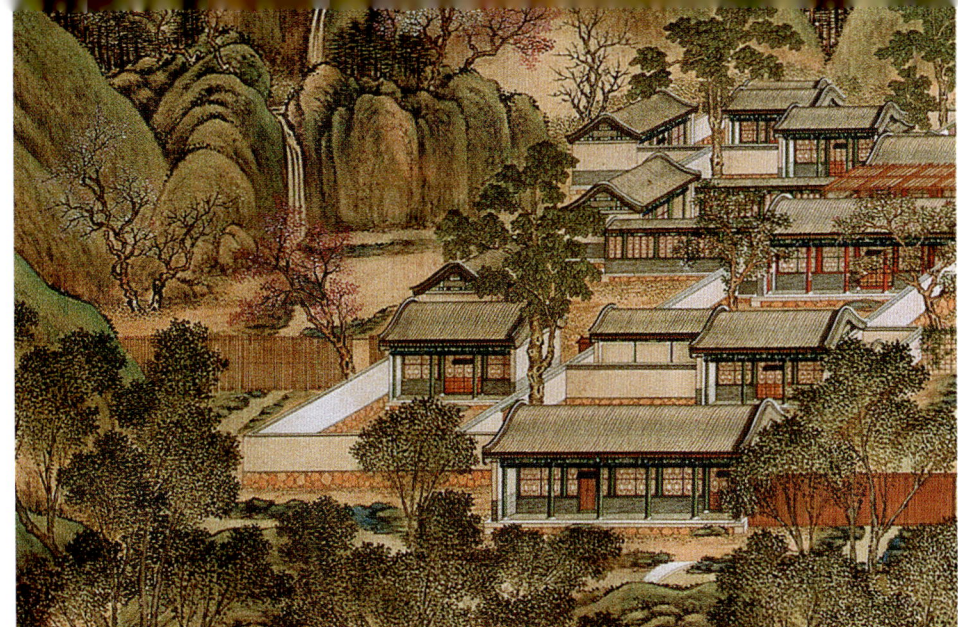

Fig. 93　Painting of Bitong Library from *Forty Scenes of the Yuan Ming Yuan*, showing waterfall, flat bridge and stream

Below
Fig. 92　Bitong Library

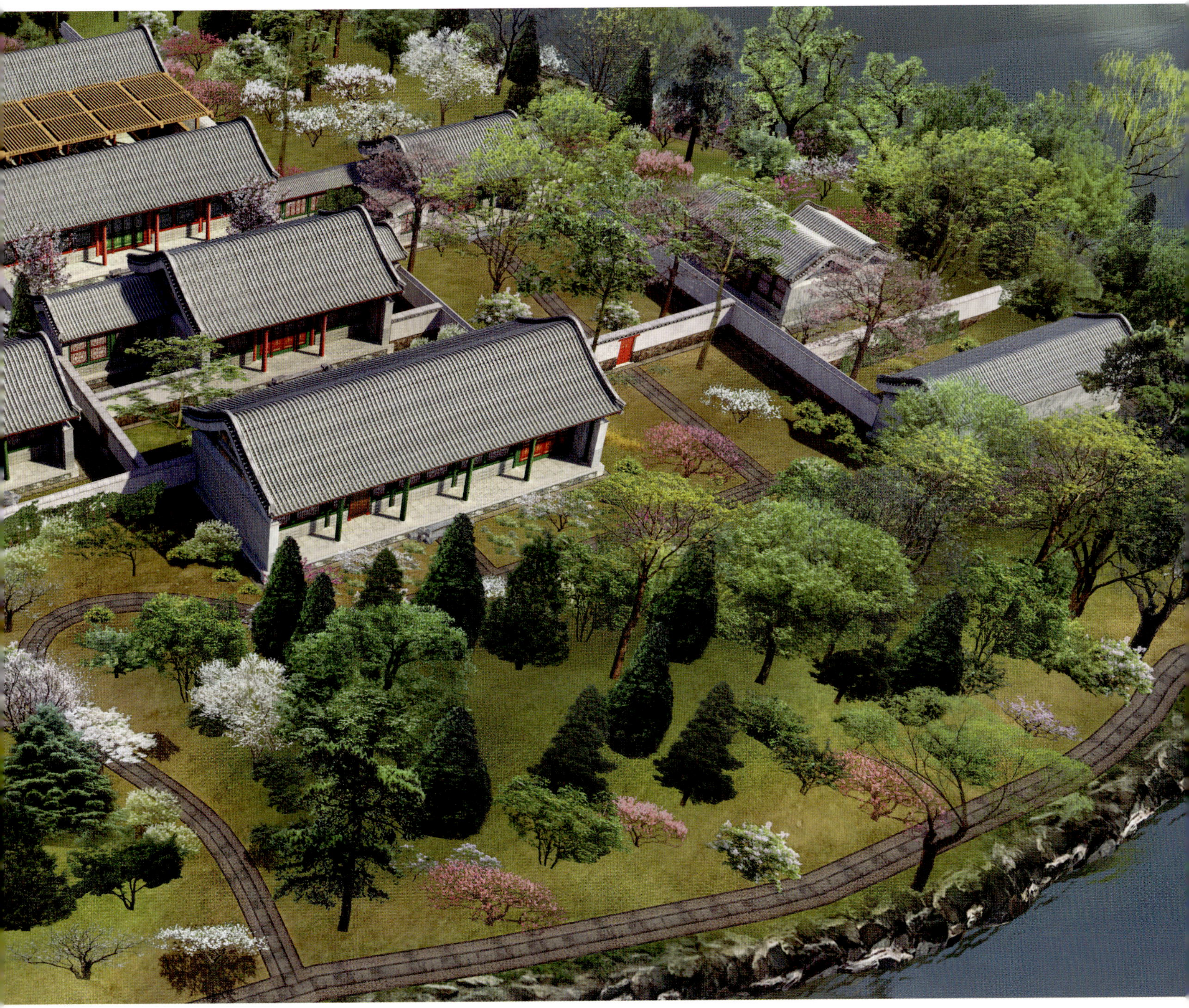

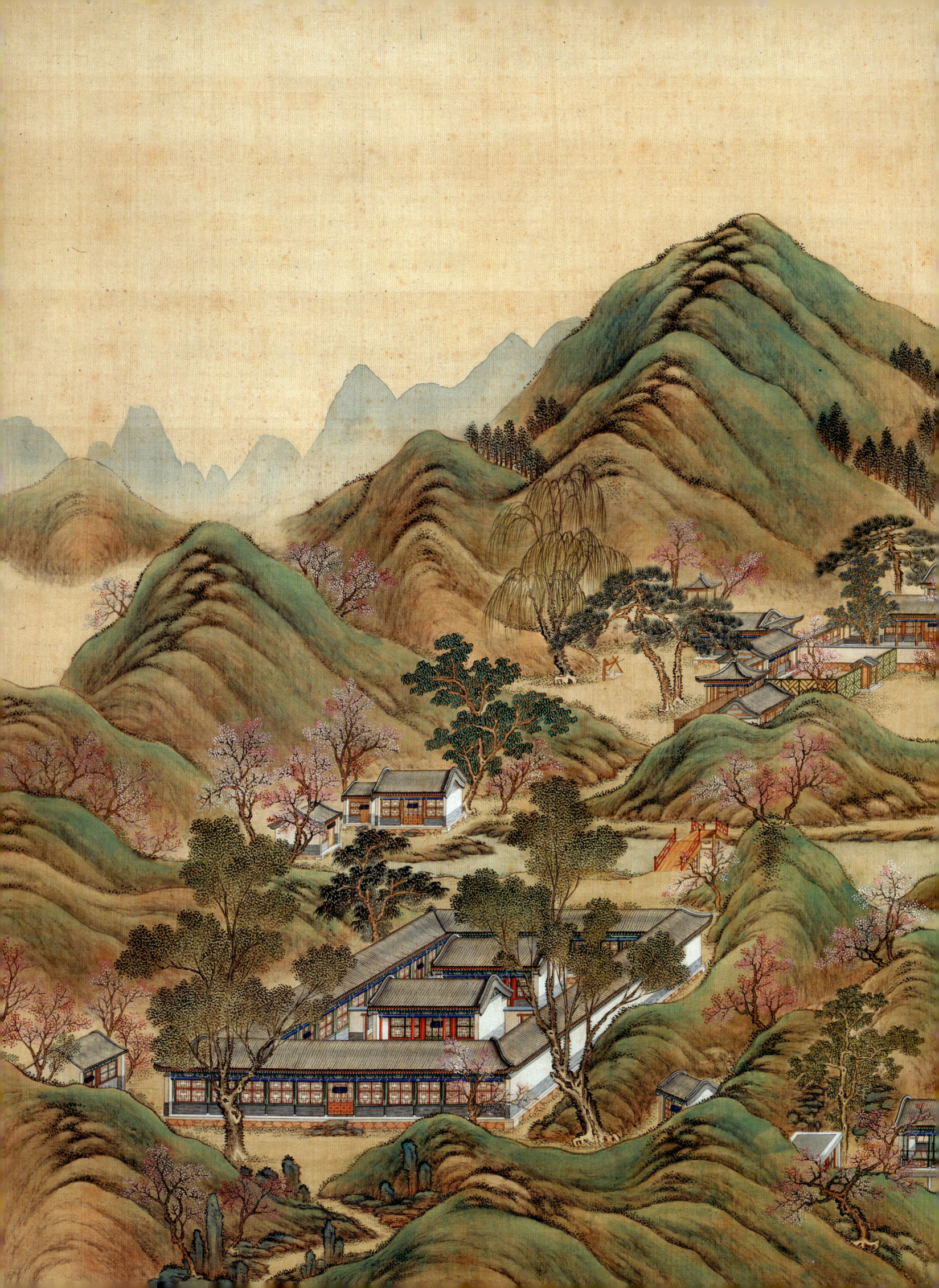

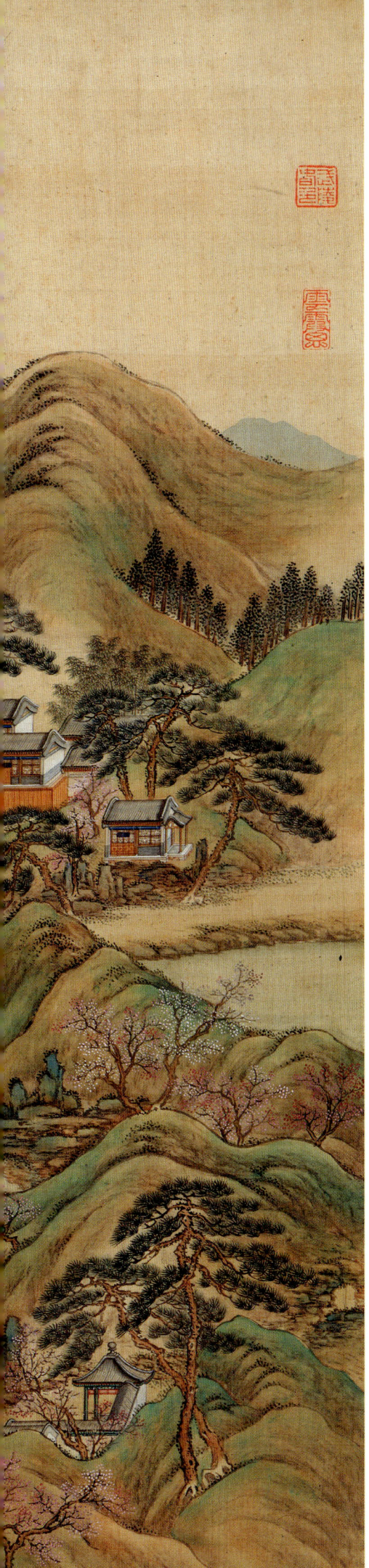

武陵春色

Wuling Chunse (Spring Color at Wuling)

The Wuling Chunse was situated in the middle of the Yuan Ming Yuan to the north of the Nine Islands area (fig. 94). It was built in the reign of Emperor Kangxi and was known then as Taohua Hollow.

This scenic section was surrounded by hills and was embellished at its south by artificial hills, stone grottos, streams and groves of peach trees, sprinkled with a few windowed verandas and small pavilions (fig. 95). When one approached this place by boat, one would, just as described in *The Peach Blossom Spring* written by Tao Yuanmig, first cross a stream and the introductory space in front of an artificial hill and pass through a stone grotto before arriving at the area where the main buildings were. If one went by land, one would start from the Wanfang Anhe Complex (Complex of Universal Peace and Harmony) of the park and cross a bridge to the north before coming to a group of buildings called the Quanbi Hall (Hall of All Green) on the south side. The Quanbi Hall was an enclosed courtyard with two small halls in the middle. At the north end of the Wuling Chunse was another group of scattered

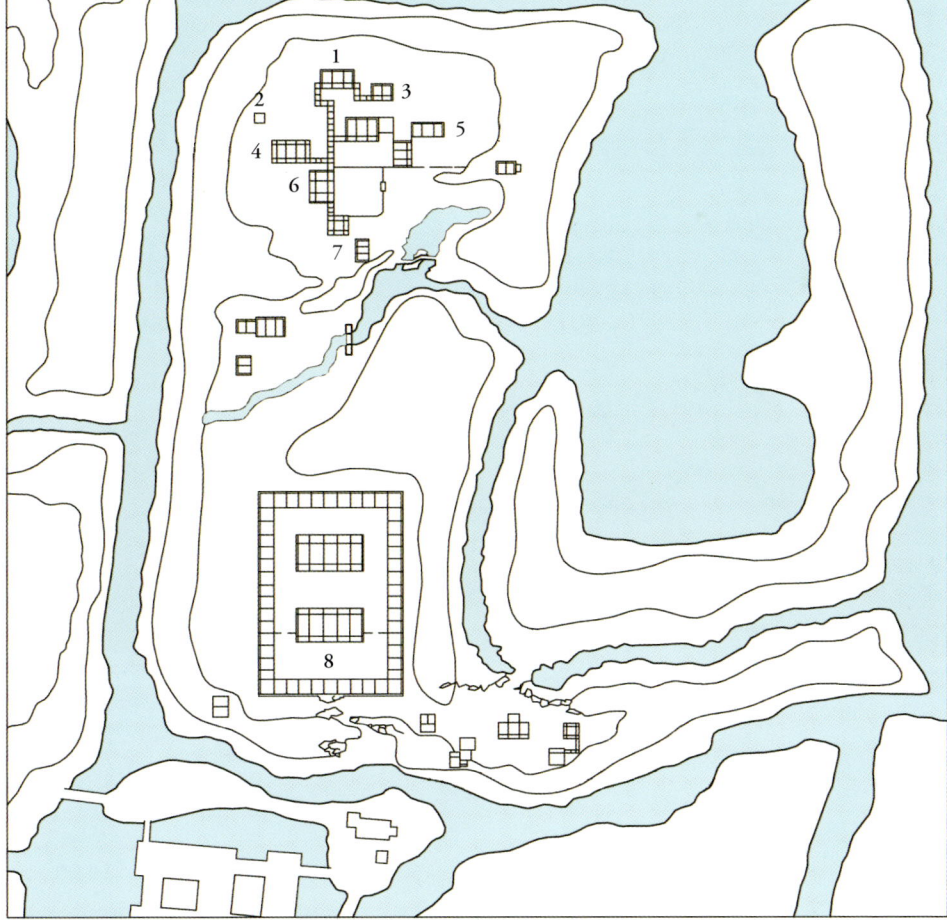

Fig. 95 Plan of Wuling Chunse
1. Qingshui Zhuoying Hall 2. Qinghui Pavilion 3. Wanchun Pavilion 4. Taoyuan Shenchu Hall 5. Pinshi Hall
6. Leshan Hall 7. Qingxiu Pavilion 8. Quanbi Hall

Fig. 94 Painting of the Wuling Chunse from the album *Forty Scenes of the Yuan Ming Yuan*

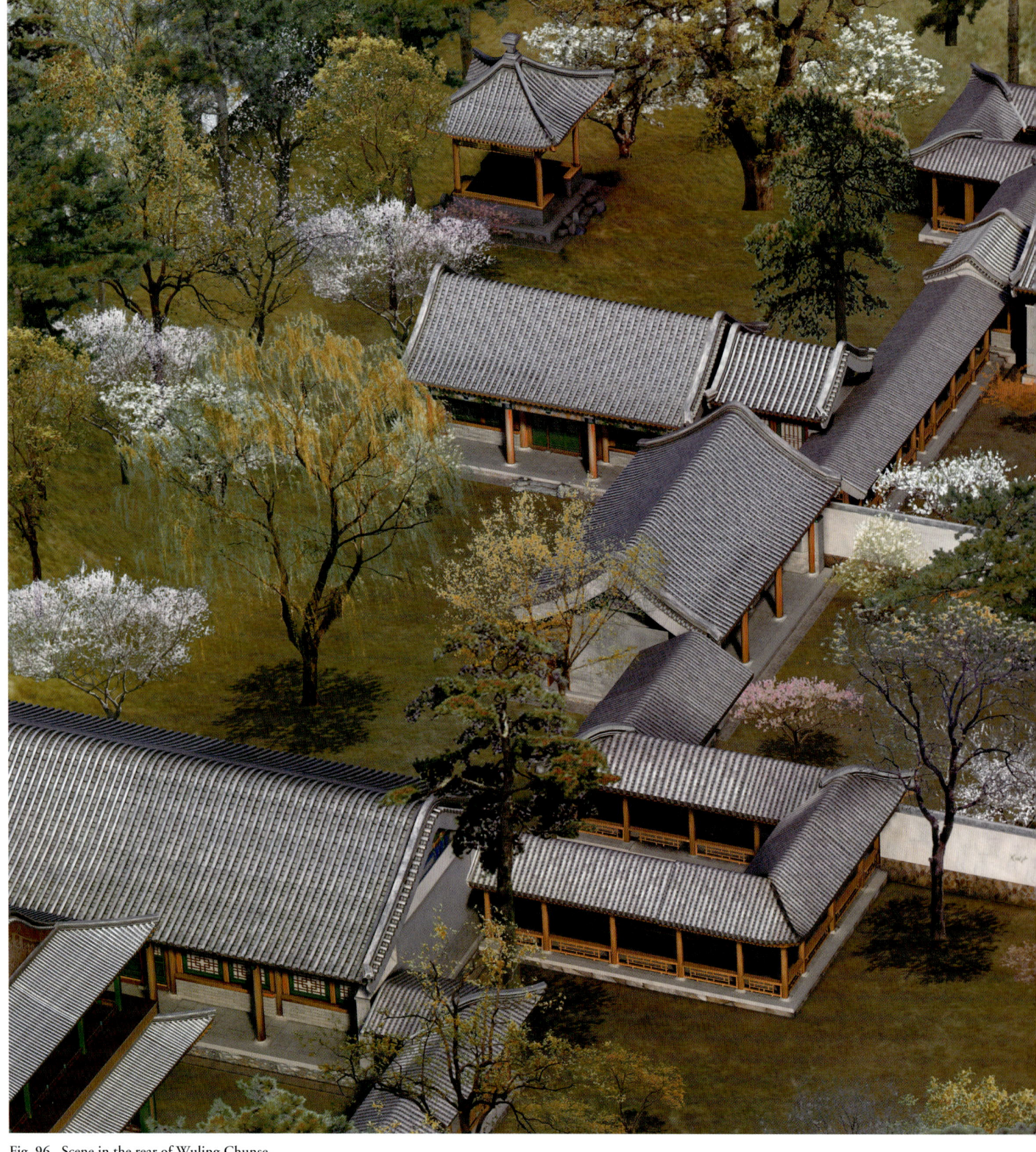

Fig. 96 Scene in the rear of Wuling Chunse

buildings, the largest of which was called the Taohua Hollow. The Qingshui Zhuoying Hall (Hall of Washing Hat Tassels in Clear Water) stood behind it and the Taoyuan Shenchu Hall (Hall of Deep in the Peach Blossom Spring), the Leshan Hall (Delight in Doing Good Deeds Hall) and the Qinghui Pavilion lay to the west of the Taohua Hollow, bordering on which to its east was a small courtyard enclosed with a wooden fence. A small windowed veranda the Wanchun Pavilion stood in the middle of the courtyard and a small hall the Pinshi Hall lay to its northeast. This group of buildings in the north of the Wuling Chunse were all unpainted and uncarved, keeping the original color of the wood used in their construction. The Leshan Hall, which had an east-west orientation, had at its west a well and was fenced in with bamboo pickets at its east; these gave it a rustic air. Emperor

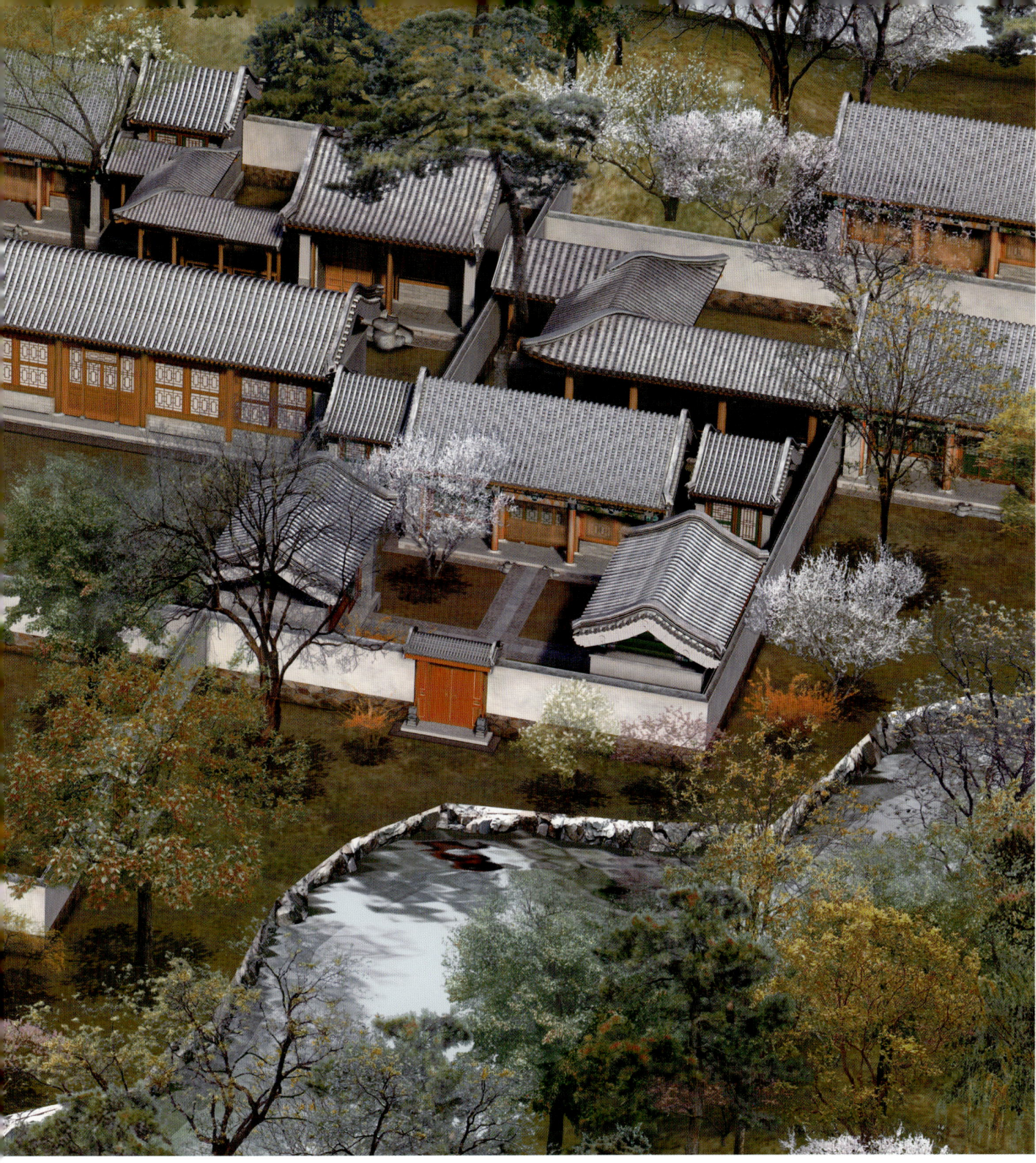

Qianlong wrote: "It has a number of studies. It is quiet and cool and has a bucolic atmosphere. I am often accompanied by herons and a lute, surrounded by patches of vegetables and blossoming peach trees. It is a delightful sight (fig. 96)."[1]

The Leshan Hall served as Qianlong's study in his youth. As an imperial son, Hongli spent a prodigious amount of time in this study reading classics, which helped form his philosophy and his character. He sought wisdom in reading and was already at the time producing articles commenting on current affairs and politics. These writings were collected in an anthology entitled *Le Shan Tang Wen Ji*, which gave a vivid account of the lives of the imperial sons during their stays at the Wuling Chunse.

---

1 *Leshantang Ji* (*Record of the Leshantang*) in *Yuzhi Leshantang Quanji Dingben*, by Emperor Qianlong, Volume 8.

四宜書屋 Siyi Library (Library of the Four Seasons)

The Siyi Library, situated north of the Lake of Happiness in the Yuan Ming Yuan, was tucked behind a hill. The Chunyu Shuhe (Soothing Spring Rain), the Qiujin Changyuan (Autumn Clarity) and the Xiaguan Hanqing (Summer Cool) were buildings that dated back to the Yongzheng era; in the ninth year of the Qianlong era the Chunyu Shuhe was renamed Siyi Library. The significance of Siyi (literally "four favorables") in the name of this complex can been seen in a prefatory note Emperor Qianlong wrote in the collections of his poems: "Spring is a season favorable for flowers, summer is a season favorable for breezes, autumn is a season favorable for the moon and winter is a season favorable for snow" and "All four seasons are favorable times for the pleasure of reading."[1]

The album of paintings *Forty Scenes of the Yuan Ming Yuan* from the ninth year of the Qianlong era (1744) shows that this group of buildings spread out east and west with the structures scattered about. There were almost no courtyards enclosed by buildings. The main buildings the Yanyue Qingzhen Building (Veiled Moon Building), the Siyi Library, the Xiuyuan Mountain House (Mountain House with a View of Distant Hills) and the Hanqiu Hall (Autumn Reflections Hall) were linked by galleries. It had hills and stalagmite-like rocks in front and back; the buildings had a simple, unadorned style and exuded a free and relaxed character.

After the rebuilding subsequent to a fire in the 20th year of the Qianlong era (1755) the new Siyi Library comprised a number of irregular courtyards crisscrossed by streams, thus assuming more of a resemblance to the gardens of Jiangnan, south of the Yangtze River (fig. 97).

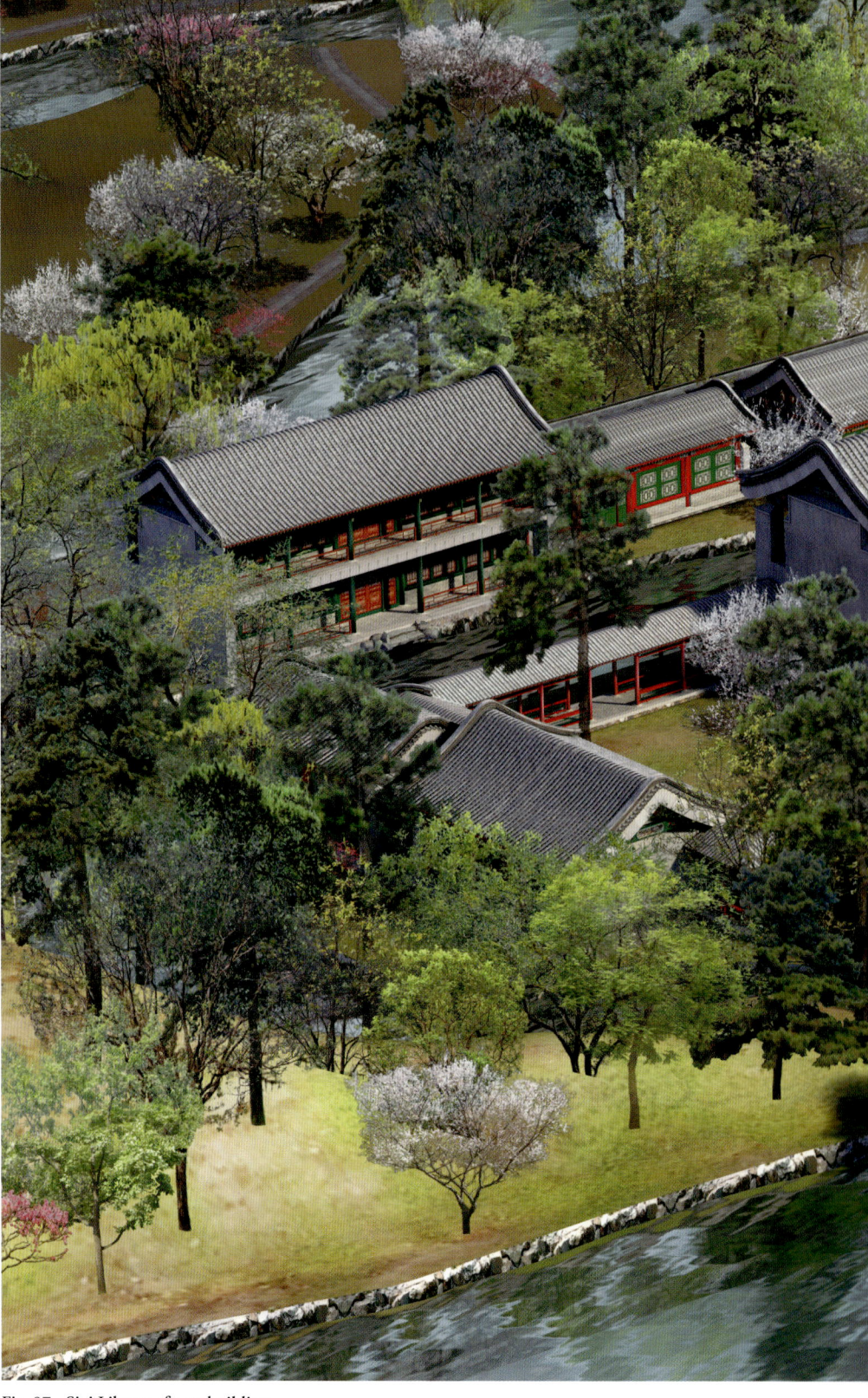

Fig. 97 Siyi Library after rebuilding

Water access to the Siyi Library was from its west and the Hanqiu Hall, situated at the water inlet, formed a small "water courtyard." The Hanqiu Hall, situated at the water outlet, formed, with the Siyi Library, a small water courtyard that had an extremely pleasant open feeling. As expressed by Emperor Qianlong in his poetry:

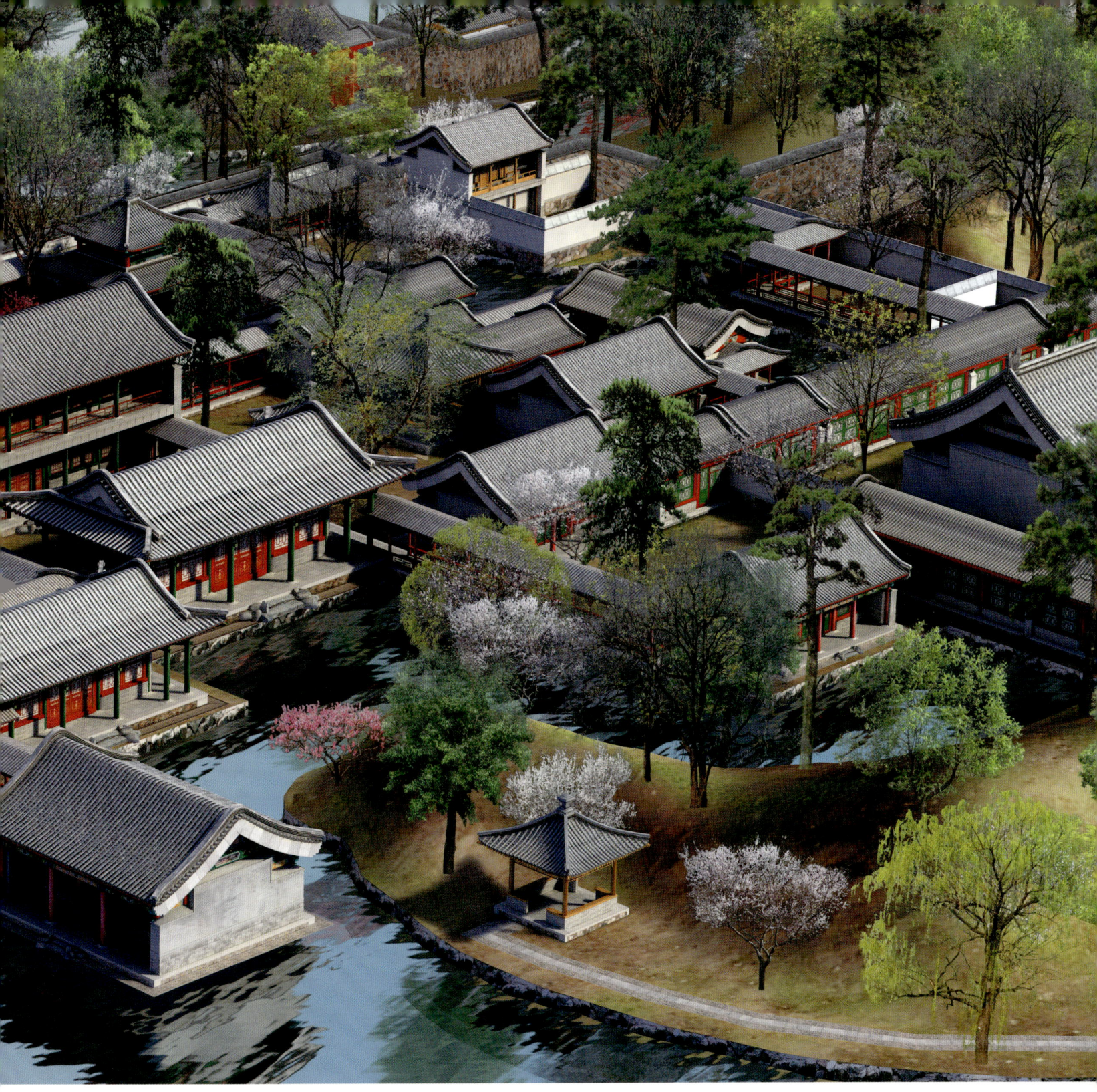

"Whenever I had occasion to visit this spot, I invariably felt enveloped in a refreshing coolness."[2] In the north of the Siyi Library stood the Yanyue Qingzhen Building, which, with its five-bay width and two stories, was the biggest of the buildings in this complex. The view from this two-storied building often reminded Emperor Qianlong of the Anlan Garden (Pacifying Tidal Bores Garden) in the residence of the Grand Secretary Chen Yuanlong in Haining when the emperor was inspecting the seaside dike reinforcement project in that locality on one of his southern tours. This name recalled the weighty responsibility of disaster management, which prompted the emperor to give the Siyi Library in the Yuan Ming Yuan the name of Anlan Garden as well.

1 *Yuzhi Shi*, by Emperor Qianlong, Book III, Volume 39.
2 Ibid.

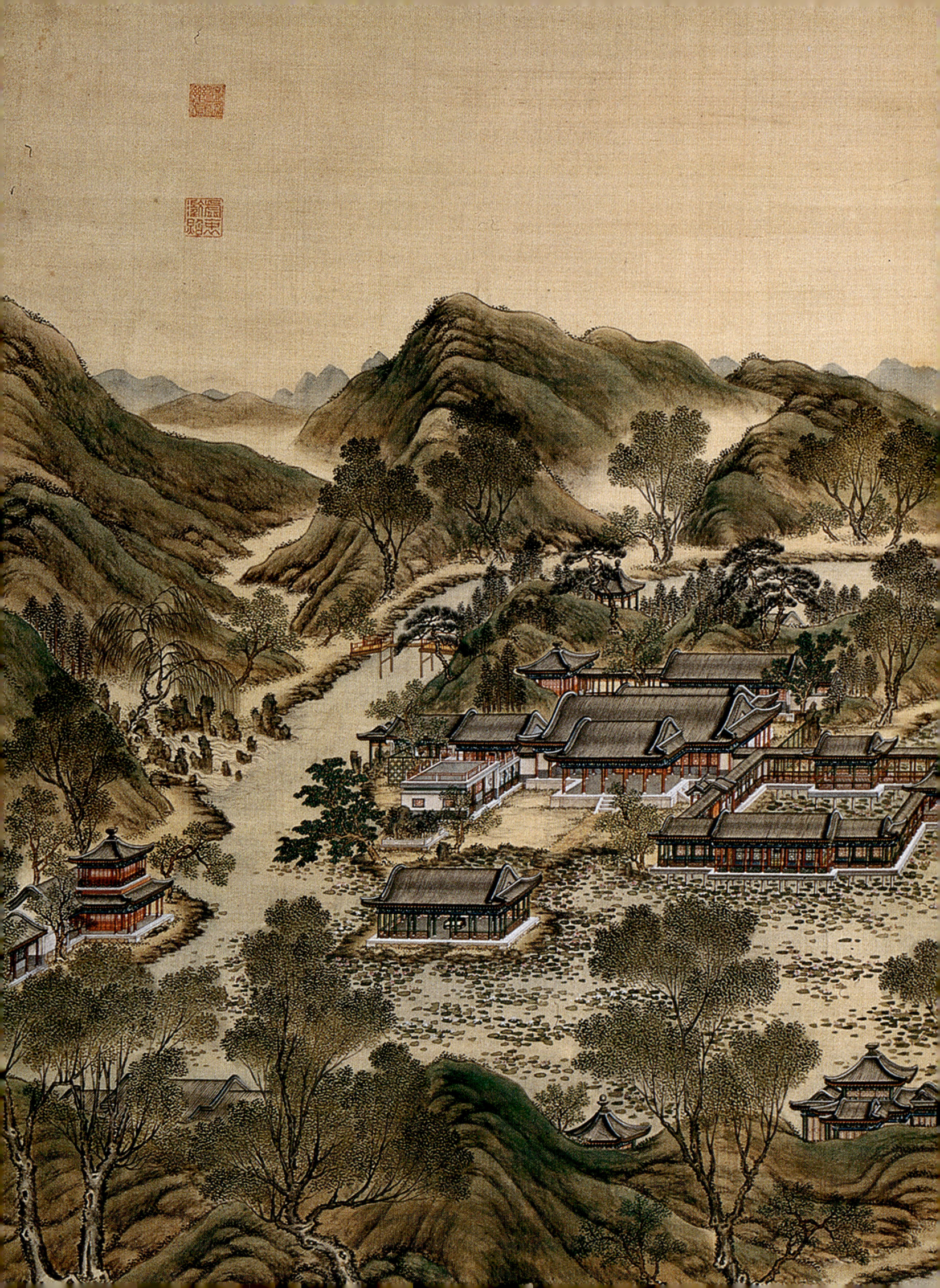

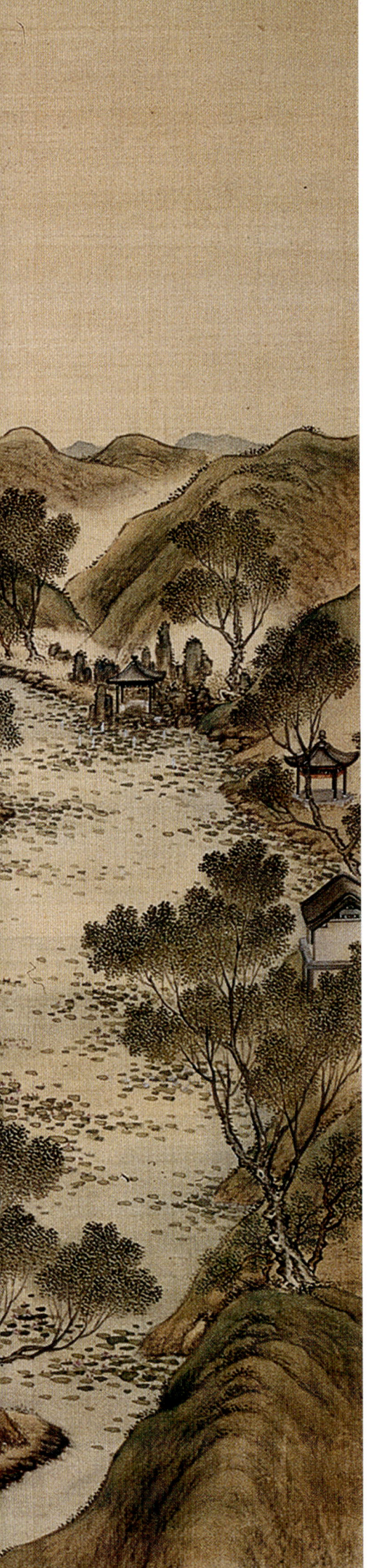

濂溪樂處 Lianxi Lechu Complex (Complex of Happy Place of Lianxi)

The Lianxi Lechu Complex was a landscaped section in the northwest of the Yuan Ming Yuan. Lianxi was the art name of Zhou Dunyi, a Neo-Confucian philosopher in the Song dynasty. He believed that the ancient sages created *renji* modeled on *taiji* (supreme polarity). He believed that following the *taiji* and inspired by the five elements of yin and yang, he who maintained integrity and governed benevolently and justly could hope to attain sagehood. In his *On the Love of the Lotus*, he writes that the best quality of life is that of a pure lotus growing out of dirty waters. Emperor Qianlong believed that the Lianxi Lechu Complex, surrounded by hills and embraced by streams and ponds overgrown with lotuses, tended to cleanse impure desires and bring tranquility, creating a favorable environment for inner reflection and self-improvement. He considered it a pleasure to be able to improve himself by reading Zhou Lianxi. The Lianxi Lechu Complex had a relatively free layout and comprised three clusters of buildings (fig. 98). On the islet stood the main building the Shenxiu Siyong Hall (Hall of Improving Oneself So that the Country Will Enjoy Eternal Peace and Prosperity) and the rear hall the Yunxiang Qingsheng Hall (Hall of Exquisite Clouds); a gallery extended from its southwest to link up with the Shuiyun Pavilion (Water and Clouds Pavilion). At the east end of the islet a water courtyard was enclosed by the Jihe Shenchu Open Hall (Open Hall of Deep among Water Chestnuts and Lotuses), Hexiang Pavilion (Lotus Scent Pavilion) and Xiangxue Gallery (Snow of Fragrance Gallery). The temple Huiwan Zongchun Zhimiao (Temple of Flower Goddesses) stood at the south end of the lotus pond; it enshrined the flower goddesses and was also known as the Huashen Temple. Its main hall Fanyu Qunfang (Hall of Abundance of Flowers) had a courtyard of its own, with other halls around it. At the northeast stood the Xiangyuan Yiqing Hall (Hall of Fragrance is Subtler with Distance), and to the northwest were smaller halls such as the Letianhe and the Weizhen Library and an east-facing, T-shaped hall called Chishui Gongxin Yuetongming Hall (Hall of Pond and Water Shining with the Moon). A number of small pavilions were scattered about.

Access to the Lianxi Lechu Complex was mostly by boat along the canals in the southeast of the Yuan Ming Yuan. To reach it by land one would have to cross a small bridge at the northwest of the islet.

The Hall of Shenxiu Siyong was nine bays wide. It had an open porch of five bays on its front façade. On its back it had a five-bay wide veranda with a

Fig. 98 Painting of Lianxi Lechu Complex from the album *Forty Scenes of the Yuan Ming Yuan*

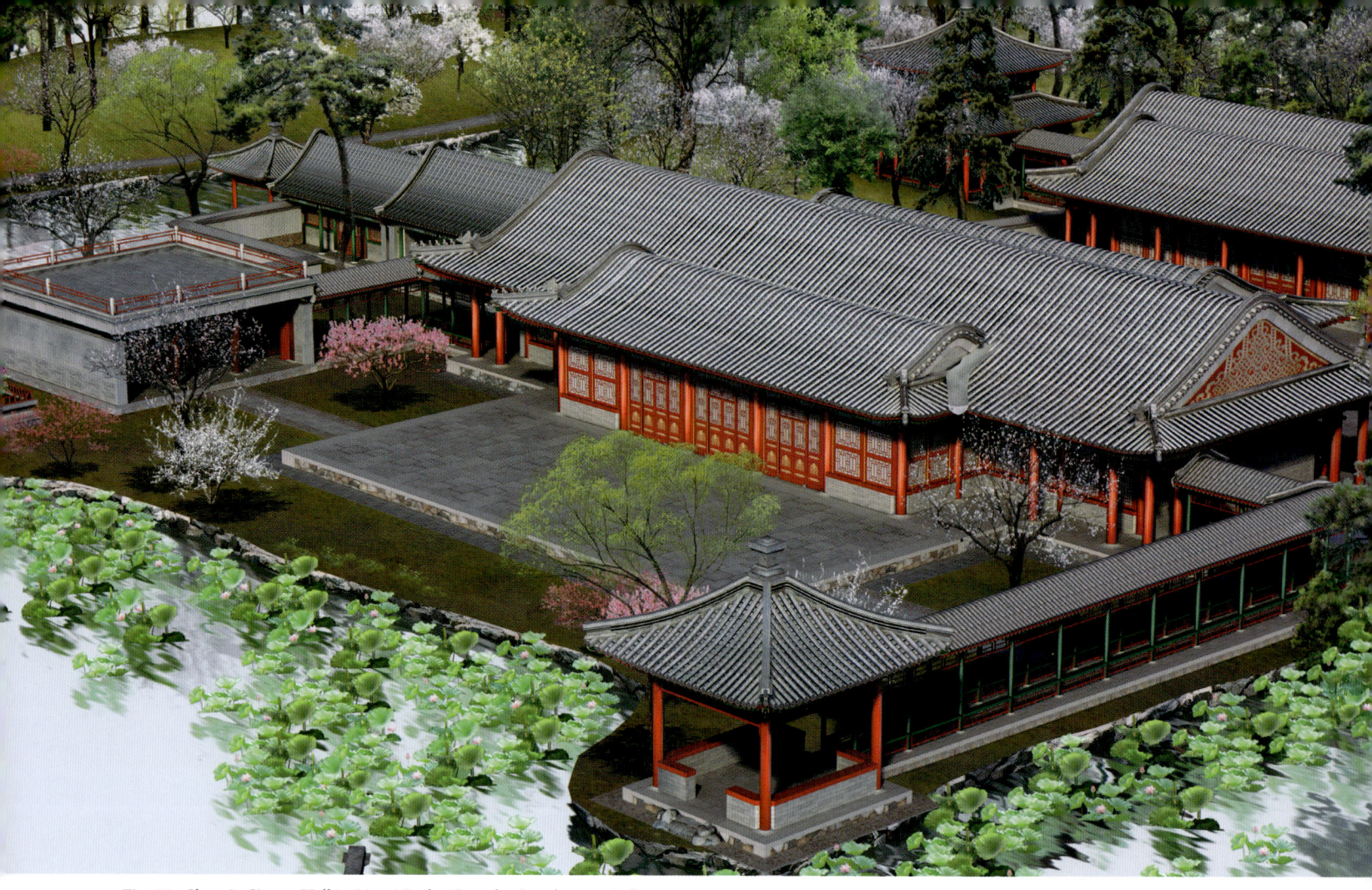

Fig. 99 Shenxiu Siyong Hall in Lianxi Lechu Complex (at a later period)

gallery. A window overlooked the north courtyard, which was only accessible from the main hall. The appearance of the building with its front porch and rear veranda and Chinese hip-and-gable roofs was interesting and richly varied (fig. 99). The interior was even more interesting and unique. According to records of the fourth year of the Qianlong era (1739) of the Imperial Household Department, a "European theater stage" was installed in the hall. The plan indicated that the stage and the throne from which the emperor viewed the performances were located in the rear veranda, with the stage at its east end and the viewing box at the west end in the same room. The east outer bay provided entry and exit to and from the stage, the backdrop and the backstage. Although the hall of nine bays contained a theater, a throne was still placed in the hall constituted by the three middle bays in front. This room was partitioned off with silk panel screens, which added a sense of gravity that related to the name Shenxiu Siyong. It was a motto that warned Emperor Qianlong against becoming lax before his abdication. To maintain an aura of imperial authority visiting ministers were not allowed to venture beyond this three-bay front hall.

The rear hall Yunxiang Qingsheng Hall was at one time a five-bay hall surrounded by a gallery. In the 47th year of the Qianlong era (1782) it was rebuilt as a palace with contiguous front and back roofs and was named Zhiguo Hall (Recognition of One's Mistakes Hall). The rebuilding followed Emperor Qianlong's censure of the provincial governor of Shandong for presenting the emperor with gifts including carved lacquer screens, which was considered a corrupt and wasteful practice. But the gifts had been given and it was wasteful to destroy them and it was improper to build a big hall to house them. The decision was therefore made to expand the Yunxiang Qingsheng Hall for the purpose of housing the gifts and for the purpose of reflecting upon the legacy of his governance. In the 46th year of his reign, Emperor Qianlong wrote *Zhiguo Lun* (*On Recognizing One's Mistakes*). The Zhiguo Hall symbolized his effort to set an example in correcting one's mistakes.

Wenyuan Pavilion (Pavilion of the Source of Literature)

In the fourth year of the reign of Emperor Yongzheng the *Gujin Tushu Jicheng* was published. The 10,000-volume tome covered topics including natural phenomena, geography, history, literature, philosophy and government. In the 37th year of his reign, Emperor Qianlong commissioned the *Siku Quanshu* (*Complete Library of the Four Treasuries*), an expansion on the *Yongle Dadian* (*Yongle Encyclopedia*) of the Ming dynasty, based on 79,330 books in 3,503 categories collected from across the country. The *Siku Quanshu* collection was divided into four repositories, in reference to the imperial library divisions used since the Tang dynasty. These fell under the rubrics of *Jing* (Chinese classic texts), *Shi* (Histories), *Zi* (philosophy, arts, sciences) and *Ji* (anthologies from Chinese literature), hence the name *Siku Quanshu*. It took ten years to complete the compilation of the collection, and four manuscript copies were produced. In the meantime construction started of a building to house the collection. In the 39th year of the Qianlong era (1774) the construction of the Wenyuan Pavilion (fig. 100) in the Yuan Ming Yuan was completed[1]. The subsequently published *Siku Quanshu Huiyao* and *Siku Quanshu Zongmu Tiyao* (*Annotated Catalogue of the Siku Quanshu*) analyzed and commented on a vast range of ancient texts. The Xiazhu Building was built in the Hanjing Hall of the Changchun Garden to house the *Siku Quanshu Huiyao* and the ceremonial hall Danhuai Hall of the Changchun Garden held the

---

1 *Rixia Jiuwen Kao*.

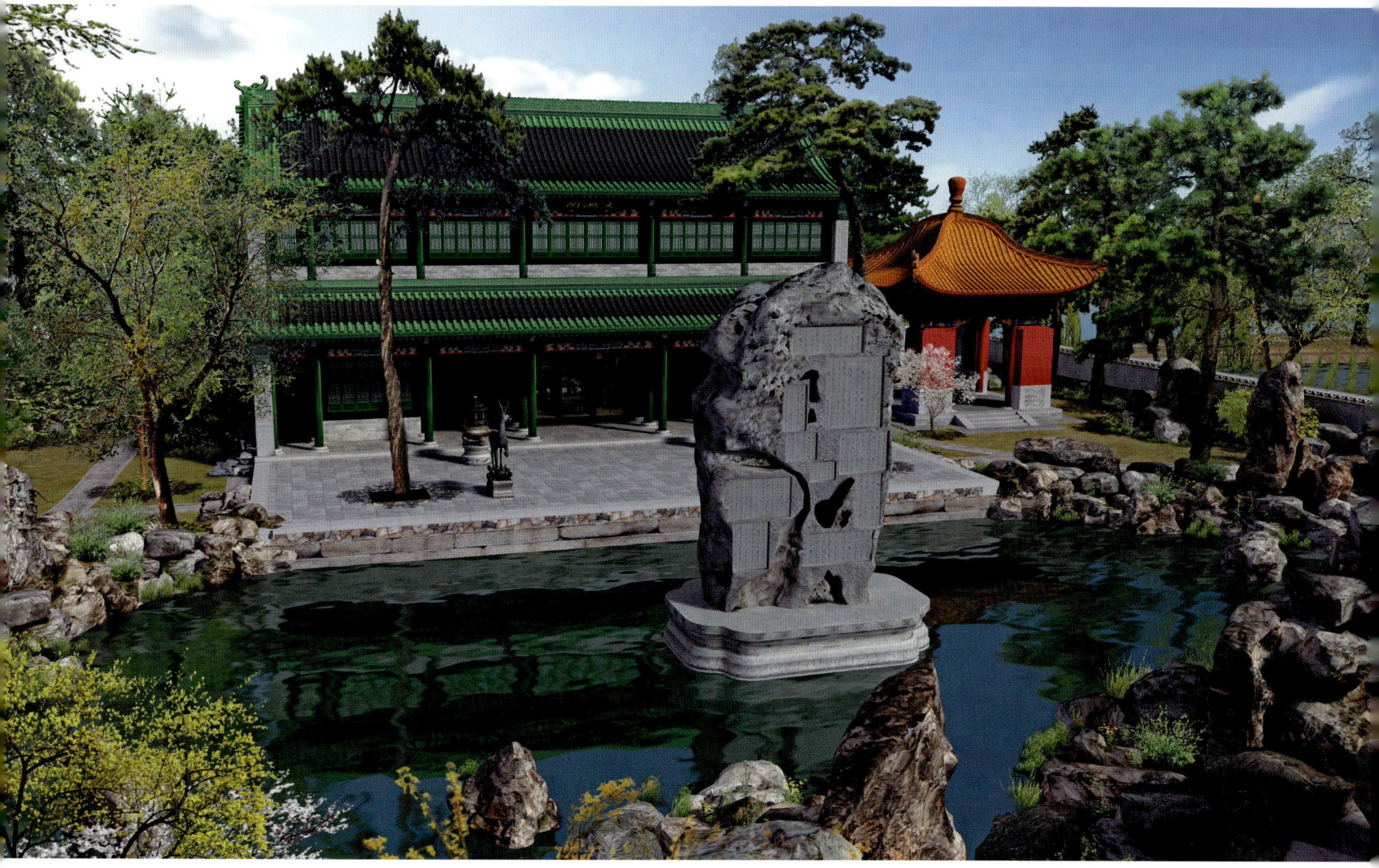

Fig. 100 Wenyuan Pavilion and the Lingfeng Rock (Dainty Rock) in a pool

PART II SCENERY OF THE YUAN MING YUAN | 113

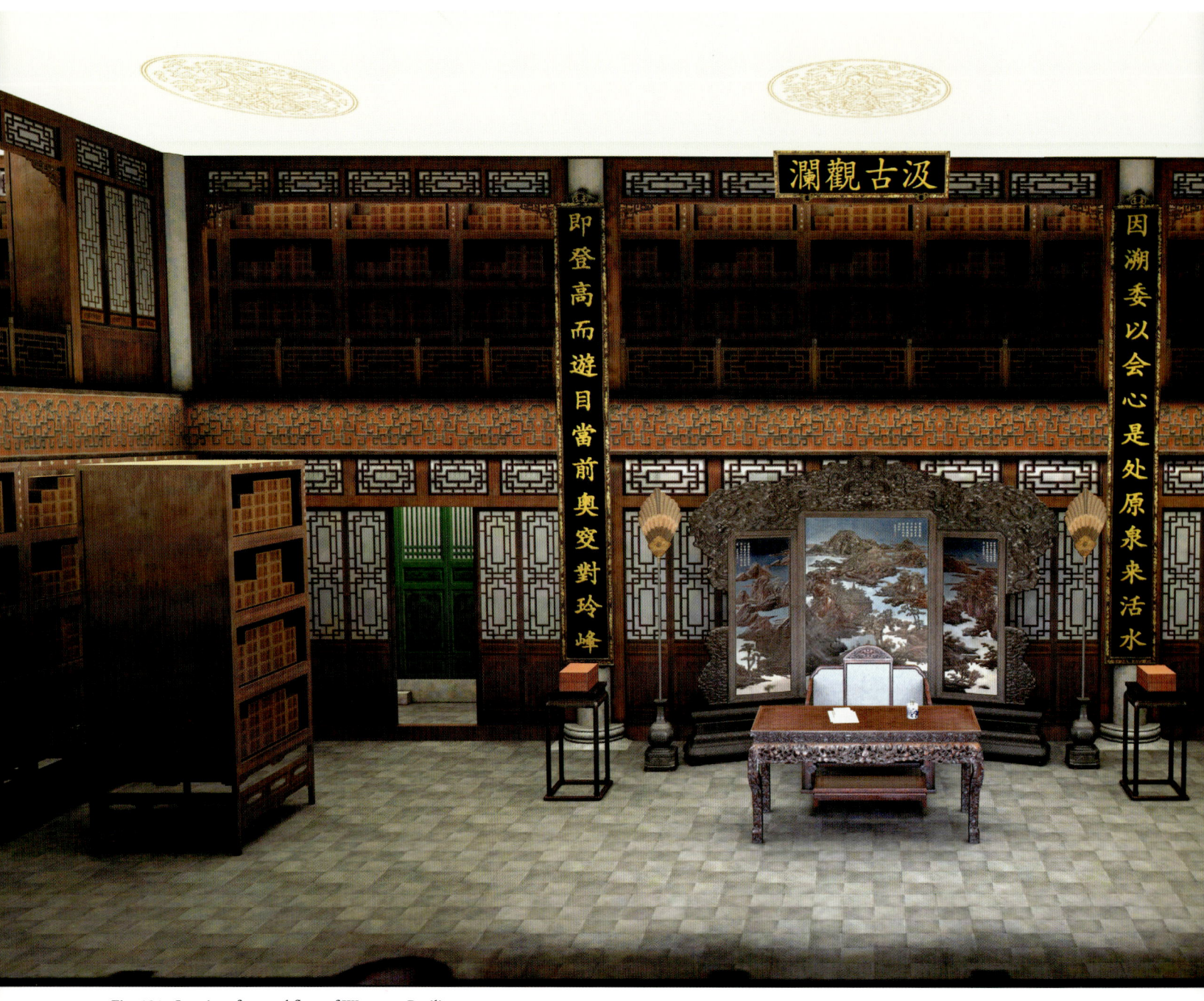

Fig. 101 Interior of ground floor of Wenyuan Pavilion

Gujin Tushu Jicheng, but the Library of the Source of Literature was dedicated to the *Siku Quanshu*. This enterprise demonstrated the determination of the emperor to become a learned, well-read "sage monarch."

The Wenyuan Pavilion, situated north of the Nine Islands area, was modeled upon the Tianyi Pavilion (One Sky Pavilion) in Ningbo both in site layout and in architectural style of the individual buildings such as the Cangshu Pavilion (Pavilion of Book Collections Library), the gate of entrance, the pavilion covering tablets and the moon terrace. Ponds and artificial hills were also to be found in the complex, which was enclosed by a fence, which was unusual in the Yuan Ming Yuan and seemed an indication of the extra care taken about security. The Cangshu Pavilion stood in the north of the rectangular courtyard. It was fronted by a pond, at the south of which a large artificial hill extended from east to west. The gate of entrance, aligned with the Cangshu Pavilion on a central axis, was placed at the south side of the artificial hill. After entering the

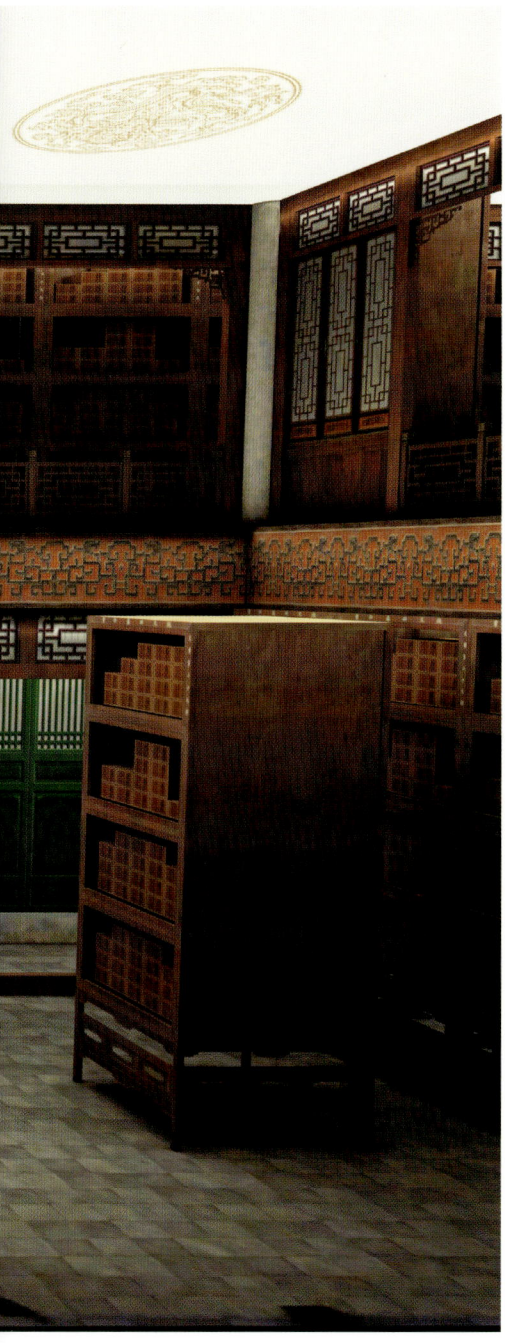

gate, one passed through a tunnel or followed a winding flight of steps and rounded a pond to reach the Cangshu Pavilion. Another artificial hill lay to the north of the Cangshu Pavilion, shielding from view the moon gate in the northern wall of the courtyard.

In a departure from the rule of an odd number of bays in building widths in traditional Chinese architecture, the Wenyuan Pavilion was six bays wide and had two stories, a front and a back porch, closely emulating the Tianyi Pavilion of Ningbo. The building was designed with a six-bay width for *feng shui* considerations. In the theory of yin and yang, odd numbers symbolize "yang" and even numbers symbolize "yin," which is associated with water and water is good for preventing and putting out fires. Judging from the Wenyuan Pavilion in the Forbidden City and the Wensu Pavilion (Pavilion of the Origin of Literature) in the Imperial Palace of Shenyang, which were coeval with the Wenyuan Pavilion (Pavilion of the Source of Literature) in the Yuan Ming Yuan and which have survived to this day, black glazed tiles with a green edge were used for the roofs. Again these colors associated with "yin" further reinforced the fire-prevention qualities of the buildings.

The four manuscript copies of the *Siku Quanshu* were not completed at the same time.[1] The first completed copy was deposited in the Wenyuan Pavilion in the Forbidden City. The copy stored in the Wenyuan Pavilion in the Yuan Ming Yuan was not completed until the 48th year of the Qianlong era (1783). The Wenyuan Pavilion in the Yuan Ming Yuan made wide use of *nanmu* wood to craft the bookshelves and the binding of the tome was color-coded with yellow, red, blue and gray for the *Jing*, *Shi*, *Zi* and *Ji* sections respectively. There was an account of this in one of Emperor Qianlong's poems: "The book was completed last year and placed on *nanmu* wood shelves, each section being assigned one of four colors (fig. 101)."[2]

In the Wenyuan Pavilion a tall North Lake Tai rock with more than 80 "grottos" stood in the middle of the pond in the courtyard. Emperor Qianlong was quite pleased with it and named it "Lingfeng Rock." Unfortunately this giant rock has not escaped destruction.

West of the artificial hill in front of the Wenyuan Pavilion was a small pavilion where one could take a break from reading. East of the artificial hill was a moon terrace. In the pavilion covering tablets east of the library stood a tablet inscribed with the characters *Wenyuange Ji* (Record of the Wenyuan Pavilion) in Emperor Qianlong's hand. This tablet survived the rape of the Yuan Ming Yuan and has become a holding of the Beijing Library since its opening in the Nationalist era.

Besides the *Siku Quanshu*, the Wenyuan Pavilion also had the *Gujin Tushu Jicheng* among its holdings. Unfortunately both of them were lost in the aftermath of the torching and pillaging of the Yuan Ming Yuan.

---

1 *Yuzhi Shi*, by Emperor Qianlong, Book V, Volume 12.
2 Ibid.

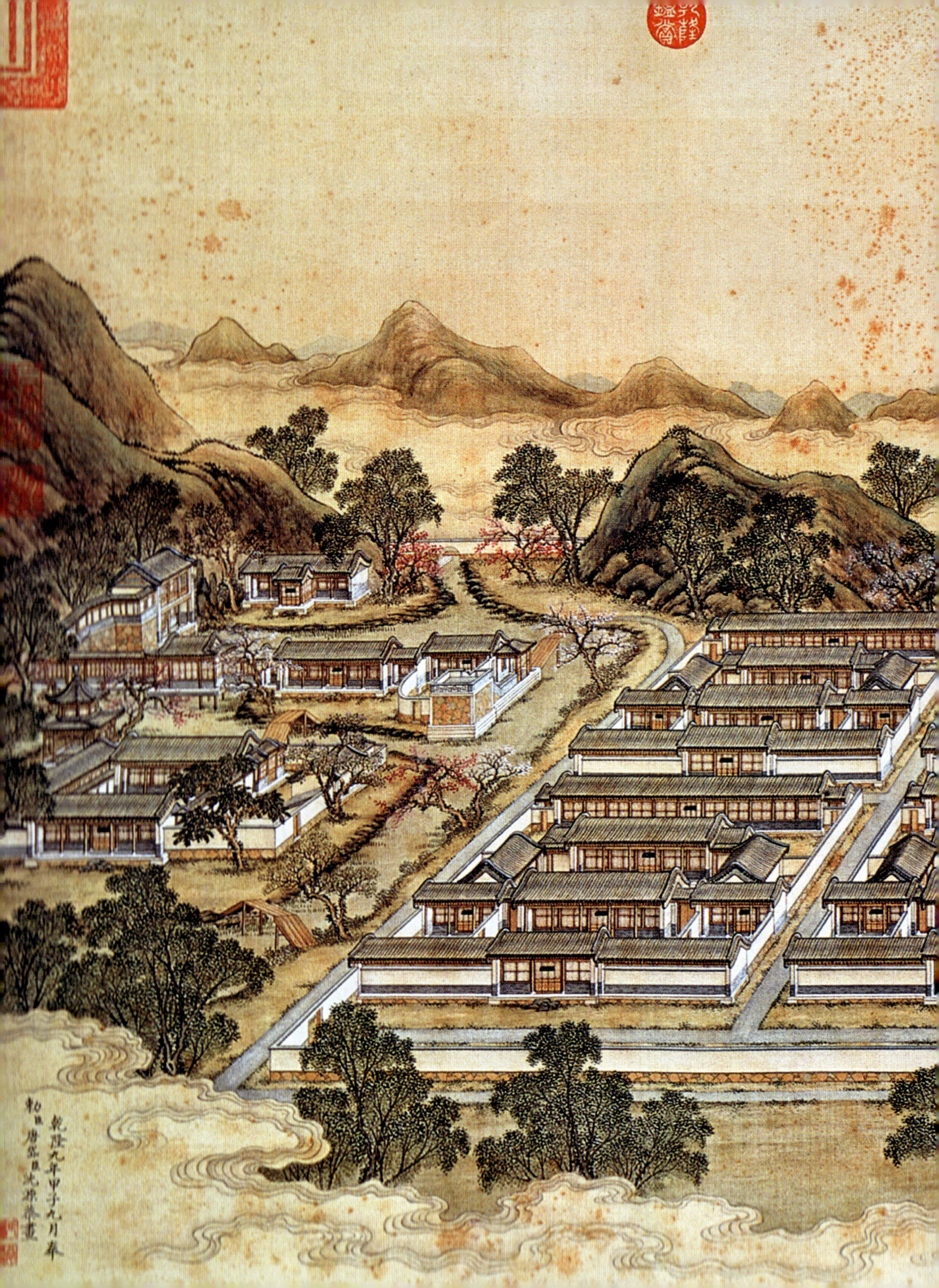

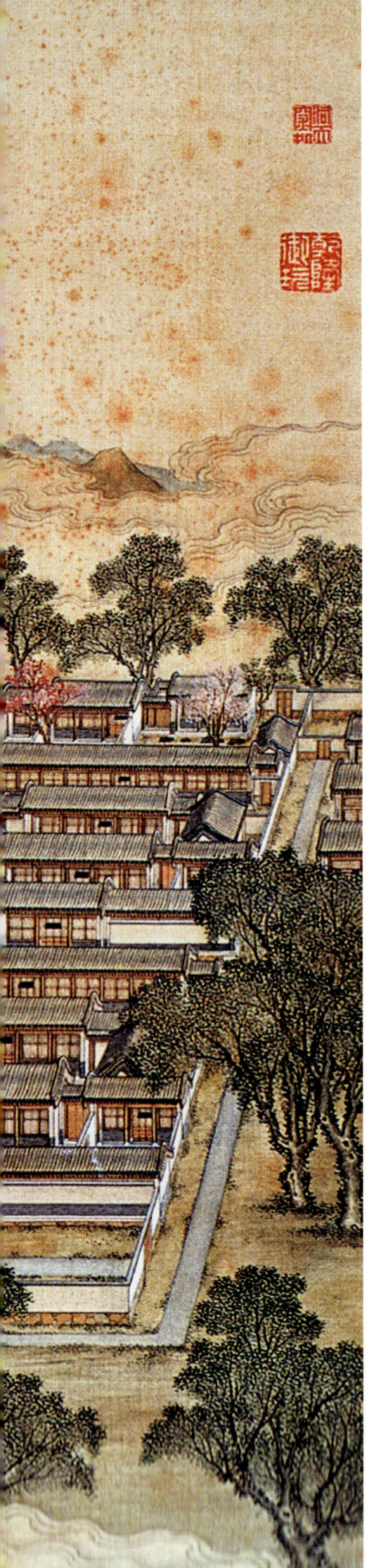

Dongtian Shenchu Complex (Deep in the Grotto Complex)

The Dongtian Shenchu Complex was situated east of the Qinzheng Qinxian Complex, close to the eastern wall of the Yuan Ming Yuan. It was built in the reign of Emperor Yongzheng (fig. 102). This complex comprised three sections, i.e. the princes' study hall in the west, the Si Suo (Four Living Quarters) in the east, where the princes lived and a courtyard called Ruyi Pavilion in the northeast. The Si Suo consisted of four courtyards with identical layouts that indicated equality among the siblings. This was where the princes lived. At the time of its construction, there were not a great number of princes. Extant records show that Emperor Yongzheng had 10 sons and 4 daughters. The first, second, seventh, eighth, ninth and tenth sons died before maturity.[1] It therefore seems that the Si Suo had enough room for the young princes and princesses (fig. 103).

The princes' school was situated west of the Si Suo. It had a courtyard in front called Qianchui Tiankuang (Gift of Heaven), located on an islet. It had a small hall that housed a shrine to Confucius. North of the islet was another cluster of staggered buildings, also serving as a place for the princes' study purposes. The two parts were linked by a bridge. In his *Analects*, Confucius cautioned: "Be a 'gentlemanly scholar' (*junzi ru*), not a 'petty' one (*xiaoren ru*)." The gentlemanly Confucian scholar has the wellbeing of society in mind; the petty Confucian scholar may be erudite and well-read but has only his own interests at heart. Emperor Qianlong exhorted his sons to be gentlemanly Confucian scholars

---

1 *Qingdai Gongting Shi (History of the Qing Court)* by Wan Yi, Wang Shuqing and Liu Lu, Baihua Literature and Art Publishing House, page 212.

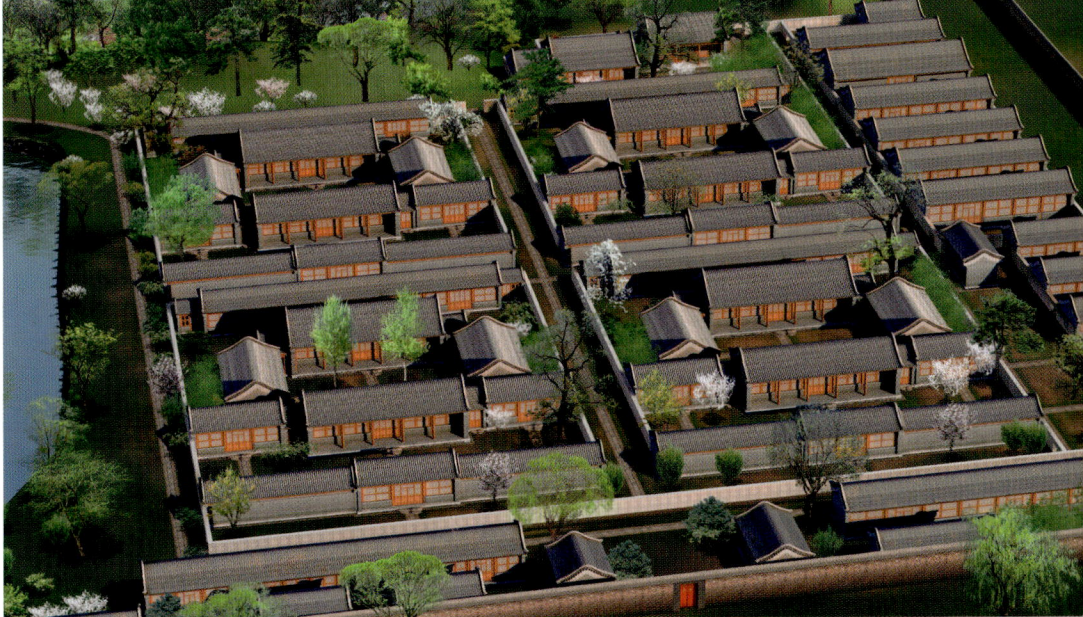

Fig. 103   Apartments of the princes

Fig. 102   Painting of Dongtian Shenchu Complex from the album *Forty Scenes of the Yuan Ming Yuan*

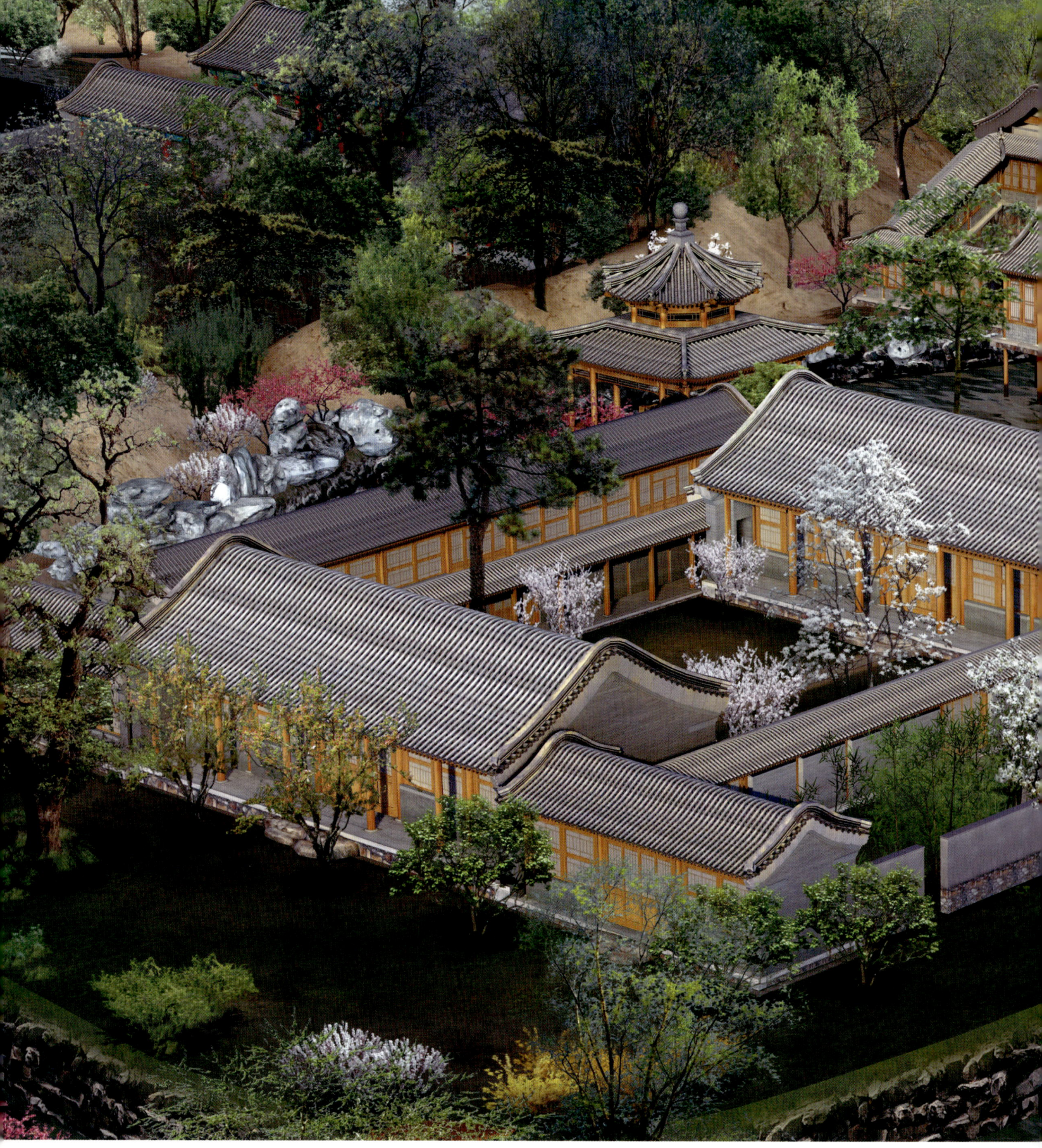

Fig. 104 School for the princes

118 CHINA'S LOST IMPERIAL GARDEN

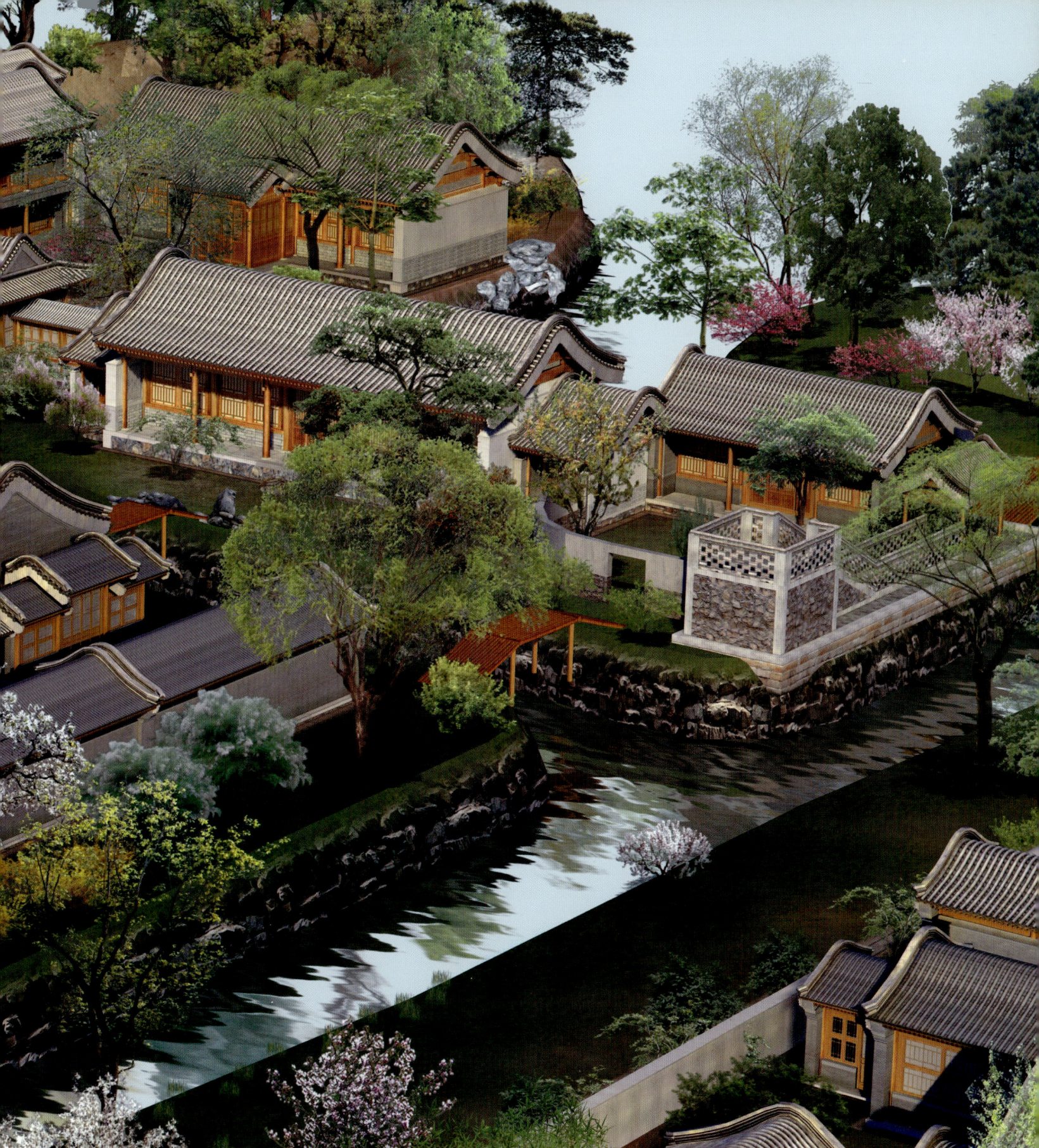

and not indulge in indolence. He expected his sons to adhere to the highest standards of Confucianism and warned that "he who governs does so not by force but by virtue. Therefore he who excels in virtue will govern well and he who loses virtue loses his right to govern."[1]

The Ruyi Pavilion located to the northeast of the Si Suo was a studio for painting artists. Its buildings were not numerous, since the artists did not reside there but only used the premises for work (fig. 104).

---

1 *Yuzhi Leshantang Quanji*, by Emperor Qianlong, Volume 8.

CHAPTER X
Observing Farming Activities and Monitoring the Agricultural Cycle

Only when all the peoples of his realm had been visited with good fortunes could an emperor have a solid economic foundation for his rule and achieve "Wanfang Anhe" or universal peace and harmony and "Jiuzhou Qingyan" or calm and clarity across all nine continents of his empire. This was the earnest hope of the emperor holding court in the imperial garden. Therefore the imperial policy of economic development driven by agriculture found an eminent place in the design of the Yuan Ming Yuan.

Quite a few themed areas of the Garden had agricultural elements; some were explicitly called "villages," as the Beiyuan Mountain Village. Some themed areas were adjacent to ploughing fields to facilitate the emperor's discussions with the peasants about farming matters. Some areas might not have buildings that were designed to be rustic but had an environment that was conducive to understanding farming and following the agricultural cycle. There were areas that were so designed as to evoke a vision of agriculture; here are some of the typical ones (fig. 105).

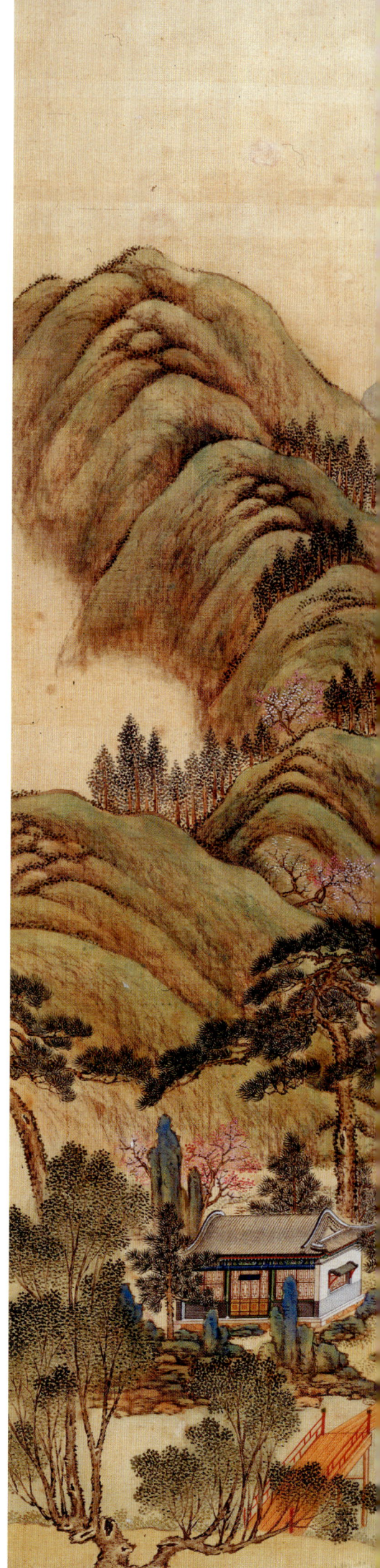

Fig. 105 Painting of Shuimu Mingse Complex (Complex of Sounds of Trees and Water) from the album *Forty Scenes of the Yuan Ming Yuan*

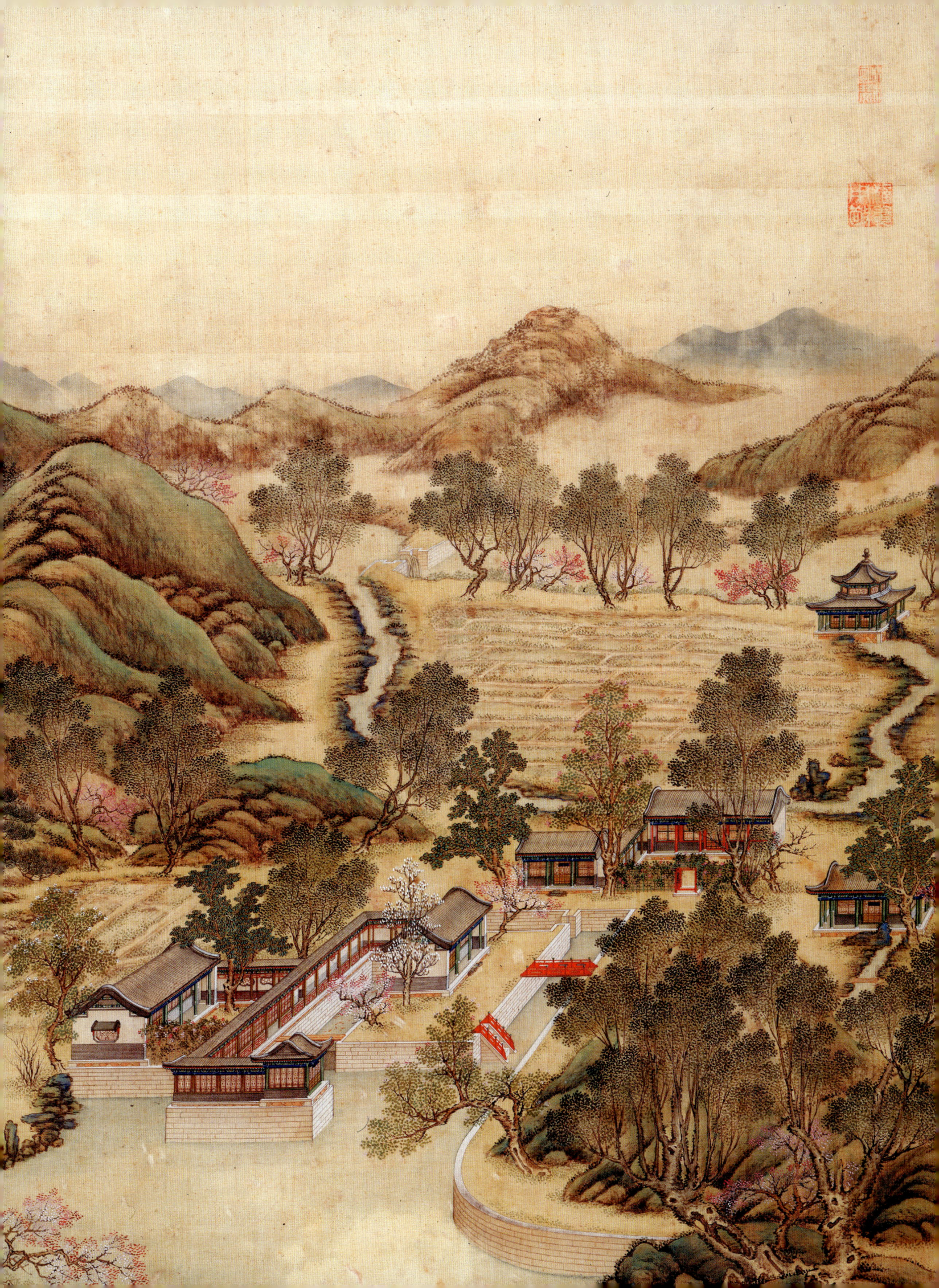

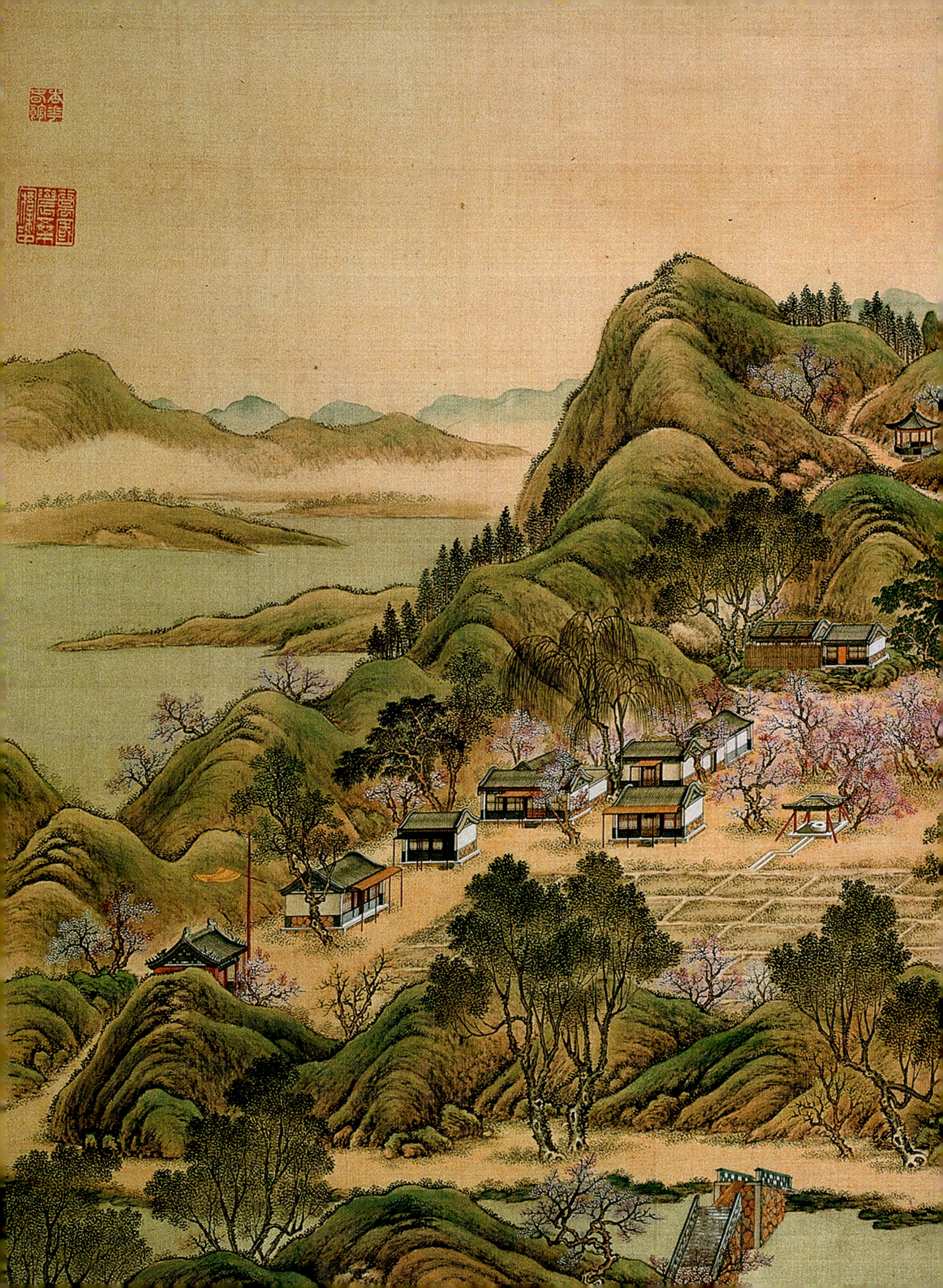

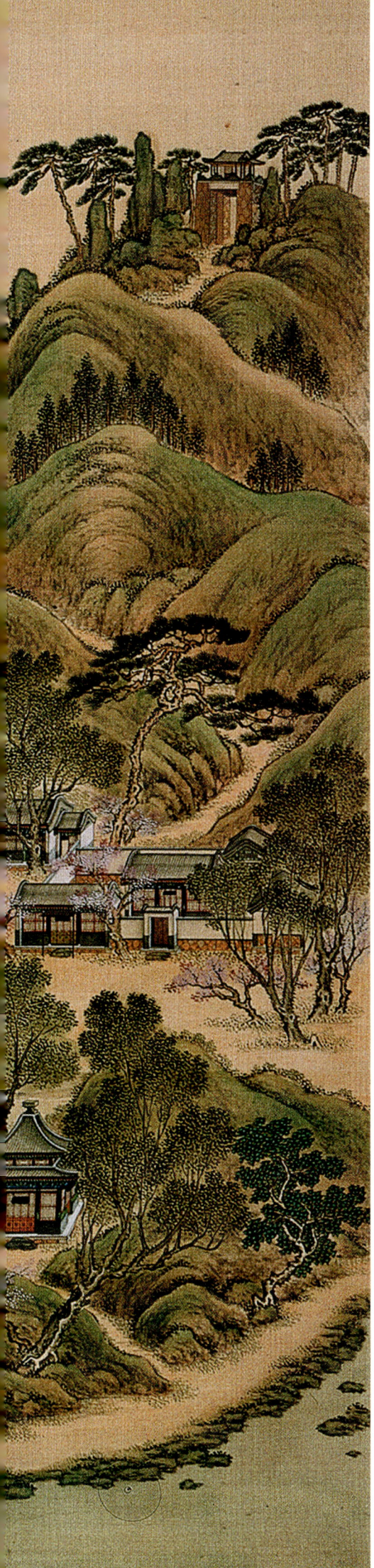

杏花春館 Xinghuachun Pavilion (Apricot Blossom Spring Pavilion)

The Xinghuachun Pavilion was located in the northwest corner of the Back Lake. It was called "Vegetable Patch" when it was first built and was renamed Xinghuachun Pavilion in the fifth year of the Yongzheng era (1727). The album of *Forty Scenes of the Yuan Ming Yuan* affords us a vision of its appearance in the early days (fig. 106): it was surrounded on four sides by earthen hills; up near the gap between the peaks "One descends a winding trail from the pavilion on the mountain and is greeted by the sight of a scattering of low buildings, some of which are surrounded by crude fences. The numerous apricot trees that blossom in late spring create a mass that evokes the rose-colored reflected glory of a sunrise sky. In front of the huts is a plot planted with a variety of leafy vegetables and melons; it gives the whole place the look of a farm village."[1] The "low buildings" mentioned in the quote included the Xinghuachun Pavilion, the Xinghua Village (Apricot Blossom Village), the Cuiwei Hall (Green Hill Hall), the Tudi Temple (Land God Temple) and Jianhe Yuqing Hall (Hall of Lingering Cool of a Mountain Book). These buildings were scattered around. The vacant lot south of the hamlet was developed into a vegetable patch, which was bordered on its north by a pavilion covering a well. A small ditch ran south from the well to irrigate the patch. A small shrine to the land god stood to the southwest of the patch. A winding trail on the hill to the north led to a small hexagonal pavilion midway up the hill. On the peak of the hill to the northeast stood a small gatehouse at which hung tablets respectively inscribed with the characters *Ping Yan* (barrier rock) and *Pan Jing* (waterside mirror); this was another point of access to the hamlet. The buildings here were of modest size; some of them featured slate roofs and walls faced with granite that gave them a simple, rustic look.

In the 20th year of the Qianlong era (1755), the area was rebuilt. The vegetable plot was removed. A winding canal was dug in the southeast that cut across the hills to connect with the Back Lake, thus bringing the lake water into the low land in the small valley. The "low buildings" in the middle were rebuilt into a courtyard compound that faced water to its east and to its south. At the south end of the courtyard was a small five-bay hall with a surrounding gallery called Jianhe Yuqing, which also served as entry to the compound. The hall had a terrace in front, which gave direct access, through a bridge to its south, to the grotto in the artificial hill in the north of the Tantan Dangdang Complex; in the north

---
1 *Yuzhi Shi*, by Emperor Qianlong, Book I, Volume 22.

Fig. 106 Painting of Xinghuachun Pavilion from the album *Forty Scenes of the Yuan Ming Yuan*

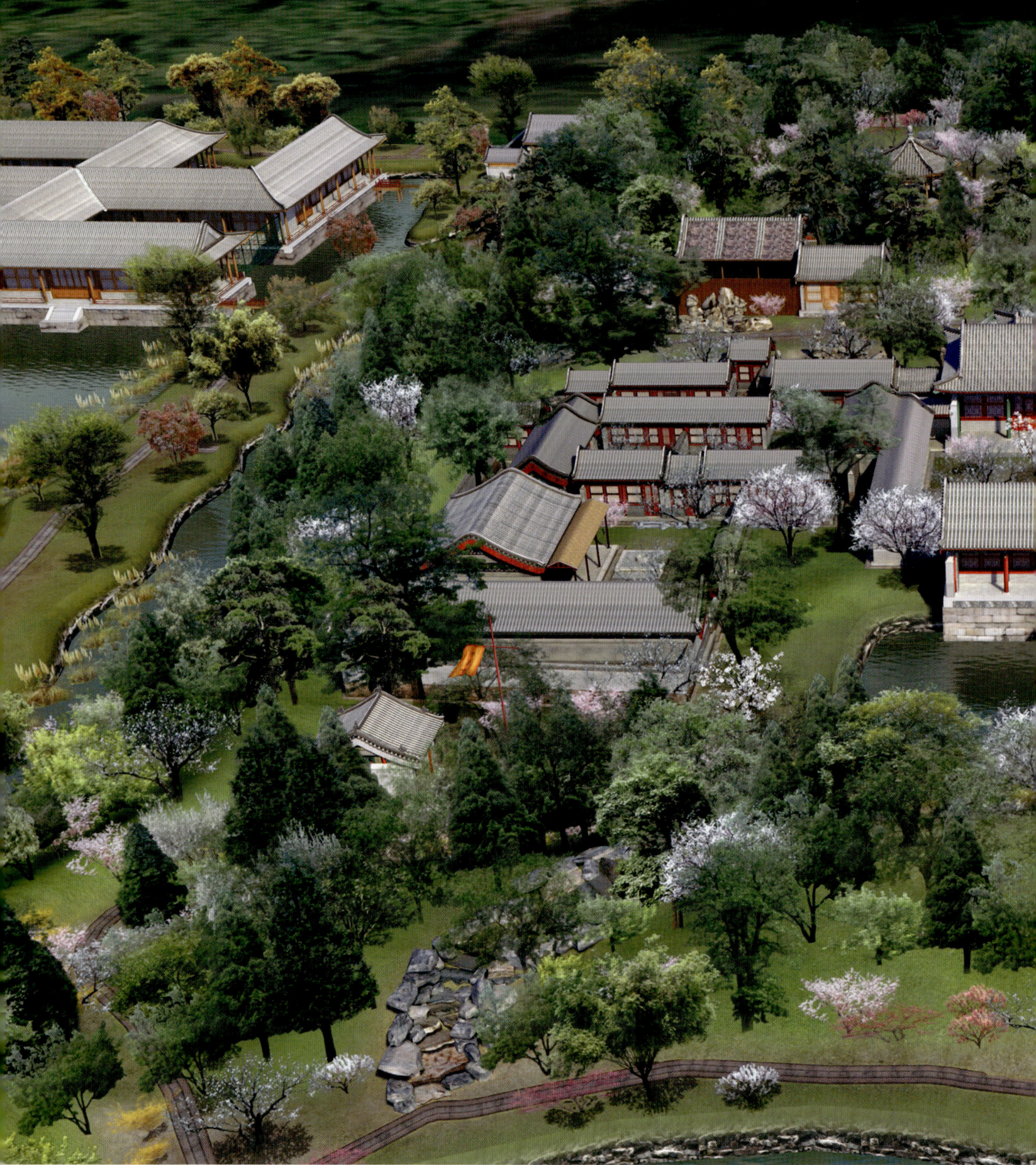

Fig. 107 Chunyu Pavilion

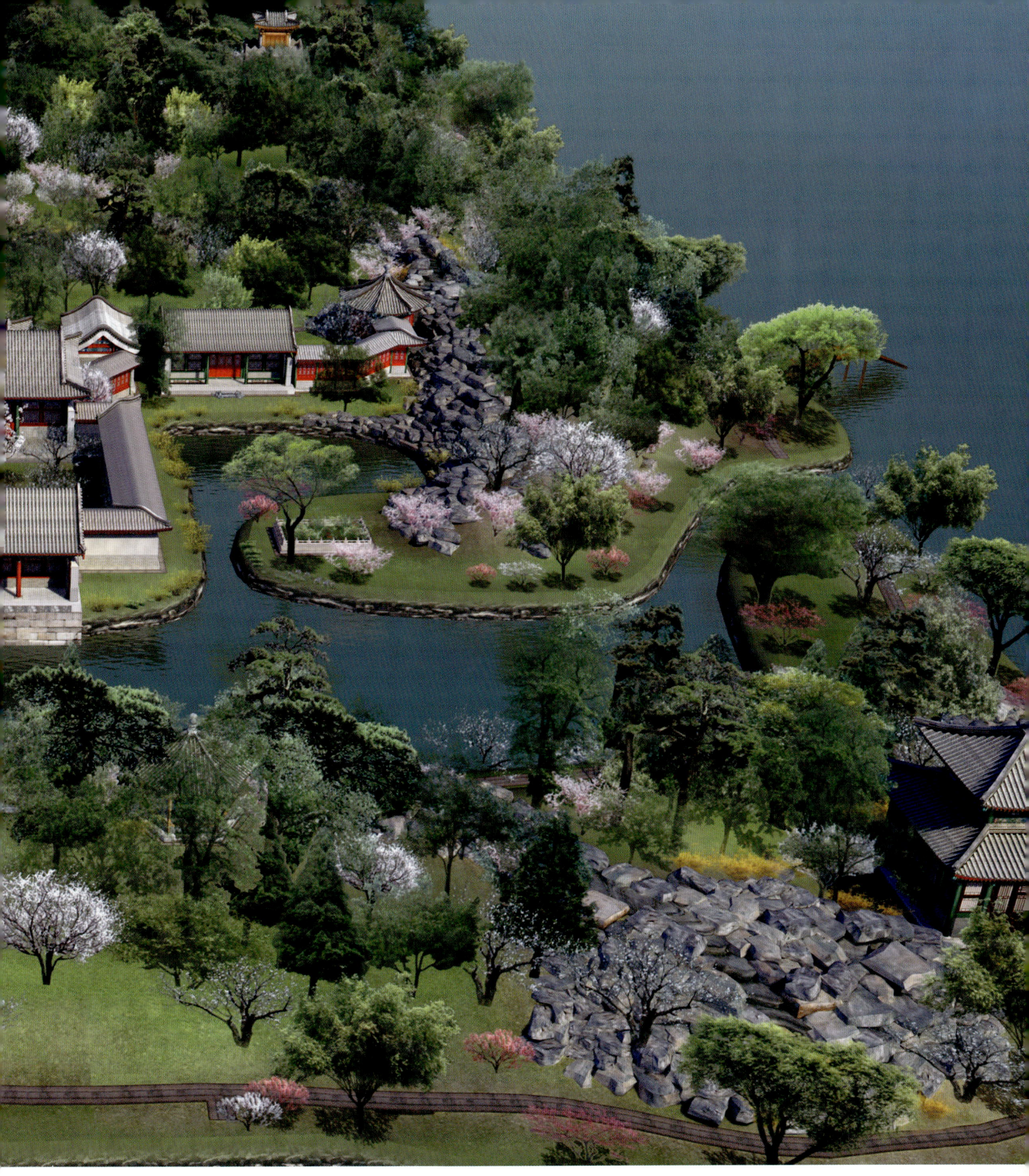

of the court was the main hall Chunyu Pavilion, five bays wide, that featured a three-bay veranda in its rear; the Jianhe Yuqing Hall and the Chunyu Pavilion were linked by a gallery (fig. 107). In the north of the Chunyu Pavilion, a number of small buildings—Jingshui Study (Water Mirroring Study), Shangqu Hall (Pleasing Vista), Yi Study and Cuiwei Hall—dotted the hills to the west and the east at different elevations. Only the Tudi Temple in the southwest corner was kept and formed, with a duty room and the well pavilion, another small courtyard compound called Xinghua Village. The erstwhile vegetable patch and crude fences were no longer there. In the 34th year of the Qianlong era (1769), another tall rocky hill was thrown up behind the Chunyu Pavilion, which became the tallest peak[1] round the Back Lake and had a transformative effect on the surrounding landscape. By that time the compound had shed its previous bucolic look to become a garden in its own right, featuring not only a main hall, but also secondary buildings, with a clear hierarchy assigned to each; together they formed a whole that conformed to a "differential mode of association." One can see here a difference in the effects that Qianlong and Yongzheng strove to achieve with these buildings. In recent years remnants of the hexagonal pavilion west of the artificial hill and traces of the small gatehouse in the east have been unearthed and they tracked with the information provided by the album *Forty Scenes of the Yuan Ming Yuan* (fig. 108).

The Chunyu Pavilion was an important venue for Emperor Qianlong to observe the weather and monitor the agricultural cycle. In an agricultural society, spring rainfall was pivotal for the year's harvest. As emperor, Qianlong had to worry about agriculture, and rain and snow fall were uppermost on his mind. In the face of the unpredictability of nature he could only pray for the blessing and protection of the gods. Therefore whenever rainfall fell short he would go to the hall that housed the shrine to the Dragon King to "pray for rain," and when rain did fall, he would return to the shrine to "give thanks for the rain." Thus on the 23rd day of the fourth month of the 21st year of his reign (1756), Qianlong, having had breakfast at the Huai Qingfen Building of the Qinzheng Qinxian Complex, rode in a "cool" (uncurtained) sedan chair carried by four bearers that exited the side gate near Zao Garden in the southwest of the Yuan Ming Yuan and took him to the Dragon King Temple in the Jingming Garden on the Jade Spring Mountains to burn joss sticks and pray for rain.[2] And lo and behold, five days later it rained! Qianlong composed an ebullient poem about this timely rain that enabled him to finally have a good night's sleep.

On the 13th day of the fifth month of the same year, he again made a trip to the Black Dragon Pool north of Beijing to burn joss sticks and pray for rain. Some rain did fall afterwards, but it was so little that he had to make another trip up the Jade Spring Mountains to pray for rain. A good rain finally fell on the 20th day of the month, which in his judgment promised a good harvest that year.

The naming of the Chunyu Pavilion reflected Emperor Qianlong's strong interest in agriculture. The construction of the Chunyu Pavilion was followed by years of copious spring rain. That so pleased him that he wrote in a poem that the Chunyu Pavilion worked wonders and brought years of good spring rain, that it came especially at a propitious time that year, right before the blossoming season.[3] Consequently the Xinghuachun Pavilion became one of his favorite haunts in the Garden. Whenever he came, even for a short visit, he would often observe with feeling that all the propitious rains could be attributed to the apt naming of the buildings.

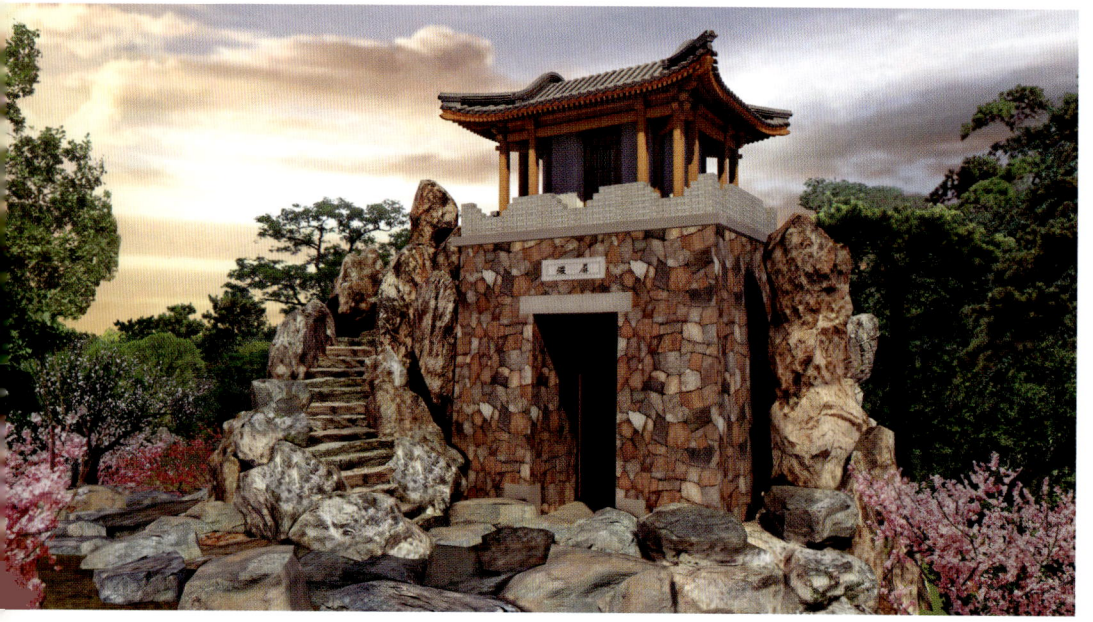

Fig. 108 Small gatehouse called *Ping Yan* (Barrier Rock)

---

1 According to a survey map of 2002, the highest point of the north hill in this area has an elevation of 54.6 meters and the hill itself is 9.8 meters high.
2 *Wardrobe Log for the 21st Year of the Qianlong Era* as referenced in the *Yuan Ming Yuan* compiled by the First Historical Archives of China, published by Shanghai Ancient Books Publishing House, 1991.
3 *Yuzhi Shi*, by Emperor Qianlong, Book III, Volume 37.

北远山村 Beiyuan Mountain Village (Mountain Village in the Distant North)

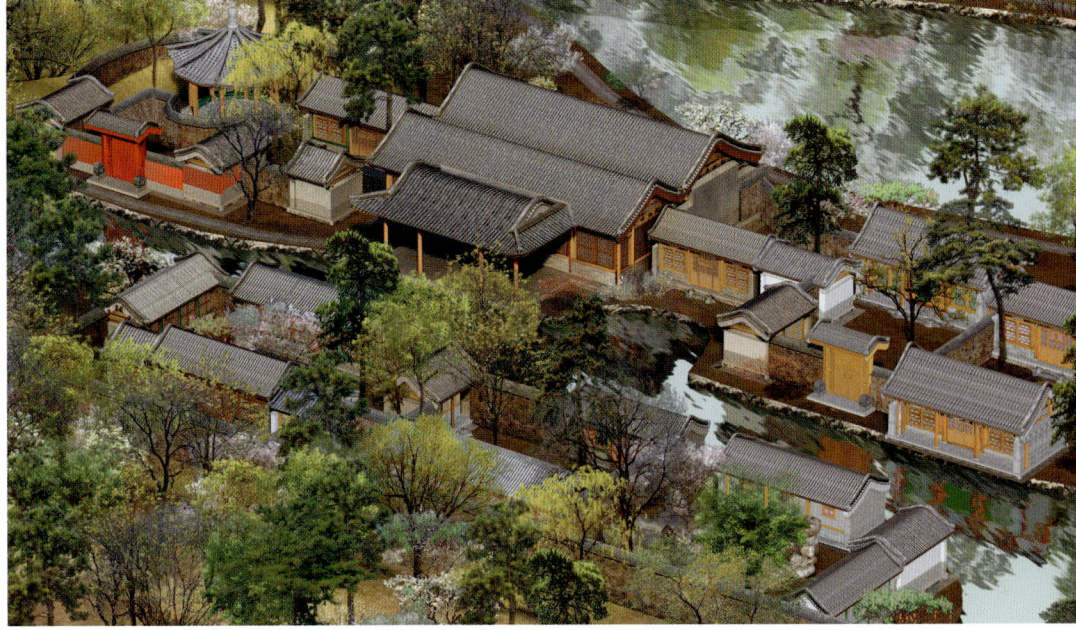

Fig. 109 Beiyuan Mountain Village

The Beiyuan Mountain Village lay just inside the north section of the enclosure wall of the Yuan Ming Yuan (fig. 109). It was built in the late period of the Yongzheng era. "The little village comprised rows of houses, featuring bamboo fences and thatched roofs, crisscrossed with streets and alleys. Breezes blowing in from afar across the level fields carry on them a symphony of shepherds' flutes, fishermen's chants and the pounding of pestle and mortar."[1] This was a setting modeled on a village by the water. The village was built along a stream, with buildings of a variety of styles and sizes on its two banks and crop fields stretching to the distance. On the north bank one can see, from east to west, a courtyard, a farm house, thatch-roof huts, a two-storied building, a temple; at the east end where the village started there was a small pavilion with a slate roof and a front porch that extended over the stream. Behind it lay a small courtyard with a main hall called Huiyu Jingshe (Hall of Depicting Rain) and a small west hall called Lanye (Hall of Orchid Field). To the west of the courtyard was a small three-bay hall with a front porch; it was set back a few feet from the stream as if in humility. Two-storied buildings stood to its west. The front one, called Jiechun Pavilion, was the largest as well as the main building in the village; behind it stood the Daoliang Building. The Jiechun Pavilion was flanked by huts with a thatched roof on either side. It was fronted by a dock that gave access from the water. West of the Jiechun Pavilion were the Shequ Building, the Zhanxu Library and the Guanyin Monastery. The latter stood out among the rest of the buildings in the hamlet, which were built with unpainted wood, whitewashed walls and black roof tiles; it was constructed with wood pillars painted red, red doors and windows and beams colored with green patterns; its walls were also painted dark red. Inside the monastery one found an octagonal main hall flanked by two side halls. A small hip-and-gable roof surmounted the entry gate in the wall, sight unseen in the other buildings. A few clusters of buildings sat on the south bank of the stream. In later drawings some of these buildings underwent changes and some of them were designated by the designers as ornamental structures to embellish the landscape.

Mulberry trees were planted outside the hamlet and farmers and silk-processing women worked here every season, lending substance to the simulated water village.

This was the most successful simulation of a rural scene in the Garden and added an idyllic touch to the imperial park. But the Beiyuan Mountain Village was after all not a real farming village where farmers and silk makers lived and worked but the emperor's studies, libraries and private apartments. The main building of the hamlet—the Jiechun Pavilion—was, for instance, a library; the Guanyin Monastery was no place for village women to pray to the Guanyin goddess for fertility, but an auspicious building in which the emperor could find spiritual solace. To better simulate a village on the water, the garden creators dotted the village with willows, peach and plum trees, elms, bamboos and red-flower apricot trees, creating a rustic setting.

---

1 *Yuzhi Shi*, by Emperor Qianlong, Book I, Volume 22.

澹泊寧静

Danbo Ningjing Complex (Complex of Detachment and Serenity)

This themed area located in the middle of the Yuan Ming Yuan was separated from the Back Lake (Nine Islands area) by earthen hills and streams. It was surrounded by large areas of rice paddies. In the fifth year of the Yongzheng era, a 田-shaped building was constructed here and named the 田 ("Field")-Character Building (fig. 110).

Here the building served as a metaphor for how much the emperor took agriculture to heart for it was in the form of a Chinese character to do with ploughing. The square with a connecting cross in the middle dividing it into four squares is the Chinese character for a planting field. In the *Tianzifang Ji* (*Record of the Field Character Building*) written by him before his accession to the throne, Qianlong stated clearly: "… several acres of rice paddies lie north of it, the fragrance of the rice plants wafting into the building … My imperial father was committed to agricultural development and never for a moment forgot its importance even when he betook himself to this park of pleasure."[1] In *Forty Scenes of the Yuan Ming Yuan* of the ninth year of the Qianlong era (1744) the Field Character Building was renamed "Danbo Ningjing." The change was meant as a further elaboration on the foregoing statement. The motto *Danbo Ningjing* or "detachment and serenity" originated from Zhuge Liang's advice to his son: "Without detachment, there is no way to clarify one's purpose; without serenity, one will not go far." Qianlong was making a statement by the name change that his apparent detachment, serenity and lack of ambition in an idyllic setting such as the Yuan Ming Yuan belied a higher purpose.

---

1 *Yuzhi Leshantang Quanji Dingben* by Qianlong, Volume 8.

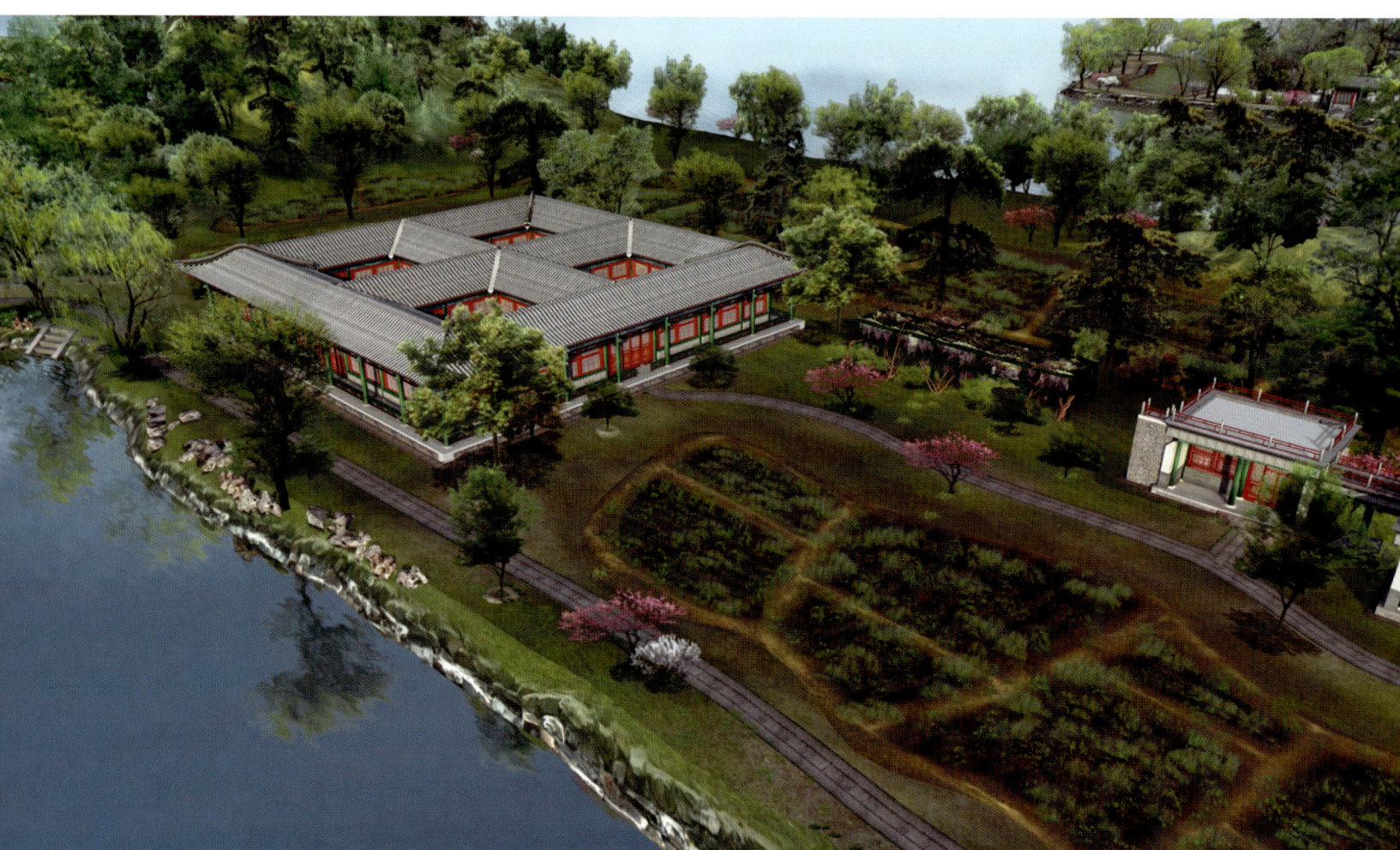

Fig. 110 Danbo Ningjing Complex

映水蘭香 Yingshui Lanxiang Complex (Complex of Water Reflections and Orchid Fragrance)

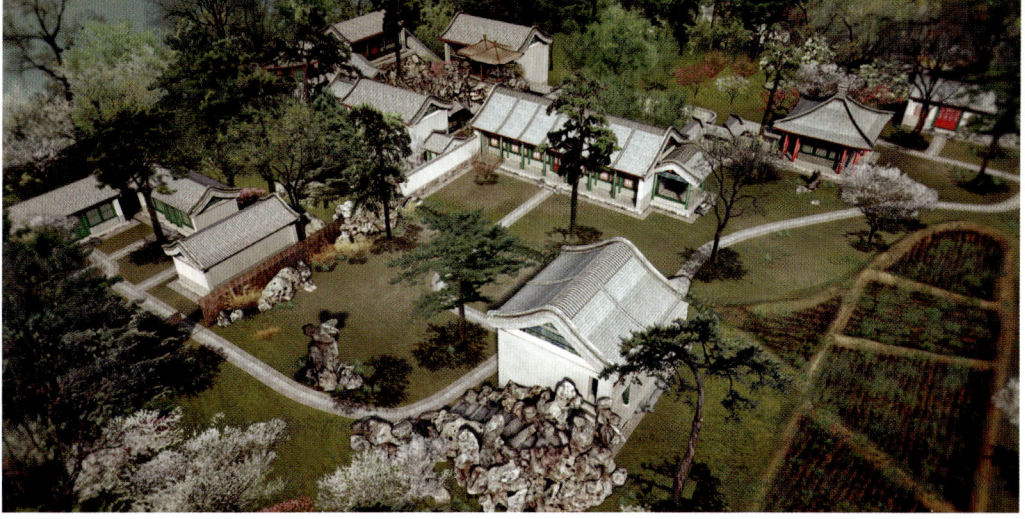

Fig. 111 Aerial view of Yingshui Lanxiang Complex

The themed area Yingshui Lanxiang Complex was located to the west of the Danbo Ningjing Complex. According to descriptions in the *Rixia Jiuwen Kao* (Study of Ancient Accounts Heard in the Precincts of the Throne), this group of buildings centered around the Duojia Pavilion (Bountiful Crop Pavilion), which was surrounded by artificial hills, streams, bamboo-roof kiosks, galleries and raised pavilions. To its east the Guanjia Pavilion (Crop Watching Pavilion) stood close to a rice field. The buildings Yiqing Yuemu (Soothes the Mind and Pleases the Eye) and Daoxiang (Rice Fragrance) stood in its rear; west of the Duojia Pavilion were the Shuijing Land (Unspoiled Land), Jingxiang House (Subtle Fragrance House), Zhaohe Deng (Terrace to Attract Cranes), Cunbi (Inch of Green), Yinsheng (Ushers in Beauty) and Humiao Building (Mutual Enhancement Building) (fig. 111).

The Duojia Pavilion, with its slate roof, was a picture of rusticity. The window in its east gable wall looked out on the rice field and the veranda underneath the window brought the building into more intimate contact with the field. The sight of this little pavilion once prompted Qianlong to say feelingly that this old house with a window on the several paddies of rice plants epitomized his single-minded concern for a good harvest across his realm. His observation of the farming activities in the Garden attested to his empathy for the welfare of the peasants of the country. A poem he composed in the 41st year of his reign (1776) entitled "Inscription for the Duojia Pavilion"[1] stated that his farming activities in the field, such as ploughing, channeling water into the rice paddies, etc. were aimed at setting an example for his subjects and at teaching them to treasure cereal crops. In a prefatory note to another poem about the Duojia Pavilion he stated that "the pavilion's east window overlooked the rice paddies; I sat with the farm folks discussing the weather, the rainfall …", which explained that monitoring and harnessing the agricultural cycle was the purpose of his observation of farming activities.

The Guanjia Pavilion, situated to the east of the Duojia Pavilion and much closer to the rice field, was an open-sided building. Qianlong wrote in one of his poems that there were no window sashes between pillars so that one could observe farming activity unhindered and follow the agricultural cycle.[2] In another poem he wrote that he was not in the imperial garden solely for pleasure and sightseeing, that he enjoyed watching farming activity from the house, the acres of millet ripening into masses of yellow after a season of good rain and rice in green watery paddies whose color was comparable to jade and whose fragrance was unsurpassed by the orchids. He went on to say that he always had a feeling of walking in a painting illustrating *Odes of Bin* and that he would not for a moment forget the instructions given to the agricultural officials in the *Hymns of Zhou* in the *Book of Songs*.[3] Bin is the name of a place in antiquity; it was in the area of present-day Bin county and Xunyi county of Shaanxi province. The "Painting illustrating the *Odes of Bin*" was one that depicted the activities of agriculture and sericulture around Bin. It has eventually become an appellation for all paintings with a similar subject. The *Hymns of Zhou*, which is part of the *Book of Songs*, records the ritual songs and dances used in the ancestral shrine of the Zhou dynasty (1046–256 BC). Qianlong hoped to be blessed by the same kind of joy over a good harvest depicted in the ancient painting and in folk music by observing farming activities and monitoring the agricultural cycle in his imperial garden.

---

1 *Yuzhi Shi*, by Qianlong, Book IV, Volume 37.
2 Ibid., Book V, Volume 62.
3 Ibid., Book II, Volume 87.

水木明瑟 Shuimu Mingse Complex (Complex of Sounds of Trees and Water)

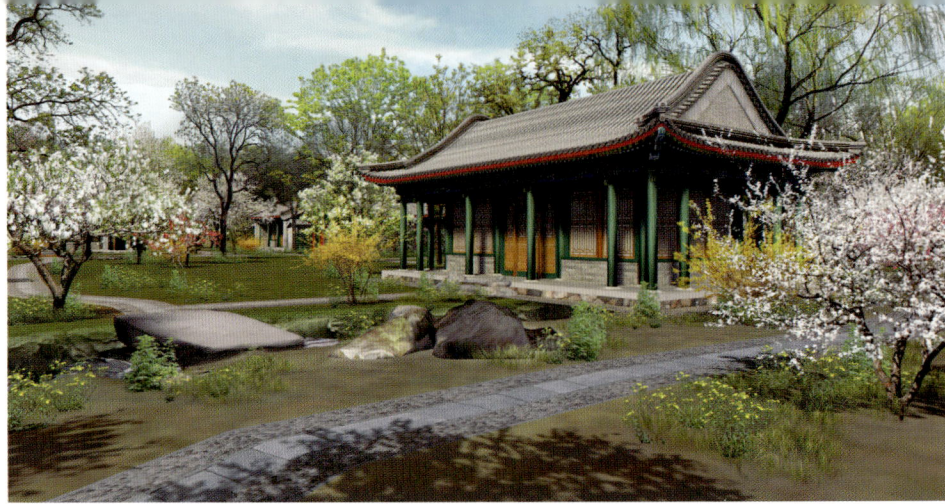

Fig. 112 The Shuimu Mingse Hall

Going north from the Danbo Ningjing Complex and crossing a bridge one arrived at the Shuimu Mingse Complex. The album *Forty Scenes of the Yuan Ming Yuan* shows (fig. 113) that this building complex consisted of two parts. One comprised the small hall called Shuimu Mingse straddling a stream in the east, the other comprised a group of buildings that spread out from a west-facing five-bay building. The westernmost of this group of buildings was the Fengle Pavilion (Joy of Plenty Pavilion), an east-facing five-bay hall ringed by a veranda. A gallery stretched from the north of the Fengle Pavilion to the long gallery to its east so that the courtyard was enclosed on three sides by galleries. The east gallery continued south to link up with the Diaoyu Jetty (Angling Jetty) and north to the Yinyue Pond (Moon Reflecting Pond). North of the pond was a three-bay building called Zhi Gengzhi (Understanding Ploughing and Weaving), which was connected by a gallery with a building to its northeast called Zhuolin Pond (Swimming Fish Pond). The two buildings formed a courtyard compound together with a fence.

The Shuimu Mingse Hall, a building for entertainment purposes, straddled a stream that ran east of the Yinyue Pond. It employed a Western technique of driving a fan by water power. It produced a cool draught and a pleasing note that sounded like "ling, ling," the sound of flowing water, and "se, se," the sound of wind soughing through the trees. This was a favorite place for the emperor and his consorts to escape summer heat.

The group of buildings was surrounded by large tracts planted to rice. It is worth noting that southwest of the Fengle Pavilion was a small three-bay hall called Guizhi Mountain Hall (Mountain Hall of the Importance of Weaving), which was a shrine to the goddess of sericulture, and attested to the importance given to sericulture and weaving in the Garden.

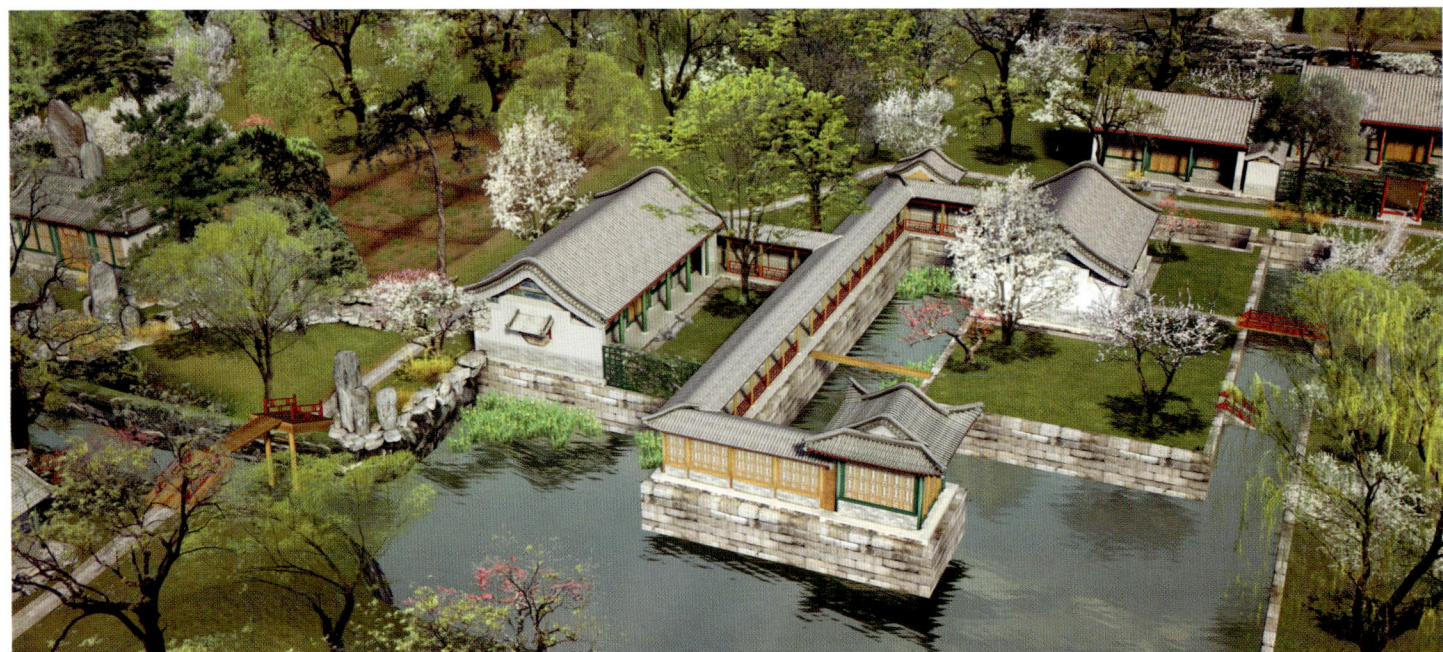

Fig. 113 Aerial view of Shuimu Mingse Complex

耕
耘
堂

Gengyun Hall (Hall of Crop Cultivation)

The rural scene of the Beiyuan Mountain Village extended eastward and northward, though in the east there were no more streams. In those days the area outside the north enclosure wall of the Yuan Ming Yuan was covered by paddy fields and looking out from the Gengyun Hall that perched on a small earthen hill in the Garden, the beholder could see peasants toiling in the fields outside. A little to the west of the Gengyun Hall, near the north wall, another group of buildings was constructed in the 29th year of the Qianlong era (1764), namely the Ruofanzhi Pavilion (Boat-Like Pavilion) and the Anzhi Building (Building of Stability), both of which were two-storied buildings and were linked by a gallery. Its north face was girt by an exterior veranda with a balustrade that afforded a view to the distance. The building was erected right next to a stream and commanded a view of billowing rice plants, giving the beholder an impression of riding in a boat, hence the name Ruofanzhi Pavilion or a two-storied building like a boat. Qianlong often described a feeling of being transported to a fairyland when he was there. Qianlong's interest in looking out on the scene outside the Yuan Ming Yuan from this building lay less in the pleasure of an agreeable, idyllic sight, than in monitoring the farming progress outside.

An elevation drawing from the Imperial Office of Architectural Design of the Ruofanzhi Pavilion (fig. 114) shows an unconventional design: there was symmetry on the ground level while on the second level the three bays in the east of the exterior gallery were kept open to the outdoors, with the windows set back, leaving only a balustrade, leaning against which the beholder could command a view of the distance.

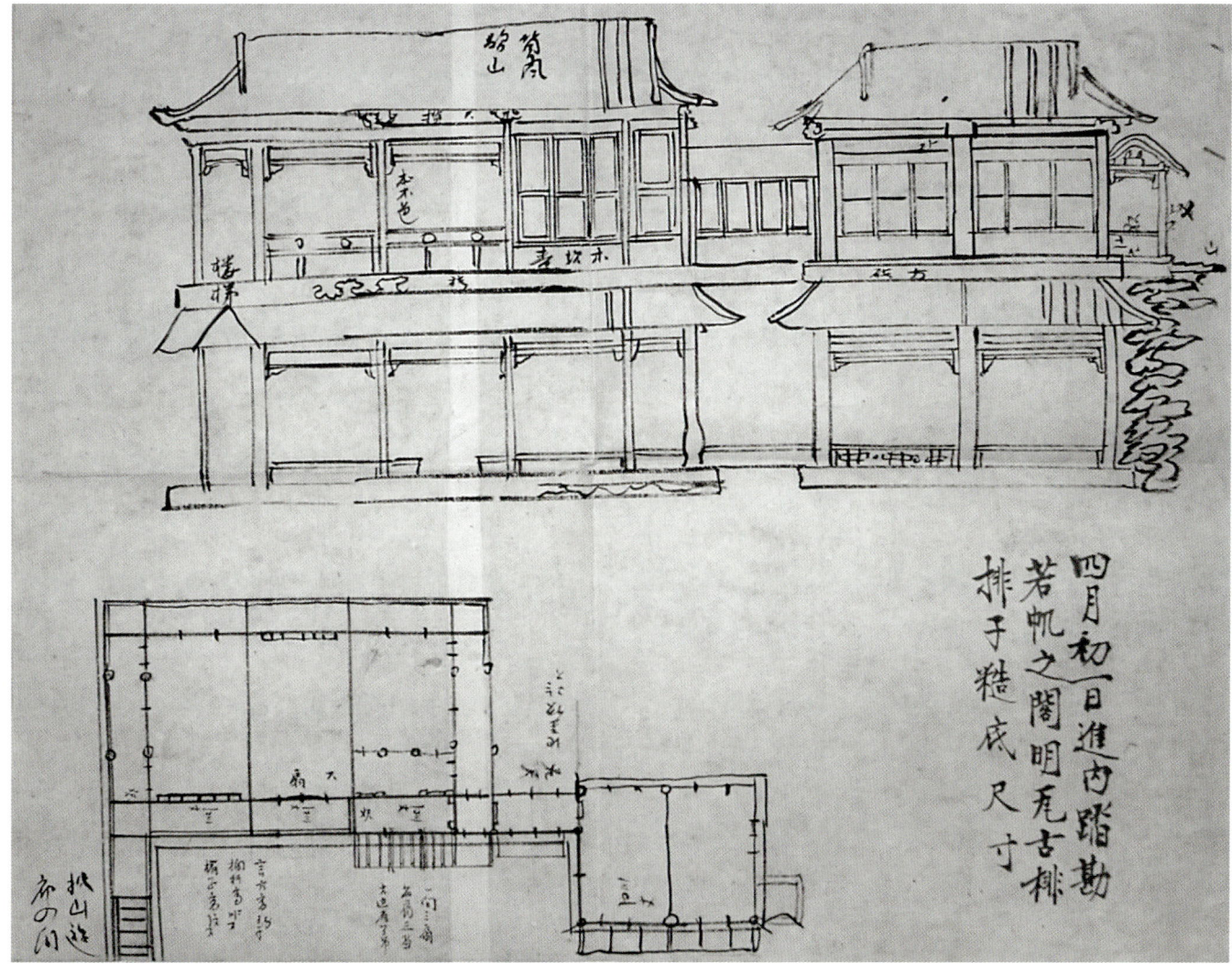

Fig. 114　Ruofanzhi Pavilion

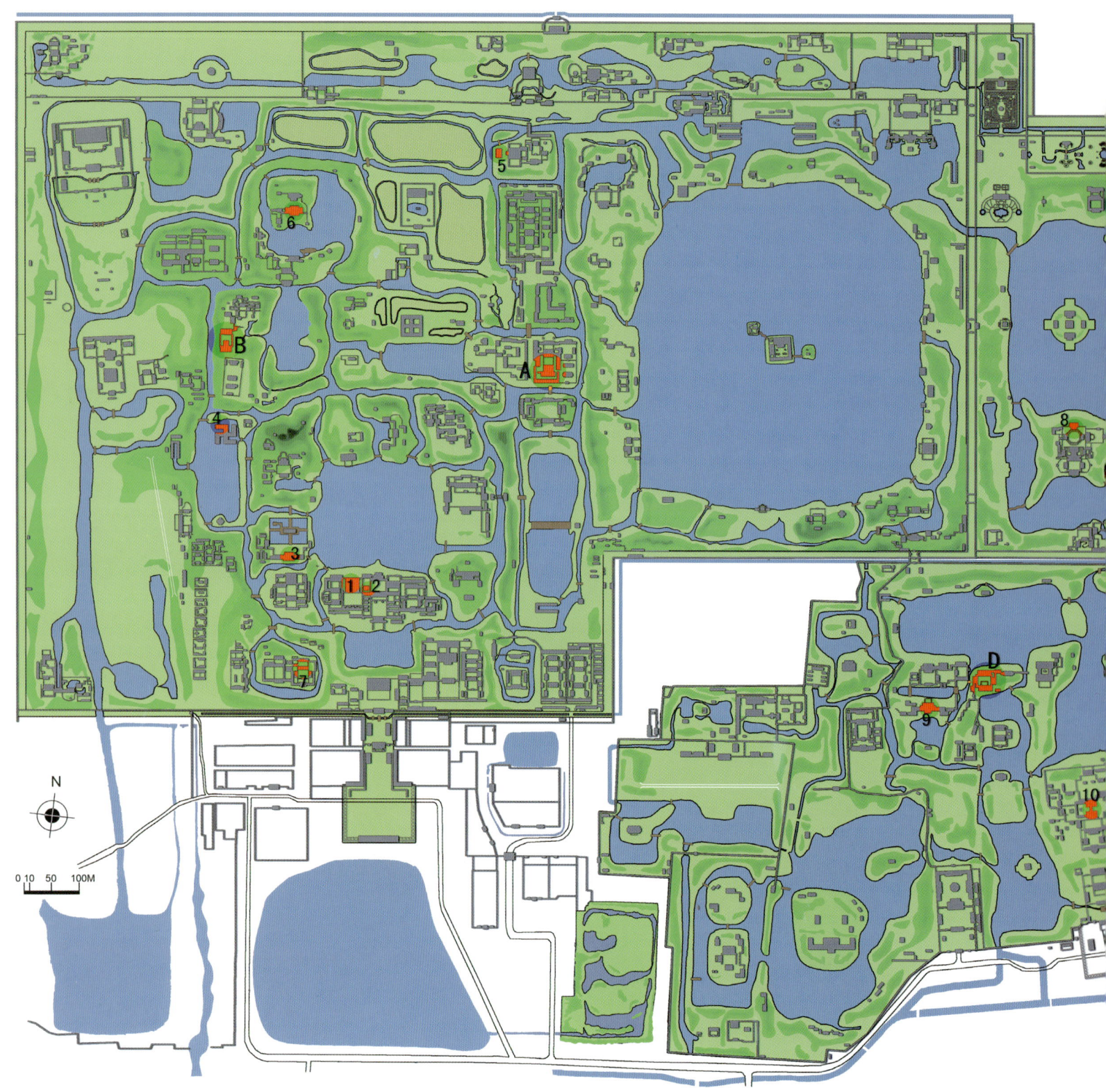

Fig. 115 Sketch map of theatrical stages in Yuan Ming Yuan

132 CHINA'S LOST IMPERIAL GARDEN

CHAPTER XI
Theatrical Buildings

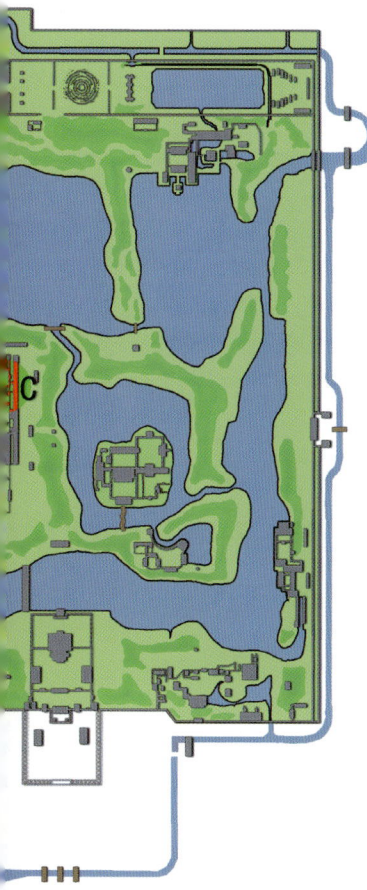

There were two types of theatrical buildings in the Yuan Ming Yuan, one was the alfresco type used for acrobatic performances and fireworks displays of which there was only one, i.e. the Shangao Shuichang Complex. The other was the stage type. There were a dozen such stages at different times in the three gardens of the Yuan Ming Yuan; at least five were stand-alone stages not attached to other buildings, including the larger ones such as the Qingyin Pavilion (Clarion Notes Pavilion) stage in the Tongle Garden of the Zuoshi Linliu Complex (Complex of On a Rock by the River) area, the Huzhong Xianlai (Divine Sound in a Pot) stage of the Hengchun Hall (Permanent Spring Hall) in the Wuling Chunse area and the Yuezou Juntian (Music Reaching Heaven) stage in the Chunhua Pavilion area in the Changchun Garden, not to mention the smaller ones. These included the Tongdao Hall stage in the Yuan Ming Yuan and the Qingyue Shengping stage in the Zhanshi Yinglü Complex in the Qichun Garden. The rest were small indoor stages.

The so-called small indoor stages were performance spaces inside a building; the Yuan Ming Yuan boasted at various times the Shende Hall (Hall of Strict Virtue Cultivation) stage in the Jiuzhou Qingyan Complex, the Fengsan Wusi stage, the Banmu Garden (Half Acre Garden) stage in the Tantan Dangdang area, the Wanfang Anhe stage, the stage in the Xifeng Xiuse Open Hall and the Shenxiu Siyong stage in the Lianxi Lechu Complex. Then there was the Siyong Study stage in the Changchun Garden and the Shengdong Room (Room of Winter Scenery) stage and the Fuchun Hall stage in the Qichun Garden. These small stages set indoors often were only a space partitioned off in a room for the performance. Sometimes the stage was defined simply by a carved wooden affair serving as the proscenium arch hanging from the ceiling and a wooden guardrail; in some places a small kiosk was placed in the room to serve as stage.

The Tongle Garden was the largest theatrical building group in the Yuan Ming Yuan. It was situated to the northeast of the Back Lake in the Nine Islands area of the Yuan Ming Yuan and fell within the Zuoshi Linliu Complex. The Huzhong Xianlai stage in the Wuling Chunse area, located to the north of the Wanfang Anhe area, had at its north a five-bay hall called Hengchun Hall for seating the spectators, which was completed in the Jiaqing era. The Yuezou Juntian stage, located in the Hanjing Hall group of buildings in the middle of the Changchun Garden, had a viewing hall at its north called Shenxin Miaoda, completed in the 19th year of the Jiaqing era (1814); it had the attribute of an imperial private apartment. The Tongdao Hall stage in the Jiuzhou Qingyan area in the Yuan Ming Yuan was modest in scale. The viewing hall at its north, called Tongdao Hall, was connected by a gallery to the Shende Hall, very close to the Jiuzhou Qingyan Hall. The Zhanshi Yinglü Complex, located in the north of the Qichun Garden, had a stage called Qingyue Shengping, situated at the south side of the courtyard, with a viewing hall at its north. The small indoor stages were distributed evenly among buildings in the three Gardens (fig. 115).

山高水長 Shangao Shuichang Complex (Complex of High Hills and Long Waters)

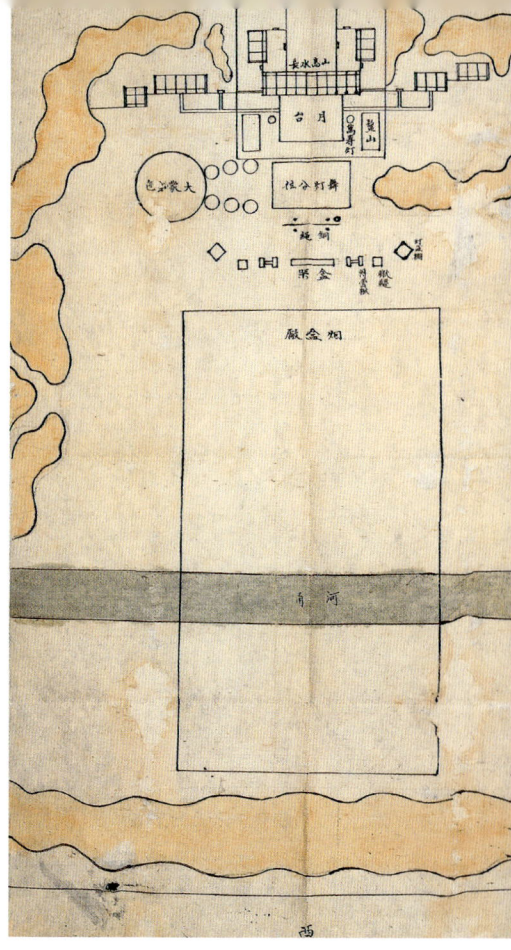

Fig. 116 Yurts and plan of the plaza from the Imperial Office of Architectural Design

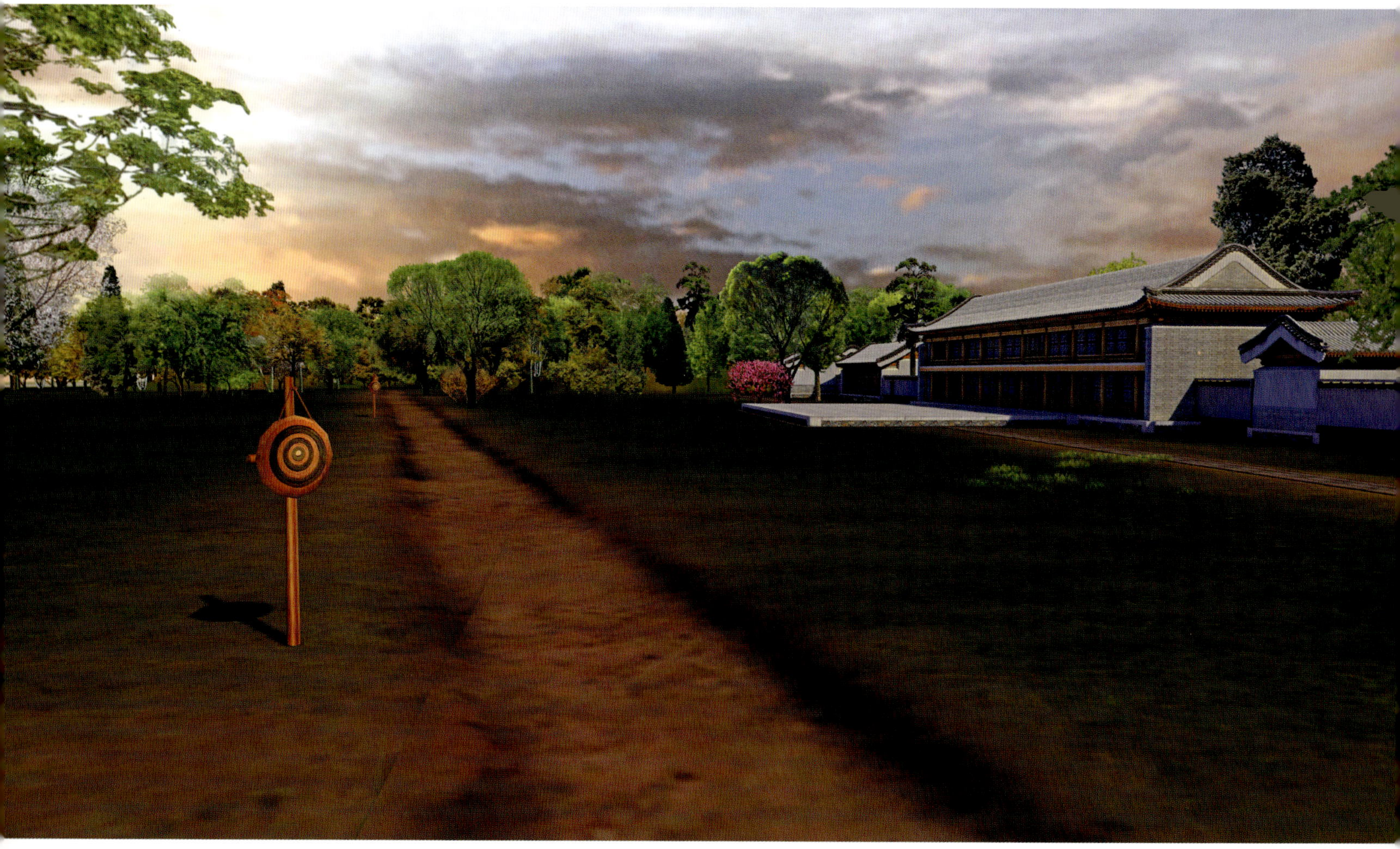

The anchor of this themed area was a long two-storied building that faced east. It was nine bays long and its east façade formed a courtyard compound with two smaller three-bay halls that faced south and north respectively. The west façade of the long building faced a vast open space and commanded a view of the distant hills. This open space served as venue for archery contests and in front of the building there was a run for horses (fig. 117).

In Yongzheng's day this place was called the Yinjian Building (Audience Building). Qianlong also used it to wine and dine foreign legates and envoys of vassal states, usually on the 13th day of the first month of every year, i.e. shortly before the Lantern Festival. The guests were treated to a display of fireworks and a lantern show.

Such banquets normally were not held indoors but in a number of yurts put up in front of the building. The bigger yurts measured 24 meters in diameter and the smallest ones measured 4 to 5 meters across. A Daoguang era drawing gave details of the buildings of the Shangao Shuichang Complex, the big yurts as well as the placement of

Fig. 117 Shangao Shuichang Complex

134 CHINA'S LOST IMPERIAL GARDEN

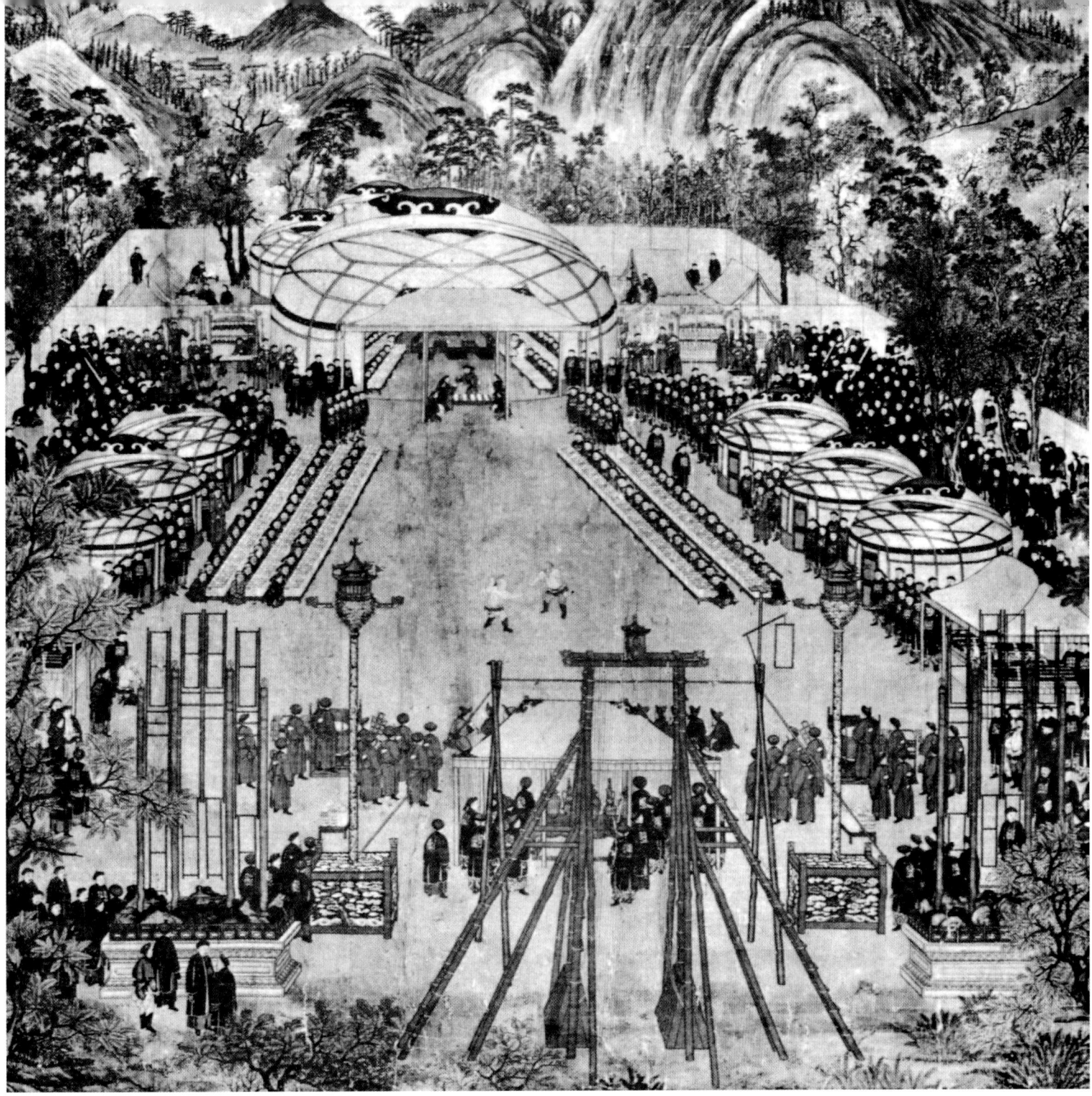

Fig. 118 Giuseppe Castiglione's painting *The Imperial Banquet in the Garden of Ten Thousand Trees*
Colored inks on silk
221.2 × 419.6 cm

the lanterns and fireworks setup (fig. 116). The setup of the yurts was similar to that shown in Giuseppe Castiglione's painting *The Imperial Banquet in the Garden of Ten Thousand Trees* (fig. 118).

Architectural arches were erected for the launching of the fireworks. On the day of the exhibition of fireworks the emperor took his seat outside the building door, with members of the royal family, chiefs of vassal states and court officials seated on either side of him. The lanterns were exhibited on the terraces on either side of the Shangao Shuichang Complex. Early in his reign Emperor Qianlong laid down the rule that the viewing of the lanterns would start on the 13th day of the first month and end on the 19th. There were simultaneous performances of acrobats and jugglers. During the feast officials from the imperial kitchen would come before the emperor on their knees bearing delicacies which the emperor then granted those accompanying him.

In the Qianlong era the Feast of Lanterns was a very elaborate affair with myriad lanterns. Of all the invited guests he showered the greatest attention and affection on the empress dowager his mother in a display of filial piety.

同樂園 Tongle Garden (Garden of Shared Pleasure)

The Tongle Garden was bordered by water on the south, north and east. It stood opposite the Sravasti and the Quyuan Fenghe Complex across the water. To the west it faced the bustling market street that stretched before the Shewei City (fig. 119).

The Tongle Garden was built before the fourth year of the Yongzheng era (1726). It consisted of a stage, a viewing hall, a viewing gallery and a lounge. According to *Yangjizhai Conglu* (*Historical Notes of the Qing Dynasty*) by Wu Zhenyu of the Qing dynasty: "In the Qianlong era the Festival was celebrated annually in the Garden starting from the 13th of the first month. Princess, members of the imperial family, vassals, Mongolian princes, taijis, princes' spouses, ministers of dependencies were invited by the emperor to partake of the good food and attend theatrical performances. In the days preceding and following the imperial birthday, theatrical performances were also offered here." Besides serving as theater, this place was a main dining facility. In the 21st year of his reign (1756) Emperor Qianlong stayed

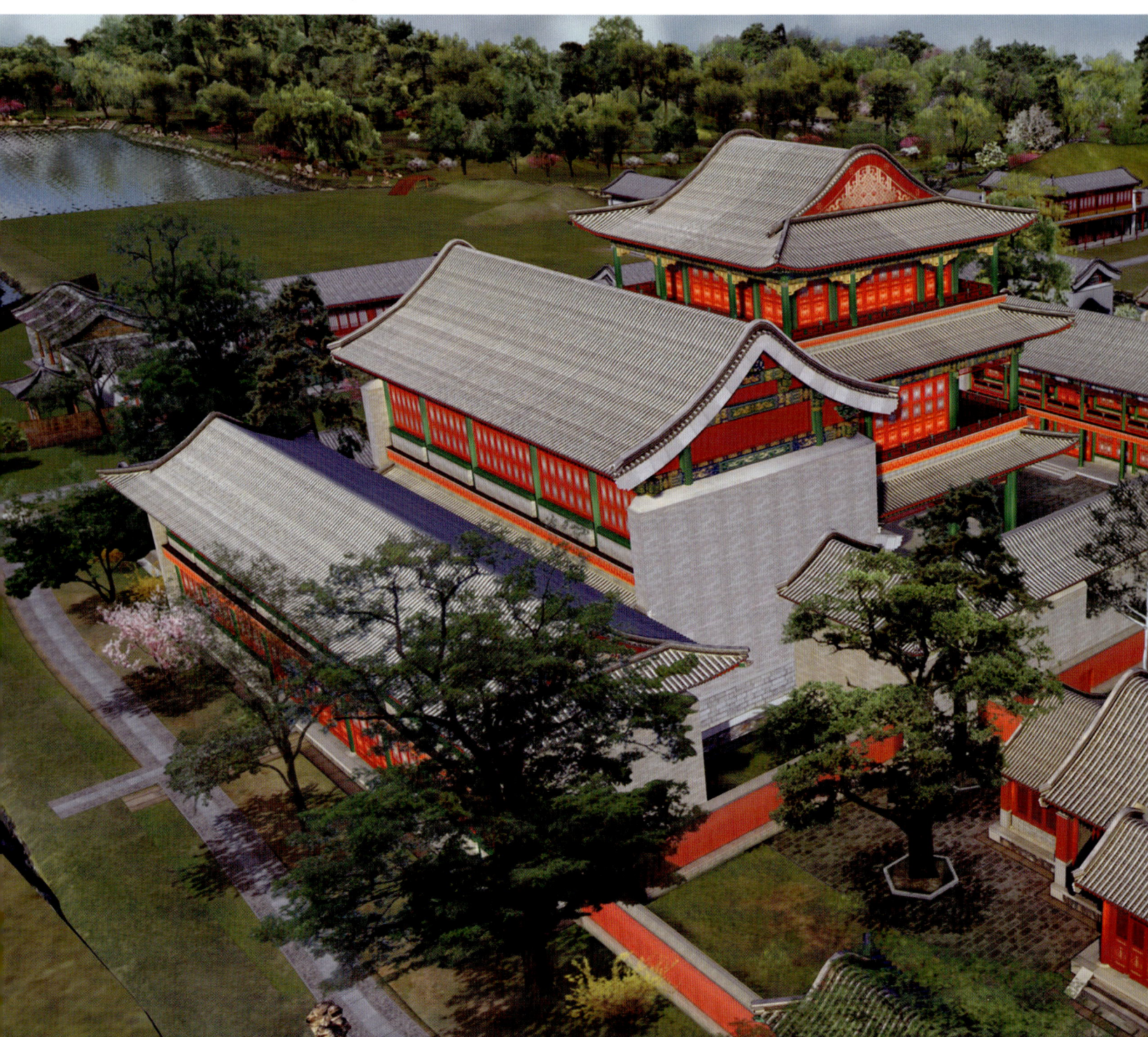

158 days in the Yuan Ming Yuan and had as many as 82 meals at the Tongle Garden.

The Tongle Garden was a major venue for court entertainment in the Yuan Ming Yuan. It was the normal practice to stage lavish theatrical performances in the days around the 15th day of the first lunar month. These performances offered more an opportunity for the emperor to socialize with his court officials and dole out rewards and favors than real theatrical entertainment for the emperor, for which he depended on his court musicians in the Forbidden City.

The stage at the Tongle Garden was named Qingyin Pavilion. It was a large three-storied theatrical building surmounted by a hip-and-gable roof, with in its back a five-bay two-storied dressing room building. At its north was the viewing hall and a back building; two-tiered viewing galleries were attached to the viewing hall at its two sides. It was a full-fledged theater. As one of the more important theatrical stages of the Qing court, it was built with the best available construction technology and equipment. Due to the complex and strict requirements of theatrical performances, the design and structure of the Tongle Garden differed from that of other buildings, and involved ingenious devices unique to such buildings.

(1) Layout of the Tongle Garden

To the east of the theatrical buildings of the Tongle Garden stood a small Buddhist temple called the Yongri Hall; at its west stretched the market street. There were entry and exit doors giving direct access from the theater to the street (fig. 120 on page 138).

From front to back there were three courtyard compounds to the Tongle Garden. The first had a two-storied building at its south side and a north building containing dressing rooms. The second courtyard compound was the anchor of the entire complex, with at its south the stage called Qingyin Pavilion and a viewing hall at its north called Tongle Garden Hall interconnected with galleries around the courtyard. The dressing room building, the stage building, the viewing hall and the back building north of it sat along a north-south axis. The stage building stood directly opposite the viewing hall and an east and a west gallery connected it with the viewing hall and the dressing

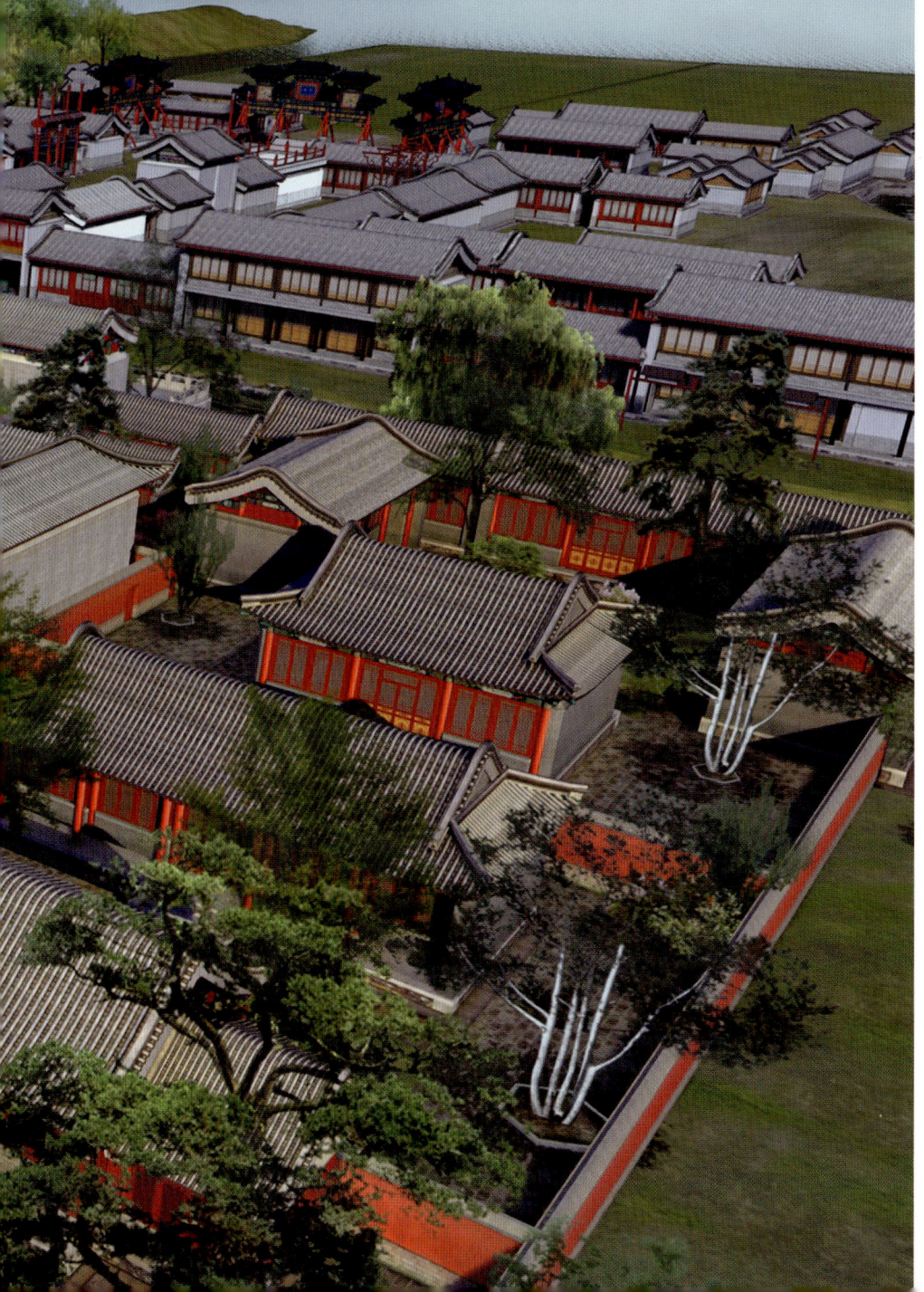

Fig. 119 Aerial view of Tongle Garden

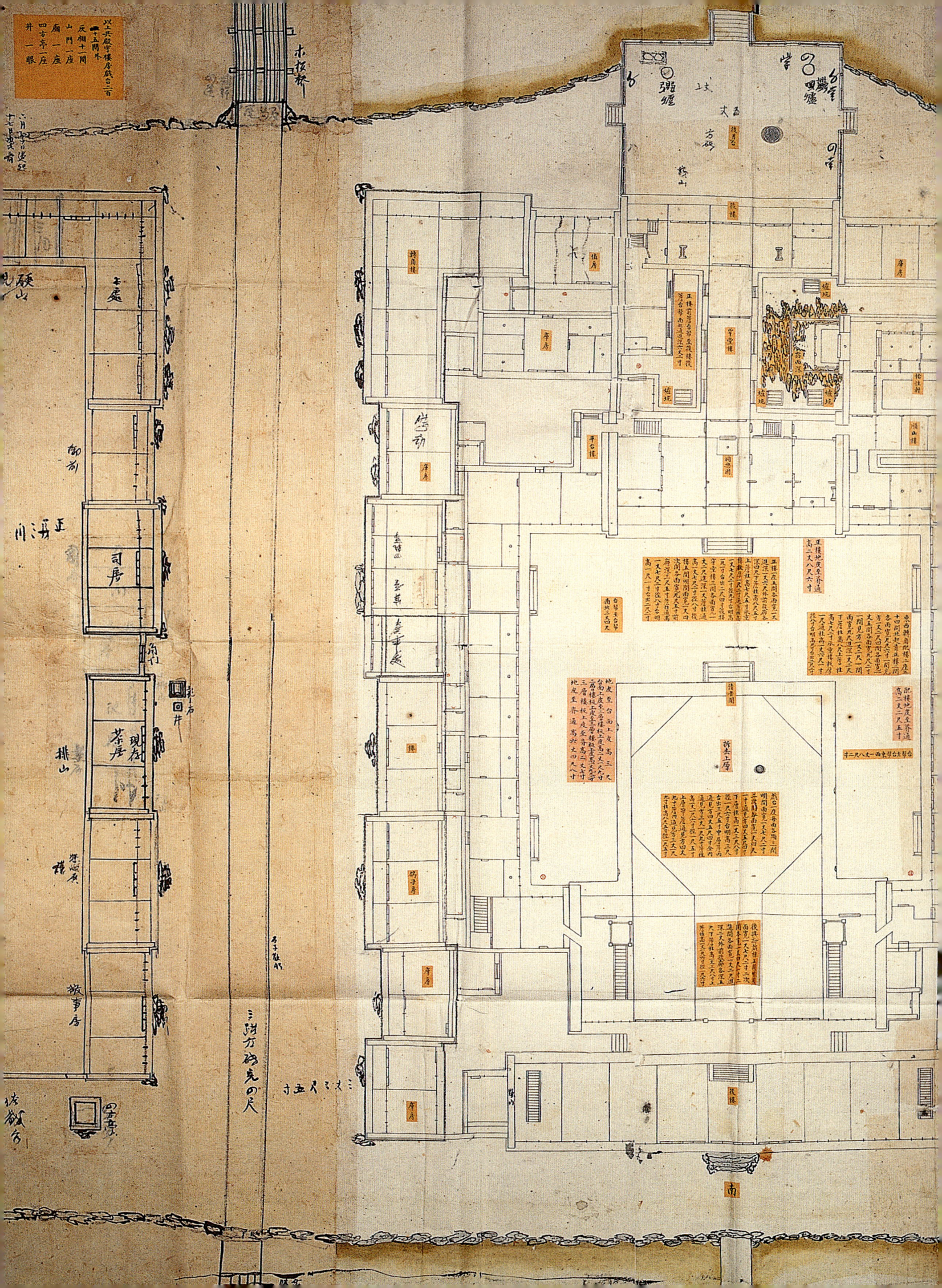

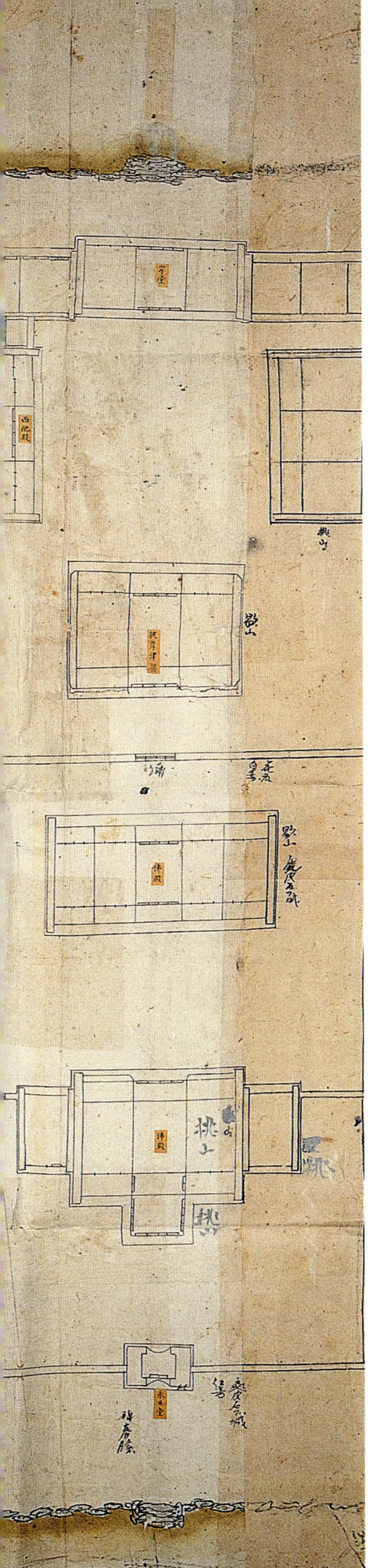

room building to form a courtyard around the stage. The spectators were seated according to their rank in the main hall, the east and west side halls or the side galleries. Guards were stationed on the steps outside the halls. The third courtyard was the back building behind the Tongle Garden, which served as a lounge for the emperor and his consorts and for socializing between the emperor and his ministers. There was a gallery on the north face of the back building and a north-facing terrace with a balustrade which commanded a view of the waterside scenery and surrounding vistas to the north.

The stage was located in the center of the courtyard, with the surrounding buildings all oriented toward it and the spectators focusing their attention on the stage from three sides, so there was a great sense of cohesion.

(2) The Stage Building and the Dressing Room Building

The stage building consisted of the stage for theatrical performances and the dressing room building consisted of the backstage, the dressing room for the actors and the storeroom. The stage building was three-storied and three bays wide; it was square-shaped in plan and the roof was in the Chinese hip-and-gable style; the dressing room building was two-storied and five bays wide and had an overhanging gable roof. The dressing room building and the stage building were constructed on the same base

Fig. 120 Plan of Tongle Garden

and the two structures were linked to each other.

The stage building was very different from the ordinary multi-story buildings; each of its three stories was a stage in its own right and they were named the Fu (Happiness) Stage, the Lu (Prosperity) Stage and the Shou (Longevity) Stage. But there was actually another, smaller stage on a mezzanine behind the Longevity Stage on the bottom level; therefore this three-storied theater comprised four performing spaces, each of which had its own stage entrance and exit and could be easily reached from the others, making for flexible use of the spaces as required by circumstances.

To facilitate communication between the stages on various levels, openings called sky wells were created in the floors. The sky well in the floor between the Happiness Stage on the third level and the Prosperity Stage on the second level was normally kept closed but could be opened when necessary. The actors could ascend or descend to different stages when required by the script to enact a scene of ascending to heaven or descending to earth.

There were a total of seven sky wells between the Prosperity Stage and the lower ones: a big opening in the middle and smaller ones. Some gave access to the Longevity Stage, others to the small stage in the mezzanine. For instance the stage directions in the script of the court drama entitled *Shengping*

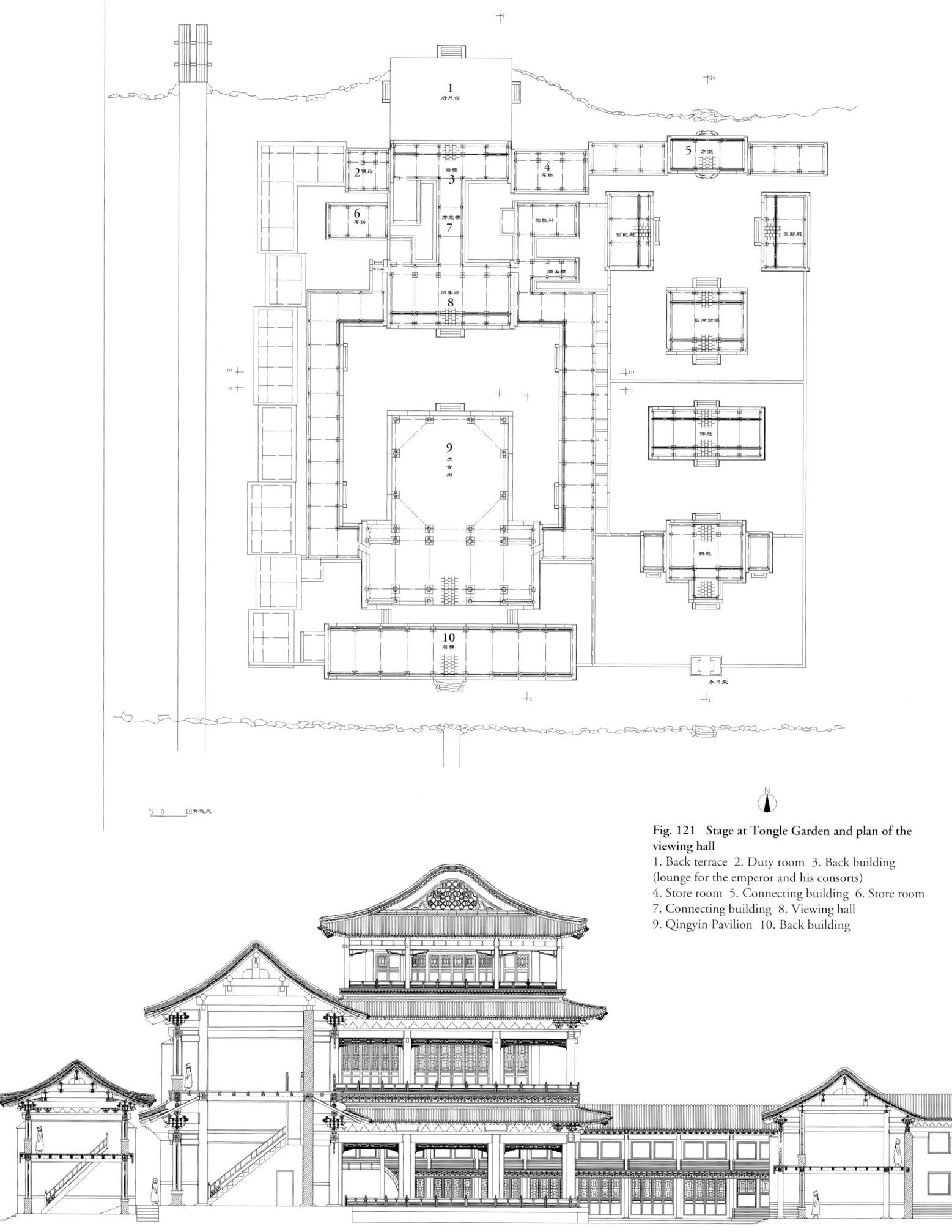

Fig. 121 Stage at Tongle Garden and plan of the viewing hall
1. Back terrace 2. Duty room 3. Back building (lounge for the emperor and his consorts)
4. Store room 5. Connecting building 6. Store room
7. Connecting building 8. Viewing hall
9. Qingyin Pavilion 10. Back building

Fig. 122 Section of the stage at Tongle Garden

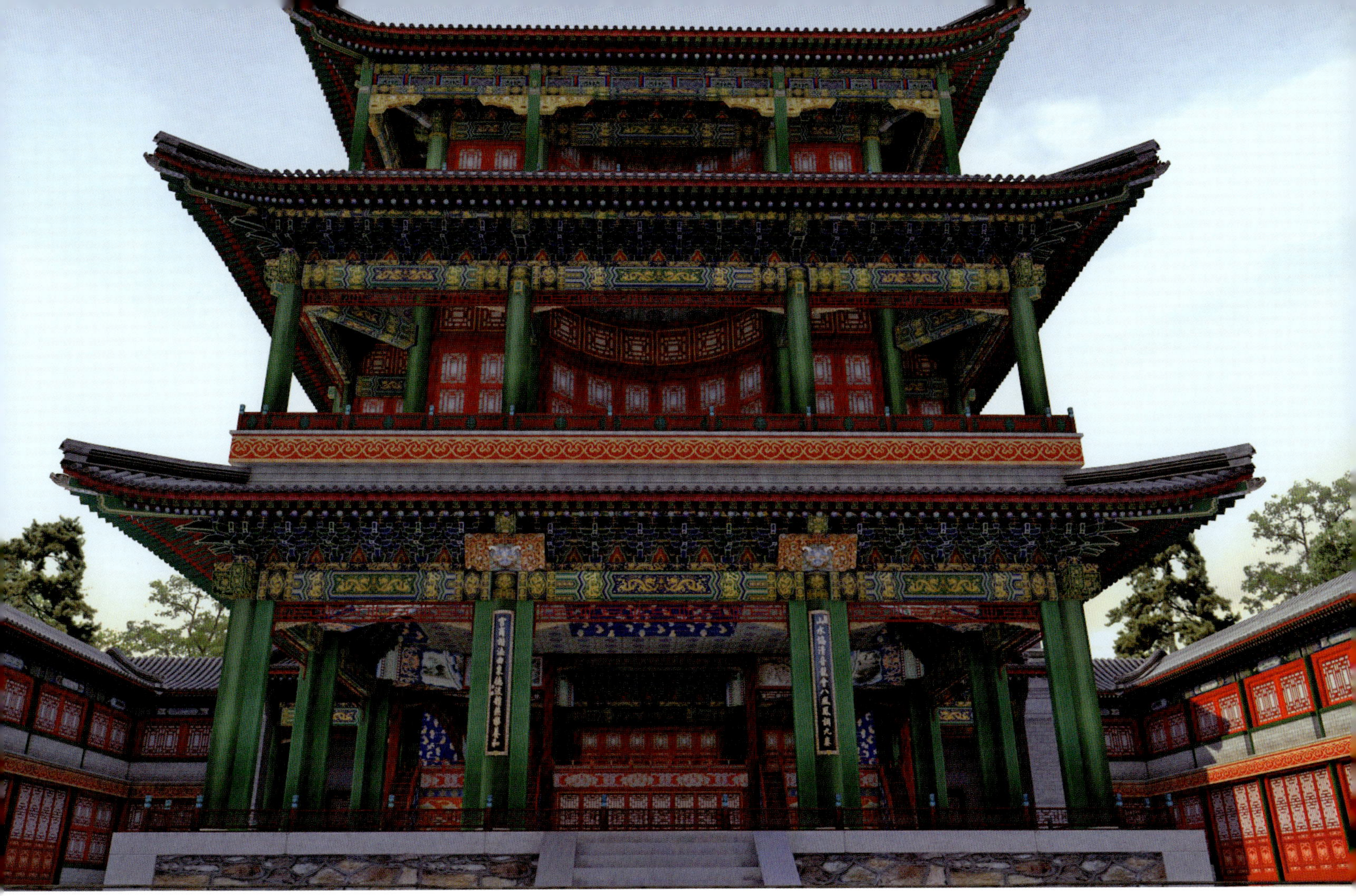

Fig. 123   Stage at Tongle Garden

Baofa (*Precious Raft of Supreme Peace*) called for "descent from west sky well," "four comical immortals descend from central sky well, eight immortals descend from sky well in four corners," etc., making full use of these openings between the stages on different levels.

There was more than one sky well between the Happiness Stage on the third level and the lower ones. To prevent accidents, the wells in the middle of all the stages were fitted with a railing. The sky well on the Happiness Stage on the third level had at its four corners thick wooden pillars surmounted by a wooden frame on which was mounted a copper pulley. The east, north and west sections of the railing around the sky well were fitted with wooden windlasses which could lower and raise props needed by the actors.

The stage building of the Tongle Garden had special structural requirements because it had to meet the need of simultaneous performances on three different levels. Numerous sky wells and staircases were necessary for this purpose; at the same time the number of pillars must be reduced to minimize obstruction of the view. The complexity of the props required the installation of special equipment (figs. 121, 122).

The first level (the Longevity Stage) was the main stage (fig. 123); it measured 16.8 meters in width and in length, with a surface area of 282 square meters. At its back was another smaller stage on a mezzanine reached by ascending four steps. Seven sky wells were visible in the ceiling above the first-level stage. The sky well in the middle was larger, those on the two sides were slender and four more were in the four corners. Some planks on the Longevity Stage were movable, indicating that there might have been a performing space below. There was no specific mention of any floor well in extant records. Archaeological work at the site of the Chunhua Pavilion stage in recent years found only a cellar underneath the stage and no floor

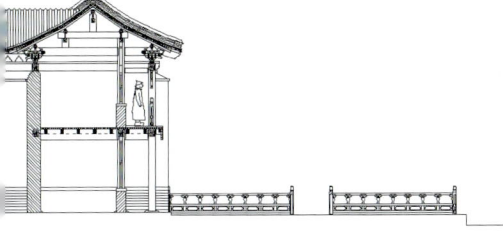

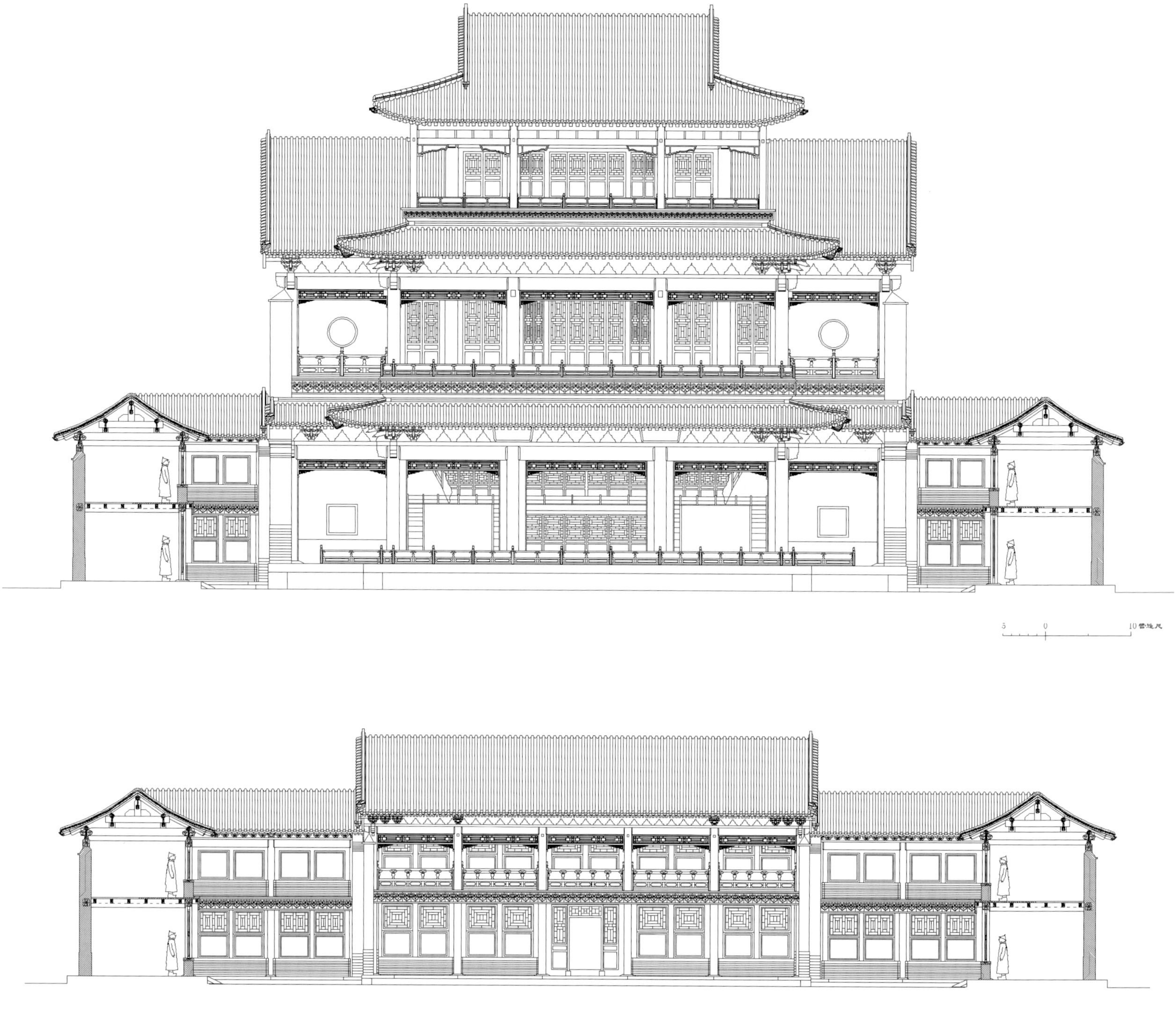

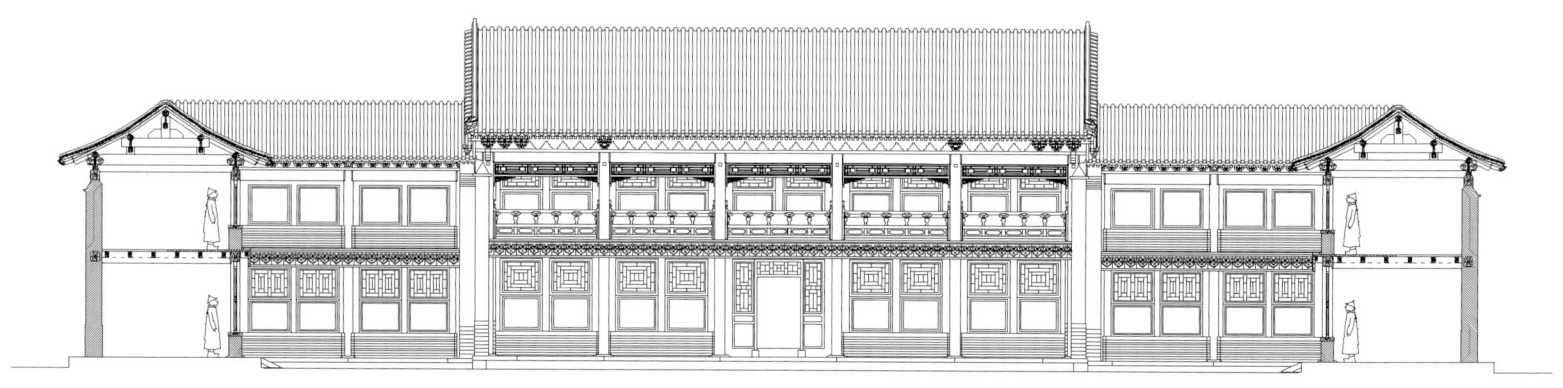

Fig. 124 Elevation of the stage (up) and the viewing hall (below)

well was found. The net height in the cellar was 2.47 meters[1] and its walls and floor were all faced with granite. Apparently the cellar was used solely for occasions when actors were required by the script to "burrow into the ground."

On the middle level (the Prosperity Stage), the area within the eave pillars was 210 square meters and comprised an indoor and an outdoor part. The outdoor part was primarily on the north side of the stage, with an area of about 40 square meters, or 1/5 of the total area of the second level. This was where the performances took place. As the spectators' line of sight would be partially obstructed by the stage structure, the performing space on the higher stages had to be moved closer to the front edge of the stage. While a guardrail 48 centimeters high was built at the edge, it was too low to effectively protect the actors from falling off the stage and could at most serve as a warning against overstepping it. The outdoor and indoor parts were divided by lattice doors, which were arranged in a concave U shape in the middle bay, thus increasing the outdoor performing area and its depth. The setback lattice doors flared outward to give directionality to the performing area. The most important element in the indoor part of the stage was the sky well in the middle, which afforded access to all three levels. On the second-level stage there were two staircases that led to upper floors.

On the upper level (the Happiness Stage), the pillars were further set back, giving an area within the pillars of 104 square meters. It also comprised an indoor and an outdoor part. The higher elevation meant that the spectators looking up could see an even smaller area of the stage. The two parts were also partitioned by lattice doors that were arranged in a concave arc facing the viewing hall directly opposite the stage. The Happiness Stage had three openings in its floor: there were the two openings at the left and the right for the two staircases and there was the middle well, where the machinery to lower and raise objects and people was concentrated. At the four corners of the middle well were thick pillars with a square cross section that were surmounted by a wooden frame to which was attached a copper pulley. On the east, north and west sections of the railing around the well were wooden windlasses with a handle that served to lower and hoist props or actors to any of the stages. In those days the actors and props were moved from the dressing room building at its south to the middle well, therefore there was no windlass at the south of the middle well.

(3) The Spectators' Seats in the Tongle Garden

The spectators' seats were placed in the viewing hall called Tongle Garden Hall and in the galleries at the two sides of the courtyard (fig. 124). The emperor and his consorts were seated in the viewing hall and the nobility and ministers were assigned by rank to seats at the sides in the hall all the way down to the two side galleries. According to *Yangjizhai Cong Lu* (*Historical Notes of the Qing Dynasty*) by Wu Zhenyu of the Qing dynasty, "the Tongle Garden Hall was five bays wide. When the emperor arrived he would watch the performances … the nobility, princes and ministers were seated by rank in the east and west wings in seats that were preassigned. Then tea, wine, fruits and pastry were served." Depending on where one sat in this kind of courtyard setting, the viewing and auditory experience would vary greatly. Acoustic tests conducted at the grand stage of the Dehe Garden (Garden of Virtue and Harmony) in the Yihe Yuan (the Summer Palace) have shown that the acoustics were best at the location of the throne.[2]

The east and west galleries, each fourteen bays long, connected the viewing hall and the dressing room building. The galleries had two stories to them and were about 3.84 meters deep, which was much greater than the 1.3 meters for most galleries that enclosed a courtyard, and therefore spacious enough to accommodate tables around which spectators could drink tea while watching the performance. Doors in the galleries at ground level facilitated entry and exit.

The viewing hall and the back building were not unlike other two-storied buildings in exterior shape and form; one difference was that the windows in these theatrical buildings were set lower than those in other buildings so that there would be less obstruction of the view. In the mid-Qing period the plan of the Tongle Garden shows the back building, the viewing hall and the connecting hall forming an H-shaped cross section.

The interior design of the viewing hall was unlike that of other buildings. Its main functional space was toward the front near the windows. Except for the central bay, in which was placed a throne, the other bays were all furnished with a front *kang* (traditional long platform for sleeping and entertaining). The throne was oriented toward the stage for the emperor's opera viewing pleasure. The empress and other imperial consorts could only watch the performance from the front *kangs* by the windows.

The exterior environment of the H-shaped viewing hall was enriched by the complexity of its structural mass, being divided into a right and a left courtyard, which added to the attractiveness of the grounds and enhanced the pleasure of watching the stage performance (fig. 125 on pages 144 and 145).

---

1 "2001–2002 *Summary Report on Work at the Ruins of the Hanjing Hall in the Yuan Ming Yuan*", by the archaeological team working on the Yuan Ming Yuan, of the Beijing Municipal Institute of Cultural Relics, second issue of *Archaeology* in 2004.
2 *Formation and Evolution of the Theatrical Stage in Chinese Antiquity*, by Luo Deyin, 2000.

Pages 144 and 145
Fig. 125 **North aerial view of Tongle Garden**

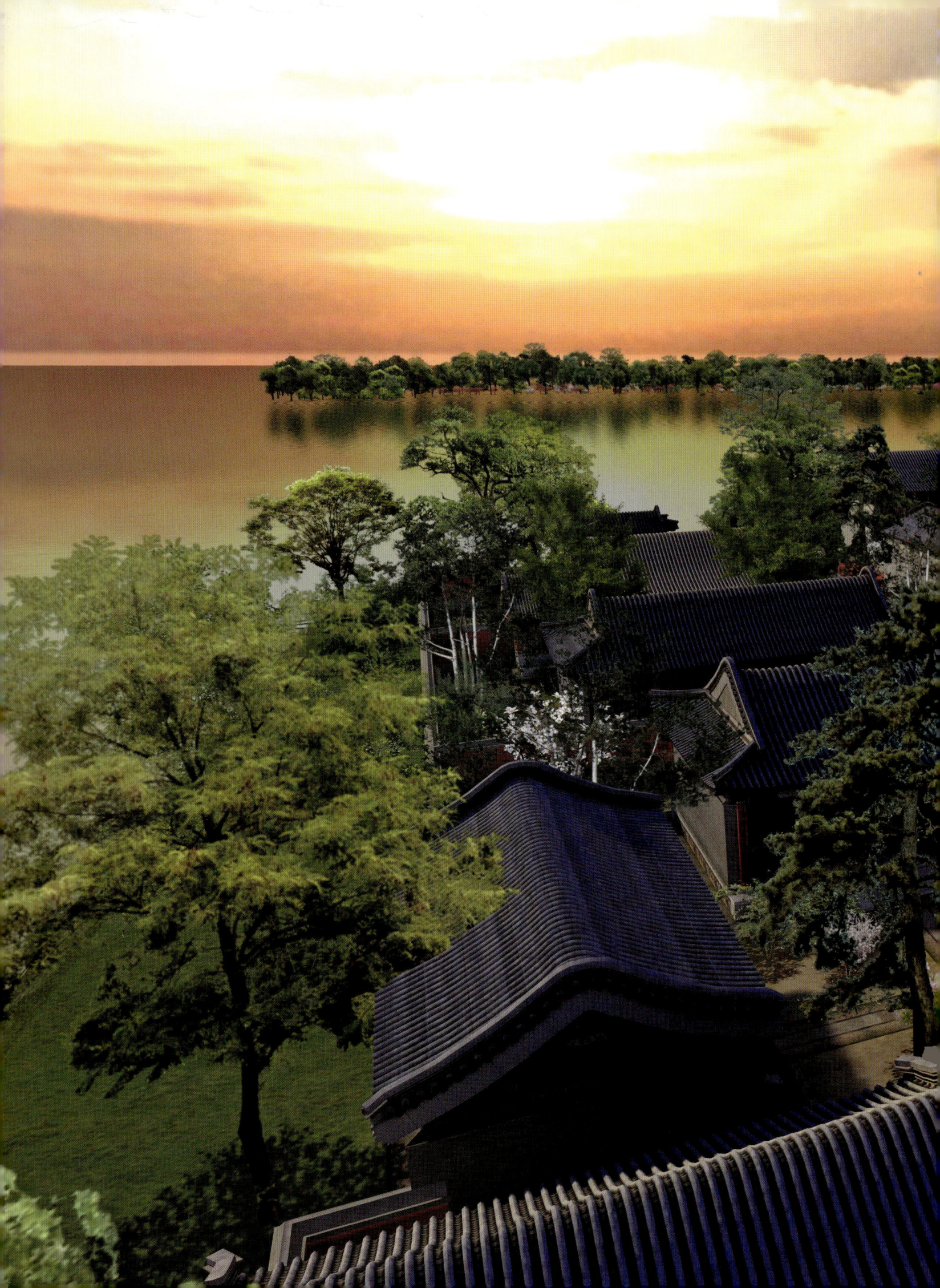

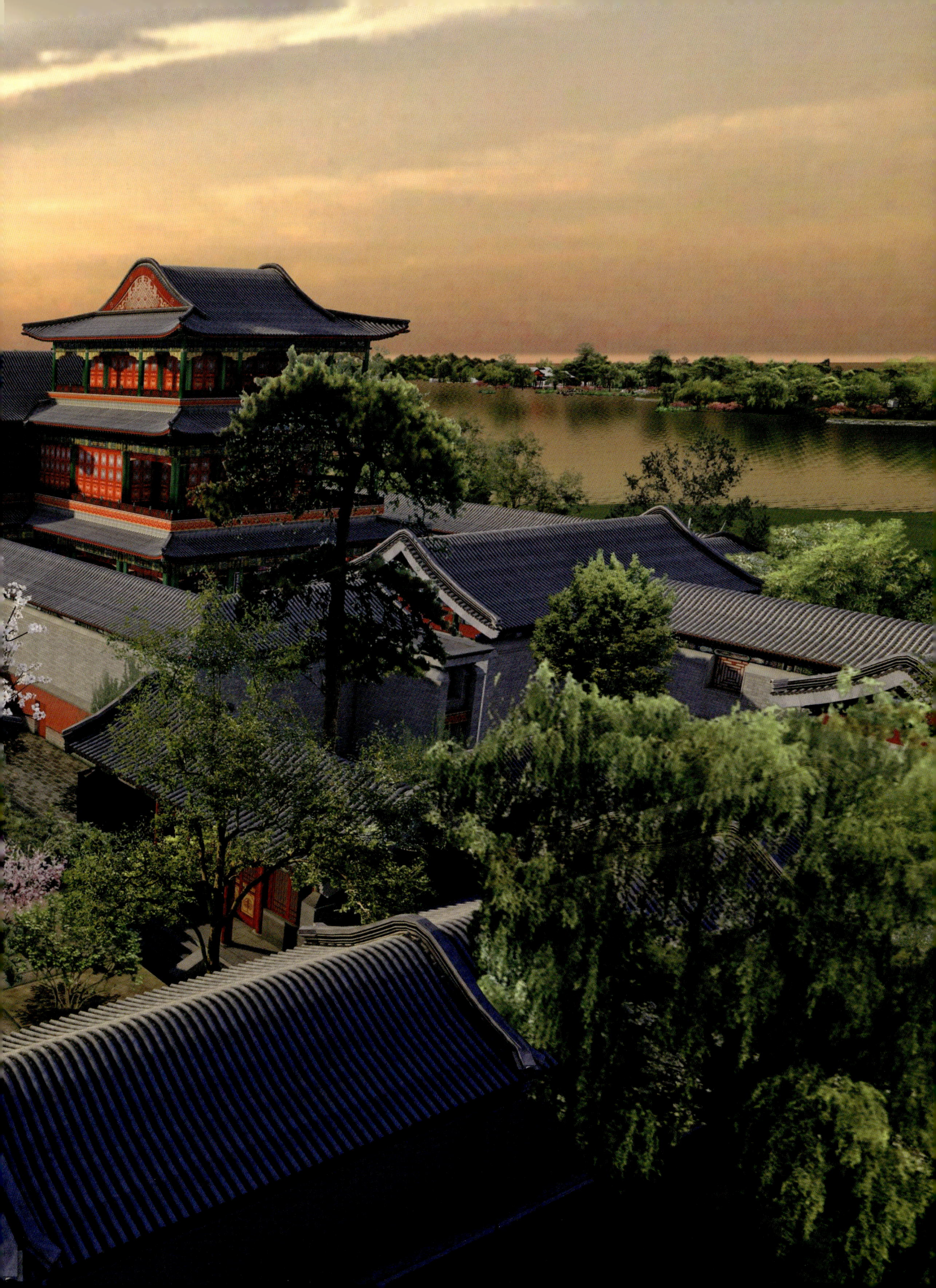

展詩應律 Zhanshi Yinglü Complex (Complex of Verse and Rhyming)

The Zhanshi Yinglü Stage, built in the sixth year of the Jiaqing era (1801), was located on a peninsula a little north of the central sector of the Qichun Garden and was the only outdoor stage in the Garden that could be used for performances. The grounds measured 108 meters east and west, and 60 meters north and west, giving an area of about 0.54 hectares. On the occasions of the annual Lantern Festival on the 15th day of the first lunar month, the Bathing the Buddha Day (Shakyamuni Buddha's Birthday) on the eigth day of the fourth lunar month, the Dragon Boat Festival on the fifth day of the fifth lunar month and the empress dowager's birthday, performances were offered here. The general plan of the Qichun Garden shows that this complex was situated in a beautiful environment, with water on three sides, particularly the Back Lake to its north. Here one could watch the opera performances sitting indoors or enjoy the scenery going outdoors. It was one of the special venues in the Garden for entertainment and leisure activities.

The plan of the Zhanshi Yinglü Complex shows that it consisted primarily of a stage (fig. 126) and a viewing hall, which comprised the main hall called Zhanshi Yunlü Hall, the east side hall Yinyu Pavilion (Gem of a Poem Pavilion) and a west side hall that served only as a passage space with no spectator facilities.

The viewing hall was of modest scale. Since the Qichun Garden became the private residence of the empress dowager and the consort dowager in the Daoguang era, they were the main spectators of the drama productions there and therefore the seating area need not be very large, given that the retinue accompanying them to the performances was not as numerous as for the emperor. This group of buildings basically formed a symmetrical *siheyuan* courtyard, the only difference being the "ear hall" and gallery added between the main hall and the east side hall to facilitate communication between them. The ear hall was a service room with access to both the main hall and the gallery.

Fig. 126 Small stage at Zhanshi Yinglü Complex

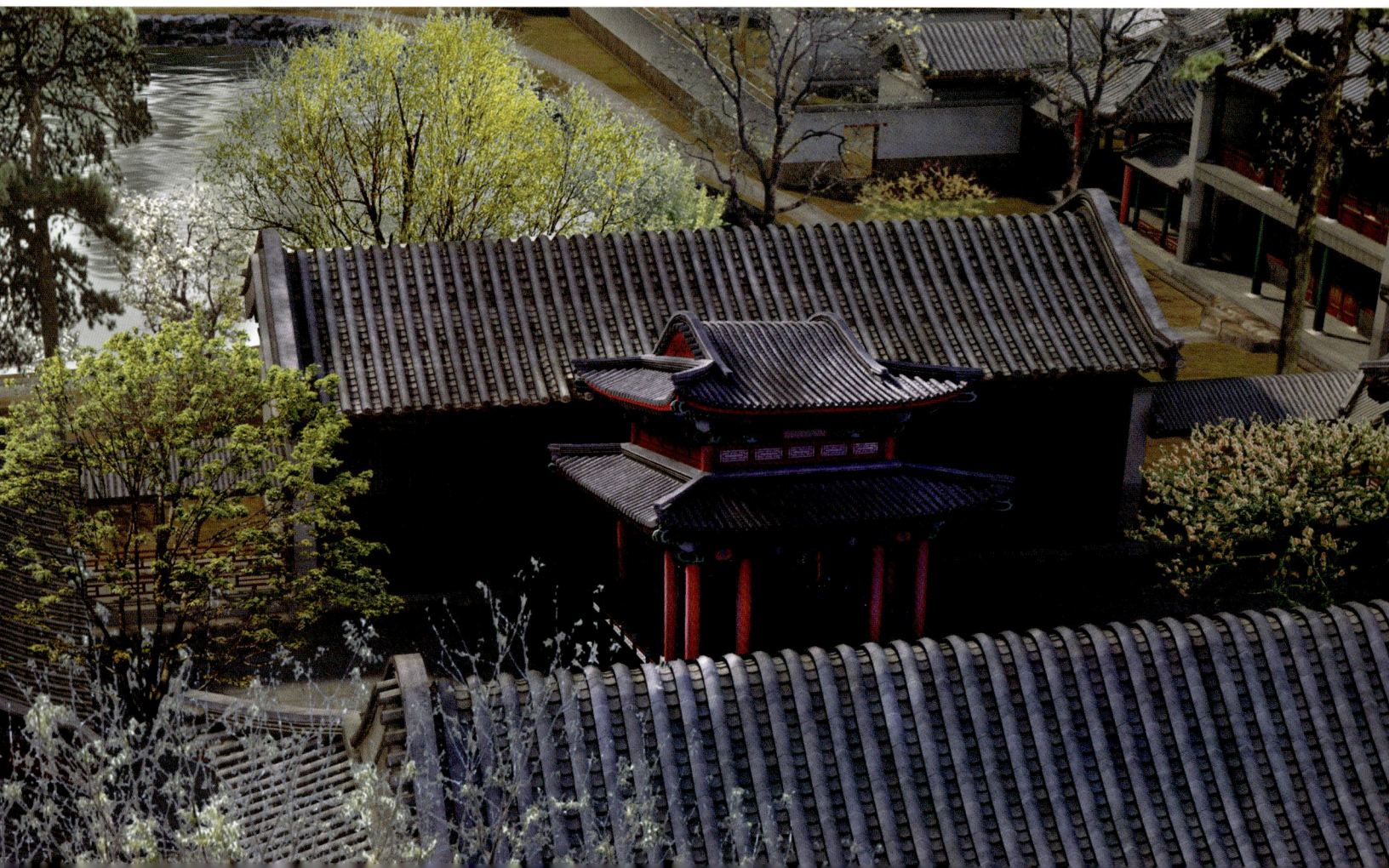

坦
坦
荡
荡

Tantan Dangdang Complex (Complex of Clear Conscience and Broad Mind)

The Tantan Dangdang Complex, located on the west shore of the Back Lake in the Yuan Ming Yuan, was one of the nine islands around the Back Lake. There was a large fish pond on the island. The Suxin Hall (Pure Mind Hall), Banmu Garden and Danhuai Hall lined the south side of the pond. In the middle of the pond stood the Guangfeng Jiyue Hall (Hall of Breeze and Moon after a Rain) with causeways in its east, west and north connecting it to shore, dividing the pond into three parts.

At the northwest corner of the pond a square kiosk sat in the water. At its southeast corner were the Zhiyu Pavilion (Know Your Fish Pavilion) and the Cuijing Study (Collection of Scenes Study) and at the southwest the Shuangjia Study (Double Beauty Study) (fig. 128 on pages 148 and 149). The small stage of the Banmu Garden was unique among the indoor stages of the Yuan Ming Yuan (fig. 127).

The buildings of the complex were widely spaced and the hierarchy of the buildings was obvious. When Qianlong stayed in the Yuan Ming Yuan, he often came here to feed the fish and to watch opera performances.

The main building Suxin Hall, five bays wide, featured a front porch and an overhanging gable roof and a three-bay veranda on the façade facing the pond with a hip-and-gable roof. The Suxin Hall held books for the emperor's perusal when he visited. Both the Banmu Garden building and the Danhuai Hall flanking the main hall were five bays wide; only, the bay size in these two buildings was somewhat reduced (fig. 129 on page 150). An L-shaped gallery extended north respectively from the Banmu Garden building and the Danhuai Hall, with the east gallery linking up the Zhiyu Pavilion with a pyramidal roof and the Cuijing Study with a hip-and-gable roof, and the west gallery connecting with the Shuangjia Study with a flat roof.

The small stage at the Banmu

Fig. 127 South view of Danhuai Hall, Suxin Hall, Banmu Garden

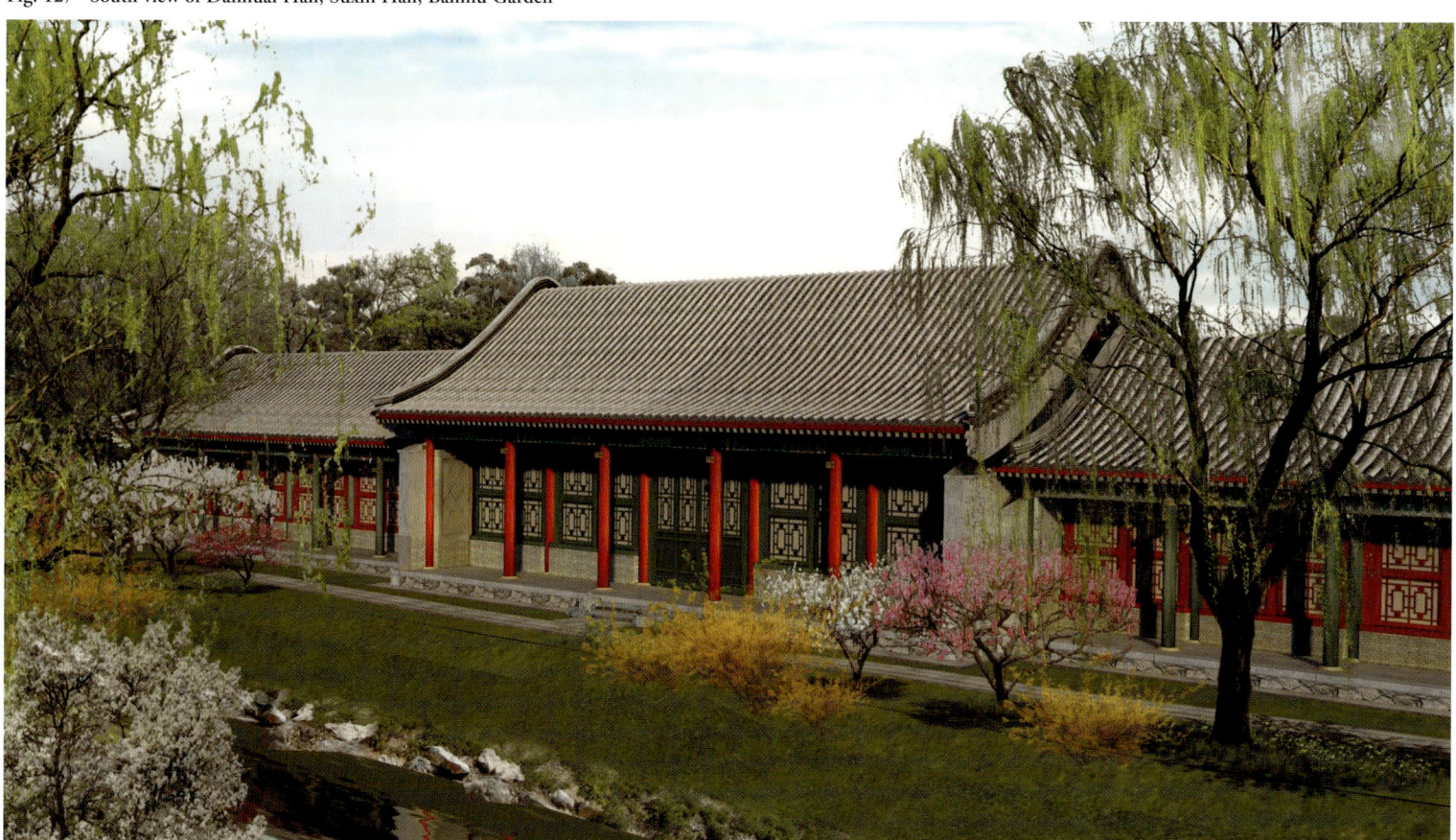

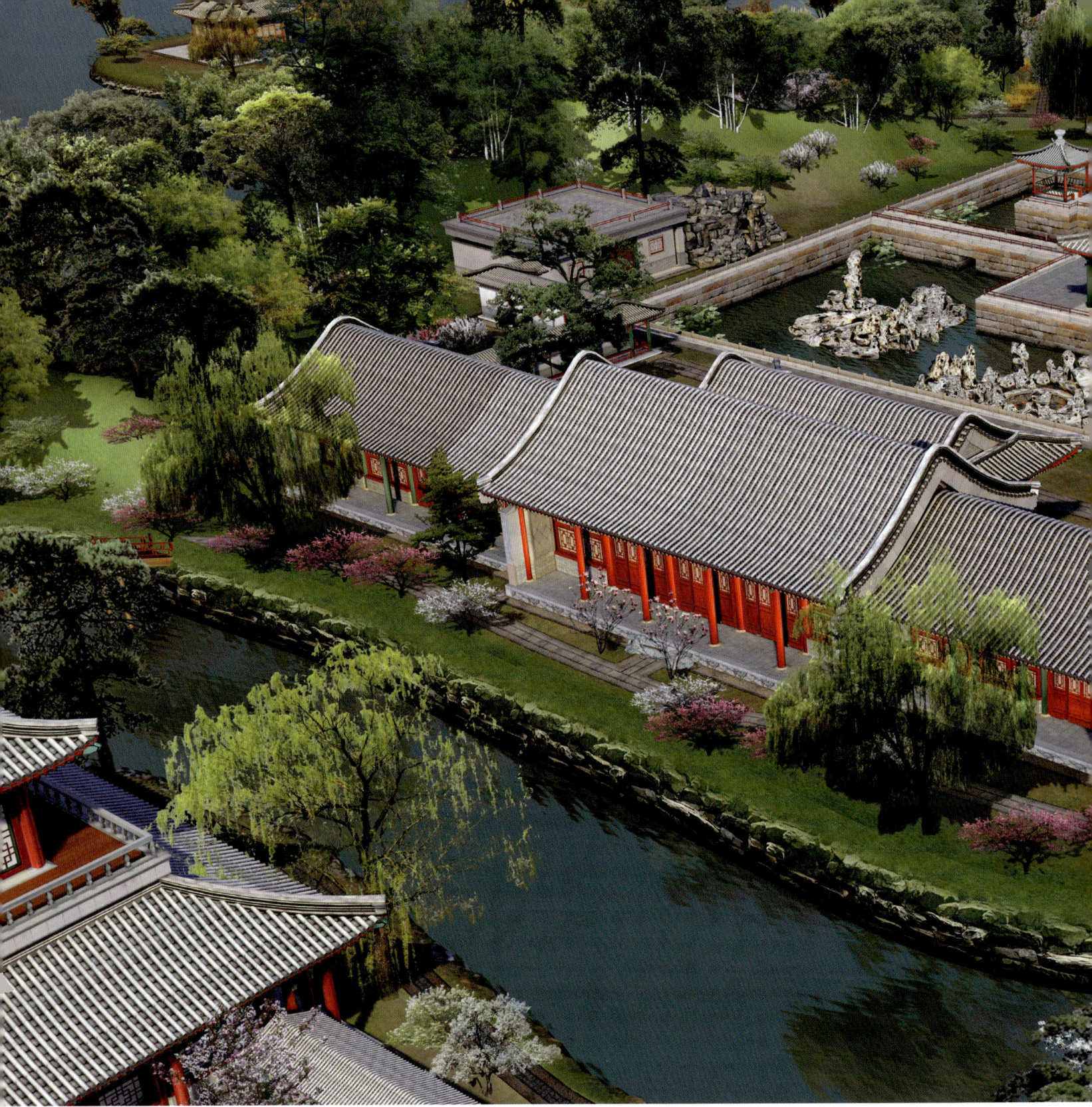

Fig. 128 Aerial view of Tantan Dangdang Complex

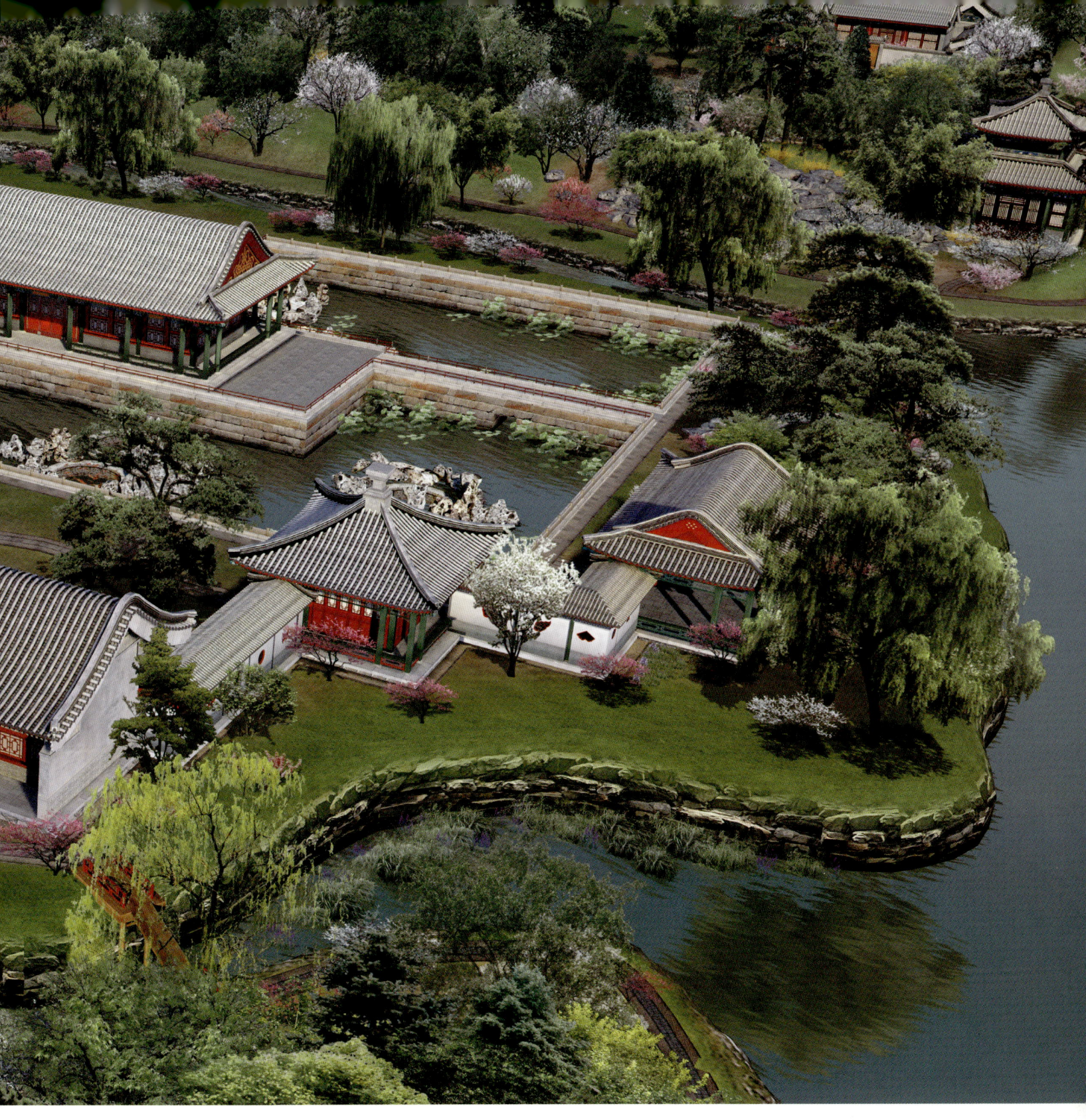

PART II SCENERY OF THE YUAN MING YUAN

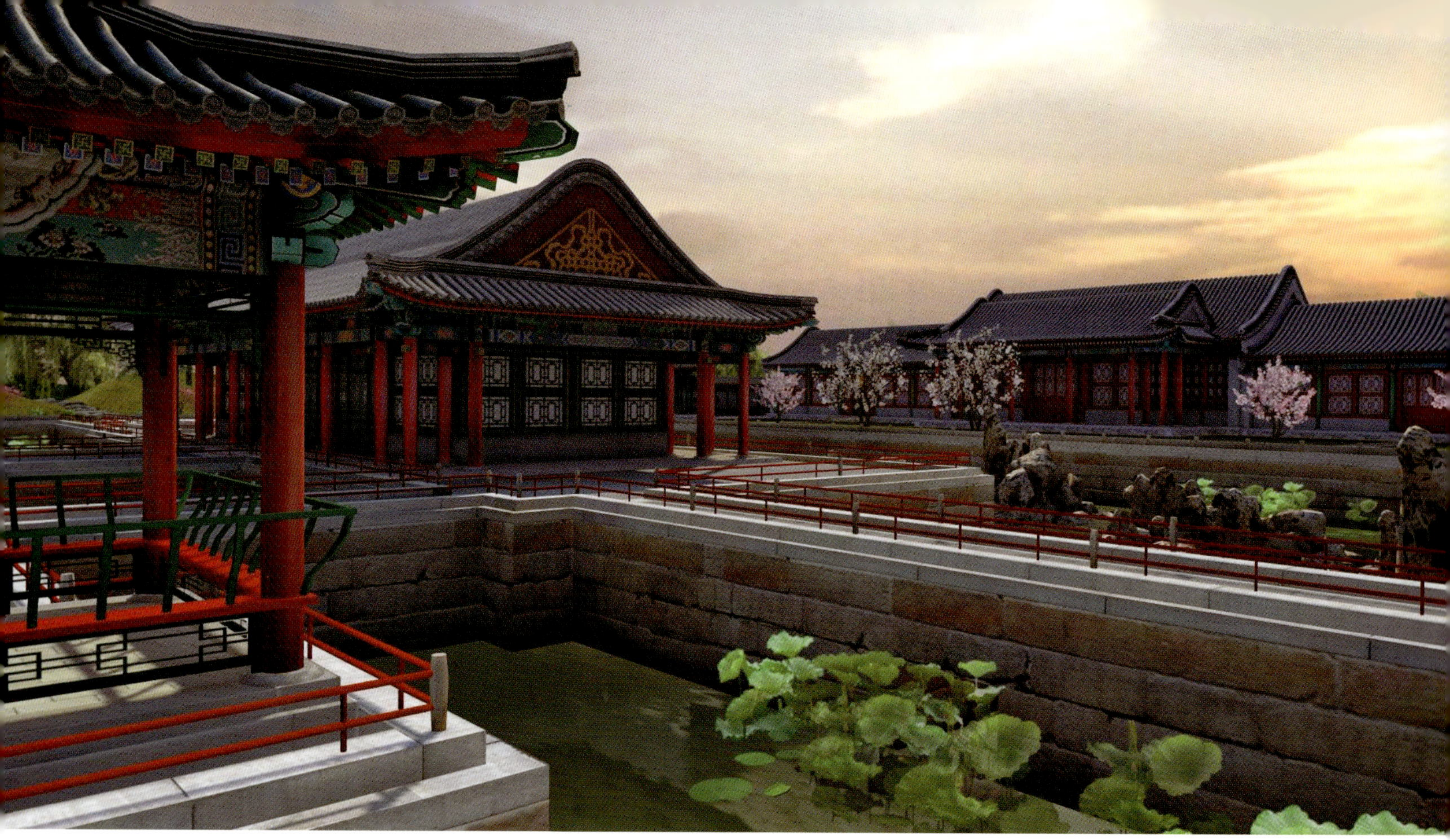

Fig. 129 Courtyard at north of Suxin Hall

Garden was very unique. It took the form of a small kiosk placed in the east end of a room (fig. 131). The throne from which the emperor watched the performance sat at the west end of the room (fig. 132). A second tier was built in the back of the throne to accommodate more seating for the spectators. The actors had to use a passageway between the stage and the gable wall to make their entrance. This small hall was elaborately decorated: at its south end stood a section of simulated bamboo fence as a semi-translucent partition; the ceiling was pasted with paper painted with a profusion of vines, giving the interior the feel of a small garden outdoors under a pergola trailing with vines, and suggesting the origin of the name of Banmu Garden. The small, intimate setting made for active interchanges between the spectators and the performers, an interesting feature.

In the Tantan Dangdang Complex ruins a number of remnants of the fish pond and of the buildings have been uncovered by archaeologists and afforded a glimpse of its past. The fish pond was lined with huge pieces of granite and had artificial hills in its midst. Some of these mock hills had water wells in them, where the fish could swim around or linger to escape summer heat and winter cold (fig. 130).

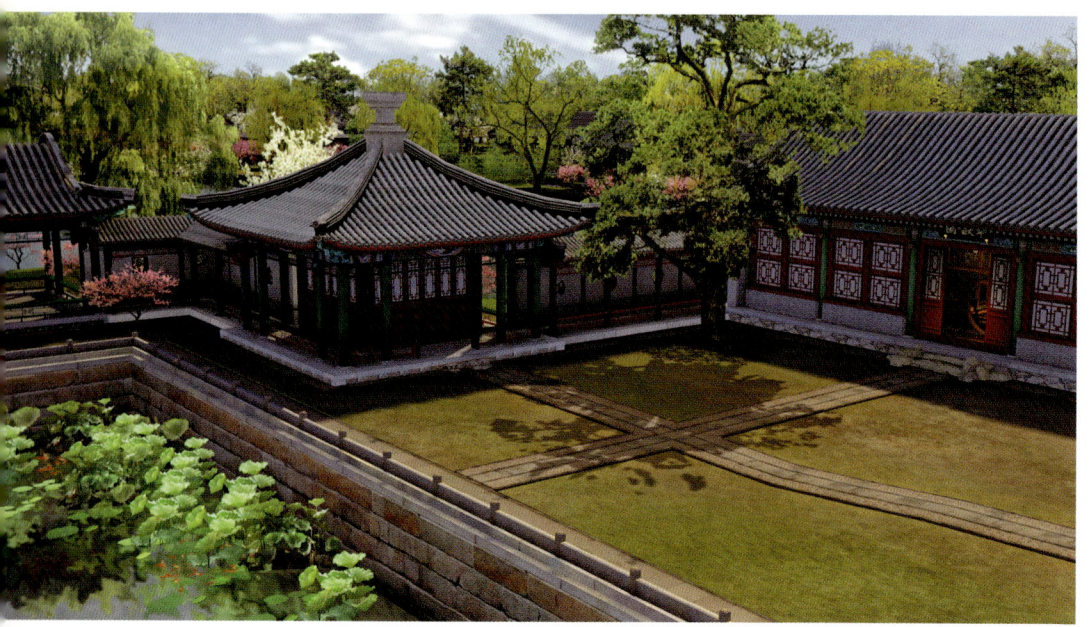

Fig. 130 View of Zhiyu Pavilion and Banmu Garden from the north courtyard

150   CHINA'S LOST IMPERIAL GARDEN

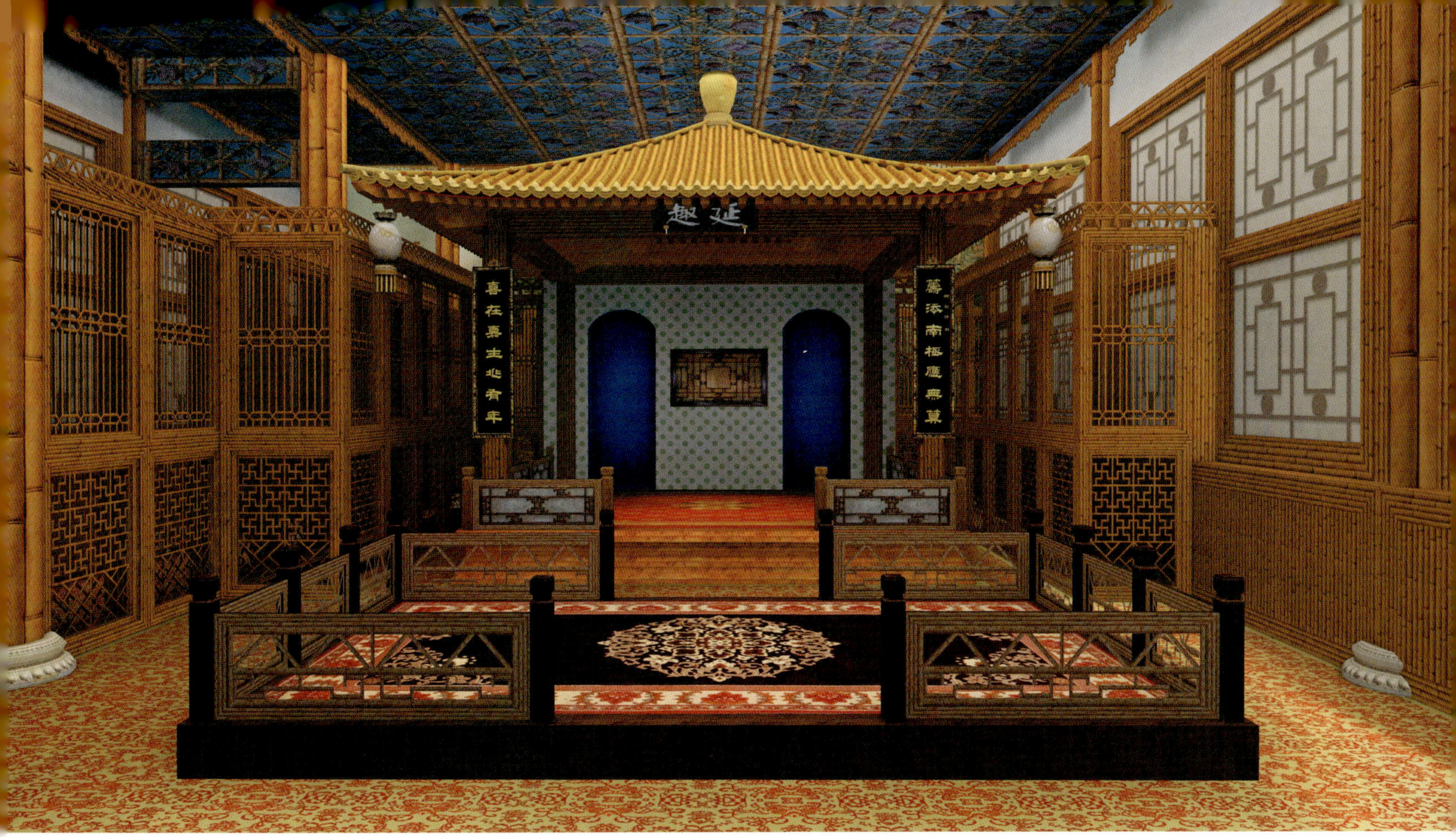

Fig. 131 Small indoor stage in Banmu Garden

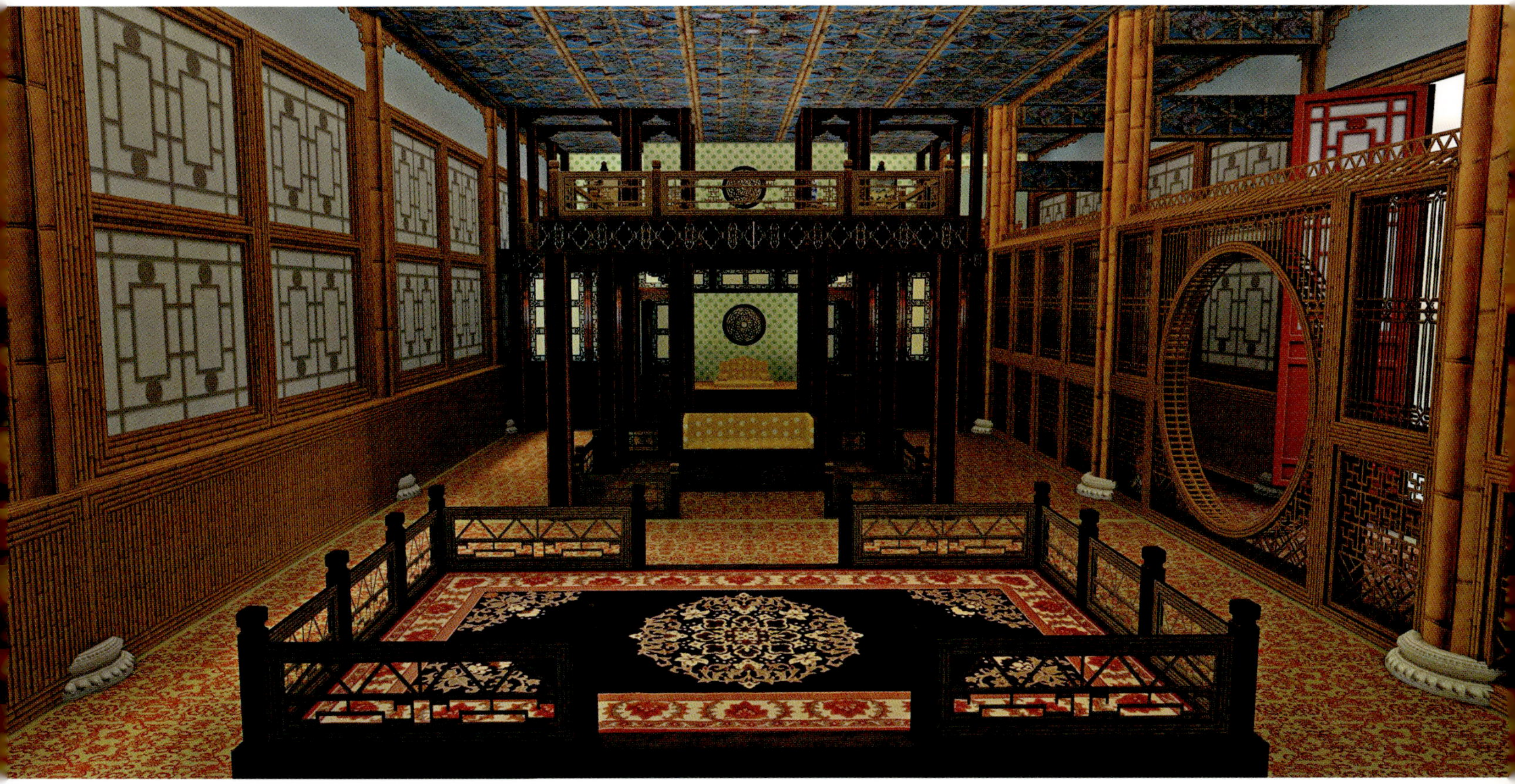

Fig. 132 Throne for indoor opera viewing in Banmu Garden

PART II SCENERY OF THE YUAN MING YUAN

萬方安和 Wanfang Anhe Complex (Complex of Universal Peace and Harmony)

The Wanfang Anhe Complex was situated west of the Nine Islands area of the Back Lake. It sat in a large, isolated pond. The building complex was a swastika in plan; it was built in the Yongzheng era (fig. 135). This building with an intriguing shape reflected the emperor's aesthetic vision and his hope for peace and harmony in his realm; the decor was richly varied with the small indoor stage attracting the most notice and interest.

To facilitate an explanation of the special features of the Wanfang Anhe Complex, this swastika-shaped building will be described in several sections (fig. 133):

(1) Section A: The south-facing, southeastern section of five bays surrounded by a gallery, called the Southeast Main Hall.

(2) Section B: the east-facing, northeastern section of five bays surrounded by a gallery.

(3) Section C: the west-facing, southwestern section of five bays surrounded by a gallery.

(4) Section D: the north-facing, northwestern section of five bays surrounded by a gallery.

(5) Section E: the 3-bay corridor from Section A to Section O (swastika center).

(6) Section F: the 3-bay corridor from Section D to Section O (swastika center).

(7) Section G: the 3-bay corridor from Section C to Section O (swastika center).

(8) Section H: the 3-bay corridor from Section B to Section O (swastika center).

(9) Section O: the center of the swastika, called the Middle Hall.

In traditional Chinese buildings hanging tablets were mostly placed above the door. Extant records show that there were four tablets hung outdoors here. The first, inscribed with the four characters *Wanfang Anhe*, was hung in the south-facing main hall in the southeast and gave the name of the complex. The second, inscribed with *Bixi Yidai* (Green Belt of a Stream), hung above the east-facing door of a room of Section B. The *Forty Scenes of the Yuan Ming Yuan* shows this long stream along the north-south running dike, with a stone bridge at its north end. This section was

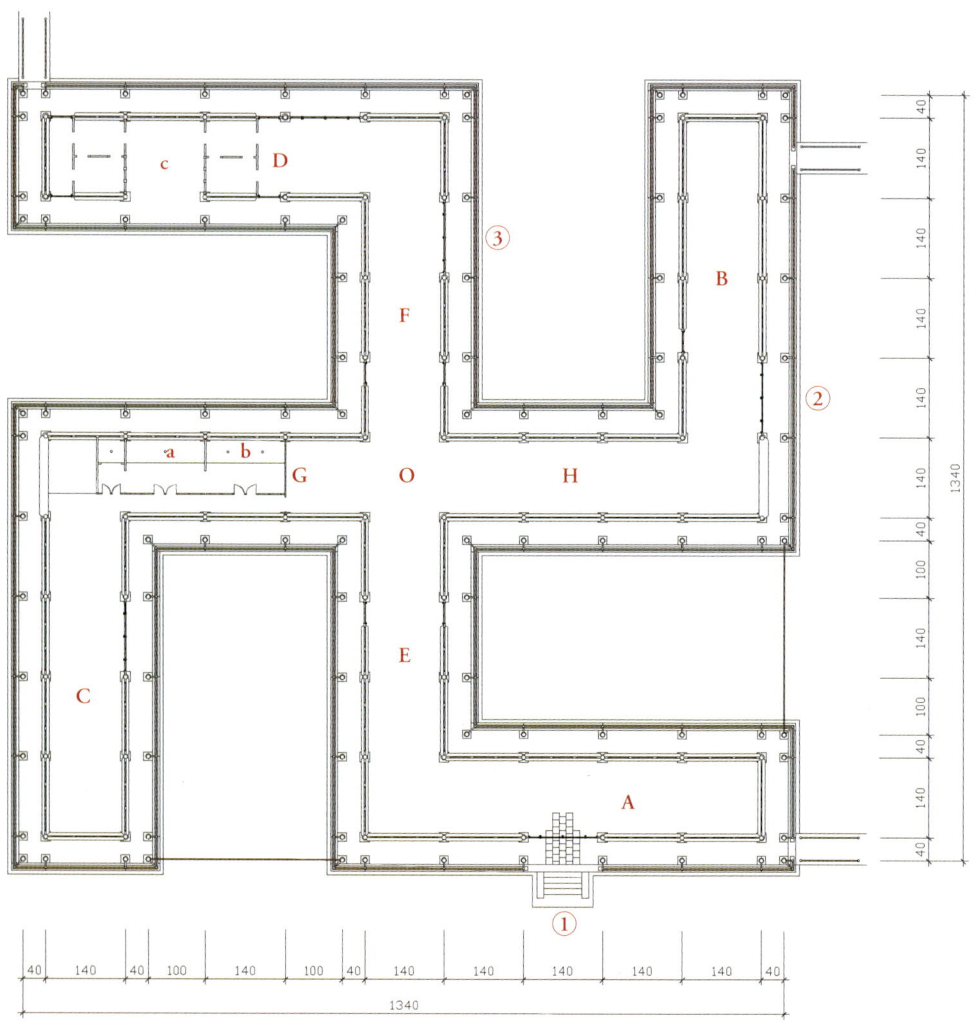

a. Emperor's throne
b. Viewing room for the use of the empress and other imperial consorts
c. Stage

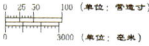

Fig. 133 Plan of Wanfang Anhe Complex

152 CHINA'S LOST IMPERIAL GARDEN

furnished with a triptych screen with the left and right panels at an angle and a throne from which to look out at the scenery. The third tablet, *Shenzhou Sandao* (Three Islands of Legend), hung outside the east-facing eaves of the second room from the north of Section F. The interior of the room was furnished as two levels; such a setup was called a *xian lou*, meaning a room inside a room. The fourth tablet, *Guan Miaoyin* (Looking at the Wonderful Voice), presumably hung on the west-facing façade of Section C, opposite a hill with a stream and a waterfall[1] that one could view from a window in the section.

The other five tablets were all hung indoors. A plan kept by the Imperial Office of Architecture Design[2] helps further our understanding of the locations of the interior hanging tablets, the decor and furnishings. It was specifically recorded that a tablet inscribed with *Sifang Ningjing* (Universal Calm) hung in the Middle Hall (or Section O).

Of special interest in the interior space of the Wanfang Anhe Complex were the small stage and a viewing area across the water (fig. 134). The small stage was located in the second room from the west in Section D; the stage was flanked by auxiliary stages and spaces for actors waiting to enter or entering and exiting. The stage had no windows but only a guardrail on its south side, although the auxiliary stages had windows on their south sides. The seating areas were located in Section G. The second room from the west was the viewing hall for the emperor and was furnished with a throne and a screen at its south end. The third room, with a couch at its north side by the window, was for the use of the empress and other imperial consorts. Watching performances across the water is like watching before a standalone stage in that in both cases there is an outdoors space separating the players from the spectators, except that the in the former mode of viewing the spectators get the interesting bonus of also seeing the reflections of the actors in the water.

Archaeological digging is in progress at the ruins of the swastika building.

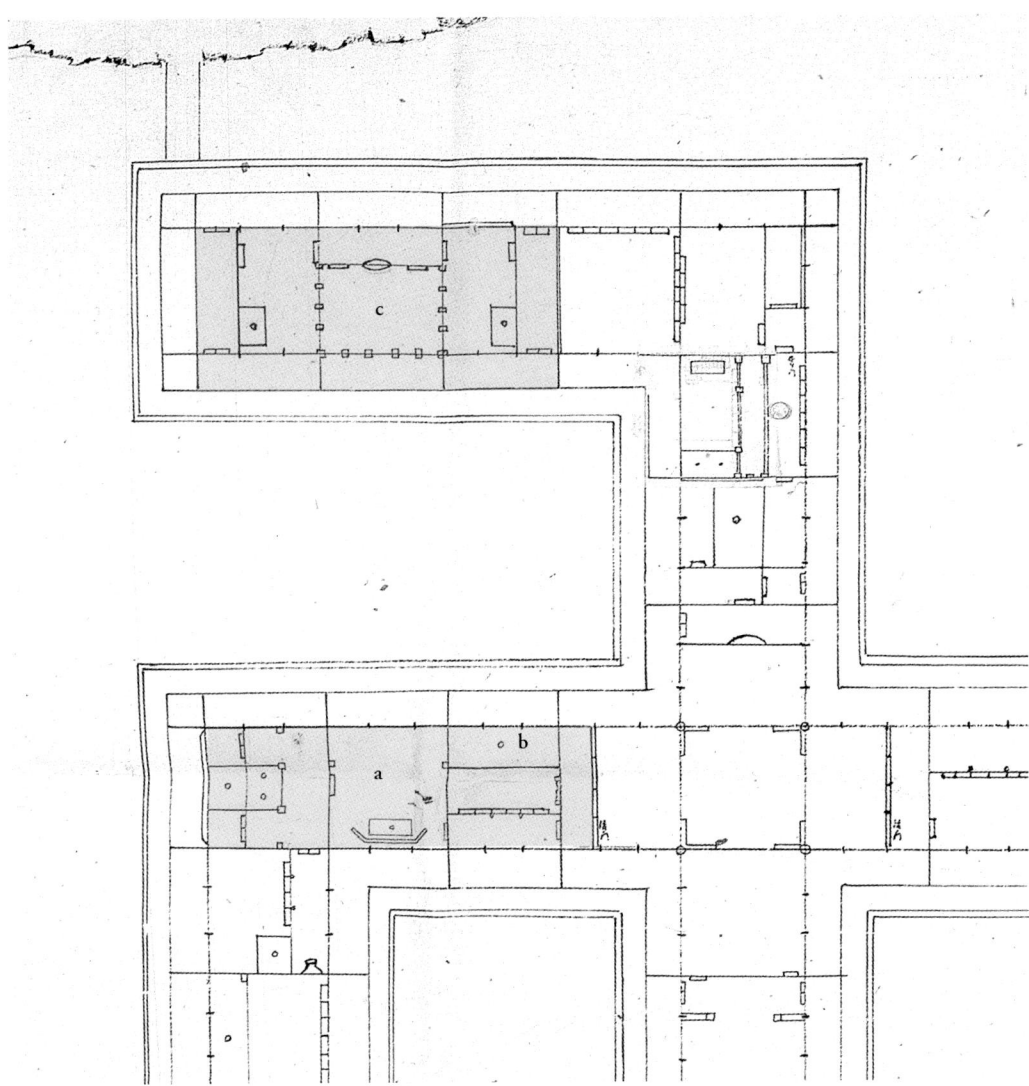

Fig. 134 Plan of the small stage

---

1 Reference was made to "a room facing the waterfall in the swastika building" in *Yuan Ming Yuan*, compiled by the First Historical Archives of China, published by Shanghai Ancient Books Publishing House, May 1991.
2 This plan was post-Qianlong, but could still yield important information.

PART II SCENERY OF THE YUAN MING YUAN   153

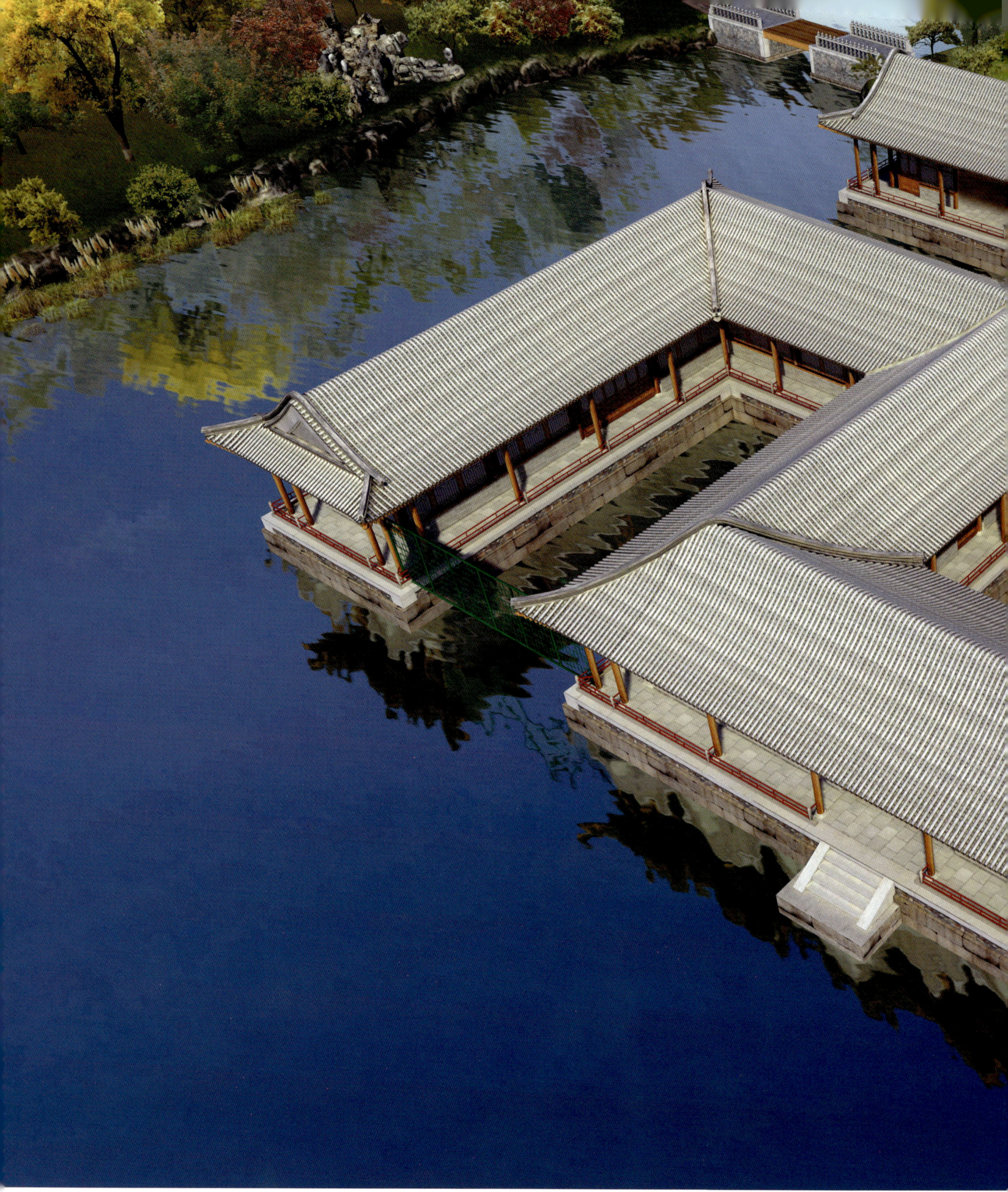

Fig. 135 Wanfang Anhe Complex

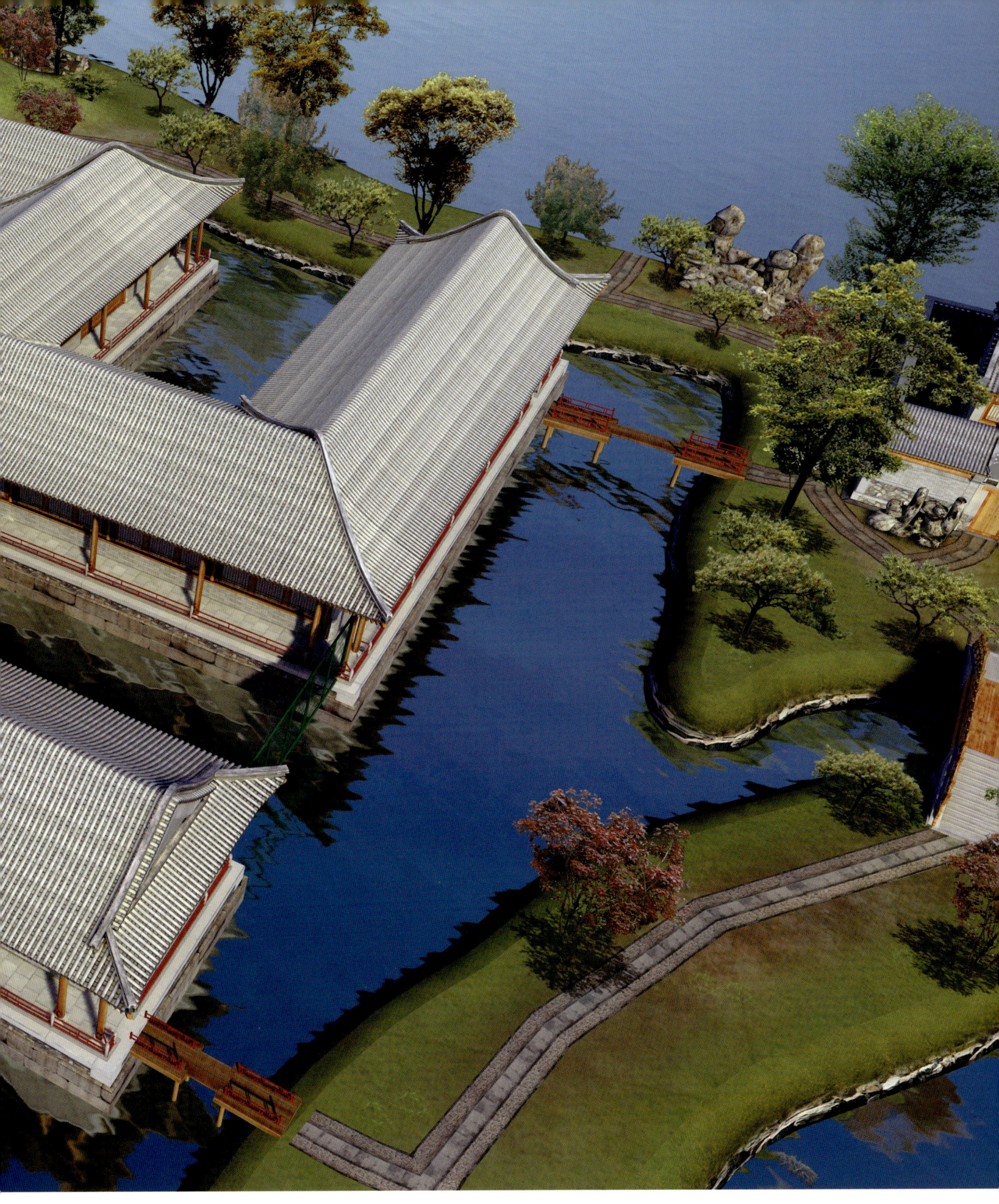

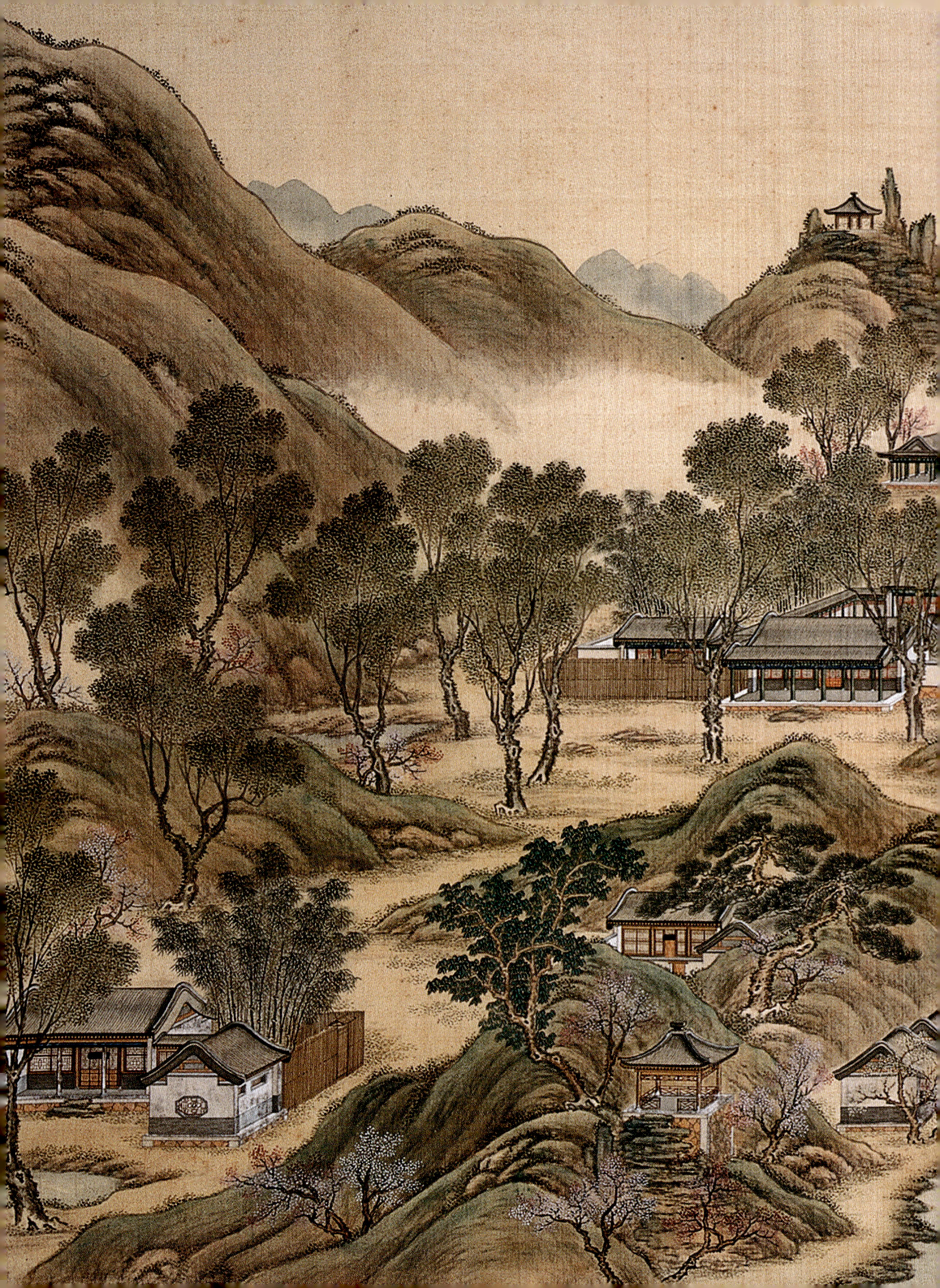

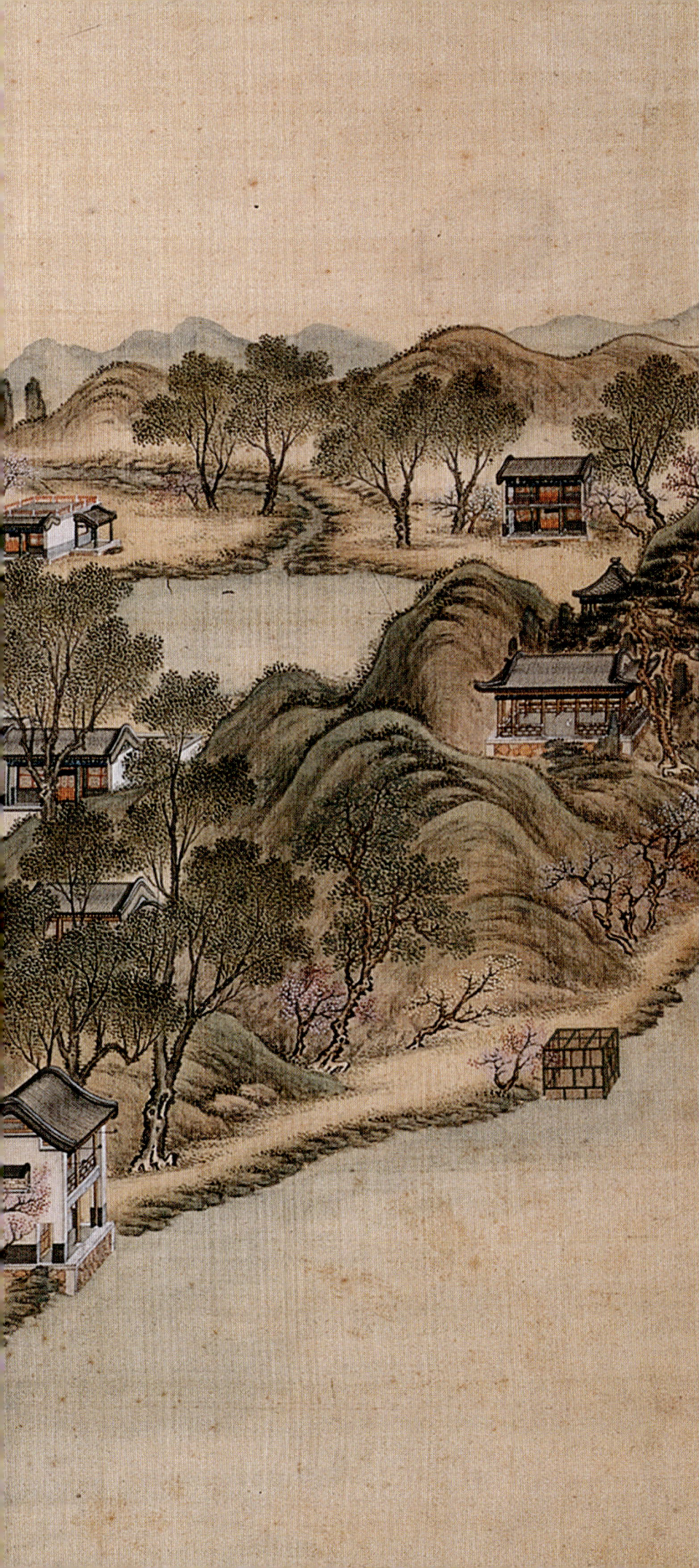

CHAPTER XII
Landscape Architecture

There were several types of landscape architecture in the Yuan Ming Yuan. The first type included those complexes with a special metaphorical significance, such as the fairyland-evoking Fanghu Shengjing and Pengdao Yaotai complexes. The second type covered those with a profound cultural dimension and an inspirational message, such as the Kuoran Dagong Complex (fig. 136) and the Lianxi Lechu Complex. The third type consisted of those well situated to view the beautiful scenery outside the Yuan Ming Yuan, such as the Jiexiu Mountain House and the Xifeng Xiuse Complex (Complex of Elegant Color of the Western Peaks). The fourth type involved those vistas and complexes that emulated the scenery and landscape of a certain location, such as those modeled on the Jiangnan gardens south of the Yangtze River. Some illustrative examples follow.

Fig. 136 Painting of Kuoran Dagong Complex from the album *Forty Scenes of the Yuan Ming Yuan*

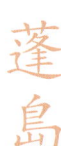

Pengdao Yaotai Complex (Complex of the Jade Terrace of Paradise Island)

The Pengdao Yaotai Complex was situated in the middle of the Lake of Happiness, the largest lake in the Yuan Ming Yuan (fig. 138). It was built in the Yongzheng era and named Penglai Island, which consisted of three islands of varying sizes in emulation of the three sacred mountains in the East Sea—Penglai, Fangzhang and Yingzhou. The largest of the three was in the middle; to its northwest lay the West Island, which was the next in size, and the smallest island sat in the southeast of the largest island.

The three islands were connected by bridges. There were buildings on the islands: an enclosed courtyard compound on the island in the middle and a few buildings dotting the west (fig. 137) and the east island. The entrance gate hall, called Jingzhong Pavilion, of the courtyard compound on the middle island was three bays wide and the main hall, called Pengdao Yaotai Hall, was seven bays wide. "In front of the hall at its east is the Changjin Building (Venting of Feelings Building) and at its west the Shenzhou Sandao building. It is flanked on its east by the Sui'an Room, and on its west by the Riri Ping'an Baohaoyin Pavilion (Pavilion of Good Tidings of Peace Everyday)," "Crossing a bridge at the southeast of the Pengdao Yaotai Hall, one reaches the east island, on which stands the kiosk called the Yinghai Sacred Mountain, and crossing a bridge at the northwest one arrives on the north island, on which stands a courtyard compound with a three-bay main hall."[1] There were a number of secondary buildings on the big island. The architecture of this group of buildings was distinguished by rich and varied forms and bright colors.

Legend had it that in the eastern seas of China were to be found the sacred mountains, that had gripped the imagination of the people of antiquity, "the three sacred mountains are reportedly found in the sea of Bohai, not far from shore and once visited by humans ... where the palaces were

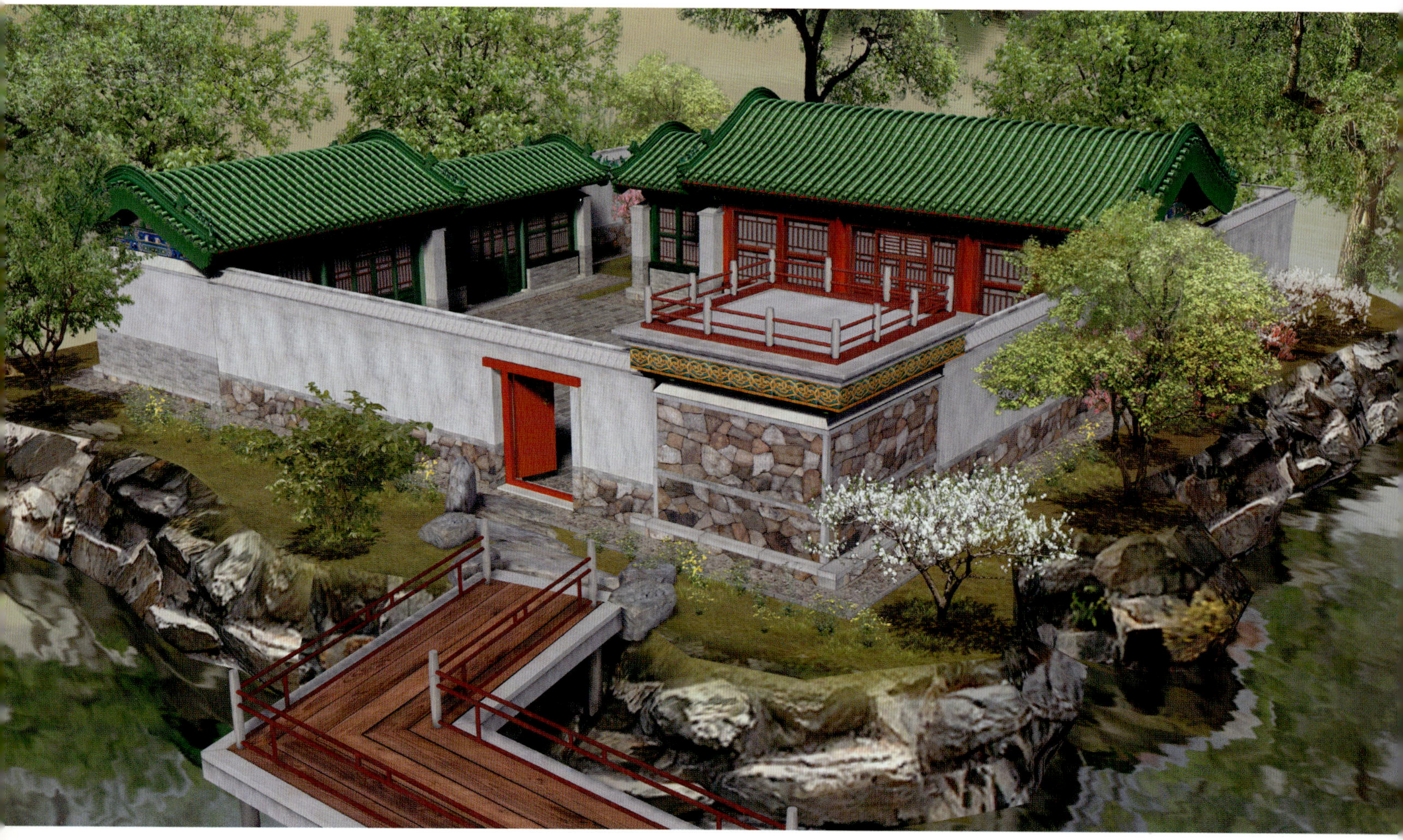

Fig. 137 Courtyard compound on west island

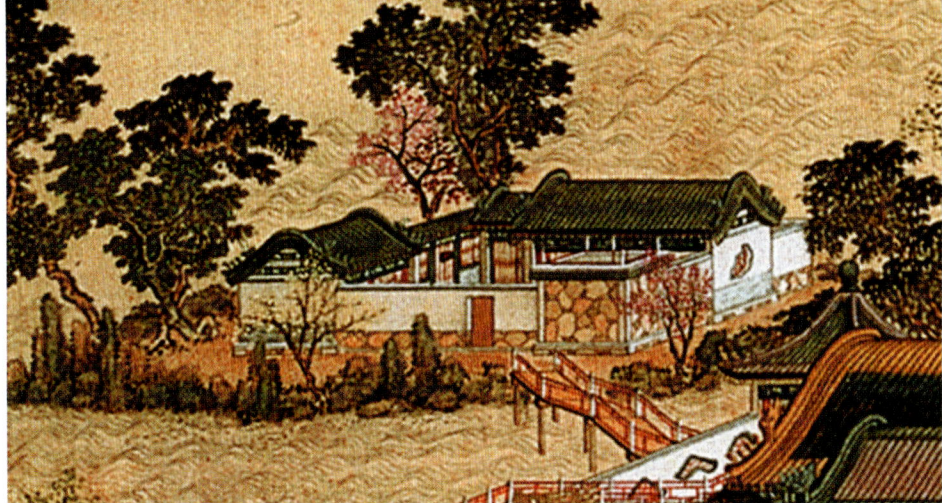

Fig. 138 Courtyard compound on west land from the album of *Forty Scenes of the Yuan Ming Yuan*

made from gold and platinum, and where they had seen the immortals and their immortality pills."[2] Shihuangdi, emperor of the Qin dynasty, once sent "Xu Fu out to sea to search for the immortals … and to find the legendary longevity drug."[3] The landscape of the three holy mountains in the sea had subsequently found favor with the emperors of succeeding dynasties, although later emperors did not follow Shihuangdi's example in looking for the immortals' immortality pills but only consistently followed the practice of assimilating the landscape of the legendary three mountains in the sea into their imperial park, hence the reincarnation in the Pengdao Yaotai Complex in the Yuan Ming Yuan. This immortals' abode on earth was perfected by the craftsmen of the imperial garden to the great satisfaction of Emperor Qianlong.

The Pengdao Yaotai's fairyland quality was partly attributable to its location in the midst of a large expanse of water and the consequent sharp contrast between the tiny size of the islands and the vastness of the Lake of Happiness in which they were situated. The visual distance from shore to islands was 200 to 300 meters and the islands were so miniscule that in the early morning light the islands would look like a mirage to a beholder on the lake shore and evoke an immortals' abode in the ethereal sphere.

Contributing to the fairyland atmosphere was the unusual architecture of the buildings on the big island, which consisted of palatial halls, multi-story buildings, kiosks and galleries of varying sizes in a clear hierarchical order judiciously arranged in the grounds. Jingzhong Pavilion, the entry gate in the south, of three bays and surmounted by a flush gable roof, was flanked by five-bay buildings with an overhanging gable roof on either side. To attract attention to the three-bay gate hall in the middle, a small superstructure of only one bay was erected on its roof, which was akin to the eye added by a painter to his unfinished dragon that gave it instant life (fig. 139). The Pengdao Yaotai Hall at the center of the big island was the largest building of the group. In order to reduce the mass of the building, this hall of seven bays was surmounted by a double round-ridge roof; it had a five-bay front porch with a hip-and-gable roof. The two-storied building called Changjin Building at the east of the big island commanded an exquisite view of the scenery in the distance. There were also the flat-roofed Shenzhou Sandao and the hexagonal kiosk Yinghai Sacred Mountain. The architectural variety and the lavish colors dazzled the eyes. All the roofs were covered with yellow, green and blue glazed tiles; different colors were used for the ridges and the eaves than for the roof surface and there was a varied permutation of color schemes in the complex, creating a striking effect of a lavish palace complex. With the enhancement of the artificial hills and the pines, the whole scene evoked an immortals' abode. In his *Eight Odes to Pengdao Yaotai*,[4] Qianlong elaborated on the beauty of this fairyland on earth and revealed some details about its architecture, for example, the use of glass panes for the windows that "drew in myriad vistas," jade screens in the rooms and the gilt bird on the rooftop serving as a weather vane.

The Changjin Building was a library at the Pengdao Yaotai Complex. Qianlong liked to go up the building to compose poetry to give vent to his feelings. An emperor's ability to freely vent his feelings did not depend on the scenery, even in a paradise on earth!

The Pengdao Yaotai Hall was a venue in the imperial garden for viewing waterside scenery and water activities; every year Emperor Qianlong brought the empress dowager here to watch the dragon boat race, with "heavenly music" playing in the air.

---

1 *Rixia Jiuwen Kao*, Volume 82.
2 Ban Gu: *History of the Former Han Dynasty* (206 BC–220 AD).
3 *Records of the Grand Historian*, Volume 118.
4 *Yuzhi Shi*, by Emperor Qianlong, Book III, Volume 74.

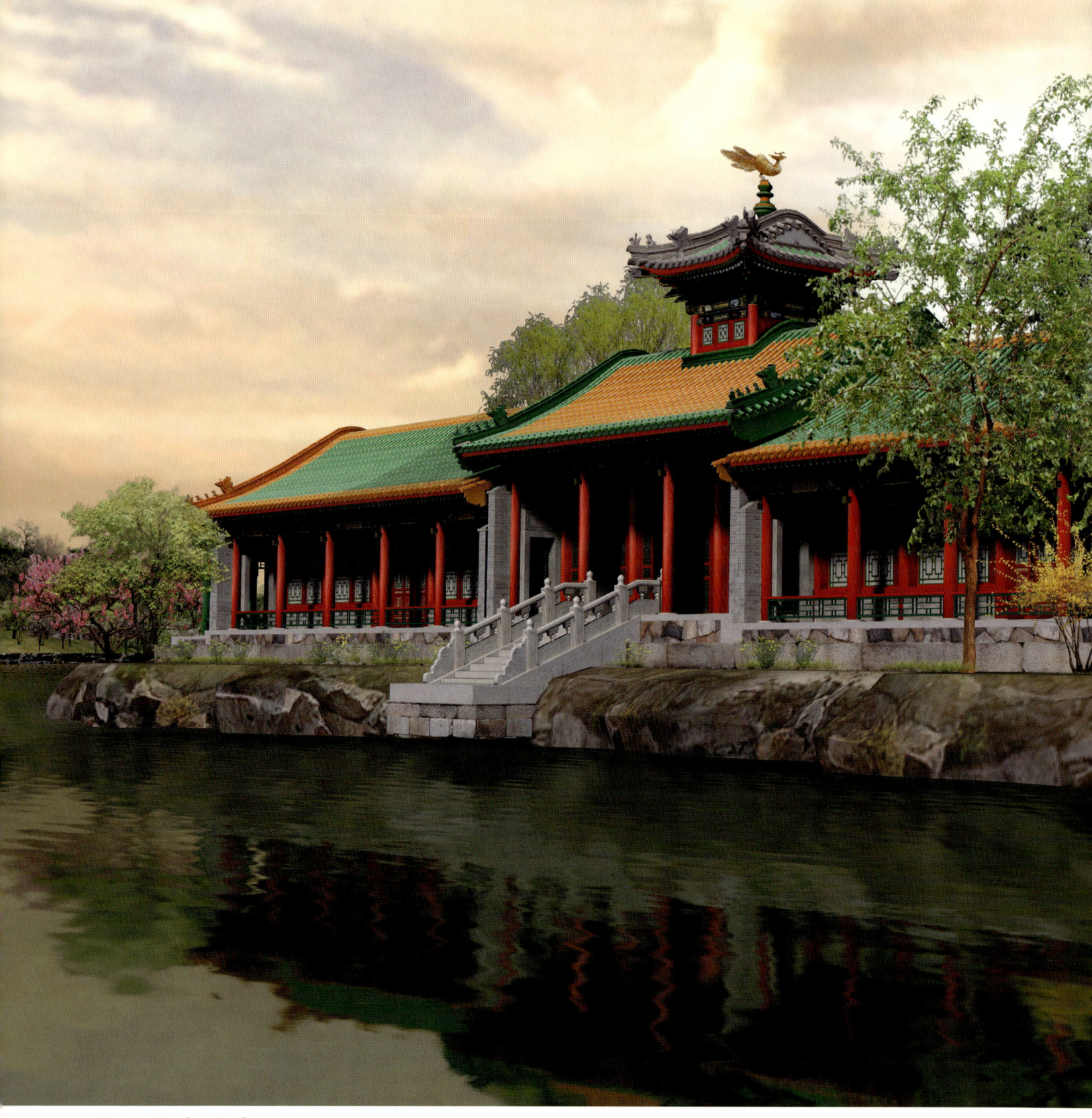

Fig. 139   Jingzhong Pavilion

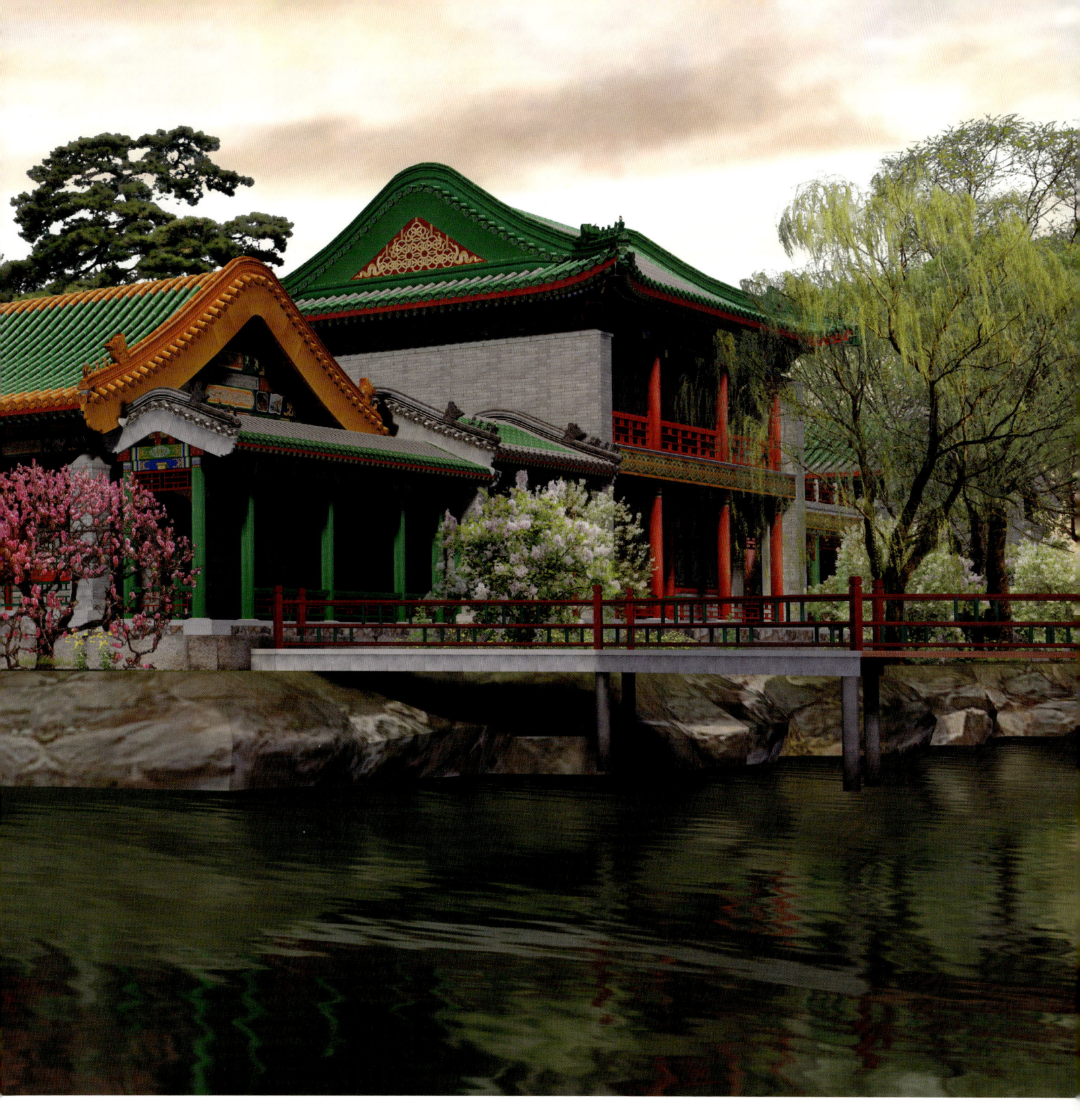

PART II SCENERY OF THE YUAN MING YUAN

方壺勝境 Fanghu Shengjing Complex (Complex of the Beautiful Scene of the Square Pot)

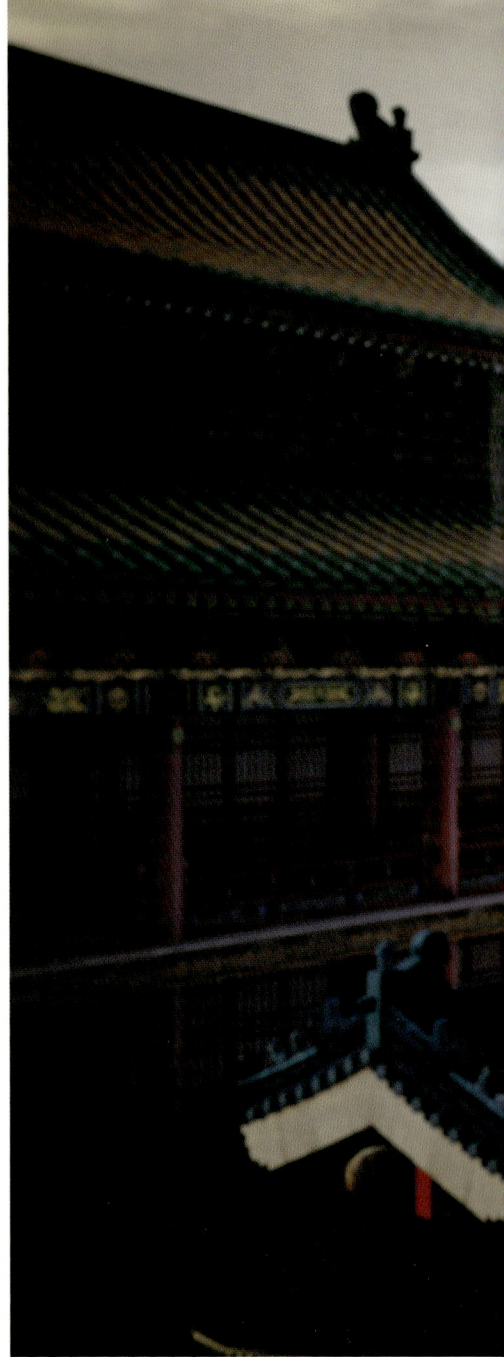

The Fanghu Shengjing Complex, built in the third year of the Qianlong era (1738), was located on the north shore of a small lake in the northeast of the Lake of Happiness and north of the Hanxu Langjian Complex (Complex of the Vast Empty Clear Mirror). The complex consisted of nine two-storied buildings and three kiosks and pavilions; some of the buildings extended well out over the water. It was one of the groups of buildings constructed on a grandiose scale in the Yuan Ming Yuan. Here the traditional layout of courtyard compounds was abandoned: there were three rows of buildings from front to back, each row consisting of three buildings standing side by side. The first row of buildings came up to the pond, its main hall Yichun Hall facing south, while the Jinqi Building and the Feicui Building (Jade Building) at its left and right facing east and west respectively; the three buildings were connected by galleries running left and right and turning south to connect with the two kiosks out on the water called "Huiyuan" and "Jirui." Crossing a three-arch stone bridge from the Yichun Hall, one came to the kiosk on water called Yingxun Pavilion. The second row of buildings had at its center the Huiluan Hall, flanked by Zixia Building and Biyun Building (Building of Azure Clouds). The third row of buildings had at its center the Qionghua Building, flanked by Qianxiang Hall and Wanfu Pavilion, which were connected by a gallery (fig. 140).

These buildings all adopted the style of official structures of the Qing dynasty. In an indication of the high ranking given to this complex, it comprised nine two-storied buildings and three kiosks, with covered walkways above ground level linking up the buildings. Seven buildings projected double-eave hip-and-gable roofs. Two pavilions on the water were cruciform in plan and consequently featured a cross-ridge roof on the upper tier and the verandas on four sides were topped by hip-and-gable roofs; the kiosk Yingxun Pavilion at the forefront was surmounted by a double-eave pyramidal roof. No comparable building complex could be found in the world.

Another distinguishing mark of this complex was its resplendent colors: all the roofs were covered with yellow, green, blue and purple, and other colored glazed tiles in vivid contrast with the red of the wooden pillars and beams, and doors and windows. Glazed tiles were not normally used in the buildings of the Yuan Ming Yuan. The few that did use them, such as the Hongci Yonghu and the Pengdao Yaotai complexes, employed only one or two colors. Only the Fanghu Shengjing Complex boasted glazed tiles in seven colors. Every roof here had a two-tone combination and the colors differed from building to building. Some had roof surfaces covered with yellow tiles and ridges and eaves covered with green ones, others with green surface and yellow trim and still others had blue or purple surfaces with yellow ridges and eaves. The combinations were myriad and helped create an atmosphere of a mountain inhabited by immortals with fabulous buildings. Hence Qianlong's observation that "if the palaces of legend were made of gold and platinum, what's so different from the human world? That kind of fairyland is right here, why go far for it? Therefore I name this place Fanghu (one of the three holy mountains of legend)."[1]

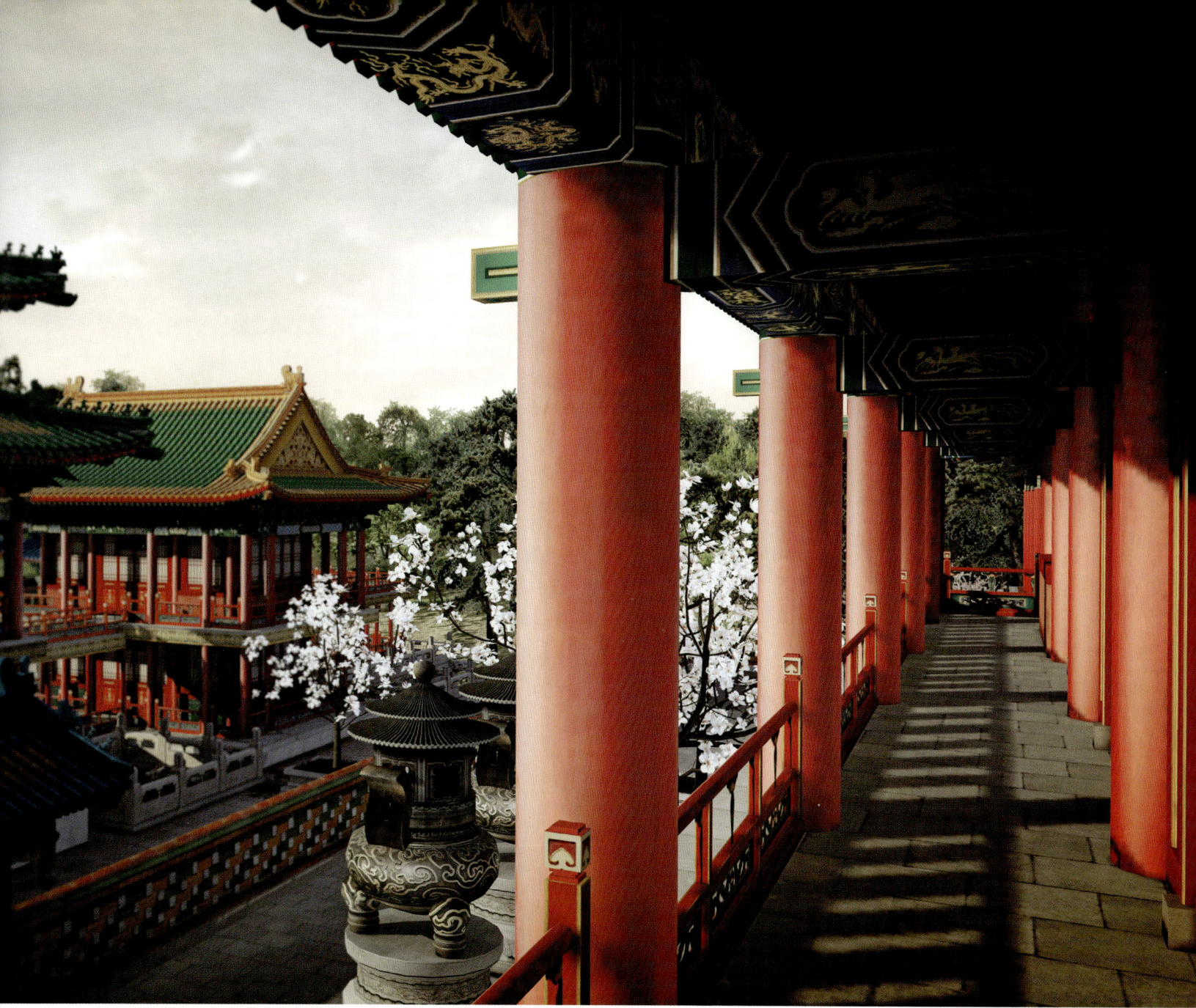

Fig. 140　Interior of gallery on second story of Qionghua Building

The siting of this largest building complex was an exception to the norm. Instead of being built on the shore of the largest lake—the Lake of Happiness—in the Yuan Ming Yuan, it was constructed next to a medium-sized pond and was separated from the Lake of Happiness by a range of low earthen hills. Through a gap in the hills, riders on a boat cruising on the Lake of Happiness would be able to descry a corner of these fabulous buildings, which tantalizingly revealed their charm like a *pipa*-playing noble lady half veiling her face. The Fanghu Shengjing Complex was situated on the north shore of this small water body that represented a northern finger of the Lake of Happiness; at its east stood a group of smaller buildings called Ruizhu Palace. At its west were scattered a few kiosks, bridges and waterside pavilions and a Three Ponds Reflecting the Moon à la West Lake, with three small stone jars in the water and kiosks and waterside pavilions around them. These two groups of buildings were much dwarfed in scale by the Fanghu Shengjing Complex proper.

Emperor Qianlong more than once praised the beauty of this fairyland-like building complex since its completion in quite a few poems. Regrettably the "fairyland-like palaces built with gold and platinum" are no more today; only remnants of the hard-to-burn stone terraces are left for people's sad and nostalgic contemplation (figs. 141, 142).

1　*Rixia Jiuwen Kao*, Volume 81.

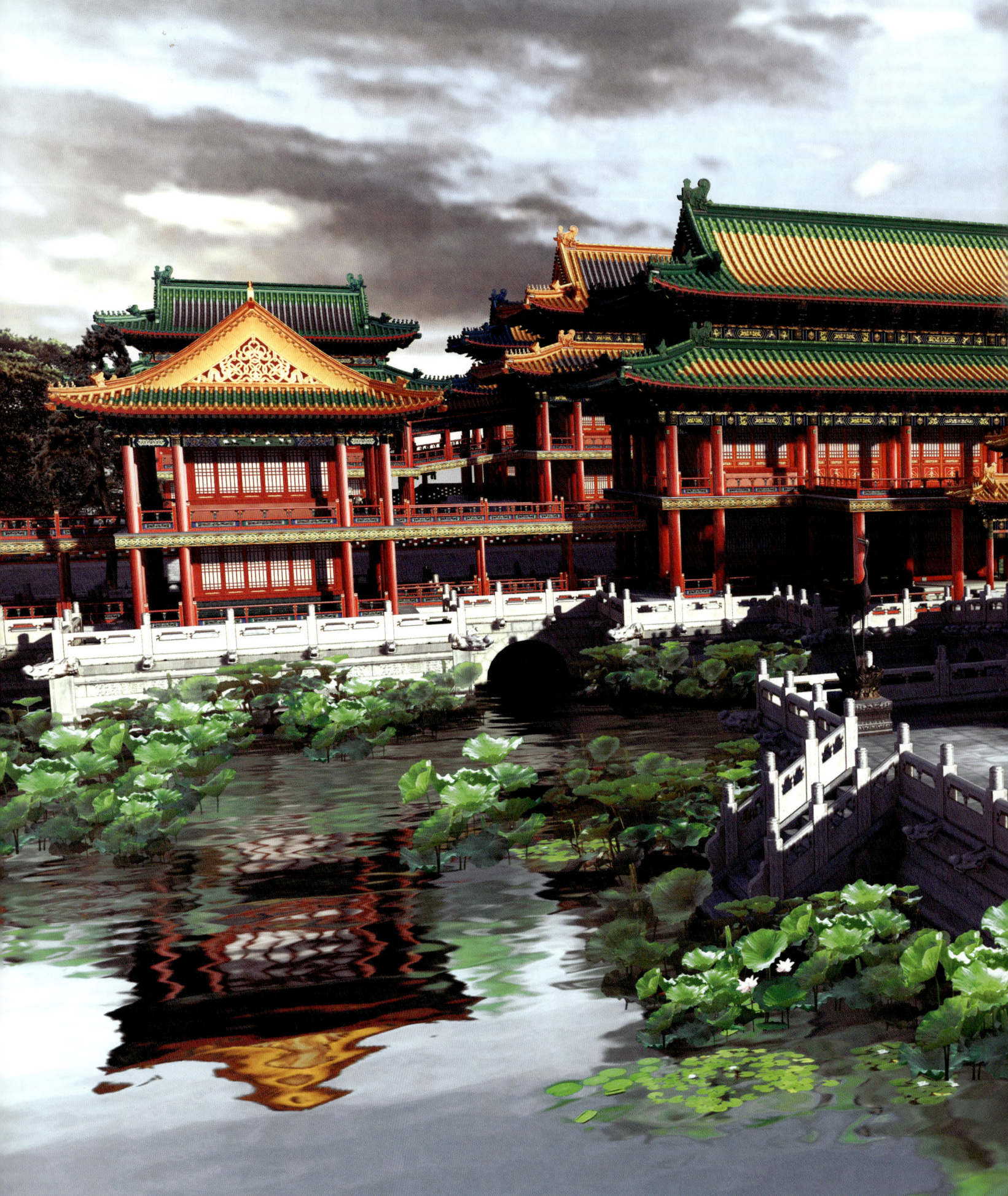

Fig. 141 Fanghu Shengjing Complex

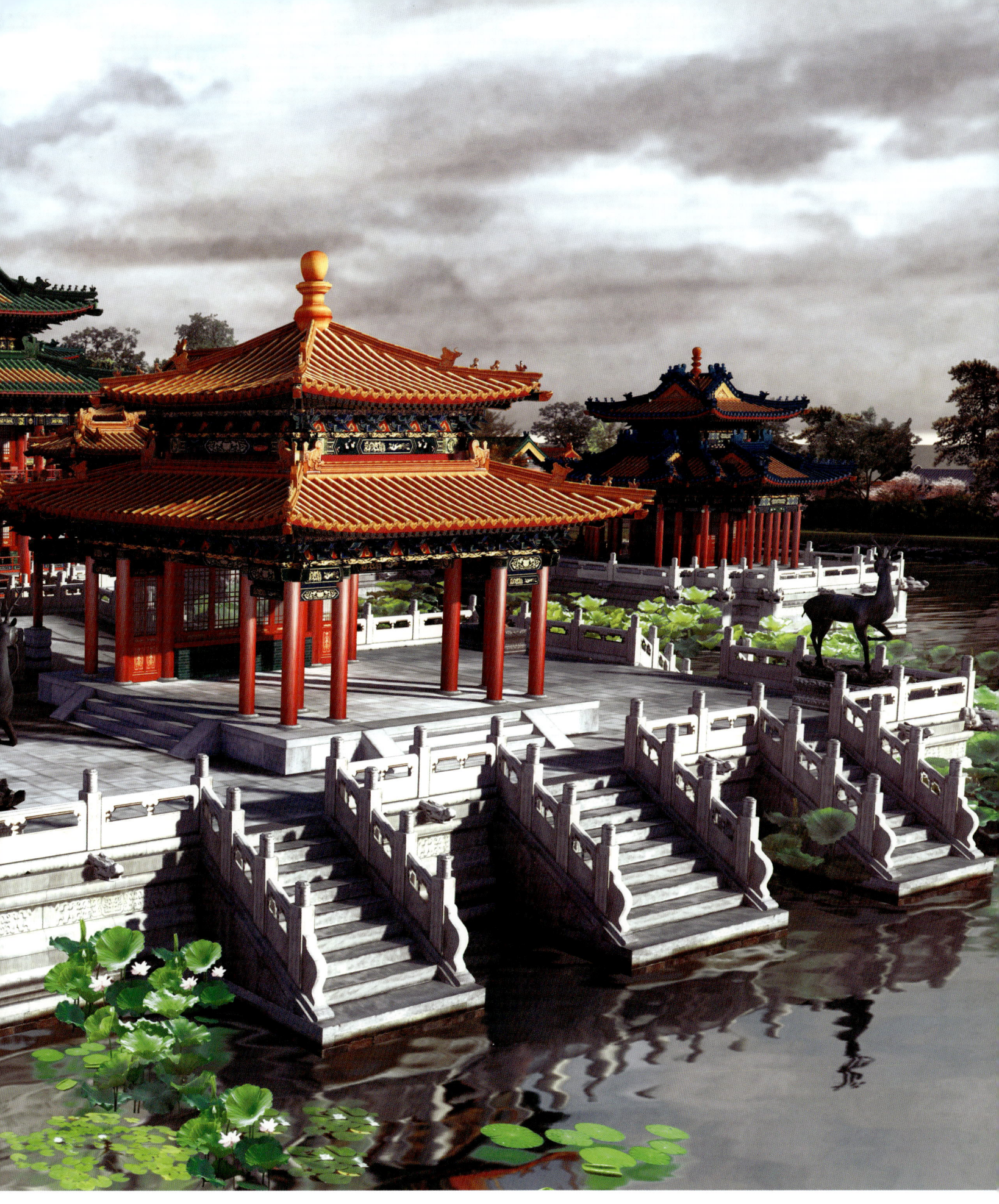

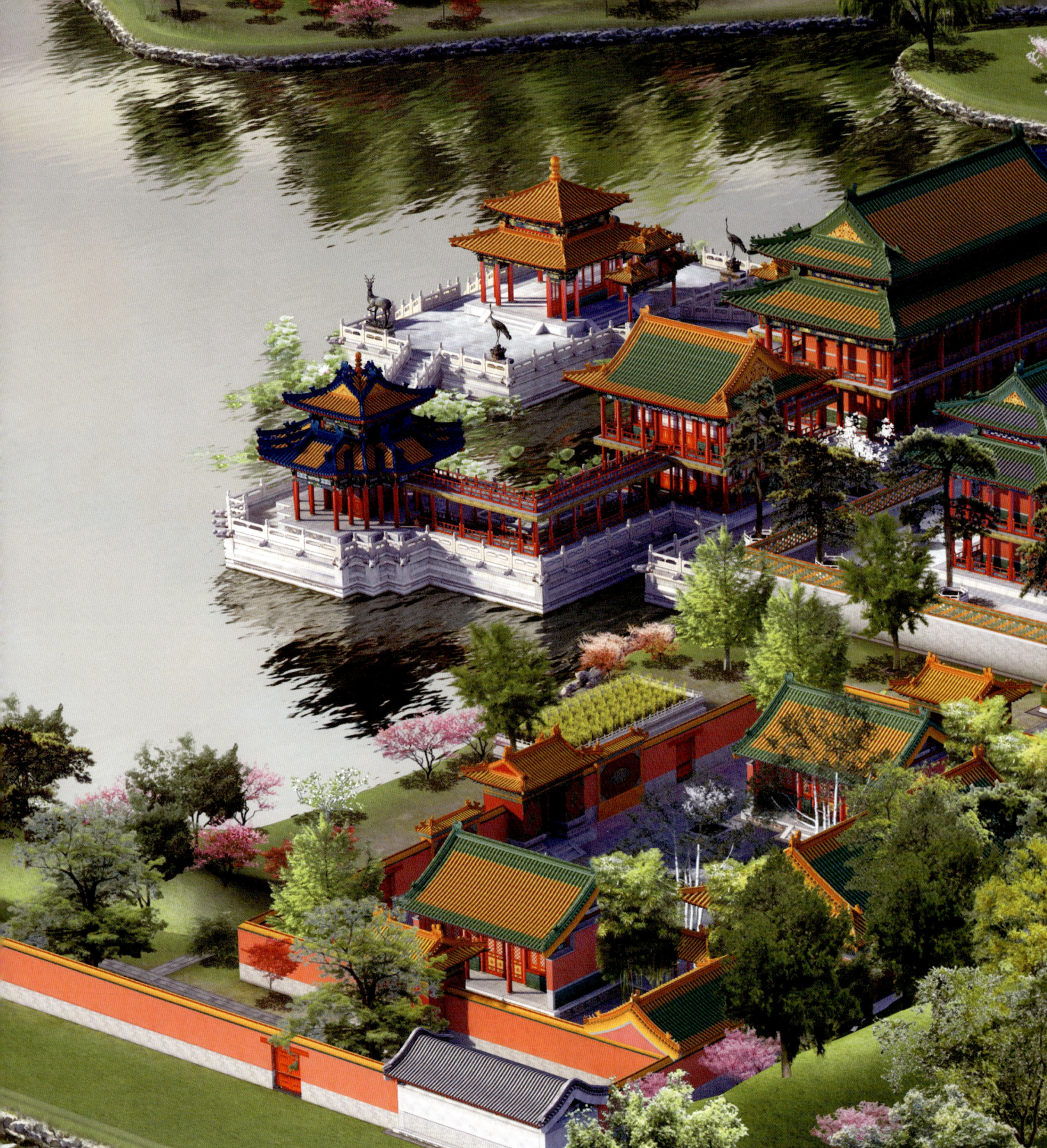
Fig. 142 North view of Fuanghu Shengjing Complex

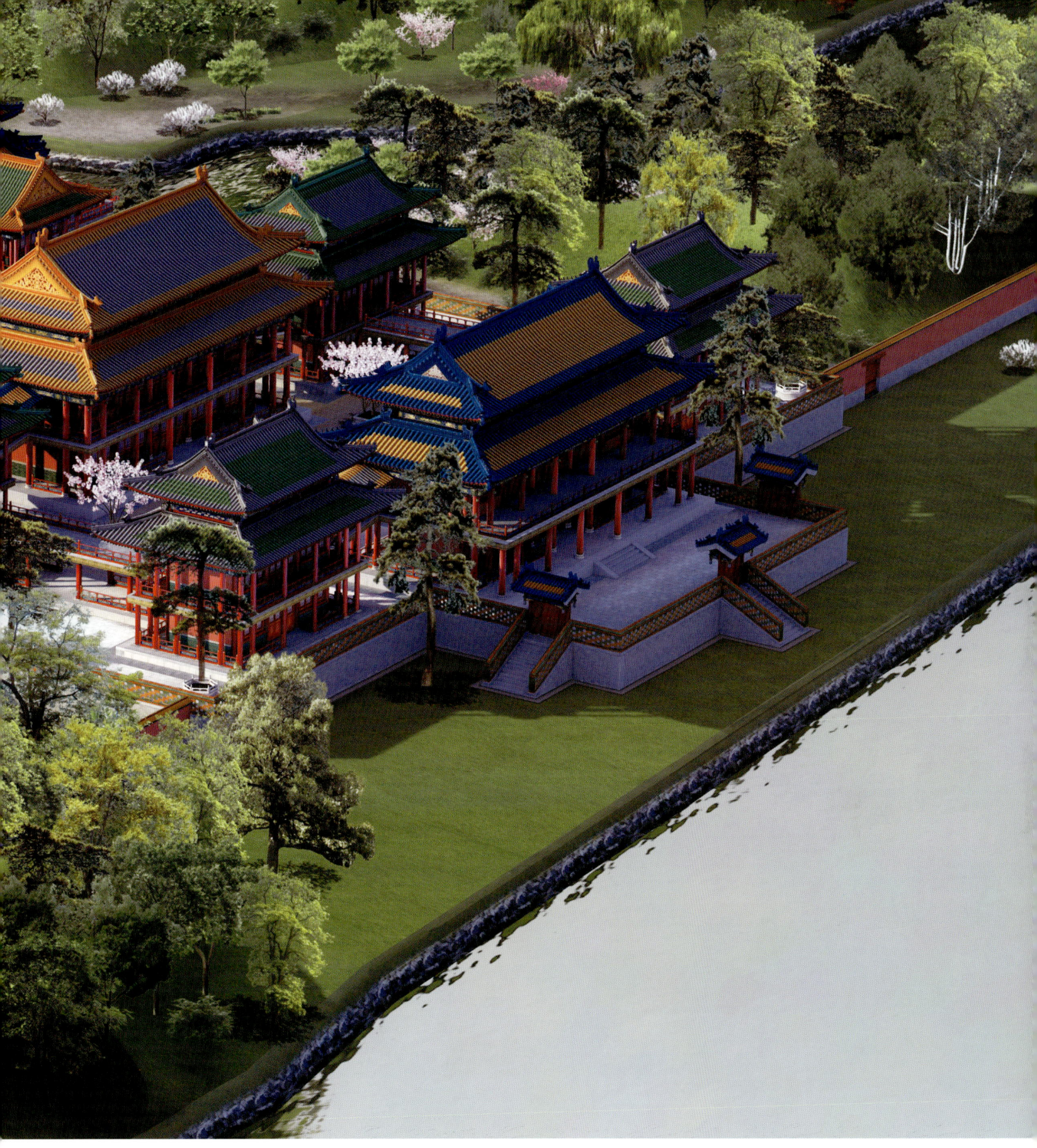

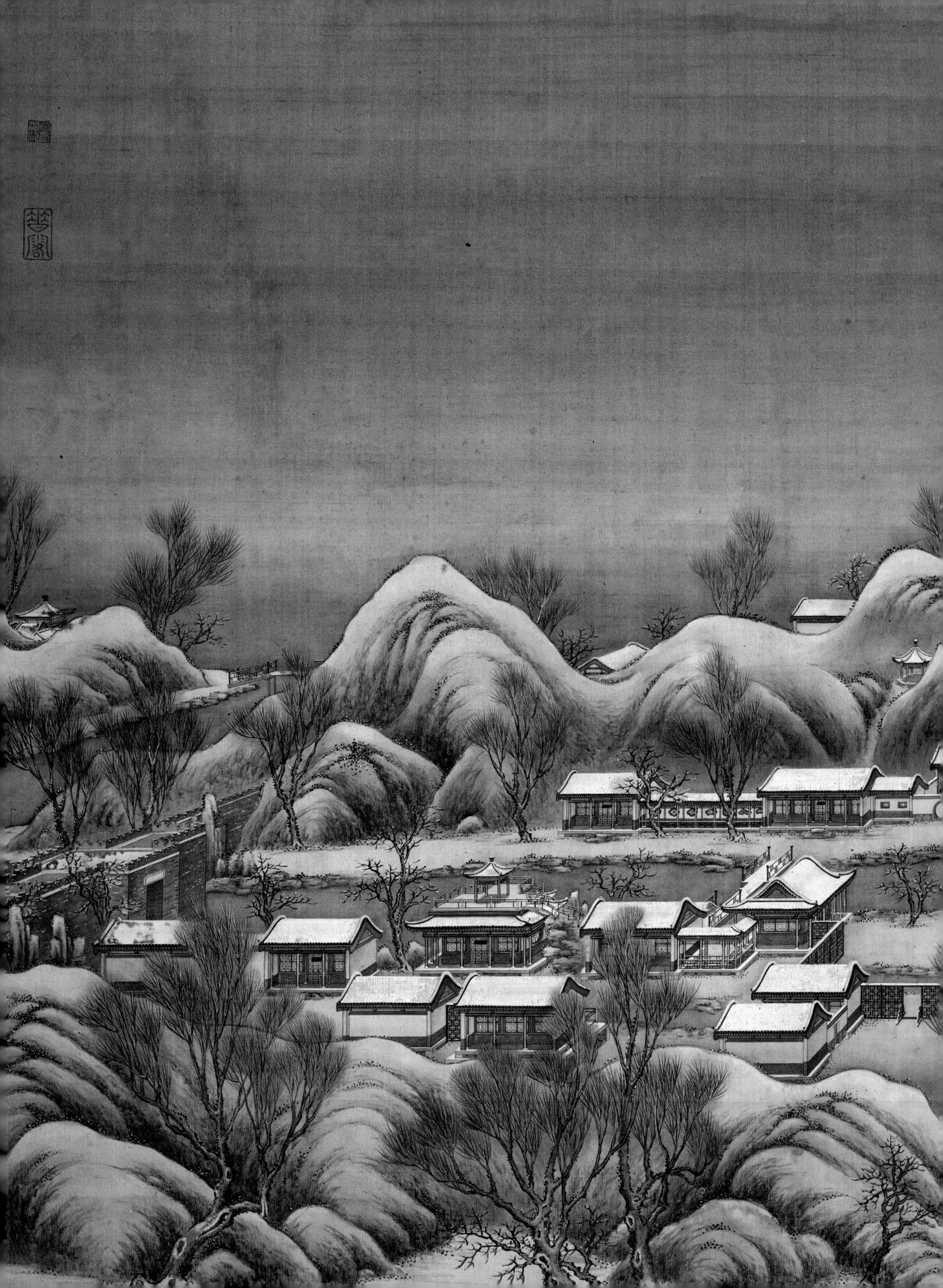

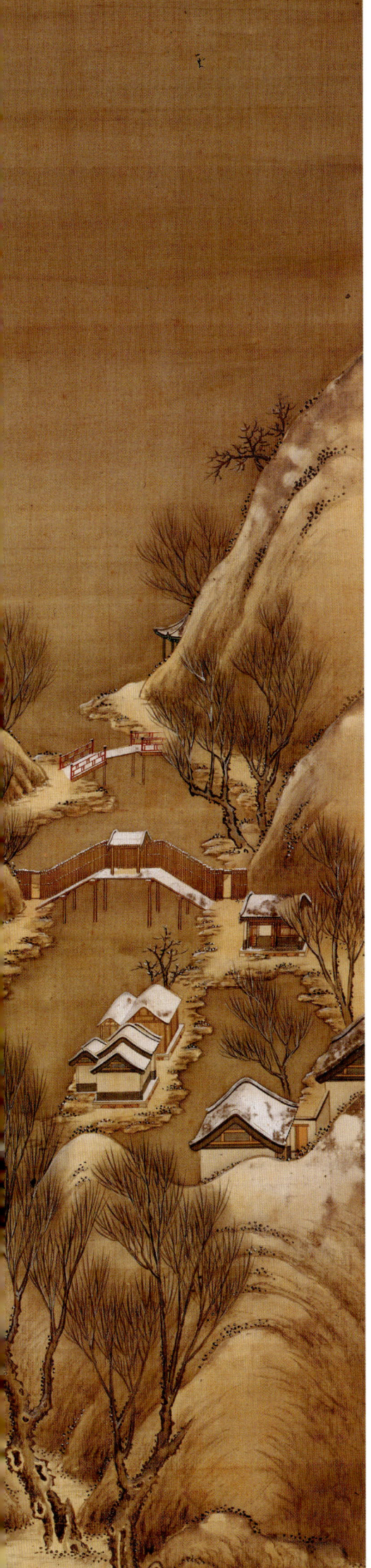

别有洞天 Bieyou Dongtian Complex (Complex of a Whole New World within a Grotto)

The Bieyou Dongtian Complex, located in the southeast of the Lake of Happiness, was built in the Yongzheng era. Being separated from the Lake of Happiness by small hills at its north and insulated from the rest of the Garden at its south and east by hillocks, woods and streams, with only a small gatehouse on an earthen hill at its west, the Bieyou Dongtian Complex gave the impression of a small garden unto itself (fig. 3-7-C-1). In Qianlong's eyes this little garden kept out the stir and bustle of the outside world and let refreshing nature run free, surrounding the beholder with scenic beauty.

The buildings in this group lined the two banks of a stream flowing east then north. The *Forty Scenes of the Yuan Ming Yuan* (fig. 143) shows the buildings on the north bank, centered about the main hall Bieyou Dongtian, spread out left and right, each with one or two small halls; more buildings lined the south bank in a staggered fashion and featured elegant hip-and-gable roofs or, in one case, a roof shaped like a truncated rectangular pyramid, surmounted on its flat top surface by a four-cornered kiosk with a pyramidal roof, which, interestingly, could be reached by ascending a rock-stacked hill next to the building (figs. 144, 145).

Major rebuilding took place starting in the 16th year of the Qianlong era (1751). Drawings from the Imperial Office of Architecture Design show that numerous buildings were added, and as a result there were now on the north bank the Bieyou Dongtian Hall, the Shuimu Qinghua Zhi Pavilion, the Nacui Building, the Shishang Study and the Jieye Pavilion, and on the south bank the Huohua Stone Boat (Living Painting Stone Boat) and the Tiaoshuang Building, as well as the Zhumi Mountain House (Mountain House of Dense Bamboo Grove), the Yanzao Building and the Shanxun Gazebo at the east. Additionally there were the Danxian Room (Room of Tranquility and Leisure), the Yunsong Study and the Zida Pavilion.

The scenery here was exquisite and Emperor Qianlong visited often during his stays at the imperial garden. Thus, in the 21st year of his reign (1756) he visited the Bieyou Dongtian Complex 25 times, with 8 visits in May alone. Sometimes he came for a short stay after supper and at other times he took his repast here; but mostly he came here to read and to look at paintings for self-improvement and for relaxation.

Some of the unique vistas in this area included the Shishang Study, a hall of three bays built on a terrace surrounded by a gallery, with at its front a cascading

Fig. 143 Painting of Bieyou Dongtian Complex from the album *Forty Scenes of the Yuan Ming Yuan*

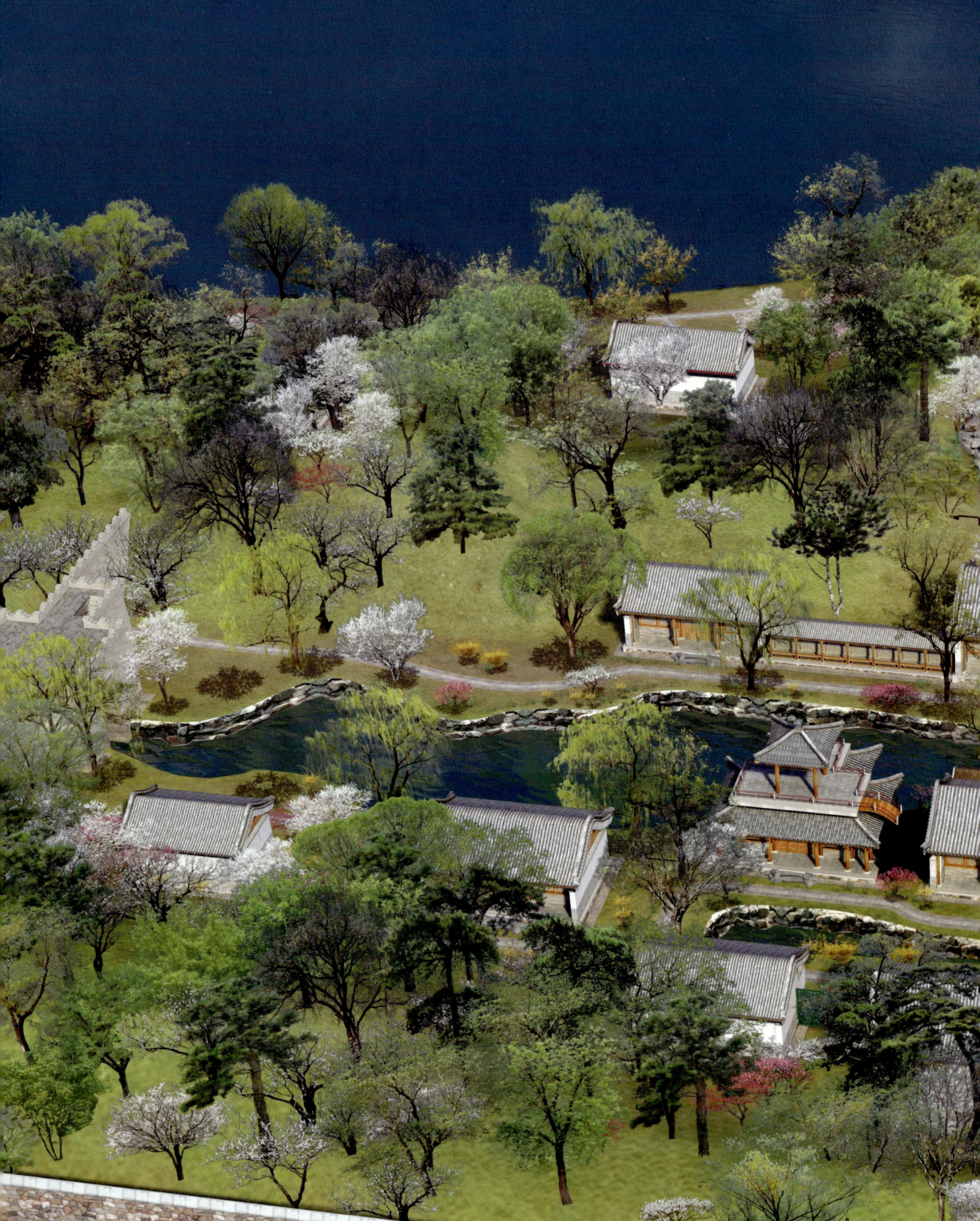
Fig. 144   Aerial view of Bieyou Dongtian Complex

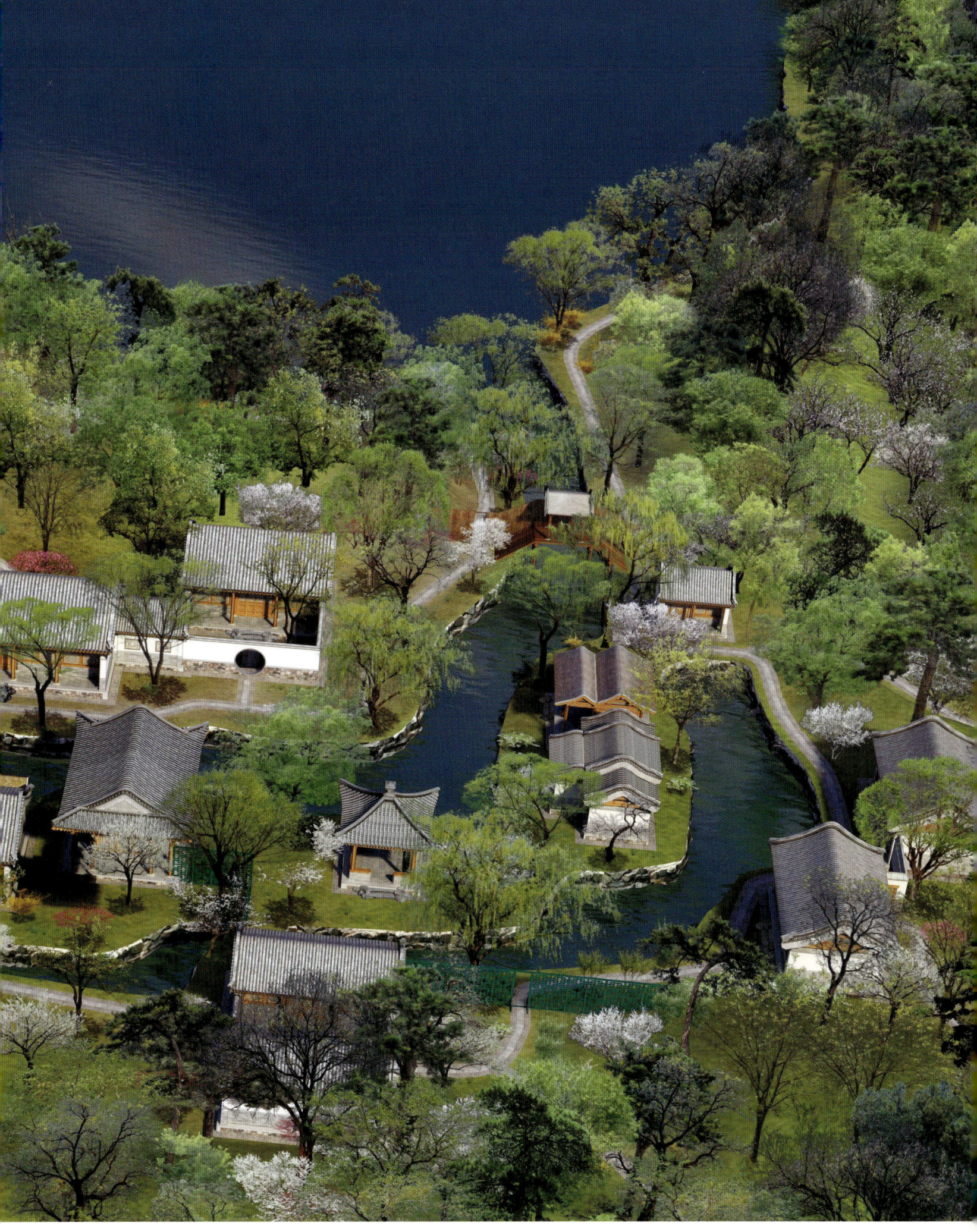

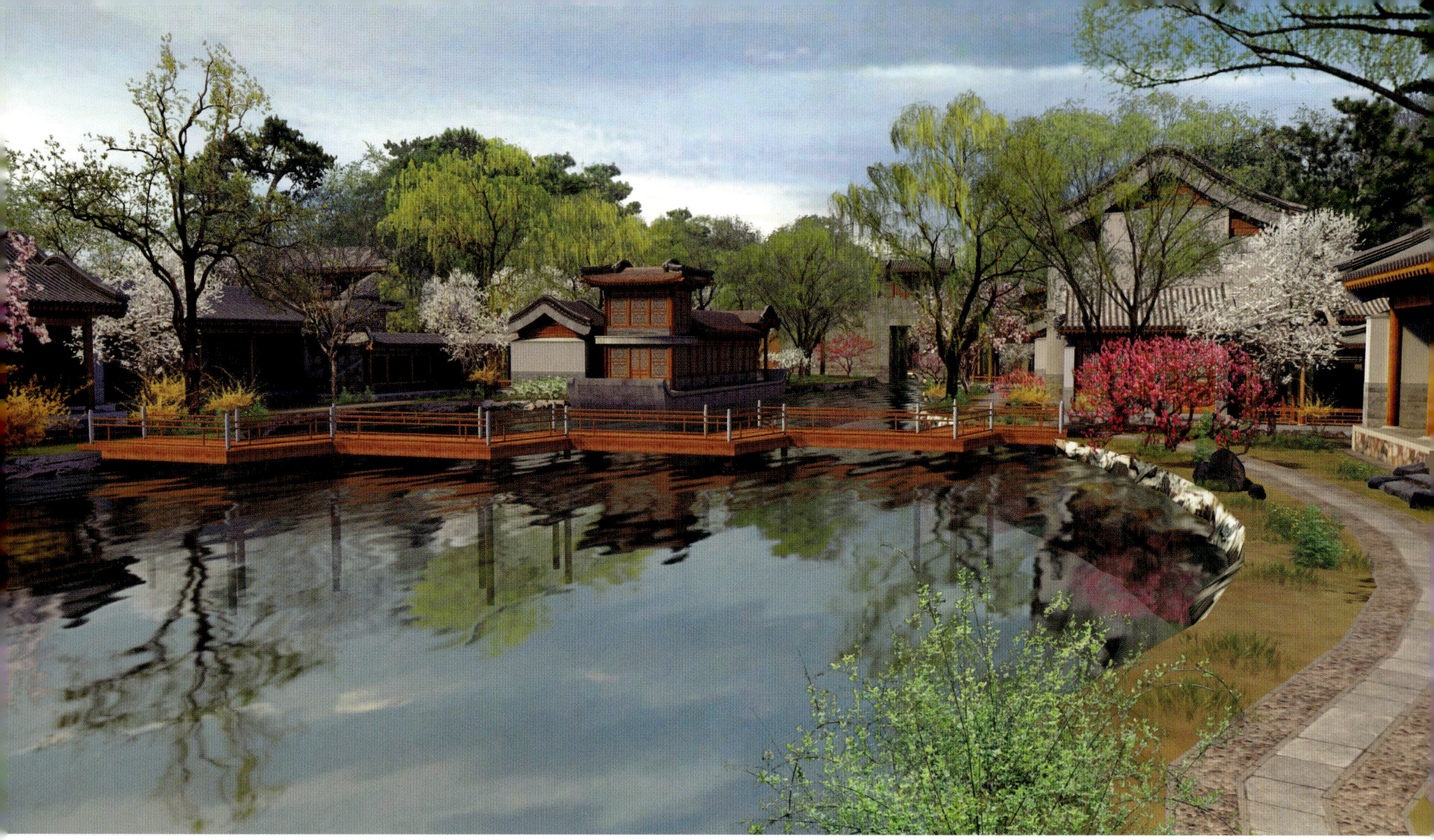

Fig. 145 Groups of buildings along two banks of stream

gallery that completed an enclosed courtyard exhibiting at its center a Lake Tai rock given the name of Qing Yun Pian. The harvester of this Lake Tai rock was the late Ming painter Mi Wanzhong, who had intended it for his Shao Garden (Peony Garden) in Beijing, but was unable to overcome logistic difficulties and was forced to abandon it in Liangxiang County 20 kilometers southwest of Beijing. In the Qing period it was moved to the Yuan Ming Yuan.

Another attraction was the Huohua Stone Boat on the south bank of the stream, which featured a base in the shape of a boat, surmounted by a long building. Qianlong mentioned in one of his poems that he named this stone building by the stream a living painting.[1] This stone boat, which has survived to this day, is an invaluable architectural relic in the Garden (fig. 146). Although the superstructure is no longer there, the stone boat has been well preserved. The Huohua Stone Boat was built about the 27th year of the Qianlong era (1762); the conception of the building is perhaps not unrelated to the impressions formed on the two southern tours he had undertaken by that time.

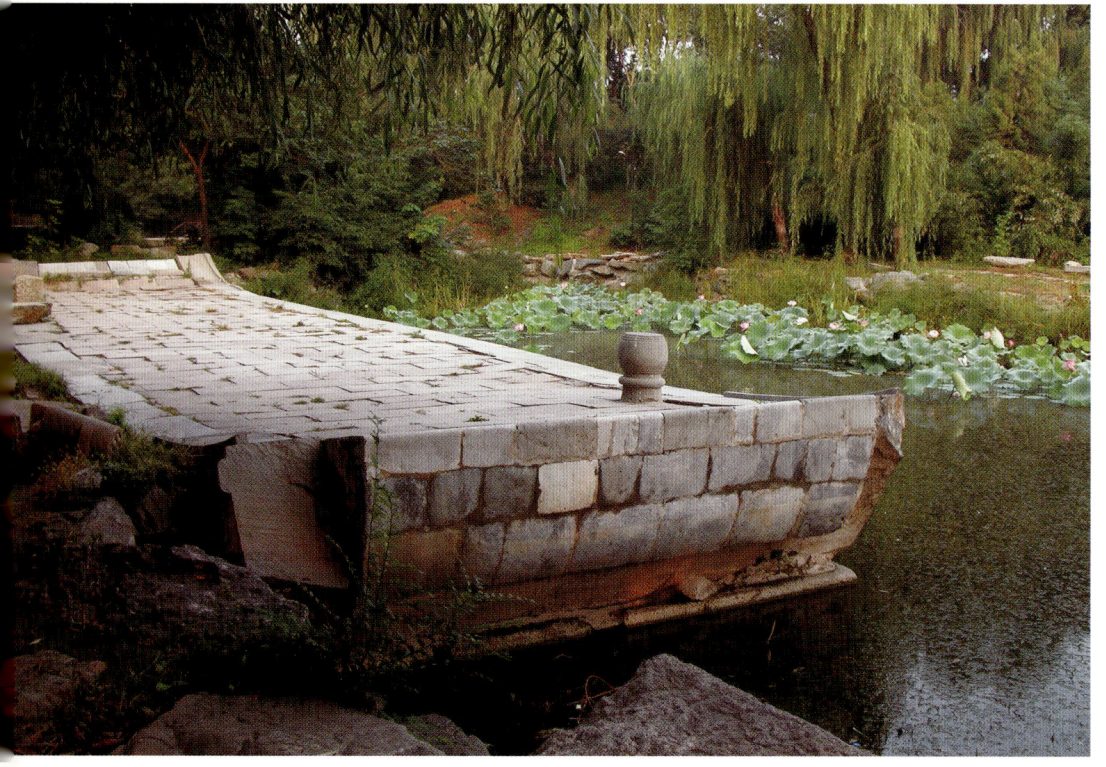

Fig. 146 Remnants of Huohua Stone Boat

---

1 *Yuzhi Shi*, by Emperor Qianlong, Book V, Volume 28.

172 CHINA'S LOST IMPERIAL GARDEN

廊然大公 Kuoran Dagong Complex (Complex of Boundless Impartiality)

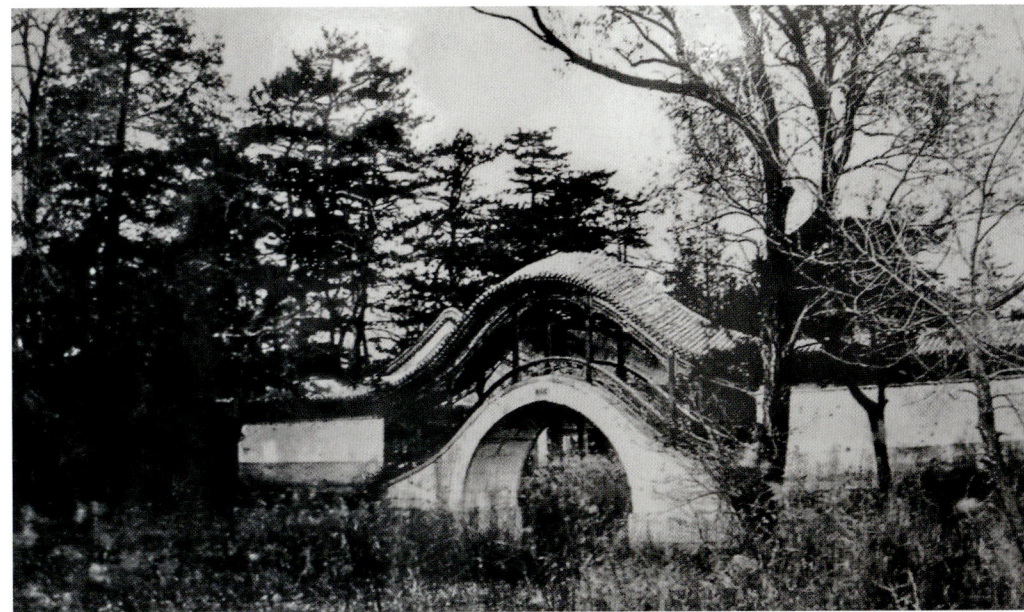

Fig. 147 Guiyue Bridge in southwest corner

The Kuoran Dagong Complex, situated at the northwest corner of the Lake of Happiness, was a small garden. Its construction started when the Yuan Ming Yuan was still a prince's garden; in the third year of Qianlong's reign (1738) it was given the name of Kuoran Dagong. The garden grounds were ringed by hills, with a pond in the middle and the buildings spread around the pond. The *Forty Scenes of the Yuan Ming Yuan*, drawings from the Imperial Office of Architecture Design and a 3-D model that has survived combine to give a general idea of the buildings of the time.

The main building in this garden—the Kuoran Dagong Hall—was situated on the south side of the pond (fig. 148 on pages 174 and 175). It was seven bays wide and featured a front and a back porch, and an overhanging gable roof. A veranda of three bays in the middle of its north façade extended over the water and there were galleries at the hall's two sides that ran south to connect with the Shuanghe Study of five bays projecting a double round-ridge overhanging gable roof. A winding gallery extended eastward from the Kuoran Dagong Hall, passed the Linhe Hua Hall (Riverside Painting Hall) and the Qiyin Hall (Elegant Verse Hall), and climbed up the hill to reach the small pavilion Caizhi Jing (Pavilion of Ganoderma Picking) with a pyramidal roof at the top of the hill. A trail along the hill ridge led north to the Danti Pavilion (Red Ladder Pavilion), then west to the Qixiu Pavilion. On the north side of the pond in front of the artificial hill stood the Qiaoqianju Gazebo, a small three-bay pavilion surrounded by a gallery and topped with a hip-and-gable roof; it had a veranda on its east gable wall. To its northwest was the Miaoda Pavilion.

At the northwest of the pond stood a two-storied building called Yingshan Building (Reflection of the Hill Building) and a hexagonal kiosk called Qixiu Pavilion. At the west side of the pond was a three-bay building with a gallery around it called Jingjia Pavilion; it had a moon terrace at its east and a vestibule of one bay at its west. Another waterside building was the Zhancun Study of only three bays, with an overhanging gable roof. At the southwest of the pond an L-shaped gallery connected the Zhancun Study and the Kuoran Dagong Hall. Where the gallery turned west a covered bridge with a crescent-shaped arch spanned the stream; it was named Guiyue Bridge (Full Moon Bridge) (fig. 147). Its form was unique among the more than a hundred bridges in the Yuan Ming Yuan. South of the Shuanghe Study there was a swan coop.

The Kuoran Dagong Hall, with its surrounding hillocks, its pond overgrown with sweet flag irises and lotuses and mountain birds and waterfowl thriving and coexisting peacefully in their respective habitats, reminded Qianlong of the generosity and impartiality of nature that allowed all livings things to live each in its own niche and made him reflect on the fact that ancient sages must have been inspired by such generosity and impartiality.

Emperor Qianlong was so attracted by the charms of the Kuoran Dagong Complex that he often took a boat from the Qinzheng Qinxian Complex to go there when he had some free time from transacting the business of government. He also composed a number of poems in its praise.

The pond and the rock-stacked hills of the Kuoran Dagong Complex remain but the buildings were totally destroyed. Further archaeological digging is expected at the building foundations.

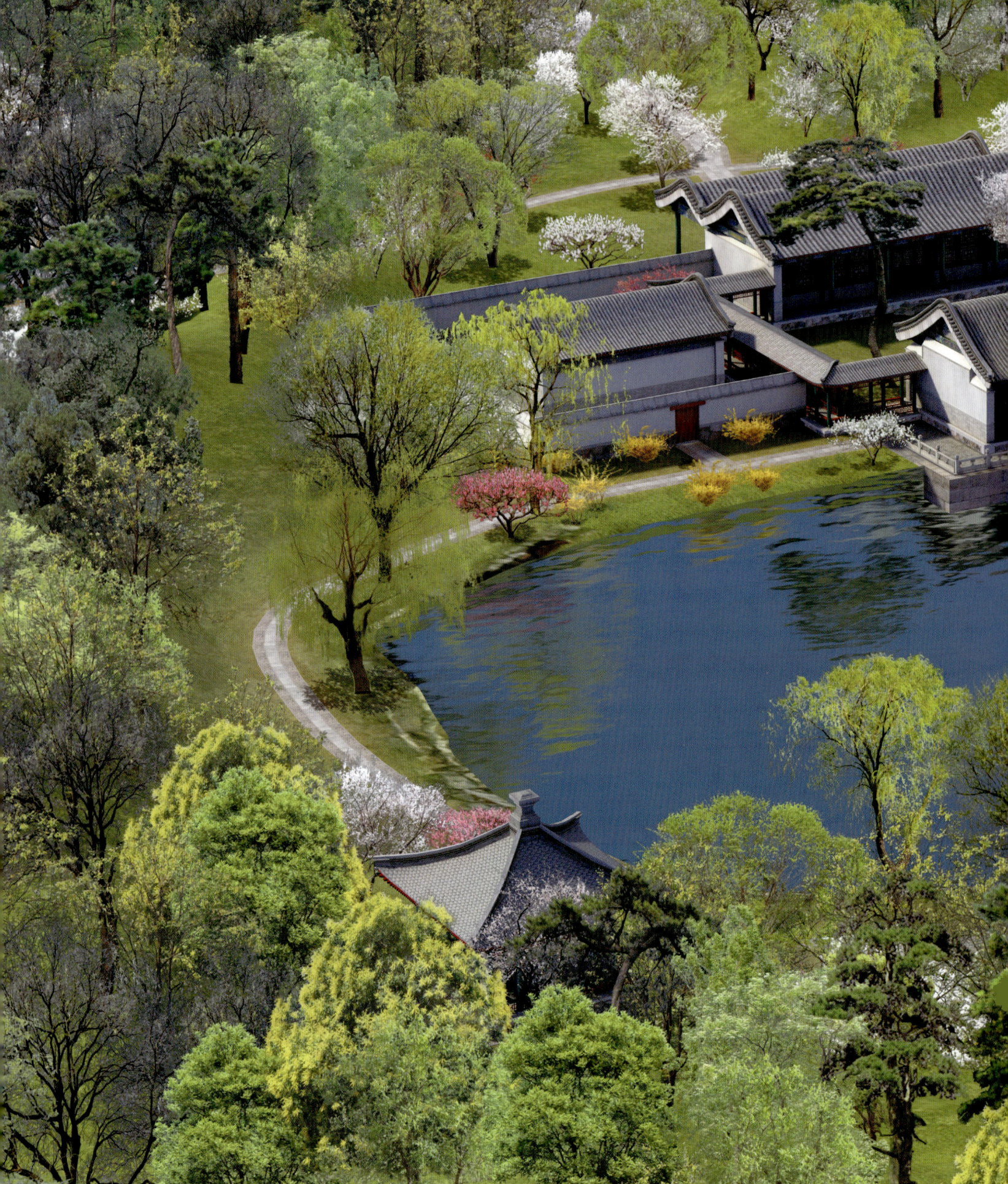

Fig. 148 North view of Kuoran Dagong Complex

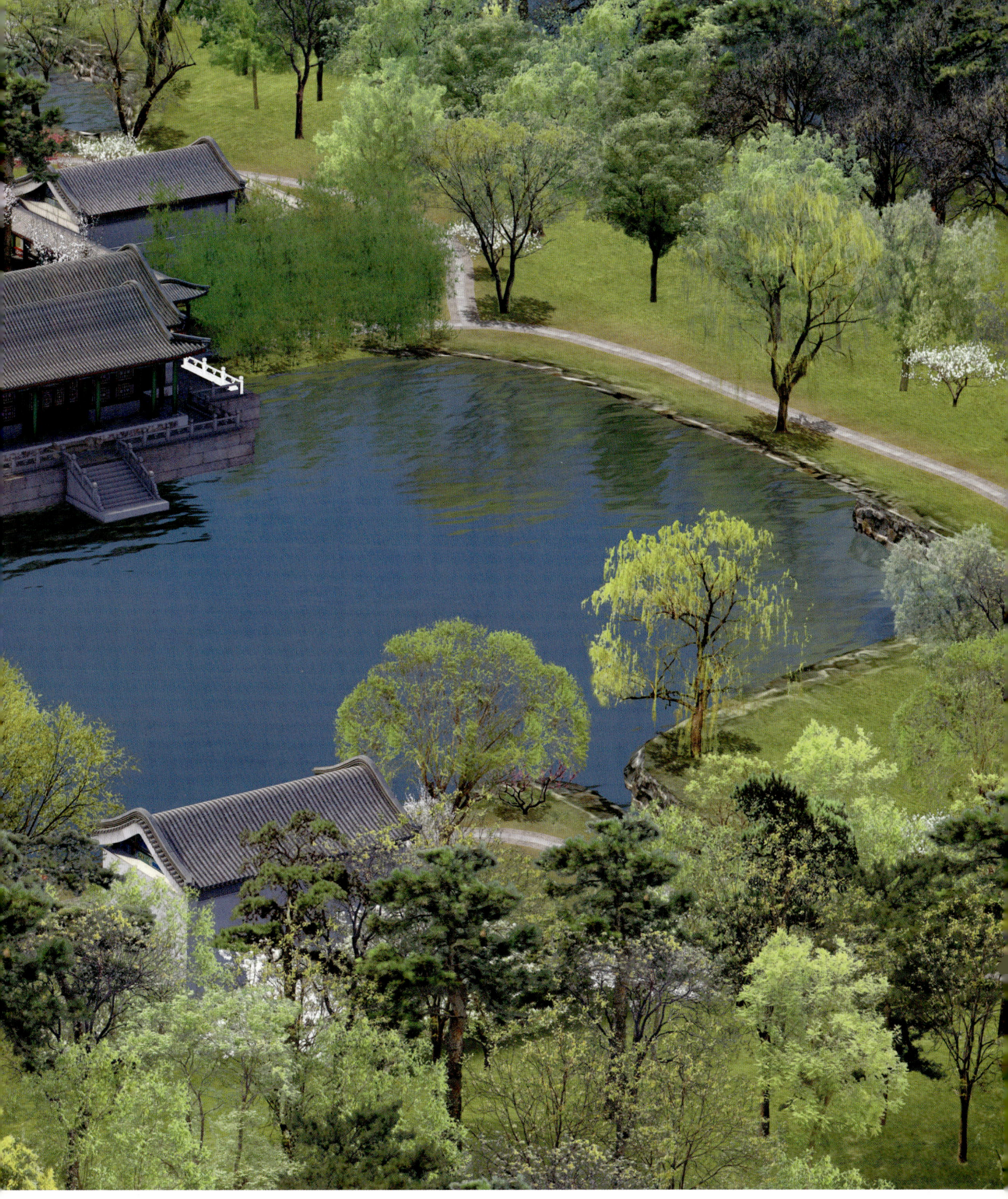

接秀山房 Jiexiu Mountain House (Mountain House Greeted by the Beauty of the Hills)

The Jiexiu Mountain House, located on the east shore of the Lake of Happiness, was built in the Yongzheng era. It included the buildings called the Jiexiu Mountain House and Lancui Pavilion (Take in the Green Hills Pavilion). According to *Rixia Jiuwen Kao*, "The Jiexiu Mountain House, situated in the east of the Lake of Happiness, had a west-facing main hall of three bays. A little to its east was the Qinqu Pavilion (Pleasure of the Lute Pavilion); at its north was the Xunyun Building (Building of Following the Clouds) and at its southeast was the Chenglian Building (White Silk Building), behind which stood the Yiran Library. A little east of the Xunyun Building was the Buddhist building Anyin Chuang (Dhvaja of Peace). The Lancui Pavilion stood south of the Jiexiu Mountain House." The group of buildings adopted a scattered layout, with kiosks, terraces, galleries and pavilions arranged along the lake shore in a staggered fashion (fig. 149).

From here the beholder had a view of the beautiful western hills outside the Yuan Ming Yuan in the distance; this is the so-called *jie jing* or "borrowed view" in Chinese garden design. Ji Cheng, a garden designer of the Ming period, pointed out that when designing a garden "one must be good at borrowing from exterior landscapes and excel in adapting to the topography and environment and attaining the right proportionality, so that the beholder would take it for the work of Nature." The Jiexiu Mountain House was a good example of the application of Ji Cheng's theory.

The vista here underwent a major change in the Jiaqing era. The relics at this site were from the buildings of this later period.

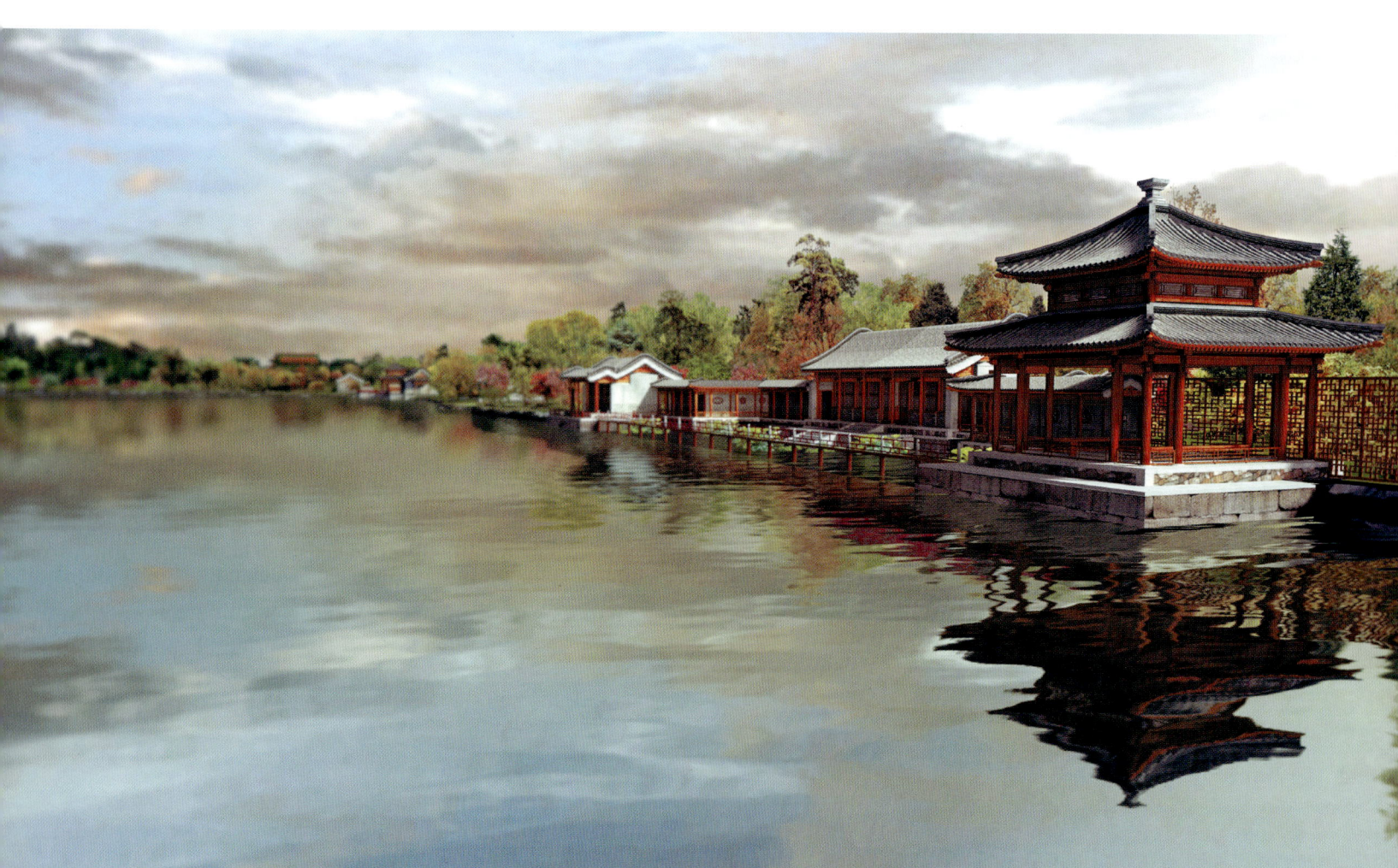

Fig. 149 Aerial view of Jiexiu Mountain House

蒨园 Qian Garden in the Changchun Garden (Garden of Eternal Spring)

As a small garden in the Changchun Garden, the Qian Garden (fig. 150 on pages 178 and 179) was not geographically and space-wise well-endowed and the garden creators designed it as three separate sections extending from east to west. For the middle section, water was introduced from the lake around the area to create a small lake in a lake, which was surrounded by the buildings the Langrun Study, Biaosheng Pavilion (Pavilion of Noble Morality), Cizhong Dayou Jiachu Pavilion, Raoyeyi Hall, Taixu Room, Yunxia Si Pavilion, Bieyou Tian Open Hall and Yuntianqin Pavilion (Pavilion of Music of a Celestial Lute), and was spanned by a bridge. By harnessing the water resources, the garden designers were able to create a landscape rich in interest. The Yuntianqin Pavilion at the northeast of the interior lake was a small kiosk surrounded by rockeries. In one of his poems,[1] Qianlong wrote that when the water lapped against the rocks of the artificial hills, the wavelets made a pleasing musical sound, hence the name given the kiosk. The Biaosheng Pavilion, a kiosk that perched on a hilltop at the west of the interior lake, afforded a view to the distance. There stood at one time the Zhanjing Building, which was described in one of Qianlong's poem[2] as overlooking both the interior and the exterior lakes and commanding a view to the distance. It must have been one of the landmark buildings ringing the interior lake in the period. Regrettably the original Zhanjing Building disappeared in the rebuilding undertaken in the Jiaqing era and that has left a gap in our understanding of the original conception of the garden designers.

The interior lake and its immediate environs were the core of the Qian Garden. The landscape at its east consisted primarily of elements of natural scenery, such as rockeries; at its north was a square kiosk called Lingxiangpan (Shore of Water Chestnut Fragrance Pavilion), which marked the end of the garden. A string of small courtyard compounds were placed in the western part to form an interesting, layered space characterized by quiet seclusion.[3]

The garden once boasted an unusual Lake Tai rock, which had belonged in the Deshou Palace garden (Palace of Virtue and Longevity) (now in the Zhejiang Province) of the retired Emperor Gaozong of the Southern Song dynasty in Hangzhou and was originally called the "Furong Shi" (Lotus Rock). At the time the rock was placed next to a plum tree to make an idyllic pair. In the late Ming period, a stone tablet carved with a painting of the rock and the plum tree was set down by the Lotus Rock. When Emperor Qianlong visited the garden on his first southern tour in the 16th year of his reign (1751), the plum tree had already died but the stone tablet still stood. Emperor Qianlong, struck by the dilapidation and decay, felt the surroundings did not do enough justice to the rock. The local officials, seeing that the emperor was much taken with the huge rock, sent it by boat and by land to Beijing as a gift to the emperor. It was later placed in the Qian Garden of the Changchun Garden and given the name "Qinglian Duo" (Green Lotus Petal). In the 30th year of his reign (1765) when Emperor Qianlong revisited the Desheng Palace in Hangzhou on his fourth southern tour, he had a replica of the old, now crumbling tablet made and erected next to it. Two years later another tablet engraved with the same rock and plum tree was erected in the Qian Garden. This rock bore an inscription of Emperor Qianlong's explanation of the history of the rock.

In the early period after its construction the garden exhibited the characteristics of the private gardens of the Jiangnan area south of the Yangtze River, i.e. modest size and compact spacing as well as a staggered layout. These characteristics were watered down in the rebuilding undertaken in the 13th year of the Jiaqing era (1808). In the aftermath of the rebuilding the Jingbi Hall, a hall of five bays with a veranda became the dominant feature of the garden, but it had only a winding gallery at its east side that connected it to the Lingxiangpan Pavilion at the northeast. There were no structures of appropriate proportions that could serve as companion buildings to the five-bay main hall. The added straight bridge appeared redundant given the zigzag bridge already in the garden and it detracted from the aesthetic appeal of the landscape around the interior lake.

---

1 *Yuzhi Shi*, by Emperor Qianlong, Book II, Volume 42.
2 Ibid.
3 Ibid.

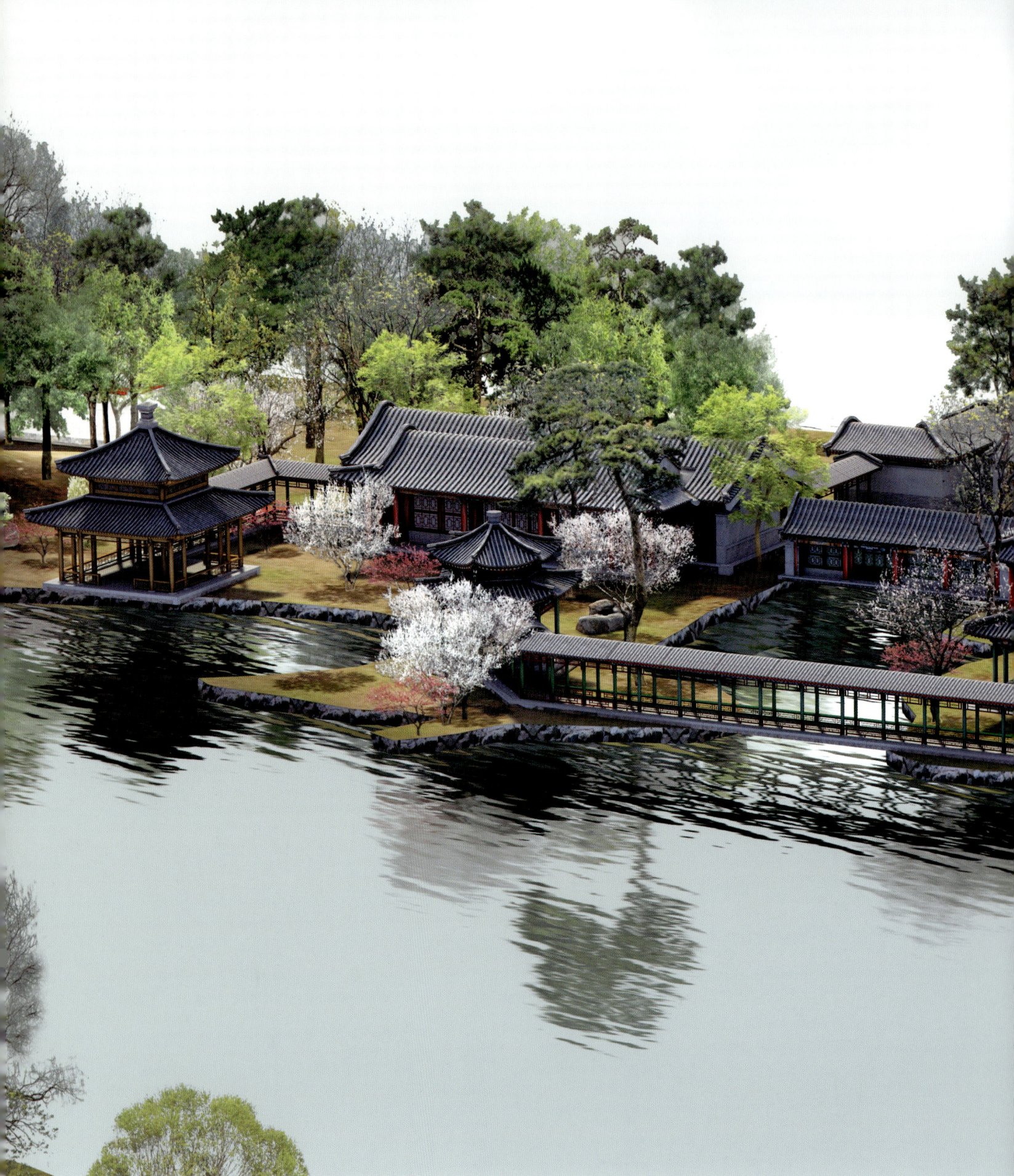

Fig. 150 Aerial view of Qian Garden (seen from north)

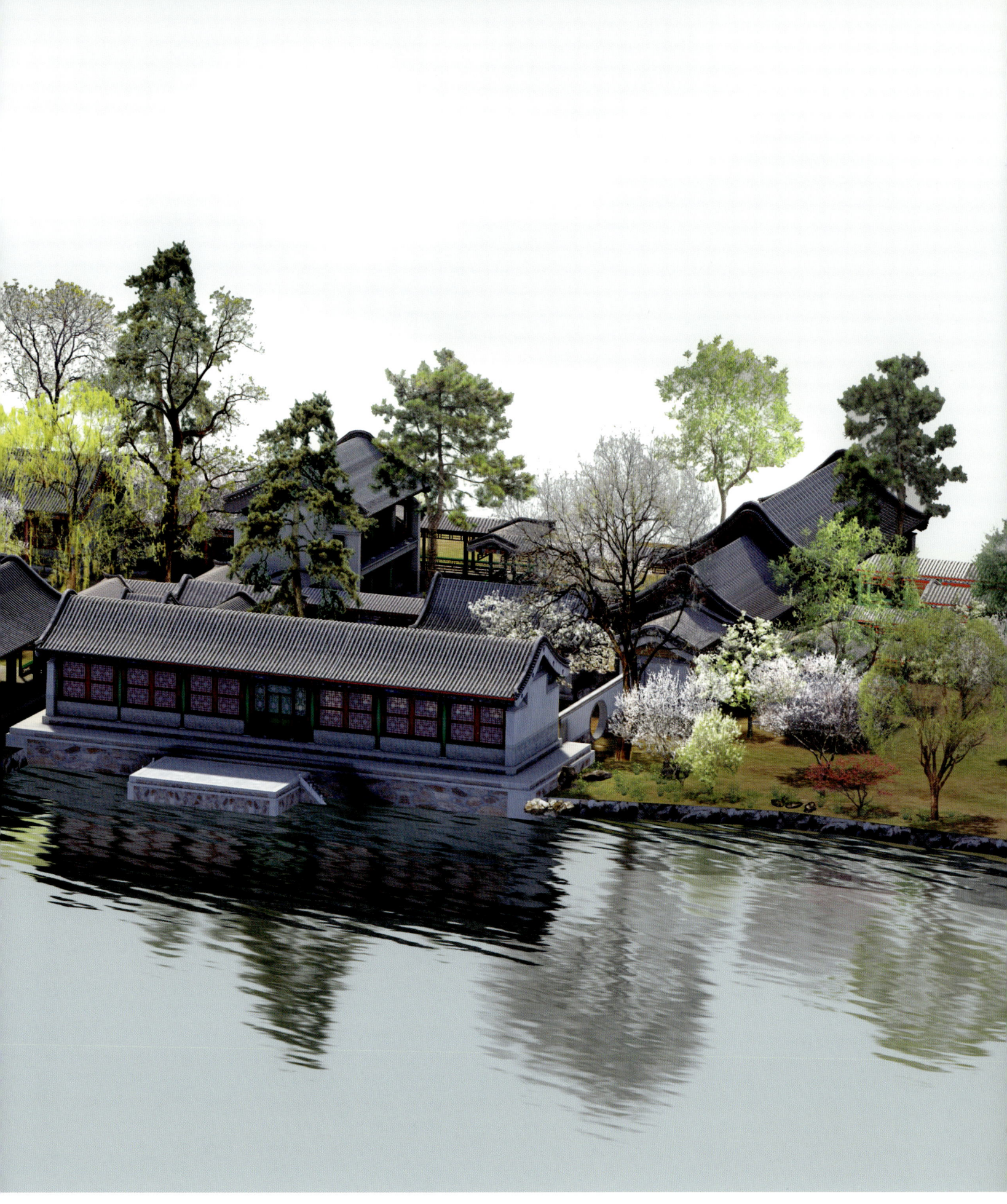

獅子林 Shizi Grove (Lion Grove) in the Changchun Garden

The Changchun Garden was Emperor Qianlong's creation and incorporated all his favorite sceneries. The Shizi Grove, situated in the northeast of the Changchun Garden, was modeled on the Shizi Grove in Suzhou (now in Jiangsu Province), which was one of the four renowned gardens in that town and a classical example of the private gardens of China. Because of his liking for Ni Zan's *Lion Grove Painting* and because he believed that the Shizi Grove in Suzhou was built with that painting as a blue print, Qianlong commissioned the Shizi Grove in the Changchun Garden. It was not until the 49th year of his reign (1784) when he went on his fifth southern tour that he found out the genesis of the Shizi Grove in Suzhou and realized that the original Shizi Grove was not based upon Ni Zan's painting.

After the completion of the Lion Grove in the Changchun Garden, Qianlong was not satisfied with the result even though the rockeries were made by professional craftsmen specially hired from Suzhou. The Shizi Grove in the imperial garden was different from the Shizi Grove in Suzhou in that they were situated in entirely different environments and the placement of the kiosks, terraces and pavilions in them also differed from one to the other. Eight scenes named by Qianlong in the 38th year of his reign were: the Shizi Grove, the Rainbow Bridge, the artificial hill, the Najing Hall (Hall of Collected Scenery), the Qingbi Pavilion, the vine trellis, the stone-paved trail in the hill and the Zhanfeng Pavilion. Later he named another eight scenes in the Shizi Grove: the Qingshu Study, the Xiaoxiang Chuang Hall, the Tanzhen Library, the Yanjing Building (Building of Extensive Scenery), the Huahuang (Gaily Decorated Boat), the Yunlinshi Room, the Hengbi Pavilion and the sluice gate. These sixteen scenes made for a building complex of rich and varied forms (fig. 153 on pages 182 and 183).

These sixteen scenes described by Qianlong were all situated in the east of the garden. The replicated part had artificial hills in the east and a pond in the west,

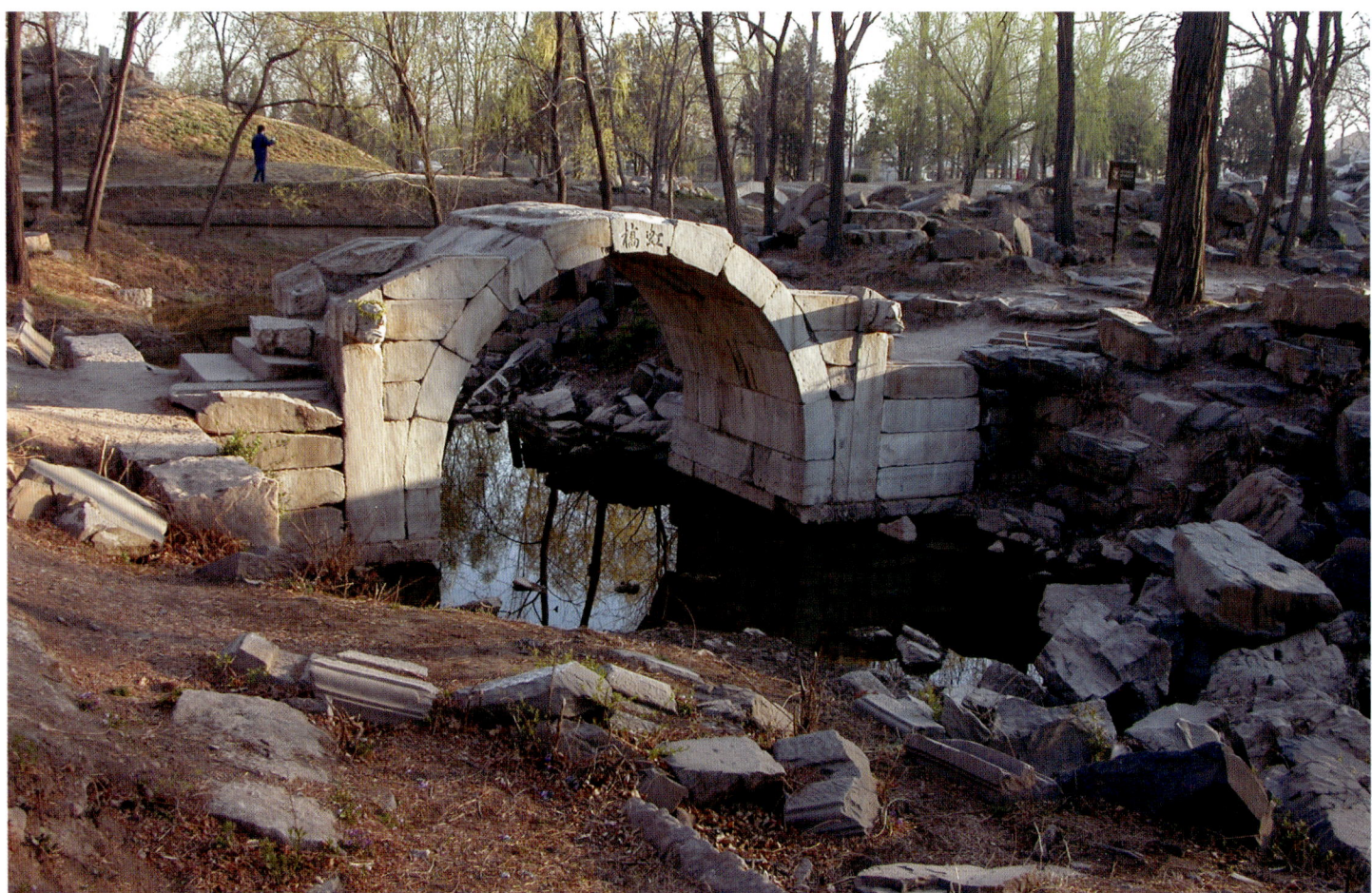

Fig. 151 Remnants of stacked rocks

CHINA'S LOST IMPERIAL GARDEN

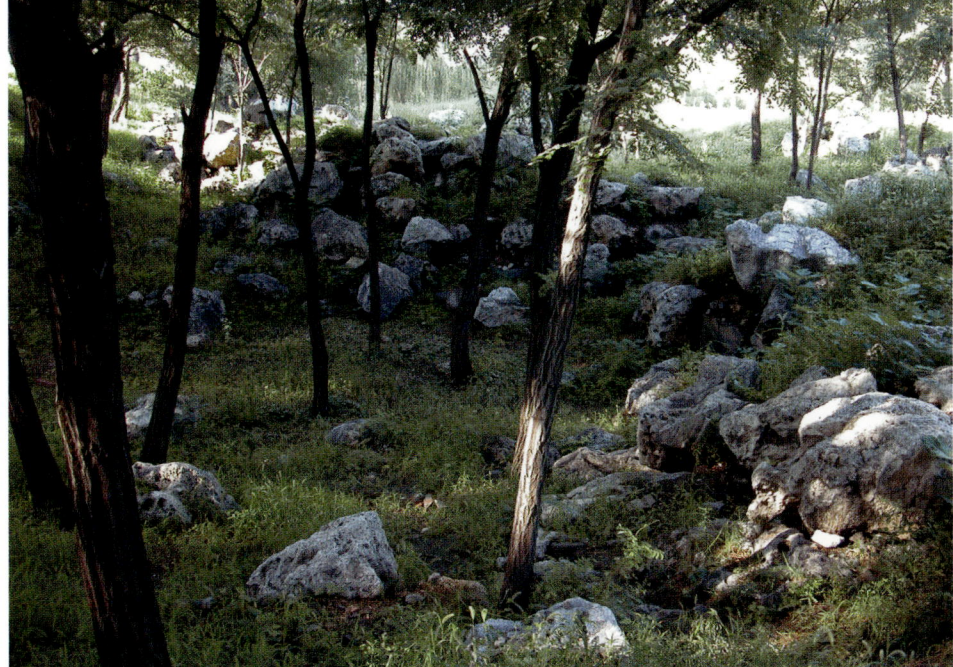

Fig. 152 Remnants of Rainbow Bridge

which formed, together with the buildings around it, a water courtyard. The Qingshu Study, the main building in the water courtyard, was open-sided, three bays wide and girt by a veranda, but the hall, bounded by hills on its north, east and west, was not directly on the water except at its south where it overlooked a small pool, which in turn was bounded on its south by an artificial hill topped by the kiosk the Zhanfeng Pavilion. In a poem Qianlong described this artificial hill with a peak on which perched a four-pillared kiosk.[1] The creation of an artificial hill in an exiguous space with limited north-south extendibility attested to the superb skill of the craftsmen.

The Qingbi Pavilion north of the water courtyard was a two-storied building of five bays. The name originated from the name of the library of Ni Zan, a famous painter of the Yuan dynasty. This building once held Ni Zan's paintings[2] and a long scroll painting of the newly built Shizi Grove in the imperial garden emulating Ni Zan's *Lion Grove Painting*.[3]

There was a vine trellis at the east of the water courtyard. It was integrated with the stone bridge. At the northwest corner of the water courtyard was a small bridge called Rainbow Bridge, which linked the Qingshu Study and the Hengbi Pavilion to the west. Judging from the drawing it appeared that the boat route must circumvent the artificial hill surmounted by the Zhanfeng Pavilion, and allowed the passage of only smaller boats (fig. 152).

At the northwest of the Qingbi Pavilion, the small Tanzhen Library perched on an earthen hillock and was linked to the Qingbi Pavilion by a cascading gallery.

Due west of the water courtyard, a five-bay pavilion called the Hengbi Pavilion featuring a front and a back porch sat facing a stream over which arched the Rainbow Bridge. This building, together with other buildings in the western part, such as the Congfan Gazebo (Gazebo of Bountiful Flowers) and the Qinqing Study, and the Shizi Grove added at a later period, formed an organic whole. The Hengbi Pavilion appeared to be a wing hall of the Congfang Gazebo and was also a scene of interest from the Rainbow Bridge.

At the east side of the Qingshu Study was a courtyard enclosed by a gallery, with the main building of three bays called Najing Hall. Further east was the Yanjing Building, in the midst of an artificial hill.

North of the artificial hill, close to the enclosure wall was the Yunlinshi Room. To the west of the Yunlinshi Room, opposite the vine trellis and the zigzag bridge, a building called Xiaoxiang Chuang stood close by an artificial hill with stone steps. Artificial hills were the main distinction of this garden; professional hill builders were hired from Suzhou to craft these rockeries with stone harvested from nearby Yanshan Mountains. These rocks from the Yanshan Mountains were publicly praised by Emperor Qianlong and as a result became a brand name among stone materials used to build artificial hills (fig. 151).

The sluice gate found here was not found in the Shizi Grove in Suzhou. There were numerous interconnecting water bodies in the vast imperial garden, and a sluice gate was built in the enclosure wall in the north of the Shizi Grove, beyond which was the Rectangular River in the Xiyang Building Complex. It must have been a pleasant experience in those days to ride in a boat on a stream lined with rocky banks, pass through the sluice gate and be greeted by the novel sight of a European landscape.

---

1 *Yuzhi Shi*, by Emperor Qianlong, Book IV, Volume 5.
2 Ibid., Book V, Volume 20.
3 Ibid., Book IV, Volume 4.

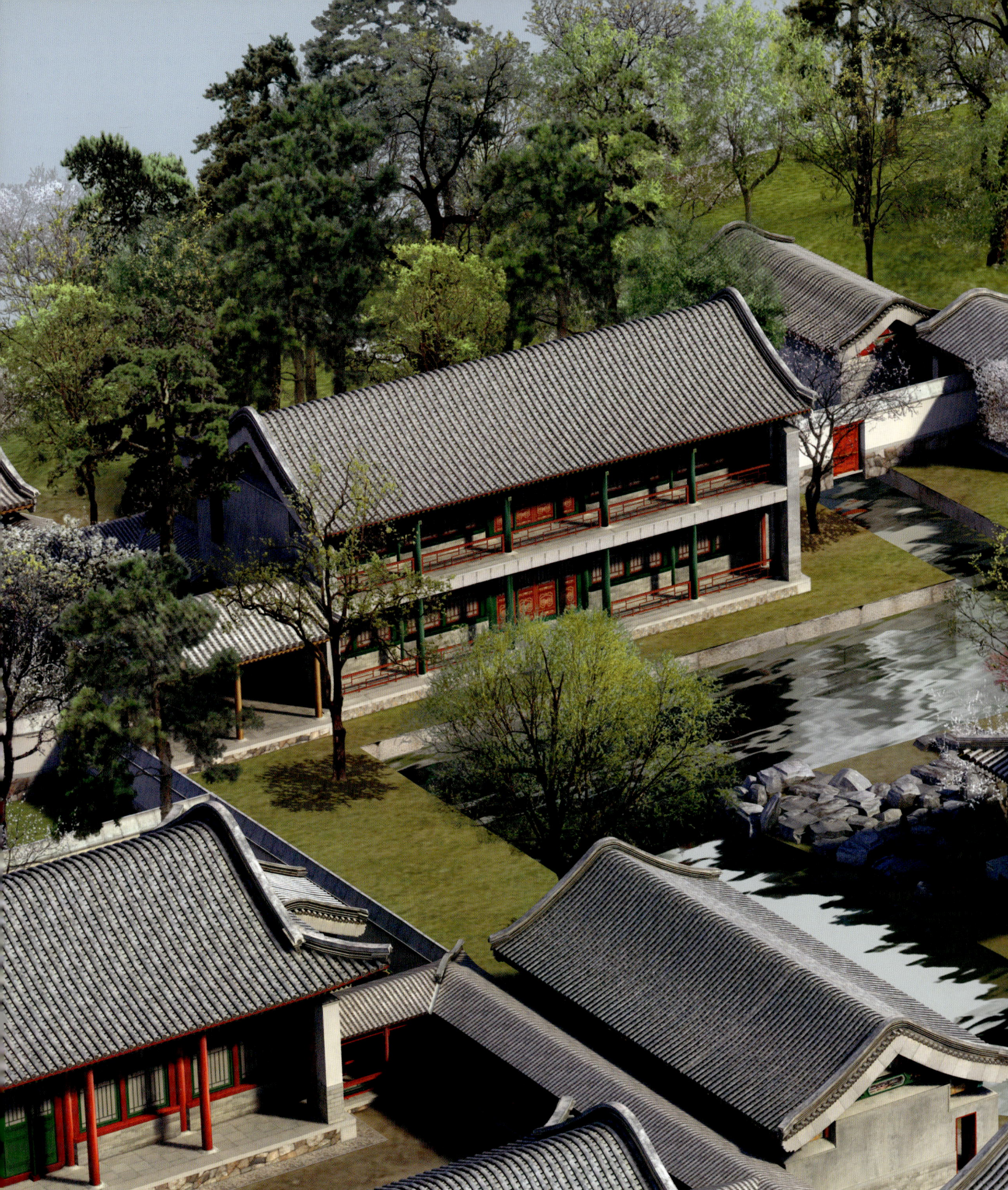

Fig. 153 Aerial view of the Shizi Grove (seen from southwest)

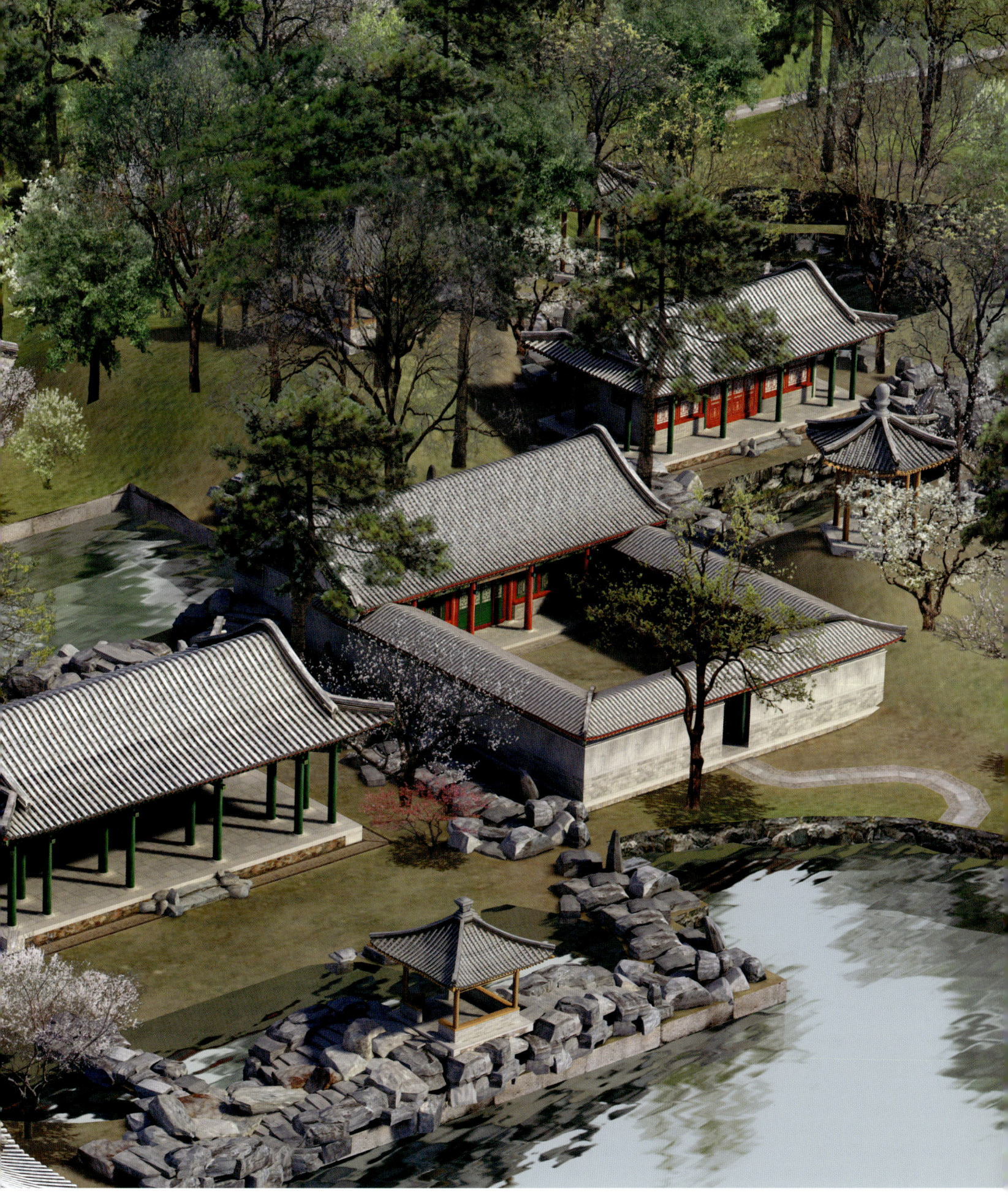

鑒園 Jian Garden (Garden of Mirror) in the Changchun Garden

The Jian Garden, located in the east of the Changchun Garden, was bounded in the east by the enclosure wall and in the west by a slender lake. It was situated on a long narrow strip of land. It was a small garden built in imitation of the Qu Garden (Interesting Garden) by the Slender West Lake in Yangzhou after Qianlong's fourth southern tour. The name Qu Garden was given to it by Qianlong, who was much impressed by its landscape during his southern tour. After he revisited the Qu Garden in the 49th year of his reign (1784) on his sixth southern tour, he explained in a poem why he gave that name to the garden, writing that the interest lay in its bamboo and plum trees, the bamboo breaking into lush green after winter and the plum blossoms ushering in another spring.[1]

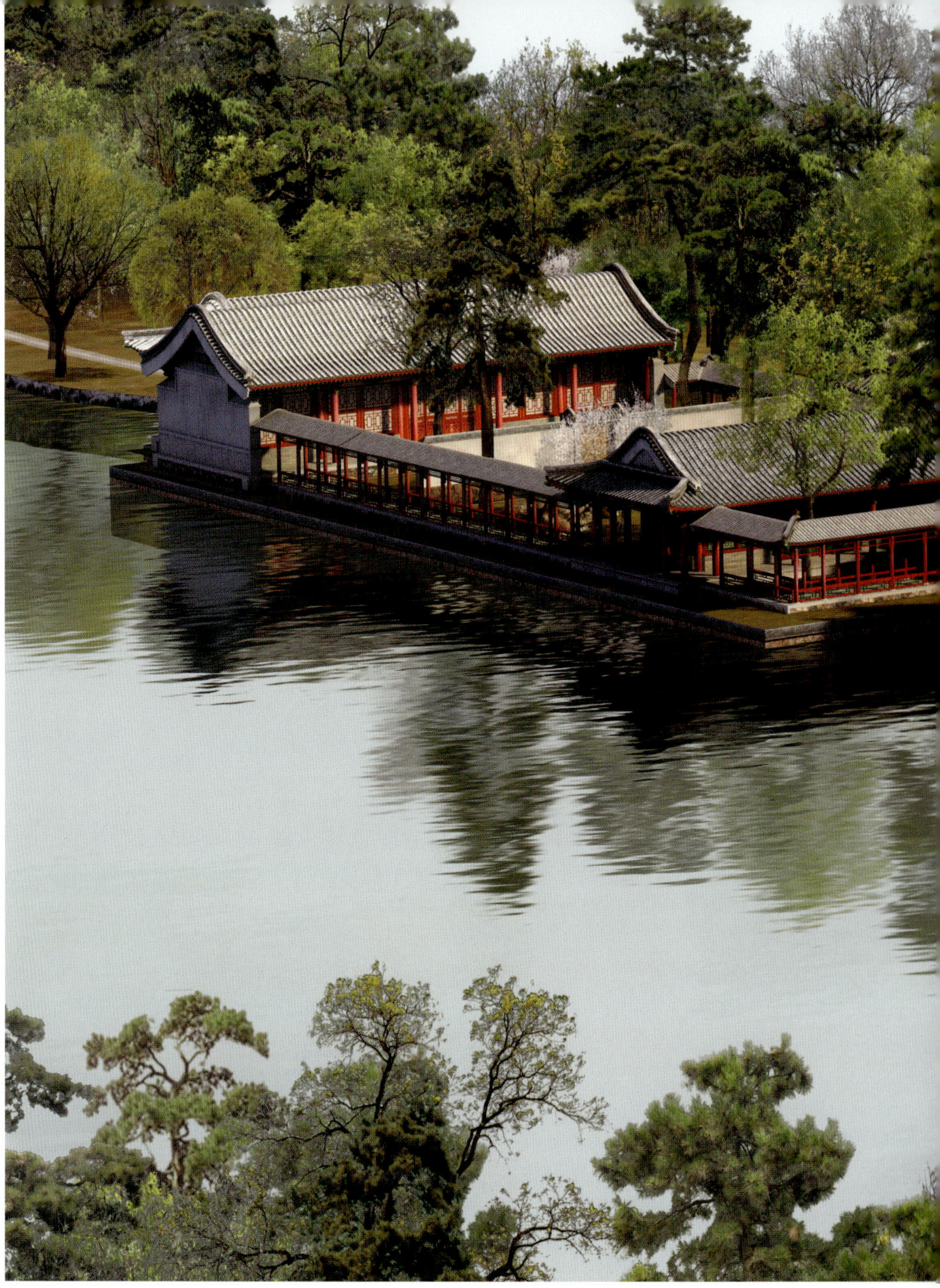

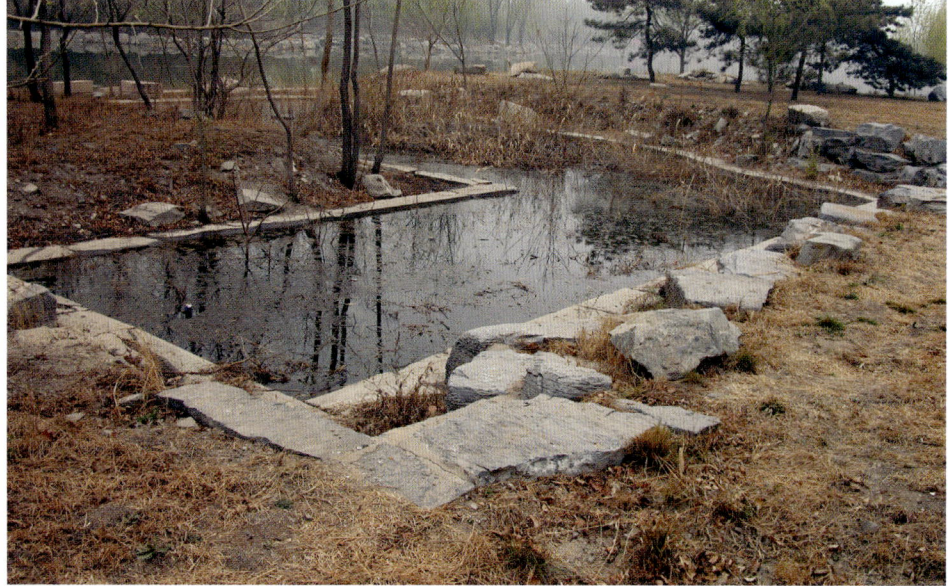

Fig. 154 Aerial view of Jian Garden (seen from southwest)

Fig. 155 Remnants of a pond

Therefore in addition to the attractions of the rockeries, winding galleries, kiosks and pavilions typical of gardens of Jiangnan, there was also the unique charm of the bamboo and plum blossoms. The imitation Qu Garden in the Changchun Garden was completed in the 32nd year of the Qianlong era (1767). In the Jobs Records kept by the Imperial Household Department at the time, it was still referred to as Qu Garden but the following year it was mentioned by the name of Jian Garden.

184 CHINA'S LOST IMPERIAL GARDEN

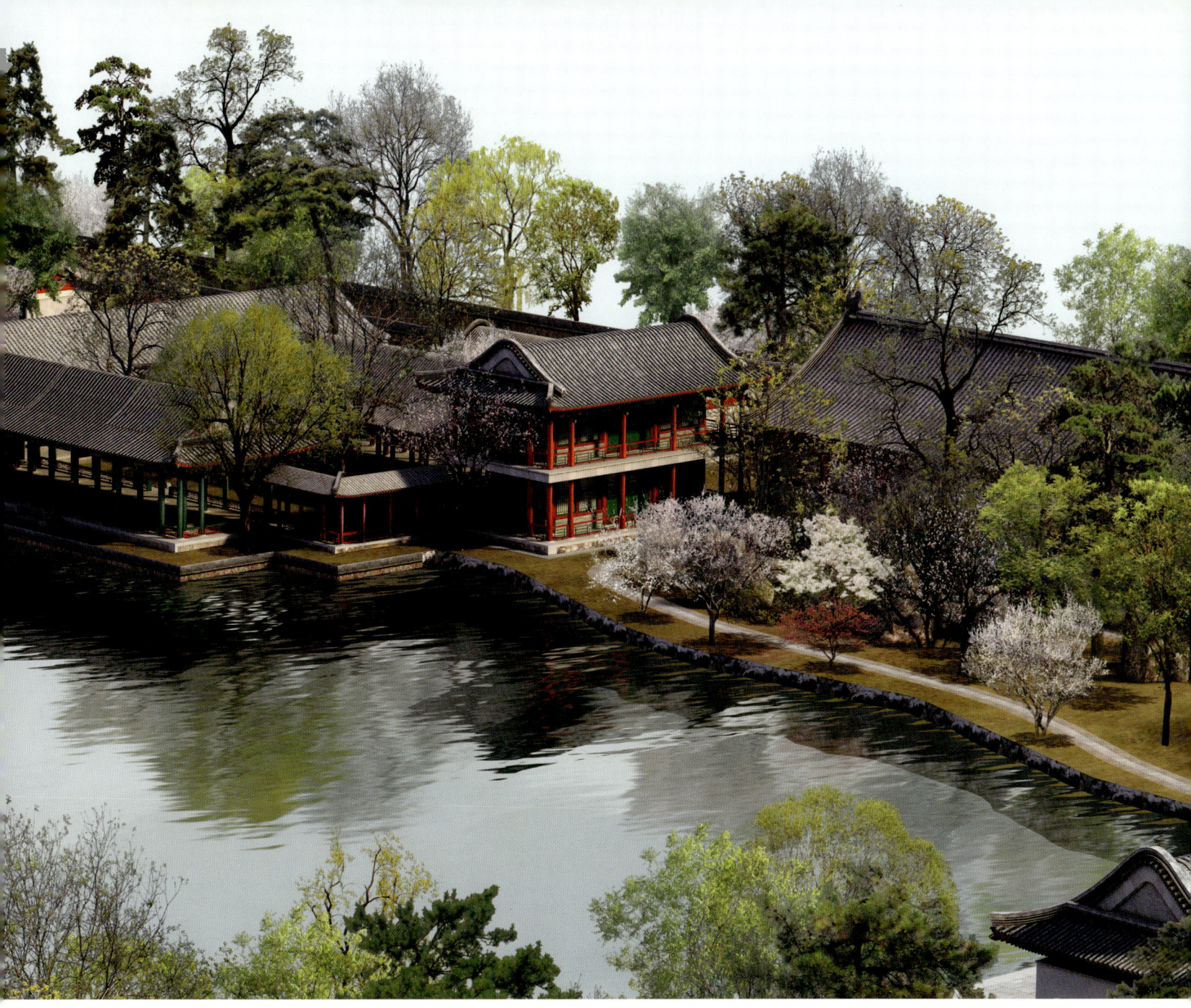

The Jian Garden was a strip running north-south (fig. 154). The northernmost hall called Shuqiong Study constituted a small courtyard with a Hanging Flowers Gate on the south side of the courtyard and a small L-shaped pond in front. The north shoreline of the pond described an arc (fig. 155) and a small pavilion called Kaiyi Pavilion on the south shore occupied the area in the hollow of the L shape. Further south was another courtyard, which faced west; a hall of five bays with open sides overlooked the water outside, "it is surrounded by water; the pavilions and terraces are reflected in the water as in a mirror. It's a pristine pure land like a glass structure."[2] In the courtyard to the east of the open-sided hall stood the Shishan Hall, the Fanghui Building and the Lüjing Gazebo. A figure painting by the missionary Jean-Denis Attiret hung in the Shishan Hall.[3] In front of the Fanghui Building was an artificial hill stacked with rocks and peonies were planted in the yard. Willows lined the long dike at its west; while unlike the Qu Garden it didn't have any bamboo or plum trees, these willows embellished this cold spot in northern China. Close to the Jian Garden at its south was a boat house; to break the monotony of the dockyard, a building of three bays called Lüjing Gazebo was built at its west.

---

1 *Yuzhi Shi*, by Emperor Qianlong, Book V, Volume 4.
2 Ibid., Book IV, Volume 35.
3 *Yuan Ming Yuan* compiled by the First Historical Archives of China, published by Shanghai Ancient Books Publishing House, May 1991, P1458.

Qingxia Study of the Qichun Garden (Garden of Elegant Spring)

清夏齋

The Qingxia Study complex (fig. 20 on page 26) occupied an area of about three hectares. Its buildings included the Qingxia Study, the West Palace Gate, the Jinghong Pavilion, the Tianlin Haijing Pavilion and the Jiqing Xianchang Pavilion.

The Qingxia Study, the main building, was a hall with an H shape in plan. It fronted a small pond and had a front hall of seven bays and a rear hall also of seven bays, both of which featured front and back porches. The front hall was used for receiving guests; the rear hall with an extended depth was furnished with beds and couches and served as a private apartment.

The front porch of the front hall led eastward to the small kiosk Tianlin Haijing, and connected at its west with a winding gallery that led to the palace gate in the west. A small kiosk called "Jiqing Xianchang" stood by the gate close to the southwest corner of the pond.

East of the rear hall of the Qingxia Study was a small hall of three bays called Jinghong Pavilion. It had a charm that was not obvious in a plan drawign. The small kiosk Tianlin Haijing facing it at its south had an interesting, visually appealing form, with its double-eave pyramidal roof and a wraparound veranda under the lower eave featuring hip-and-gable roofs.

Of special interest in the small garden was the small kiosk Jiqing Xianchang. This was a "floating cups pavilion," with a narrow water channel cut into the floor of the kiosk and linked with the pond. The water was kept flowing by the difference in elevation (fig. 156). Cups of wine were placed in the channel and friends gathered around the kiosk would drink from the cups, take in the scenery and compose verses.

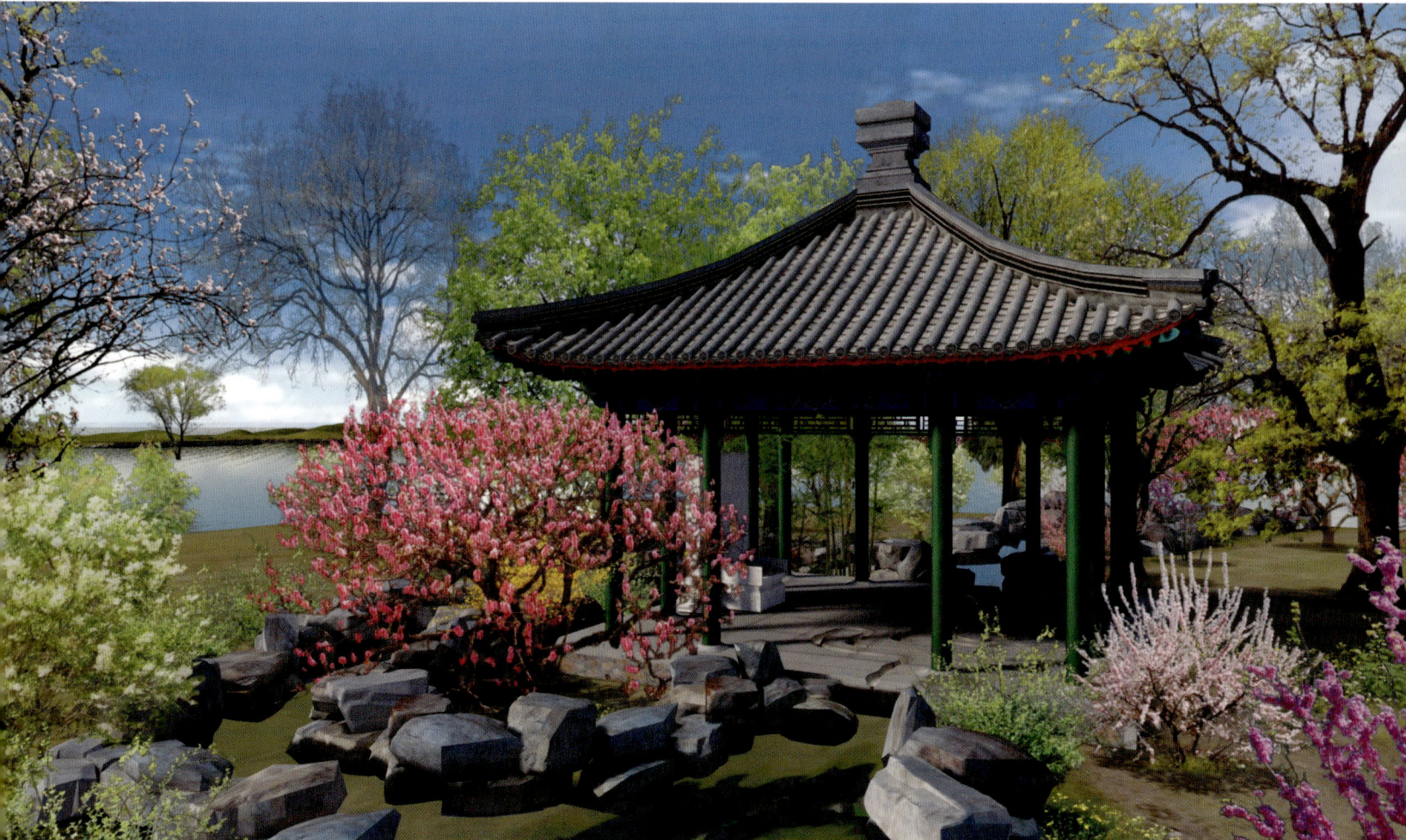

Fig. 156 Floating cups pavilion (situated in southwest corner of Qingxia Study)

Chengxin Hall (Hall of Cleansing the Mind) of the Qichun Garden

The Chengxin Hall was built in the Jiaqing era when Emperor Jiaqing undertook rebuilding in the Yuan Ming Yuan (figs. 157, 158). According to his *Record of the Chengxin Hall*, "there used to be an abandoned lot in the southwest corner of the Qichun Garden with the name of Bamboo Garden. The buildings there were crumbling and the ponds silted up. The whole place was overrun by weeds and brambles. When I chanced to pass the spot, I found the sight quite offensive. I therefore ordered that funds of the treasury be used to clean up the place and it was done. Water was introduced from a new spring outside the garden to fill the old ponds and soon they swelled into vast expanses of water. On the island in the middle of the lake a hall of five bays was erected. It was kept light and simple, with no carved or painted structural elements. It was surrounded by

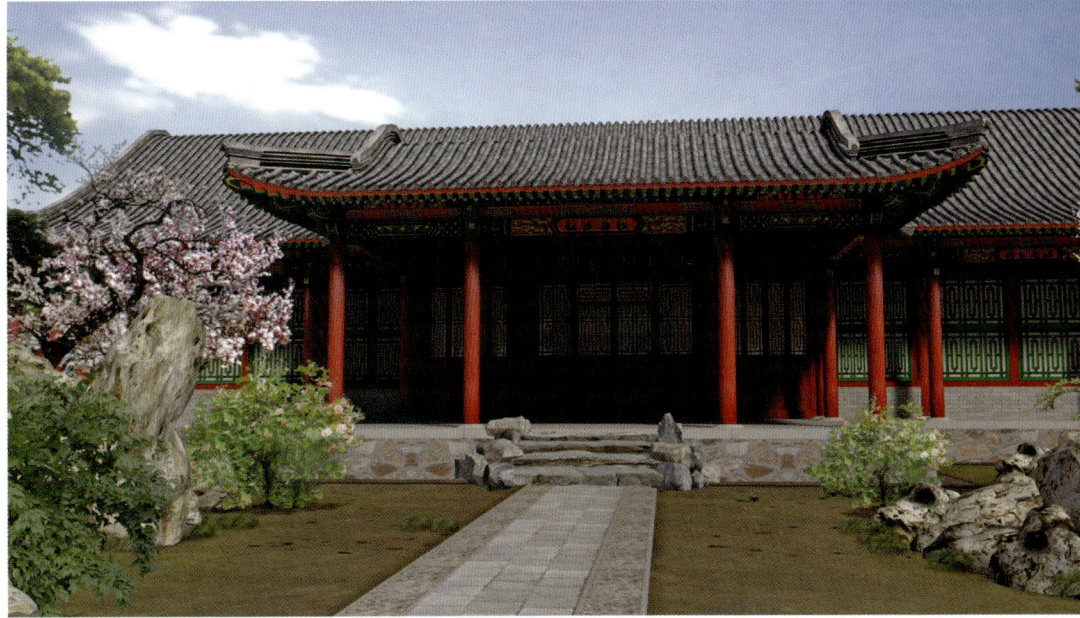

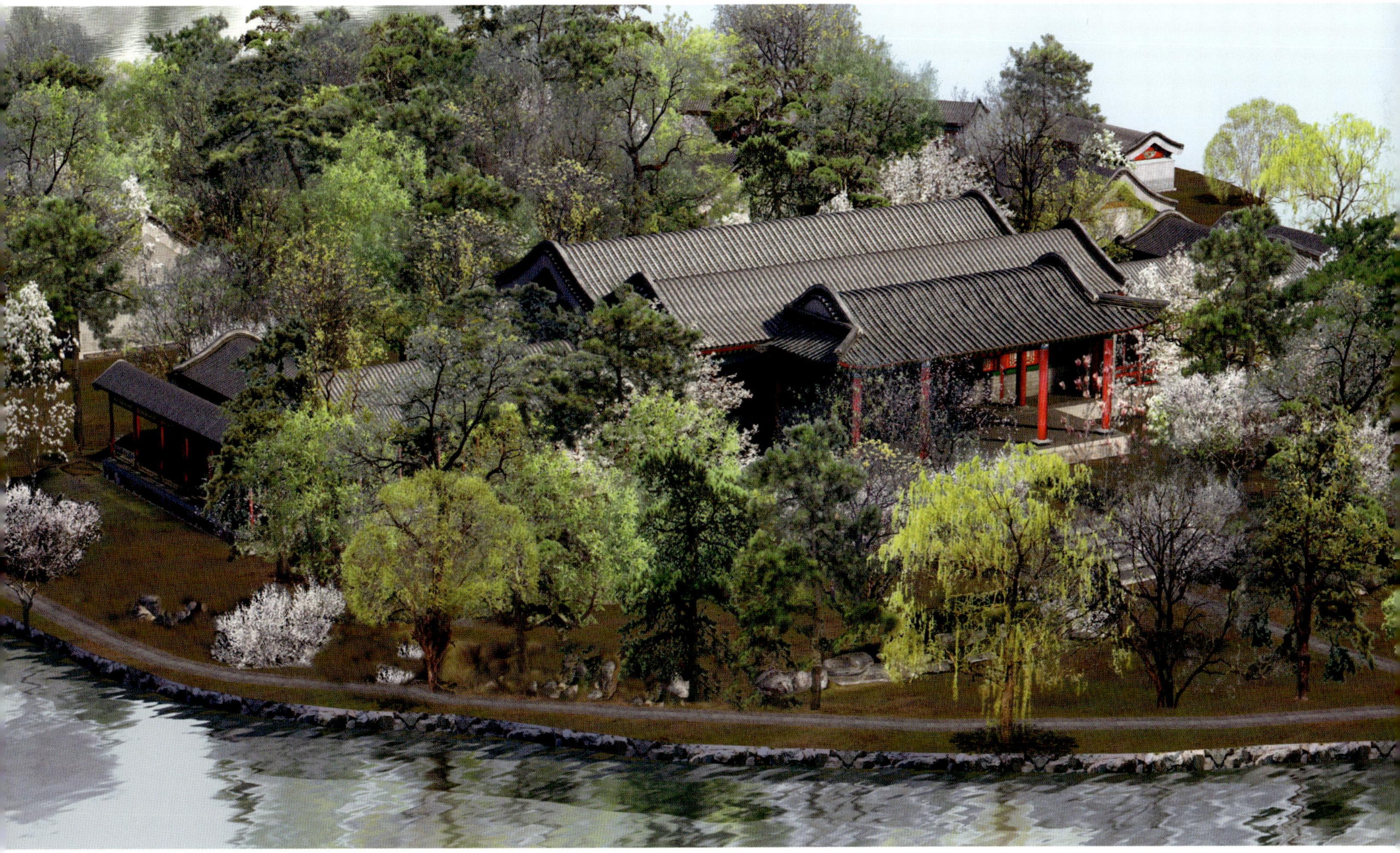

Fig. 157 Front of Chengxin Hall

Fig. 158 Chengxin Hall

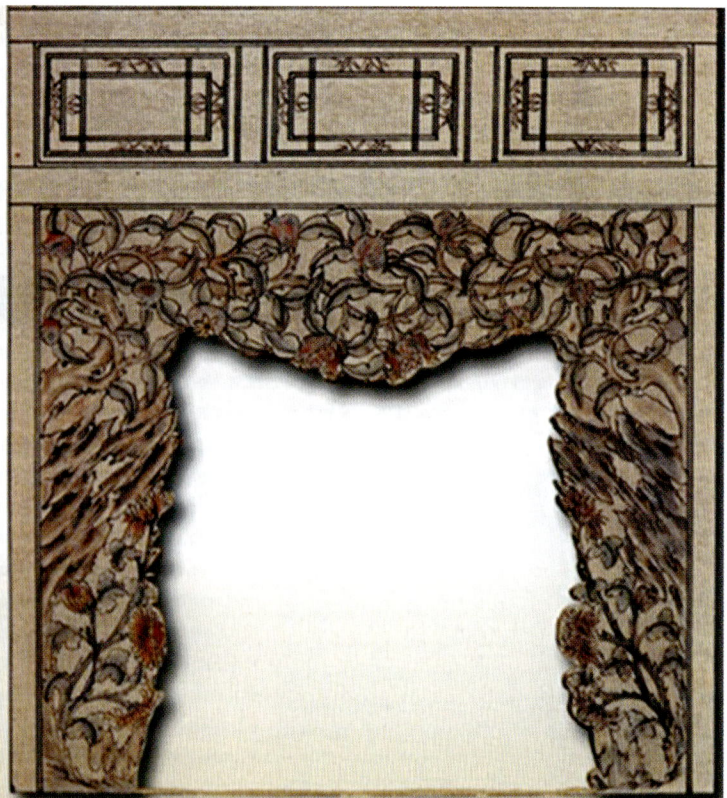
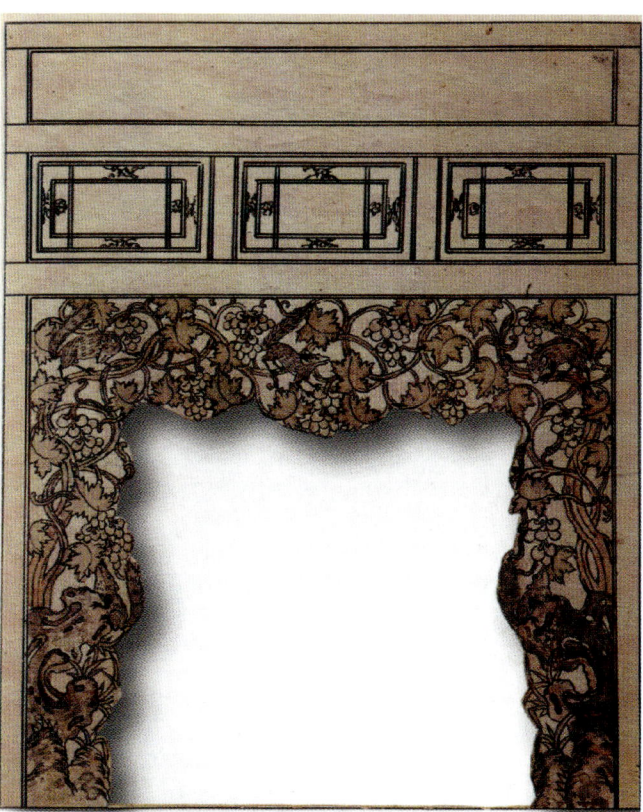

Fig. 159 Lattice partition with motif of the pomegranate

Fig. 160 Lattice partition with motif of long lineage of descendants, from drawing of Imperial Office of Architectural Design

streaked rocks. The flat bridge was a little narrow but was passable by treading carefully. It is a pleasure to tour the place in a boat. The tablet above the door is inscribed with the characters *Chengxin* (Cleansing the Mind)."[76]

The Chengxin Hall was situated on an island in the southwest of the Qichun Garden. The island measured about 125 meters east and west and 150 meters north and south, with an area of about 1.79 hectares. The Chengxin Hall comprised a main hall and the east and west ear halls, and an east and a west side hall to the north. The main hall of five bays consisted of a front and a rear hall. The east and west ear halls of six bays each extended three bays northward. The two northernmost bays were open-sided, and the one on the east side was called Qixu Pavilion and the one on the west was Chuihong Gazebo (Gazebo of Rainbow). Surrounding the east and west ear halls at the front and the left and right were terraces and galleries of 12 bays each.

The Chengxin Hall was architecturally rich and varied. The front hall of the main hall had a flush gable roof, while the rear hall projected an overhanging gable roof. The east and west verandas of the rear hall were also topped with an overhanging gable roof, while the front veranda of the front hall and the three verandas of the Qixu Pavilion and the Chuihong Gazebo had hip-and-gable roofs. The main hall and the east and west ear halls were structurally independent of one another, with the gable walls of the main hall flush against the gable walls of the ear halls. The terraces and galleries were attached to the front of the east and west ear halls.

A plan drawing of the interior furnishings of the Chengxin Hall shows a richly varied decor achieved by using various techniques of interior decoration. Around the space of the main hall, 14 subspaces were created by the use of partitions. They consisted of a door hall, passage halls, bedrooms and lounges. These subspaces fulfilled myriad functions and set off the scale of the main hall. Decorative motifs created and enhanced the atmospheres in the various spaces. Thus in the front hall one found elements carved with auspicious symbols of longevity and fertility and long lineage and the rear hall was decorated with motifs of the pomegranate, an auspicious symbol of fertility because of its many seeds and the gourds and their long vines symbolizing long life and good fortune (figs. 159, 160).

西湖十景 Ten Scenes of the West Lake in the Yuan Ming Yuan

The beautiful scenery of Jiangnan fascinated Emperor Qianlong. He might have had more noble reasons for undertaking six southern tours, but there is no denying that his fondness for the Jiangnan landscape was one motivation behind those trips, as attested by the numerous scenes emulating the scenic and landscape attractions of Jiangnan in his imperial gardens. Long before his southern tours he already named some vistas in the Yuan Ming Yuan the Ten Scenes of West Lake.

The vistas emulating the Ten Scenes of West Lake in the Yuan Ming Yuan were of disparate sizes and forms and were built at different periods. They included complete building complexes, such as the Pinghu Qiuyue (Autumn Moon over a Calm Lake) and the Quyuan Fenghe Complex (fig. 161), which were themed areas in the Yuan Ming Yuan; then they might form part of a themed area; in some cases it was just a name given to a building without an actual physical representation of the scene emulated. Those that constituted a themed area were built in a setting that bore some resemblance to the West Lake scenes emulated. Thus the Pinghu Qiuyue Complex had a large expanse of lake water at its south and the buildings were interlaced with pavilions and galleries. In the case of the Quyuan Fenghe Complex, it featured an ordinary farm house that was in imitation of a wine-making cottage; a pond overgrown with lotuses in front was a reminder of the association with the "distillery" and the "lotus pond." Those imitation scenes that were represented by a building, such as the Sudi Chunxiao Open Hall, Leifeng Xizhao Open Hall (Open Hall of Sunset on Leifeng Pagoda), Huagang Guanyu Open Hall (Open Hall of Fish Watching in Flower Cove), Nanping

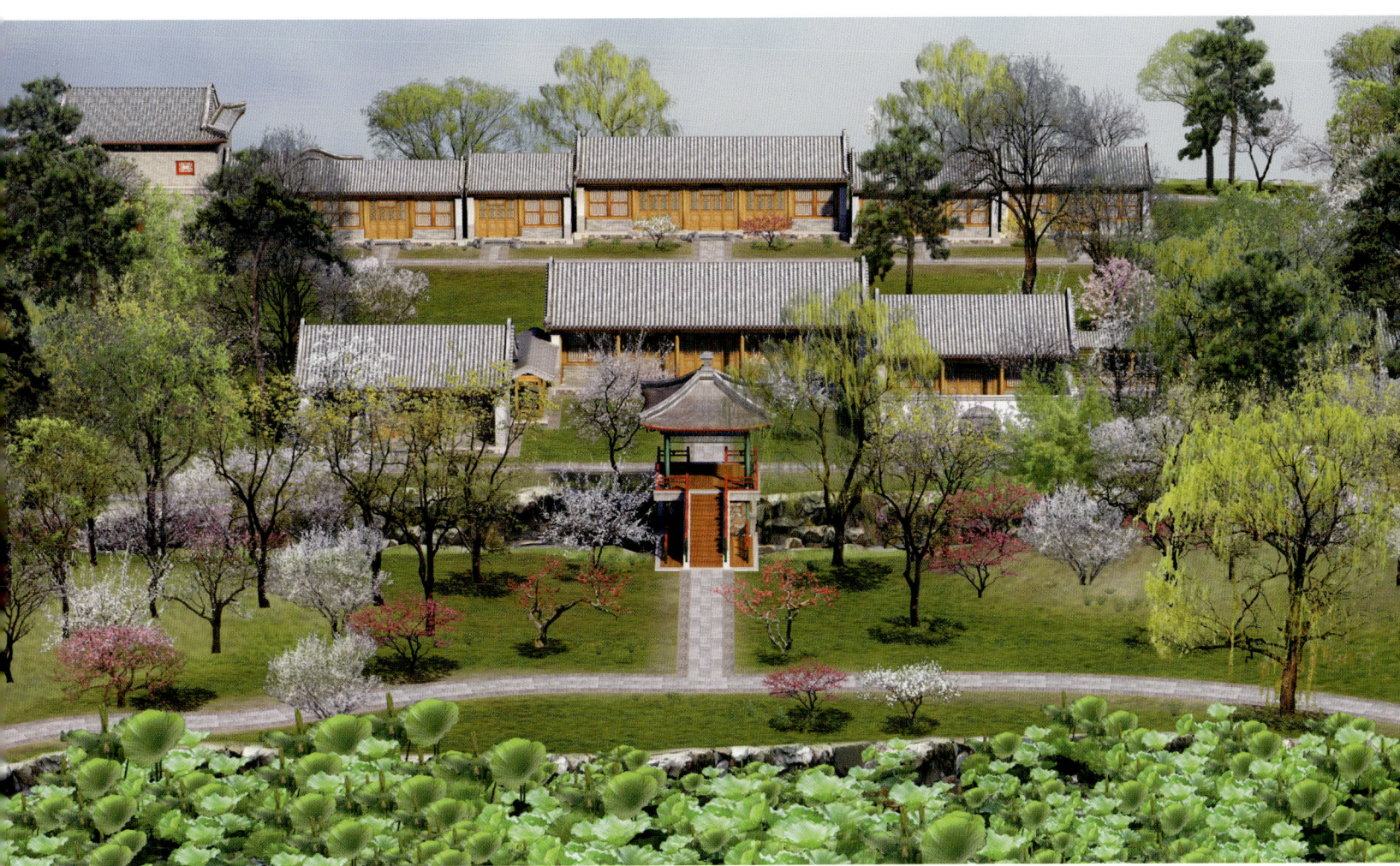

Fig. 161 Quyuan Fenghe Complex

Wanzhong Pavilion (Evening Bell on Mount Nanping), were all situated where a scene similar to its namesake could be viewed. Thus at the Leifeng Xizhao Open Hall on the east shore of the Lake of Happiness the observer had a view of glorious sunsets. The Sudi Chunxiao Open Hall, situated on a long dike in the Tianran Tuhua Complex, commanding a view of the pond of the Quyuan Fenghe Complex on its east and the pond in the Tianran Tuhua on its west and ornamented by trees and flowers, looked very much like the Sudi Chunxiao landscape in Hangzhou. Some of the Ten Scenes were merely a stone architectural arch, such as the Liulang Wenying (Orioles Singing in the Willows) (fig. 20 on page 25), the Liangfeng Chayun (Twin Peaks Piercing the Clouds) and the Duanqiao Canxue (Melting Snow on a Broken Bridge), and the Santan Yingyue (Three Ponds Reflecting the Moon) (fig. 162); they served mainly to stir the imagination of the observer and evoke associations, to humor the wish to replicate beautiful West Lake—reputed paradise on earth—in the Yuan Ming Yuan.

The construction of the Ten Scenes of West Lake in the Yuan Ming Yuan started early in the Yongzheng era. Yongzheng accompanied Emperor Kangxi on his fourth southern tour and had an intimate encounter with the Ten Scenes of West Lake in Hangzhou. After his southern tour in the 16th year of his reign (1751) Emperor Qianlong too had his first taste of the West Lake. It was unrealistic to try to make an exact replica of the scenery of the West Lake in the Yuan Ming Yuan, for the Ten Scenes of West Lake needed the native natural environment and landscape to set them off. The Yuan Ming Yuan, an artificial park made by man from scratch, could not compete with West Lake in scale and landscape and water resources and therefore the creators of the imitation Ten Scenes had to make choices and settle for less.

During the sixty years of his reign Emperor Qianlong undertook a total of six southern tours, in the course of which he visited many places in Jiangnan, including Huai'an, Yangzhou, Suzhou, Hangzhou, Huizhou and Jiangning. He considered his southern tours as one of the two most important things he accomplished in his life. Some of his ministers, though, were privately

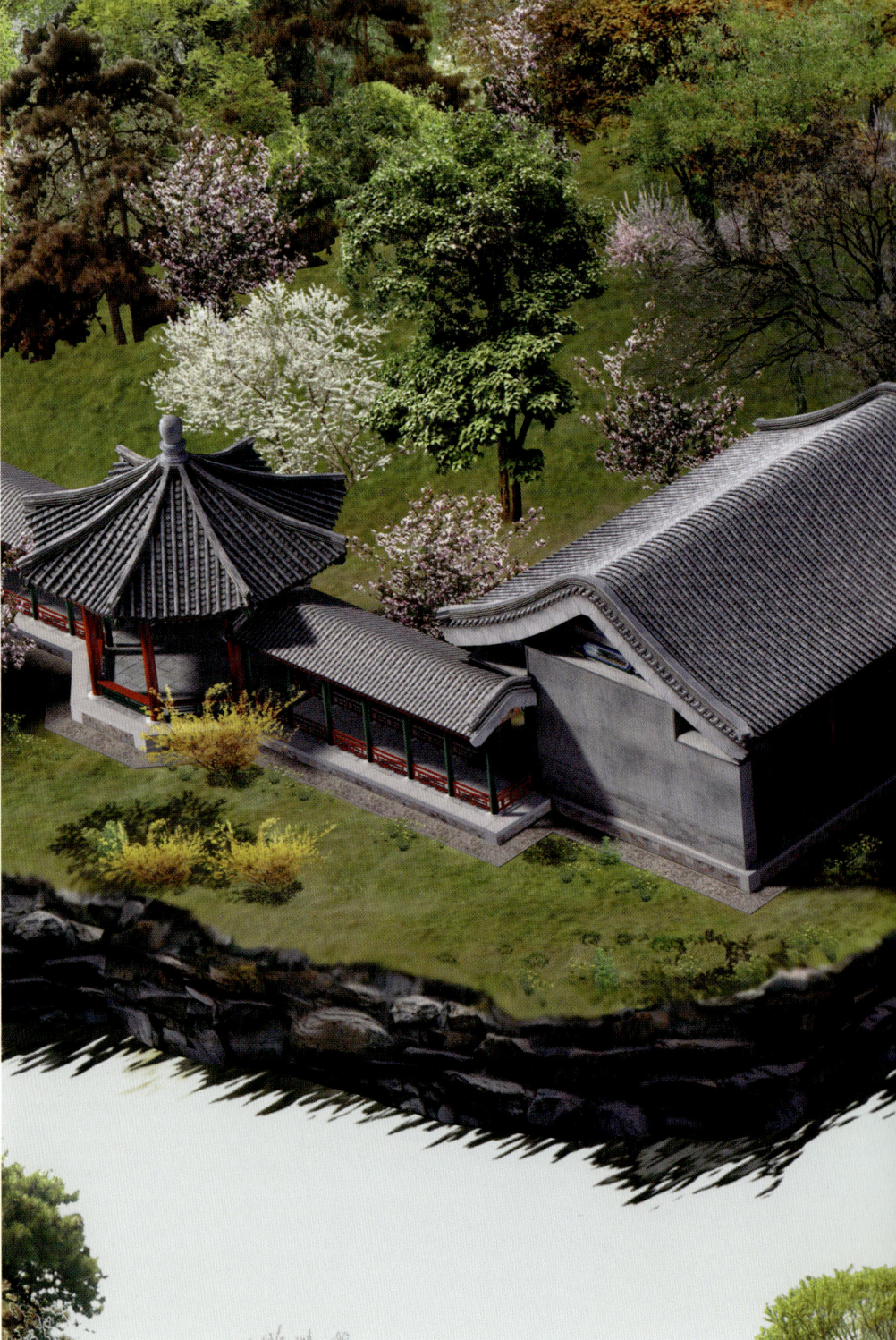

Fig. 162 Santan Yingyue

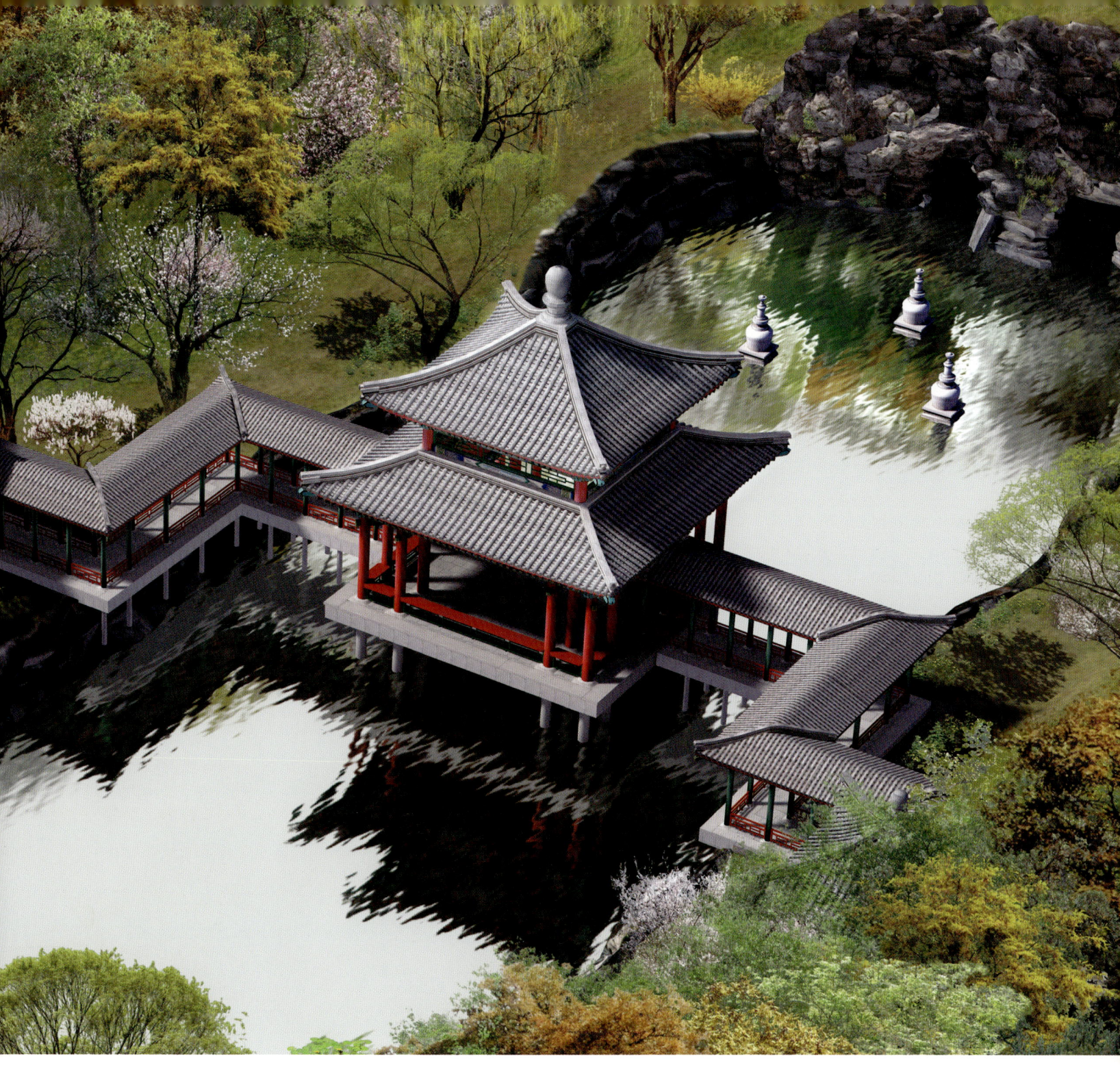

critical of Qianlong's sightseeing tours in the name of inspecting the southern precincts of his realm, at great cost to the coffers of the state, but they could only offer passive, silent resistance and some were known to have been removed from office for this resistance. A huge amount of resources was consumed in receiving the imperial visits on Qianlong's southern tours. Thus just the prefecture of Suzhou alone had to spend 300 thousand taels of silver on road repairs. The round trip was 3340.8 kilometers. While Qianlong emphasized the need to constantly bear in mind the financial burden and counsel against extravagance and demanded that local governments practice thrift in receiving the emperor and his retinue, the reality was that no expenses were spared in his reception. In his old age Qianlong conceded that "in my sixty years of rule, I have never had any moral lapse, but my six southern tours were a burden on my subjects and were indeed counterproductive."[1]

---

1 *Langji Congtan* by Liang Zhangju, Volume 3, quoted in *Emperor Qianlong*, by Sun Wenliang, Zhang Jie and Zheng Chuanshui.

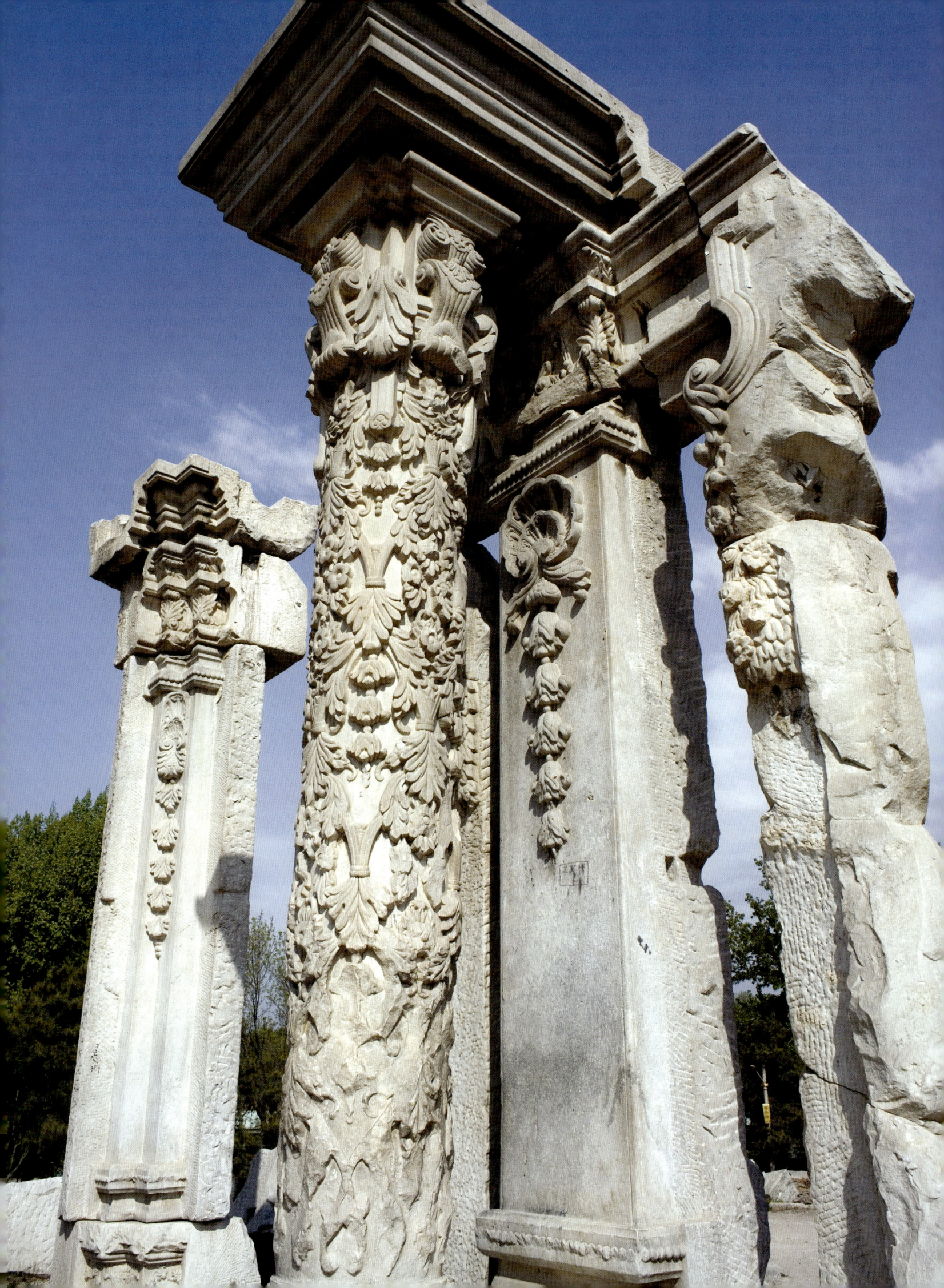

CHAPTER XIII
Xiyang Building Complex (Complex of European Buildings)

The Xiyang Building Complex, situated in the north of the Changchun Garden next to the north enclosure wall, measured 850 meters east-west and 115 meters north-south with an area of about 8.13 hectares. It included the Xie Qiqu Pavilion (Pavilion Harmonizing Surprise and Delight), the Wanhua Zhen Complex (Complex of the Maze), the Yangque Long (Aviary), the Bamboo Pavilion, the Fangwai Observatory (Observatory of Lands Beyond), the Haiyan Hall (Hall of Calm Seas), the Yuanying Observatory (Immense Ocean Observatory), the Da Shuifa Fountain (Great Fountain), the Xianfa Hill (Perspective Hill) and the Xianfa Wall (Perspective Wall) at the Rectangular River (fig. 164). The planning of the Xiyang Building Complex started in the 12th year of the Qianlong era (1747) and construction began in the 15th year of Qianlong's reign (1750). In the 17th year of the Qianlong era (1752) the main building the Xie Qiqu Pavilion was completed; in the second month of the following year interior decoration and the execution of paintings began in its main hall, galleries and kiosks. In the 24th year (1759) the Haiyan Hall, the Fangwai Observatory and the Da Shuifa Fountain were completed. Not until 24 years later, in the 48th year of Qianlong's reign (1783), was the Yuanying Observatory completed in the north of the Da Shuifa Fountain.

The Xiyang Building Complex were built at a time when European architecture was gradually moving away from late Baroque into the Rococo style and therefore Giuseppe Castiglione, the architectural designer of the Xiyang Building Complex in the early stage, adopted both the Baroque and the Rococo styles in those buildings and covered them with Chinese-style glazed roof tiles and glazed tile decorative patterns, with details varying from building to building. The Xie Qiqu Pavilion, the Fangwai Observatory and the Haiyan Hall featured ornate outside staircases that led down to fountains outside, a typical feature of 18th century European gardens. Castiglione died in the 31st year of Qianlong's reign (1766) and the design of the Yuanying Observatory was entrusted to other artists (fig. 163).

Facing page
Fig. 163 Close view of remnants of Yuanying Observatory

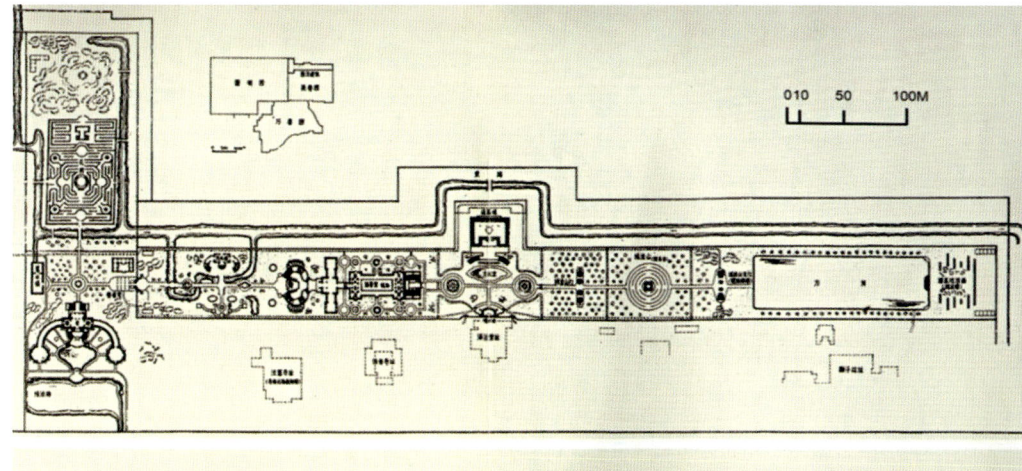

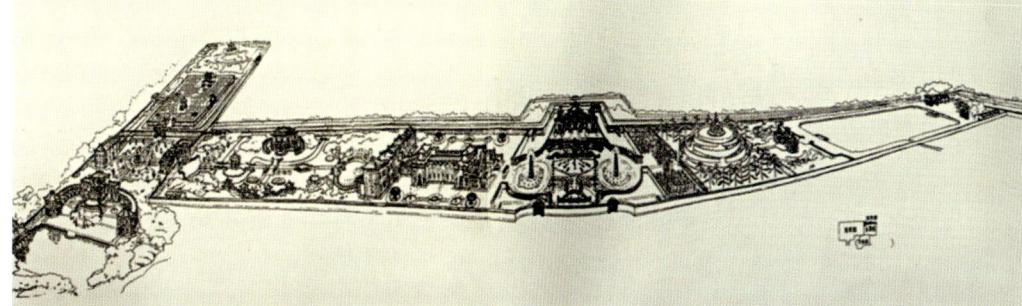

Fig. 164 General map of the Xiyang Building Complex in Yuan Ming Yuan

諧奇趣 Xie Qiqu Pavilion (Pavilion Harmonizing Surprise and Delight)

The Xie Qiqu Pavilion, located at the western end of the Xiyang Building Complex, was the earliest building group in the complex (fig. 166). Its main building, rectangular in plan, was joined by curved galleries in the shape of splayed arms to two octagonal pavilions at its southeast and southwest. The central part of the main building was three-storied, with three windows on each floor in section (fig. 169 on pages 196 and 197), indicating a width of three bays. It had a four-slope roof; at either side the section of the building shows two stories and two windows on each floor, indicating a width of two bays and the roof was flat. Each of the two galleries was five bays long, one story in height and covered with flat roofs. The octagonal pavilions were two stories high and topped with octagonal roofs; the width of each of the eight sides of the pavilions was approximately the same as that of the galleries. On its south side curved staircases led down from the second story directly to a pool; the two staircases on the north side, also leading down from the second story, were regular-shaped two-flight stairs. The physical mass of the building group went from the three-story height of the central section down to the two stories at either side and descended further to the one-story galleries before climbing back up to the two-story height of the octagonal pavilions, much as a musical tune dropping gradually from a high note before rising to end in a forte note (fig. 165). This building was richly decorated, with niches in the exterior walls and glazed tile decorated door and window frames. The octagonal pavilions featured columns of a modified Ionic design; the four-slope roof in the central section of the building was an imitation of the Chinese hip roof, whose ridges and rooftop railing were all decorated with glazed tiles. Interestingly not only the roof was inspired by a Chinese architectural style, even the stone lions by its doors combined Chinese and Western elements, with a Western head and freehand decorative patterns on its back all the way to the tail that resembled the auspicious knots seen on Chinese lion sculptures (figs. 167, 168).

In the embrace of the two curved galleries was a water basin in the middle of a court. The pool's periphery consisted of 14 curved sections and the balustrades by the water were ornamented with animal sculptures such as hounds and sheep. In the water basin were spouts in the shape of crabs, shrimps, ducks, geese, fish and lotuses. A reservoir building in the northwest supplied the water for the fountains via steel pipes.

Fig. 165　North side of Xie Qiqu Pavilion

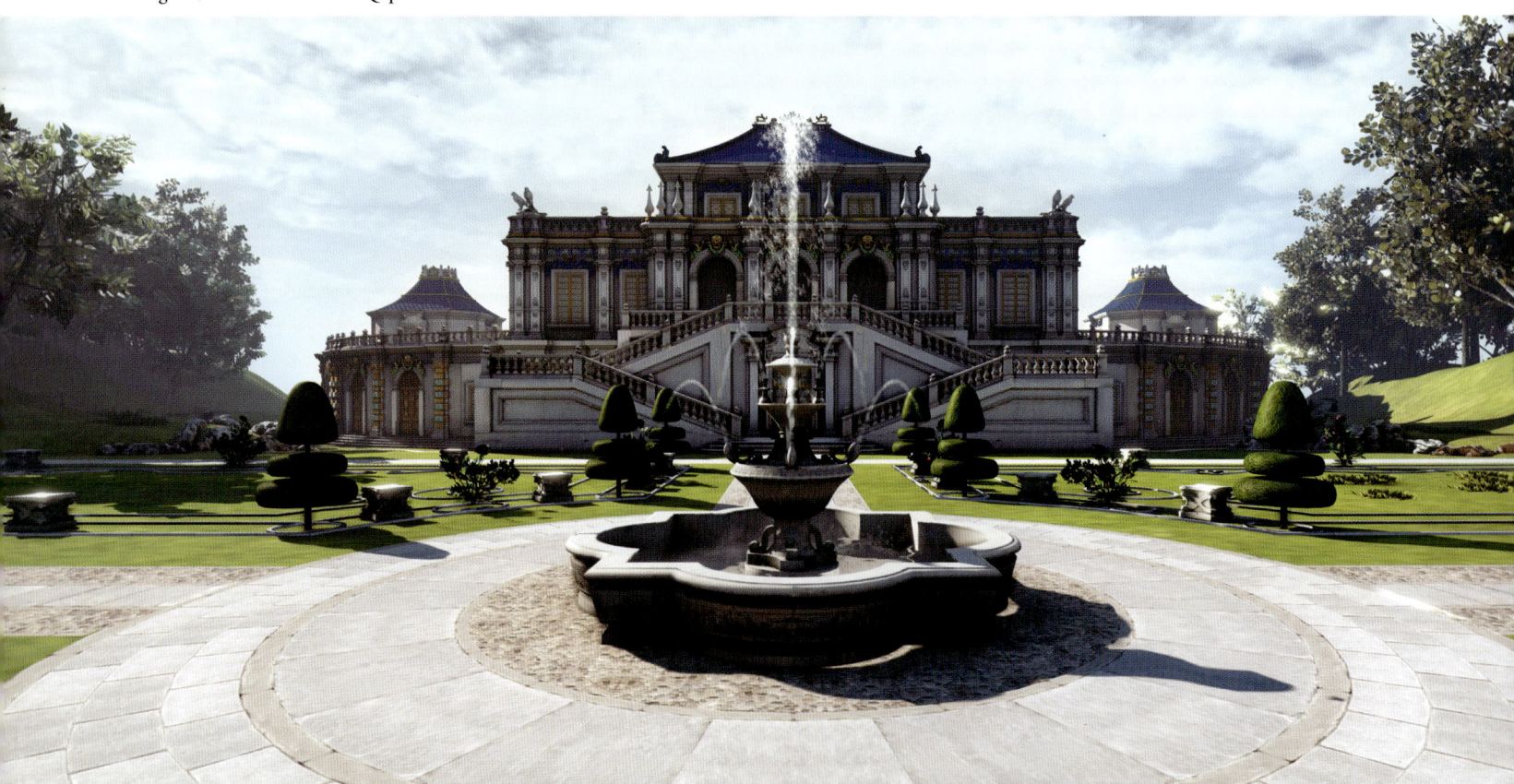

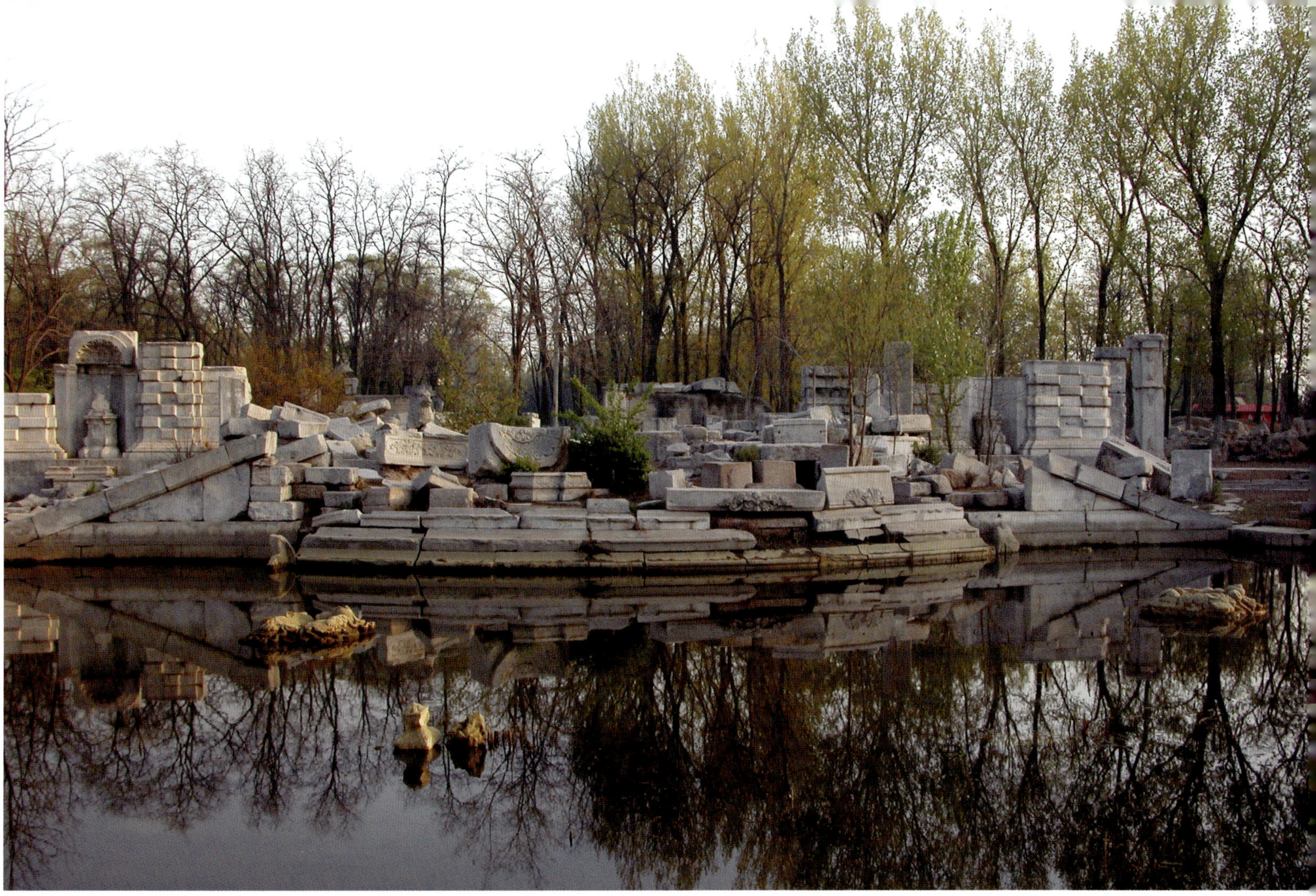

Fig. 166 Ruins at a glance

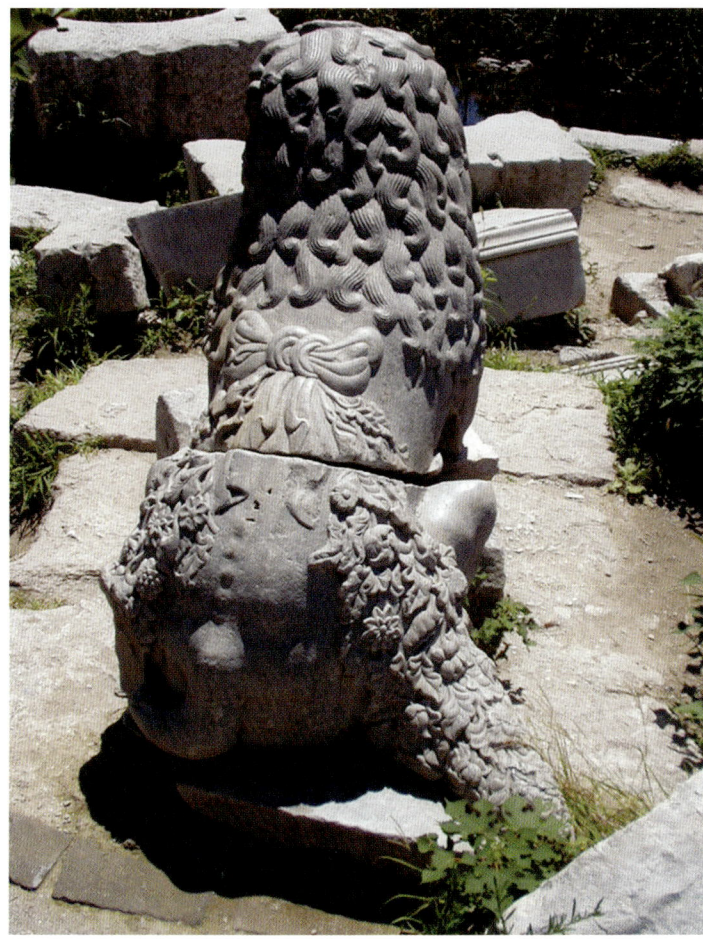

Fig. 167 Back of stone lion

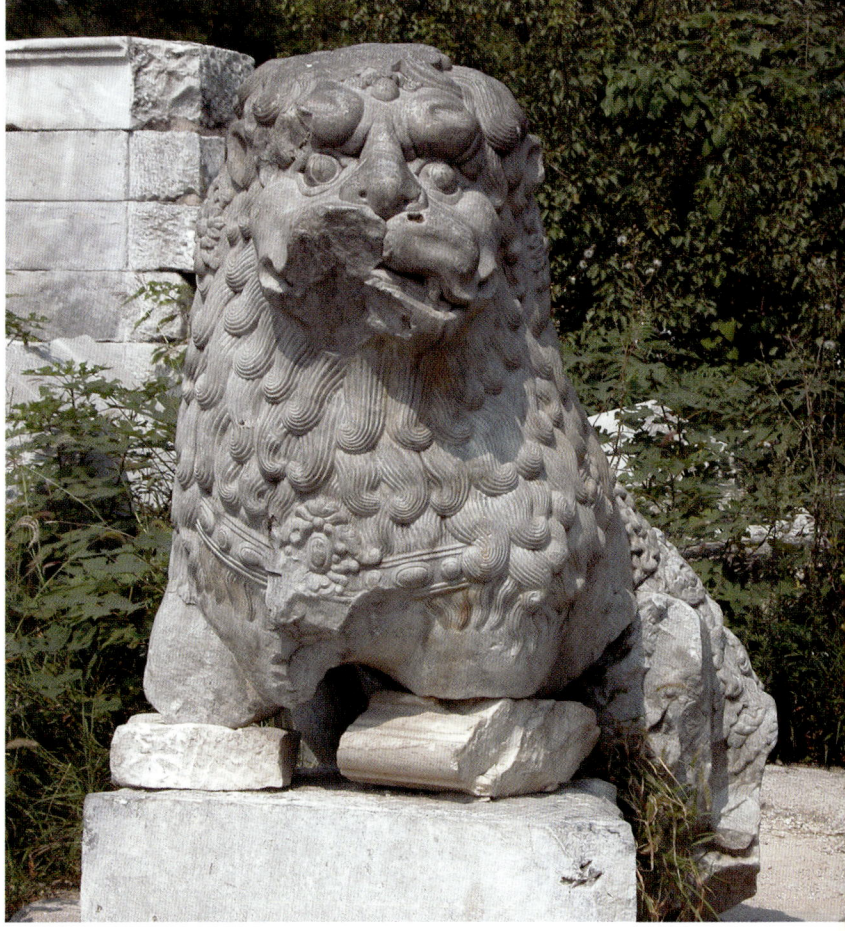

Fig. 168 Front of stone lion

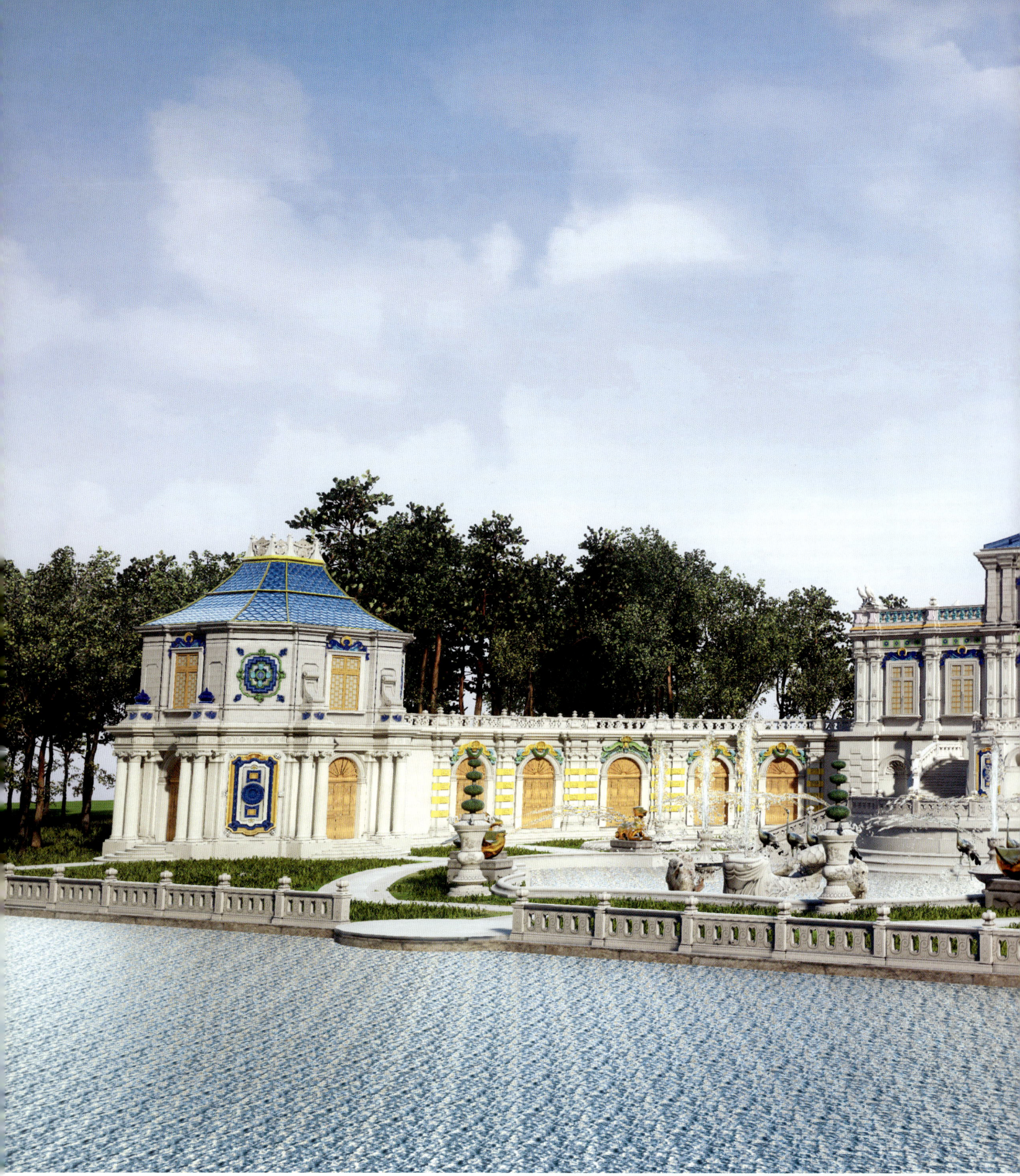

Fig. 169 Picture of reconstituted Xie Qiqu Pavilion

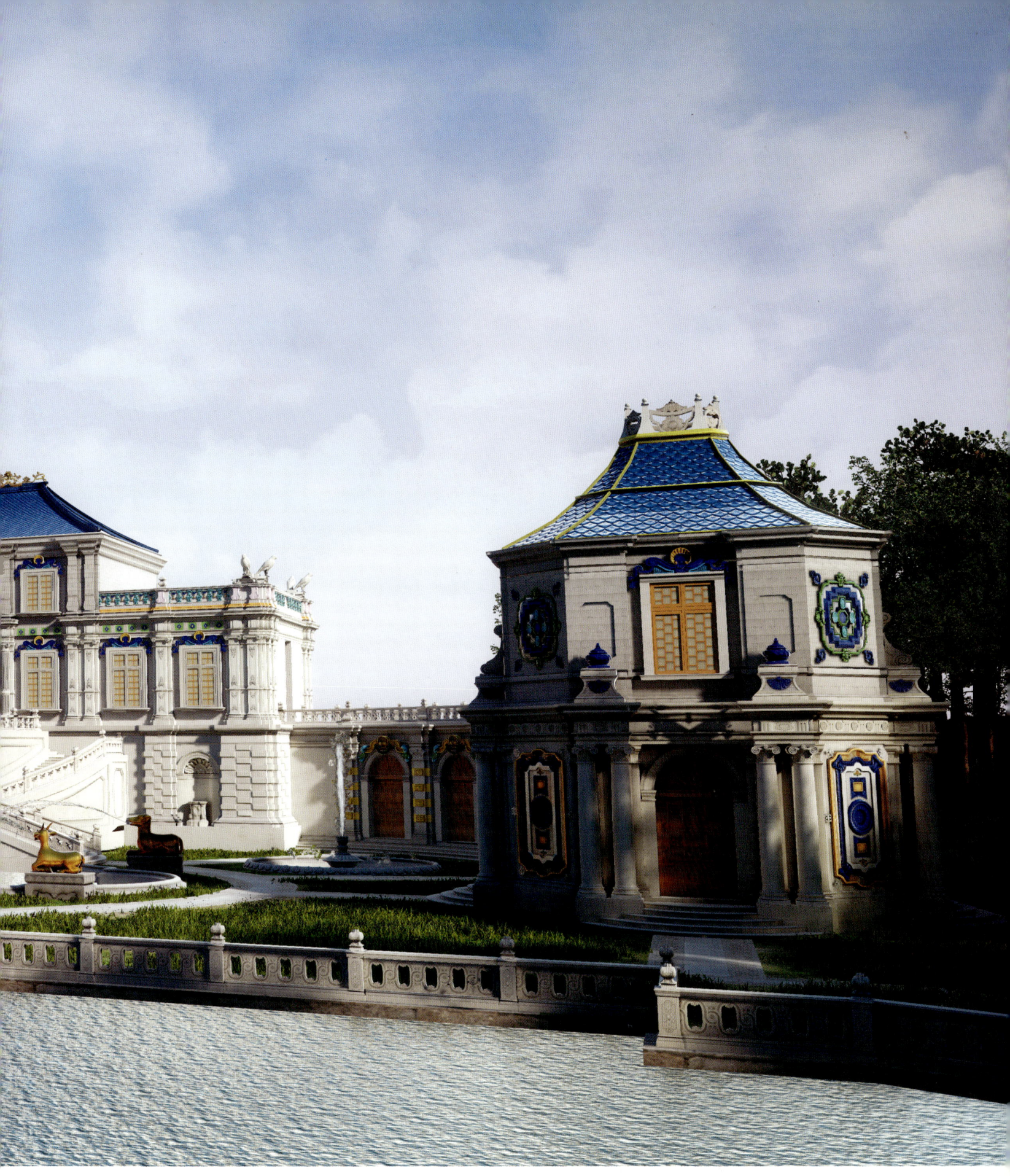

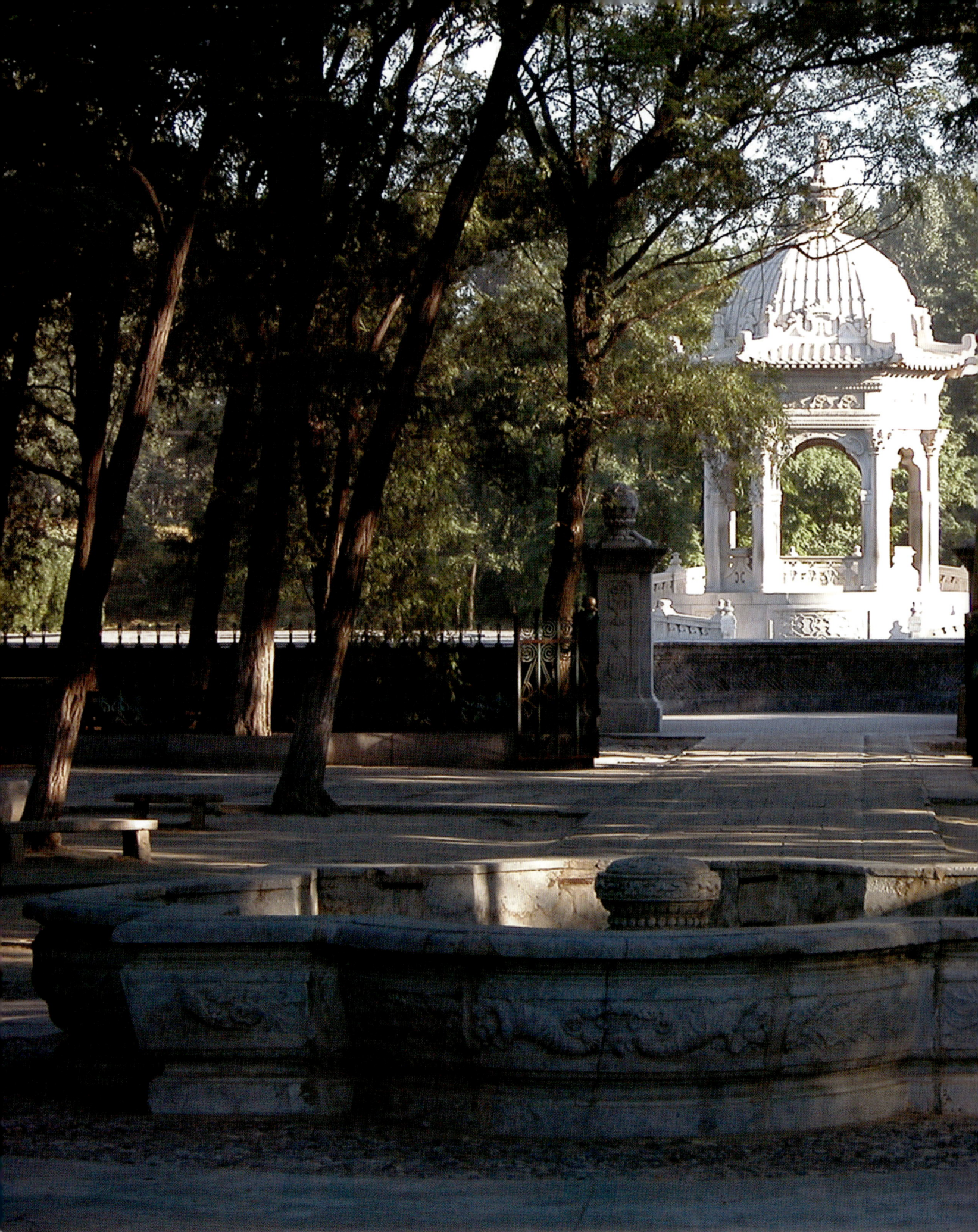

Fig. 170 Wanhua Zhen Complex

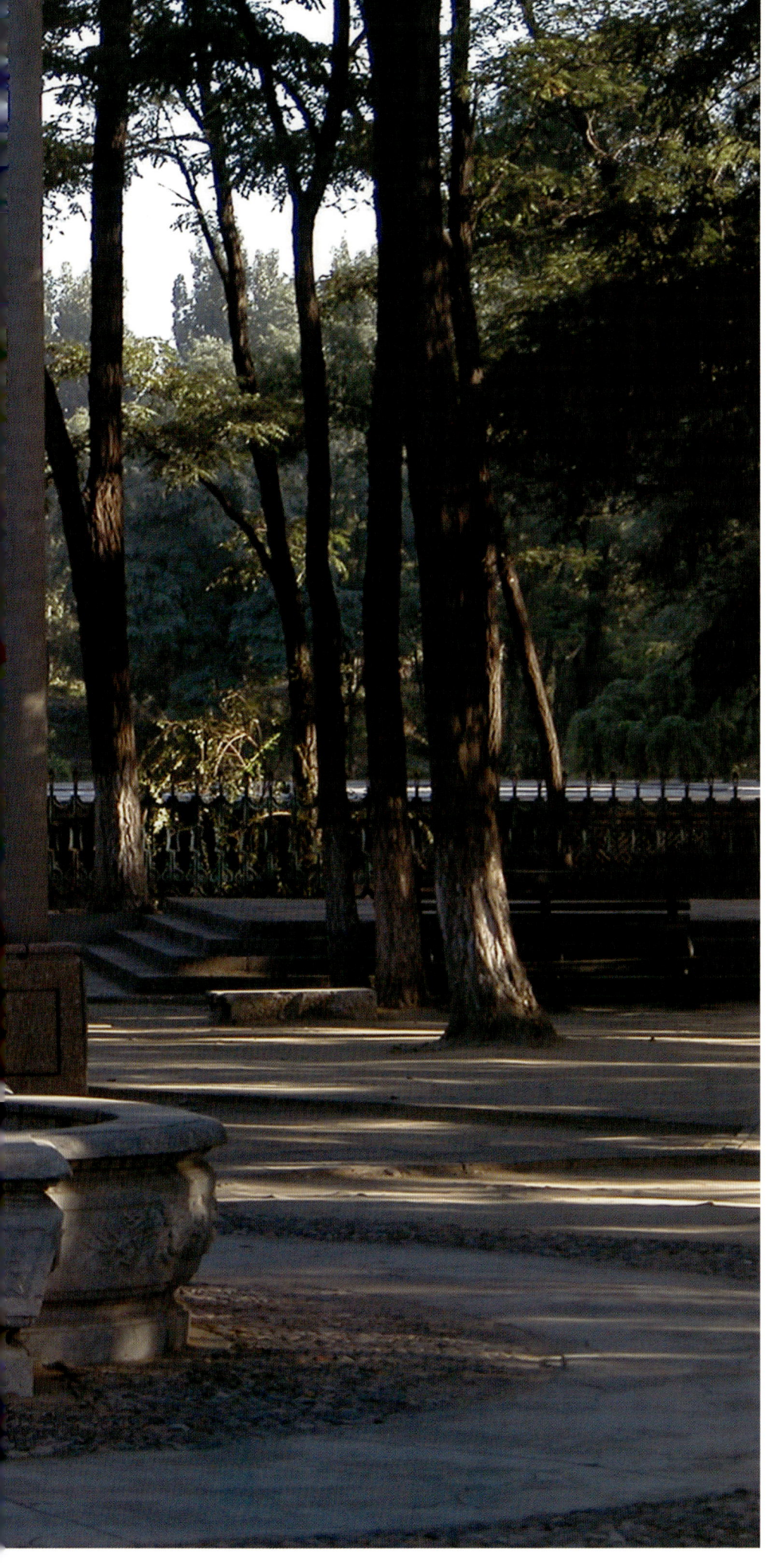

萬花陣 Wanhua Zhen Complex (Complex of the Maze)

The Wanhua Zhen Complex, located due north of the Xie Qiqu Pavilion along a central axis, was a maze garden (fig. 170). At its center was a round pavilion surrounded by sections of low walls about a meter high, creating paths with uncertain issues. In the periphery of the area of low wall sections were openings or entrances; once inside these entrances a visitor had to navigate a maze to try to reach the pavilion at the center.

The round pavilion in the maze was seated on a round base. It was round in plan and was supported on eight round pillars; the beams and tie-beams between pillars were all rectilinear and the roof consisted of an octagonal apron with short Chinese style slopes and eaves and, above it, a dome terminating in an ornamental cap. It was a very small round kiosk.

The low walls of the Wanhua Zhen Complex bore swastika patterns and were ornamented with plants on top, hence the name "Wanhua Zhen," literally "swastika and flowers maze." At the openings of the low walls stood columns sculpted with pineapples. These columns once functioned as structural support for iron grille gates.

In European gardens, this type of mazes would be constructed with manicured hedges, which had a particular charm. In the Yuan Ming Yuan, climatic conditions were not suited for a topiary maze and low walls were used instead.

PART II SCENERY OF THE YUAN MING YUAN

海晏堂 Haiyan Hall (Hall of Calm Seas)

A path that ran east-west from between the Xie Qiqu Pavilion and the Wanhua Zhen Complex, dotted all the way with architectural elements such as fountains, pools and bridges, led to the Haiyan Hall. This was a building group of some magnitude, consisting mainly of two buildings and a large pool. The main building of the Haiyan Hall faced west and had in front of it a large elliptical pool (fig. 171). The building behind it housed a reservoir.

The Haiyan Hall was two stories high. In plan it consisted of five rectangular sections of varying dimensions. In section it had a grand western façade; the middle three bays, with one door and two windows, projected out in front; two grand curvilinear staircases descended from the second story and embraced a pool. The two bays at either end of the building also projected forth slightly with the ground-level portions extending sufficiently out to accommodate a rooftop terrace that served as a balcony, to which access could be had from the second story through a door for anyone desiring to enjoy an outdoor view. The roof was covered with glazed tiles; the three sections in the middle were two-sloped, with a parapet above the three central bays. At either end of the building the roof was four-sloped for a change. The building was particularly ornate in its ornamentation. At the sides of the bronze door on the second story were two columns with modified Ionic capitals supporting

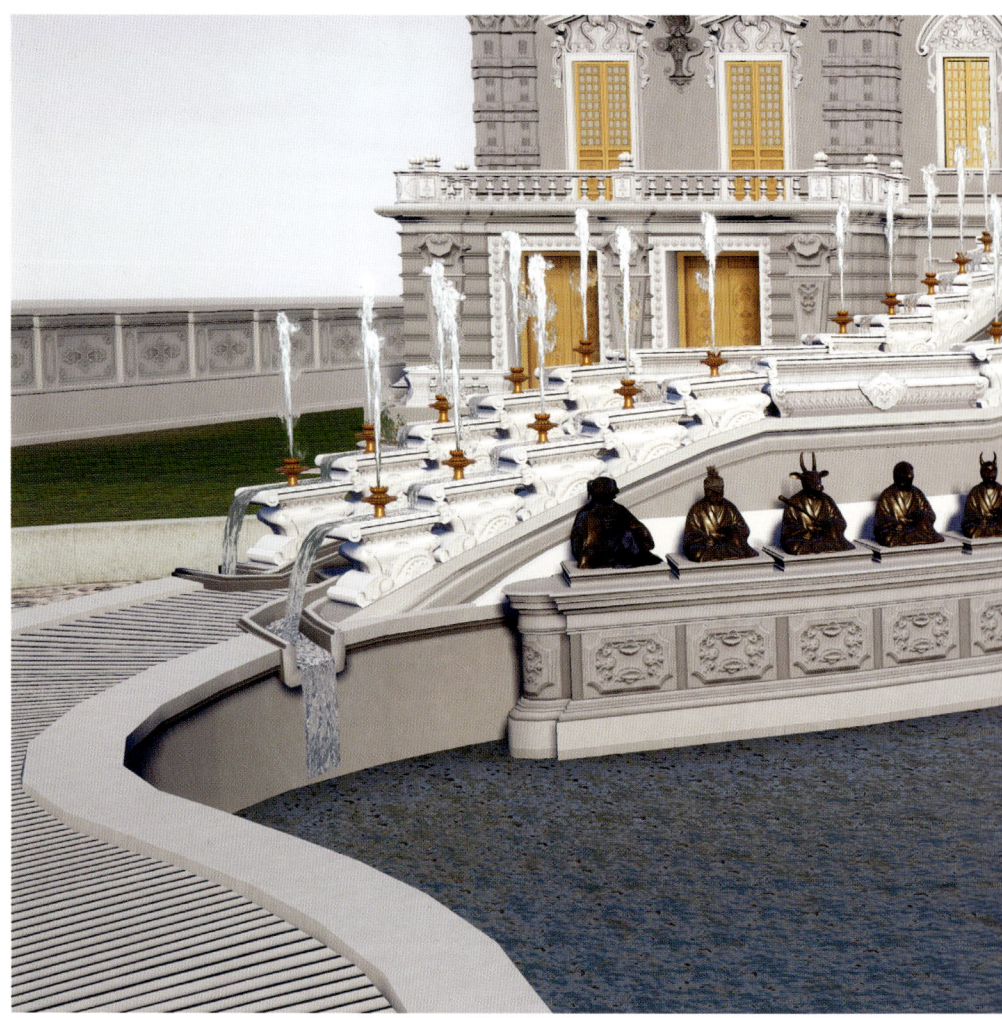

Fig. 171 Picture of reconstituted Haiyan Hall

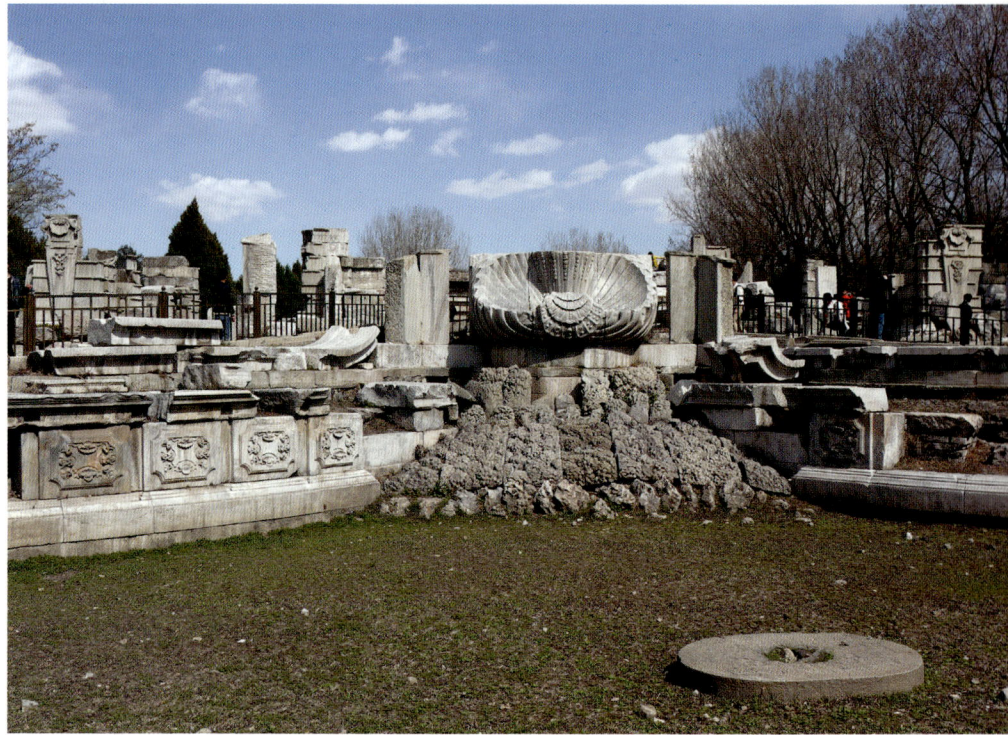

Fig. 172 Ruins

200 CHINA'S LOST IMPERIAL GARDEN

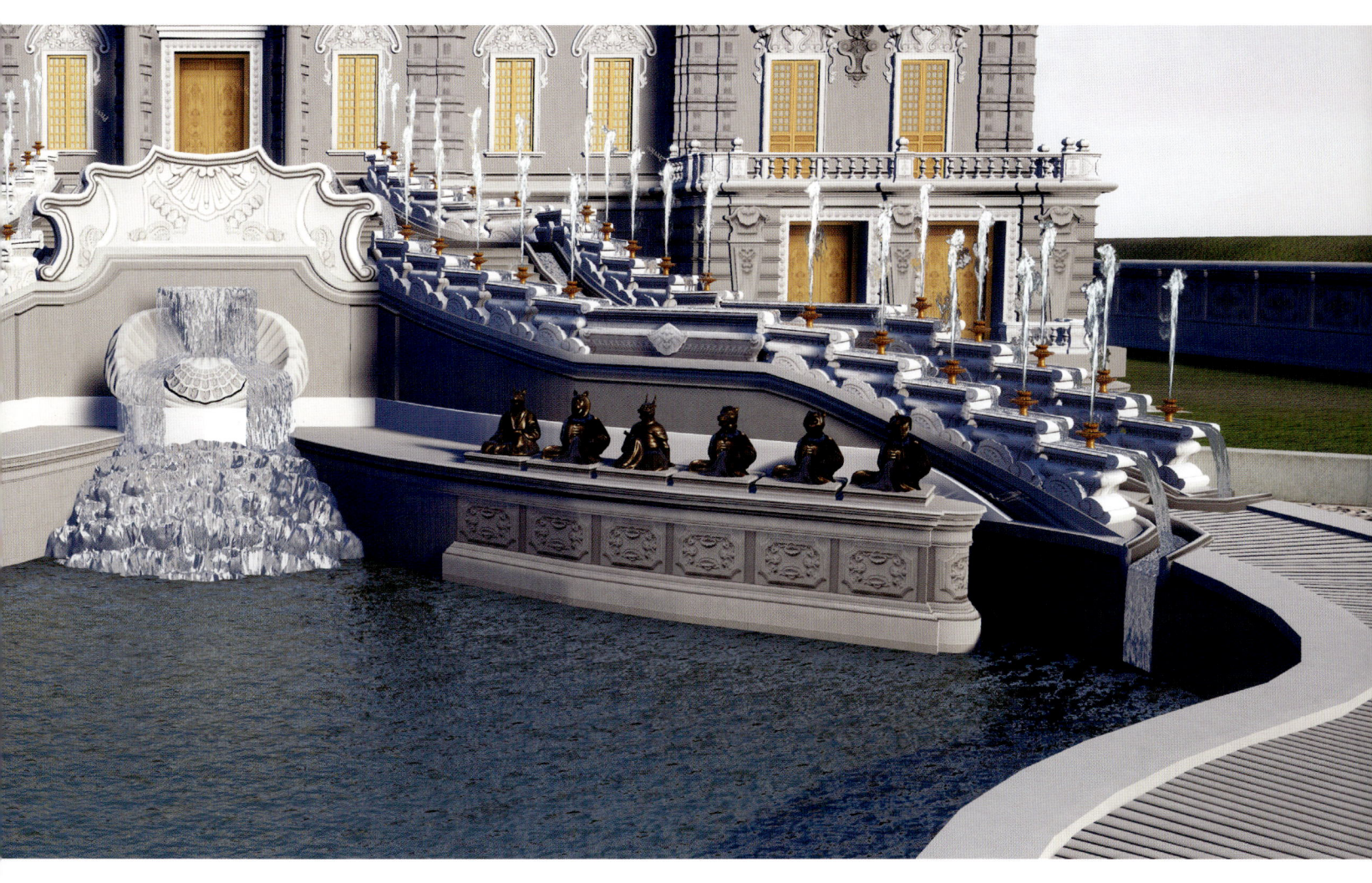

overhanging eaves.

Two other features that stood out were the sweeping curvilinear ramps and the spring fountains in front. The balustrades of the two ramps were made up of descending water receptacles; the water welling out of the twin stone fish cascaded down the successive water receptacles on the inside balustrades into the pool. On the outside balustrades the water receptacles carried water spouted out from a pair of stone lions down into smaller pools on the outside of the stairs. A large clam shell was built under the pair of stone fish to collect the water from the spouts and brimming water would overflow into the basin. The design of the fountain in the water basin was very ingenious, with water spouts in the form of the twelve zodiac animal statues. The fountain also doubled as a clock, with water shooting out from a different animal every hour and with all twelve spouting water at noon. At the west end of the water basin was a big, vase-like spring fountain. Traces of these are visible among the ruins , including parts of the crumbled walls of the main building and of the foundation (fig. 172).

The water for the fountains of the Haiyan Hall was supplied by the reservoir building east of the main hall. A large reservoir sat on top of the building; to further elevate the water level, the reservoir was built on a high platform on a base made with *sanhe tu* (building material traditionally used in China, containing sand, lime and clay) and faced with stone to make it look like a row of buildings complete with pillars and faux windows. The water reservoir was lined with a layer of "tin" for waterproofing purposes. The water that sprang from the fountains was power-driven by a machine. After the death of Michel Benoit, who designed the machine, the mechanism stopped working and whenever the emperor came to watch the water plays, water had to be hand carried to the reservoir. Remnants of the stone walls of this building and of the foundation of the tin-lined reservoir are still visible today; the stone facing, however, is gone, with only a few fragments of stone door frames remaining.

方外觀 Fangwai Observatory (Observatory of Lands Beyond)

Another building to the west of the Haiyan Hall was the Fangwai Observatory, a rectangular two-story building of three bays. The ground-level central bay with the entrance door projected forth. At either side of the building a semicircular external staircase led up to the second story. The building was supported on stone pillars and the brick walls between pillars. The placement of the pillars was somewhat random, and the styles of the doors and windows, the door and window frames and lintels differed from floor to floor (figs. 173, 174). On the second story the left and right bays featured floor-length rectangular windows and the middle bay featured a door that led out onto a balcony surrounded by a stone balustrade on the roof of the ground-level porch; the windows at either side were also fronted by a balustrade. The two windows on the ground level, however, abandoned the rectangular logic and went for the elliptical shape and their frames featured bas-reliefs. "The banded pilasters and the oval windows of the ground floor are typical elements of picturesque Baroque

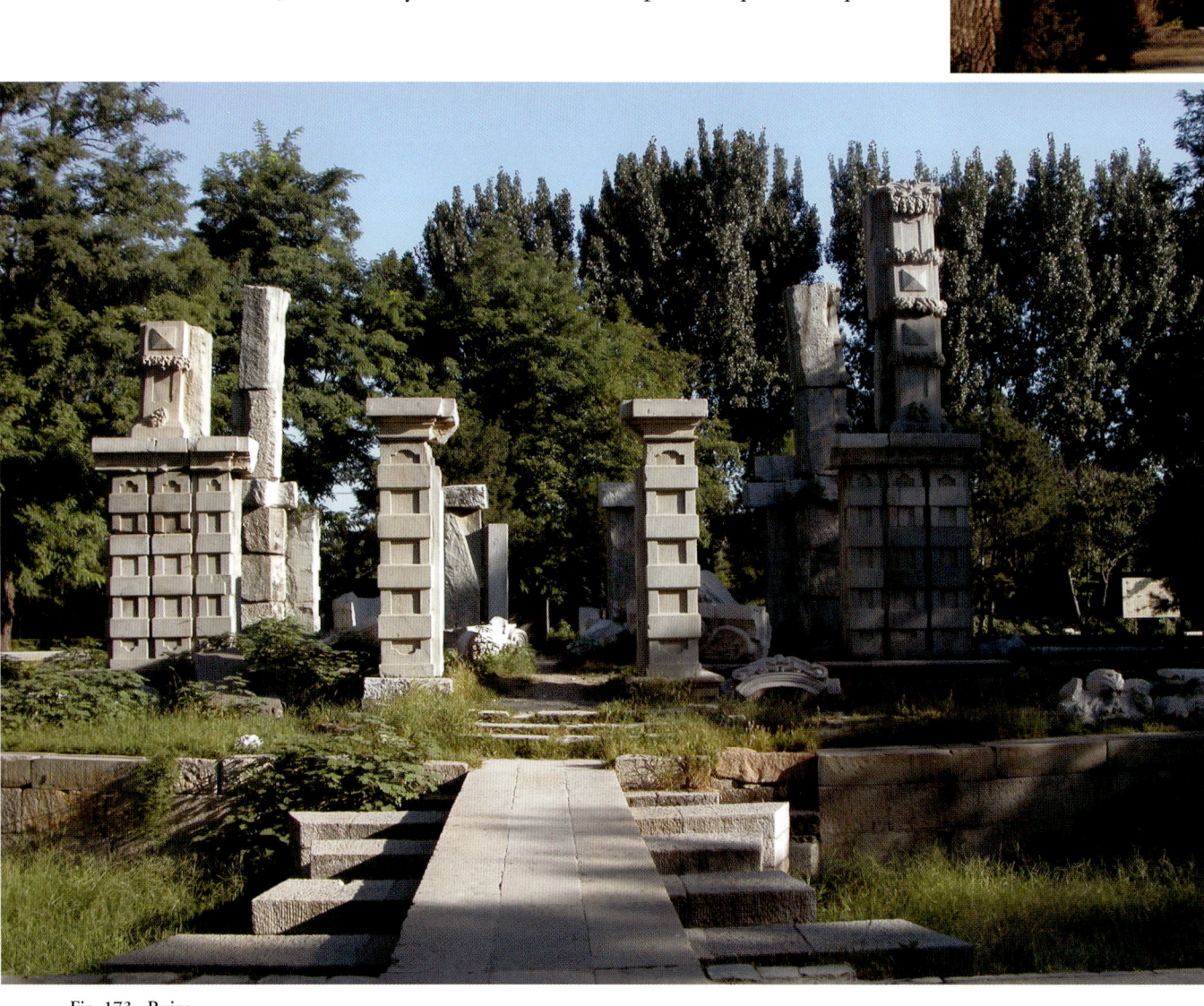

Fig. 173 Ruins

202 CHINA'S LOST IMPERIAL GARDEN

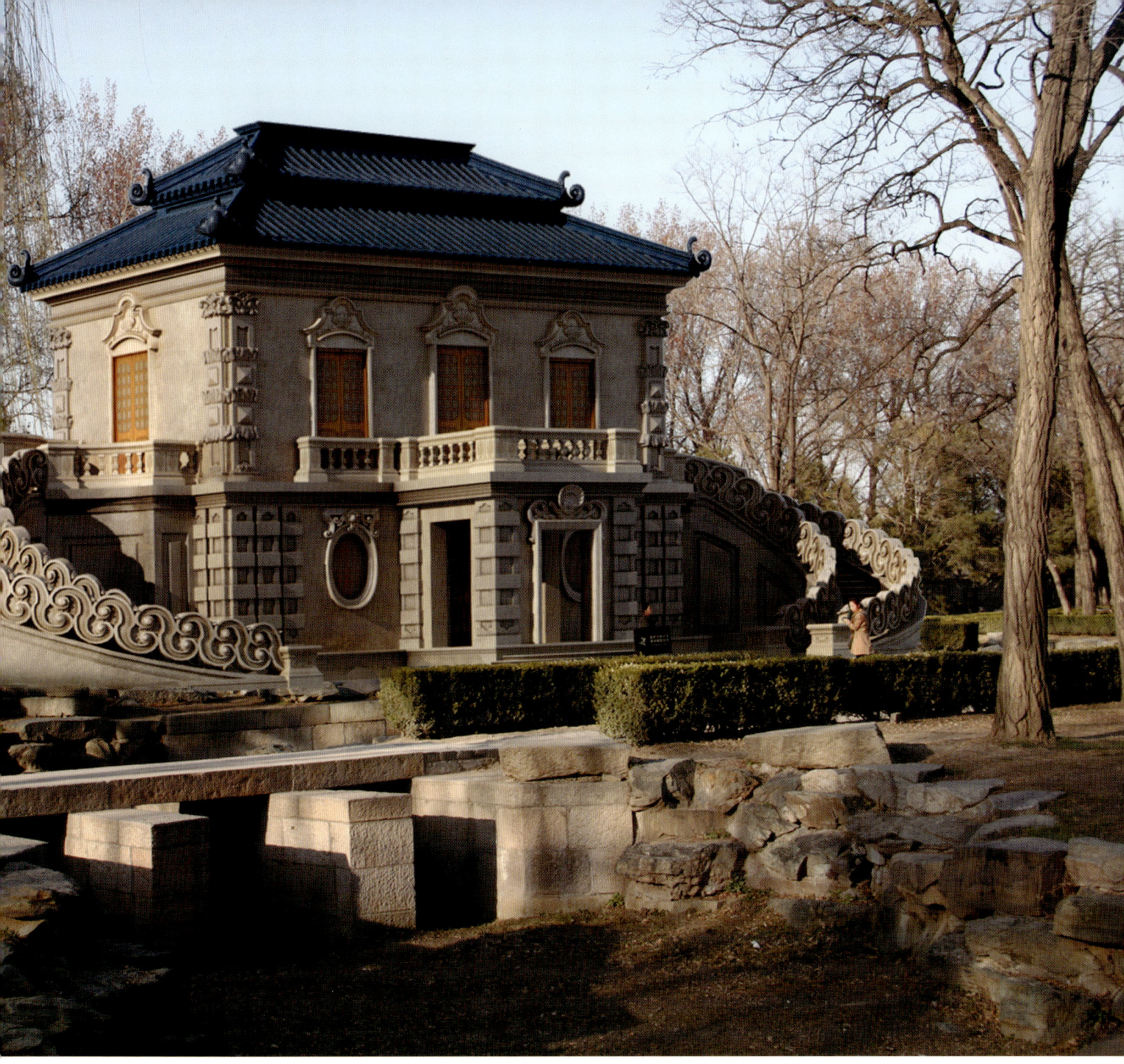

Fig. 174　Picture of reconstituted Fangwai Observatory

architecture."[1] Hardly any trace of Chinese architectural style could be found beneath the roof level; even the balustrades of the two sweeping staircases outside the building were pierced in S-shaped patterns popular in European buildings from the 15th to the 18th century. The roof, however, was similar to the double-eave hip roof of Chinese architecture. The roof's four corners and the two ends of the main ridge were ornamented with carvings of Chinese curly grass patterns; the middle of the ridge was also decorated. These were similar to the zoomorphic roof ridge ornaments in Chinese traditional architecture called *wenshou* and *jiaoshou*.

This building had an unusual function: it was said that the place was made into the worship hall of Qianlong's favorite consort Imperial Consort Rong, also known as the Fragrant Consort. In order to please the Fragrant Consort, who was a Muslim and to show respect for the Uighurs' Islamic faith, Qianlong designated this building as the Fragrant Consort's place of worship in the Yuan Ming Yuan.

1　*Gardens of China* by Osvald Siren (Sweden), Chapter 9.

遠瀛觀與大水法 Yuanying Observatory (Immense Ocean Observatory) and Da Shuifa Fountain (Great Fountain)

The Yuanying Observatory, located in the eastern part of the Xiyang Building Complex, was constructed more than twenty years after the other buildings of the area had been completed. It had a significant mass and scale. It had a direct line of sight to the Zelan Hall on a hillock in the Changchun Garden; a north-south axis linked up the Zelan Hall and the Guan Shuifa Fountain (Throne for Observing the Great Fountains), the Da Shuifa Fountain and the Yuanying Observatory to its north. The two obelisks in front of the Yuanying Observatory happened to be aligned with the east-west axis extending eastward from the Haiyan Hall.

The Yuanying Observatory, a palatial building of five bays, sat on a high terrace. With the two bays at the ends projecting out toward the front the building formed an inverted U in plan. Although the building had only one story, its dimensions were grander than those of the other buildings in the area; the three central bays featured three bronze doors separated from one another by two white marble columns carved with exquisite *mao gen* (Japanese buttercup) leaf patterns (fig. 175). Every bay was ornamented with pilasters; the three doors in the middle were decorated with small pilasters and arched door frames, with ornate decoration on the archivolts. Above the detached columns in front of the central bay was a 凸-shaped parapet projecting from the façade that was decorated with volutes of various sizes around its border. The two side bays projecting forward from the building featured long windows framed by pilasters and carved decorative lintels on their south-, east- and west-facing sides in a style reminiscent of late Baroque. The middle section of the building had a triple-eave hip roof; the left and right sections were surmounted by a small kiosk in front of the sloped roof. The roofs were covered with glazed barrel tiles and flat tiles on the first and third tier roofs and the second tier was covered with fish scale tiles. The roof ridges were decorated with scrolling flowers and leafy sprays in glazed tiles of different colors. The ornamental cap of the building was also in colored glazed tiles.[1] The ceiling in the main hall was decorated with a figure painting bordered with a floral pattern. Similar figure and landscape paintings were also

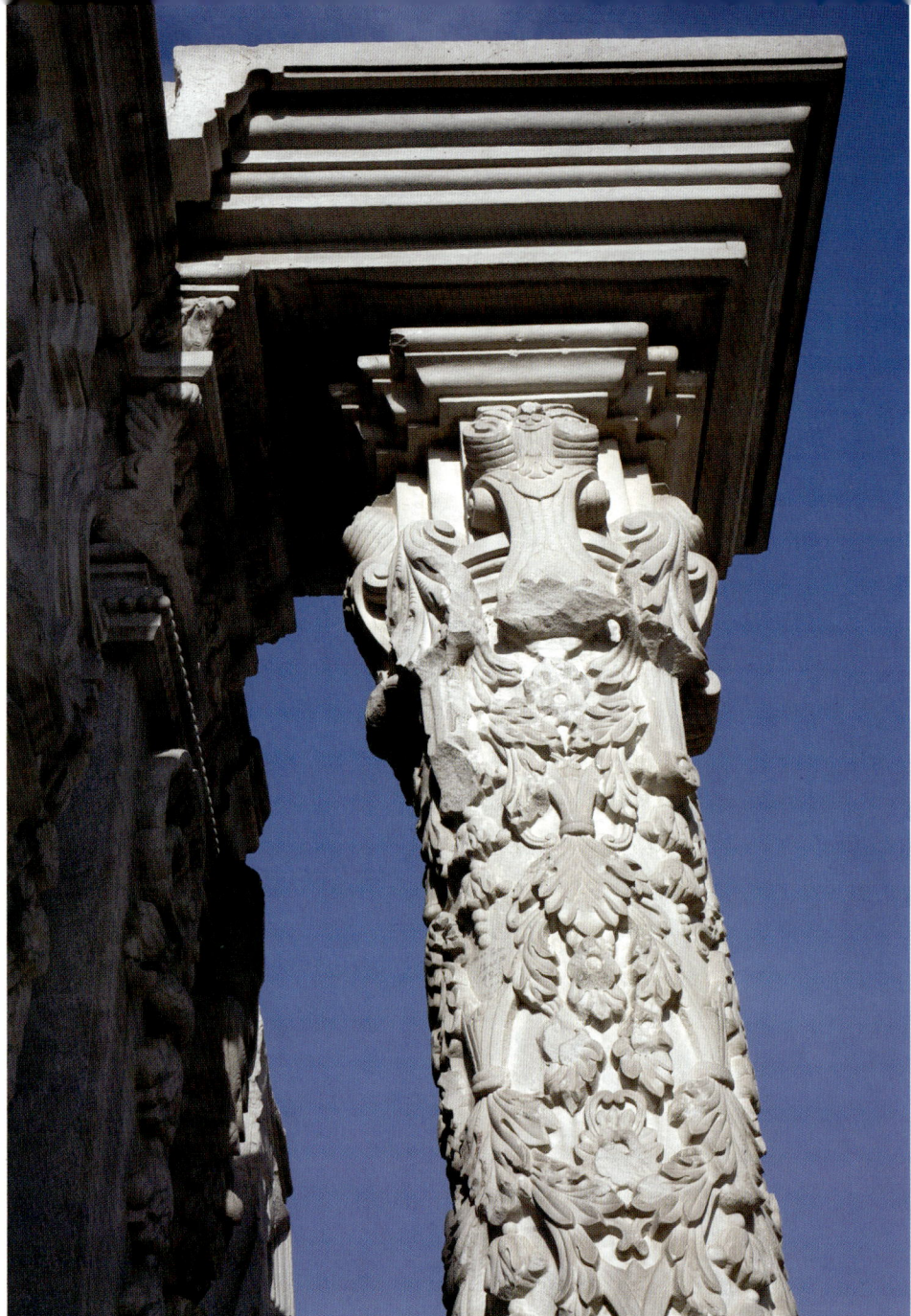

Fig. 175   Close view of remnants

204   CHINA'S LOST IMPERIAL GARDEN

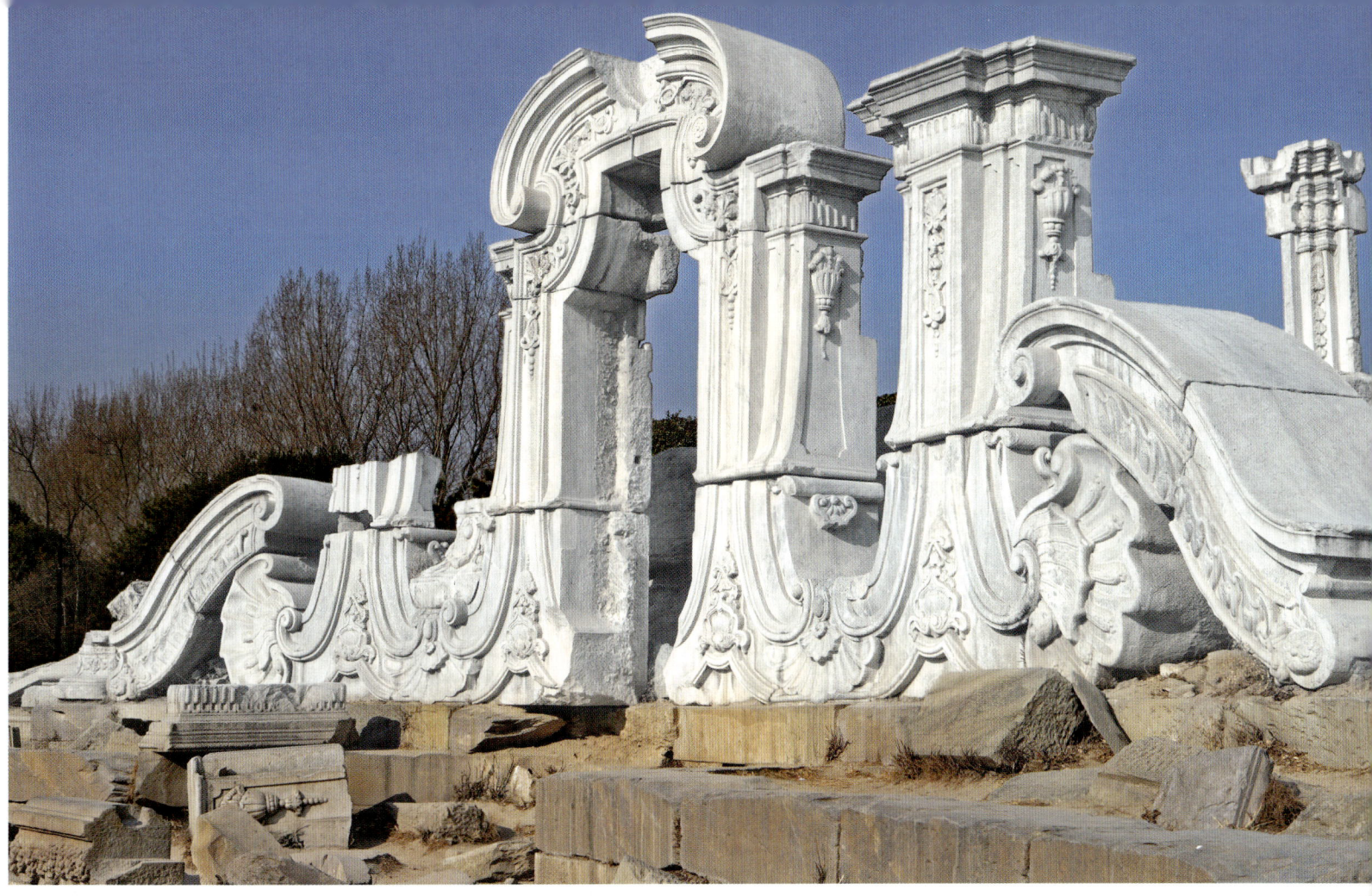

Fig. 176 Ruins of the Da Shuifa Fountain

present in the rear hall.[2]

The Yuanying Observatory had a spacious terrace in front that overlooked the Da Shuifa Fountain, which was situated at the base of the terrace. Behind the water basin stood a large central niche of marble from which animal heads spouted water. This served as backdrop for the water plays. This great background motif was supported by large, deeply profiled and sculptured double volutes, whose flowing and billowing forms doubtless harmonized well with the movement of the gushing water (fig. 176). The water basin was in the shape of a fan in plan but its border was composed of curvilinear sections. In the pool there were the animal figures of a deer and ten hounds, with the latter flanking the former. During the water plays water jets played out of the antlers of the deer and the mouths of the hounds. The show was popularly called "Ten Hounds Chasing a Deer."

At either side (east and west) of the basin, "water cascaded down from the top of two 13-tier pagodas."[3] The pagodas stood in their respective fountain basins.

South of the Da Shuifa Fountain was a low terrace about 40 centimeters in height paved with marble surmounted at its south side by a five-panel stone screen. This was the so-called Guanshuifa Fountain or the Throne for Observing the Da Shuifa Fountain. At the time a throne was placed on the terrace so that the emperor could watch the water shows from there. Curiously the screen was adorned with reliefs representing Western armorial festoons consisting of swords, guns, shields and arrows (fig. 177 on page 206). It is hard for us today to imagine how Emperor Qianlong could have tolerated these Western weapons behind his throne.

East of the Da Shuifa Fountain were to be found the Xianfa Hill, Zhuanma Tai (Carousel), Xianfa Wall and Rectangular River all the way to the eastern enclosure wall of the Changchun Garden, but no more buildings of any bulk to speak of. The stone plinths at the entrance to the small structure of Xianfa Hill can still be seen today (fig. 178 on page 207). The designers of the Xiyang Building Complex ingeniously achieved a

---

1 Journal *Yuan Ming Yuan*, third collection, "Data on the Buildings and Trees and Flowers in the Garden of Eternal Spring" by Zhao Guanghua, quote from Jin Xun's memory.
2 *Yuan Ming Yuan*, compiled by the First Historical Archives of China, published by Shanghai Ancient Books Publishing House, 1991, page 1578.
3 Journal *Yuan Ming Yuan*, third collection, "Data on the Buildings and Trees and Flowers in the Garden of Eternal Spring" by Zhao Guanghua, quote from Jin Xun's memory.

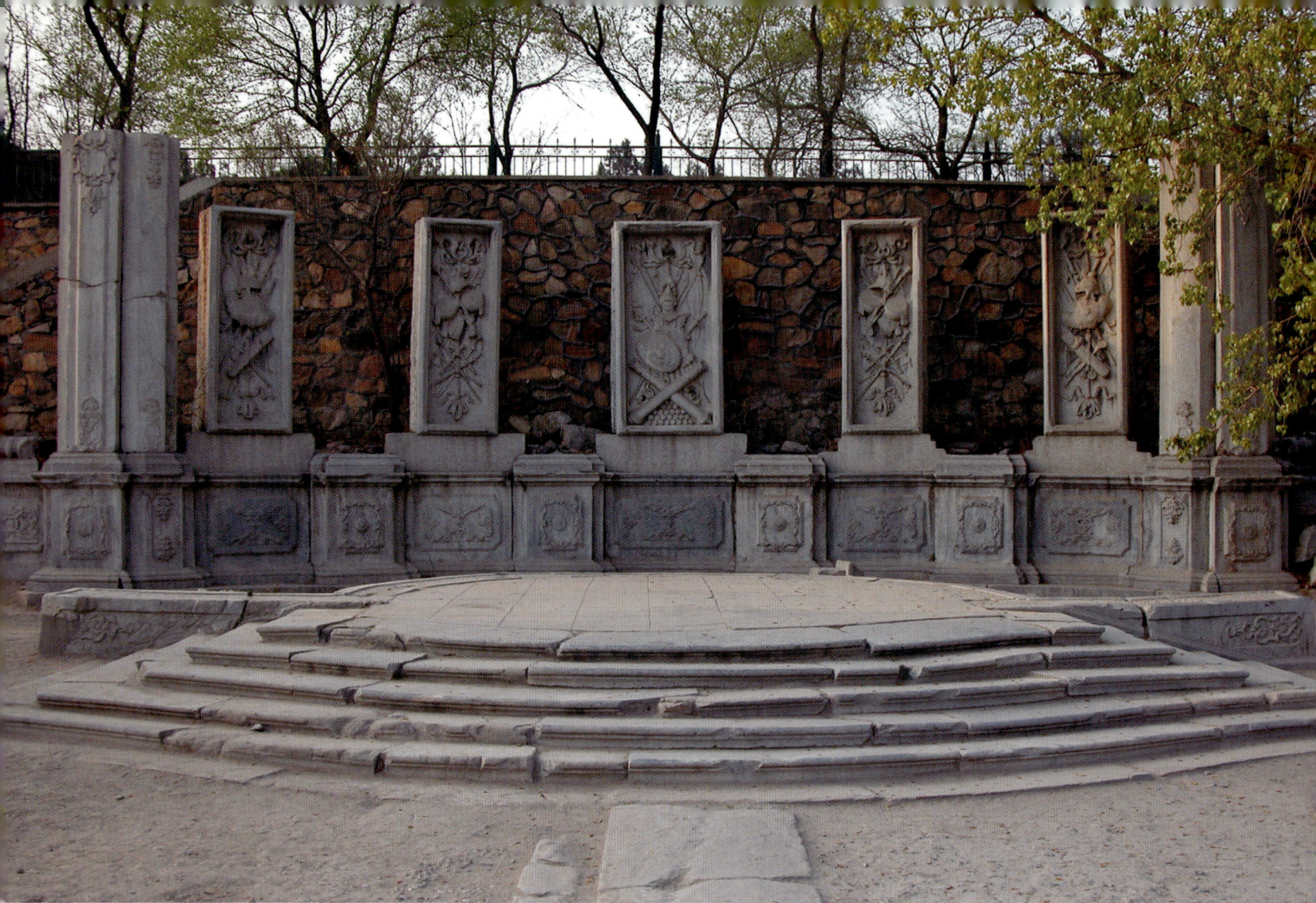

Fig. 177　Remnants of the Guanshuifa Fountain

kind of balance by the placement of earthen hills and the spacious rectangular lake in the eastern sector to contrast with the west section, which was more densely populated with buildings. This approach put the Yuanying Observatory in a central position.

While the Xiyang Building Complex was constructed mainly for the purpose of creating a special vista in the Yuan Ming Yuan, it sometimes hosted the imperial family's events and activities. The Haiyan Hall was used to give banquets; the Xie Qiqu Pavilion hosted musical performances and the Fangwai Observatory served as the Fragrant Consort's place of worship. All these buildings were occasionally used to hold gifts received by the emperor.

The siting of the Xiyang Building Complex in the northeast corner of the Changchun Garden indicated a realization by its planners that a Western garden was constituted differently from a traditional Chinese garden. Therefore a separate site was found for it and a range of earthen hills going from east to west was built between the two gardens. The Xiyang Building Complex was situated on a narrow strip of land with a width of 70 meters and a length of 800 meters. By the standards of European gardens this was rather an exiguous space to put buildings in and these had to be lined up in a row. It was only with the construction of the Yuanying Observatory north of the Da Shuifa Fountain in the 48th year of the Qianlong era (1783) that some north-south depth was gained and the monotony of the 800 meter east-west stretch was broken by new vertical variety; the previous appearance of the sector as merely a combination and permutation of building and landscape elements was thus ameliorated. The studied ornate effects of the Yuanying Observatory catapulted the latecomer to a position of top contender for preeminence in the sector. As the buildings were designed by painters and missionaries who were not professional architects, the non-adherence to orthodox rules of Western architecture was sometimes inevitable, as in the case of the column orders and the motifs and patterns for the carved

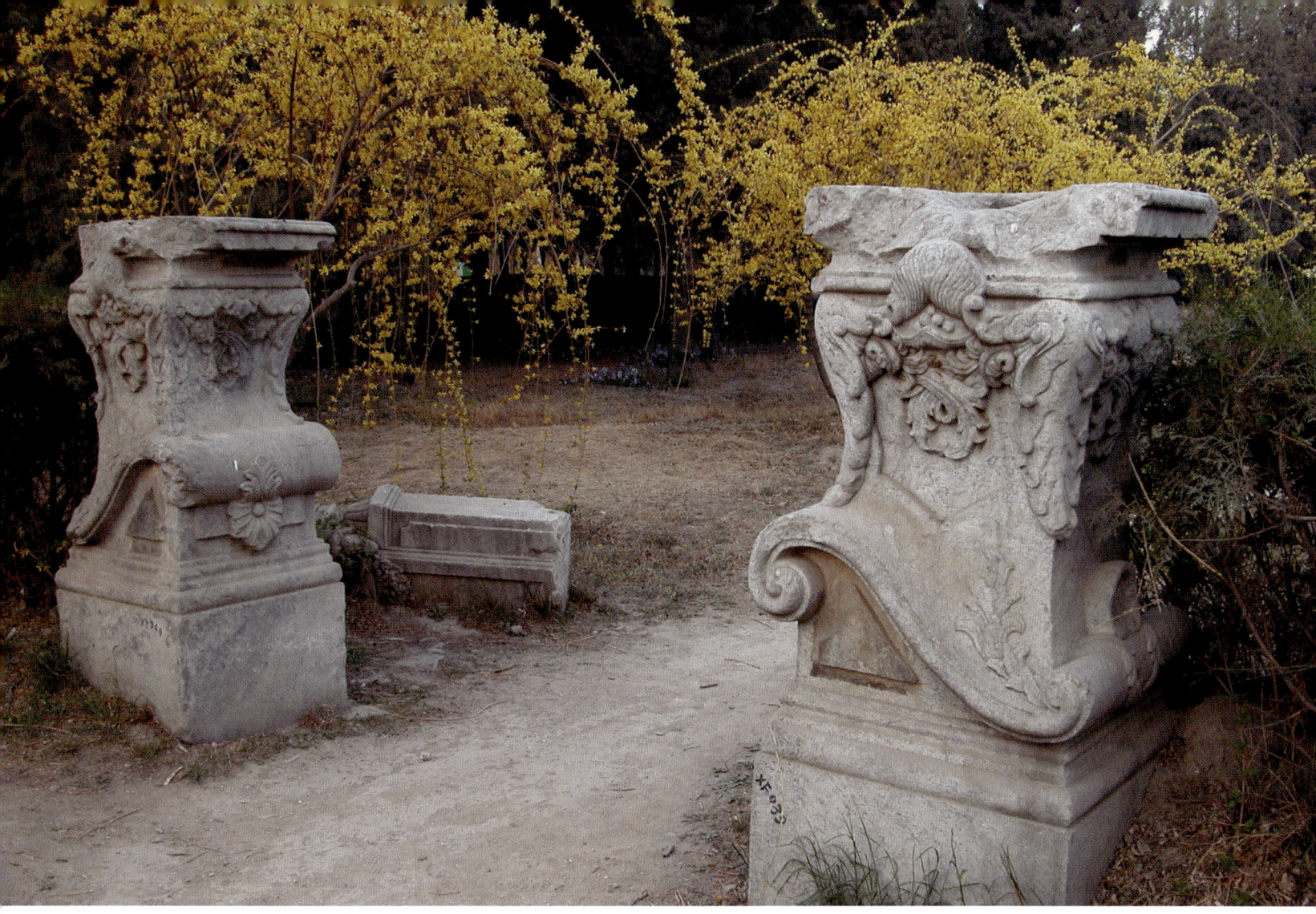

Fig. 178 Stone base at west entrance of Xianfa Hill

ornaments. But on the whole the sector reflected the architectural style of 18th century Europe. The designers also incorporated Chinese architectural elements as much as they could; thus they mounted roofs covered with glazed tiles on weight-bearing wall systems. The eave overhang in these buildings was much shorter than for traditional Chinese roofs and therefore reduced the aesthetic appeal of the buildings, which lacked both the virility of Western architecture and the natural grace of Chinese architecture, and struck the observer as an inorganic merging of the two styles.

But to a Chinese emperor many of these had never been seen by him before, such as the fountains, the pools and the stone buildings brimming with decorative carvings and therefore found favor with him. The Xiyang Building Complex was the first group of Western buildings ever constructed in China by the wish of its ruler and this attested to Qianlong's willingness to accept novelties from foreign countries and his trail-blazing spirit.

This curiosity about Western architecture is further borne out by certain activities in the imperial court. Thus in the 55th year of the Qianlong era (1790) on the occasion of the 80th birthday of the emperor, 16 scenes of Western buildings, triumphal arches and fountains lined the way from the Yuan Ming Yuan to the Forbidden City in the form of theatrical drops.

The construction of the Xiyang Building Complex satisfied Emperor Qianlong's curiosity about novel things. Even as he imported Western architecture, he couldn't hide the arrogance and conceit of the ruler of a great power. He considered the fountains merely the gadget of a craftsman. "In a country as big as China, there's nothing it cannot produce." In his view the great Qing dynasty could manufacture anything, and therefore he had the Xiyang Building Complex built to show off his prowess; he once invited the British ambassador George Macartney to view the fountains, not realizing that they represented nothing novel to the British. Seventy years hence British troops torched them with the rest of the Yuan Ming Yuan.

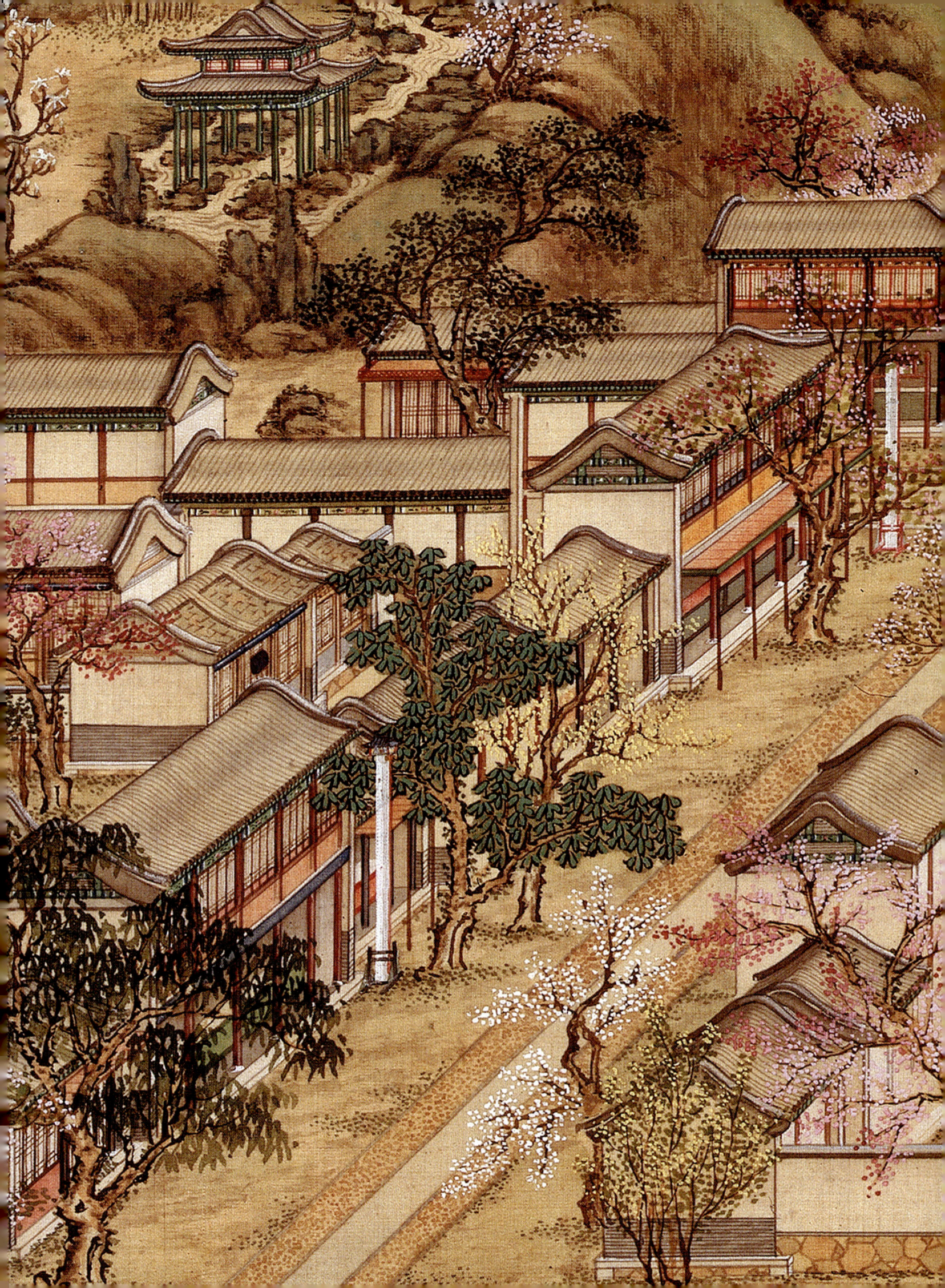

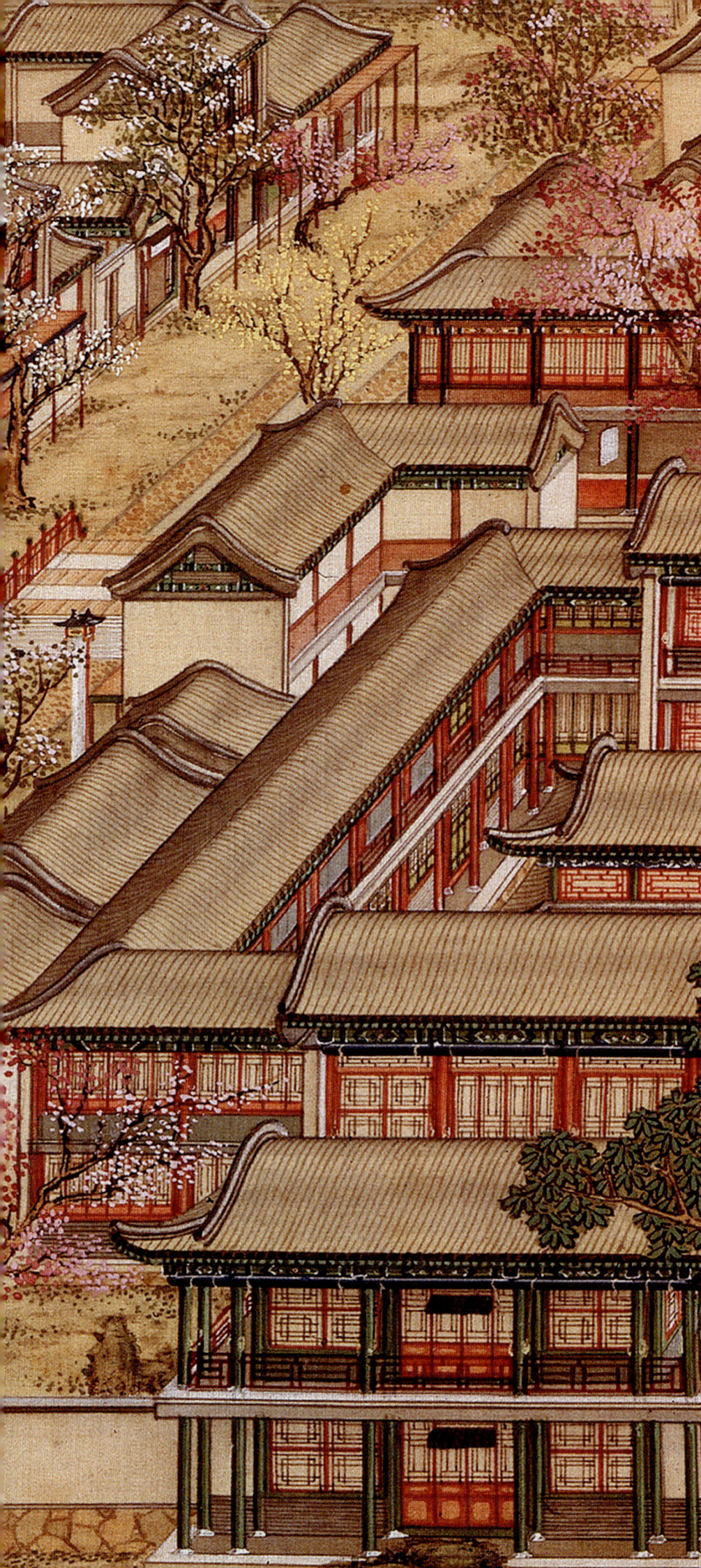

CHAPTER XIV
Market and Pleasure Grounds

The introduction of a market or a fair into the imperial garden soothed the longing of those long cooped up in the restricted precincts of the imperial garden for a taste of town life. Besides even those living in the Yuan Ming Yuan had needs in their daily lives and in the time of traditional festivals, buildings that catered to these mundane needs went up and they became an important part of the garden design of the Yuan Ming Yuan (fig. 179).

Fig. 179 Market Street shown in painting of Zuoshi Linliu Complex from the album of *Forty Scenes of the Yuan Ming Yuan*

買賣街

Market Street

Although members of the imperial family and the nobility enjoyed the idyllic environment of the imperial garden, they missed the pleasure of living just like ordinary people in a town setting. "As the Emperors of China find themselves obliged to live in this strange fort of solitude, they have always endeavoured to supply the loss of all public diversions, (which their high station will not suffer them to partake,) by some other means or inventions, according to their different tastes and fancies."[1] Therefore a scene simulating the bustle and hustle of town life was created in the imperial garden, with shops lining a street, called Market Street. There were two market streets in the Garden; one was located in front of the Shewei City, west of the Lake of Happiness, next to the Tongle Garden (fig. 180), the other was on the east side of the Hanjing Hall groups of buildings in the Changchun Garden.

"At the New Year a street fair would be set up in the Garden, where one could find everything, curios, clothing, teahouses and restaurants and daily necessities. Anything available in town was available here. There were even peddlers selling roasted pumpkin seeds out of small baskets they carried."[2] At the fair the "vessels arrive at the port; the shops are opened; and the goods are exposed for sale. There is one quarter for those who sell silks, and another for those who sell cloth; one street for porcelain, and another for varnish-works … This man sells furniture of all sorts; that, clothes and ornaments for the ladies, and a third has all kinds of books, for the learned and curious. There are coffee-houses too, and taverns, of all sorts, good and bad, beside a number of people that cry different fruits about the streets, and a great variety of refreshing liquors. The mercers, as you pass their ships, catch you by the sleeve; and press you to buy some of their goods."[3] The French missionary Jean-Denis Attiret also recorded that there was a street lined with shops in the Garden, where the most novel and precious articles from China, Japan and Europe could be found, as in a bazaar.[4] On Market Street, eunuchs acted as merchants or workmen. According to the *Zhuyeting Zaji* (*Random Notes of the Bamboo Leaf Pavilion*), "The eunuchs doubled as shopkeepers. The superintendent of customs and octroi at the Chongwen Gate would pick out curios from shops in town beforehand and agree on the prices. They would be recorded in a book. For those articles sold, the sale proceeds would go to the merchant and those that remained unsold would be returned to the merchant. The high ministers visiting the Garden would vie in buying the articles. After the withdrawal of the officials in the afternoon, the ladies of the imperial harem would also come to the market to make purchases. The officials would gather in wine shops and restaurants just as they would in town. The waiters in the restaurants were picked from regular waiters in town who had a good voice and were capable of articulate speech. Whenever the emperor passed by, some waiters would yell out the orders, others would settle the tabs and the manager would handle the bills. There was a general hum and din from all the people talking at the same time. It made for great fun at the New Year. This would go on for nine days … The practice stopped in the fourth year of Jiaqing's reign."[5] Attiret also gave an account of market activities: "and you can scarce distinguish the Emperor himself, from the meanest of his subjects. Everybody bawls out what he has to sell; some quarrel, others fight, and you have all the confusion of a fair … The public officers come and arrest the quarrelers; carry them before the judges, in the courts for justice; the cause is tried in form; the offender condemned to be bastinadoed; and the sentence is put in execution, and that so effectually, that the diversion of the Emperor sometimes costs the poor actor a great deal of real pain. The mystery of thieving is not forgotten, in this general representation. That noble employ is assigned to a considerable number of the cleverest eunuchs; who perform their parts admirably well. If any one of them is caught in the fact, he is brought to shame; and condemned, to be stigmatized, bastinadoed, or banished; according to the heinousness of the crime, and the nature of the theft. If they steal cleverly, they have the laugh on their side; they are applauded, and the sufferer is without redress. However, at the end of the fair, everything of this kind is restored to the proper owner.

"This fair, (as I told you before,) is kept only for the entertainment of the Emperor, the Empress, and his mistresses. It's very unusual for

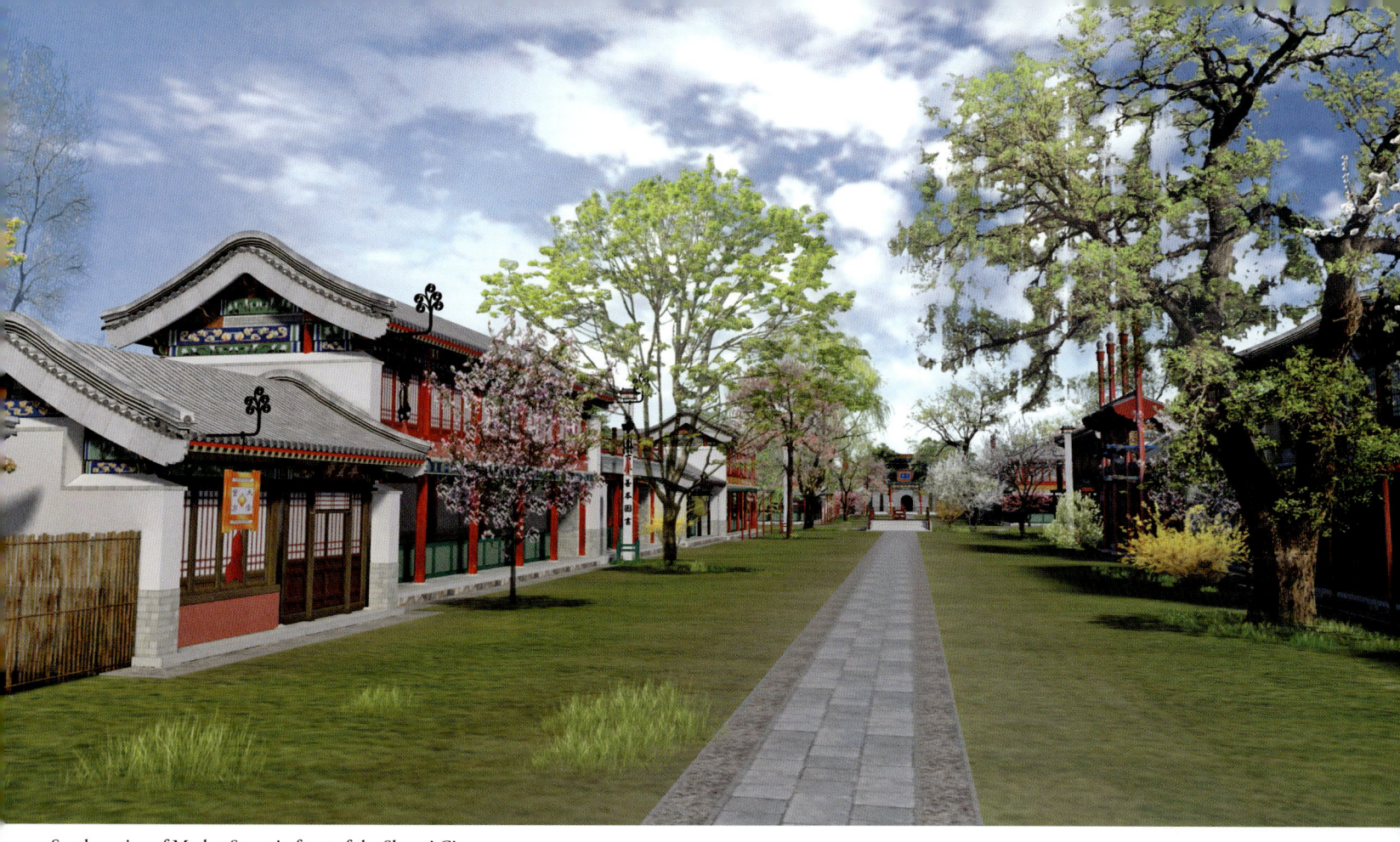

South section of Market Street in front of the Shewei City

any of the princes, or Grandees, to be admitted to see it, and when any have that favor, it is not till after the women are all retired to their several apartments. The goods which are exposed and sold here, belong chiefly to the merchants of Pekin; who put them into the hands of the eunuchs, to be sold in reality, so that the bargains here are far from being all pretended ones. In particular, the Emperor himself always buys a great many things; and you may be sure, they ask him enough for them. Several of the ladies too make their bargains; and so do some of the eunuchs. All this trafficking, if there was nothing of real mixt with it, would want a great deal of that earnestness and life, which now make the bustle the more active, and the diversion it gives the greater."

There was an anecdote in the *Zhuyeting Zaji* about shopping done by Emperor Qianlong and Gurun Princess Hexiao on the market street next to the Tongle Garden. Gurun Princess Hexiao was the youngest daughter of Qianlong and the latter doted on her. At the period she was already promised to Fengshen Yinde, a son of He Shen, the Grand Councilor, and He Shen accompanied the Emperor to the market. "When Emperor Gaozong (Qianlong) saw a bright red quilted blouse offered for sale by a used clothing purveyor, he said to Princess Hexiao: 'You can ask your father-in-law for it.' And He Shen had to buy it for 28 *jin*."

The uniqueness of the buildings on Market Street was the tall architectural arches of varying heights in front of the shops, on which hung shingles giving the name of the establishment, just like the shops in old Beijing. In front of every shop a long pole stuck out on which hung samples of their ware. The myriad colorful signs and shingles gave the impression of a bustling market, and dazzled the eyes of the emperor and his consorts, who felt as if they were shopping in town (fig. 181 on pages 212 and 213).

---

1 *A Particular Account of the Emperor of China's Gardens near Pekin: In a Letter from F. Attiret*, by Jean-Denis Attiret.
2 *Zhuyeting Zaji* (*Random Notes of the Bamboo Leaf Pavilion*), by Yao Yuanzhi of the Qing dynasty, published by Zhonghua Publishing House, 1982, page 5.
3 *A Particular Account of the Emperor of China's Gardens near Pekin: In a Letter from F. Attiret*, by Jean-Denis Attiret.
4 Translation of *A Particular Account of the Emperor of China's Gardens near Pekin: In a Letter from F. Attiret*, Beijing Publishing House, 1999, page 890.
5 *Zhuyeting Zaji* by Yao Yuanzhi of the Qing dynasty, published by Zhonghua Publishing House, 1982, page 5.

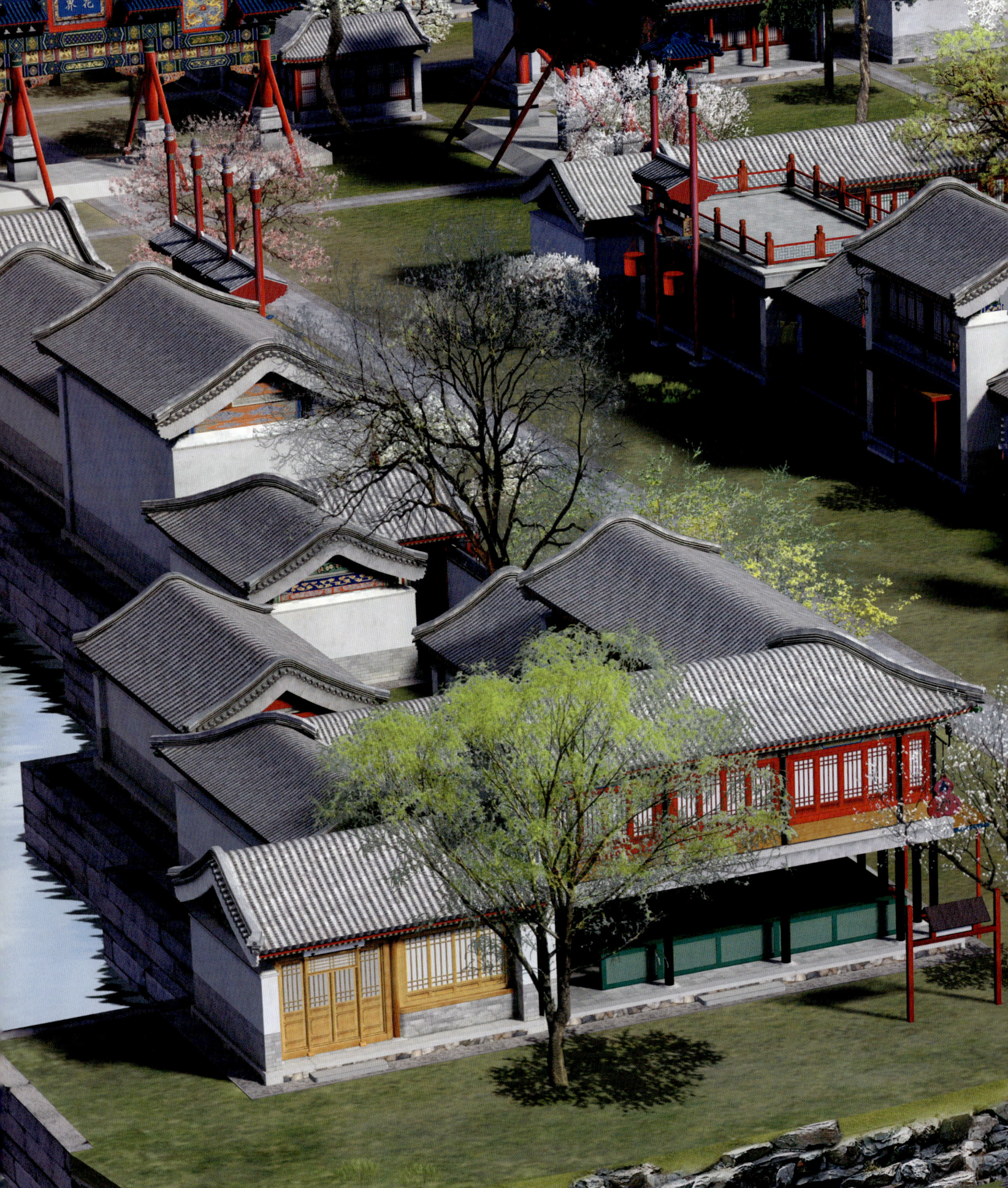

Fig. 181　North section of Market Street in front of the Shewei City

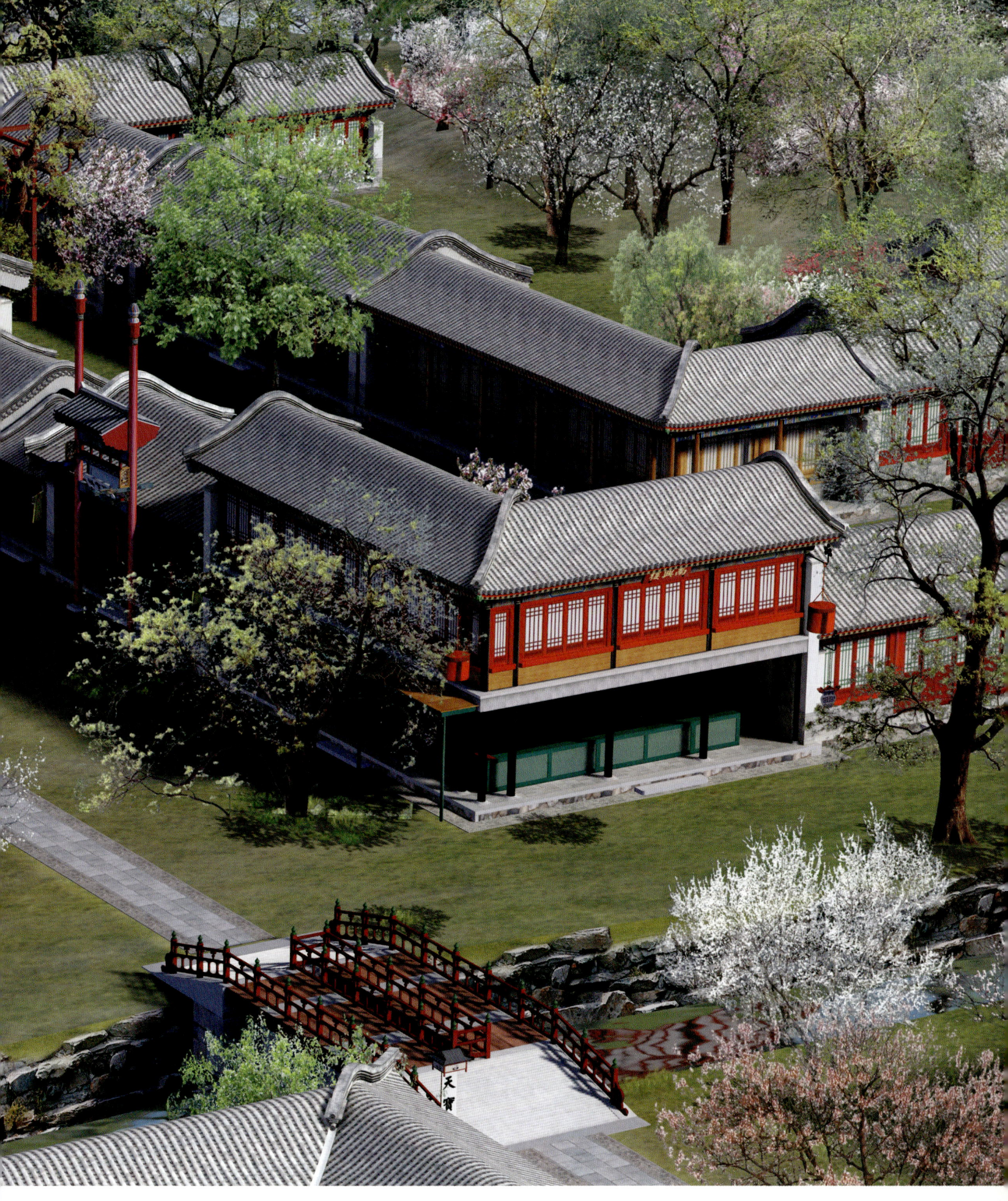

曲水流觞 Qushui Liushang Complex (Complex of Wine Cups Floating on a Winding Channel)

The core building in the Zuoshi Linliu Complex was the Zuoshi Linliu Pavilion. It sat to the northeast of the Tongle Garden and was known also by the name of the Lan Pavilion (Orchid Pavilion). The pavilion was completed in the Yongzheng era. In a poem entitled *Zuoshi Linliu* composed by Emperor Qianlong in the ninth year of his reign (1744), he described white rocks in a clear spring with trailing vines and gilt lotus blossoms and how he enjoyed going there on a day in the third month devoted to the cleansing of evil spirits just as a famous poet did in the Yonghe era of the Jin dynasty.

The poem alluded to the Shangsi Festival (third day of the third lunar month) in the ninth year of the Yonghe era (353) of the Eastern Jin dynasty (317–420), a day in which Wang Xizhi, Xie An and some other literati went to the Lan Pavilion to drink from wine cups floating in a winding channel in the kiosk, composed poetry and enjoyed revels by a stream. This was a long-standing custom: on the annual Shangsi Festival people would flock to a stream to wash themselves and cleanse themselves of evil spirits and shed ill luck, a custom eventually adopted by the literati, who would gather to compose poetry while they drank wine on the occasion. With the spread of the *Lanting Xu* (*Preface to the Poems Collected from the Orchid Pavilion*), Qushui Liushang became a favorite motif for garden designers in succeeding generations. It not only was featured in imperial gardens but became a landscaping element of lasting appeal in private gardens and temple grounds. The relic of the earliest pavilion with a channel for floating wine cups is found in the Chongfu Palace (Palace of Praying for Fortune), a Daoist temple dating to the Song dynasty in Dengfeng of Henan Province.

Early in the Qing dynasty a number of such "floating cups" pavilions were built, such as the Liushui Yin Pavilion (Sound of Flowing Water Pavilion) in the Shuchun Garden (Gentle Spring Garden) in the West Imperial Park, the Qushui Hexiang Pavilion (Pavilion of Lotus Fragrance in

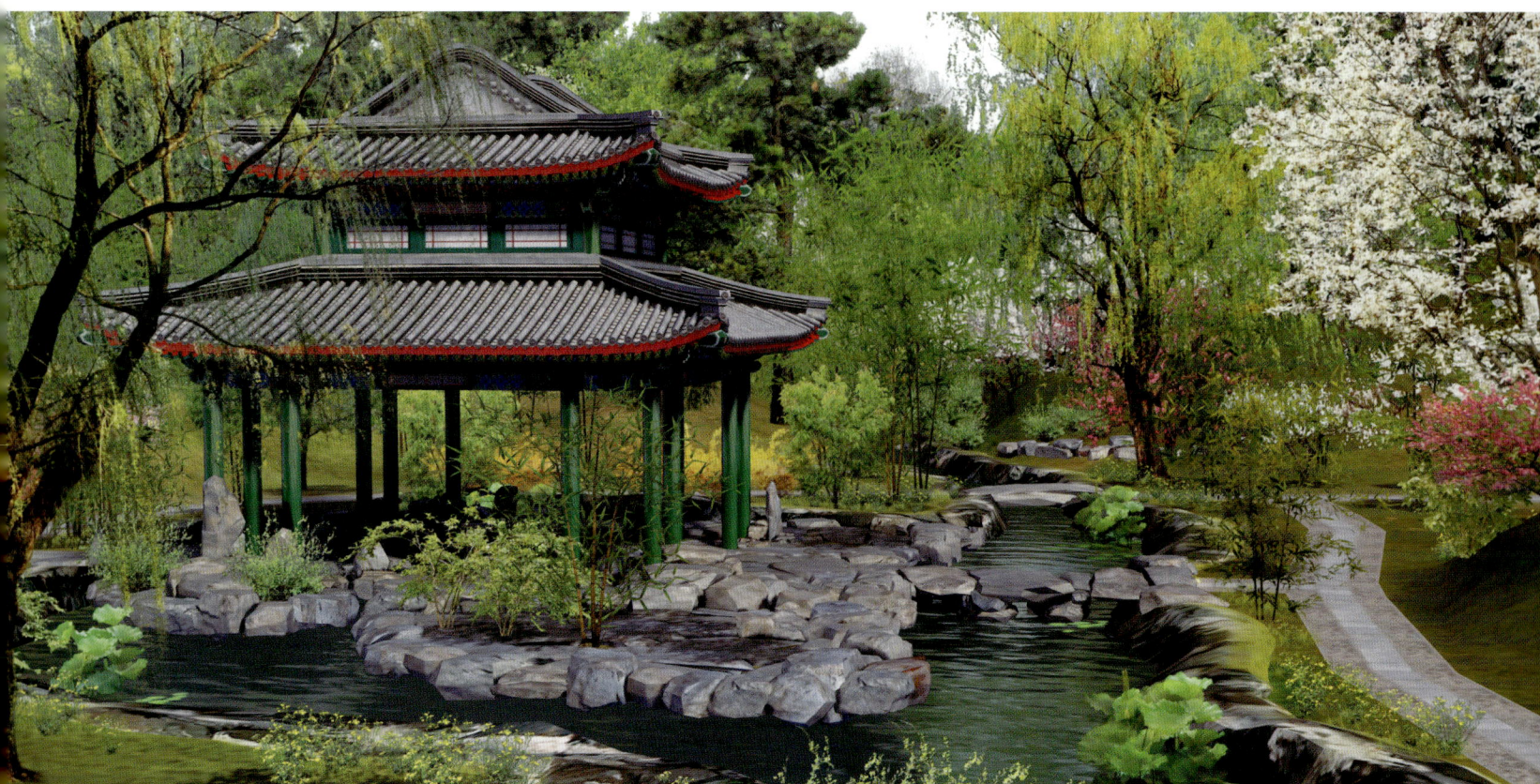

Fig. 182 Square floating cups pavilion built in 1744 in Zuoshi Linliu Complex

Meandering Water) in the Bishu Mountain Resort in Chengde and the Xishang Pavilion in the Qianlong Garden in the Forbidden City. In these pavilions a water channel was dug in the floor in an exiguous space. The Zuoshi Linliu Complex in the Yuan Ming Yuan was different: low hills sat to the east and the north of the pavilion, which looked out across the water on a tract of rice paddies. Water spurted out from a grotto in the rock-stacked hill on its north, creating a babbling mountain brook. The water passed through the kiosk to flow into a rock-lined stream.

The album of *Forty Scenes of the Yuan Ming Yuan* of 1744 (ninth year of the Qianlong era) shows that the Zuoshi Linliu was a rectangular west-facing pavilion of three bays, with a double-eave roof (fig. 182).

In the 44th year of the Qianlong era (1779) the pavilion was rebuilt into an octagonal pavilion with a double-eave roof and on its stone pillars was engraved with the famous "Lanting Xu". Pavilions with a thatch or bamboo roof were added on the grounds. Traces of a pavilion covering a floor carved with a water channel are still visible in the ruins of the Zuoshi Linliu Pavilion (fig. 183). When the octagonal pavilion was built, no change was made to its base, which was native rock. There might be another foundation that would match the dimensions of the space on which the eight stone pillars had stood. The eight stone pillars of the octagonal stone pavilion inscribed with the *Lanting Xu* of Wang Xizhi in the hand of famous calligraphers have become objects of art and were moved to the Zhongshan Park in 1860.

The Zuoshi Linliu Pavilion was unique not only for the wine cups borne on the water of a winding channel under its roof; Qianlong also wrote appreciatively about the beauty of the plants in the environs: white rocks in a clear spring with trailing vines and gilt lotus blossoms. Here "gilt lotus blossoms" could plausibly have meant the lotus petals borne away by the flowing water, just like the floating wine cups. However the Shangsi Festival does not fall in the flowering season for lotuses; therefore the reference was apparently to the beauty of the floating cups after all. It cannot be ascertained if there ever were events at Zuoshi Linliu Complex that involved floating wine cups.

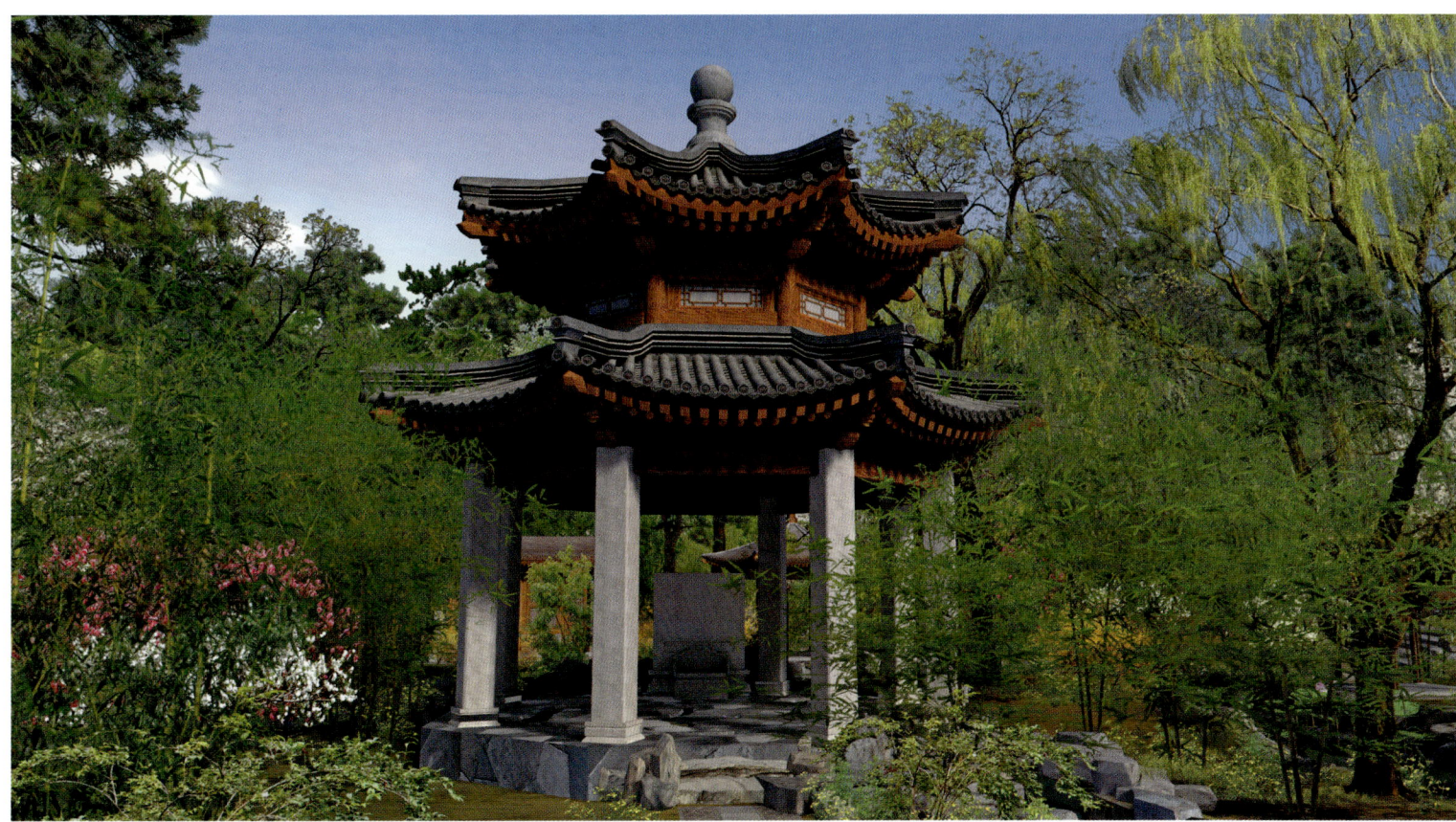

Fig. 183　Octagonal floating cups pavilion built in 1799 in Zuoshi Linliu Complex

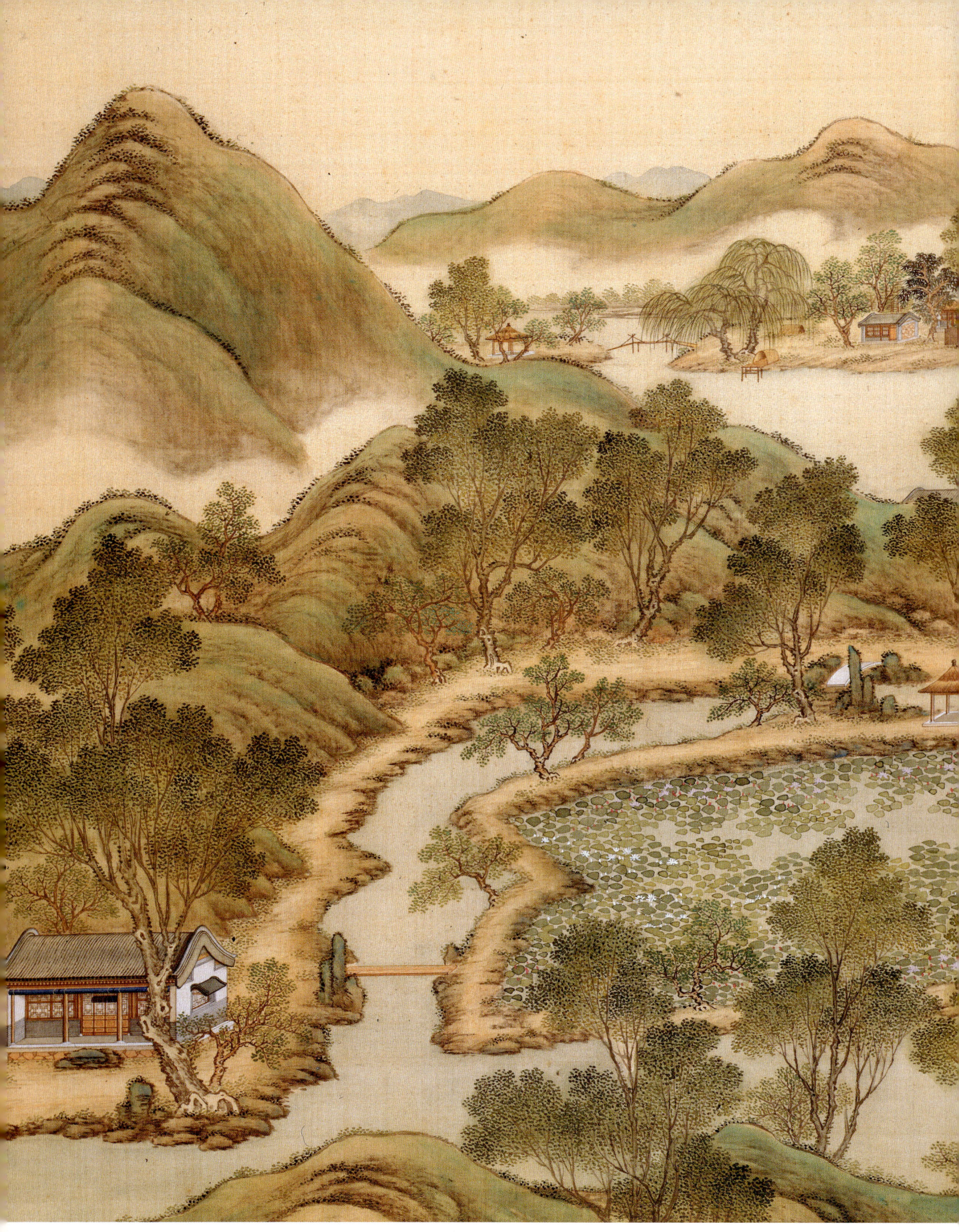

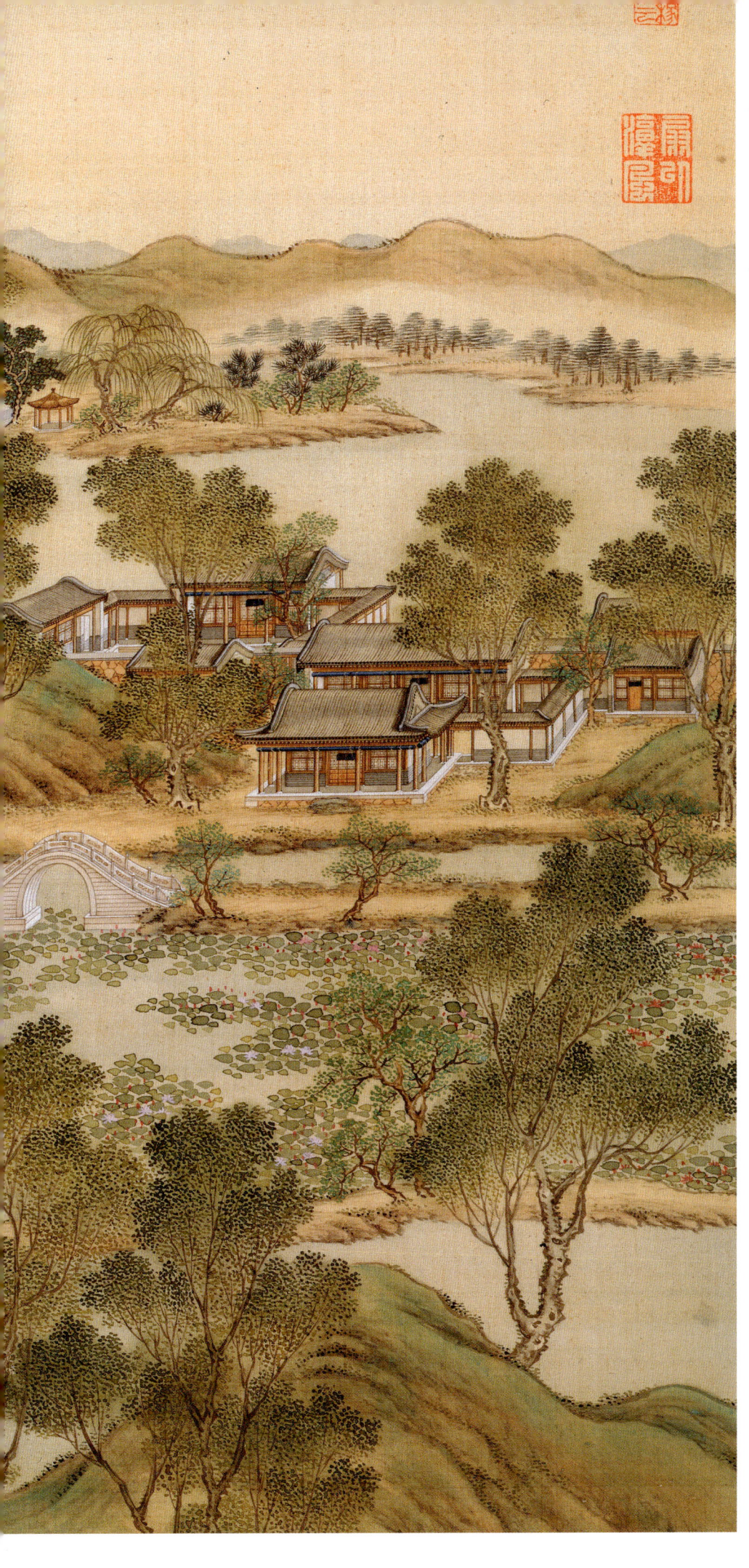

御園賞荷

Viewing Lotus Blossom in the Imperial Garden

As early as the Yongzheng era, "on the occasion of festivals banquets were given in honor of princes and ministers, who would take boat tours of the Lake of Happiness, take in the beauty of lotus blossoms and fish in the lake until late in the day. In such moments there was such conviviality that those attending the event would pour out their heart to each other."[1]

In the Qianlong era the viewing of lotus blossoms became even more important. This had to do with the emperor's personal admiration of lotus blossoms, which became an important feature of the landscape in the imperial garden. Qianlong took a personal interest in how well the lotus plants were doing and when they went into bloom. As the lotus flower first burst its bud, Emperor Qianlong would compose a poem about its purity and untainted character, writing that he was once more riding in a boat to revisit the lotus blossoms on the imperial lake, where he had his own fairyland mountain and the lotus blossoms untainted by human foibles.[2] In autumn, reminded of the change of

---

1 *Xiaoting Zalu* (*Random Notes from Roaring Pavilion*) by Zhao Lian, Zhonghua Publishing House, 1980.
2 *Yuzhi Shi*, by Emperor Qianlong, Book I, Volume 5.

Fig. 184 Lotus viewing site in Duojia Ruyun Hall, from the album *Forty Scenes of the Yuan Ming Yuan*

PART II SCENERY OF THE YUAN MING YUAN

season by the sight of the lotuses, he would write that there was a crispness in the air about the pavilions and the clothes on him were not enough to keep warm, and that the red of the lotuses was now tinted with purple and the willows began to show yellow leaves among the green.[1]

When the lotuses were in full bloom Emperor Qianlong would invite the empress dowager to the imperial garden to view them. The empress dowager would travel from the Changchun Garden (Joyful Spring Garden), where she lived, in an ornately decorated boat and be met by Emperor Qianlong at the Zaoyuan Gate in the southwest of the Yuan Ming Yuan. The empress dowager would usually go to the Duojia Ruyun Hall (Hall of Crops as Bountiful as the Clouds) to view the lotus blossoms (fig. 184 on pages 216 and 217), where the Jihexiang Pavilion (Pavilion of Fragrant Lotus) had before it several acres planted to lotuses in a pond, which was surrounded by a long embankment. The streams and hills dotting the landscape provided a pristine environment for viewing the lotus blossoms. Every year Qianlong composed poems that mentioned viewing lotus blossoms with the empress dowager. In one poem he wrote about this crystal palace quiet and unsullied by dirt and dust … viewing summer blossoms of the lotuses and smelling their subtle scent borne on light breezes … their color refreshed by a recent shower … the longevity peaches of the legendary Queen Mother of the West were indeed nice to have but the spring-like smile of the empress dowager was even better.[2]

中元河燈 Floating River Lanterns on Zhongyuan Festival

In the Chinese lunar calendar, the Zhongyuan or Ghost Festival is on the 15th night of the seventh month. In olden times sacrificial rites and prayers for blessings would be performed in Daoist temples and at Buddhist temples rituals would be performed where the Ullambana Sutra was chanted to transmute and absolve the sufferings of the deceased. The common people accomplished the same purpose by placing lanterns on rivers and lakes. In the Yuan Ming Yuan waterborne lanterns were usually placed in the Lake of Happiness on the annual occasion of the Zhongyuan Festival.

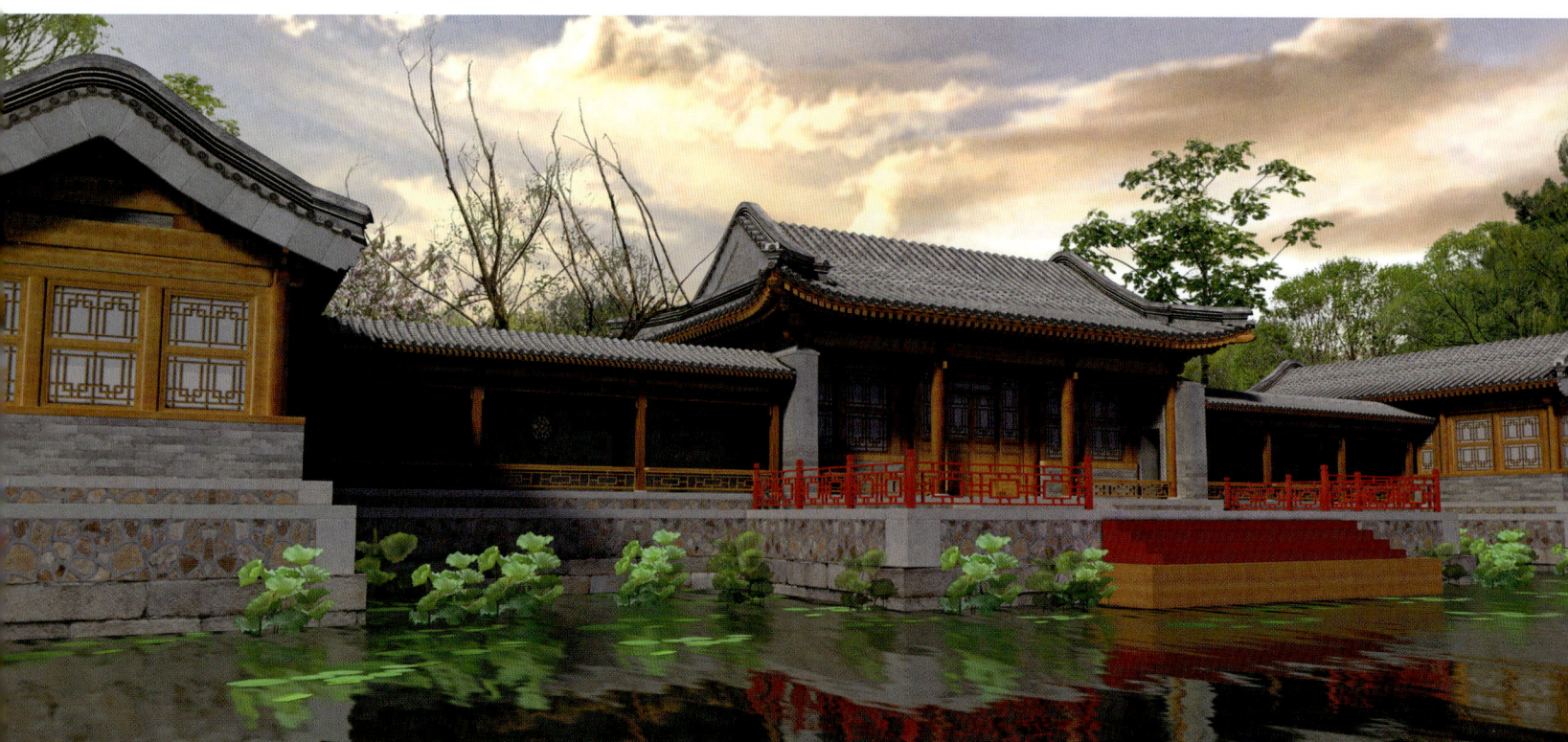

Fig. 185 Chengxu Gazebo in the Zaoshen Yude Complex

Qianlong composed a number of poems on such activities.

In the poem entitled *Launching Lanterns in the Imperial Garden on Zhongyuan Festival*[3] composed in the 15th year of his reign (1750) Qianlong wrote that the chanting of the Ullambana Sutra at night reminded him that for two years running no river lanterns had been floated in the imperial garden because of the death of Empress Xiaoxian the year before last and also because of his stay at the Bishu Mountain Resort on the occasion of the Zhongyuan Festival the previous year. He said that he had fond memories of the scenes of the Chengde Mountain Resort and he revisited the poems he composed in previous years. In the poem *Floating River Lanterns on the Eve of Zhongyuan*[4] of the 32nd year of his reign (1767) Qianlong wrote that because of the later arrival of autumn in a leap year he had to postpone his planned tour; and since he happened to stay in the Yuan Ming Yuan at the time of the Zhongyuan Festival he was able to see myriad lanterns on the imperial lake.

In the poem entitled *Placement of River Lanterns on Zhongyuan Festival*[5] of the 38th year of his reign (1773) Qianlong wrote that there was a light rain at dawn which later cleared and that river lanterns were floated in accordance with custom.

These poems tell us that the floating of river lanterns was not strictly a ritual to transmute and absolve the sufferings of the deceased but had evolved into a form of entertainment.

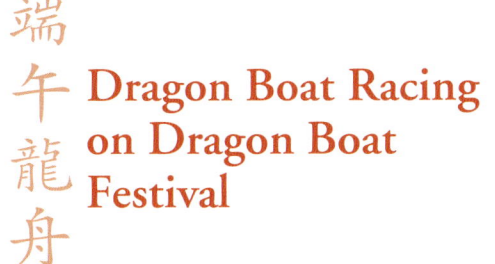

Dragon Boat Racing on Dragon Boat Festival

At the annual Dragon Boat Festival the emperor would invite close aides and princes and members of the nobility to watch the dragon boat race on the Lake of Happiness. It was also an opportunity for bonding between the emperor and his retinue as well as for showing filial devotion to his mother the empress dowager. In the 30th year of his reign Qianlong wrote that it was a time of harvest and guests were invited as usual on this Dragon Boat Festival to view the dragon boat race; that there was really no competition in the so-called race and that he was glad his mother was pleased with it.[6] Not a year passed without Qianlong writing a poem like that; after the death of the empress dowager he would be filled with sadness at the Dragon Boat Festival. A decade after the death of his mother he composed a poem in which he expressed his sense of loss. He wrote that "Dragon Boat Festival being in the middle of summer it would be a time to pray for rain, but it was lucky that the boat race could go forward today (in late spring and early summer rain was scarce in the north of China and festive events had often been canceled on Dragon Boat Festival in previous years because of a dearth of rain. Because of the copious rain falling all day the previous day the boat race could now be held as per custom) ... (it has been ten years now that I have not been able to go to Pengdao Yaotai Complex to ask after the health of the empress dowager), with sadness I remember her ..."[7]

The boat race was watched from the Pengdao Yaotai Complex, where the best seats were at the building on the south side called the Jingzhong Pavilion and the galleries at its sides. Another good spot for viewing lake scenes was the Wangyingzhou Pavilion of the Zaoshen Yude Complex (fig. 185), which had a waterfront terrace and a stone balustrade on the lake shore.

Floating wine cups, the viewing of lotus blossoms and the dragon boat races were conventional events at the time of traditional festivals in the Qing period and the imperial garden was not to be deprived of such entertainment. These festivals provided an opportunity for the amusement of the emperor, his consorts and high officials and for bonding between the emperor and his family as well as his ministers. The premises hosting such events were both functional and aesthetic.

---

1 *Yuzhi Shi*, by Emperor Qianlong, Book I, Volume 6.
2 Ibid., Book II, Volume 10.
3 Ibid.
4 Ibid., Book III, Volume 67.
5 Ibid., Book IV, Volume 16.
6 Ibid., Book III, Volume 50.
7 Ibid., Book V, Volume 40.

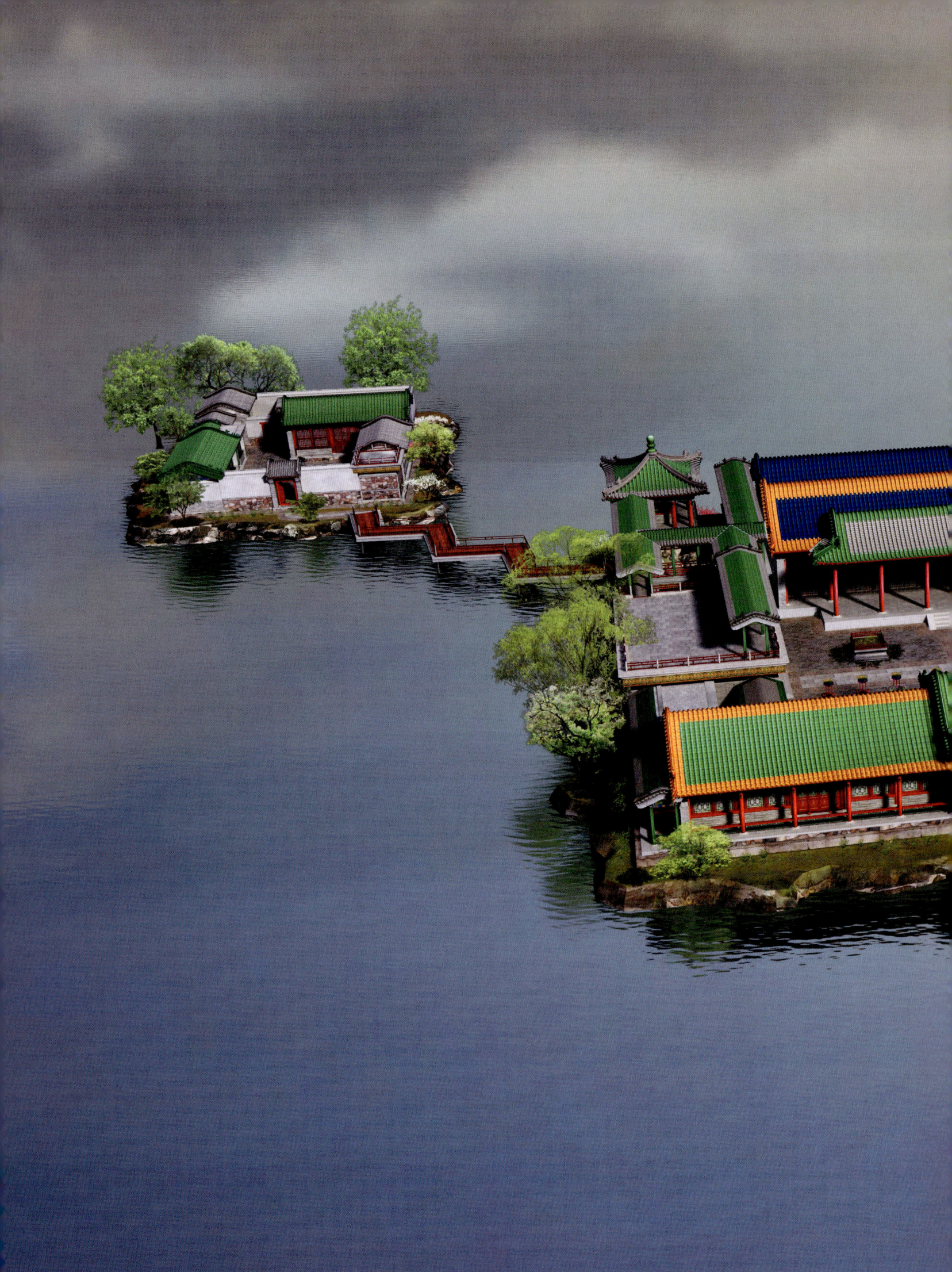

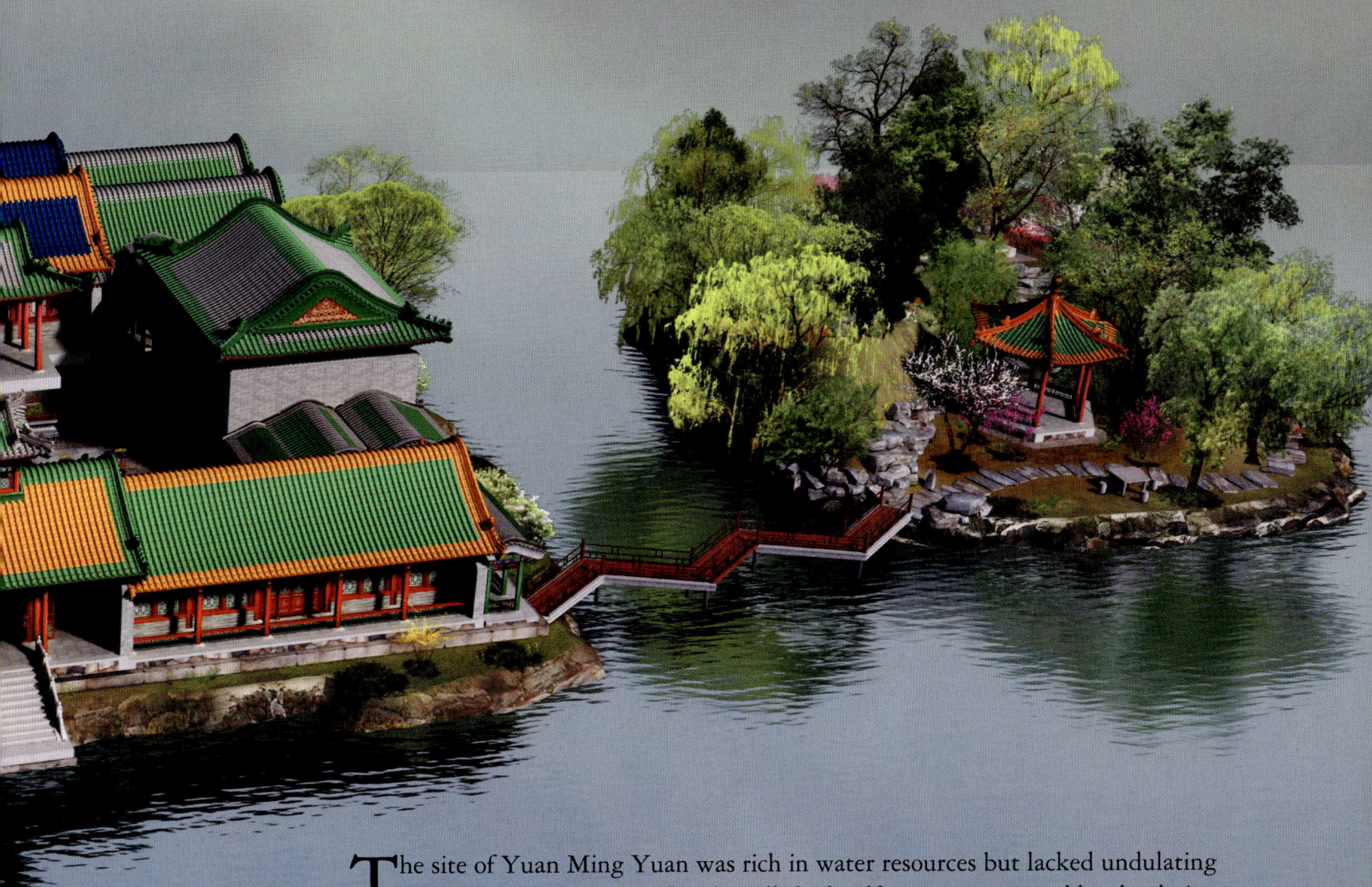

PART III
THE DESIGN APPROACH OF THE GARDEN CREATORS

The site of Yuan Ming Yuan was rich in water resources but lacked undulating terrain. The land was so flat that all the landforms were created by the designers. In the planning stages the garden architects had already visualized the hills and dales. By transforming the topography of the site and thoughtfully arranging newly created hills and water bodies, and by varying the configurations of groups of buildings, they created a garden that not only provided functional spaces but also expressed the aesthetic taste of the emperor. These features distinguished the Yuan Ming Yuan as an imperial pleasure park.

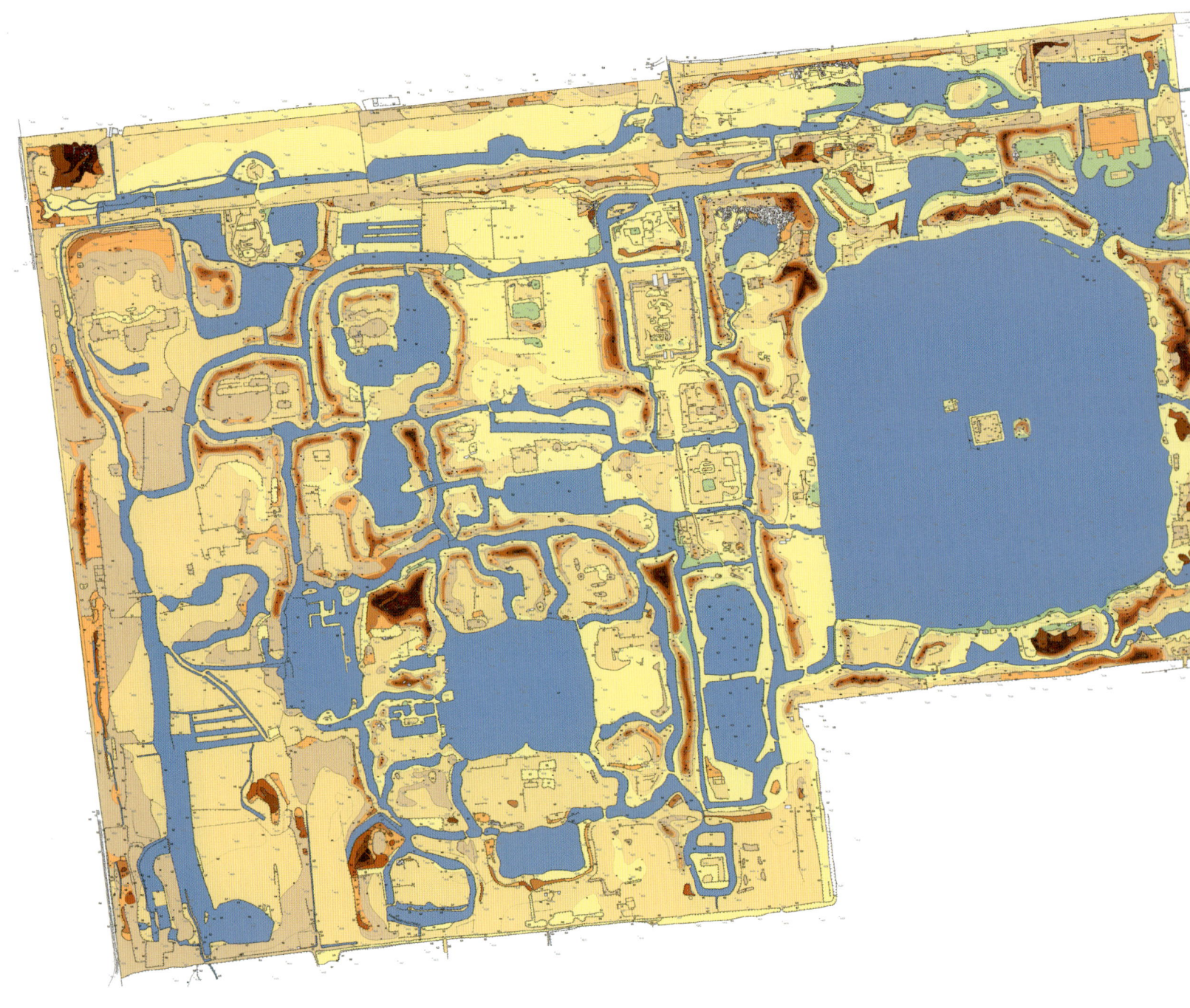

Fig. 187 Topographic model of Yuan Ming Yuan

Pages 222 and 223
Fig. 186 Aerial view of Pengdao Yaotai Complex

CHINA'S LOST IMPERIAL GARDEN

CHAPTER XV
Recreating Landscape Spaces

The ground on which the Yuan Ming Yuan was built had originally been rural wetland. It was chosen as a site for a prince's garden because of its proximity to the imperial garden of Emperor Kangxi. The Yuan Ming Yuan started as a prince's garden granted by the emperor; it continued to be developed through the eras of Yongzheng, Qianlong and Jiaqing to become the Yuan Ming Yuan, the Changchun Garden and the Qichun Garden that we know today. The landscape spaces evolved as different emperors took possession of the Garden.

The building that went on during the period when it was a prince's dwelling granted by the emperor was concentrated around the Jiuzhou Qingyan Complex on the Back Lake. The main theme was "water landscape," with streams everywhere and bridges linking the various groups of buildings. There were not many hills; only the Peony Terrace had a semblance of a hill in the form of a stack of stones and rocks. After his accession to the throne, Emperor Yongzheng undertook rebuilding that developed the Nine Islands area centered around the Back Lake, the nine islands symbolizing the nine continents of his realm. He named the main island Jiuzhou Qingyan. The islands were surrounded by low earthen hills that ran in different directions. Some were relatively closed, such as those around the Bitong Library and the Xinghuachun Pavilion; others were semi-closed, such as at Tantan Dangdang Complex and the Ciyun Puhu Complex; still others, such as those around the Jiuzhou Qingyan Complex and the Shangxia Tianguang Complex, were completely open. The landscape was rich and varied. The building activity radiated out from the Nine Islands area. In the north and the west the grounds were modeled by the excavation of ponds and the building of mounds to create different types of landscape spaces. These included gardens with artificial hills and ponds, waterside houses and archery grounds interspersed with crop fields. One could take a boat ride on the streams and canals, past gorges or across lakes; compounds—the Quyuan Fenghe, the Lianxi Lechu, or the Yingshui Lanxiang and Duojia Ruyun Hall and others—within sight of each other across fields, had each their own attractive qualities. These themed landscaped areas had low earthen hills as their boundaries. In some places two hills bounded a river or pond; in other places the hills lay on one side of a stream; there were gorges and peaks; zonal spaces and large lakes alternated, with the beholder being greeted by a new vista at every turn of his footsteps.

The excavation of the Lake of Happiness in the eastern part of the Yuan Ming Yuan started in the Yongzheng era. Three islands were thrown up in the middle of the lake to create a mirage-like illusion with the aid of the contrast between the vast expanse of the lake and the smallness of the islets. In the northwest of the Garden a mountain of considerable height was thrown up to symbolize the Kunlun Mountains (fig. 187).

The planning and design adopted in the building of the Changchun Garden in the Qianlong era differed from the approach used in the construction of the Yuan Ming Yuan. Its focus was bodies of water, whose total area exceeded that of the land areas. There were five lakes in it of varying sizes and shapes, separated from each other by earthen hills. There were a total of five islands, on the largest of which was situated the private residence of the emperor; the four smaller islands with their buildings and garden structures were satellites to the main island. The islands of different morphologies and shapes had more often than not earthen hills on them to shield the buildings from idle eyes, leaving only a few waterside pavilions visible to casual sightseers. The overall landscape structure and layout were tiered and layered and gave the sense of a coherent whole.

Under Emperor Jiaqing, the newly integrated Qichun Garden acquired the character of a collection of mini-parks. These "mini-parks" varied in size and style, thereby resulting in an uneven distribution of vistas and sceneries. The different treatments of the land and water spaces in these areas in previous times left their mark in the renovated Garden. The main means of communication in the Garden remained the waterways.

CHAPTER XVI
Control of the Architectural Layout with a Grid System

Among extant documentation is a plan of the Yuan Ming Yuan bearing the number of 043-1. A grid is drawn on the plan and each square of the grid, it has been determined by experts, is equivalent to 10 *zhang* by 10.4 *zhang*, or 32 meters by 33.3 meters on the ground.[1] It is not yet possible to know from available literature how this grid was applied at the time to the design of the Garden, but if the grid is laid over the number 1704 drawing made in the Qianlong era and now held by the library of the Palace Museum in Beijing, one finds that it relates closely to the general distribution of the groups of buildings and the treatments of the landscape spaces in the Garden, therefore presumably the grid was used as a basis for determining the general layout of the Garden (fig. 188).

Some squares on the grid happened to fall along the central axis of the themed area; thus the central axis of the Zhengda Guangming Complex coincides with the right side of square number 19 and extends northward past the Jiuzhou Qingyan Complex to end at the bell tower in the Ciyun Puhu Complex; the total distance is 566 meters. The Shewei City, as another example, sits in the middle of grid square number 28, with its central axis reaching the little dock on the small stream at the south end of Market Street; the total distance is 366 meters. The central axis of the Hongci Yonghu Complex lies on the line going through the right side of square number 4.

The courts of some groups of buildings fall completely within the grid squares, while in some others a deliberate shifting out of grid lines is done to seek variation. The grid is important for determining the layout of the Garden, as can be seen from the drawing, in the following ways.

1. Building Groups Whose Courtyards Spread out Transversely

The Jiuzhou Qingyan is the widest group of buildings, spanning 6.5 grid squares transversely and 4 squares longitudinally. The area taken up by the building group is 208 meters wide and 133 meters deep.

The Qinzheng Qinxian Complex extends 5 grid squares across and 4 squares up and down, with a width of 160 meters and a depth of 133 meters.

The Changchun Xianguan Complex takes up only a little over 3 squares across and 2 squares up and down, with a width of 100 meters and a depth of 66 meters.

The Ritian Linyu Complex extends 3 squares across and a little over 2 squares up and down, with a width of close to 100 meters and a depth of close to 80 meters.

These are examples of building groups that spread out sideways, with a depth of two or three courtyards longitudinally. The size of these courtyards varies according to the dimensions of the halls in them, with different degrees of privacy and openness as appropriate.

2. Building Groups that Extend in One Direction

Building groups that follow the natural contours of a stream flowing across the garden include, among others, the Bieyou Dongtian Complex and the Beiyuan Mountain Village, whose widths range between 160–130 meters across and whose depths range between 90–70 meters. They sprawl along the stream for up to 100 meters, while extend in the other direction only for less than 66 meters.

In these building groups the buildings on the two banks of the stream recede or advance freely, with no enclosed outdoor spaces. They are scattered about; the main and secondary buildings can be told by their different masses.

3. Large Building Groups that Extend Longitudinally

The Hongci Yonghu Complex spans 4 grid squares across and 8 up and down. The distance from the memorial columns in the south to the north wall reaches 266 meters; the introductory space is an impressive 130 meters. The longitudinal space comprises 4 tiers.

In this type of building groups there are not a great number of individual buildings; the arrangement of the architectural elements and the hierarchical treatment of the spaces are all geared toward showcasing the courtyard containing the main hall of Anyou Palace.

4. Cluster Type Building Groups

This type of building groups is found primarily among small and medium-sized ones. They normally take up 3 grid squares across, or about 100 meters, and 2 to 3 squares up and down. They consist mostly of courtyards, with scattered pavilions. Examples are the Dongtian Shenchu Complex, the Rugu Hanjin Hall (Hall of Harmony of the Present with the Past), the Xifeng Xiuse Complex and the Zibi Mountain House. They are typically modest in size and consist of two or three courtyards.

5. 品-Shaped Building Groups

These are comparable to the cluster type in scale, with a transverse span of 3 grid squares and 2.5 to 3.5 squares up and down, or 100 meters wide and 80–130 meters deep. Examples are the Yuyue Yuanfei Complex (Complex of Leaping Fish and Flying Kites), the Yuedi Yunju Complex and the Fanghu Shengjing Complex. This type of building groups tends to dwarf the surrounding landscape.

6. Building Groups that Surround a Large Courtyard or a Pond

This type of building groups typically enclose a space of about two grid squares across and up and down, or 60–70 meters each way. Some feature a pond in the middle, others stand out with the plants on the grounds, with the buildings of

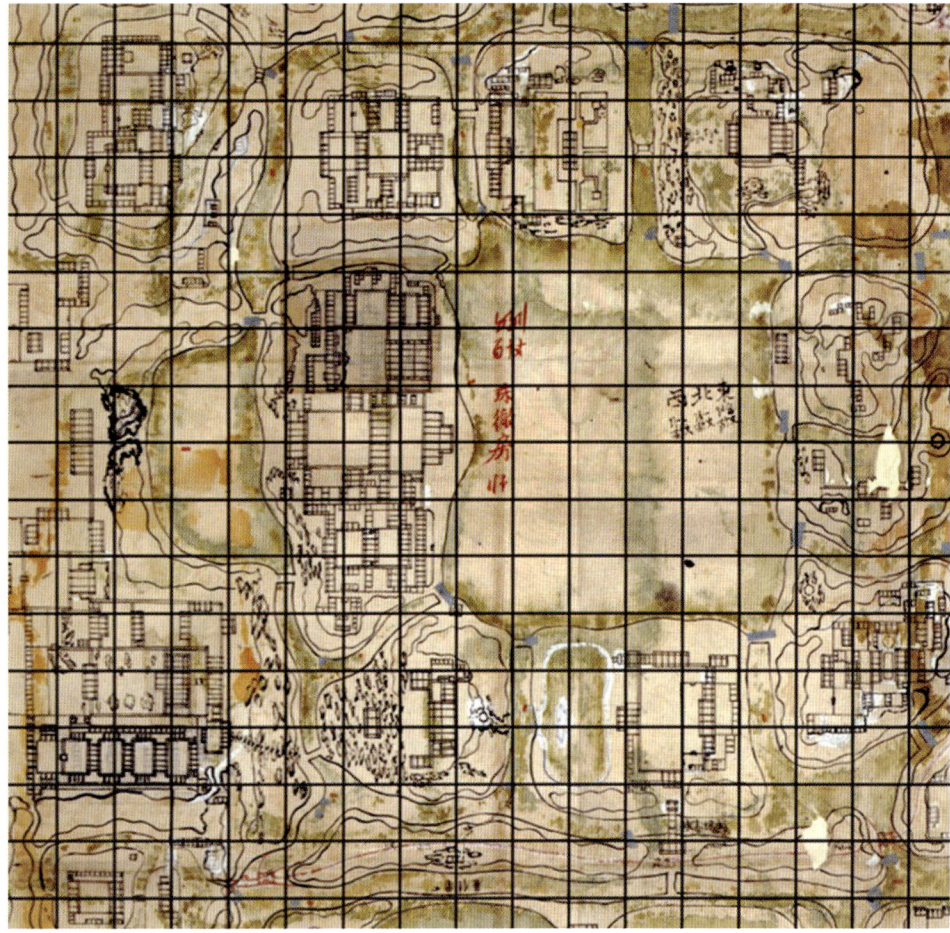

Fig. 188 Gridded plan of the Nine Islands area of Yuan Ming Yuan

different heights and masses freely arranged around them.

Some special single structures, such as the Wanfang Anhe Complex and the Danbo Ningjing Complex, typically occupy one grid square, i.e. their area is kept in the range of 32 meters by 33.3 meters. Small courtyards enclosed by auxiliary structures such as waiting rooms are kept in the range of half a grid square.

The foregoing analysis indicates that the grid square equivalent to 10 *zhang* by 32 meters represented a guide for controlling the size and scale of the building groups in the Yuan Ming Yuan. Through variation in the number of grid squares assigned to each group of buildings and the placement of the buildings in the grid, the garden designers created a rich variety of vistas.

The grid was also used as a guide in arranging the landscape that distinguished the various building complexes. This is particularly evident in the Nine Islands area, where the construction of the Yuan Ming Yuan started. Streams and low earthen hills were used in this area to divide the land into nine islands. The distance between buildings of two neighboring islands was normally one grid square; where ponds or hills fall in the square, this criterion could be slightly relaxed to adapt to the topography. There are other examples where one grid square or two was adopted as the distance between buildings in arranging the landscape. Only in the north of the park, where large agricultural fields were kept for imperial observation and inspection, was the criterion for controlling the distance between building groups considerably relaxed.

---
1 He Yan, *From a Prince's Garden to an Imperial Park*, Master's Thesis, Tsinghua University.

CHAPTER XVII
Water Courses as the Dominant Means of Transport

To satisfy the imperial predilection for the gardens of Jiangnan south of the Yangtze River, the Yuan Ming Yuan was crisscrossed with water courses. Wherever a boat could be used, the emperor and empress would take the boat in the Garden. Records in the *Chuandai Dang* (*Log of the Costumes the Emperor Wore*) of the 21st year of the Qianlong era (1756) show that as early as the latter half of March the emperor had begun to ride in boats in the Garden. Earlier in the cold season when boat riding was not an option the warm sedan chair was used instead. When water courses froze over, the "pulled couch" was used. It was a winter-proofed flat-bottom boat that was pulled across the ice by men (fig. 189).

The logged boat rides included:

Fourth day of the fourth month: entered the Churu Xianliang Gate, stayed shortly at the Jiuzhou Qingyan Hall, took the boat at the rear dock to go to the Tongle Garden; after supper, took the boat to tour the East Garden, returned to the Jiuzhou Qingyan Complex.

Fifth day of the fourth month: rode in a *liang jiao* (uncurtained sedan chair) carried by four to the Goldfish Pond to feed the fish, took a boat ride; went to Jiuzhou Qingyan Complex for supper, took the boat to Xiuqing Village for a short visit; rode in a cool sedan chair carried by four to return to Jiuzhou Qingyan Complex from the Ruyi Pavilion.

Sixth day of the fourth month: went to work at the Qinzheng Hall, gave audiences. Took the sedan chair to Shangao Shuichang Complex for a short visit, rode in a cool sedan chair carried by four to Wanfang Anhe Complex for a boat tour, went to the Goldfish Pond to feed the fish, went to Jiuzhou Qingyan Complex for supper, took the boat for a tour in the East Garden before returning to Jiuzhou Qingyan Complex.

Seventh day of the fourth month: toured Wanshou Hill (Longevity Hill); on return, entered Zaoyuan Gate to take the boat to kowtow at Qingjingdi Complex. Took a *liang jiao* carried by four to Wanfang Anhe Complex, changed into a thick red and blue silk-filled satin jacket and stayed for a short visit. About noontime, changed into a thick red and blue silk-filled jacket embroidered with gilt dragons, put on a few gharu wood beads, took the boat to Shengqiu Court to light incense sticks at the altar; rode in a *liang jiao* carried by four to Jiuzhou Qingyan Complex, took off the beads and changed into a light red and blue silk-filled satin jacket; after supper, rode in a *liang jiao* carried by four for a tour, rested at Shuanghe Study, took the boat to the Goldfish Pond to feed the fish and returned to Jiuzhou Qingyan Complex.

Eighth day of the fourth month: exited the southwest gate in a warm sedan chair carried by four and went to the Yongning Temple to pay homage to the Buddha, entered the Zaoyuan Gate to kowtow (perform prostrations) at Qingjingdi Complex, proceeded to Wanfang Anhe Complex to take the boat to Shewei City to pay homage to the Buddha and stroll about; went to the Tongle Garden, took off the beads, changed into a heavy red and blue silk-filled satin jacket. After supper, took a boat for a tour in the Changchun Garden before returning to Jiuzhou Qingyan Complex.

Ninth day of the fourth month: took a boat to Qinzheng Hall for work; went on a *liang jiao* borne by four to the Shuanghe Study for a short visit, took a boat to Wanfang Anhe Complex for supper; took a sedan chair to Qingjingdi Complex to light joss sticks before returning to Jiuzhou Qingyan Complex.

Tenth day of the fourth month: returned to Jiuzhou Qingyan Complex for supper; took a boat for a tour in the east garden before returning to Jiuzhou Qingyan Complex.

Eleventh day of the fourth month: exited the Churu Xianliang Gate on a warm sedan chair borne by four, entered the northwest gate of the front garden to take a boat inside the Yuanguang Gate, went to the Shouxuan Chunyong Hall to ask after the health of the empress dowager; took a sedan chair, left the Wuyi Study gate to the Taoyuan Library to have breakfast, transact official business and give audiences; rode in a *liang jiao* carried by four for a tour; took a boat at the dock by the west gate of Wanshou Hill to the Jingming Garden, took a tour on a *liang jiao* carried by four before returning by retracing steps.

Nineteenth day of the fourth month: went to Wanshou Hill for breakfast, official business and audiences; returned after taking a tour on a *liang jiao* carried by four; entered Zaoyuan Gate to take a boat to Huifang Library, changed into a light red and blue silk-filled satin jacket, went by a *liang jiao* carried by four to Shenxiu Siyong Hall for a short visit, took a boat to Qinzheng Hall to transact official business. After supper at Jiuzhou Qingyan Complex, walked to the Goldfish Pond to feed the fish, took a boat for a tour in the Changchun Garden before returning to Jiuzhou Qingyan Complex.

Thirteenth day of the fifth month: took a boat at the rear dock to Pengdao Yaotai Complex, had supper there and took a boat to Xiuqing Village, changed into a light red and blue voile jacket, stayed for a while, then took a boat tour before returning to Jiuzhou Qingyan Complex.

From these log entries it is clear that Emperor Qianlong traveled by boat nearly every day. Some trips could have been made by taking a sedan chair all the way through, but he still preferred to alternate the chair with the boat.

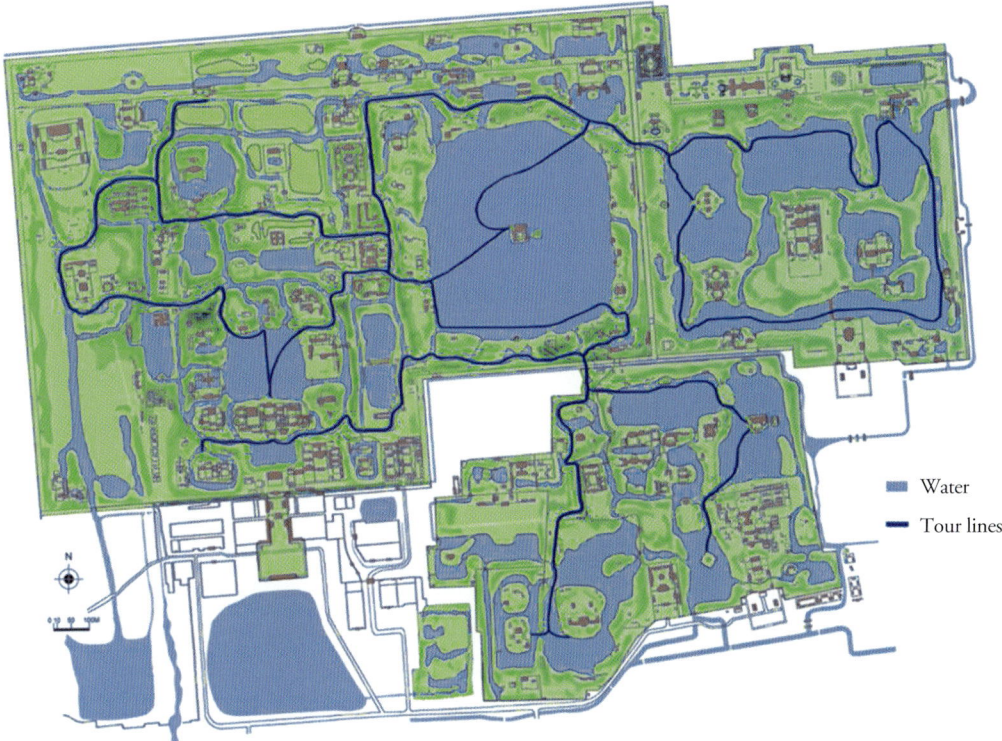

Fig. 189 Water courses as the dominant means of transport

This shows how much Emperor Qianlong enjoyed the water routes, a number of which are listed below, with the sceneries and vistas along the routes noted.

(1) From his private apartments at Jiuzhou Qingyan Complex to Tongle Garden (a theater). Vistas along the route included the Tianran Tuhua Complex and the Bitong Library.

(2) From Jiuzhou Qingyan Complex to Xiuqing Village (later named Bieyou Dongtian Complex). Sights worth seeing along this route included the Peony Terrace, Quyuan Fenghe Complex, Jiajing Mingqin Complex and a view of Pengdao Yaotai Complex in the distance.

(3) From Jiuzhou Qingyan Complex to the Ciyun Puhu Complex. The views along this routed included the seven islands around the Back Lake.

(4) From Wanfang Anhe Complex to the Jiuzhou Qingyan Complex and on to the East Garden (i.e. the Xichun Garden on the south side of the Changchun Garden). The views along this route included the Tantan Dangdang Complex, scenery around the Back Lake, the Tongle Garden, scenes around the Lake of Happiness, the Fanghu Shengjing Complex, the Xie Qiqu Pavilion of the Changchun Garden, the Haiyue Kaijin Complex, Siyong Study, the north side of Danhuai Hall, the Ru Garden and the East Garden.

(5) From Shuanghe Study (also named Kuoran Dagong) to the Tantan Dangdang Complex and on to the Jiuzhou Qingyan Complex.

(6) From the Chunyu Pavilion of the Xinghuachun Pavilion to the Qinzheng Hall. Views on this route included the islands of the Back Lake. The route led across the Zongting Bridge, the Great South Bridge and the Ruyi Bridge to reach the dock on the north side of the Qinzheng Qinxian Complex, where one could continue on land.

(7) From Zaoyuan Gate to Huifang Library. The route ran

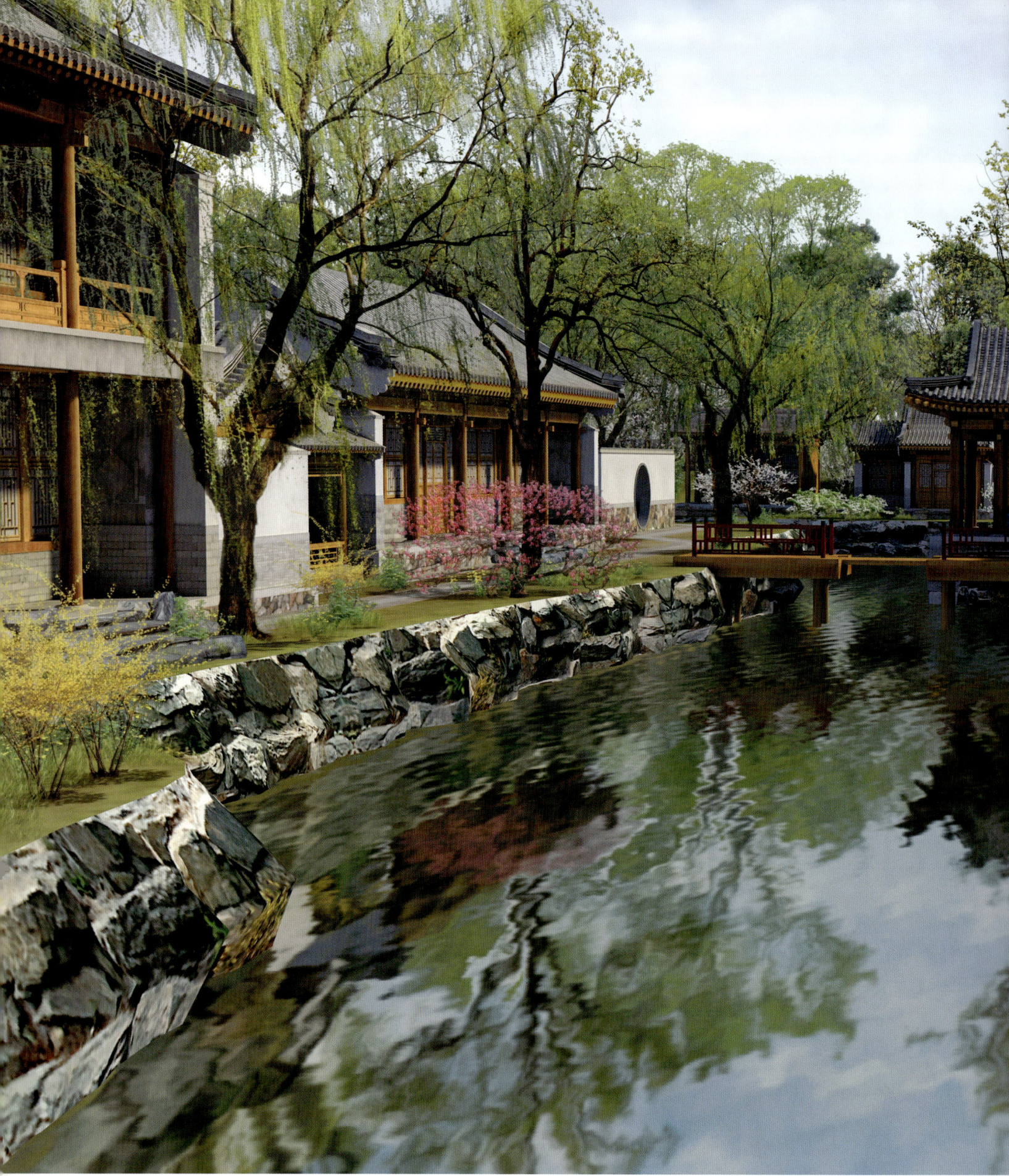

Fig. 190 View of the waterways in the Bieyou Dongtian Complex

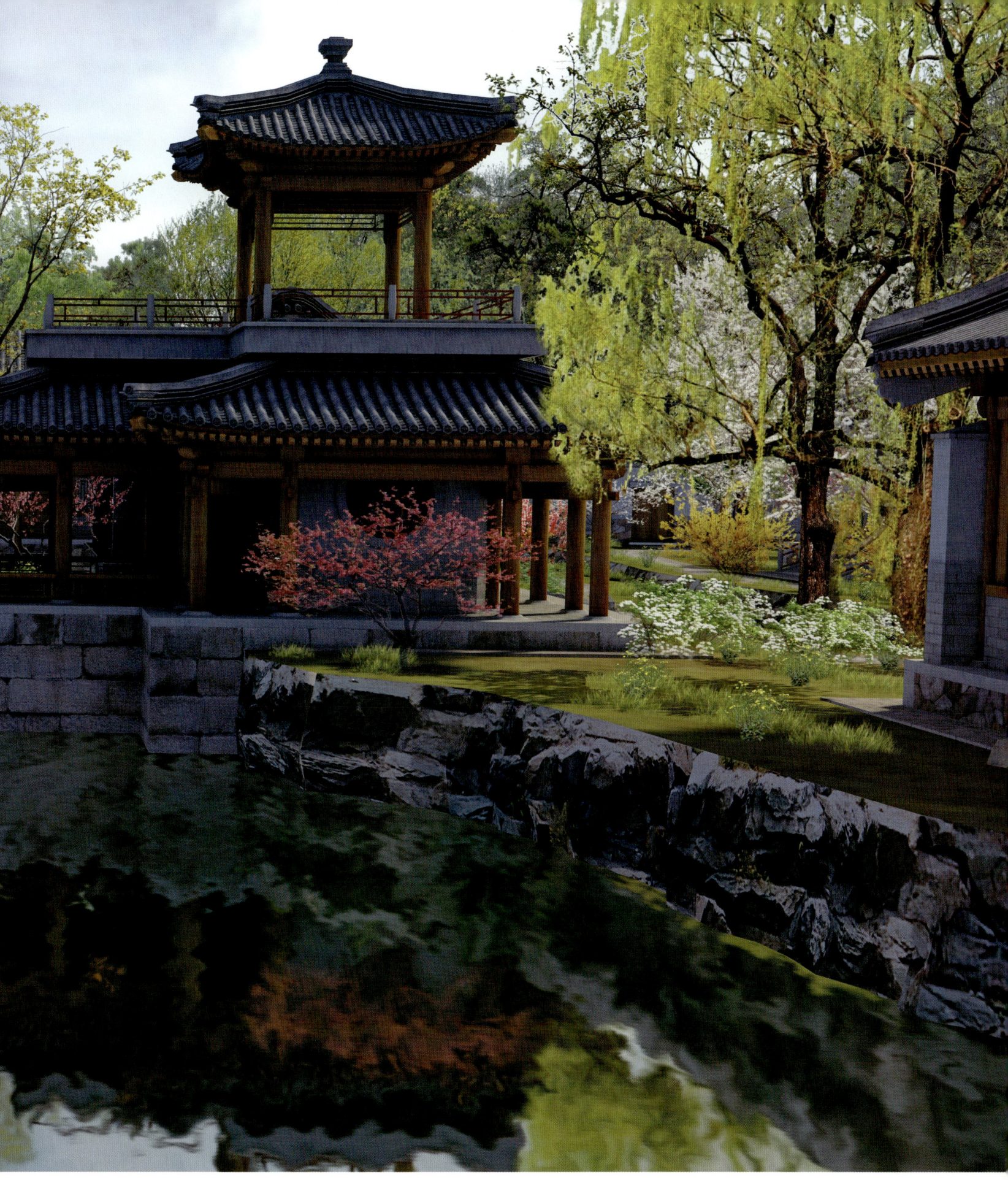

north, past Yuedi Yunju Complex and Ritian Linyu Complex to reach Wenjin Pavilion, where one could disembark.

(8) From Shenxiu Siyong Hall (also called Lianxi Lechu) to the Qinzheng Hall. It passed through the Yingshui Lanxiang Complex, the Ciyun Puhu Complex, the islands of the Back Lake and the small stream west of the Jiuzhou Qingyan Complex to reach the dock on the north side of the Qinzheng Qinxian Complex, where one could disembark.

(9) From the Goldfish Pond (i.e. Tantan Dangdang) to the Changchun Garden. Views included scenery around the Back Lake, Tongle Garden, scenes around the Lake of Happiness, and the Fanghu Shengjing Complex.

(10) From Jiuzhou Qingyan Complex to the Pengdao Yaotai Complex and on to Xiuqing Village. It ran past the Peony Terrace, the north side of the Dongtian Shenchu Complex, the southwest corner of the Lake of Happiness and the Pengdao Yaotai Complex to reach Xiuqing Village.

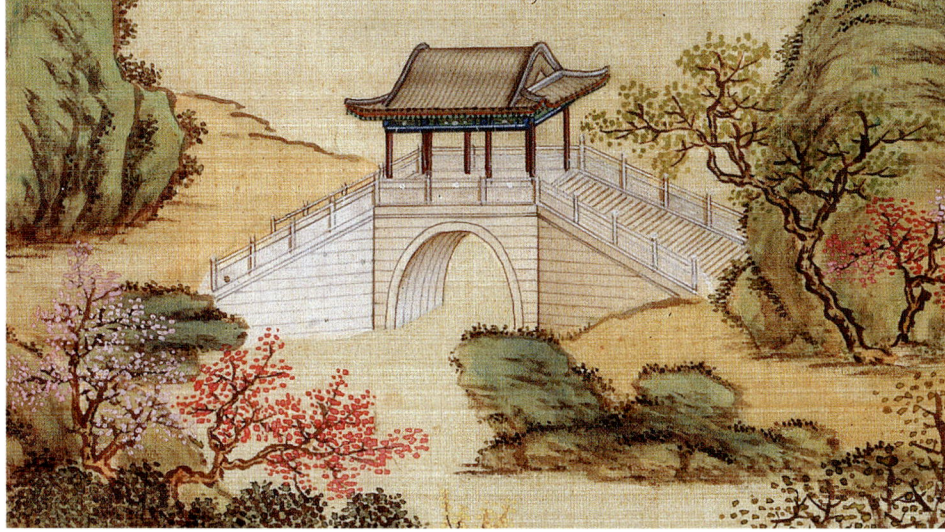

Fig. 191 Mingyuxi Bridge at northwest corner of Changchun Xianguan Complex (from *Forty Scenes of the Yuan Ming Yuan*)

Every one of these water routes was rich in scenery (fig. 190 on pages 228 and 229).

Then there were the land routes. Over a hundred bridges spanned the streams, rivers and canals in the Garden; they were indispensable for travel over land. Depending on the building materials, these could be wood bridges, stone bridges, brick bridges or wood and stone bridges. Structurally they could be beam bridges, arch bridges or moveable bridges. In length they could have as many as nine arches or as few as one arch. Some bridges, such as the Zongting Bridge (fig. 193) and the Mingyuxi Bridge (fig. 191), were surmounted by a pavilion. There was an impressive variety in shapes and forms. Some were one of a kind as far as garden bridges are concerned. They were exquisitely crafted; examples are the Ruyi Bridge (fig. 194) in the Nine Islands area, the zigzag bridge in Shangxia Tianguang Complex (fig. 192), Bilan Bridge (Green Wave Bridge) in Tantan Dangdang Complex (fig. 195), curiously no mention of any of these bridges could be found among Emperor Qianlong's poems.

Bridges are transport structures and vary greatly with the different means of transport. The means of imperial transport in the Yuan Ming Yuan consisted primarily of boats and sedan chairs; they came in a bewildering variety: *feng ge* (elaborately ornamented boat), *tuo chuang* (pulled couch), *feng yu* (phoenix vehicle), *liang jiao*. In winter the emperor used warm sedan chairs on land and pulled couches on ice, which "resembled a bed and a vehicle." Emperor Qianlong's indifference to the bridges in his imperial pleasure park was necessarily related to the use of these means of transport. We will take a random two days of Qianlong's activities in the Garden in the 21st year of his

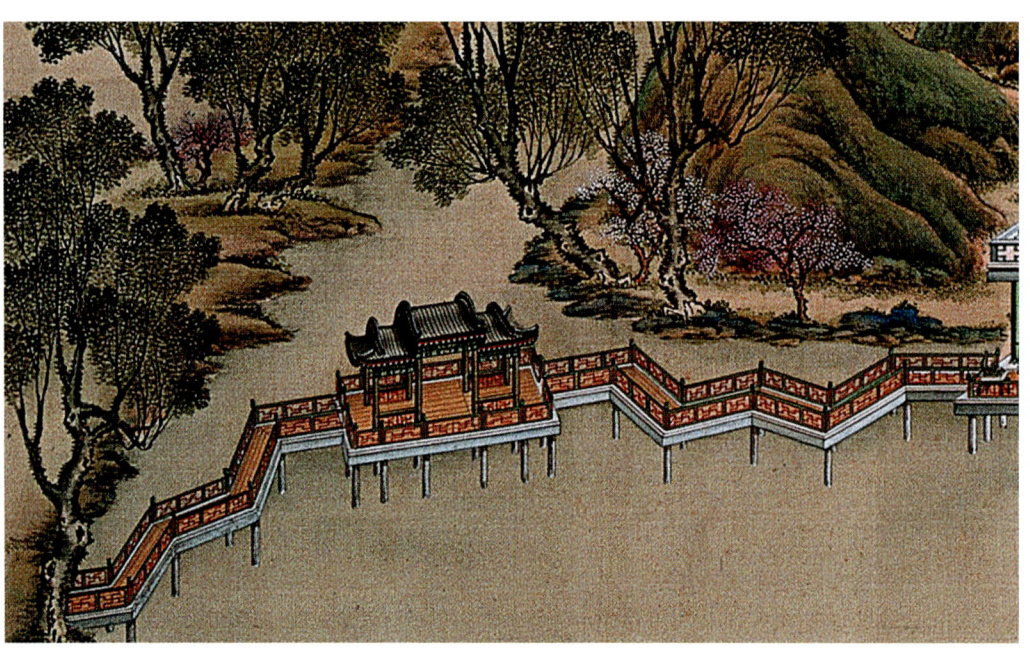

Fig. 192 Zigzag bridge in front of Shangxia Tianguang Complex (from *Forty Scenes of the Yuan Ming Yuan*)

reign (1756) for illustration. On the eighth day of the first month of the lunar calendar, he returned from the Forbidden City. It was wintertime and he "entered the Churu Xianliang Gate on a sedan chair … at the rear dock he rode in a pulled couch to the Ciyun Puhu Complex, the Qingjingdi Complex, the Anyou Palace and the Buddhist Complex to pay homage to the Buddha. He took a warm sedan chair carried by four to go to the Changchun Xianguan Complex to ask after the health of the empress dowager … then to the Jiuzhou Qingyan Complex … at the rear dock he went on a pulled couch to go to the Tongle Garden for supper." On the 23rd day of the sixth month, he mainly traveled by boat: from Jiuzhou Qingyan Complex he "took a cool sedan chair carried by four to go to Huai Qingfen Building (also called Qinzheng Qinxian) for breakfast … then took a cool sedan chair carried by four to the Goldfish Pond to feed the fish, went to the Jiuzhou Qingyan Complex to sit for a while, then traveled by boat to the East Garden to fish …" The log entries did not vary much from day to day. Only rarely does one find an entry like "a walk from the Jiuzhou Qingyan Complex to the Chunyu Pavilion." On most days he traveled either by boat or by sedan chair and therefore he rarely had occasion to walk across a bridge on his royal feet. This could possibly explain the dearth of odes to these bridges among his imperial poems.

Regardless of that fact, these variegated bridges were beautiful sights on the water and land routes in the Garden.

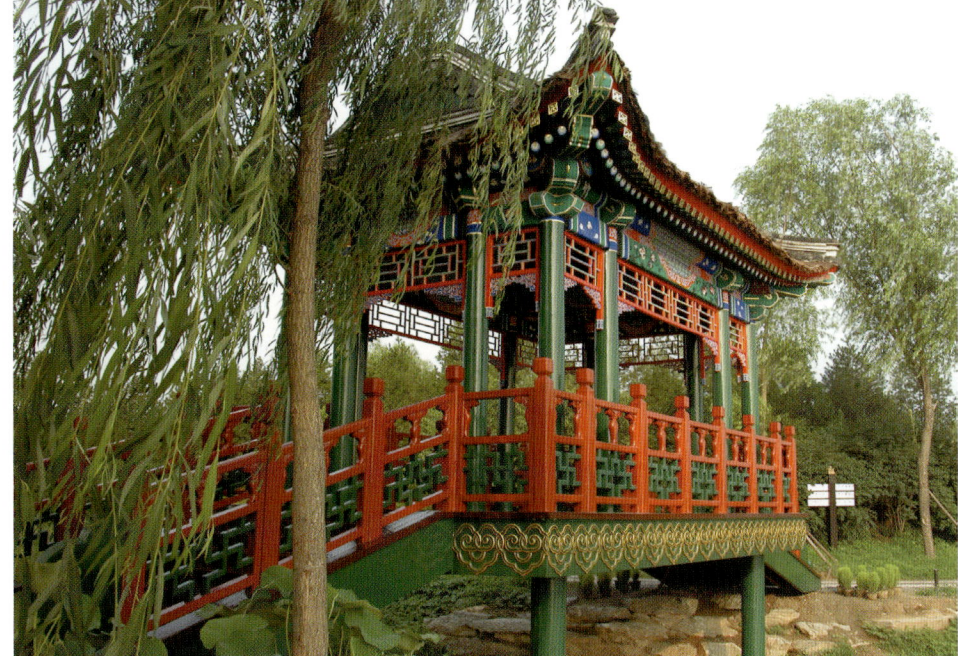

Fig. 193 Zongting Bridge at northwest corner of Jiuzhou Qingyan Island (restored in 2007)

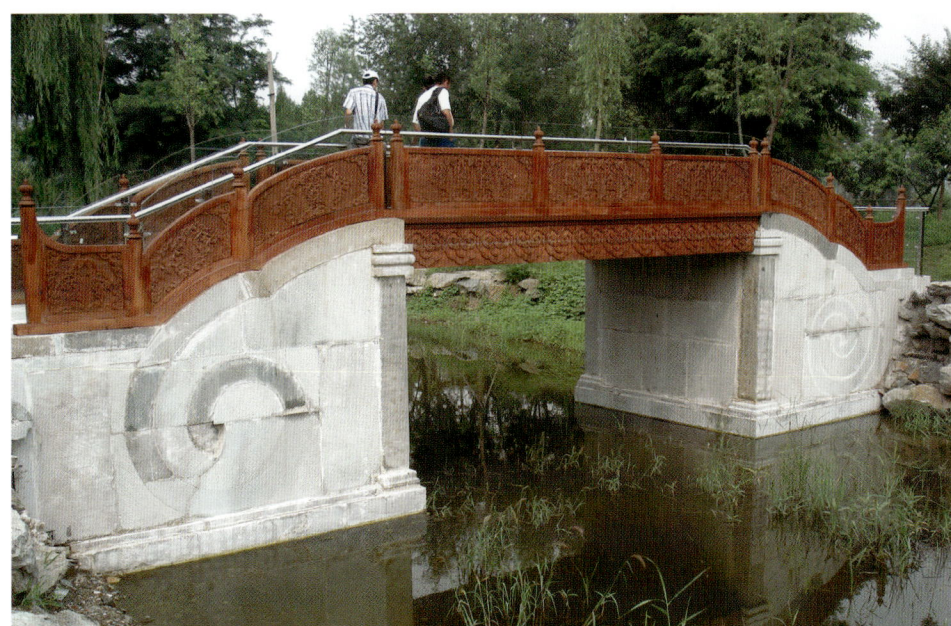

Fig. 194 Ruyi Bridge at southeast corner of the Jiuzhou Qingyan Island (restored in 2007)

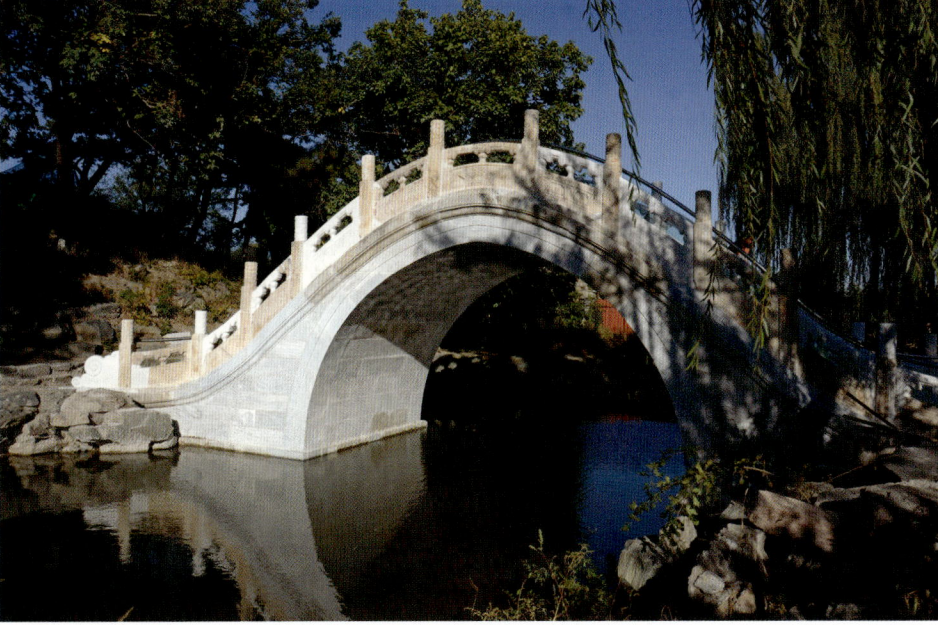

Fig. 195 Bilan Bridge at north of Tantan Dangdang Complex (restored in 2015)

PART III THE DESIGN APPROACH OF THE GARDEN CREATORS   231

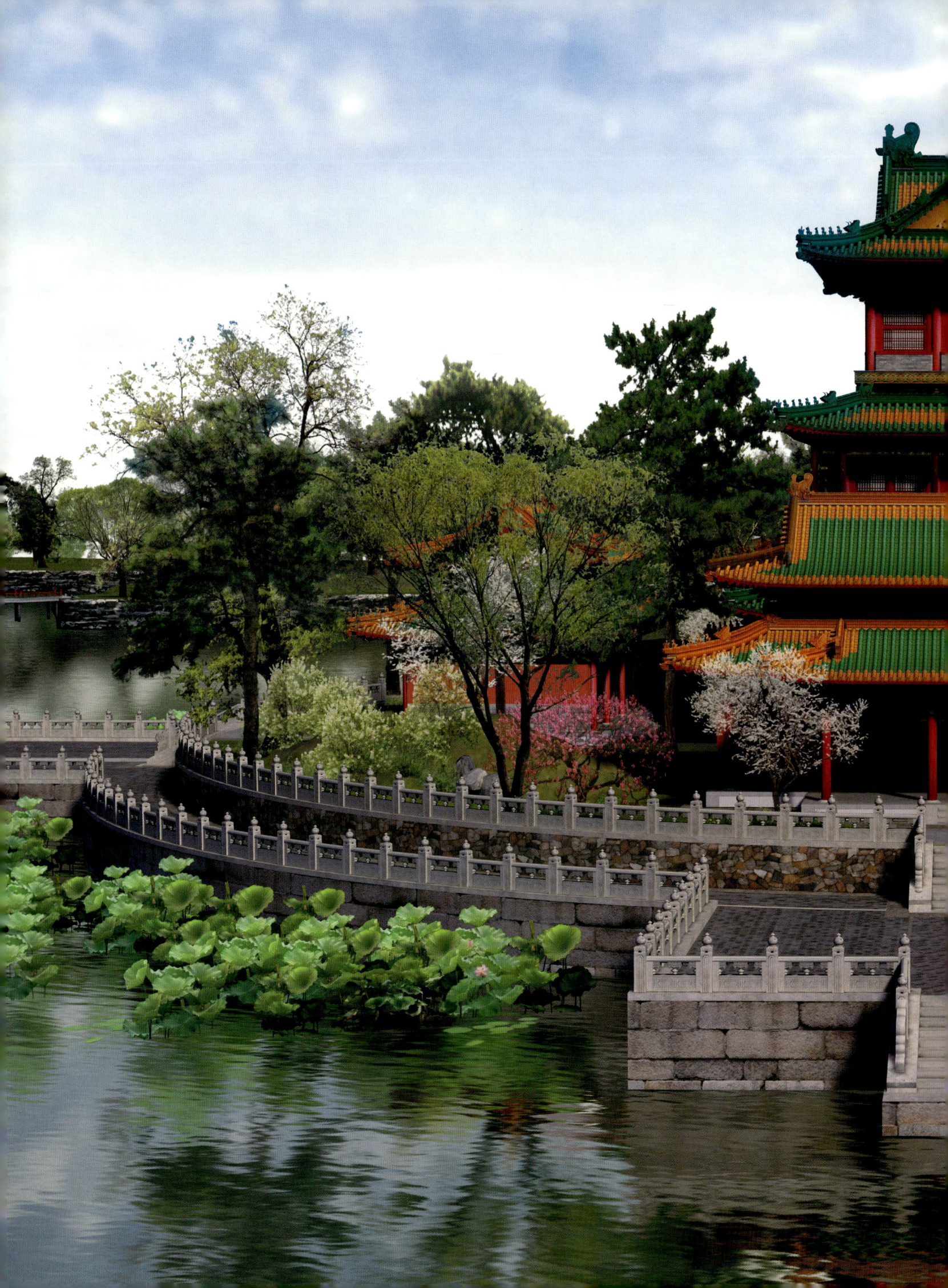

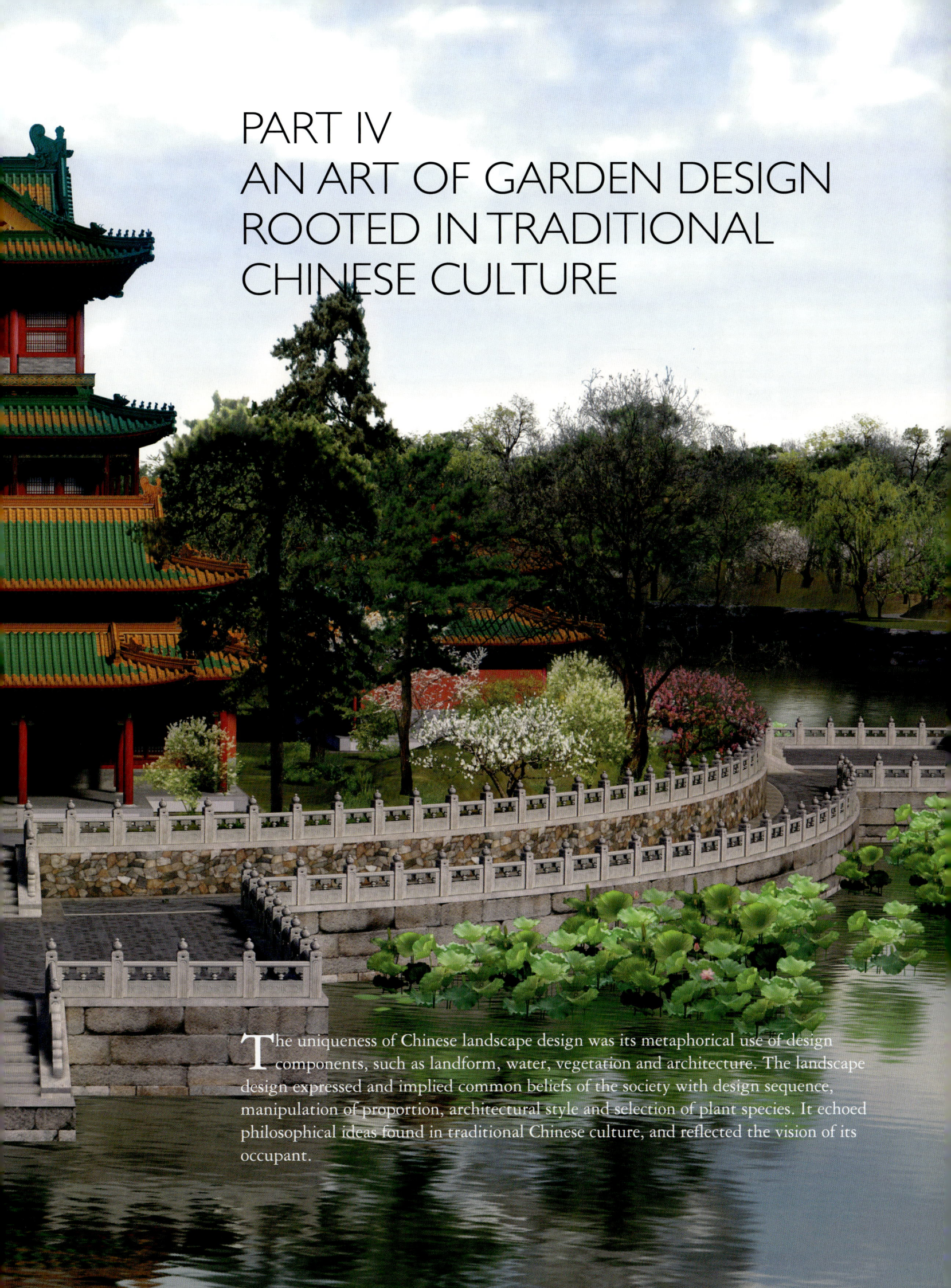

PART IV
AN ART OF GARDEN DESIGN ROOTED IN TRADITIONAL CHINESE CULTURE

The uniqueness of Chinese landscape design was its metaphorical use of design components, such as landform, water, vegetation and architecture. The landscape design expressed and implied common beliefs of the society with design sequence, manipulation of proportion, architectural style and selection of plant species. It echoed philosophical ideas found in traditional Chinese culture, and reflected the vision of its occupant.

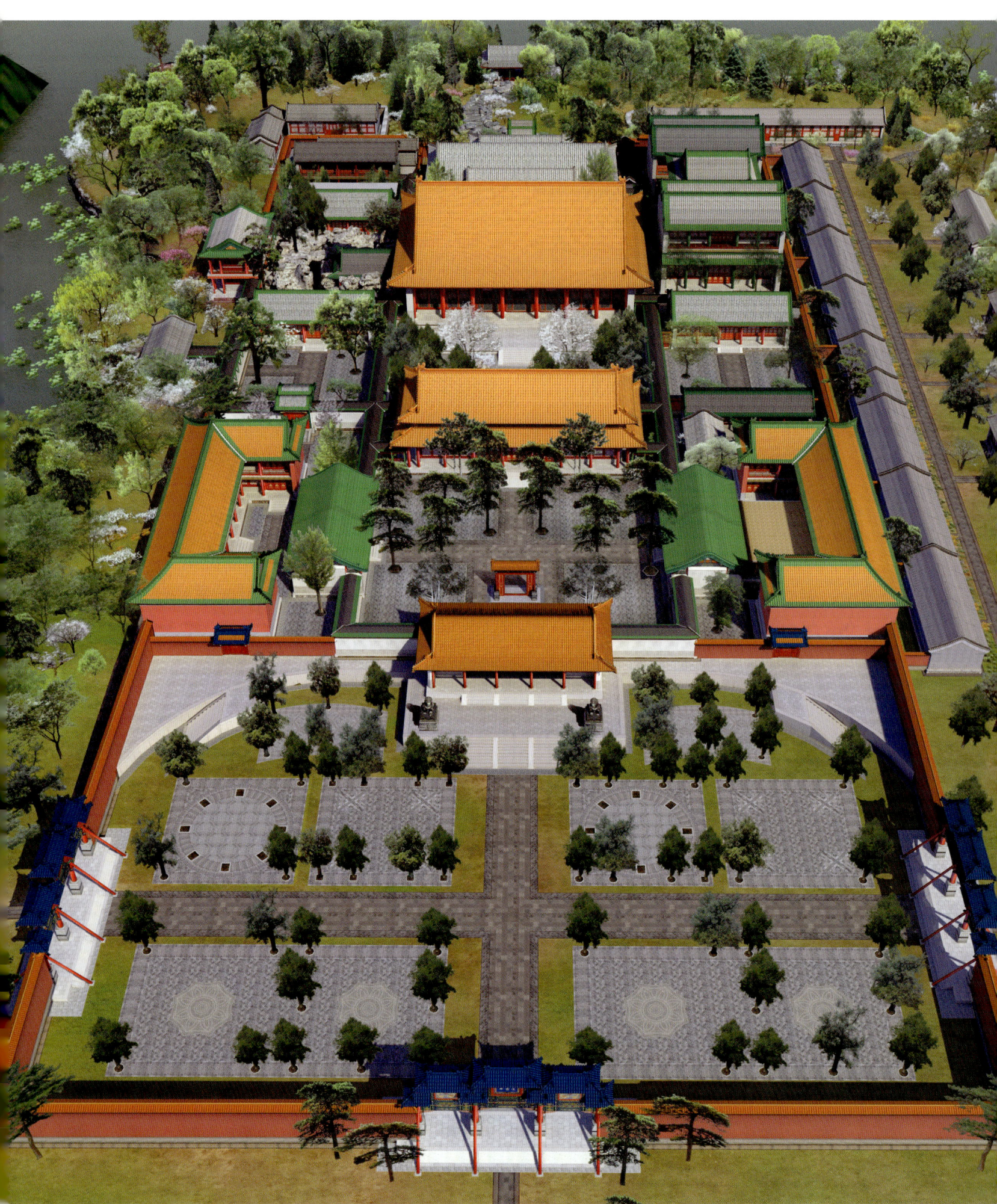

CHAPTER XVIII
Configuration of Building Groups that Conforms to a Culture Based on Ethics

A culture that is based on ethics fosters a social organization that is characterized by a "differential mode of association" and a strict hierarchy in society. This was particularly evident in the buildings of the Yuan Ming Yuan that had a front section devoted to the transaction of official business and a rear section that served as imperial apartments. The palace gate areas of the three gardens of the Yuan Ming Yuan adopted this kind of layout without an exception.

The front section, used for the transaction of court business and ceremonial activities, including imperial audiences, the reception of leaders of vassal states and foreign legates, was built strictly along a central axis with meticulous attention to the observance of hierarchy and precedence. The Yuan Ming Yuan started out with a spirit wall, after which came the main gate, the Churu Xianliang Gate, the main audience hall, the side halls, the officials' waiting rooms and service facilities … everything in its place.

The imposing Zhengda Guangming Hall—the main audience hall not in the Forbidden City—dominated the scene; it was preceded by a long introductory space in front, two palace gates and a Moon River and was shielded in the rear by an artificial hill. The hall was furnished only with a throne, which was a symbol of the emperor and affirmed the unique attribute of the hall. The emperor's presence was felt even if he was not physically occupying that space at any particular moment.

The artificial hills and walls around this group of buildings created a secluded and closed ambience that attested to the control exercised by the emperor over his palaces.

The Hanjing Hall (fig. 197) and Chunhua Pavilion in the Changchun Garden—a group of more than 20 buildings—was another typical illustration of the "differential mode of association." Hierarchy was established via building location, mass and materials.

The Hongci Yonghu Complex was most successful in its affirmation of ethics and in the management of its introductory space. Hierarchy was clearly established among the not too numerous main buildings of the complex. The introductory space was designed in a way that was different from the standard approach used for ceremonial buildings. Through the symmetrical placement of successive architectural elements, a strong sense of solemnity and formality was created and enhanced in a natural park setting. The earthen hill at the front end, the three architectural arches and the two pairs of memorial columns erected at the four corners represented the first nodal point of the introductory space; it was not clearly marked off from the surrounding landscape. After the three stone bridges one came to a virtual space enclosed by three architectural arches standing on three sides of a square outside the compound walls; this was the second nodal point of the introductory space, where trees and other elements of natural landscape were kept out by those three architectural arches. The sense of solemnity was ratcheted up a notch here. When one entered the glazed-tile-ornamented architectural arch-style gate in the outer wall, one came to a platform on which the main gate was located; after passing this gate in the inner wall one finally arrived at the main hall seated on a high terrace. Here the sense of solemnity reached its zenith.

Pages 232 and 233
Fig. 196   Haiyue Kaijin Complex

Fig. 197   Hanjing Hall

CHAPTER XIX
Planning the Garden with an Eye to "Centrality"

The ancient Chinese legalist text *Guanzi* advised that the emperor would do well to situate himself at the center. The *Lüshi Chunqiu* (*Annals of Lü Buwei*) also espoused the principle of establishing one's country at the center of the world and situating the capital at the center of the country (fig. 198). The planning of the Changchun Garden gave prominence to this concept of "centrality" (fig. 199) by locating the main buildings of the Hanjing Hall and the Chunhua Pavilion at the center of the garden. Given its function, scale and location, the Hanjing Hall was the most important building in the entire garden. The buildings like the

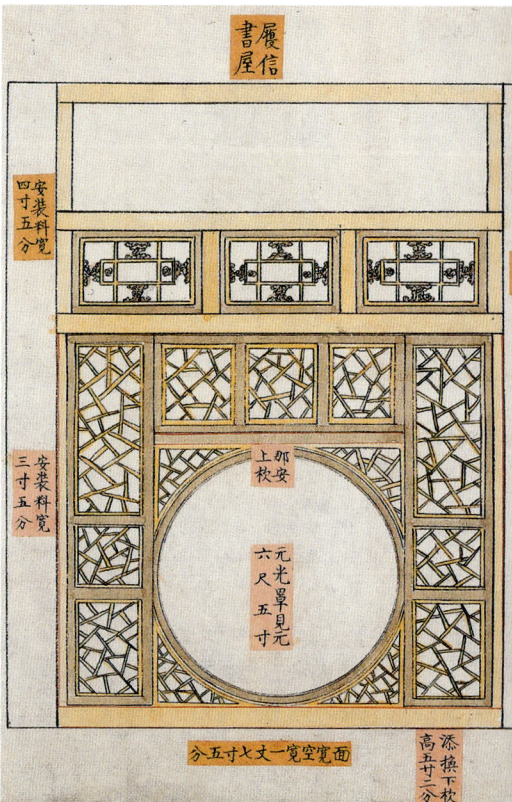

Fig. 198 The entrance of Lüxin Library in the Shende Hall imperial residence

Siyong Study, the Haiyue Kaijin Complex, the Yulinglong Pavilion and the Zelan Hall were evenly distributed around it. The central axis of the Hanjing Hall extended north past the Zelan Hall to reach the Yuanying Observatory of the Xiyang Building Complex. This planning approach gave expression to the concept of "centrality." The landscaping also observed a left-right balance, with only minor variations.

The central axis of the Hanjing Hall failed to extend further at its front because it was blocked by a privately owned garden at the time of the construction of the Yuan Ming Yuan. It was not until the 34th year of Qianlong's reign (1769) that the private garden was taken back by the Qing court and formed a part of the Qichun Garden in its northeast corner.

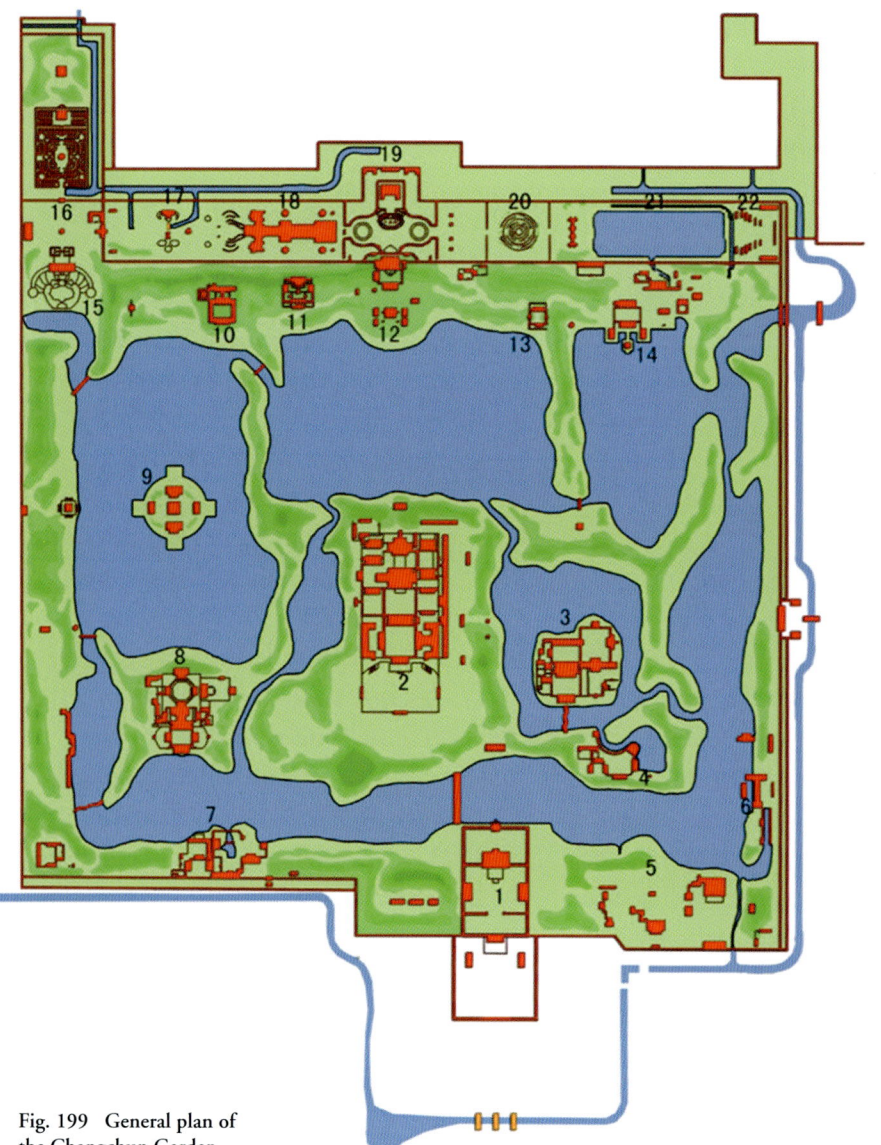

Fig. 199 General plan of the Changchun Garden

236 CHINA'S LOST IMPERIAL GARDEN

CHAPTER XX
Objectification of the Vision of Governance

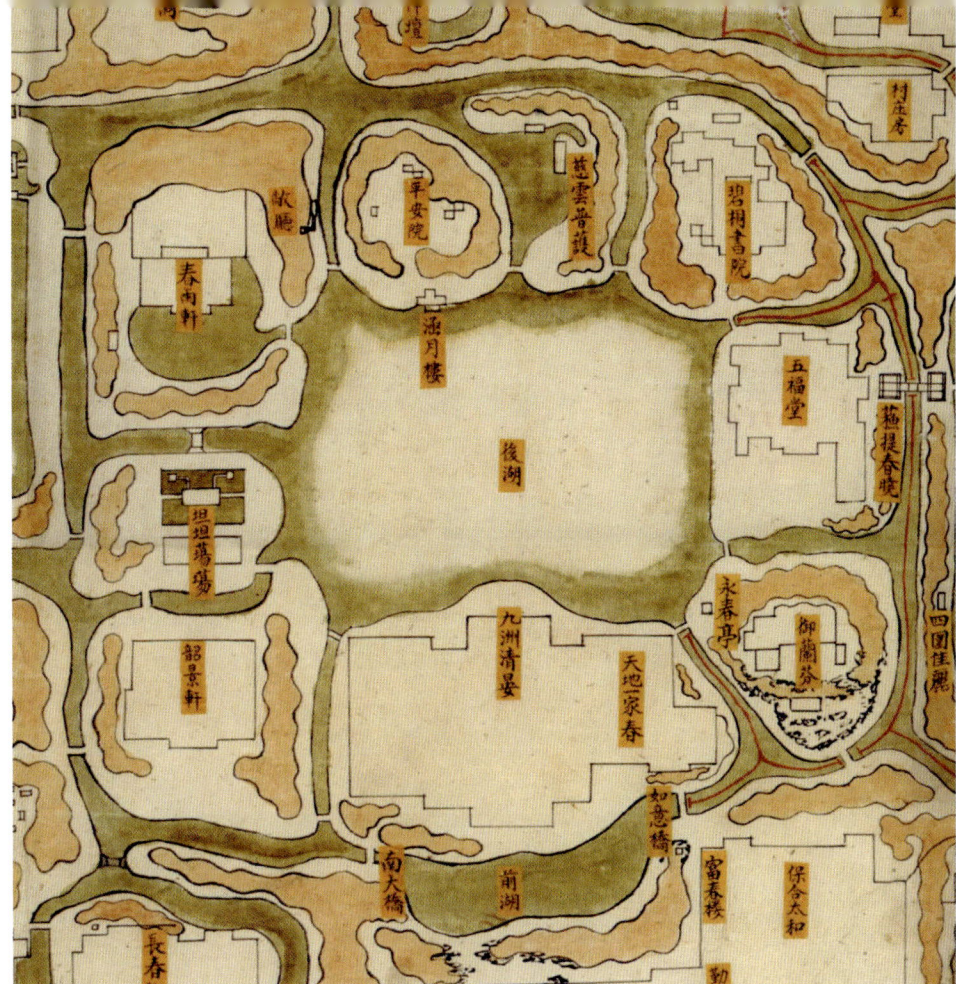

Fig. 200 Plan of the Nine Islands area of Yuan Ming Yuan (from the Imperial Office of Architectural Design)

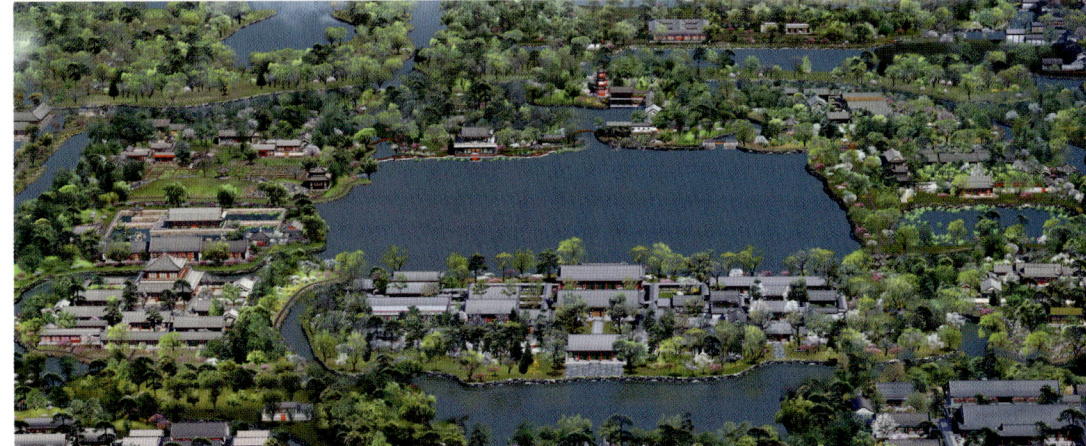

Fig. 201 Aerial view of the Nine Islands area of Yuan Ming Yuan

The Nine Islands area at the center of the Yuan Ming Yuan was intended to symbolize the nine continents of the imperial realm. It was a reflection of the vision of Emperor Yongzheng, who lived in the Yuan Ming Yuan but was ever mindful of the wellbeing of the state and therefore directed the creation at the center of the imperial park of nine islands populated with groups of buildings (figs. 200, 201). The nine islands were configured into a 3 by 3 grid and reminded people of the article titled *Yu Gong* (*Tribute of Yu*) in the *Shang Shu* (*Book of Documents*), which divided China into nine continents. The words "Nine Continents" has since become a symbol of the Chinese nation. The nine islands distributed around the Back Lake were crisscrossed with canals as a nod to Zou Yan's theory of nine big continents surrounded by sea. The design of the Yuan Ming Yuan took advantage of the bountiful water resources in its environs, erecting buildings and pavilions "on the heights and in the dales, on the hills and by the water" around the Back Lake and named it "Jiuzhou Qingyan" or Nine Continents Clear and Calm. "Qingyan" or "Clear and Calm" expressed a fervent hope for peace in the country. It was the same with Wanfang Anhe Complex. It was a reflection of the sentiment of Emperor Yongzheng expressed in these words: "What I wish for is not only my own peace of mind but peace and calm everywhere in my realm" and it gave a cultural dimension to the scenery and landscape. Names given to the buildings, such as Zhengda Guangming and Qinzheng Qinxian were the emperor's slogans for clean and good government. The Danbo Ningjing Building (once Field Character Building), Guanjia Pavilion, Duojia Pavilion, Gengzhi Pavilion and Beiyuan Mountain House (Mountain House in North Garden) were an objectified vehicle for giving expression to the importance accorded by the emperor to farming in an agricultural society.

CHAPTER XXI
From Aesthetic Pursuit to *Nei Sheng Wai Wang*

The Yuan Ming Yuan abounded in academies, libraries and studies. Emperor Qianlong gave the reason for equipping his imperial park with so many buildings related to reading in these words: "I have always loved reading and therefore libraries are everywhere."[1] In a poem about the Tianran Tuhua Complex, Emperor Qianlong wrote that he had no use for songs and dances, that instead he'd much rather read." In another poem he wrote that one acquired knowledge of antiquity not because one desired to be able to show off one's erudition but because the books passed down through the ages contained pearls of wisdom about governing in difficult times.[2] For Emperor Qianlong "reading" was not merely a hobby but afforded a way of *nei sheng wai wang* (becoming an emperor who is a sage at heart) through an aesthetic pursuit.

The ultimate purpose of learning is to appreciate the true meaning of the Dao or enlightenment. To be a sage-like emperor was to inherit the orthodoxy of the Dao. Since the Dao is inherent in Nature one needs only to seek enlightenment directly in nature. This is an inevitable path of learning. The Yuan Ming Yuan was a meticulously crafted imperial park but not at the expense of nature. Its design allowed nature to show its "true colors" not merely for the purpose of enabling the appreciation of its beauty and soothing the beholder's mind but more importantly for the purpose of the emperor's enlightenment. To be an emperor who was a sage at heart was the life ambition of Emperor Qianlong. He wrote that "he who governs does so not by force but by virtue. Therefore he who excels in virtue will govern well and he who loses virtue loses his right to govern." As an imperial "pleasure" park, the Yuan Ming Yuan naturally abounded in exquisite views and sceneries, but instead of rhapsodizing about these sceneries and expressing his personal sentiments, he mostly cited classic texts, reminded himself about moral behavior, reflected upon his legacy and tried in general to improve himself. He often left handwritings in some buildings, warnings to himself such as *wu yi* (No indolence!) and *wei jun nan* (Not easy to be a ruler!) (fig. 202). He even named one building "Zhiguo Hall." He clearly wanted to be an enlightened, sage-like ruler.

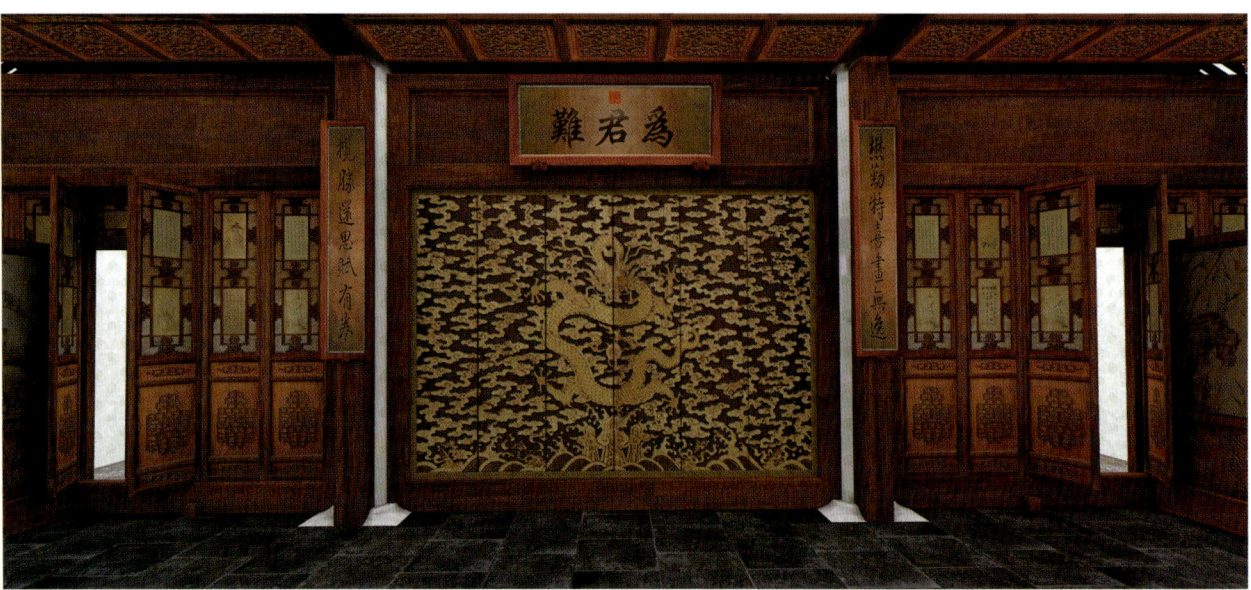

Fig. 202 The horizontal name tablet with the characters *wei jun nan* in the Qinzheng Hall

CHAPTER XXII
An Unusual Sight Removed from the Realm of Reality

There were a number of descriptions of abodes for immortals in ancient literature. The *Shi Ji* (*Records of the Grand Historian*) mentioned three sacred mountains called Penglai, Fangzhang and Yingzhou, where the palaces were made from gold and platinum. The *Han Shu* (*Book of the Han*) also described three mountains on the sea located in the Gulf of Bohai, not far from shore and once visited by humans who reported having seen the immortals and their immortality pills. This is the origin of the landscaping motif of three mountains surround by a sea or lake, which appeared as early as the Zhou dynasty and became popular in the Qin and Han periods. It was a product of primitive worship of spirits, mountain worship and Daoism.

In order to highlight the unique nature of the Yuan Ming Yuan as an imperial garden, the motif of three mountains surrounded by sea in traditional Chinese gardens was introduced, with three hills symbolizing Penglai, Fangzhang and Yingzhou placed at the center of the Lake of Happiness to create a vista of the legendary abode of immortals so much sought after by emperors of antiquity. This was called Pengdao Yaotai. Another simulation of an abode of immortals was the Fanghu Shengjing Complex (fig. 203), which stood out with its magnificent buildings. The complex comprised ten two-storied buildings and three kiosks. It was a colorful, complex group of structures of various styles that evoked a magic mountain graced by beautiful pavilions found only in a fairytale.

---
1 *Yuzhi Shi*, by Emperor Qianlong, Book III, Volume 62.
2 Ibid., Volume 87.

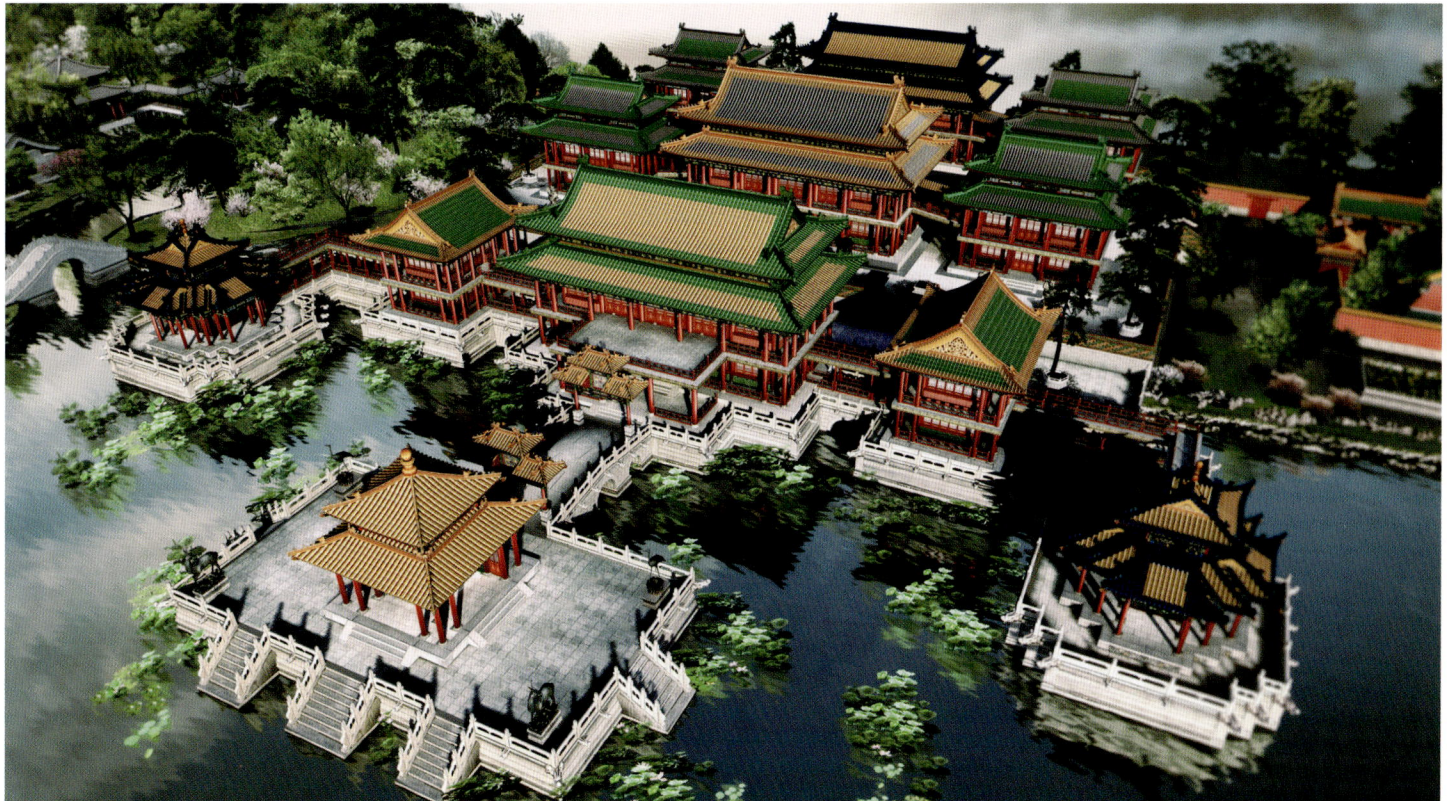

Fig. 203 Aerial view of Fanghu Shengjing Complex

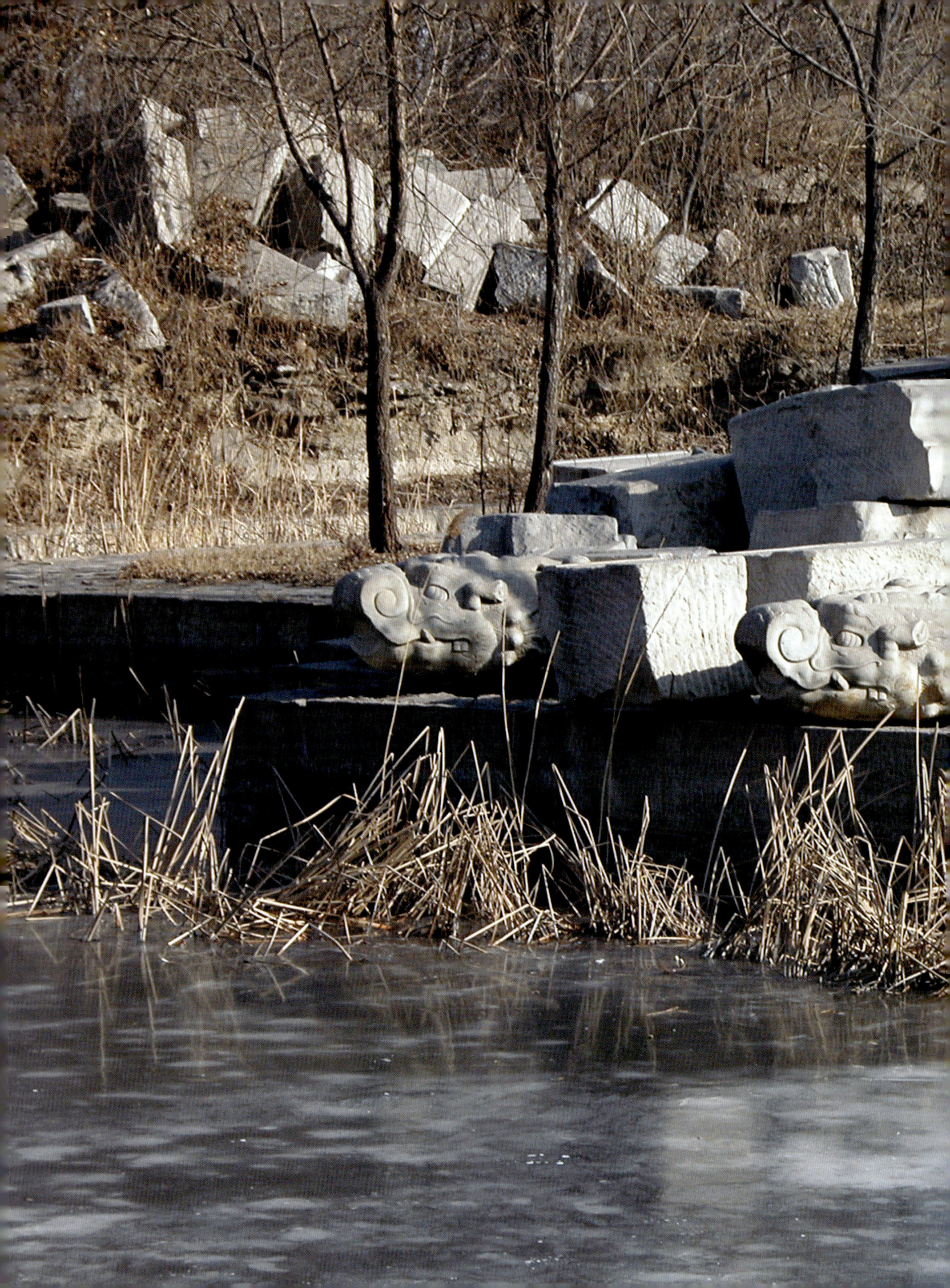

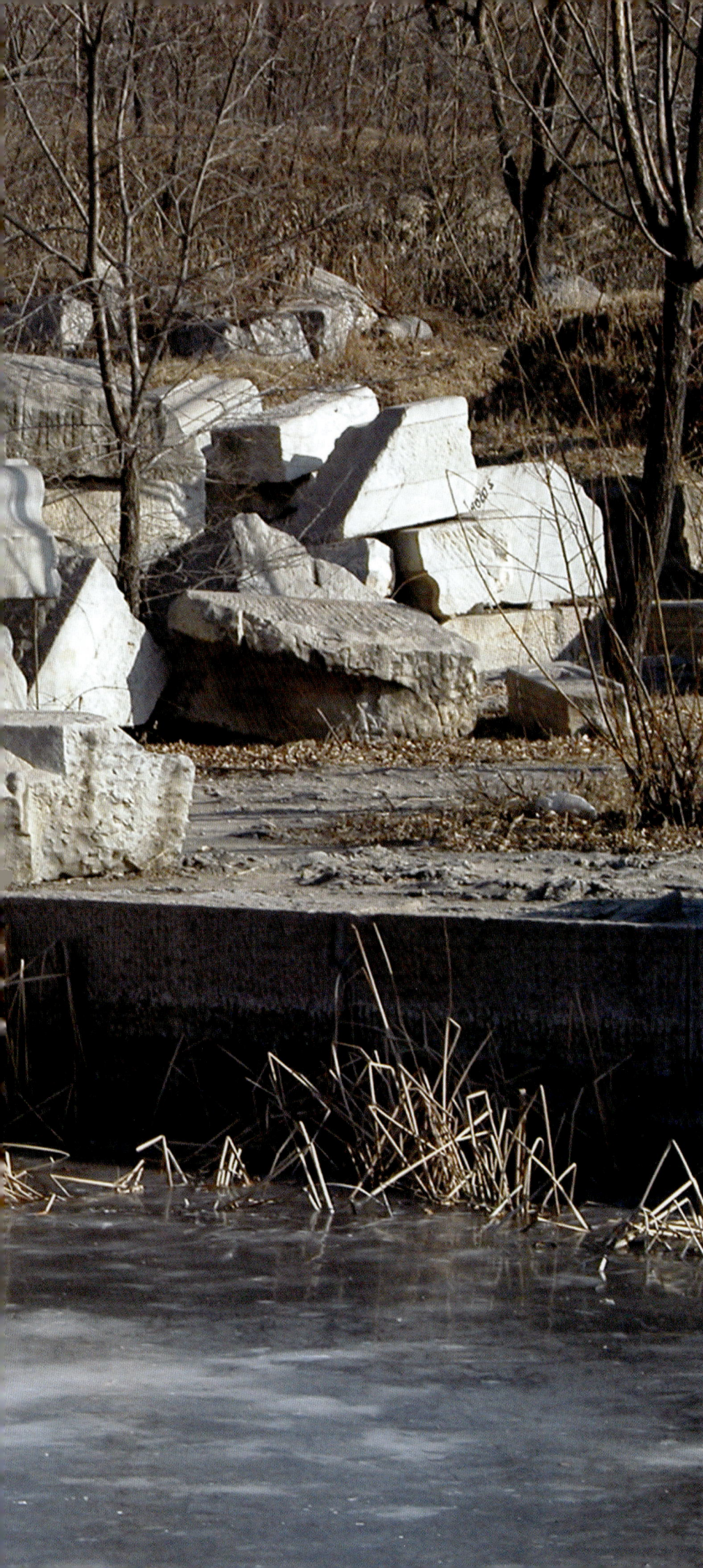

CONCLUSION

The Yuan Ming Yuan was a masterpiece that drew on the best of the art creation of classical Chinese gardens. It was pregnant with the history of the Chinese art of garden design. It reflected the development and evolution of society in the Qing period. Its outstanding achievement called world attention to the art of Oriental garden design and inspired enthusiasm for Chinese gardens in 18th century Europe. The great French writer Victor Hugo wrote: "All that the imagination can spawn from an almost superhuman people was there." The Yuan Ming Yuan's destruction by fire was a national tragedy that should never be forgotten by the Chinese people. It motivated the Chinese people to strive for greater achievements.

When you visit the Yuan Ming Yuan today you can download an application on to your phone at the entrance, go into the park, stand in front of the ruins and the application will display the past glory of the Yuan Ming Yuan before your very eyes. The Yuan Ming Yuan is now a major part of China's cultural heritage and recorded in history for ever.

Fig. 204 Ruins of the Fanghu Shengjing Complex

APPENDICES

GLOSSARY

English Name	Explanation	Chinese Pinyin	Chinese Name
Anlan Garden	Pacifying Tidal Bores Garden	an lan yuan	安澜园
Anyin Chuang	Dhvaja of Peace	an yin chuang	安隐幢
Anyou Palace	Palace of Peaceful Protection	an you gong	安佑宫
Anzhi Building	Building of Stability	an zhi lou	安止楼
Bamboo Courtyard		zhu zi yuan	竹子院
Bamboo Garden		zhu yuan	竹园
Bamboo Pavilion		zhu ting	竹亭
Banmu Garden	Half Acre Garden	ban mu yuan	半亩园
Baohe Taihe Hall	Preserving and Conserving the Primordial Harmony	bao he tai he	保合太和
Baoxiang Temple	Jeweled Image Temple	bao xiang si	宝相寺
Beiyuan Mountain House	Mountain House in North Garden	bei yuan shan fang	北苑山房
Beiyuan Mountain Village	Mountain Village in the Distant North	bei yuan shan cun	北远山村
Biaosheng Pavilion	Pavilion of Noble Morality	biao sheng ting	标胜亭
Bieyou Dongtian Complex	Complex of a Whole New World within a Grotto	bie you dong tian	别有洞天（建筑群）
Bieyou Dongtian Hall		bie you dong tian	别有洞天（厅）
Bieyou Tian Open Hall		bie you tian	别有天
Bilan Bridge	Green Wave Bridge	bi lan qiao	碧澜桥
Bishu Mountain Resort in Chengde	Imperial Summer Resort in Chengde	cheng de bi shu shan zhuang	承德避暑山庄
Bitong Library	Green Wutong Tree Library	bi tong shu yuan	碧桐书院
Biyun Building	Building of Azure Clouds	bi yun lou	碧云楼
Buddhist Complex	Buddhist Complex	fo lou	佛楼
Cai Pu	Vegetable Patch	cai pu	菜圃
Caizhi Jing Pavilion	Pavilion of Ganoderma Picking	cai zhi jing	采芝径
Cangjing Building	Building of Scriptures	cang jing lou	藏经楼
Cangshu Pavilion	Pavilion of Book Collections Library	cang shu ge	藏书阁
Changchun Garden	Garden of Eternal Spring	chang chun yuan	长春园
Changchun Garden	Joyful Spring Garden	chang chun yuan	畅春园
Changchun Library	Eternal Spring Library	chang chun shu wu	长春书屋
Changchun Xianguan Complex	Complex of Eternal Spring Immortals Hall	chang chun xian guan	长春仙馆
Changjin Building	Venting of Feelings Building	chang jin lou	畅襟楼
Cheng'en Hall	Hall for Grace Received	cheng en tang	承恩堂
Chengbo Xizhao Pavilion	Clear Ripples in Sunset Pavilion	shui xie cheng bo xi zhao	水榭澄波夕照
Chengguang Pavilion	Pure Light Pavilion	cheng guang ge	澄光阁
Chenglian Building	White Silk Building	cheng lian lou	澄练楼
Chengxin Hall	Hall of Cleansing the Mind	cheng xin tang	澄心堂
Chishui Gongxin Yuetongming Hall	Hall of Pond and Water Shining with the Moon	chi shui gong xin yue tong ming	池水共心月同明
Chongfu Palace	Palace of Praying for Fortune	chong fu gong	崇福宫
Chongwen Gate		chong wen men	崇文门
Chuihong Gazebo	Gazebo of Rainbow	chui hong xie	垂虹榭
Chunhua Pavalion		chun hua xuan	淳化轩
Chunxi Courtyard	Courtyard of Harmonious Light in Spring	chun xi yuan	春熙苑（春熙院）
Chunyu Pavilion	Spring Rain Pavilion	chun yu xuan	春雨轩
Chunyu Shuhe Library	Library of Soothing Spring Rain	chun yu shu he	春雨舒和
Churu Xianliang Gate	Gate for the Departure and Entrance of Virtue and Goodness	chu ru xian liang men	出入贤良门
Ciyun Puhu Complex	Complex of Merciful Clouds Protect All	ci yun pu hu	慈云普护（建筑群）
Ciyun Puhu Temple	Temple of Merciful Clouds Protect All	ci yun pu hu	慈云普护（佛寺）
Cizhong Dayou Jiachu Pavilion		ci zhong da you jia chu	此中大有佳处
Congfang Gazebo	Gazebo of Bountiful Flowers	cong fang xie	丛芳榭

CHINA'S LOST IMPERIAL GARDEN

English Name	Explanation	Chinese Pinyin	Chinese Name
Cuijing Study	Collection of Scenes Study	cui jing zhai	萃景斋
Cuiwei Hall	Green Hill Hall	cui wei tang	翠微堂
Cuizhao Building	Green Glow Building	cui zhao lou	翠照楼
Cunbi (pavilion)	Inch of Green	cun bi	寸碧
Da Shuifa Fountain	Grand Fountain	da shui fa	大水法
Daiyue Building	Waiting for the Moon Building	dai yue lou	待月楼
Dajue Temple	Temple of Enlightenment	da jue si	大觉寺
Danbo Ningjing Building	Building of Detachment and Serenity	dan bo ning jing	澹泊宁静（楼）
Danbo Ningjing Complex	Complex of Detachment and Serenity	dan bo ning jing	澹泊宁静（建筑群）
Danhuai Hall	Simple Needs Hall	dan huai tang	澹怀堂
Danti Pavilion	Red Ladder Pavilion	dan ti ting	丹梯亭
Danxian Room	Room of Tranquility and Leisureness	dan xian shi	澹闲室
Daoliang Building		dao liang lou	稻凉楼
Daoxiang Pavilion	Rice Fragrance Pavilion	dao xiang ting	稻香亭
Dehe Garden	Garden of Virtue and Harmony	de he yuan	德和园
Deshenggai Pavilion	Victory Pavilion	de sheng gai ting	得胜概亭
Deshou Palace	Palace of Virtue and Longevity	de shou gong	德寿宫
Diaoyu Jetty	Angling Jetty	diao yu ji	钓鱼矶
Dongtian Shenchu Complex	Deep in the Grotto Complex	dong tian shen chu	洞天深处
Duanqiao Canxue (stone architectural arch)	Melting Snow on a Broken Bridge (stone architectural arch)	duan qiao can xue	断桥残雪（石牌坊）
Duobao Liuli Pagoda	Abundant Treasures Pagoda with Glazed Tiles	duo bao liu li ta	多宝琉璃塔
Duobao Pavilion	Abundant Treasures Pavilion	duo bao ge	多宝阁
Duojia Pavilion	Bountiful Crop Pavilion	duo jia xuan	多稼轩
Duojia Ruyun Hall	Hall of Crops as Bountiful as the Clouds	duo jia ru yun	多稼如云
East Garden		dong yuan	东园
Eastern Quarters		dong suo	东所
Fahui Temple	Dharma Wisdom Temple	fa hui si	法慧寺
Fangbi Cong (Open Hall)		fang bi cong	芳碧丛
Fanghu Shengjing Complex	Complex of the Beautiful Scene of the Square Pot	fang hu sheng jing	方壶胜境
Fanghui Building		fang hui lou	芳晖楼
Fangwai Observatory	Observatory of Lands Beyond	fang wai guan	方外观
Fanxiang Building	Buddhist Incense Pavilion	fan xiang lou	梵香楼
Fanyu Qunfang Hall	Hall of Abundance of Flowers	fan yu qun fang	蕃育群芳
Fayuan Building		fa yuan lou	法源楼
Feicui Building	Jade Building	fei cui lou	翡翠楼
Feiyun Pavilion	Flying Cloud Pavilion	fei yun xuan	飞云轩
Fengle Pavilion	Joy of Plenty Pavilion	feng le xuan	丰乐轩
Fengsan Wusi Hall	Hall of Pursuing Selflessness	feng san wu si dian	奉三无私殿
Fu Stage	Happiness Stage	fu tai	福台
Fuchun Building		fu chun lou	富春楼
Fuchun Hall	Blossoming Spring Hall	fu chun tang	敷春堂
Fuyou Daqian (gate)	Gate of Blessed Is the World	fu you da qian	福佑大千
Gengyun Hall	Hall of Crop Cultivation	geng yun tang	耕耘堂
Gengzhi Pavilion	Ploughing and Sericulture Pavilion	geng zhi xuan	耕织轩
Goldfish Pond		jin yu chi	金鱼池
Great South Bridge		nan da qiao	南大桥
Guande Hall	Hall of Observing Virtue	guan de dian	观德殿
Guangfeng Jiyue Hall	Hall of Breeze and Moon after a Rain	guang feng ji yue	光风霁月
Guangming Xinghai (hall)	Hall of Brightness and Ocean of Original Nature	guang ming xing hai	光明性海
Guangyu Temple	Fertility Temple	guang yu gong	广育宫
Guanjia Pavilion	Crop Watching Pavilion	guan jia xuan	观稼轩
Guanlian Pavilion	Pavilion for Lotus Viewing	guan lian suo	观莲所
Guanshuifa Fountain	Throne for Observing the Great Fountains	guan shui fa	观水法
Guanyin Hall		guan yin dian	观音殿
Guanyin Monastery		guan yin an	观音庵
Guiyue Bridge	Full Moon Bridge	gui yue qiao	规月桥

English Name	Explanation	Chinese Pinyin	Chinese Name
Guizhi Mountain Hall	Mountain Hall of the Importance of Weaving	gui zhi shan tang	贵织山堂
Guxiang Study		gu xiang zhai	古香斋
Haiyan Hall	Hall of Calm Seas	hai yan tang	海晏堂
Haiyue Kaijin Complex	Complex of Sea of Magnanimity	hai yue kai jin	海岳开襟
Hanbi Hall		han bi tang	含碧堂
Hande Lirary	Virtue-Steeped Library	han de shu wu	涵德书屋
Hanguang Room	Room of Lightness	han guang shi	涵光室
Hanjing Hall	Tripataka Hall	han jing tang	含经堂
Hanqiu Hall	Autumn Reflections Hall	han qiu tang	涵秋堂
Hanxu Langjian Complex	Complex of Vast Empty Clear Mirror	han xu lang jian	涵虚朗鉴
Hanyuan Study	Mirror Reflection of the World Study	han yuan zhai	涵远斋
Hengbi Pavilion		heng bi xuan	横碧轩
Hengchun Hall	Permanent Spring Hall	heng chun tang	恒春堂
Hexiang Pavilion	Lotus Scent Pavilion	he xiang ting	荷香亭
Hongci Yonghu Complex	Complex of Vast Compassion and Eternal Blessing	hong ci yong hu	鸿慈永祜
Huagang Guanyu Open Hall	Open Hall of Fish Watching in Flower Cove	hua gang guan yu	花港观鱼
Huai Qingfen Building	Building of Embracing Subtle Fragrance	huai qing fen	怀清芬
Huashen Temple	Temple of Flower Goddesses	hua shen miao	花神庙
Huifang Library	Library of Collected Fragrances	hui fang shu yuan	汇芳书院
Huiji Ancestral Temple	Ancestral Temple of Mercy	hui ji shen ci	惠济神祠
Huiluan Hall		hui luan dian	哕鸾殿
Huiwan Zongchun Temple	Temple of Flower Goddesses	hui wan zong chun zhi miao	彙万总春之庙
Huiyu Hall	Hall of Depicting Rain	hui yu jing she	绘雨精舍
Humiao Building	Mutual Enhancement Building	hu miao lou	互妙楼
Huohua Stone Boat	Living Painting Stone Boat	huo hua fang	活画舫
Huzhong Tian	Universe in a Pot	hu zhong tian	壶中天
Huzhong Xianlai (stage)	Divine Sound in a Pot (stage)	hu zhong xian lai	壶中仙籁
Inner Gatehouse		nei gong men	内宫门
Jiajing Mingqin Complex	Complex of A Double Mirror and the Sound of the Lute	jia jing ming qin	夹镜鸣琴
Jian Garden	Garden of Mirror	jian yuan	鉴园
Jian Pavilion	Pavilion by a Mountain Stream	jian ge	涧阁
Jianhe Yuqing Hall	Hall of Lingering Cool of a Mountain Book	jian he yu qing	涧壑余清
Jiechun Pavilion		jie chun ge	皆春阁
Jiexiu Mountain House	Mountain House Greeted by the Beauty of the Hills	jie xiu shan fang	接秀山房
Jieye Pavilion		jie ye ting	接叶亭
Jihe Shenchu Open Hall	Open Hall of Deep among Water Chestnuts and Lotuses	ji he shen chu	菱荷深处
Jihexiang Pavilion	Pavilion of Fragrant Lotus	ji he xiang ting	菱荷香亭
Jing Room	Quiet room	jing shi	静室
Jingbi Hall		jing bi tang	静碧堂
Jinghong Pavilion		jing hong guan	镜虹馆
Jingjia Pavilion		jing jia xuan	静嘉轩
Jinglian Study	Quiet Lotus Study	jing lian zhai	静莲斋
Jingming Garden		jing ming yuan	静明园
Jingshui Study	Water Mirroring Study	jing shui zhai	镜水斋
Jingxiang House	Subtle Fragrance House	jing xiang wu	静香屋
Jingyu Library	Quiet Pleasure Library	jing yu shu wu	静娱书屋
Jingzhi Chunshi Jia Hall	Hall of Quietly Comes the Good News of Spring	jing zhi chun shi jia	静知春事佳
Jingzhong Pavilion		jing zhong ge	镜中阁
Jinqi Building		jin qi lou	锦绮楼
Jiqing Xianchang Pavilion		ji qing xian chang	寄情咸畅
Jiuzhou Qingyan Complex	Complex of Nine Continents Clear and Calm	jiu zhou qing yan	九洲清晏（建筑群）
Jiuzhou Qingyan Hall		jiu zhou qing yan	九洲清晏（殿）
Jixiang Suo Pavilion	Auspicious Pavilion	ji xiang suo	吉祥所
Kaiyi Pavilion	Improvement by Reading Pavilion	kai yi xuan	开益轩
Kenong Pavilion		ke nong xuan	课农轩
Kuoran Dagong Complex	Complex of Boundless Impartiality	kuo ran da gong	廓然大公（建筑群）
Kuoran Dagong Hall		kuo ran da gong	廓然大公（殿）

English Name	Explanation	Chinese Pinyin	Chinese Name
Lan Pavilion	Orchid Pavilion	*lan ting*	兰亭
Lancui Pavilion	Take in the Green Hills Pavilion	*lan cui ting*	揽翠亭
Langrun Study		*lang run zhai*	朗润斋
Langyin Pavilion	Verse Reciting Pavilion	*lang yin ge*	朗吟阁
Lanye Hall	Hall of Orchid Field	*lan ye*	兰野
Le Anhe Palace		*le an he*	乐安和（寝宫）
Leifeng Xizhao Open Hall	Open Hall of Sunset on Leifeng Pagoda	*lei feng xi zhao*	雷峰夕照
Leshan Hall	Delight in Doing Good Deeds Hall	*le shan tang*	乐善堂
Letianhe Hall		*le tian he*	乐天和
Lezhi Mountain Village	Mountain Village for Gladdening the Heart	*le zhi shan cun*	乐志山村
Liangfeng Chayun (stone architectural arch)	Twin Peaks Piercing the Clouds (stone architectural arch)	*liang feng cha yun*	两峰插云（石牌坊）
Liangxiang County		*liang xiang zhen*	良乡镇
Lianhua Facang Hall	Lotus Fazang Hall	*lian hua fa cang dian*	莲花法藏殿
Lianhua Pavilion	Lotus Pavilion	*lian hua guan*	莲花馆
Lianxi Lechu Complex	Complex of Happy Place of Lianxi	*lian xi le chu*	濂溪乐处（建筑群）
Lianxi Lechu (hall)		*lian xi le chu*	濂溪乐处（殿）
Lijing Pavilion		*li jing xuan*	丽景轩
Lingxiang Pan Pavilion	Shore of Water Chestnut Fragrance Pavilion	*ling xiang pan*	菱香泮
Linhe Hua Hall	Hall of Riverside Painting	*lin he hua*	临河画
Linxu Guijing Courtyard		*lin xu gui jing*	林虚桂静
Liulang Wenying (stone architectural arch)	Orioles Singing in the Willows (stone architectural arch)	*liu lang wen ying*	柳浪闻莺（石牌坊）
Liumeng Jiangjun Temple	Temple to General Liu Meng	*liu meng jiang jun miao*	刘猛将军庙
Liushui Yin Pavilion	Pavilion of Sound of Flowing Water	*liu shui yin*	流水音
Lixin Building	Ordering One's Thoughts Building	*li xin lou*	理心楼
Louyue Kaiyun Complex	Complex of the Engraved Moon and Unfolding Clouds	*lou yue kai yun*	镂月开云
Lu Stage	Prosperity Stage	*lu tai*	禄台
Luxiang Study	Dew Fragrance Study	*lu xiang zhai*	露香斋
Lüjing Gazebo		*lü jing xie*	绿净榭
Lüyin Pavilion	Green Shade Pavilion	*lü yin xuan*	绿荫轩
Mahavira Hall	Mahavira Hall	*da xiong bao dian*	大雄宝殿
Market Street	Market Street	*mai mai jie*	买卖街
Meiyue Pavilion	Crescent Moon Pavilion	*mei yue xuan*	眉月轩
Miaoda Pavilion		*miao da xuan*	妙达轩
Mingyuxi Bridge		*ming yu xi qiao*	鸣玉溪桥
Mochiyun Courtyard	Courtyard of Ink Pond Clouds	*mo chi yun*	墨池云
Nacui Building		*na cui lou*	纳翠楼
Najing Hall	Hall of Collected Scenery	*na jing tang*	纳景堂
Nanfu Garden	South Garden	*nan fu*	南府
Nanping Wanzhong Pavilion	Pavilion of Evening Bell on Mount Nanping	*nan ping wan zhong*	南屏晚钟
Pengdao Yaotai Complex	Complex of the Jade Terrace of Paradise Island	*peng dao yao tai*	蓬岛瑶台（建筑群）
Pengdao Yaotai Hall		*peng dao yao tai*	蓬岛瑶台（殿）
Peony Terrace		*mu dan tai*	牡丹台
Pinghu Qiuyue Complex	Complex of Autumn Moon over a Calm Lake	*ping hu qiu yue*	平湖秋月
Pinshi Hall	Poetry Appreciation Hall	*pin shi tang*	品诗堂
Pufu Palace	Universal Happiness Palace	*pu fu gong*	普福宫
Putao Courtyard	Grape Courtyard	*pu tao yuan*	葡萄院
Qian Garden		*qian yuan*	倩园
Qianchui Tiankuang	Courtyard Gift of Heaven Courtyard	*qian chui tian kuang*	前垂天贶
Qianlong Garden		*qian long hua yuan*	乾隆花园
Qianqing Palace	Palace of Heavenly Purity	*qian qing gong*	乾清宫
Qianxiang Hall		*qian xiang dian*	千祥殿
Qiaoqianju Gazebo		*qiao qian ju*	峭倩居
Qichun Garden	Garden of Elegant Spring	*qi chun yuan*	绮春园
Qingbi Pavilion		*qing bi ge*	清閟阁
Qinghui Pavilion	Clear Light Pavilion	*qing hui ge*	清晖阁

English Name	Explanation	Chinese Pinyin	Chinese Name
Qinghui Pavilion		qing hui ting	清绘亭
Qingjingdi Complex	Complex of Pure Land	qing jing di	清净地（月地云居）
Qingshu Study		qing shu zhai	清淑斋
Qingshui Zhuoying Hall	Hall of Washing Hat Tassels in Clear Water	qing shui zhuo ying	清水濯缨
Qingxia Study		qing xia zhai	清夏斋
Qingyin Pavilion	Clarion Notes Pavilion	qing yin ge	清音阁
Qingyue Shengping (stage)		qing yue sheng ping	庆乐升平（戏台）
Qinqing Study		qin qing zhai	琴清斋
Qinqu Pavilion	Pleasure of the Lute Pavilion	qin qu xuan	琴趣轩
Qinzheng Hall	Hall of Diligent Governance	qin zheng dian	勤正殿
Qinzheng Qinxian Complex	Complex of Diligent Government	qin zheng qin xian	勤政亲贤
Qionghua Building		qiong hua lou	琼华楼
Qiujin Changyuan Building	Autumn Clarity Building	qiu jin chang yuan	秋襟畅远
Qixiu Pavilion		qi xiu ting	启秀亭
Qixu Pavilion		qi xu xuan	绮旭轩
Qiyin Hall	Elegant Verse Hall	qi yin tang	绮吟堂
Qiyun Building	Clouds-Lined Building	qi yun lou	栖云楼
Qu Garden	Interesting Garden	qu yuan	趣园
Quanbi Hall	Hall of All Green	quan bi tang	全碧堂
Quanshi Ziyu Hall	Hall of Self-Entertainment with Stones in a Spring	quan shi zi yu dian	泉石自娱殿
Qushui Hexiang Pavilion	Pavilion of Lotus Fragrance in Meandering Water	qu shui he xiang	曲水荷香
Qushui Liushang Complex	Complex of Wine Cups Floating on a Winding Channel	qu shui liu shang	曲水流觞
Quyuan Fenghe Complex	Complex of Distillery and Lotus Pond	qu yuan feng he	麯（曲）院风荷
Rainbow Bridge	Rainbow Bridge	hong qiao	虹桥
Raoyeyi Hall		rao ye yi	饶野意
Renci Hall	Mercy Hall	ren ci dian	仁慈殿
Riri Ping'an Baohaoyin Pavilion	Pavilion of Good Tidings of Peace Everyday	ri ri ping an bao hao yin	日日平安报好音
Ritian Linyu Complex	Complex of Dazzling Eaves under Heaven	ri tian lin yu	日天琳宇（建筑群）
Ritian Linyu Temple	Temple of Dazzling Eaves under Heaven	ri tian lin yu	日天琳宇（寺庙）
River God Temple		he shen miao	河神庙
Ru Garden		ru yuan	如园
Rugu Hall	Embracing Antiquity Hall	ru gu tang	茹古堂
Rugu Hanjin Hall	Hall of Harmony of the Present with the Past	ru gu han jin	茹古涵今
Ruiying Palace		rui ying gong	瑞应宫
Ruizhu Palace		rui zhu gong	蕊珠宫
Ruofanzhi Pavilion	Boat-Like Pavilion	ruo fan zhi ge	若帆之阁
Ruyi Bridge		ru yi qiao	如意桥
Ruyi Pavilion		ru yi guan	如意馆
Sanshifo Hall	Buddhas of the Three Generations Hall	san shi fo dian	三世佛殿
Santan Yinyue (stone architectural arch)	Three Ponds Reflecting the Moon (stone architectural arch)	san tan yin yue	三潭印月
Sanyou Pavilion	Three Friends Pavilion	san you xuan	三友轩
Shangao Shuichang Complex	Complex of High Hills and Long Waters	shan gao shui chang	山高水长
Shangqu Hall	Pleasing Vista Hall	shang qu	赏趣
Shangxia Tianguang Complex	Complex of Heavenly Light above and below	shang xia tian guang	上下天光
Shanxun Gazebo		shan xun xie	扇薰榭
Shao Garden	Peony Garden	shao yuan	芍园
Shende Hall	Hall of Strict Virtue Cultivation	shen de tang	慎德堂
Shengdong Room	Room of Winter Scenery	sheng dong shi	生冬室
Shengqiu Court	Court of Autumn Air	sheng qiu ting	生秋庭
Shenliu Dushu Hall	Hall of Study Among Willows	shen liu du shu tang	深柳读书堂
Shenxin Miaoda Hall		shen xin miao da	神心妙答
Shenxiu Siyong Hall	Hall of Improving Oneself so that the Country Will Enjoy Eternal Peace and Prosperity	shen xiu si yong	慎修思永
Shequ Building		she qu lou	涉趣楼
Shewei City	Sravasti	she wei cheng	舍卫城
Shishan Hall		shi shan tang	师善堂
Shishang Study		shi shang zhai	时赏斋

English Name	Explanation	Chinese Pinyin	Chinese Name
Shizi Garden	Lion Garden	shi zi yuan	狮子园
Shizi Grove	Lion Grove	shi zi lin	狮子林
Shou Stage	Longevity Stage	shou tai	寿台
Shouguo Shoumin Hall	Long Live the Country and the People Hall	shou guo shou min dian	寿国寿民殿
Shouxuan Chunyong Hall		shou xuan chun yong	寿萱春永
Shuanghe Study	Two Herons Study	shuang he zhai	双鹤斋
Shuangjia Study	Double Beauty Study	shuang jia zhai	双佳斋
Shuchun Garden	Gentle Spring Garden	shu chun yuan	淑春园
Shuijing Land		shui jing yu	水精域
Shuimu Mingse Complex	Complex of Sounds of Trees and Water	shui mu ming se	水木明瑟（建筑群）
Shuimu Mingse Hall		shui mu ming se	水木明瑟（殿）
Shuimu Qinghua Zhi Pavilion		shui mu qing hua zhi ge	水木清华之阁
Shuiyun Pavilion	Water and Clouds Pavilion	shui yun xuan	水云轩
Shuqiong Study		shu qiong zhai	漱琼斋
Shuzao Pvilion	Display of Literary Talent Pavilion	shu zao xuan	抒藻轩
Si Suo	Four Living Quarters	si suo	四所
Simianyan Building	Quadrangle Building	si mian yan lou	四面延楼
Siyi Library	Library of the Four Seasons	si yi shu wu	四宜书屋
Siyong Study		si yong zhai	思永斋
Songyun Building	Pine Cloud Building	song yun lou	松云楼
Sudi Chunxiao Open Hall	Open Hall of Spring Dawn on the Su Dike	su di chun xiao	苏堤春晓
Sui'an Room	Contentment with One's Lot Room	sui an shi	随安室
Suxin Hall	Pure Mind Hall	su xin tang	素心堂
Taixu Room		tai xu shi	太虚室
Tanfei Pavilion	Clouds Pavilion	tan fei ge	昙霏阁
Tantan Dangdang Complex	Complex of Clear Conscience and Broad Mind	tan tan dang dang	坦坦荡荡
Tanzhen Library		tan zhen shu wu	探真书屋
Taohua Hollow	Peach Blossoms Hollow	tao hua wu	桃花坞
Taoyuan Library		tao yuan shu wu	讨源书屋
Taoyuan Shenchu Hall	Hall of Deep in the Peach Blossom Spring	tao yuan shen chu	桃源深处
Tengying Huacong Courtyard	Courtyard of Vine Shadows and Flowerbeds	teng ying hua cong	藤影花丛
Tiandi Yijia Chun Palace	Palace of Spring for One Family under Heaven and Earth	tian di yi jia chun	天地一家春
Tianlin Haijing Pavilion		tian lin hai jing	天临海镜
Tianran Tuhua Complex	Complex of the Nature's Own Painting	tian ran tu hua	天然图画（建筑群）
Tianran Tuhua (hall)		tian ran tu hua	天然图画（殿）
Tianwang Hall	Hall of Heavenly Kings	tian wang dian	天王殿
Tianyi Pavilion	One Sky Pavilion	tian yi ge	天一阁
Tiaoshuang Building		tiao shuang lou	眺爽楼
Tongdao Hall		tong dao tang	同道堂
Tongle Garden	Garden of Shared Pleasure	tong le yuan	同乐园
Tongle Garden Hall	Garden of Shared Pleasure Hall	tong le yuan dian	同乐园殿
Tudi Ancestral Temple	Ancestral Temple of Land	tu di ci	土地祠
Tudi Temple	Land God Temple	tu di miao	土地庙
Wanchun Pavilion		wan chun xuan	绾春轩
Wanfang Anhe Complex	Complex of Universal Peace and Harmony	wan fang an he	万方安和
Wanfu Pavilion		wan fu ge	万福阁
Wangyingzhou Pavilion		wang ying zhou	望瀛洲
Wanhe Songfeng Complex	Complex of Windy Pines among a Myriad Valleys	wan he song feng	万壑松风
Wanhua Zhen Complex	Complex of the Maze	wan hua zhen	万花阵
Weiyu Library	Rich Flavor Library	wei yu shu wu	味腴书室
Weizhen Library	True Flavor Library	wei zhen shu wu	味真书屋
Wenjin Pavilion	Pavilion for Asking Directions to the Ford	wen jin ting	问津亭
Wenshu Hall	Hall of Manjusri	wen shu dian	文殊殿
Wensu Pavilion	Pavilion of the Origin of Literature	wen su ge	文溯阁
Wenyuan Pavilion	Pavilion of the Source of Literature	wen yuan ge	文源阁
Wenyue Building	Asking the Moon Building	wen yue lou	问月楼

English Name	Explanation	Chinese Pinyin	Chinese Name
West Palace Gate		xi gong men	西宫门
Western Quarters		xi suo	西所
Wufu Hall	Five Blessings Hall	wu fu tang	五福堂
Wufu Wudai Hall	Five Blessings and Five Generations Hall	wu fu wu dai tang	五福五代堂
Wuling Chunse (Complex)	Complex of Hollow of Spring Color at Wuling	wu ling chun se	武陵春色
Wutong Courtyard	Wutong Tree Courtyard	wu tong yuan	梧桐院
Wuyi Study		wu yi zhai	无逸斋
Xiaguan Hanqing Hall	Summer Cool Hall	xia guan han qing	夏馆含清
Xianda Yuanjing Hall	Hall of Display of Great Perfect Mirror Wisdom	xian da yuan jing	现大圆镜
Xianfa Hill	Perspective Hill	xian fa shan	线法山
Xianfa Wall	Perspective Wall	xian fa qiang	线法墙
Xiangxue Gallery	Snow of Fragrance Gallery	xiang xue lang	香雪廊
Xiangyuan Yiqing Hall	Hall of Fragrance is Subtler with Distance	xiang yuan yi qing	香远益清
Xianxiang Courtyard	Courtyard of Fragrance of Immortals	xian xiang yuan	仙香苑
Xiaoxiang Chuang Hall		xiao xiang chuang	小香幢
Xiazhu Building		xia zhu lou	霞翥楼
Xichun Garden		xi chun yuan	熙春园
Xie Qiqu Pavilion	Pavilion Harmonizing Surprise and Delight	xie qi qu	谐奇趣
Xifeng Xiuse Open Hall	Open Hall of Elegant Color of the Western Peaks	xi feng xiu se	西峰秀色
Xinghua Village	Apricot Blossom Village	xing hua cun	杏花村
Xinghuachun Pavilion	Apricot Blossom Spring Pavilion	xing hua chun guan	杏花春馆
Xishang Pavilion		xi shang ting	禊赏亭
Xiumu Jiayin Hall	Hall of Fine Shade under Handsome Tree	xiu mu jia yin	秀木嘉荫
Xiuqing Village		xiu qing cun	秀清村
Xiuyuan Mountain House	Mountain House with a View of Distant Hills	xiu yuan shan fang	秀远山房
Xiyang Building Complex	Complex of European Buildings	xi yang lou	西洋楼
Xuming Room	Clarity by Cleansing Room	xu ming shi	虚明室
Xunyun Building	Building of Following the Clouds	xun yun lou	寻云楼
Yangsu Library	Cultivating the Essential Self Library	yang su shu wu	养苏书屋
Yanjing Building	Building of Extensive Scenery	yan jing lou	延景楼
Yanshang Pavilion	Transferred Favors Pavilion	yan shang ting	延赏亭
Yanyue Qingzhen Building	Veiled Moon Building	yan yue qing zhen lou	烟月清真楼
Yanzao Building		yan zao lou	延藻搂
Yi Study		yi zhai	抑斋
Yichun Hall		yi chun dian	宜春殿
Yihe Yuan	Summer Palace	yi he yuan	颐和园
Yinghai Sacred Mountain (kiosk)		ying hai xian shan	瀛海仙山
Yingshan Building	Reflection of the Hill Building	ying shan lou	影山楼
Yingshui Lanxiang Complex	Complex of Water Reflections and Orchid Fragrance	ying shui lan xiang	映水兰香
Yingxun Pavilion		ying xun ting	迎薰亭
Yinjian Building	Audience Building	yin jian lou	引见楼
Yinsheng (gazebo)	Ushers in Beauty	ying sheng	引胜
Yinyu Pavilion	Gem of a Poem Pavilion	yin yu xuan	吟玉轩
Yinyue Pond	Moon Reflecting Pond	yin yue chi	印月池
Yiqing Shushi Hall	Hall of Books that Give Pleasure Library	yi qing shu shi	怡情书史
Yiqing Yuemu Hall	Hall of Soothes the Mind and Pleases the Eye	yi qing yue mu	怡情悦目
Yiran Library	Serene Contentment Library	yi ran shu wu	怡然书屋
Yishou Pavilion	Longevity Nurturing Pavilion	yi shou xuan	颐寿轩
Yixiu Pavilion	Taking in the Scenery Pavilion	yi xiu ting	挹秀亭
Yonghe Palace	Palace of Peace and Harmony	yong he gong	雍和宫
Yongning Temple		yong ning si	永宁寺
Yongri Hall		yong ri tang	永日堂
Yuan Ming Yuan	Garden of Perfect Brightness	yuan ming yuan	圆明园
Yuan Ming Yuan Hall		yuan ming yuan dian	圆明园殿
Yuanfei Yuyue Hall	Hall of Leaping Fish and Flying Kites	yuan fei yu yue	鸢飞鱼跃
Yuanying Observatory	Immense Ocean Observatory	yuan ying guan	远瀛观
Yuanying Study	Lake Reflections Study	yuan ying zhai	渊映斋

English Name	Explanation	Chinese Pinyin	Chinese Name
Yuedi Yunju Complex	Complex of Dwelling of the Moon, Earth, and Clouds	yue di yun ju	月地云居（建筑群）
Yuedi Yunju Temple		yue di yun ju	月地云居（佛寺）
Yueji Pavilion	Pavilion of the Joy of Clearing after Snow	yue ji ting	悦霁亭
Yuezou Juntian (stage)	Music Reaching Heaven (stage)	yue zou jun tian	乐奏钧天（戏台）
Yulan Fen Hall	Hall of Orchid Scent	yu lan fen	御兰芬
Yulinglong Pavilion		yu ling long guan	玉玲珑馆
Yunlinshi Room		yun lin shi shi	云林石室
Yunsong Study		yun song zhai	韵松斋
Yuntianqin Pavilion	Pavilion of Music of a Celestial Lute	yun tian qin	韵天琴
Yunxia Si Pavilion		yun xia si	云霞思
Yunxiang Qingsheng Hall	Hall of Exquisite Clouds	yun xiang qing sheng	云香清胜
Yunzhen Study		yun zhen zhai	蕴真斋
Yuyue Yuanfei Complex	Complex of Leaping Fish and Flying Kites	yu yue yuan fei	鱼跃鸢飞
Zaoshen Yude Complex		zao shen yu de	澡身浴德
Zaoyuan Gate		zao yuan men	藻园门
Zelan Hall		ze lan tang	泽兰堂
Zhancun Study		zhan cun zhai	湛存斋
Zhanfeng Pavilion		zhan feng ting	占峯亭
Zhanjing Building		zhan jing lou	湛景楼
Zhanran Room		zhan ran shi	湛然室
Zhanshi Yinglü Complex	Complex of Verse and Rhyming	zhan shi ying lü	展诗应律（建筑群）
Zhanshi Yinglü (hall)		zhan shi ying lü	展诗应律（殿）
Zhanxu Library	Hollowness Belying Profundity Library	zhan xu shu wu	湛虚书屋
Zhaohe Deng (pavilion)	Terrace to Attract Cranes	zhao he deng	招鹤磴
Zhengda Guangming Complex	Complex of Rectitude and Honor	zheng da guang ming	正大光明（建筑群）
Zhengda Guangming Hall	Hall of Rectitude and Honor	zheng da guang ming	正大光明（殿）
Zhengjue Temple	Temple of Supreme Perfect Enlightenment	zheng jue si	正觉寺
Zhi Gengzhi	Understanding Ploughing and Weaving	zhi geng zhi	知耕织
Zhifu Hall	Achieving Trust Hall	zhi fu dian	致孚殿
Zhiguo Hall	Recognition of One's Mistakes Hall	zhi guo tang	知过堂
Zhiyu Pavilion	Know Your Fish Pavilion	zhi yu ting	知鱼亭
Zhongle Pavilion	Shared Joy Pavilion	zhong le ting	众乐亭
Zhuke Building		zhu ke lou	竹萪楼
Zhumi Mountain House	Mountain House of Dense Bamboo Grove	zhu mi shan zhai	竹密山斋
Zhuolin Pond	Swimming Fish Pond	zhuo lin zhao	濯鳞沼
Zhuoyun Building	Lofty clouds Building	zhuo yun lou	倬云楼
Zhushen Hejing Hall	Hall of Dense Bamboos and Quiet Lotuses	zhu shen he jing	竹深荷净
Zibi Mountain House	Purple Green Mountain House	zi bi shan fang	紫碧山房
Zida Pavilion		zi da xuan	自达轩
Zixia Building		zi xia lou	紫霞楼
Zongting Bridge		zong ting qiao	棕亭桥
Zuisheng Pavilion	Golden Light Sutra Pavilion	zui sheng ge	最胜阁
Zuojing Pavilion	Books as Pillow Pavilion	zuo jing guan	葄经馆
Zuoshi Linliu Complex	Complex of On a Rock by the River	zuo shi lin liu	坐石临流（建筑群）
Zuoshi Linliu Pavilion		zuo shi lin liu	坐石临流（亭）

BIBLIOGRAPHY

Ban Gu, *Qian hanshu* [History of the Former Han Dynasty].

Brizay, Bernard, Gao Faming, Li Quan and Li Hongfei, trans. *1860: yuanmingyuan da jienan* [The Looting of Summer Palace, Second Opium War]. Hangzhou: Zhejiang guji chubanshe (Zhejiang Ancient Books Publishing House), 2005.

Chen Minglei, ed. *Gujin tushu jicheng* [Complete Collection of Illustrations and Writings from the Earliest to Current Times].

Daqing gaozong chunhuangdi shilu [Chronicles of the Qianlong Emperor].

Gugong zhoukan [Palace Museum Weekly].

Hong Li, *Yuzhi leshantang quanji dingben*.

Hong Li, *Yuzhi shi* [Imperial Poems].

Jiangyouren shu yuanmingyuan shi [Translation of *A Particular Account of the Emperor of China's Gardens near Pekin: In a Letter from F. Attiret*]. Beijing: Beijing chubanshe (Beijing Publishing House), 1999.

Kaogu [Archaeology]. Beijing: zhongguo shehui kexueyuan (Chinese Academy of Social Sciences).

Lai Zhide, *Zhouyi jizhu* [Variorum of the *Book of Changes*].

Lang Shining, *Qingaozong wanshuyuan ciyan tu* [Imperial Banquet in the Garden of Ten Thousand Trees].

Li Fang, Li Mu and Xu Xuan, comps. *Taipingt yulan* [Imperial Readings]. 983.

Liang Zhangju, *Langji congtan*. Fujian: Fujian renmin chubanshe, 1983.

Lü Buwei, *Lüshi chunqiu* [Annals of Lü Buwei].

M'ghee, R. J. L, *How We Got into Pekin: A Narrative of the Campaign in China of 1860*. London: Richard Bentley, 1862.

Macartney, George, *1973 qianlong yingshi jinjianji* [British Embassy to China 1793]. Tianjin: Tianjin renmin chubanshe, 2006.

Qiju zhuce [Chronicles of Imperial Activities].

Qing huidian [Official Journal of the Qing Dynasty]. Beijing: zhonghua shuju (Zhonghua Publishing House), 1991.

Renzong yuzhi wenji [Collection of Emperor Jiaqing's Writings].

Si Maqian, *Shiji* [Records of the Grand Historian].

Siren, Osvald, *Gardens of China*. New York: The Ronald Press, 1949.

Staunton, George, Ye Duyi, trans. *Yingshi yejian qianlong jishi* [An Authentic Account of an Embassy from the King of Great Britain to the Emperor of China]. Beijing: shangwu yinshuguan, 1963.

Sun Wenliang, Zhang Jie and Zheng Chuanshui, *Qianlong di* [Emperor Qianlong]. Nanjing: Jiangsu jiaoyu chubanshe, 2005.

Tang Wenji and Luo qingsi, *Qianlong zhuan* [Biography of Emperor Qianlong]. Beijing: renmin chubanshe (People's Publishing House), 1994.

Wan Yi, Wang Shuqing and Liu Lu, *Qingdai gongting shi* [History of the Qing Court]. Tianjing: baihua wenyi chubanshe (Baihua Literature and Art Publishing House), 2004.

Wang Zhicheng, *Yuan Ming Yuan jishi shuzha* [A Particular Account of the Emperor of China's Gardens Near Pekin: In a Letter from F. Attiret].

Wei Kaizhao, *Yonghegong manlu* [Random Notes on the Yonghe Gong]. Henan: Henan renmin chubanshe (Henan People's Publishing House), 1985.

Wu Zhenyu, *Yangjizhai conglu* [Historical Notes of the Qing Dynasty]. Beijing: Beijing guji chubanshe, 1983.

Yao Yuanzhi, *Zhuyeting zaji* [Random Notes of the Bamboo Leaf Pavilion]. Beijing: zhonghua shuju (Zhonghua Publishing House), 1982.

Yong Zheng, *Shizong xianhuangdi yuzhi wenji* [Anthology of Emperor Yongzheng's Writings].

Yu minzhong, Ying Lian, et al., *Rixia jiuwen kao* [Study of Ancient Accounts Heard in the Precincts of the Throne]. 1788.

Yuan Ming Yuan changchunyuan hanjingtang kaogu fajue baogao [Archaeological Report on the Hanjing Tang of Changchun]. Beijing: wenwu chubanshe, 2006.

Yuan Ming Yuan. Shanghai: Shanghai guji chubanshe (Shanghai Ancient Books Publishing House), 1991.

Zhang Tingyu, Ji Huang and Liu Yong, comps., Ji Yun, ed. *Huangchao wenxian tongkao* [Encyclopedia of the Historical Records of the Imperial Dynasty]. 1787.

Zhao Lian, *Xiaoting zalu* [Random Notes from Roaring Pavilion]. Beijing: zhonghua Shuju (Zhonghua Publishing House), 1980.

Zhu Chengru, *Qingshi tudian* [Illustrated Dictionary of the History of the Qing Dynasty]. Beijing: zijincheng chubanshe, 2002.

DATES OF THE CHINESE DYNASTIES

Xia Dynasty （夏）	2070 – 1600 BC
Shang Dynasty （商）	1600 – 1046 BC
Zhou Dynasty （周）	1046 – 256 BC
Western Zhou Dynasty （西周）	1046 – 771 BC
Eastern Zhou Dynasty （东周）	770 – 256 BC
Spring and Autumn Period （春秋）	770 – 476 BC
Warring States Period （战国）	475 – 221 BC
Qin Dynasty （秦）	221 – 206 BC
Han Dynasty （汉）	206 BC – 220 AD
Western Han Dynasty （西汉）	206 BC – 25 AD
Eastern Han Dynasty （东汉）	25 – 220
Three Kingdoms （三国）	220 – 280
Wei （魏）	220 – 265
Shu Han （蜀）	221 – 263
Wu （吴）	222 – 280
Jin Dynasty （晋）	265 – 420
Western Jin Dynasty （西晋）	265 – 316
Eastern Jin Dynasty （东晋）	317 – 420
Northern and Southern Dynasties （南北朝）	420 – 589
Southern Dynasties （南朝）	420 – 589
Liang Dynasty （梁）	502 – 557
Northern Dynasties （北朝）	439 – 581
Sui Dynasty （隋）	581 – 618
Tang Dynasty （唐）	618 – 907
Five Dynasties and Ten Kingdoms （五代十国）	907 – 960
Five Dynasties （五代）	907 – 960
Ten Kingdoms （十国）	902 – 979
Song Dynasty （宋）	960 – 1279
Northern Song Dynasty （北宋）	960 – 1127
Southern Song Dynasty （南宋）	1127 – 1279
Liao Dynasty （辽）	916 – 1125
Jin Dynasty （金）	1115 – 1234
Xixia Dynasty (or Tangut) （西夏）	1038 – 1227
Yuan Dynasty （元）	1279 – 1368
Ming Dynasty （明）	1368 – 1644
Qing Dynasty （清）	1644 – 1911

INDEX

A

Anlan Garden   20, 109, 242
Anyin Chuang   176, 242
Anyou Palace   20, 67–69, 225, 231, 242
Anzhi Building   131, 242
arched door frame   204
architectural arch   20, 43, 51, 54, 68, 69, 87, 135, 190, 211, 235, 243, 245, 246

B

Back Lake   20, 47, 64, 84, 123, 126, 128, 133, 146, 147, 152, 223, 227, 230, 237
Bamboo Courtyard   13, 14, 242
Bamboo Garden   75, 187, 242
Bamboo Pavilion   193, 242
Banmu Garden   133, 147, 150, 151, 242
Baohe Taihe Hall   20, 44, 45, 242
Baoxiang Temple   24, 81, 93, 242
Bathing the Buddha Day   146
bay
 central   55, 56, 58, 143, 200, 202, 204
 end   55, 56
 outer   55, 56, 112
 secondary   56
bed chamber   49
Beiyuan Mountain House   237, 242
Beiyuan Mountain Village   32, 95, 120, 127, 131, 224, 242
bell tower   84, 86, 91, 224
Biaosheng Pavilion   177, 242
Bieyou Dongtian (Complex, Hall)   169, 170, 227, 228, 242
Bieyou Tian Open Hall   177, 242
Bilan Bridge   230, 231, 242
Bishu Mountain Resort in Chengde   39, 40, 63, 64, 215, 219, 242
Bitong Library   20, 102, 103, 223, 227, 242
Bixia Yuanjun   90
Biyun Building   162, 242
Black Dragon Pool   126
bridge
 arch   230
 beam   230
 moveable   230
 zigzag   177, 181, 230
Buddha chapel   48
Buddhist Complex   85, 87, 231, 242

C

Cai Pu   13, 14, 242
Caizhi Jing Pavilion   173, 242
Cangjing Building   91, 242
Cangshu Pavilion   114, 115, 242
cascading gallery   169, 181
central niche   205
Changchun Garden (Garden of Eternal Spring)   24, 28, 32, 42, 43, 51, 55, 81, 92, 93, 113, 133, 177, 180, 184, 193, 204–206, 210, 223, 226, 227, 230, 235, 236, 242
Changchun Garden (Joyful Spring Garden)   11, 28, 58, 71, 218, 242
Changchun Library   95, 242
Changchun Xianguan Complex   20, 32, 71, 72, 224, 230, 231, 242
Changjin Building   158, 159, 242
Chen Yuanlong   109
Cheng'en Hall   50, 242
Chengbo Xizhao Pavilion   51, 53, 242
Chengguang Pavilion   93, 242
Chenglian Building   176, 242
Chengxin Hall   187, 188, 242
Chishui Gongxin Yuetongming Hall   111, 242
Chongfu Palace   214, 242
Chongwen Gate   210, 242
Chongyang Festival   71
Chuandai Dang   226
Chuihong Gazebo   188, 242
Chunhua Pavilion   51–57, 133, 141, 235, 236, 242
Chunxi Courtyard   25, 28, 242
Chunyu Pavilion   20, 32, 124–126, 227, 231, 242
Chunyu Shuhe (Library)   108, 242
Churu Xianliang Gate   31, 226, 231, 235, 242
Ciyun Puhu (Complex, Temple)   20, 81, 82, 84, 223, 224, 227, 230, 231, 242
Cizhong Dayou Jiachu Pavilion   177, 242
concubine/imperial consort   13, 50, 58, 143, 152, 153, 203
changzai   50
daying   50
guifei   50
guiren   50
huangguifei   50
pin   50
Confucian   15, 61, 67, 95, 111, 117, 119
Confucius   117
Congfang Gazebo   181, 242
corbel bracket   38, 68
courtyard enclosed by a gallery   44, 92, 181
crown prince   13, 14, 21, 44, 45
Cuijing Study   147, 243
Cuiwei Hall   123, 125, 243
Cuizhao Building   97, 243
Cunbi   129, 243

D

Da Shuifa Fountain   193, 204–206, 243
Daiyue Building   51, 53, 243
Dajue Temple   81, 243
Danbo Ningjing (Building, Complex)   20, 24, 128, 129, 130, 225, 237, 243
Danhuai Hall   24, 42, 43, 113, 147, 227, 243
Danti Pavilion   173, 243
Danxian Room   169, 243
Daoliang Building   127, 243
Daoxiang Pavilion   129, 243
Dehe Garden   143, 243
Deshenggai Pavilion   51, 52, 243
Deshou Palace   177, 243
Diaoyu Jetty   130, 243
Dongtian Shenchu Complex   95, 117, 225, 230, 243
Dou Tan   81
dowager consort   28
Dragon Boat Festival   71, 146, 219
Dragon King Temple   126, 247
dressing room building   137, 139, 143
drum tower   86, 91
Duanqiao Canxue   98, 190, 243
Duobao Liuli Pagoda   92, 243
Duobao Pavilion   88, 89, 243
Duojia Pavilion   20, 129, 237, 243
Duojia Ruyun Hall   217, 218, 223, 243
duty room   32, 51, 54, 92, 126, 140

Dzungars   40

E

ear room   44, 64, 79, 98
East Garden   226, 227, 231, 243
Eastern Quarters   58, 243
emperor
 Daoguang   11, 28, 58
 Kangxi   11, 13–15, 63–65, 67, 79, 105, 190, 223
 Jiaqing   11, 27, 28, 46, 54, 187, 210, 223
 Qianlong (Hongli)   9, 11, 21, 24, 25, 39–47, 49, 51, 52, 55, 63–69, 71, 72, 75, 79, 81, 84–86, 89, 91, 95, 97, 102, 107–109, 111–113, 115, 117, 119, 126–129, 131, 134–136, 147, 159, 162, 163, 169, 172, 173, 177, 180, 181, 184, 185, 189, 190, 191, 193, 203, 205, 211, 214, 215, 217–219, 227, 230, 236, 238, 239
 Xianfeng   11, 29, 31, 32
 Yongzheng (Yinzhen)   9, 11, 13–15, 17, 21, 47, 63–65, 67, 71, 75, 79, 84–86, 90, 113, 117, 126, 134, 190, 223, 237
empress dowager   9, 28, 40, 58, 71, 72, 89, 135, 146, 159, 218, 219, 227, 231
 Xiaosheng   72
Empress Xiaoxian   219
era
 Daoguang   28, 29, 33, 58, 72, 134, 146
 Jiaqing   25, 45, 91, 133, 146, 176, 177, 187, 223
 Kangxi   11, 13, 50, 63
 Qianlong   21, 24, 25, 28, 29, 42, 44, 48, 54, 72, 79, 86, 90, 91, 108, 112, 113, 115, 123, 126, 131, 135, 136, 153, 162, 169, 172, 193, 206, 207, 215, 217, 223, 224, 226
 Xianfeng   11, 29, 31, 32
 Yongzheng (Yinzhen)   11, 14, 17, 21, 49, 85, 108, 123, 127, 128, 136, 152, 158, 169, 176, 190, 214, 217, 223

F

Fahui Temple   24, 81, 92, 93, 243

Fangbi Cong Open Hall   44, 243
Fanghu Shengjing Complex   20, 21, 37, 157, 162–164, 225, 227, 230, 239, 241, 243
Fanghui Building   185, 243
Fangwai Observatory   193, 202, 203, 206, 243
Fanxiang Building   51, 52, 243
Fanyu Qunfang Hall   111, 243
Fayuan Building   87, 243
Feicui Building   162, 243
Feiyun Pavilion   45, 46, 243
felt tent   54
feng ge   230
feng yu   230
Fengle Pavilion   130, 243
Fengsan Wusi Hall   47, 48, 49, 243
Fengshen Yinde   211
Field Character Building   24, 128, 237
floating cups pavilion   186, 214, 215
floor well   141
Forbidden City   8, 11, 38, 39, 42, 55, 63, 68, 115, 137, 207, 215, 231, 235
Front Lake   20, 47, 84
Fu Heng   25
Fu Long'an   25
Fuchun Building   20, 45, 243
Fuchun Hall   28, 29, 58, 133, 243
Fuyou Daqian   92, 243

G

Gengyun Hall   131, 243
Gengzhi Pavilion   13, 14, 237, 243
Giuseppe Castiglione   45, 135, 193
Goldfish Pond   13, 14, 21, 226, 227, 230, 231, 243
grand councilor   211
grand secretary   25, 48, 109
Great South Bridge   20, 227, 243
Guan Yu   81, 85, 88, 89
Guande Hall   39, 243
Guangfeng Jiyue Hall   25, 147, 243
Guangming Xinghai   92, 243
Guangyu Temple   20, 81, 90, 243
Guanjia Pavilion   129, 237, 243
Guanlian Pavilion   63, 243
Guanshuifa Fountain   205, 206, 243
Guanyin   84, 90, 127
Guanyin Hall   90, 243
Guanyin Monastery   32, 127, 243
Guiyue Bridge   173, 243
Guizhi Mountain Hall   130, 244
Guxiang Study   71, 72, 244

H

Haiyan Hall   193, 200, 201, 202, 204, 206, 244
Haiyue Kaijin Complex   24, 32, 51, 92, 227, 235, 236, 244
hall
    door   188
    open   20, 44, 85
    passage   46, 188
    side   38, 43, 47, 51, 52, 55, 58, 68, 71, 87–91, 97, 127, 139, 140, 146, 188, 235
    viewing   133, 136, 137, 140, 142, 143, 146, 153
    wing   181
Han Chinese Archives Office   32
Hanbi Hall   71, 72, 244
Hande Lirary   49, 244
Hanging Flowers Gate   51, 52, 71, 87, 185
Hanguang Room   53, 244
Hanjing Hall   42, 51, 52, 54, 55, 113, 133, 143, 210, 235, 236, 244
Hanqiu Hall   108, 244
Hanxu Langjian Complex   162, 244
Hanyuan Study   97, 98, 244
Happiness (Fu) Stage   139, 141, 143, 243
He Shen   211
heated room   55, 56
heir apparent   13, 14, 21, 65
Hengbi Pavilion   180, 181, 244
Hengchun Hall   133, 244
Hexiang Pavilion   20, 111, 244
Hongci Yonghu Complex   21, 67, 68, 86, 162, 224, 235, 244
horizontal name tablet   39, 238
Huagang Guanyu Open Hall   189, 244
Huai Qingfen Building   45, 46, 126, 231, 244
Huang Gongwang   49
Huashen Temple   20, 81, 111, 244
Huifang Library   13, 20, 21, 97, 98, 99, 100, 227, 244
Huiji Ancestral Temple   32, 244
Huiluan Hall   37, 162, 244
Huiwan Zongchun Zhimiao   111, 244
Huiyu Hall   127, 244
Humiao Building   129, 244
Huohua Stone Boat   169, 172, 244
Huzhong Tian Complex   13, 14, 244
Huzhong Xianlai   133, 244

I

Imperial Architectural Design Studio   32
imperial garden   8, 11, 17, 20, 21, 29, 47, 120, 129, 159, 169, 180, 181, 189, 209, 214, 216–219, 223, 239
Imperial Household Department   32, 55, 112, 184
imperial residence (sleeping palace)   40, 42, 46, 47, 50, 51, 56, 81
Inner Gatehouse   58, 244
introductory space   38, 99, 105, 224, 235

J

Jade Emperor   85, 93
Jade Spring Mountains   126
Jean-Denis Attiret   89, 185, 210, 211
Ji Cheng   176
jiagan shi   87
Jiajing Mingqin Complex   20, 21, 90, 227, 244
Jian Garden   24, 184, 185, 244
Jian Pavilion   13, 14, 244
Jianhe Yuqing Hall   123, 125, 244
Jiechun Pavilion   127, 244
Jiexiu Mountain House   95, 157, 176, 244
Jieye Pavilion   169, 244
Jihe Shenchu Open Hall   111, 244
Jihexiang Pavilion   20, 218, 244
Jing Room   87, 244
Jingbi Hall   177, 244
Jinghong Pavilion   186, 244
Jingjia Pavilion   173, 244
Jinglian Study   51, 53, 244
Jingming Garden   81, 126, 227, 244
Jingshui Study   125, 244
Jingxiang House   129, 244
Jingyu Library   92, 244
Jingzhi Chunshi Jia Hall   75, 79, 244
Jingzhong Pavilion   158–160, 219, 244
Jinqi Building   162, 244
Jiqing Xianchang Pavilion   186, 244
Jiuzhou Qingyan (Complex, Hall)   17–20, 32, 46–50, 72, 84, 95, 133, 223, 224, 226, 227, 230, 231, 244
Jixiang Suo   45, 244

K

Kaiyi Pavilion   95, 185, 244
Kenong Pavilion   20, 32, 244
King Cheng of Zhou   39
Kunlun Mountains   223
Kuoran Dagong Complex   32, 157, 173, 174, 244
Kuoran Dagong Hall   21, 173, 244

L

Lake of Happiness   20, 90, 108, 158, 159, 162, 163, 169, 173, 176, 190, 210, 217–219, 223, 227, 230, 239
Lake Tai   44, 51, 56, 115, 172, 177
Lan Pavilion   214, 245
Lancui Pavilion   176, 245
Langrun Study   177, 245
Langyin Pavilion   75, 78, 79, 245
Lantern Festival   40, 47, 49, 71, 134, 135, 146
Lanye Hall   127, 245
Le Anhe Palace   49, 245
Leifeng Xizhao Open Hall   20, 189, 190, 245
Leshan Hall   105–107, 245
Letianhe Hall   111, 245
Lezhi Mountain Village   86, 245
liang jiao   226, 227, 230
Liangfeng Chayun   190, 245
Liangxiang County   172, 245
Lianhua Facang Hall   87, 245
Lianhua Pavilion   13, 14, 245
Lianxi Lechu (Complex, hall)   95, 111, 112, 133, 157, 223, 230, 245
Lijing Pavilion   71, 245
Lingfeng Rock   113, 115
Lingxiangpan Pavilion   177, 245
Linhe Hua Hall   173, 245
Linxu Guijing Courtyard   71, 245
Liulang Wenying   20, 25, 190, 245
Liumeng Jiangjun Temple   20, 81, 245
Liushui Yin Pavilion   214, 245
Lixin Building   53, 245
Longevity (Shou) Stage   139, 141, 247
Louyue Kaiyun Complex   61–65, 95, 245
Lüjing Gazebo   185, 245
Luxiang Study   49, 245
Lüyin Pavilion   71, 245

M

Mahavira Hall   91, 245
Main Audience Hall   38
Main East Gate   32
Manchu Archives Office   32
Manjusri Bodhisattva   91
Market Street   88, 89, 209–212, 224, 245

Meiyue Pavilion   97–99, 245
memorial   17, 44, 45
memorial column   68, 69, 224, 235
Mi Wanzhong   172
Miaoda Pavilion   173, 245
Mid-Autumn Festival   71
Ming Shan   32
Mingyuxi Bridge   230, 245
Minning   28
Mochiyun Courtyard   71, 72, 245
moon gate   115
Moon River   69, 235
moon terrace   43, 56, 69, 114, 115, 173
multiform window   79, 84

N

Nacui Building   169, 245
Najing Hall   180, 181, 245
Nanfu (garden)   28, 245
Nanping Wanzhong Pavilion   20, 189, 245
Ni Zan   49, 180, 181
Nine Islands   64, 65, 71, 79, 85, 97, 105, 114, 128, 133, 152, 223, 225, 230, 237
Nine Ministers   48
North Lake Tai rock   115

O

octagonal hall   87

P

Palace Museum   15, 55, 65, 224, 250
Palace School for Prince   95
parapet   89, 200, 204
pavilion covering tablet   68, 114, 115
Pengdao Yaotai (Complex, Hall)   20, 32, 157–159, 162, 219, 222, 227, 230, 239, 245
Peony Terrace   13, 14, 63–65, 223, 227, 230, 245
peripheral room   71
Pinghu Qiuyue Complex   20, 189, 245
Pinshi Hall   95, 105, 106, 245
pipa   163
Prince Gong   31, 32
princess
    Kurun Princess Hejing   40
    Kurun Princess Hexiao   40, 211
princess' spouse   136
private garden   11, 15, 17, 24, 27, 177, 180, 214, 236
Prosperity (Lu) Stage   139, 142, 245
Pufu Palace   88, 89, 245
pulled couch   226, 230, 231
Putao Courtyard   13, 14, 245

Q

Qian Garden   24, 177, 178, 245
Qianchui Tiankuang Courtyard   117, 245
Qianlong Garden   215, 245
Qianqing Palace   21, 39, 245
Qianxiang Hall   162, 245
Qiaoqianju Gazebo   173, 245
Qichun Garden   25, 27–29, 32, 58, 81, 91, 133, 146, 186–188, 223, 236, 245
Qingbi Pavilion   180, 181, 245
Qinghui Pavilion   49, 105, 245
Qinghui Pavilion   106, 246
Qingjingdi Complex   20, 32, 86, 226, 231, 246
Qinglian Duo   177
Qingming Day   68
Qingshu Study   180, 181, 246
Qingshui Zhuoying Hall   105, 106, 246
Qingxia Study   27, 186, 246
Qingyin Pavilion   133, 137, 140, 246
Qingyue Shengping   133, 246
Qinqing Study   181, 246
Qinqu Pavilion   176, 246
Qinzheng Hall   20, 39, 44–46, 226, 227, 230, 246
Qinzheng Qinxian Complex   44, 117, 126, 173, 224, 227, 230, 231, 237, 246
Qionghua Building   162, 163, 246
Qiujin Changyuan Building   108, 246
Qixi Festival   71
Qixiu Pavilion   173, 246
Qixu Pavilion   188, 246
Qiyin Hall   173, 246
Qiyun Building   64, 246
Qu Garden   184, 185, 246
Quanbi Hall   105, 246
Quanshi Ziyu Hall   50, 246
Queen Mother of the West   218
Qushui Hexiang Pavilion   214, 246
Qushui Liushang Complex   214, 246
Quyuan Fenghe Complex   20, 21, 79, 136, 189, 190, 223, 227, 246

R

Rainbow Bridge   180, 181, 246
Raoyeyi Hall   177, 246
Rear Buddhist Complex   85, 87
Rectangular River   181, 193, 205
Ren Liang   31

Renci Hall   88, 246
Riri Ping'an Baohaoyin Pavilion   158, 246
Ritian Linyu (Complex, Temple)   81, 85, 224, 230, 246
River God Temple   32, 246
roof
    double round-ridge overhanging gable   173
    double-eave hip-and-gable   79, 162
    flush gable   45, 159, 188
    four-slope   194, 200
    hip   194, 203, 204
    hip-and-gable   38, 44, 45, 58, 79, 86, 112, 137, 147, 162, 186, 188
    overhanging gable   45, 58, 84, 139, 147, 159, 173, 188
    pyramidal   86, 147, 162, 169, 173, 186
round pavilion   199
Ru Garden   24, 227, 246
Rugu Hall   49, 95, 246
Rugu Hanjin Hall   225, 246
Ruiying Palace   20, 85, 246
Ruizhu Palace   20, 163, 246
Ruofanzhi Pavilion   131, 246
Ruyi Bridge   20, 117, 227, 230, 231, 246
Ruyi Pavilion   20, 117, 119, 226, 246
Ruyi Zhou   63

S

sanhe tu   201
Sanshifo Hall   88, 89, 246
Santan Yinyue   20, 246
Sanyou Pavilion   53, 57, 246
Shakyamuni   88, 146
Shangao Shuichang Complex   20, 32, 133–135, 226, 246
Shangqu Hall   125, 246
Shangsi Festival   214, 215
Shangxia Tianguang Complex   32, 223, 230, 246
Shanxun Gazebo   169, 246
Shao Garden   172, 246
Shen Yuan   48
Shende Hall   133, 236, 246
Shengdong Room   133, 246
Shengqiu Court   45, 46, 226, 246
Shenliu Dushu Hall   13, 14, 21, 246
Shenxin Miaoda Hall   133, 246
Shenxiu Siyong Hall   20, 111, 112, 227, 230, 246
Shequ Building   127, 246
Shewei City   20, 88, 89, 136, 210–212, 224, 226, 246
Shihuangdi   159

Shishan Hall   185, 246
Shishang Study   169, 246
Shizi Garden   64, 247
Shizi Grove   24, 91, 180–182, 247
Shouguo Shoumin Hall   88, 89, 247
Shoushan   38, 47
Shouxuan Chunyong Hall   227, 247
Shuanghe Study   20, 32, 173, 226, 227, 247
Shuangjia Study   147, 247
Shuchun Garden   214, 247
Shuijing Land   129, 247
Shuimu Mingse (Complex, Hall)   120, 130, 247
Shuimu Qinghua Zhi Pavilion   169, 247
Shuiyun Pavilion   111, 247
Shuqiong Study   185, 247
Shuzao Pvilion   97, 98, 247
Si Suo   117, 119, 247
siheyuan   45, 146
Simianyan Building   92, 247
Siyi Library   95, 108, 109, 247
Siyong Study   24, 51, 133, 227, 236, 247
sky well   139, 141, 142
Slender West Lake   184
sluice gate   180, 181
Songyun Building   49, 247
South Fruit Storeroom   32
spirit wall   38, 54, 235
stone screen   205
stone-paved trail   180
Sudi Chunxiao Open Hall   20, 75, 189, 190, 247
Sui'an Room   13, 72, 98, 99, 158, 247
Suxin Hall   147, 150, 247

T

taiji   111
taiji   136
Taixu Room   177, 247
Tanfei Pavilion   93, 247
Tang Dai   48
Tantan Dangdang Complex   20, 21, 25, 123, 133, 147, 148, 150, 223, 227, 230, 231, 247
Tanzhen Library   180, 181, 247
Tao Yuanmig   24, 105
Taohua Hollow   13, 14, 21, 105, 106, 247
Taoyuan Library   227, 247
Taoyuan Shenchu Hall   105, 106, 247
temple gatehouse   88, 91–93
Tengying Huacong Courtyard   71, 247
three mountains   159, 239
    Fangzhang   158, 239

APPENDICES   255

Penglai 158, 239
Yingzhou 158, 239
Tiandi Yijia Chun Palace 20, 50, 247
Tianlin Haijing Pavilion 186, 247
Tianran Tuhua (Complex, hall) 75, 76, 79, 102, 190, 227, 238, 247
Tianwang Hall 86, 91, 247
Tianyi Pavilion 114, 115, 247
Tiaoshuang Building 169, 247
tile
  barrel 204
  fish scale 204
  flat 204
titled prince 28, 47
Tongdao Hall 133, 247
Tongle Garden (Hall) 20, 32, 43, 88, 133, 136, 137, 139–141, 143, 210, 211, 214, 226, 227, 230, 231, 247
Tudi Ancestral Temple 32, 247
Tudi Temple 123, 125, 247

U

Ullambana Sutra 218, 219

V

veranda 48, 52, 79, 99, 105, 106, 111, 112, 125, 129–131, 147, 162, 173, 177, 181, 186, 188

W

waiting room 32, 38, 43, 54, 69, 225, 235
Wanchun Pavilion 105, 106, 247
Wanfang Anhe Complex 105, 133, 152–154, 225–227, 237, 247
Wanfu Pavilion 90, 162, 247
Wang Xizhi 214, 215
Wangyingzhou Pavilion 219, 247
Wanhe Songfeng Complex 64, 247
Wanhua Zhen Complex 193, 198–200, 247
Wanshou Hill 226, 227
warm sedan chair 226, 230, 231
water clock 84
Wawa Hill 90
Weiyu Library 95, 247
Weizhen Library 95, 111, 247
well pavilion 51, 69, 126
Wenjin Pavilion 98, 99, 230, 247
Wenshu Hall 91, 247
Wensu Pavilion 20, 115, 247
Wenyuan Pavilion 113–115, 247
Wenyue Building 58, 247
West Lake 25, 164, 189, 190
West Palace Gate 186, 248
Western Hills 79
Western Quarters 58, 248
Winter Solstice 39
wood
  gharu 226
  nanmu 64, 65, 115
  rosewood 47
Wu Zhenyu 136, 143
Wufu Hall 20, 75, 78, 79, 248
Wufu Wudai Hall 78, 79, 248
Wuling Chunse (Complex) 21, 95, 105–107, 133, 248
Wutong Courtyard 13, 14, 248
Wuyi Study 27, 248

X

Xiaguan Hanqing Hall 108, 248
Xianda Yuanjing Hall 93, 248
Xianfa Hill 193, 205, 207, 248
Xianfa Wall 193, 205, 248
Xiangxue Gallery 111, 248
Xiangyuan Yiqing Hall 111, 248
Xianxiang Courtyard 86, 248
Xiaoxiang Chuang Hall 91, 180, 181, 248
Xiazhu Building 54, 55, 113, 248
Xichun Garden 25, 28, 227, 248
Xie An 214
Xie Qiqu Pavilion 193, 194, 196, 199, 200, 206, 227, 248
Xifeng Xiuse (Complex, Open Hall) 20, 133, 157, 225, 248
Xinghua Village 123, 126, 248
Xinghuachun Pavilion 15, 32, 123, 126, 223, 227, 248
Xishang Pavilion 215, 248
Xiumu Jiayin Hall 45, 248
Xiuqing Village 20, 226, 227, 230, 248
Xiuyuan Mountain House 108, 248
Xiyang Building Complex 9, 24, 92, 181, 193, 194, 204–207, 236, 248
Xuming Room 95, 248
Xunyun Building 176, 248

Y

Yangque Long 193
Yangsu Library 64, 95, 248
Yanjing Building 180, 181, 248
Yanshan Mountains 11, 181
Yanshang Pavilion 98, 99, 248
Yanyue Qingzhen Building 108, 109, 248
Yanzao Building 169, 248
Yi Study 71, 72, 125, 248
Yichun Hall 162, 248
Yihe Yuan 143, 248
yin and yang 111, 115
Yinghai Sacred Mountain (kiosk) 158, 159, 248
Yingshan Building 173, 248
Yingsheng 129
Yingshui Lanxiang Complex 129, 223, 230, 248
Yingxun Pavilion 162, 248
Yinjian Building 134, 248
Yinreng 13, 14
Yinsheng 129, 248
Yinyu Pavilion 146, 248
Yinyue Pond 20, 130, 248
Yiqing Shushi Hall 49, 95, 248
Yiqing Yuemu Hall 129, 248
Yiran Library 95, 176, 248
Yishou Pavilion 27, 58, 248
Yixiu Pavilion 13, 98, 99, 248
Yong Yan 25
Yonghe Palace 85, 90, 91, 248
Yongning Temple 81, 226, 248
Yongri Hall 137, 248
Yuan Ming Yuan Hall 47, 248
Yuanfei Yuyue Hall 49, 248
Yuanguang Gate 227
Yuanying Observatory 31, 193, 204–206, 236, 248
Yuanying Study 54, 248
Yuedi Yunju (Complex, Temple) 81, 86, 87, 225, 230, 249
Yueji Pavilion 88, 89, 249
Yuezou Juntian (stage) 133, 249
Yulan Fen Hall 20, 64, 65, 249
Yulinglong Pavilion 24, 32, 51, 236, 249
Yunlinshi Room 180, 181, 249
Yunsong Study 169, 249
Yuntianqin Pavilion 177, 249
Yunxia Si Pavilion 177, 249
Yunxiang Qingsheng Hall 111, 112, 249
Yunzhen Study 51, 52, 56, 249
Yuyue Yuanfei Complex 20, 225, 249

Z

Zaoshen Yude Complex 218, 219, 249
Zaoyuan Gate 20, 218, 226, 227, 249
Zelan Hall 51, 204, 236, 249
Zen 89
Zhancun Study 173, 249
Zhanfeng Pavilion 180, 181, 249
Zhanjing Building 177, 249
Zhanran Room 88, 89, 249
Zhanshi Yinglü (Complex, hall) 133, 146, 249
Zhanxu Library 95, 127, 249
Zhaohe Deng 129, 249
Zhaohui (General) 40
Zhengda Guangming (Complex, Hall) 20, 21, 32, 37–40, 41, 44, 47, 84, 224, 235, 237, 249
Zhengjue Temple 25, 29, 32, 81, 91, 249
Zhi Gengzhi 130, 249
Zhifu Hall 69, 249
Zhiguo Hall 112, 238, 249
Zhiyu Pavilion 147, 150, 249
Zhongle Pavilion 43, 249
Zhongshan Park 215
Zhongyuan Festival 71, 218, 219
Zhou Dunyi 64, 111
Zhuanma Tai 205
Zhuge Liang 24, 128
Zhuke Building 75, 78, 79, 249
Zhumi Mountain House 169, 249
Zhuolin Pond 130, 249
Zhuoyun Building 97, 98, 249
Zhushen Hejing Hall 75, 79, 249
Zibi Mountain House 20, 32, 48, 225, 249
Zida Pavilion 169, 249
Zixia Building 162, 249
Zongting Bridge 227, 230, 231, 249
zoomorphic roof ridge ornament 203
Zou Yan 237
Zuisheng Pavilion 88, 249
Zuojing Pavilion 95, 249
Zuoshi Linliu (Complex, Pavilion) 20, 133, 209, 214, 215, 249